THE FIRST EUROPEAN

THE FIRST EUROPEAN

A History of Alexander in the Age of Empire

PIERRE BRIANT

Translated by
Nicholas Elliott

Harvard University Press

Cambridge, Massachusetts
London, England
2017

First published as *Alexandre des lumières: Fragments d'histoire européenne*
by Pierre Briant © Editions Gallimard, Paris, 2012.

Library of Congress Cataloging-in-Publication Data
Names: Briant, Pierre, author.
Title: The first European : a history of Alexander in the age of empire /
Pierre Briant ; translated by Nicholas Elliott.
Description: Cambridge, Massachusetts : Harvard University Press, 2017. |
"First published as Alexandre des lumières. Fragments d'histoire européenne
by Pierre Briant © Editions Gallimard, Paris, 2012."—Title page verso |
Includes bibliographical references and index.
Identifiers: LCCN 2016009269 | ISBN 9780674659667 (hard cover : alk. paper)
Subjects: LCSH: Alexander, the Great, 356 B.C.—323 B.C. | Hellenism—Influence. |
Hellenism—Historiography. | History, Ancient—Historiography. |
Europe—Intellectual life—18th century. | Greece—History—Macedonian
Expansion, 359–323 B.C.—Historiography.
Classification: LCC DF234.2 .B74713 2017 | DDC 938/.0707204—dc23
LC record available at http://lccn.loc.gov/2016009269

Contents

IV. THE SENSE OF HISTORY

10. Alexander, Europe, and the Immobile Orient   305

     Conclusion   340

     Bibliography   *349*
     Notes   *411*
     Acknowledgments   *471*
     Index   *473*

Preface to the English-Language Edition

This book for English readers differs slightly from the volume published in Paris by Gallimard in 2012 under the title *Alexandre des Lumières: Fragments d'histoire européenne*. Like that one, this volume focuses on the figure of Alexander as "First European" from the Introduction onward. The book's general structure, which is in four parts, is identical. However, in order to conform to the format planned by Harvard University Press, I have trimmed parts of the text, particularly in the first part of the French edition. The first four chapters have been condensed into a single chapter (Chapter 1), without—I hope—altering the coherence of the argument. The next two chapters of the French edition (5 and 6) have been combined into Chapter 2. Chapters 7 and 9 of the French edition have been cut, but some of their arguments have been included in Chapters 3, 5, and 7 of the American edition. Chapters 3–10 of this edition can thus be considered identical to those in the French edition (4 and 6–10) or extremely close to it (3, 5, 7; the same is true of Chapter 2, with the exception of a few changed details. In the French edition, the numerous quotations were presented in French, including those taken from English and German works, either because I had used preexisting translations or had translated them myself. For this American edition, I have returned to the original texts of those works published in English. I have used English translations of French and German works when they were available, which was most often the case.

Concerning my text in and of itself, the only notable addition is a passage on the representations of Alexander at the court of Philip V of Spain in Chapter 1. Other than that, I have added references in the Notes and Bibliography to studies that have appeared since 2011, but did not attempt to

go overboard in completing what was already very abundant documentation. To my knowledge, very few of the books and articles published recently
deal directly with the subject I am addressing—outside, of course, of the reviews of the French edition.[1] I will primarily mention the biography of the
Baron de Sainte-Croix by Stefania Montecalvo,[2] in which one can now find
exhaustive documentation of one of the greatest erudite writers of the
eighteenth century, a man who made a fundamental contribution to the
history of Alexander and its interpretation, as I show in Chapters 2 and 7.
Another book deserves to be mentioned at this point, despite the fact that it
deals with an earlier period: Vincent Barletta's *Death in Babylon,* which,
though published in 2010, had previously escaped my attention.[3] As the
subtitle indicates (*Alexander the Great and Iberian Empire in the Muslim Orient*),
the author discusses issues close to those I have addressed, in the context of
the expansion of Spain and Portugal against the Islamic powers of Africa
and Asia during the fifteenth and sixteenth centuries: "The ghost of Alexander is intricately related to European, and more specifically Iberian, colonial adventures that took place in Muslim Africa and Asia during the
fifteenth and sixteenth century" (201). In a way, the author traverses the
Iberian fifteenth and sixteenth centuries on the trail of the images of Alexander constructed and imagined by the people of the time, as I do for the
European long eighteenth century.[4] This comparison does not detract from
the specificity of the Alexander of the Enlightenment largely constructed
by Montesquieu and those historians and philosophers whom he influenced in England, Scotland, Germany, and France (the four countries at the
heart of my investigation), but it serves as a reminder that the use of the
Macedonian king as a precedent for European expansion began in Europe
in the Middle Ages, including in the context of the Crusades led or imagined
against the "Infidels"—particularly at the court of the dukes of Burgundy.

Given the proliferation in recent years of studies both partial and innovative,[5] a most interesting future project would be to provide a synthesis of
the "European" Alexander from the Middle Ages to the present day, without
omitting to include such a study in a global perspective, given the extent to
which the figure of Iskender/Aliksandar/Sikandar has remained alive in
the literatures and imagination of people from Egypt to Java. I will attempt
to make my own modest contribution to this effort in a forthcoming volume.[6]

THE FIRST EUROPEAN

Now that commerce has connected the entire universe,
that politics are enlightened regarding its interests,
and that humanity extends to every people,
there is no sovereign in Europe who
does not think like Alexander.

JAUCOURT, *Encyclopédie,* 6(1756): 51.

Introduction

Fragments of European History

Alexander, Europe, and the "Rest of the World" from Antiquity to the Enlightenment

An author customarily begins his book by stating its genesis and objectives. This type of explanation is especially necessary when a historian of antiquity writes a book that falls into a historical and cultural context outside his original field of expertise—in this case, the Enlightenment or, if you will (I will come back to this), the long eighteenth century.

The direction of my research evolved radically from the initial impulse to the book you hold before you. I initially sought to study the genesis of the modern historiography of Alexander the Great. Some of my findings have been described in a previous volume (*Darius in the Shadow of Alexander*, 2015) and in preparatory and subsequent articles in which I considered representations of the history of the Achaemenid empire through its intersections with the history of its European conqueror. At this point, I had already decided to continue my research after uncovering a paradoxical gap of which I had initially not suspected the full extent or significance. I found that a moment in this history of history has regularly been undervalued, if not completely eclipsed: the Age of Enlightenment.[1] I decided to rediscover Alexander through the Enlightenment while discovering the Enlightenment through Alexander.

In opening such an approach (which is not as narrow as it may seem), the historian in me is perfectly aware that my method here is an extension of my previous work. Through the figure of Alexander and the vastly differing opinions on his role in history, I have long had a sustained interest in the

forms and meaning(s) of the dialogue between the past and the present in-
strumentalized as mirrors (particularly in European colonial literature), as
well as the question of European views of the Orient (which naturally calls
to mind Edward Said's *Orientalism*), including through the analysis of the
slow emergence of a Persian history "in equal parts," in which Alexander no
longer appears as a deus ex machina casting a deep shadow over the history
of the Great Kings.[2] In an article published in 1979, I discussed the use of the
figure of Alexander as a "colonial model" based on a corpus of manuals and
popular histories dating from approximately 1850 to 1950. I have since continued adding to the case file on "history in the past and in the present,"
picking up the thread of my historian's obsessions in prior close examinations
of the literatures of the Enlightenment.[3]

My approach has also been inspired by the growing rediscovery of
Aufklärungshistorie initiated by contemporary German historiography,[4] and
incorporates an investigation of the writing of history in the Age of Enlightenment not in a global form (that would be another book, which it is not my
place to write), but through the examination of a specific case. The example
in question was a response to a competition launched by the Académie
Royal des Inscriptions et Belles-Lettres in 1769, which is all the more remarkable for the fact that it led to the first comprehensive reflection on the
sources of the history of Alexander. Submitted by the Baron de Sainte-Croix
in 1771 and published in two editions from 1775 to 1804, the *Examen critique
des anciens historiens d'Alexandre* clearly raises the central question of the
hierarchization of sources. Voltaire had appealed in 1776 for a critical
reading of Quintus Curtius Rufus's *The History of Alexander* and, referring
again to the ways of writing the history of the king of Macedon, denounced
the "modern parrots who repeat ancient words" (*La Bible enfin expliquée*).

It is important to understand the circle(s) and context(s) in which a critical history of Alexander began to be established as a distinct field in European countries over the course of the long eighteenth century, as well as the
methods and perspectives according to which it was developed and the existing movement(s) against which it was formulated—for it did not come into
being without polemics or contradictions. Such an inquiry allows one to
tackle a large number of issues, which are not exclusively raised by the historiography of Alexander: these are the links between history, education,
and political morality, between critical examination of the sources and
historical synthesis, between scholarship, philosophy, and history, between

scholarly literature and popular literature, and between text and image. In this sense, my study brings to fruition a suggestion independently made both by Elias Bickerman (1944–1945) and Arnaldo Momigliano (1952): namely, that the beginnings of the history of Alexander should be situated in the eighteenth century, long before Johann Gustav Droysen (born in 1808) began his university studies in Berlin under eminent professors and went on to publish his *Geschichte Alexanders des Grossen* (*History of Alexander the Great*) in 1833.

My inquiry was naturally shaped by the recent and rich contributions made by eighteenth-century historians to the history of European expansion and the intense political and philosophical struggles that characterized it. Their work is practically devoid of references to Alexander, with the exception of scattered, random, and anecdotal allusions. The same is more or less true of the work of scholars of antiquity and specialists in reception.[5] Even if other examples from antiquity are taken into account (particularly those from the Roman empire), this silence or lack of interest is detrimental, for the figure of Alexander the Conqueror became an increasingly noteworthy and frequent reference in the discourse of men of the Enlightenment who directly connected him to the concerns of their time. This is most apparent in the attention he attracted from French philosophers who were among the most prestigious and respected in Europe (Voltaire and Montesquieu) and from every philosopher-historian from other countries (Scotland, England, and Germany) who was heavily influenced by Montesquieu's *The Spirit of the Laws* (*L'esprit des lois*), Voltaire's *Essai sur les mœurs et l'esprit des nations*, and many less renowned works. My aim is to complement rather than work against the analyses of modernist historians (who have significantly taught and stimulated me), precisely by showing that an approach through the Enlightenment's use of the Alexandrine past can singularly enrich the corpus, refine questions, and clarify ongoing debates about the political uses of history in the relationships that Europe established and / or imposed with foreign lands transformed into lands of conquest opened wide to European commerce. While not necessarily made explicit in these exact words, the questions asked by Enlightenment political analysts, moralists, philosophers, and historians fragment into multiple echoes: What can we learn from Alexander and his way of conquering and organizing his empire, and to what extent and in what form(s) is his (variously estimated) experience specific to the ancients or transposable to the moderns? At the very moment when the philosophers were engaged in a heated debate over the legitimacy of European attempts to impose their laws on what Raynal referred to as the Two Indies—a debate that included complete rejection— they found a source of inspiration in the ancients who, in speaking of Alexander, had already shared the arguments that would fuel the moderns' thought and serve as a partial basis for their antagonistic conclusions regarding the "modernity" of the man who would be considered (in both good and bad lights) the first European conqueror of the Orient.

As the object of a clearly identified reflection on the "great man" and the "hero," which intersected with another line of thought on war and peace but did not completely merge with it (see Chapter 3), the figure of Alexander as it took shape in the modern camp over the course of the long eighteenth century is that of a conqueror who came from Europe to bring to heel the lands of the Great King, which were themselves assimilated (implicitly or more often explicitly) into the world referred to as the Orient (or Asia).[6] It will therefore not be a surprise to find that in this book current events are obsessively present in the formation of historical representations. Through the image of Alexander represented (for better and for worse) as a "modern" precedent to European conquests, the history of the Macedonian conquest was a part of the polemics between French, British, and German philosophers and political analysts over the conquest of extra-European areas and their moral and political justifications, while simultaneously being elaborated in the form of monographs and finding its place in Greek and universal histories. It will therefore also not come as a surprise that observers based their estimated assessments of Alexander's imperial adventure on contemporary events and their own prejudices, nor that throughout these debates one can easily distinguish the implicit figure of a despotic Orient, which had "stood still" from Darius III to the Ottoman sultans and to which Alexander the European brought renewal and revitalization.

My wish is that coming from a historian of antiquity this very specific focus on the figure and images of Alexander through the literatures of the Enlightenment will contribute to the thinking of eighteenth-century specialists (among whom I do not claim to include myself, though I have spent eight years immersed in their sources and documents). My responsibility was to identify and collect the pertinent information, analyze it, and offer a synthesis, in hopes that this would generate critical reflection and conceptual developments among Enlightenment specialists, followed by a constructive and enriching dialogue between the two fields—and perhaps, in the best of cases, within what would become a shared field. This dialogue goes to the heart of the histories of European identity and of encounters between Europeans and the lands that they imagined, roamed, inventoried, and conquered as they moved from the East Indies to the West Indies and from antiquity to the Enlightenment.

History, Geography, Navigation, and Commerce

I have referred to the literatures of the Enlightenment. The plural expresses linguistic diversity, but also indicates that my inquiry was not limited to major works by the most famous philosophers nor to those historians traditionally included in historiographic studies. I also wanted to include far more trivial books and articles, which do not necessarily qualify as "history books" in the strict sense of the term and have largely been forgotten, but nonetheless contributed in their own genres to constructing and spreading images of Alexander among various European audiences.

Yet it was not conceivable nor would it be reasonable to claim to provide an introduction to all the authors who, at one time or another, in one context or another, took up the history of Alexander or expressed their outlooks on the more or less distinct views they had of a figure initially encountered through their own reading and the lessons well-born youth received from their instructors and private tutors.

However, I would like to explain the principles that guided me in the process of assembling a corpus. Such an enterprise can only be accomplished by making a preliminary choice between two options: to conduct the research according to the method of the representative sample (subject to defining its criteria) or the imperative of exhaustiveness (appearing a priori to exclude nothing). My choice is indicated both by the number of titles collected (over six hundred) and their thematic and linguistic diversity.

This type of compilation has been attempted twice before, close to two centuries apart, in the form of excerpts from works considered representative, collected according to methodological principles based on dramatically different standards. In 1988, Chantal Grell and Christian Michel collected forty-nine "contemporary accounts," ordered chronologically from Yves Duchat (1624) to Cousin-Despréaux (1786).[7] For reasons owing to the purpose of the research (which dealt with changes in the instrumentalization of the myth of Alexander under Louis XIV), the majority (31 of 49) of the documents cited date from the seventeenth century.

Close to two centuries earlier (in 1802), Jean-Baptiste Chaussard (1766–1823) had accompanied his now long-forgotten annotated translation of Arrian's *Anabasis of Alexander* with a selection of quotations from writers of antiquity and the sixteenth, seventeenth, and eighteenth centuries, organized in extremely debatable categories: "historians" (Bossuet, Rollin, Barthélemy, Bougainville); "politicians" (Bodin, Naudé, Montesquieu); "moralists" (Montaigne, Bayle, Fénelon, Voltaire, Rousseau, Vauvenargues); "poets" (Racine, Boileau, Lemercier). Others appear (or, in some cases, reappear) in the "parallel" category (Mably, Tourreil, Montaigne, Saint-Evremond, La Fontaine, Folard, Bougainville, Fontenelle).[8] The "fourth class" of these authors, ranging from Gauthier de Châtillon (twelfth century) to William Vincent (1797), is gathered under a heading worthy of a Jacques Prévert list poem: "Modern historians. Compilers with or without choice. Military research. Geographic clarifications. Critical philosophy" (1: xxix–xlviii). Chaussard was attuned to a specific type of publications on Alexander, the study of war. He provides a selection of such studies (see 1:xli–xlvii, lxix–lxxvi; 3:219–278) and devotes a significant part of his fourth volume to the subject. Indeed, images of Alexander in the seventeenth and eighteenth centuries were also developed through the period's countless treatises on the military arts.

Such anthologies have the advantage of providing the general public with immediate access to works sometimes difficult to identify and consult. However, they are also subject to the shortcomings inherent to the form. Even when passages are quoted at length, the citations are removed from their context of production and enunciation, which often makes internal edits of excerpts acutely frustrating. Additionally, the selection is subjective and inevitably partial. It is particularly unfortunate that the only works included are those considered history books, a type of book whose definition remains vague.

In fact, the observer wishing to follow the genesis of images and representations of Alexander must considerably enrich his palette. Anyone studying scholarly research presented and published in France (for instance) must not only comb through the registers and publications of the Académie Royale des Inscriptions et Belles-Lettres, but also those of the Académie Royale des Sciences, since findings in research on the closely related fields of astronomy, navigation, and geometry were primarily presented in the latter institution.[9] In 1873, the well-known geographer Vivien de Saint-Martin (who also referred to *The Spirit of the Laws*, 10.13) proclaimed: "Alexander's expeditions were no less useful to science than to civilization.... In fact, war makes demands that particularly benefit geography," and, "In the history of geographic discoveries, there are five or six crucial periods that particularly contributed to progress in the knowledge of the globe in civilized nations. Alexander's expeditions defined one of these great periods, and not the least important one."[10] With this, Vivien de Saint-Martin was doing little more than repeating an opinion well established by the beginning of the eighteenth century and reinforced throughout the next hundred years.[11] Its recurring themes were that Alexander had opened Asia to European eyes; that his conquests had also served to discover countries unknown or lost in the fog of legend; that he was a geographer; that he was an explorer and that certain texts from his period belonged to one of the most popular literary genres, travel books. A particularly notable case was Nearchus's *Indica* (known through Arrian), which led to a flood of publications by philologists and translators, as well as authors fascinated by travel, geographic discoveries, and the conquest of modern India (especially William Vincent in 1797, who reached a considerable audience in Europe).

I once suggested that one should study not only the historiography of Alexander, but his *geo-historiography*.[12] The fact is that the history of geography is closely connected to the history of nations' identities,[13] but also to the history of European expansion and dominion over territories now declared "open," which naturally means "open to European commerce." While "colonial geography" was more narrowly codified by Albert Demangeon in 1923, it had in fact existed throughout the modern era: it is a constituent element of imperial ideology, which explains why beginning in the late seventeenth century, Alexander was both object and subject of the history of geography, cartography, and explorations, and why famous explorers (Delisle and d'Anville in France; Rennell in England; Mannert in Germany) were leading figures in the history of the history of Alexander on the same level as the erudite-historian Sainte-Croix, who read and referred to them extensively. Travelers' narratives and historical geography studies, which were most often connected—sometimes even organically—to European diplomatic and military enterprises in India and the countries of the Orient, make up an important part of the corpus I have assembled and analyzed.

Navigation and journeys naturally also imply commerce. Countless histories of commerce regularly identify Alexander's reign as a decisive stage,[14] while just as many books introduce him to the reader as an opener of trade routes seen through the eyes of European travelers to Alexandria and the Levant or British military personnel and diplomats crisscrossing the routes between India, Central Asia, and Persia.[15] In Chapter 4, we will see that it would be inconceivable to comment on the passage in *The Spirit of the Laws* (21.8) concerning Alexander and commerce with India without making the connection with Bishop Huet's treatment of the subject in his 1716 *Histoire du commerce et de la navigation des Anciens* (translated into English in 1717 as *The History of the Commerce and Navigation of the Ancients*). The subject also frequently comes up in the (often polemic) literature related to Franco-British competition between Egypt and India up to and including the Napoleonic era.[16] The inclusion of this protean literature extends the list of pertinent works and considerably enriches and diversifies the information available to the observer, who can consequently orient his own reflection on Alexander's history toward closely interconnected cross-disciplinary subjects, such as geography, travel, navigation, commerce, colonization, and European conquests (Chapters 4–8).

Republic of Letters; Europe; Nations and Languages

My choices were also based on another principle and another conviction, which was that restricting my work to national production (of any kind) would create a frustrating limit and an insurmountable handicap.[17] Any research on the genesis of European images of Alexander during the Age of Enlightenment must necessarily extend to all of Europe (and beginning in the 1780s to the United States), at least in the fields of publishing, translation, and the reissuing of works originally published in Europe. For reasons that will easily be understood (the desire to be exhaustive has its limits, which are the author's limits), my research does not devote equal attention to every country. In particular, one might consider that Italy and Spain are underrepresented in the corpus I have assembled.[18] The Netherlands is primarily represented by its philologists, publishers, translators, and commentators;[19] the same is true of Switzerland, in the form of interpolated remarks rather than thorough discussions, through the philologist Daniel Wyttenbach and the philosopher Isaac Iselin. To these countries, one must add Greece, initially under Ottoman rule, then independent, where Enlightenment endeavors in the fields of translation and historiography have recently inspired innovative studies.[20] Additionally, the tsar and tsarina's territorial ambitions ranging from the Straits to Central Asia and their particular interest in Orthodox Greece (including through a close connection with ancient Greece)[21] leave no doubt that it would be important to research Alexander's presence in political and historiographic reflections in the Russian literature of the long eighteenth century. But in this instance, I did not learn of any specific study that could have even partially compensated for my lack of knowledge of Peter and Catherine's language.[22]

The protagonists of the new history of Alexander are France, England, Scotland, and Germany (or the Germanies). This is due to their philologists, translators of Greek and Latin works, scholars, and philosophers, but also their geographers and travelers and (particularly in Great Britain) those colonizer-diplomat-soldiers who were convinced that they were walking in the Macedonian's footsteps.[23] Though German scholars were not involved in the conquest of land and sea territories, they did participate in carrying on Alexander's legacy of appropriation, both through their own works and through translations, and sometimes by taking part in journeys organized by other nations (the Forsters, father and son, were enrolled on Cook's second expedition under the dual title of "naturalists and philosophers").[24] The questions I have referred to in the previous pages are considered on a European scale. Reflections and responses can therefore only be offered based on a multilingual European corpus. In this sense, my book also represents a contribution (however fragmentary) to the political and cultural history of Europe in its unity and diversity.

At the same time, while many historians and philosophers referred to Europe and shared standards of civilization, the eighteenth century and the first third of the nineteenth century also saw them acting and thinking in increasingly differentiated and specific national contexts[25] with the emergence of the question of nationalities (as can so clearly be seen in the Balkans but also in the Germanies). Eighteenth-century scholars indiscriminately (or compatibly) published studies of ancient, medieval, or contemporary history, reveled in their use of analogy (between past and present),[26] and never hesitated to take a direct position on the burning issues of the day (whether national or international). They were anything but indifferent to political concerns—to the point that the inspiring fraternity supposed to govern the Republic of Letters sometimes vanished.[27] This is yet another reason not to reduce the diversity of Alexander's images to a single thing, however European.

These observations led me to make a very clear distinction between national fields of research on Alexander, particularly in the first third of the nineteenth century (Chapters 8–10), all the while noting incontestable convergences and borrowings in multiple directions. Indeed, one can say that there emerges an image of a "European Alexander"—one that is especially coherent in contrast to the Orient (as will particularly be seen in Chapter 10)— while distinct national images are elaborated in parallel and can conflict or compete with each other. In each national space, these images can coexist in hostile confrontation (as is the case in France: Chapter 7) or change considerably over time (as with Germany—Chapter 8—or Greece—Chapter 10 § "The First of the Hellenes?"). There is no single Alexander of the Enlightenment, just as there is no single philosophy or history of the Enlightenment.

This necessity to consider things from a European perspective also explains why I have risked weighing down the corpus by including translations. Some will ask why, for instance, I cite five translations (in English, German, Dutch, Italian, and Spanish) of the same French book written by Pierre-Daniel Huet and published in 1716, the aforementioned *Histoire du commerce*. Doesn't that needlessly prolong the list of works consulted? Yes, if one follows the original edition to the letter, given that faithful translations do not add anything and those that distort the original are of no importance. Yet the problem is more complex than this sweeping generalization would suggest. On the one hand, it is risky to blindly rely on translations when analyzing foreign literature; it is useful and even indispensable to conduct synoptic checks of the original text, which I did systematically (in those instances where there is a translation, which is obviously not generally the case). Additionally, multiple translations of individual French works attest to the fact that the full diversity of volumes published in the language of Molière was not immediately accessible to European readers. At the same time, the linguistic variety of European publications reveals that the members of the Republic of Letters did not generally use French to publish their works. The case of Frederick of Prussia and his court was an exception in the Germanies, as was his nephew Frederick Augustus's use of Italian in his *Alessandro Magno* (*Alexander the Great*) in 1764; the use of French at the Berlin

1. Title pages of *Histoire du commerce et de la navigation des Anciens* by Pierre-Daniel Huet (1716) and those of five translations.

Academy did not last beyond Frederick's death.[28] In Göttingen, Latin was no longer a real alternative, despite the voluntarist policy encouraged by Heyne. Admittedly, doctoral candidates' dissertations and oral presentations made before academies such as the one in Göttingen[29] continued to be published in Latin, particularly in Germany and the Netherlands. Yet in Göttingen, Gatterer, who was very concerned with the development of a historical science in native languages in the face of the prestige of French publications, advocated publishing articles and books in German,[30] while Heyne himself was ultimately forced to recognize that he had to publish in German if he wanted his work to be read by the general public and students.[31] Many years earlier in England, John Selden published his *Mare Clausum* in Latin in 1635 but quickly decided to provide an English version (*Of the Dominion of Ownership of the Sea*, 1652) because, as he explained in his "Epistle Dedicatorie to the Parliament of the Commonwealth of England," "Latin is a language unknown to the greatest part of the Nation whom it most concern's.... It is necessary to let the People have a clear understanding of their nearest interest." Despite the resistance expressed by the upholders of the classical tradition, readers in various countries clearly preferred to read foreign books translated into their own languages.[32] The abundance of translations is a good indicator of the diffusion of books and the circulation of ideas throughout Europe. One can evaluate this phenomenon by consulting footnotes, despite the often patchy nature of the references. Johann Isaac Berghaus's 1792 volume provides a very rare example of a classified bibliography (2:137–186). The author's reading material on Alexander and his time illustrates the variety and diffusion of translations: aside from Rollin, Montesquieu (1767), Buache (1731), and Sainte-Croix (1775), who are cited in the original French, he refers to Huet (in the Dutch translation, with questions about its accuracy), Schlözer (in the Swedish original), Gillies (in a German translation), as well as Robertson (in a German translation),[33] Raynal, and a German version of the *Universal History*.

The translators are themselves sometimes very interesting characters (Georg Forster and Christian Garve in Germany, for example, or Rigas in Greece), who played an important role as cultural intermediaries, either in bilateral relations or on a European scale.[34] There is much to be learned from the prefaces they wrote to introduce their translations. In some cases, they illustrate the fact that a certain translation has a particular political significance (for instance, Billecocq's 1800 translation of William Vincent's

The Voyage of Nearchus, 1797) and / or that the book in question is aimed at a specific audience (the anonymous translation of Huet into English is addressed "to the Chairman, the Deputy-Chairman and to the other Directors of the East India Company"). Failed attempts at translation are equally informative, as with the double failure of the German translation of *The Voyage of Nearchus,* which can be pieced together through the contemporary German press and the English author's unpublished manuscript notes.[35]

Two other indicators are available to analyze books' reception in their native countries and abroad. One is intrinsic and does not cause the bibliography to swell, though it imposes a certain kind of reading. Many of the works I consulted do not present original ideas. Yet just like more innovative texts, these works can spark interesting reflections so long as one reads the dedications, prefaces, forewords, and other introductory materials and methodically goes through the footnotes. The other indicator available lengthens the list of works consulted: I am referring to reviews. These are nearly systematically anonymous, though in some cases the author can be identified. The journals in question can be intended for scholars (for instance, the *Journal des Savants* or the *Göttingische gelehrte Anzeigen*),[36] but one can also find very interesting reviews in more or less mass market periodicals (*Magazin encyclopédique, Mercure de France, Journal de l'empire, Journal de Trévoux, British Critique, Gentleman's Magazine, Edinburgh Review, Allgemeine Literatur-Zeitung,* etc.). Circulated in private distribution networks through subscription, other periodicals such as the *Correspondance Littéraire* edited by Friedrich Melchior Grimm and Bachaumont's *Mémoires secrets* regularly reported on new releases. Even through a random sampling, collecting and comparing reviews allows us to piece together a type of erudite and philosophical intra-European conversation that dynamically enriched the debates on the history of Alexander from which it arose.

A (Very) Long Eighteenth Century

The chronological demarcation of my research was somewhat imposed on me by the nature and composition of the corpus collected. As the outcome of an approach marked by a kind of empiricism (that of the outsider), my book finds itself included in what specialists have become accustomed to calling "the long eighteenth century."

On the early side, Pierre Bayle's *Alexandre de Macédoine* (1697) could have served as a perfectly acceptable starting point. Nevertheless, two considerations led me to go further back in time. First, with respect to the history of criticism and the critical apparatus, it seemed appropriate to include the studies, commentaries, and translations published around 1645–1650 (e.g., Gaudenzio 1645; La Mothe Le Vayer 1646; Perrot d'Ablancourt 1646), which can better contextualize the Baron de Sainte-Croix's work in the following century (Chapters 1–2). One can also add that the first book (or pamphlet) about Alexander was published in 1665, by Samuel Clarke. Another observation was far more decisive: while published in 1716, the completely unprecedented view of Alexander in Pierre-Daniel Huet's book *Histoire du commerce* was actually composed in the fall of 1667 as a handwritten report submitted to Colbert. The book was distributed in France and throughout Europe, where it exercised a considerable long-term influence, which I attempt to uncover through its various networks of circulation.[37] From 1667 to 1716, Huet's report remained a kind of "nonbook" kept in the ministry's archives and in the author's personal papers. Nonetheless, the manuscript needed to be included in my analysis. Huet did include a few excerpts on Alexander in his book on the *Paradis terrestre* in 1691. In a more general manner, an explanation of the French and European political context in which Huet conceived his image of Alexander is required. This can only be accomplished by considering as a whole the period that extends from the handwritten report to the printed book (1667–1716) and that predates Rollin, Voltaire, and Montesquieu's first contributions to the subject.

On the later side, 1789 is not a pertinent caesura in the field under discussion, particularly since the careers and thinking of many scholars continued uninterrupted by the political changes.[38] The first third of the nineteenth century needed to be included to study the transition from the Enlightenment to Historicism. One will first note that the body of information about Alexander was barely modified until the end of this period, with the exception of two statuettes representing Alexander (the Azara herm found near Tivoli in 1779 and later given to Bonaparte, then to the Musée Napoléon; and another found in Herculaneum in 1751)[39] and a sarcophagus found in Memphis on the Egyptian Expedition, which, once transported to London, was interpreted (rather boldly) as being Alexander's first tomb in Egypt.[40] The situation changed on October 24, 1831, when a marvelous mosaic was discovered in Pompeii in what was then referred to as the House of Goethe, and later known as the House of the Faun. After brief discussions among Italian specialists, it was quickly recognized that the scene depicted an armed confrontation between Alexander and Darius and their soldiers and that it could either represent the Battle of Issus or Gaugamela.[41]

In an entirely different vein, 1831 also saw the deaths of Niebuhr and Hegel, two great scholars who had played an active part in discussions of Alexander's historical role in their respective fields in Bonn and Berlin, and the beginning of the career of the young Berlin student Johann Gustav Droysen mentioned above, who would publish his *Geschichte Alexanders des Grossen* (1833) two years later. Aside from isolated references, this book (the subject of an overabundant literature primarily dealing with the 1877 edition, which there is no need to cite here) will remain outside of my discussion—with the exception that, in this field as in others, the reassessment of the historiography of the long eighteenth century casts serious doubts on the traditional view that historians of antiquity in the 1820s to 1840s, such as Niebuhr in Germany and Grote in England,[42] were key innovators. Droysen should also be included in this group; when he began writing his book in the fall of 1831, he was extremely skillful (though he did not openly admit it) at making full use of more than a century's worth of European research and thought on the history of Alexander, to the point that his Alexander has a few striking similarities with the one in *The Spirit of the Laws*.[43]

The period 1790–1830 was marked by the publication in 1804 of the second edition of the Baron de Sainte-Croix's *Examen critique* and the fascinated and fascinating discussions of the book among the various juries convened to attribute one of the Decennial prizes in 1810, as well as in accounts in the press (Chapters 2 and 7). In a more general manner, the period 1790–1830 saw a flood of publications in Great Britain, France, Germany, and the Netherlands (Chapters 2 and 6–8). This production reveals notable reorientations, which can be ascribed to the intense political and ideological struggles taking place both within Europe as a whole (particularly due to Napoleonic expansionism) and within each of the countries considered (from the revolution to the empire, then the restoration in France; British debates on Indian policy; discussions on the future of post-Napoleonic Germany), but also within an area that covered Darius and Alexander's former empire and was increasingly the stage for a European Great Game (the Egyptian Expedition and its consequences; the Russian push toward the Straits and toward Persia and Central Asia; British ambitions stretching from India to the same regions and Persia). In the Balkans, 1830 saw a radical shift in the relationship between Europe and the (Ottoman) Orient through a drastic change in political spaces. Indeed, it marked the (provisional) end of the conflict-heavy process that had allowed the Greeks to shake off Ottoman tutelage and Greece to appear in the concert of European nations. As we know, the struggle for independence aroused a tremendous solidarity movement across Europe, often colored by a romantic desire to "return to Ancient Greece," including in Greece itself and throughout the various Hellenic diasporas from Vienna to Smyrna. We will see (Chapters 9–10) that over the *longue durée* of Europeans' real and imagined relations with Greece and the Orient (from Salamis to Navarino), these events and their interpretation had a hand in the assertion of an aggressive image of Alexander the Great as a "missionary" of European values.

I

A Critical History

Chapter 1

History, Morals, and Philosophy

Prelude: The Competition of 1769

Under the date of Tuesday, November 15, 1769, the "Register of the Assemblies and Deliberations of the Académie Royale des Inscriptions et Belles-Lettres" in Paris mentions (among other things) the title of the annual competition, which would attribute its prize at Easter 1770. The candidates were to consider "The critical inquiry of the Ancient Historians of Alexander the Great," or (if one prefers the more transparent wording used by a few commentators), "Who among the historians of Alexander should be preferentially believed?" Given the mediocrity of the proposals, the call for submissions was not a great success. The prize was awarded at Easter 1772 to the dissertation by His Honor the Baron de Sainte-Croix, chosen over two other submissions. The revised version he published in 1775 included the following opinion expressed by the academy's rapporteur: "This subject had not yet been treated and was lacking in our Literature." Was this conventional phrasing an accurate reflection of the status of Alexander studies in France and Europe? Nearly fifty years later, the Englishman William Mitford, who had met Sainte-Croix in 1776–1777 on his property at Mormoiron, stated that "no part of antient profane history has been transmitted more authenticated than that of Alexander," and that consequently the choice of "the Royal Academy of Inscriptions and Polite Literature at Paris" could be explained by "the singular state and the interesting character of the history of Alexander the Great."[1] In the rather allusive and uncertain form in which it is presented, this kind of remark adds to our questions rather than answering them.

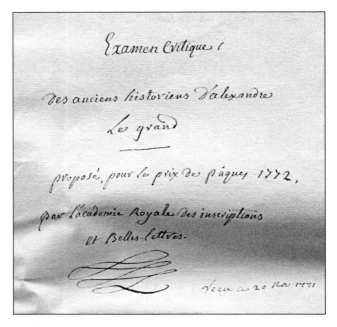

2. Title page of the manuscript of *Examen critique des anciens historiens d'Alexandre le Grand* by the Baron de Sainte-Croix, submitted to the Académie for the Easter 1771 competition. Archives de l'Institut. Photo © Patrick Imbert, Collège de France.

Without denying the book's specificity or novelty, it is important to be aware that it did not appear fully formed, suddenly, out of the brain of a scholar, however notable its successive contributions can be deemed. It was also the outcome of a long process, which was neither linear nor exempt from polemic contradictions. This scholarly research should be tied to the reflections that opened the way to new interpretations of the history of Alexander the Great long before 1771, returning it to the context of world history past and present, in the fields of politics, commerce, and "mores, literature and the fine arts." Indeed, publications and reflections on Alexander's history were already numerous and in-depth, as included in histories of ancient Greece, universal histories, histories of the Jews, and presentations made to various European academies; from 1691 to 1773, more than ten dissertations on the subject were defended in German, Swedish, and Dutch universities. In a completely different style, seven years before the competition of 1769, the unusual author and philosopher-historian Linguet had even published an entire volume on Alexander's adventure and its importance in universal history, the *Histoire du Siècle d'Alexandre avec quelques réflexions sur ceux qui l'ont précédé,* a new edition of which was published the very year of the competition; as early as 1736, Voltaire had given his opinion on Alexander's historical importance and in 1748 Montesquieu had devoted several chapters of his *The Spirit of the Laws* to the Macedonian conquest, which were further developed in the posthumous second edition (1757). The full diversity of this legacy of scholarship and of interpretative reflection must be accounted for, at least in its broad outlines.

The History of the Dauphin

Interest in Alexander had been unabated since antiquity and the Middle Ages. One need merely cite Lord Chancellor Bacon, who in 1605 had already pointed out that the narrative of Alexander's (and Caesar's) exploits had been a constant source of wonder.[2] In the shape of paraphrases from the Greek and Roman sources already familiar to the well-read, the narrative of the conquest and the references in political ethics seemed to be established once and for all, to the point that one has the impression of always reading the same book or the same chapter. One can therefore understand that authors regularly insisted upon the fact that Alexander's story was well-known to readers. In the seventeenth century and the greater part of the eighteenth century, collections of stories about the great men of antiquity were plentiful. One approached their lives and exploits through the study of the Greek and Latin authors. Alexander was no exception to the rule. Authors merely needed to paraphrase the chapters Plutarch had devoted to him—at once narratives of the life and inexhaustible treasuries of lessons in private and public morals;[3] exactly what Christina, queen of Sweden, had done in her *Diverse Reflections on the Life and Actions of Alexander the Great,* a short book in which she proposed "to endeavour to place truth in a clear light, [because] the world has not as yet done justice to his merit."[4] Since antiquity, exempla drawn from the *Lives of Illustrious Men* had regularly and abundantly nourished books of history, politics, and morals, and inspired the elaboration of collections made in the manner of the ancients.

In 1665, Samuel Clarke (1625–1669) published what can be considered the first book ever devoted to the life and conquests of Alexander the Great, paired with a Life of Charlemagne.[5] A great scholar and architypographus of Oxford University, Clarke knew Greek and Latin, as well as Hebrew and other oriental languages, and was the author of further books on great figures of antiquity and the modern era (*Tamerlane the Great; Cyrus the Great; Nebuchadnezzar the Great*). The book's title describes Alexander by the prestigious designation of "the first founder of the Grecian empire" and expressly identifies him with references from the book of Daniel (2.32; 7.6; 8.5) that evoke the succession of the four empires and the advent of the Macedonian empire. Following on from Plutarch, Clarke describes Alexander's youth and does not underplay his qualities or, naturally, the extent of his conquests. Adhering to the circumstantial narratives of the authors of antiquity, who would be piously copied and paraphrased by all the modern authors, he praises the conqueror's continence in dealing with the Persian princesses captured after the Battle of Issus. But further on, he places greater emphasis on Alexander's errors and vices. Already illustrated by the murders ordered immediately after his accession to power, the king's cruelty becomes one of the leitmotifs of Clarke's narrative, particularly beginning with the taking of Gaza, but also later when Alexander faces his own companions. The victories were not only won over a weak and decadent enemy, but they were followed by reprehensible decisions. Clarke considers that Alexander was driven by excessive ambition. He should not have rejected the offers for peace and collaboration made by Darius after the Battle of Issus. He should have accepted to reign over a vast kingdom extending between the Danube and the Euphrates, rather than launching into unreasonable conquests in Babylon, Persia, and India; this would have allowed him to prove his administrative skills and prepare a smooth succession. Instead, the taking of Babylon taught the Macedonians luxury and debauchery and the burning of Persepolis revealed that the conqueror was now in the grips of a deplorable drunkenness. As for the decisions made after Darius's death (such as requiring his intimates to bow to him), they reveal that Alexander had completely "degenerated" and that he had turned into "one of Darius' licentious courtiers." As can be seen by this belittling expression, Clarke has a firm command of the classical authors, though he does not systematically refer to them. He has clearly primarily drawn from Quintus Curtius Rufus's *History of Alexander,* which he cites several times and abundantly paraphrases, particularly to condemn Darius and Persian customs. Clarke was not the first to use Curtius to attack Alexander's "oriental degeneration": thirty years earlier, Mathias Bornegger had published a "historical-political" dissertation on the subject in Strasbourg.

Clarke's book falls neatly into the category of history as "teacher of life" (*magistra vitae*, according to Cicero's expression). It was considered indispensable for princes to study history under the tutelage of their educators. This was the spirit in which history—including ancient history and the history of Alexander—was regularly taught to young people. This was why Don Fernando de Biedma had earlier addressed his *Vida de Alexandro Magno* (*Life of Alexander*) to King Philip IV of Spain in 1634. But in the period we are concerned with here, the first figure to consider is naturally Bossuet (1627–1704). Appointed private tutor to the Dauphin in 1670, he would address his pupil in one of his major works, *Discours sur l'histoire universelle* (1681).[6] In the introduction "To the Dauphin," Bossuet describes the "general design of this Work" and acquaints his royal student with the idea of the political and pedagogical role of history, which will allow the Dauphin to reflect on "how Empires have succeeded one the other"; he explains that this is why, for example, he will speak "of Persians conquered by Alexander."

The same preoccupations can be found in the work of the Abbé Guyon (1699–1771), who, in the *Histoire des Empires* (1733), considers it necessary to have daily commerce with the illustrious men of the past. Thus we can "bring them back to life ... listen to their lessons, follow their advice, examine their approaches, adjust ourselves according to their maxims, imitate their virtues." The same is true of Rollin and his *Histoire ancienne* (vol. 1 [1730]). The tone is set by the dedicatory epistle addressed to His Serene Highness and Lord the Duke of Chartres, son of the Duke d'Orléans.[7] Rollin is pleased to note that his work was useful, for "it was principally intended for the instruction of youth. ... This is the proper learning for princes, more apt to form their mind and heart than any other studies." Here, they can find lessons from "illustrious models of all the virtues that suit them." They will also learn to distinguish and dismiss "low and unworthy vices that have tarnished the splendor [of the] good deeds and dishonored [the] reigns of Philip and Alexander his son." History is a means to give the Greats lessons they would not receive from courtiers eager to flatter them. By studying history, future kings must simply learn lessons in "the arts of empire and war, the maxims of civil society, and the conduct of life that suits all ages and conditions."[8]

This idea was tirelessly developed by teachers throughout the eighteenth century (and beyond). Let's take the example of Mably (1709–1785) and his book *De la manière d'écrire l'Histoire* (1783). The author invites young people to "[choose] as a model a regular citizen of Greece and Rome," and to move away from the model of the "greatest kings, [who] too often forget that they are merely the instrument of their people's happiness." Philip and Alexander are included in this category. Of course, one could admire "the inexhaustible resourceful genius" of the former and "the audacious courage" of the latter, but neither one made "[good] use of their great qualities": they gave in to ambition. It comes as no surprise to find the same position in the writings of Condillac (1709–1785), who was Mably's brother. Naturally, this moral orientation was not exclusive to Francophone educators and tutors. For instance, it can also be found in John Gast's *History of Greece* (1782), where the history of the Greek city states alternates between virtue and vice: "The diversities of the History of Greece, amidst the passions they excite, bespeak forcibly the superintendency of a Divine Providence, and inculcate the important truth, that happiness is the reward of virtue, and misery the consequence of vice" (1:iv).

Teachers and other educators were not the only ones to draw lessons from Alexander's history. Princes also examined the Macedonian conqueror's life and actions and contributed to reflections on royalty and power. This is evident in two books published in Italian by a pair of German (or German-speaking) princes—the Baron von Kossin in 1716 and Frederick Augustus of Brunswick-Oels, nephew of Frederick the Great, in 1764.[9] In both cases, the exempla serve to foster reflection on monarchy and the art of leadership: a king must control his passions (anger, pleasures of the table, pride, physical desire, etc.) and constantly have his subjects' well-being in mind. The latter's book was immediately translated into French, then English.[10] In his preface, the English translator "consider[s] this treatise as an useful lesson of morality, not only to such as are designed for the importance offices of government, but likewise to men of private capacity, and especially those of younger years [who] may have occasion to read the history of Alexander in the course of their classical learning" (pp. iv, vii). Thanks to a French translation, Frederick Augustus's reflections made a big impression on Frederick the Great, whose correspondence with Voltaire about Alexander the Great and Peter of Russia repeats his nephew's assessment of the murder of Cleitus by the Macedonian king practically word for word.

The History of Alexander and the History of the People of God

As illustrated by John Gast's reference to Divine Providence, morality, history, and religion went hand in hand in Europe's Christian kingdoms. God was everywhere, even in secular history. A great number of books and manuals consistently structured their narratives based on the role they recognized Providence to play in the history of the world. Providence was particularly present in Bossuet, including in the context of the history of Alexander. As Bossuet said himself, his book was "a way of Universal History," at least in its first part. This type of history book had come into existence before Bossuet and constantly developed since. In fact, it had flourished to an extraordinary extent and enjoyed exceptional circulation. One of the first examples was Sir Walter Raleigh's impressive *Historie of the World* [1614], which was published in London in 1652 and led the reader from the dawn of the world to the Roman conquest of Macedon and Asia. The history of Alexander was treated (in a very critical manner) in some forty pages of book 4 (chap. 2).

If Alexander occupies such an important place in Bossuet's work, it is because his victorious march is integrated into the history of the Jews in Bossuet's account of the Eighth Period ("Cyrus or the Jews Reestablished"). What became of the Jews, who had traditionally been protected by the Great Kings, after Darius's defeat and during the Macedonian conquest of the Phoenician coast? Bossuet does not question Flavius Josephus; he faithfully follows his accounts of the break between Samaria and Jerusalem, of Sanballat of Samaria's rallying to Alexander during the siege of Tyre, and of the Macedonian king visiting Jerusalem, "full of resolution to take his Revenge." The narrative was itself structured around a dream that Alexander allegedly had in Macedon before his expedition: the high priest was said to have appeared to him and strongly encouraged him to go on the offensive without delay, promising to guide his army and ensure his victory over Darius.[11]

With the exception of this fundamental episode in the history of the people of God, Bossuet's view of the history of Alexander is rather critical and he shares it with his illustrious pupil. Alexander may have proclaimed himself a god, but his "formidable empire" was fragile and came apart after his death.

3. *Alexander before the High Priest in Jerusalem,* in Gilbert Saunier (known as Du Verdier), *L'histoire entière d'Alexandre le Grand, tirée d'Arrien, Plutarque, Justin, Joseph, Quinte-Curce et Frensheimius* (Paris: Théodore Girard, 1671), frontispiece.

Bossuet's volume had a tremendous impact. It was translated into all the European languages. The connection between Sacred History and Secular History as clearly defined by Bossuet was adopted everywhere. To successfully be told, the history of the people of God needs to be included in the history of the empires of the Orient, with which they were constantly in contact and in conflict, between the pharaohs, the Phoenician city states, and the Mesopotamian kingdoms (Assyrian, Babylonian, Median, Persian). In these conditions, the history of the Jews merges into—or can merge into—a form of universal history that also includes the Greeks, due to their constant relations with the Persians (who had themselves been central to the history of the people of God since Cyrus) and to Alexander's conquests and the creation of the kingdoms founded after his death.

Bossuet had a pronounced influence on two French historians of the 1730s and 1740s, the Abbé Guyon and Charles Rollin. Guyon devoted more than five hundred pages to the history of Alexander in volume 4 of his *Histoire des empires* (1736). He openly aligned himself with Bossuet. Like the Egyptian conqueror Senusret, the Macedonian is condemned for his "incursions," meaning his unjustified armed invasion. Alexander displays a "contrast of the most beautiful qualities and the greatest vices," but the latter easily outweigh the former once the Macedonian king begins to imitate the ways of the Persian kings.

Bossuet's *Discours* plays a particularly significant part in Rollin's *Histoire ancienne*. In fact, Rollin closes his section on Alexander with "the admirable reflections of the bishop of Meaux on the character and government of the Persians, Greeks, and Macedonians" (15.20). Of the glorious figures of antiquity, Rollin is clearly far more sympathetic to Cyrus than to Alexander. Or rather, to be more precise, he considers that the image of Cyrus has infinitely more pedagogical and moral value than Alexander's. Cyrus is not one of those terrible conquerors like Nebuchadnezzar who are described as "cruel and savage beasts, which everywhere scatter terror and desolation, and only subsist from blood and slaughter."[12] Alexander is the perfect counterexample of the ideal king implicitly described by Rollin: his decisions are not intended for the good of his people and he does not make them happy and prosperous. Rollin's conclusions are presented as an assessment in two columns, one positive, the other negative. The side praising Alexander repeats all the ancient platitudes about his virtues, heavily emphasizing his behavior toward the Persian princesses after the battle. In the works of

Rollin, Bossuet, the Abbé Guyon, and so many others, Alexander is also and most importantly the instrument of God. Rollin uses Alexander's visit to the high priest of Jerusalem to reflect on God's presence in history: "God breaks at every interval his silence, and disperses the clouds which hide him, and condescends to discover to us the secret springs of his providence, by causing his prophets to foretell, a long series of years before the event, the fate he has prepared for the different nations of the earth" (15.7).

Let us now turn to the Englishman Humphrey Prideaux (1648–1724). One of Prideaux's main claims to fame remains his *Old and New Testament*, which was very widely circulated as of its first English edition (1715–1717) and acquired exceptional authority in Europe. In his preface, Prideaux explains why he discusses the history of Alexander in an essay devoted to the history of the Jewish people: "To make this History the more clear, I have found necessary to take in within its compass the affairs of all the other eastern nations, as well as those of the Jews, the latter not being thoroughly to be understood without the other; and as far as the Grecian affairs have been complicated with those of Persia, Syria, or Egypt, I have been obliged to take notice of them also.... How could the fulfilling of the prophecies which were delivered to Alexander, his swift victories, and his breaking by them the power of Persia be brought into a clear light, without laying before the reader the whole series of those wars whereby it was effected!" (1 [1799]: xv).

In a narrative form, the history of Alexander is thus dealt with at length (1:496–573). Prideaux takes a strong stand against the conquests. If Alexander survived all the battles he fought despite his many faults and vices ("vain glory was his predominant folly"), it was because his destiny was governed by Divine Providence: "God having ordained him to be his instrument, for the bringing to pass of all that which was by the prophet Daniel foretold concerning him, he did, by this Providence, bear him through in all things for the accomplishment of it, when it was done, did cast him out of his hand" (1:535–536).

Alexander as an Example of Royal Virtues

Alexander's royal virtues were often praised in writing because they were modeled on the virtues attributed to European princes and kings. They were also represented and exalted in other mediums, notably tapestry and

LA VERTU EST DIGNE DE L'EMPIRE DU MONDE.

Alexandre apres plusieurs victoires deffit Darius dans la bataille qu'il donna
pres d'Arbelle, et ce dernier combat ayant acheve de renverser le throsne des Perses,
tout l'Orient fut soumis à la puissance des Macedoniens.

DIGNA ORBIS IMPERIO VIRTUS.

Post multas victorias virtute sua partas ultimo ad Arbellam prælio Darium
fugat Alexander eaque clade fundithus eversô Persarum solio totus Oriens in
potestatem Macedonici cessit Imperii.

4. *Alexander's Victory at Arbela* (drawing after Le Brun). British Museum, London. Photo © Trustees of the British Museum.

IL EST D'UN ROY DE SE VAINCRE SOY MÊME.   SUI VICTORIA INDICAT REGEM.

Alexandre ayant vaincu Darius pres d'Isse, entre   *Alexander Dario ad Issum victo tabernaculum*
dans une tente ou étoient la mere, la Femme, et les   *Reginarum ingreditur ubi singulare clementiæ ac*
filles de Darius, on il donne un exemple singulier   *continentiæ præbet exemplum.*
de retenue et de clemence.

5. *Alexander and Hephaestion before the Persian Princesses after the Victory at Issus* (drawing after Le Brun). British Museum, London. Photo © Trustees of the British Museum.

painting.[13] A royal policy already frequently seen in the Middle Ages (particularly in the court of Burgundy) and the Renaissance (from Fontainebleau to Rome) increasingly frequently required seventeenth- and eighteenth-century artists to choose their subjects from the history of Alexander. We are notably aware of the young Louis XIV's orders to the painter Le Brun. Between 1661 and 1673, Le Brun would produce five large canvases, two battle scenes (Granicus and Arbela), one scene of triumph (Entry into Babylon), and two scenes depicting the king's magnanimity (Alexander-Louis XIV): Alexander and the Persian princesses after Issus[14] and Alexander and Porus. Yet Alexander was a risky choice since, as we have seen, the figure of the Macedonian king also came with a burden of many negative traits, which were hardly appropriate for representing the royal figure of Louis XIV.[15] In the 1670s, the king of France and his advisors therefore decided to abandon references to Alexander and turn instead to ancestors of the Bourbon monarchy such as Henri IV and Saint Louis.[16]

Yet the subject of "Alexander the Great" would remain a source of inspiration throughout the eighteenth century.[17] Le Brun's paintings had an exceptional impact due to the proliferation of engravings that circulated all over Europe,[18] as well as the tapestries based on cartoons they inspired.[19] In this way, "the Alexander cycle's popularity eclipsed that of the Tapestries of the Life of Louis XIV and the décor of the Hall of Mirrors, both in France and abroad."[20]

A particularly telling example can be found in Spain at the court of Philip V.[21] Born in 1683 in Versailles to the son of Louis XIV, the Duke of Anjou succeeded Charles to the Spanish throne and founded the Spanish Bourbon dynasty. Aside from an interlude when his son Louis I reigned for a few months in 1724, Philip V ruled uninterrupted for a period of close to half a century (1700–1746). Like Louis XIV, he implemented a vigorous policy as a builder and patron of the arts. Shortly before 1724, he began constructing a modest palace close to Segovia, the Palacio de La Granja, which was expanded and embellished over the following years. In 1735, the king invited the famous Italian architect Filippo Juvarra to the court. During the nine months he spent at the palace (March 1735–January 1736), Juvarra was prodigiously active, leaving a large number of plans and projects at his death. Some had been partially conceived by the queen, Elisabeth Farnese. One of Farnese's forbears was Pope Paul III (1534–1549), who had had the Sala Paolina in the Castel Sant'Angelo in Rome decorated with eleven scenes from the life of Alexander.[22] It is therefore conceivable that the queen was involved in the choice of scenes to be represented in the La Granja Gallery. Yet it was Juvarra's responsibility to recruit and commission the painters, negotiating both the subjects they were to depict and their fees. With the exception of the French painter Lemoyne (who died before he was able to deliver his painting), all the artists were Italian. The surviving memorandum by Juvarra concerns "the virtues of His Majesty in the deeds of Alexander."[23] In that light, the choice of the eight subjects is most interesting:

ROYAL VALOUR. Battle won against Darius, King of Persia.

CLEMENCY. After having vanquished Porus, he spares his life and lets him keep his kingdoms.

MODESTY. On a visit to the family of Darius, when his mother mistakes Hephaestion for Alexander, he declares there is no mistake, Hephaestion being another Alexander.

DEVOUTNESS. He goes to Jerusalem intending to chastise and sack the city, but seeing the Great Priest clad in his robes, he fears God in the figure of his Minister, and offers sacrifices in the Temple.

MAGNIFICENCE. He orders the city of Alexandria and all its buildings to be built close to the Nile.

VICTORY. Triumphal entry into Babylon with his unrivalled retinue.

TEMPERANCE. When Apelles was painting Campaspe, with whom Alexander was in love, he gives her to the painter at the latter's request.

GENEROSITY. He distributes kingdoms and provinces among his captains.[24]

Philip, Duke of Anjou, had been educated at the court of Versailles along with his brothers Louis and Charles under the direction of Fénélon for seven years beginning in 1690.[25] Fénélon was very hostile to conquerors and war kings and exposed his young students to a highly negative view of Alexander. A remarkable record of Fénélon's teaching has survived through the schoolwork written by the young prince and taken to Spain when he acceded to the crown, particularly his handwritten 168-page *Discours pour César contre Alexandre*. Closely following Fénélon, he "endeavors to attack he among all the heroes whom human praise has most elevated, and who is offered as a model to all young people. . . . Alexander is easily as [guilty as Caesar] by the enormousness of his vices, if not more."

Nonetheless, forty years after the lessons imparted by Fénélon, Philip V and his advisors chose Alexander to represent the royal virtues. This apparent contradiction is not specific to the king of Spain: outside of the condemnations of a king whose vices and failings no longer fit with the image of the good king as it prevailed in the final decades of the seventeenth century and throughout the eighteenth century, admiration for such an exceptional character never vanished and continued to inspire artists. One must also add that the young prince's education was in the hands of many tutors besides Fénélon: for instance, we know that his military education was entrusted to the Marquis of Puységur, who ardently admired the Macedonian king not only for his victories, but for his strategic and political vision.[26] Clearly, the young Duke of Anjou had developed a double image of Alexander, which was shared by all his contemporaries.

With the exception of the founding of Alexandria,[27] the scenes chosen to decorate the La Granja Gallery were well known and had been depicted many times since the Renaissance, including, in four cases, by Charles Le Brun.[28] It may be more interesting to note that, considered as a whole, the selection of themes is more illustrative of the peace-loving king than of the insatiable conqueror. Indeed, the paintings only include one history-battle subject, intended to exalt royal valour.[29] This picture bears witness to the physical courage and moral vigor of Philip V, which were also praised by one of his courtiers when he referred to the king by the invocation "El Animoso" ("The Spirited One") and compared him to the Macedonian conqueror.[30] Only one other scene is comparable: it depicts the triumphal entry to Babylon. But in this case, despite the virtue admired (VICTORY), the picture is of a scene of peace rather than war (Alexander, victorious on his chariot, is acclaimed by the population); emphasis is uniformly placed on the splendor of the cortege and therefore of the court, which is naturally understood to be an integral part of royal prestige.[31] As for the other virtues, they deal with personal ethics (TEMPERANCE), which is hard to distinguish from political ethics (CLEMENCY; MODESTY; GENEROSITY); they also illustrate obedience to the Holy Books through Alexander's trip to Jerusalem (DEVOUT-NESS) or the long-term vision of a city-builder who, like the kings of modern Europe, was surrounded by architects, masons, and artisans (MAGNIFICENCE). To a certain extent, Philip V and his advisors chose to reject the flaws and vices for which Rollin had condemned Alexander only a few years earlier,[32] opting instead to model the royal virtues on those that Rollin had himself emphasized in the first part of his assessment of Alexander's reign.[33] At the same time, the virtues depicted were those that a Catholic king always had to display.[34]

Return to the Sources

Aside from the perpetuation of the providential and moral history of Alexander the Great, one of the trends in the progression from the seventeenth to the eighteenth century is relatively easy to identify. While it has an impact on views of the Macedonian conquest, it actually concerns every field of historical knowledge. I am referring to the establishment of critical rules through the work of the erudite writers and antiquarian scholars.[35]

It is always delicate, even risky, to indicate a date or an author supposed to initiate a development judged decisive in the history of scholarship and reflection. Nonetheless, for our purposes we will consider that the development of a critical history had been germinating since Pierre Bayle had written on Alexander the Great and his sources in his *Dictionnaire historique et critique*. A master of criticism and indefatigable hunter of mistakes and errors, Bayle never took a specific interest in the history of Alexander, but the Macedonian king is included in the gallery of men and women of antiquity given an entry in the *Dictionnaire*.[36] Bayle explains that he does not intend "to give an abridgment of his life, for . . . there is nothing more known to all sorts of readers than the History of Alexander the Great." The author is obviously referring to the actual narrative of the conquest, as it could be reconstructed from the sources then available. Feigning to be uninterested in those questions previously addressed and apparently well known, Bayle states that his real objective is "to observe all the errors that people committed concerning this conqueror." He applies himself to this with delightful alacrity, claiming all the while that he is not attempting to exhaustively catalog the errors in question. Bayle therefore rejects the biases of history as "teacher of life" (which predated him and would survive him).

The *Dictionnaire*'s articles abound with references and sources, which had already inspired many other works. Beginning in the mid-seventeenth century, several books had opened the path to critical erudition, including Mascardi's *Arte Historica* (1636), La Mothe le Vayer's essay on the ancient historians (1646), and Paganino Gaudenzio's *Alessandro* (1481–1530), which the author dedicated to the eternal memory of the Great Alexander, described as an "initiator of war and promoter of peace." In his *Alessandro,* this protégé of Ferdinand II of Tuscany and professor at the University of Pisa explicitly and extensively examined the comparative value of ancient sources, choosing many of his examples from Quintus Curtius's *History of Alexander.*[37]

Historical works on the military arts are also highly informative here. Contrary to a commonly held idea, admiration for Arrian as a "military historian" is not specific to Sainte-Croix and did not start with him. The reason for this is simple: it is that the Macedonian conquests were regularly presented in reflections on war and in discussions of the unfolding of battles. The elite's interest in the conduct of military operations and the art of command explains why Arrian, of all the ancient writers who discussed Alexander, was the subject of a great number of commentaries by practitioners and theorists of war and maneuvers. While the heroic model was rejected throughout the eighteenth century and wars of conquest were nearly universally condemned, many volumes were published about the art of war. Every author insisted that it was necessary to use examples from antiquity, even if with reservations. In the *Art de la guerre* published posthumously by his son in 1748, the Marquis of Puységur (1655–1734) devotes an opening section to the ancient authors. If a practitioner of war wants to show his contemporaries the lessons they can draw from Alexander's conquests, he has to turn to Arrian, for "one cannot doubt that the author was personally skilled in the art of war." It is also through reading Arrian that Puységur "understands Alexander's design for the conquest of Asia." Charles Guischard (1724–1775) explicitly disagrees with Puységur's opinion that antiquity was the only model to be followed, but nonetheless considers that "the military art of the Ancients will always be the School for good Officers." He naturally also chooses Arrian to illustrate Alexander's campaigns, for he is "an elegant author and a man of war who had Ptolemy's memoirs in hand."

Studies and research on the art of battle and techniques of command played a major part in elevating Arrian over other ancient authors who discussed Alexander's conquests. The Baron de Sainte-Croix, whose own background was in the military profession, was particularly drawn to this aspect of things. In his view, "military science joined with experience must guide the quill of anyone who wants to describe an army's marches and a conqueror's exploits. No one possessed the talents of war to such a high degree as Arrian."

If we expand the perspective beyond the study of marches and battles, one question appears to have stood out above all others, which concerned the relative value to attribute to Arrian's *Anabasis* and *Indica* on the one hand and to Quintus Curtius's *History of Alexander* on the other. In the foreword to a study of the ancient historians (1646), Le Vayer places himself in the tradition of his predecessors, among whom he makes certain to include the illustrious Dutch philologist Vossius (1577–1649). One chapter is devoted to Arrian, another to Quintus Curtius. Le Vayer emphasizes that the geographic detail Arrian provided in *Indica* is superior to anything Quintus Curtius wrote. But his work aims to reach far beyond these remarks. Le Vayer resolutely includes himself in a modernity that heralds Bayle and critical history, which he intends to distinguish from biography. He expresses firm, precise judgments not only on the authors themselves, but on the entire field of history: "A real and legitimate History encompasses far more than the mere narrative of any single person's life," he writes. By describing Quintus Curtius as "a Historian of that great change and shift of the Empire of the Persians into the Empire of the Macedonians," he gives Alexander's conquests a historical significance greater than the man.

In 1729, John Rooke affirms in the preface to his English translation of Arrian that Arrian and Quintus Curtius are the only two authentic ancient historians of Alexander, but that the former "is the best, the truest and the most accurate." Throughout his explanatory notes, Rooke systematically seeks to show that Arrian is superior to Quintus Curtius in every respect. As we have seen, military historians agreed with him. The philosophes were not to be outdone.

Montesquieu, Voltaire, and Their Sources

As noted earlier, several French philosophers devoted in-depth studies and / or reflections to the history of Alexander and its historical significance.[38] In 1748, Montesquieu published *The Spirit of the Laws*. From then on, he would constantly revise it; a new edition based on his notes was published in 1757, two years after his death. Here, several chapters are devoted to the history of Alexander, which is subjected to highly attentive, innovative historical reflection dealing both with the Macedonian king's plans and accomplishments (10.8–14) and his place in the history of commerce (21.8). For his part, Voltaire did not publish any book or chapter specifically devoted to Alexander with the exception of the entry on "Alexander the Great" in his *Dictionnaire philosophique* (*Philosophical Dictionary*). Yet he shared his generally very positive opinion of the Macedonian king as early as 1736 (*Conseils à un journaliste*) and would tirelessly restate it in the same terms until 1776 (*La Bible enfin expliquée*). These laudatory phrases would be widely circulated.

We will have frequent occasion to return to the interpretations and theories developed by these French philosophers, as well as to their influence on the historiography of Alexander in France and Europe. At this point, I will simply consider their sources in relation to works produced and published by erudite writers during the same period. Indeed, Voltaire and to an even greater degree Montesquieu never hesitated to express their opinions on the sources of the history of Alexander and the hierarchy that should be established among them.

While Alexander's name frequently appears in many of his books and opuscules, Voltaire never took a close or specific interest in the Macedonian conquest; as he often stated, history only became truly interesting to him with the great discoveries. To make his point of view clearly understood, he offered his readers an extremely evocative metaphor by which ancient history is contrasted with modern history the way that "old medals [are] compared to everyday currency: the former stay in the cabinets; the latter circulate in the universe for man's commerce." In other words, ancient history is frozen, it belongs to the antiquarian scholars; modern history is alive and transforms before our eyes, it belongs to historians. Of course, Voltaire does admit that ancient history is better known once it begins to center on the relationship between the Greeks and Persians, particularly through the works of Herodotus and Thucydides. Unfortunately, Alexander's period is warped by the ancient authors and those in the modern era who copied them without critical mind or method (*Mensonges imprimés*, 1748).[39] Voltaire was particularly virulent about Quintus Curtius, whom he criticizes throughout chapter 9 (on the era of Alexander) of *Pyrrhonisme dans l'histoire* (1766). Yet he makes few explicit references to Arrian, Plutarch, and Diodorus Siculus. Voltaire obviously knew their books, but did not systematically consult them.

Judging the tales and legends passed down by ancient authors unusable, Voltaire shared his own conclusions about the Macedonian conqueror and proposed a firm direction for historians' reflection: "It is no longer allowable to speak of Alexander, except in order to say something new of him, or to destroy fables, historical, physical, and moral, which have disfigured the history of the only great man to be found among the conquerors of Asia." It was necessary to stick to the essentials: "He built more towns than all the other conquerors of Asia destroyed—[. . .] young as he was, he turned the commerce of the world in a new channel."[40]

For his part, Montesquieu may not have devoted an entire book to Alexander, but unlike Voltaire he was not satisfied with referring to the conqueror without focusing on him in a consistent, well-supported manner. Montesquieu cannot be described as a historian of Alexander in that he never aimed to collect all the available sources and present his readers with a synthesis. Nonetheless, his use of the sources in *The Spirit of the Laws* (1748, 1757) was seriously considered: along with the chapters specifically dealing with the Macedonian conquest (10.13–14), Alexander is also the subject of chapter 8 of book 21, about the history of commerce.[41] Montesquieu confers all the traits of an exceptional and atypical conqueror on the Macedonian, whether it was his well-thought-out strategy, his policy for dealing with the defeated, and his clear vision of the measures required to develop commercial networks.

One cannot overlook Montesquieu's oft-expressed commitment to selecting his sources based on a prior critical analysis. This was true of the chapters on Alexander in *The Spirit of the Laws*. These chapters were notably improved from one edition to the next, while the footnotes became increasingly precise. The many references to Arrian in the chapter on commerce (21.8) alternate with references to Pliny and especially Strabo, whom Montesquieu had quoted in his own reflections (see *Pensées* [*My Thoughts*], no. 2189). And while one of the chapters on the conquest (10.13) only has a single reference to an ancient text (Plutarch's *On the Fortune or the Virtue of Alexander*) in the 1748 edition, the corresponding chapter in the 1757 edition (10.14) includes seven references to the *Anabasis of Alexander*. Montesquieu clearly reconstructed Alexander's entire strategy against Darius and interpreted his policy toward the defeated by reading and following Arrian.[42] At the same time, Montesquieu devoted one of his *Pensées* (no. 2178) to Quintus Curtius, using expressions that reveal the low regard in which he held him as a historical source. Though Montesquieu's preference for Arrian should be seen in the context of a long history of criticism, it must be recognized that in this he was a pioneer.

Simon-Nicolas-Henri Linguet: Philosophy without Erudition

At this point a third author needs to be introduced, a man who was also denounced by Sainte-Croix, but is infinitely less famous than Voltaire and Montesquieu: Simon-Nicolas-Henri Linguet (1736–1794). Linguet wrote the aforementioned *Histoire du Siècle d'Alexandre*, a volume initially published in 1762 and issued in a revised second edition in 1769. It is outside the scope of this volume to provide a detailed biography of such a complex man, both a "philosophe" and an "enemy of the philosophes," "the most retrograde conservative of the eighteenth century" and "one of the most revolutionary thinkers of his time."[43] Linguet led a turbulent life worthy of a novel and produced a diverse and abundant body of work in which the figure of Alexander holds a place that could be referred to as incidental if it did not so powerfully contribute to illustrating an entire side of the Alexander of the Enlightenment. His *Siècle d'Alexandre* should instead be situated in the context of his own reflections and those of his contemporaries on an ancient history from which current events were never truly absent.[44]

Now largely forgotten, Linguet is less known for his *Siècle d'Alexandre* than for his recognized place in the history of political thought in the eighteenth century and for his studies and reflections on despotism (he died on the scaffold in 1794, accused "of having lauded the despots of Vienna and London"). Given this context, it is easy for Linguet's biographers to overlook *Siècle d'Alexandre*. Even a present-day historian might be tempted to quickly write off a volume with such blatant shortcomings. But when considering the historiography of Alexander in the eighteenth century, these misgivings hold little weight against a simple observation: no matter what we think of the author's science and conscience, *Siècle d'Alexandre* was the first book in modern Europe to be devoted not to a narrative of the Macedonian conquests but an analysis of their induced effects on world history. Once Linguet's volume is replaced in its setting and the context of the 1760s, its method, inspiration, and objectives set it apart as a milestone on the path to a new approach of the history of Alexander the Great. Following on from Voltaire, with whom he corresponded, but also from Montesquieu, Linguet was among those in the eighteenth century who reexamined and reevaluated the historical impact of the young Macedonian king's conquests.

Voltaire had an absolutely decisive influence on the genesis and organization of *Siècle d'Alexandre,* inspiring the book's very structure. As made clear by the 1762 title, the actual history of Alexander is only one of several perspectives considered by Linguet. A breakdown of the page count reveals as much. The reign and expeditions are given 78 pages of a total of 341 pages in the 1762 edition and 460 pages in the 1769 edition. Chapters 1–12 (1762) and book 1 (1769) (*Contenant un abrégé de l'histoire ancienne et l'état des différents peuples avant Alexandre [Containing a Summary of Ancient History and the State of the Different Peoples before Alexander]*) form a kind of picture of the known world, to which 78 pages are allotted in 1762 and 120 in 1769. Chapters 18–24 (1762) and books 3 and 4 (1769) provide an overview of the world's political and cultural life and of mores and customs in the period that the author refers to by the highly extensible designation of the "Age of Alexander." Linguet uses these sections to look closely at the governments of Asia (as compared to the Greek governments) and the question of despotism, particularly in the 1769 edition. This is the most developed part of the book, given that it accounts for half the pages in both editions.

In the picture of the known world, Linguet gradually introduces peoples that did not really encounter Alexander or only have a distant relationship to the history of the age of Alexander (ranging from Rome to England). Linguet predicts that readers will "justly" be able to criticize him for "having spoken, in a volume entitled *Le Siècle d'Alexandre,* of many other things that appear to have little to do with [Alexander]." But he explains that in order to measure the extent and nature of the conquests, the result of which was "to finish making all the parts [of the Persian empire] accessible," one needs to understand the state of each of the peoples that composed the empire.

Linguet therefore aims to situate Alexander in a global context. This is one aspect of the modernity of his historical vision. Linguet holds that history cannot merely be explained by the king's personality because the king is also the product of his time (and particularly of the legacy of Athens) and because his victories were also due to internal development in the Persian empire and the countries ruled by Darius. In justifying the space he devotes to considerations and analyses that sometimes only have a peripheral bearing on the history of Alexander, Linguet also seeks to display his originality compared to Voltaire's *Siècle de Louis XIV (Age of Lewis XIV).* As much as Voltaire shined a spotlight on the absolute monarch who ruled over France, he spoke differently of Alexander, who "was only the respected leader of the Greeks who had elected him." As Linguet explains to his readers, it is "less of the conqueror than of the men of his time that [he] propose[d] to give the history." This circular reasoning serves to justify the concision to which the author aspires. Primarily wanting to draw the lessons of history and "put them within easy reach," Linguet seeks to avoid getting bogged down in the details of the conquest itself.[45] He notes that "the details of Alexander's conquests are too well known today for us to endeavor to describe them with an accuracy that would tire without imparting anything new," repeating an argument used by many of his precursors (including Bayle).

Nonetheless, the method quickly runs short, for Linguet never explains his criteria for selecting information. Linguet constantly hammered home that he was contributing entirely new ideas, but like many authors of his time he was parsimonious with references to his reading in preparation for *Siècle d'Alexandre*. Aside from Bossuet and Rollin, "two respectable great men" who are both lauded and contested, and the Abbé Guyon, whose history of empires is cited in the notes and used copiously, Linguet certainly read Montesquieu's chapters on Alexander—though he often disagreed with him on the question of despotism, including in *Siècle d'Alexandre*. He has nothing but contempt for the ancient historians, but never elucidates his position. He merely repeats that they did not provide information regarding what would actually justify research on Alexander, namely "his views, his policy, the art with which he approached making newly subjected peoples love his Empire..... Quintus Curtius is full of epigrams and platitudes. The wise and judicious Plutarch only filled his Life of Alexander with little anecdotes, which are nearly always puerile. . . . The Life of a Conqueror did not appear to be destined to be warped in such a manner."[46] All that is fine and good, but Linguet himself devotes a long Plutarchian passage to Alexander's personality, to his "gentle and sensitive character," and his "soul [full] of humanity and grandeur." He repeats a series of moralizing exempla of the first water, which also provide him with an opportunity to implicitly criticize the heavy financial burden due to the kings' mistresses in his own time: "History has not even passed down the name of any of his mistresses. This is proof that if he had any, at least his passion for them was not onerous to the people."[47] This passage was omitted from the 1769 edition, perhaps because it was deemed mocking of the court at Versailles or disparaging of despotic regimes.

Alexander in the Academy: History and Geography

While commentators, historians, and philosophers expressed their opinions of the king of Macedonia, many erudite writers were also at work on the subject. Most were directly connected to the Académie Royale des Inscriptions et Belles-Lettres, which was founded at Colbert's initiative in 1663 as the Petite Académie and took its permanent name in 1717.[48] Throughout the eighteenth century, the academy sponsored a great deal of research and

publications on Roman history. Greek history in general and the history of
Alexander and the Hellenistic period in particular were not as well represented, with the (notable) exception of Sainte-Croix's volume. Surviving registers reveal only three dissertations on the history of Alexander: only one, by
Secousse, considers the expedition as a whole, but in an extremely conventional manner; a second, by Bougainville, deals with a passage from Plutarch's
Life of Alexander and the third, by Sevin, with the life and work of Callisthenes, Aristotle's nephew. In 1752, Bougainville also published a highly
rhetorical comparison of Alexander and Thamas Kouli-Khan (Nadir Shah),
whose usurpation and expedition against Delhi were abundantly recounted
by Voltaire in his *Essai sur les mœurs* (chaps. 93–94). It is apparent that at a
time when works of history remained in the hands of distinguished amateurs, none devoted all their efforts or thinking to the history of Alexander.
In most cases, it remains unclear why a writer suddenly proposed a dissertation on a given subject. There is nothing comparable here to the dissertations
prepared in German, Swedish, and Dutch universities, both in quantitative
and qualitative terms.

The subject of the 1769–1770 competition was therefore probably due
to an effort to encourage reflection on a subject relatively neglected by the
academy. Yet while the title of the 1770–1772 prize was unprecedented, it
was not the first time that the academicians had been inspired to make the
period initiated by Alexander's conquests the subject of the annual competition. Ten years earlier, in 1759, the subject had been: "What was the extent
of Egyptian navigation and trade under the Ptolemies?" Admittedly, this
competition was not specifically devoted to the history of Alexander, but as
the winner Abbé Ameilhon explained in his preface, he made certain to discuss prior developments.[49] One has to go even further back, to 1734, to find a
mention of a competition focused on Alexander the Great and his time. The
subject was: "How far had the Ancients developed their Geographic knowledge by Alexander's death?" Each of the candidates opted for a very general
and often imprecise approach, dealing with the entirety of the Greeks' geographic and cartographic knowledge, from the origins of Greece "to the
death of Alexander" and from Albion to the Indies, sometimes even going
all the way back to Moses. None sought to innovate by attempting a critical
analysis of the sources consulted.

Yet it would be inaccurate to allow this basic presentation to suggest that
research on ancient geography—and particularly the geography of Alexan-

der's conquests—remained in its infancy. To attest to this, we must momentarily leave the Académie Royale des Inscriptions et Belles-Lettres and turn to the work presented at the Académie Royale des Sciences. Founded in 1666 by Colbert (who invited the illustrious Cassini to join in 1669) and reformed in 1699, this academy heard presentations and published dissertations bearing on every aspect of the sciences (mathematics, physics, chemistry, anatomy, botany, etc.). Many dissertations were also explicitly categorized under the heading of "Geography"—no less than thirty-four from 1666 to 1720. Geography and navigation, which were closely linked to the fast-growing field of astronomy, belonged to the sciences rather than the arts, as is so clearly expressed in the introduction to the *Histoire de l'Académie* published in 1699: "The Art of navigation . . . relies on Astronomy by necessity, and Astronomy can never be pushed too far for Navigation's good" (p. viii).

It fell to the astronomer Jean-Dominique Cassini (1625–1712) to be among the first to stress the importance of the information provided by the narrators of the expeditions of Alexander, who was himself considered to have been possessed by "the passion for new discoveries." Cassini made his point in a dissertation on the history of astronomy ("invented at the dawn of the World") and its links with geography, navigation, and commerce, as well as the "propagation of Faith."[50] The passage is worth quoting in its entirety for what it tells us about the state of reflection at the end of the seventeenth century:

The precise descriptions that Alexander took care to have made of his conquests gave Geography a far more precise form. He wanted these descriptions to be worked on, not only through estimating the path, as had previously been the practice, but even through the actual measurement and observation of the stars; and he had Callisthenes follow him to make these observations. Having had this opportunity to go to Babylon, Callisthenes found astronomical observations there that the Babylonians had made over the course of one thousand nine hundred and three years, and he sent them to Aristotle.

Pliny has passed down the measurements that Alexander ordered Diognetus and Baeton to take,[51] distances of the cities and rivers of Asia, from the Caspian Gates to the Indian Sea; and also the observations Onesicritus and Nearchus made aboard the fleet he expressly gave them to go reconnoiter the coasts of the Indian Sea and the Persian Gulf. They estimated the distances not only by estimating the paths but also by the actual measurement of the stages of their journey, when that was possible; failing the actual measurement, through the observation of the stars etc. (*Œuvres diverses*, pp. 13–14)

Scholars could no longer conceive of carrying out historical research without a knowledge of geography, which in the words of the famous Lenglet-Dufresnoy, is one of those "sciences that must precede the study of history."[52]

Evaluating the measurements used by the ancient authors became the essential issue to be tackled by geographers and cartographers, who had to do so by making the most of astronomical observations. Guillaume Delisle (1675–1726), one of the founders of modern cartography, addressed the problem several times at the Académie Royale des Sciences. It fell to the researcher he had trained in geography, Philippe Buache (1700–1773) to present to the academy the findings Delisle had already established, accompanied by his own remarks. Both Delisle's findings and Buache's remarks were based on a combination of the ancient texts, modern travelers' accounts, and astronomical observations. Their work led to the publication of the first scientific map of Alexander's expeditions in 1731.[53]

Along with the Englishman James Rennell (1742–1830), Jean-Baptiste Bourguignon d'Anville (1697–1782) was the most famous European geographer of his time.[54] As a member of both academies, d'Anville is the link between the Académie Royale des Inscriptions et Belles-Lettres and the Académie Royale des Sciences. He published many scholarly articles about the ancients' measurements and geography in the compendiums of the Académie Royale des Inscriptions et Belles-Lettres, in which other literary academicians presented their research on related subjects. Close to twenty-five titles (of which seven are by d'Anville) are listed under the entry for "History / Geography / Measurements and geographic maps" in the *Table des mémoires de l'Académie*. D'Anville did not fail to address the sources that were used to reconstruct Alexander's marches. He considers Arrian "without a doubt the most judicious of the historians we have had on Alexander's expedition and the most credible" because he drew from the memoirs of Nearchus, Alexander's admiral. D'Anville provides a map of Alexander's empire (1740), which was later given a very positive evaluation by another geographer, Jean-Denis Barbié du Bocage (1760–1825).[55]

The introduction to one of d'Anville's dissertations contains statements on the consequences of the Macedonian conquest that were on the whole already banal, such as: "Alexander's expedition, which pushed his conquests to the borders of Scythia and all the way to India, gave the Greeks positive knowledge of several regions far distant from their country. This conqueror was followed by two engineers, Diognetus and Baeton, who were charged with measuring his marches etc."[56] The same phrases can be spotted in the work of Robert de Vaugondy in 1750,[57] then in the prolific Mentelle's *Encyclopédie méthodique* in 1787 (pp. iv–xiv), as well as in the *History of the Rise and Progress of Geography* (1787) by John Blair.

Between Divine Providence, Sacred Geography, and History of Commerce

In the name of the monarchic values of the time, Rollin passes severe judgment on Alexander: "He ought to have fulfilled the several duties of the sovereignty. . . . To be the father, the guardian and shepherd of his people; to govern them by good laws; to make their trade, both by sea and land, flourish, etc."[58] His tone changes singularly in some of the chapters later devoted to "the history of arts and sciences and of the persons who have eminently distinguished themselves by them."[59] In the chapter on geography (19.2.1), Alexander appears as a "positive hero." Duplicating an essay by the geographer d'Anville word for word, Rollin emphasizes that "Alexander's expedition . . . opened to the Greeks a positive knowledge of many countries very remote from their own."[60] The contrast is even more striking in chapter 2 of book 24, which is devoted to the history of commerce and finds Rollin writing that "the taking of Tyre by Alexander the Great and the founding of Alexandria, which soon followed, occasioned a great revolution in the affairs of commerce."[61] Due to his systematic recourse to nonselective compilation and the fact that the book was written over several years, Rollin did not see fit to match up the two Alexanders alternately encountered by the reader depending on whether he was reading book 14 or 15. In fact, Rollin was probably never aware of what a historian today would easily describe as an internal contradiction. His negative assessment of the conquest in book 15 was perfectly in keeping with what was then the common idea that the conquest brought a distinct and undeniable change to the Macedonian king's way of exercising power, both over his own people and the conquered populations; in the context of history as "teacher of life," this change had to be described and denounced as disastrous when addressing young people. At the same time (though the author never makes the connection with the narrative chapters), the taking of Tyre and the founding of Alexandria represent a major commercial revolution, in the positive sense of the term.

Another notable example is John Gast. Following Rollin's lead, he develops the idea that Alexander "doubtless was in the hand of Providence, for executing the vengeance on Babylon and her dependent provinces . . . which the Almighty had, by his prophets, denounced against them." But, in a sign of the times, Gast is also able to deftly include human action, since according to him Alexander "opened a more free communication between the eastern and the western worlds, in order to the gracious purposes of eternal wisdom." The source cited in support was a very well-known exegete of Isaiah, Bishop Lowth. As we can see, Gast combined biblical exegesis and the history of commerce to show Alexander's reopening of Babylonian commerce as another manifestation of Divine Providence.[62]

Rollin, Lowth, and Gast had in common that they all consulted and drew on Pierre-Daniel Huet's *Histoire du commerce et de la navigation des Anciens*. This book was first published in 1716 in Paris when its author was eighty-six, then reprinted the same year and again in 1729 (both in Paris) and in 1763 (in Lyon); it was translated into English in 1717. Born in 1630, Huet was one of the most learned of the learned men of the French seventeenth century. A fierce supporter of the ancients against Perrault, he won royal protection for the Caen Academy. After having held even greater hopes, he was appointed subpreceptor to the Dauphin (in 1670, under Bossuet), joint editor of the *Ad usum Delphini* series, member of the Académie Française, abbot of Aulnay (in 1674), bishop of Avranches (in 1685), and titular bishop of Fontenay (in 1692). In 1700, he retired to the Jesuit House in Paris, where he died in January 1721.[63]

We will have several occasions to return to the *Histoire du commerce*, which had an exceptional audience throughout the eighteenth century and even far beyond.[64] I will simply point out that in the foreword (not included in the English edition), the publisher mentions that the book dates from long before 1716; he speaks of it as a "product of youth" "snatched" from Huet by his friends. In fact, Huet's correspondence proves that he was delighted by this initiative and was awaiting the publication of his book with tremendous impatience. The book's commercial success encouraged him to put his

HISTOIRE SOMMAIRE
DU COMMERCE
ET DE LA NAVIGATION DES ANCIENS.
A MONSIEUR COLBERT
Ministre d'Estat.

6. Opening page of the manuscript of the report by Pierre-Daniel Huet, *Histoire sommaire du commerce et de la navigation des Anciens, à Monsieur Colbert, Ministre d'Estat,* 1667, MS, BnF, Suppl. fr. 5307. Bibliothèque Nationale de France, Paris.

name on the following edition. The preface, which was written as a letter addressed to Colbert, indicates that despite the research Huet was at work on (on Origen), he had been obliged to comply with a request for a report on the future book's subject from the "Inspector and Super-Intendant General of the Commerce and Navigation of this Kingdom." The report's exact date is mentioned (October 1667) at the end of a Huet manuscript in the collections of the Bibliothèque Nationale.[65]

The least one can say is that Huet embarked on what he considered a chore with a great deal of reticence. He therefore chose to refer to the 1667 final report as "summary" (the qualifier was removed in 1716, undoubtedly for commercial reasons, while the countless cumbersome notes, references, and quotes covering the back of nearly every manuscript page were also excised). It should also be added that Huet did not revise the text, which mentioned writings published between 1667 and 1716 as future publications. As for his conclusion, it mostly bears evidence to the weariness of a report-writer in a rush to finish and return to his book on Origen (which he published in 1668).[66]

Huet was able to fulfill the minister's commission because he had a profound knowledge of Greco-Latin literature, but also because he had given himself a solid education as an Orientalist; under the supervision of his teacher Bochart (with whom he would soon fall out and break all ties), he had become one of the recognized specialists in sacred geography—a discipline that sought to match biblical sites and episodes with known areas. Huet had also studied the issues of hydrography and water circulation. It was as a biblical scholar that he later published two books announced in his 1667 report. In 1692, his *Solomon's Navigations* (in Latin) attempted to prove that Africa had been circumnavigated long before the Portuguese discoveries; this volume was in the same line of research as his *Traité de la situation du Paradis terrestre* (1691), which was soon translated into English (*Situation of Paradise,* 1694). Here, for the first time in a book intended for public consumption, Huet took up the question of Persian navigation and the changes in navigation and commerce due to Alexander. Seeking to prove (against many naysayers) that Earthly Paradise had been located in Lower Babylonia, near the Shatt al-Arab, he tried to demonstrate that his commentary on Genesis was consistent with the configuration of the lands and seas "known" in antediluvian times. To reconstruct such an ancient landscape, he had to painstakingly describe the various transformations it had under-

gone due to the extensive work carried out by kings and other men. This
was the context in which he introduced the question of the "falls and cataracts" built by the Persians on the Babylonian rivers and later destroyed by
Alexander. This first direct allusion to an episode in the history of Alexander,
inspired by Huet's reading of the ancient authors (Strabo and Arrian), would
for three centuries play an essential part in discussions of the positive and
negative consequences of the Macedonian conquests.[67]

In the 1716 volume, the Macedonian king is introduced in chapter 11 ("The
Sea-Commerce of the Ancient Persians") and his decisions are detailed in
chapter 17, which is structured as follows:

> 1. The Conquests of Alexander makes [sic] many Changes in Commerce.
> 2. Tyre destroy'd by Alexander. 3. Who lays the Foundation of Alexandria.
> 4. And thereby disposes the Indian Seas to commerce. 5. He prepares to
> make War against the Arabians. 6. He forms vast Designs for an universal
> Monarchy. (*History of Commerce* [1717], p. 57)

Huet's phrase "great revolution in all affairs of commerce" was repeated
verbatim by Rollin in chapter 2 of book 24 of his *Histoire ancienne*.[68] As for
Lowth and Gast, they borrowed Huet's argument on the hydraulic works
carried out by Alexander in Babylonia, explicitly citing him. But both the
scholarly Lowth and the popularizing historians Rollin and Gast took these
episodes out of the purely secular context of Huet's *Histoire du commerce* and
reinterpreted them in the context of providential history. We will see that
thirty years later, in 1748, Montesquieu would put Huet's argument to his
own use in book 21 of *The Spirit of the Laws*.

Chapter 2

Alexander in Europe

Erudition and History

Sainte-Croix and the Critical Inquiry into the Life of Alexander the Great by the Ancient Historians (1771–1810)

Thus when the Académie Royale des Inscriptions et Belles-Lettres debated the subject of the Easter 1770 Competition in November 1769, the subject of "Alexander the Great" was neither exotic nor ignored. Baron de Sainte-Croix and his competitors had access to what was already an impressive mass of information and commentaries on which to base their own research—including in the form of secondhand but copious reflections in the "antique" articles of the *Encyclopédie, ou dictionnaire raisonné des sciences, des arts et des métiers* (1751–1765).[1] While Sainte-Croix was able to make repeated and explicit critical use of the erudite knowledge accumulated since the sixteenth century, he proved infinitely less receptive to the interpretations of those known as the philosophes or philosopher-historians: he either openly contested them or, more frequently, simply did not know about them or chose not to mention them. This observation raises many questions about the author's conception of his work and his relationships with the major intellectual and political trends of his time, from his first manuscript (1771) to the final edition (1804). We will follow reactions to this publication until 1810, when the author's friends submitted the recently reprinted book for a Decennial prize (Sainte-Croix had died in March 1809 following a cruel illness).[2]

Guillaume-Emmanuel-Joseph Guilhem de Clermont-Lodève de Sainte-Croix was born in 1747 in Mormoiron, in a province under the pope's authority, to a very old noble family. He served in the army and navy under his uncle's orders before fully devoting himself to his passion for studying and library research. He collaborated with two remarkable scholars of antiquity from the South of France, Jean-François Séguier (1703–1784) and Esprit-Claude Calvet (1728–1810). It was probably Calvet who suggested that Sainte-Croix take up the history of Alexander with a view to entering the academy competition.[3] Sainte-Croix quickly published a book based on his first dissertation, *Examen critique des anciens historiens d'Alexandre-le-Grand*. The volume appeared in 1775 under the same title as the dissertation, with no author credit.

Sainte-Croix continued publishing dozens of essays throughout his long career, winning two prizes in succession (1775, 1777). These two essays on subjects of ancient religion served as the basis for his book about the mysteries of paganism (*Mystères du Paganisme*, 1784). At a mere thirty-one, he was elected to the academy in 1777 as a foreign associate. While ancient history and literature take the lion's share of his bibliography, his body of work also includes many studies of geography,[4] as well as papers on the history of his time such as a 1780 study on the Treaty of Paris of 1763. In 1779, he published reflections on the relationship between England and its rebellious American colonies—a book in which he openly compares ancient and modern colonies. He returned to the subject of England in 1782 with a study of the development of British naval power.[5]

Despite the diversity of his work and the advent of the French Revolution, which had disastrous consequences for him, Sainte-Croix never stopped adding to his findings on Alexander. He returned to his book on Alexander and published a new edition with Delance et Lesueur in 1804. While the 1771 manuscript had been a modest 56 pages, the 1804 was an enormous quarto close to 1,000 pages long; it had nearly tripled in size since the first printed version of 1775. Sainte-Croix underlined its novelty: "Everything that appeared erroneous or defective to me has been rectified; barely a few pages have been kept in their entirety; thus what I am publishing today is less a new edition than a new book on the same subject."

A quick inspection of the three editions confirms both the consistency of the themes addressed and that they were treated with increasing depth.[6] Sainte-Croix aimed to carry out a detailed study of the ancient authors responsible for our knowledge of Alexander and his expedition, consequently establishing the value of individual authors relative to other authors and the entire body of sources. In this regard, his evaluation never

EXAMEN CRITIQUE

DES ANCIENS

HISTORIENS

D'ALEXANDRE-LE-GRAND.

A PARIS,

Chez Dessain *Junior*, Libraire, rue Gît-le-Cœur.

M. DCC. LXXV.

AVEC APPROBATION ET PRIVILÉGE DU ROI.

7–8. Title pages of the 1775 and 1804 editions of *Examen critique des anciens historiens d'Alexandre le Grand* by the Baron de Sainte-Croix.

EXAMEN CRITIQUE

DES

ANCIENS HISTORIENS

D'ALEXANDRE-LE-GRAND.

SECONDE ÉDITION

CONSIDÉRABLEMENT AUGMENTÉE.

ΑΠΟΣΚΟΤΗΣΟΝ ΜΟΥ

PARIS,

DE L'IMPRIMERIE DE DELANCE ET LESUEUR.

AN XIII. — 1804.

changed: "Despite his flaws and prejudices, Arrian deserves to be in the front rank of the surviving historians of Alexander. He nearly always outweighs the others in matters of military operations, which are only complete in his book and were only able to be told by him" (1804, p. 102). The latter sentence serves as a transition to a very critical discussion of Quintus Curtius, whose "ignorance in tactics often makes him unintelligible in

descriptions of battles, in which he makes many inexcusable mistakes."
Sainte-Croix also has significant reservations about Plutarch, "who only
gathers facts to give lessons." He is particularly critical of Plutarch's two
discourses *On the Fortune or the Virtue of Alexander.* He cannot hide his determined opposition to Plutarch's thesis in the discourses. While he accepts
that "the civilization of mankind [made] great progress under the reign of
Augustus," he refuses to agree with Plutarch "that the [Macedonian] conqueror had no other ambition than to propagate philosophy everywhere."[7]
According to Sainte-Croix, this is mere "[invented] reverie, either to please his
companions or to practice the art of writing and become famous." In saying
this, Sainte-Croix was taking a clear position in a spirited European debate on
the consequences of Alexander's conquest and more generally on potential
views of European overseas conquests in Africa, Asia, and America since
the Greek and Roman eras.[8]

These questions about sources are very present throughout the geographic inquiry in which the author always took a lively interest. From
1771 to 1804, long passages of the *Examen critique* were devoted to geographic knowledge in Alexander's era, the contribution of travelers, geographers, and cartographers of the time, and the comprehension and
reconstruction of itineraries. The chapter covering this area in the 1804
edition provides a highly elaborate synthesis of research and discoveries
in the modern era.

While Sainte-Croix recognizes his predecessors' merits, he asserts the
originality of his own research. In the 1775 preface, he states that "the history
of Alexander nonetheless appears to have been neglected." He denounces
both the "commentators" and those who spread contempt for erudition. He
proclaims that the erudite writer is never driven by the principle of pleasure,
but must constantly be possessed with a sense of duty and seriousness. In
the 1804 edition, he even describes the historian's work as a kind of genuine
asceticism, to which only a rare few can devote themselves. The erudite
writer feels all the more lonely given that, according to the reviewer of another work by Sainte-Croix, "a work of erudition is an odd phenomenon at a
time when we only dream of politics and we only want to read novels."[9]

Sainte-Croix constantly states that the "impartial reader" must be informed of the historian's methods and sources at every step. This explains
the decisive importance of footnotes; as Sainte-Croix puts it, "[without] citations, the discussion of the facts can have no solidity; and a work of erudi-

tion deprived of this support is without value" (1804, p. iv). It is also worth noting one of his arguments in defense of the *Voyage du jeune Anacharsis* published in 1787 by his friend the Abbé Barthélemy,[10] whom several critics had criticized for publishing a volume unworthy of an erudite writer: "[The notes] rule out any idea of fiction and provide an easy means of verification."[11] Footnotes were already present in Sainte-Croix's 1771 manuscript (about ten per page), but were enhanced for the 1775 edition and supplemented by longer notes referenced in the text and printed at the end of the volume, following a method developed by Scottish historian William Robertson in his *History of Scotland* (1759) and later works. By the 1804 edition, the number of footnotes had multiplied and the original footnotes were considerably expanded.

As Anthony Grafton's fascinating research has highlighted, reflection on this exuberant infrapaginal appendix was intense throughout the eighteenth century, the period during which this two-tier technique for displaying information was developed.[12] Ameilhon, Sainte Croix's fellow laureate of the academy for his *Le Commerce et la navigation des Egyptiens* (1766), justifies the use of footnotes and endnotes as short treatises. He was aware that he had to defend himself from potential criticism by readers reluctant to embrace erudition and citations in Greek and Latin. He considered it his duty to offer proof of his assertions, especially to "that Class of Readers who only like to give their trust with solid backing" (pp. xxii–xxiii).

Ameilhon was not mistaken to insist on this. A few years earlier (1762), the philosopher-historian Linguet had expressed the opposite opinion in the offhand, provocative tone he was known for: "I did not make any citations, and I included as few remarks as possible. I have often felt that that multitude of names with which one fluffs up the bottom of pages, those accumulated notes, are obstacles for readers and cause them real difficulty. Moreover, I can easily indicate here the Authors whom I used. They are Herodotus, Quintus Curtius, Plutarch, Arrian, Athenaeus, Pliny, and the moderns who copied them" (pp. xiv–xv). At about the same time, Oliver Goldsmith affirmed in the introduction to his *History of the World* commissioned for a fee of three guineas that he was wary of "the obscure erudition and scholastic conjecture" and did not hesitate to speak out against "the late, and we may add, gothic practice of using a multiplicity of notes"; instead, he pleaded for a form of history that repudiated dry erudition and was both digestible and "entertaining."[13]

What Is a Philosopher Historian?

At the same time, the baron's relationship to the history of Alexander was never defined in a clear-cut manner and thus remains difficult to establish. In the 1775 edition, he considers that philosophy and erudition are not contradictory and that "the deepest knowledge is not incompatible with the philosophical spirit" (p. v). But as he himself admitted, though his book was based on precise, flawless scholarship, it was no more than a preliminary study and his footnotes were merely "the indication of all the surviving materials from which one could compose a new life of Alexander." However, he did not plan on writing this history of Alexander himself. If many of Sainte-Croix's colleagues at the Académie Royale des Inscriptions et Belles-Lettres presented a defense of his method, it was because it was a sensitive question. After the scholar's death in 1809, the *Classe d'Histoire et de Littérature ancienne* submitted his work for a Decennial prize created at Napoleon's initiative—the emperor wanted to reward the greatest scholars and authors in all fields of knowledge every ten years on the anniversary of the coup of 18 Brumaire.[14] One of these prizes was designed to distinguish "the author of the best work of Literature that will combine at the highest level the novelty of ideas, talent in composition, and elegance of style." The jury awarded its prize to Sainte-Croix, but expressed notable reservations in its decision, mentioning in particular that it hoped that in future "a wise mind and a good reader will devote himself to giving [the subject] a historical form, by distinguishing the presentation of the facts from anything on the order of discussion and critical analysis. Such a work is lacking from all the literatures in the world."[15] The jury's choice was sharply contested, particularly by the representatives of the *Classe de Langue et Littérature française*, who issued a unanimous protest written by Marie-Joseph Chénier (1764–1811): Sainte-Croix would have done better "to write a well-reasoned history of Alexander and his century. Here, chronological and geographical notions would have merged and found a place; here, one should have found what one vainly looks for in this work: a report on the state of letters, sciences, and arts in that memorable era."[16]

These debates were undoubtedly informed by political and personal tensions. Controversy was especially decisive in shaping reflection on what Arnaldo Momigliano interpreted as "the 18th century conflict between the old-fashioned historical method of the 'érudits' and the new-fangled approach of the philosopher historians. . . . While the 'érudits' took pride in lengthy notes, the philosopher historians seldom set out their evidence and aimed at being readable." While Sainte-Croix and Edward Gibbon (1737–1794) made similar use of the footnote, the French scholar's objectives and method were otherwise just the opposite of his English contemporary's, which are so ably analyzed by Momigliano based on *The Decline and Fall of the Roman Empire*. According to Momigliano, Gibbon wanted to reconcile erudition and philosophic spirit; his originality lay in that "[he offered] the treasures of erudition to the contemplation of the philosopher historian. By doing so, he unexpectedly reconciled two methods of writing history which so far had seemed to be inevitably opposed." Thanks to him, "philosophic history ceased to be approximate and arbitrary and was submitted to the traditional rules of historical criticism."[17]

Expressed in extremely similar terms, this debate was not unfamiliar to observers and analysts in Sainte-Croix's time. To be convinced of it, one need only look at the reactions set off in England by the publication in 1818 of volume 5 of William Mitford's *History of Greece,* which was devoted to the history of Alexander.[18] The book is purely narrative, taking a highly conventional approach that follows Alexander year after year, campaign after campaign, but ends abruptly with a long quote from Arrian's funeral oration for the Macedonian king. Its anonymous reviewer for the *Quarterly Review* (vol. 25 [1821]) exposed his idea of what a philosophical history should be in twenty dense and highly critical pages. Mitford "is certainly not the least in merit amongst the modern compilers of Grecian annals" but nothing more: "He confines himself entirely to a narration of the actions of men, he gives us a recital of what they did, but never informs us how they thought. . . . He seems to imagine that the sole business of history is to narrate the prominent and obvious deeds of public men, and that the whole annals of our race are comprised in the achievements of conquerors and the intrigues of the statesmen." Consequently—according to the reviewer—"in the higher faculties and accomplishments of an historian . . . he is . . . singularly deficient. In his writings we find no trace of that philosophical comprehension which can seize remote allusions and disjointed facts, and combine them into irresistible proof or powerful illustration." Representing the opposite of what a "philosophical historian" aims to achieve, the volume is as incomplete as would be a history of France limited to the details of Bonaparte's Russian campaign. The reviewer continues to say that, all things considered, Mitford should have chosen a more limited and consequently more accurate title such as *A Narrative of Alexander's Conquest in Asia*. Referring to chapter 55 and its description of Nearchus's voyage to the Persian Gulf (in which "Mr. Mitford almost entirely follows Dr. Vincent"), the reviewer shares his annoyance at the author's penchant for limiting his account to a list of geographic locations instead of offering "general views or philosophical reflections" and regretfully muses, "How different would the story have been in the hands of such an historian as Gibbon!"

However, another English reviewer (also anonymous) saw Mitford as "assuredly one of the most philosophical of historians." His point of reference was the same: volume 5 of Mitford's *History of Greece* "is by far the first historical work which has been produced in England since Gibbon."[19] But the contradiction is only an appearance. The review's author has chosen not to deal with the narrative history of Alexander (he refers his readers to a future issue of the journal). Instead, he focuses on Mitford's discussion of the constitution of ancient Macedon under Philip and Alexander in comparison with the political situation of other Greek kingdoms and city-states and European constitutional monarchies.[20] Mitford is praised for his ability to organize a dialogue between past and present and for evaluating ancient kingdoms and republics in the light of experience from the world he himself inhabits. In so doing, according to our reviewer, Mitford reasons and acts as a "philosophical historian."

In both reviews, the term "philosophical historian" describes converging appreciations: a real historian is defined not by the accumulation of narrative details but by the intelligence of his analysis, however "speculative." Similarly, when the young Anquetil Duperron, preparing to embark for India in February 1755 on a search for rare manuscripts, exclaims, "A ship seen philosophically is an interesting thing," he merely wants to tell his readers that he does not intend to describe the ship's technical characteristics, but rather to introduce them to the diverse population that would take up residence there for the length of the crossing: "All the social stations find themselves gathered here and form a little world."[21]

Far from the ideal of the historian embodied by Gibbon, Sainte-Croix chose instead to stick to the asceticism of the critic. In the 1804 edition, he seems perfectly happy to have produced a work of erudition and is convinced that his footnotes "contain an indication of all the surviving materials from which one could compose a new life of Alexander" (p. iv). But he never ventured to write this life of Alexander. Though he was not a stranger to "the philosophical spirit," he was wary of "philosophism," which was identified with "bel-esprit" and described as the enemy of erudition.[22] He considered his primary duty to make explicit and clarify all the methodological problems related to the identification and use of the sources, and not to discourse on "the causes of the expansion and decline of Empires." This position of principle (which is sometimes also a pose) allowed him to bluntly criticize those whom he deemed little concerned with the erudite writer's work and who dared to propose cavalier views on the history of Alexander.

Sainte-Croix and the Alexander of the Philosophes

Among those he denounced, Baron de Sainte-Croix especially targeted the thinkers whom we know as the philosophes, with a particular focus on those who had given their opinion on Alexander, namely Voltaire, Linguet, and Montesquieu—though when it came to the latter, Sainte-Croix was often respectful and deferential. Voltaire's conception of history and sources was in absolute contradiction with Sainte-Croix's staunchest beliefs. The primacy given modern history by the philosophe contravened the erudite writer's basic principles. Recall the declaration that opens the 1804 *Examen critique*: "Ancient history presents the beginning, progress, and end of Nations, Empires, Republics; it allows one to easily grasp the succession from causes to effects; the picture is finished; there is nothing more to add. On the other hand, modern history is incomplete. . . . It only allows us to confusedly glimpse the latest result of the great events preparing revolutions and the repercussions of those revolutions that finish changing the face of the Universe etc." Sainte-Croix clearly expresses his certainty that his approach is superior, explaining that because of the distance established between observer and object only the historian of antiquity can claim the necessary impartiality and thus the ability "to form the upstanding tribunal of Posterity." Silvestre de Sacy would insistently return to this notion in his vigorous defense of the 1804 *Examen critique*. De Sacy aimed to show that a history prize should not go to an essay in modern history, but should honor "a work [like the *Examen critique*], for . . . the author had at his disposal all the materials that could be put to use to write it and time and new discoveries cannot add anything to it."[23]

Naturally, Sainte-Croix could only condemn the praise of "incredulity . . . the basis of all wisdom, according to Aristotle. This maxim is very good for anyone who reads history, and especially ancient history" (*Histoire de Charles XII*, 1748, preface). The baron also called upon Aristotle's authority in stating "that only the penetrating eye of criticism can separate fact from fiction and reconcile different narratives." Plausibility cannot be ruled out under the pretext that it represents error, for "not only is the truth not always plausible, but what seems to have the characteristics of the implausible is often very true!"[24]

In one passage from the 1771 *Examen critique*, Voltaire and Linguet are denounced in the same way. Linguet is easily identifiable among those whom Sainte-Croix pilloried as "real Hams of Literature, [who] move every which way to attract the attention of the multitude." It is perfectly clear why Sainte-Croix grouped Linguet with Voltaire as objects of scorn. His rejection of the footnote, contempt for research on chronology and historical geography, and open adherence to Pyrrhonism—in short, everything about *Histoire du Siècle d'Alexandre*—seemed designed to irritate and scandalize Sainte-Croix. Not only did Linguet lack any of the recognized virtues of the authentic erudite writer, but he portrayed himself as a resolute opponent of erudition. It is therefore easy to understand that he was criticized side by side with Voltaire in the *Examen critique*, first in the 1771 manuscript, then in an anonymous but transparent guise in the 1775 edition (pp. 18–19). In another passage, Sainte-Croix hits out at "a Writer of our day and age [who], famous for his productivity and his paradoxes, criticizes the narrative of Alexander's Historians" (p. 249): once again, he is referring to Linguet. Following in Voltaire's footsteps, Linguet contradicted Quintus Curtius's claim that the Greeks and Macedonians discovered the phenomenon of tides upon arriving in the Indus River Delta. Voltaire believed they had learned about tides long before.[25]

At the same time, it is noteworthy that Voltaire's contribution is practically never included in the analyses published by Sainte-Croix. Admittedly, the eighteenth-century method of citation is not the same as ours and Sainte-Croix sometimes refuted Voltaire without explicitly referring to him.[26] Rather than citing Voltaire, Sainte-Croix targeted Linguet when he joined in the debates that had actually been started by Voltaire and which Linguet drew on nearly word for word. Similarly, while Voltaire's views on the founding of cities or the expansion of commerce are diametrically opposed to his own, Sainte-Croix never explicitly takes him to task on these subjects.

It is *The Spirit of the Laws* that Sainte-Croix cites and contests when he wants to deny that Alexander ever had far-reaching policies on urbanization, colonization, and the extension of commercial relations.

From one edition to the next, Sainte-Croix makes fewer explicit references to *The Spirit of the Laws* and increasingly emphasizes his disagreements with Montesquieu's interpretation of the history of Alexander.[27] One of the major disagreements is over the conclusion of chapter 14 of book 10 of *The Spirit of the Laws,* in which Montesquieu exonerates Alexander of all the accusations weighing against him. Regarding the destruction of Persepolis and the murder of Cleitus, Montesquieu turns the charges to Alexander's favor on the grounds of the remorse he expressed in both cases and in light of Arrian's interpretation in his funeral oration for Alexander at the end of the *Anabasis.*[28] Montesquieu's absolution of Alexander for the murder (or execution) of Cleitus is violently contested by Sainte-Croix, as it had been by Mably.[29] It was also after reading Arrian that Montesquieu praised Alexander for "his own frugality and his own economy" (10.14), using words and expressions reminiscent of what he wrote elsewhere (21.18) regarding Charlemagne's economy in managing his house. This did not fail to elicit another scandalized counterattack from Sainte-Croix, directed both at Arrian and Montesquieu's use of him. Sainte-Croix wonders "how this judicious writer could have suggested that Alexander found the means to increase his power through frugality and his particular economy." He concedes that this might have been true before Issus (1775, pp. 139–140) or before Gaugamela (1804, p. 379), but that later "the conqueror of Asia was contemptuous of the customs of his homeland and gave in to all the Asian splendor." On this point, Sainte-Croix is once again in agreement with Mably, who also admired Charlemagne's economy and could not have been more critical of the Asian luxury of the man who defeated Darius.[30]

The History of Alexander in the Revolution: Sainte-Croix and Alexander's Journey to Jerusalem (1775–1804)

Despite his fundamental differences with Voltaire, Sainte-Croix occasionally shared the main thrust of some of his interpretations—without ever citing his (unavowed) adversary. This was the case with the subject of Alexander's visit to Jerusalem, which had already been discussed by Bayle and played a strategic role in the process of inserting the epic of Alexander in the heart of providential history for Bossuet, Rollin, and many other thinkers. As such, this question was one of the most intensely debated both in the contexts of secular and sacred history and in the relationship between the two. From a methodological perspective, the problem can be formulated simply: Was the silence of the classical authors sufficient to deny that Alexander's visit to Jerusalem, as described by Flavius Josephus, had ever taken place?

The question was addressed several times by Voltaire, who had criticized Flavius Josephus in works prior to 1775, including the entry on "Alexander" in *Questions sur l'Encyclopédie* (*Questions on the Encyclopedia*) (1771) and chapter 46 of the introduction to the *Essai sur les mœurs* (1753). His theory is perfectly encapsulated by the title he chose for the chapter in question: "On a Lie Told by Flavius Josephus regarding Alexander and the Jews." Voltaire does not for a moment believe that Alexander could decipher the Hebrew words on the high priest's miter. He expresses his opinion with customary irony: "Alexander, who undoubtedly had a perfect understanding of Hebrew, immediately recognized the name of Jehovah etc." He also does not believe that Alexander had changed course after Gaza. Alexander led his army against Egypt on forced marches: "This is how Arrian, Quintus Curtius, Diodorus, even Paulus Orosius faithfully report it, based on Alexander's journal." Voltaire also refuses to believe that Alexander could have laid siege to Tyre only to please the Jews: "It behooved a very wise captain not to leave Tyre mistress of the seas when he was going to attack Egypt." However, the philosophe readily admitted that after the fall of the Phoenician city, the king "went to punish Jerusalem, which was not far off his path." He returned to the question in the "Maccabees" chapter of *La Bible enfin expliquée* (1776) and reiterated his views.

As for Sainte-Croix, he forcefully asserted that the Jewish historian's version needed to be called into question beginning with his 1771 manuscript (p. 9). By making his case in an ironic tone reminiscent of Voltaire's, he underscores the improbability of an exchange between the high priest and the Macedonian conqueror. He further developed his argument in the book's first edition,[31] drawing on the chronologies established by Newton and Prideaux, who had already cast doubt upon certain aspects of Josephus's narrative, particularly that Alexander could have journeyed to Jerusalem from Gaza. Yet Sainte-Croix does not mention that Prideaux's arguments had been brushed aside by the erudite writer Walter Moyle (1672–1721) in his posthumously published correspondence with the latter. Moyle totally rejected Flavius Josephus's authority and maintained that Judea had surrendered before Alexander reached Tyre.[32]

Ultimately, Sainte-Croix's actual role was not as pioneering as his silences might suggest. Philosophical in its essence, his demonstration fit into a critical movement developing all across Europe. To this movement, Sainte-Croix contributed his authority as an erudite writer and a specialist of the sources of Alexander's history, which was not insignificant. This is why the Scottish historian John Gillies, who was also influenced by Voltaire, referred to Moyle and Sainte-Croix in tandem.[33]

In taking a position contrary to one of the dogmas of sacred history, Sainte-Croix feels the need to justify himself. He emphasizes that, in any case, "the circumstances of this event could not be as glorious to religion as some people more pious than enlightened could initially believe." Indeed, he adds, it is impossible to imagine that a pagan polytheistic conqueror ever considered adoring the real god: "Could the hand that prostituted its incense on the altars of Apis and Belus honor the cult of the real god?" Obviously not! One must therefore accept that Josephus's version was invented after the fact: "The Jews probably invented [it] after Alexander's death, in order to earn his successors' protection."

Sir Richard Clayton, the English translator of the 1775 *Examen critique,* bluntly called Sainte-Croix's interpretation into question, which led him to openly make significant changes in the English text. Regarding Sainte-Croix's ironic remark about Alexander's alleged ability to read Hebrew, he wrote, "I do not think this skeptical [remark] deserves a translation." Clayton's English version was the subject of a long critical appraisal by William Vincent in 1793, the year it was published. At one point, Vincent takes a clearly political and ideological stance. He is pleased that the "baronet" (Clayton) sternly corrected the baron (Sainte-Croix) regarding Alexander's relations with the Jews. He denounces Sainte-Croix's positions in a particularly aggressive manner,[34] going so far as to accuse him of being one of those responsible (at least from a moral perspective) for "the dreadful convulsions not yet terminated in France," along with "innumerable writers of the same school [of Voltaire]." He even suspects that "the Baron, like many others, has paid the forfeit of his errors, under the axe of the Guillotine. He certainly was arrested, which, under the reign of what the French call liberty, is, in general, a very short step from death." This was completely untrue.

Nonetheless, Vincent's position was in keeping with what could be expected of a member of the clergy wholly devoted to the monarchy and the social order (he had been "sub-almoner to the king" since 1784). On May 13 of the previous year, he had delivered a sermon clearly directed against the revolutionary hydra rampant in Paris and still finding support in London, despite Edmund Burke's recent pamphlet and the Pitt government's anti-Jacobin measures. The sermon opened with a declaration one could describe as programmatic: "It is impossible for society to exist without a class of poor." Twenty thousand copies of the sermon were distributed free of charge in London and across the kingdom by the Patriotic Association for Liberty and Property against Republicans and Levellers, which had been founded in January 1792 by John Reeves; excerpts had previously been published in reports on the association's sessions.[35]

Aside from the excesses and misguided ideas brought on by his antirevolutionary fervor, Vincent was right about one thing: in his critique of Flavius Josephus, Sainte-Croix was partially inspired by a Ferney-based philosophe to whom he did not give credit and from whom he quietly borrowed a biting expression redolent of his brand of humor. Nonetheless, the identification of this unattributed quote hardly makes Sainte-Croix "a philosophe of the Voltairian school." Though a convinced Christian and monarchist, the author of the *Examen critique* was among those aristocrats who understood certain political demands and the need for change. He was a nobleman of high standing who had never ruled over his properties in the Comtat by terror or despotism. In 1784, he supported those of the region's inhabitants who fell victim to the pontifical government's overzealousness. He was entrusted with addressing remonstrances to the pope.[36] In retaliation, the court in Rome decided to sequester his assets; Sainte-Croix only escaped the dungeons of the Castel Sant-Angelo by going into exile in France (1784–1786) and it was only through the intervention of the French government that he would later reclaim his property in Mormoiron. He would also go on to play a part in the events of the revolution. Recalling these circumstances in 1811, Dacier reticently allowed that Sainte-Croix had not been hostile to "that spirit of innovation that more or less stirred every class of society and which, tired of the present, asked the past for lessons and examples to prepare a better future." To qualify his remarks and retrospectively exonerate the memory of Sainte-Croix, he immediately added that "if [he] showed a penchant for liberty," it was not out of revolutionary fervor; it was "because it only presented itself to him under the yoke of morality, accompanied by virtue." But the facts remain: in the early 1770s and again in the first months of the revolution, Sainte-Croix was no stranger to the philosophical spirit of the time, at least in its monarchist and reforming iteration.

The steadfastness of Sainte-Croix's conclusions in the 1775 edition did not portend the complete turnaround he would make thirty years later, to the point that the 1804 edition can be seen as an attempt to "re-Christianize" the history of Alexander or, to put it another way, as a return to a kind of sacred history further than ever from Voltaire.[37]

The 1804 volume, which Sainte-Croix refers to as "a new book," opens with a long quote from Bossuet's *Discours* (pp. xxxi–xxxii) and is noteworthy for a very thorough entry on "Universal and special Providence" in the index—a subject to which the Baron had devoted particular attention over the previous years. In 1803, he had reissued the translation of a British book by Jenyns on the same subject (1797) and his library included a great number of works on Providence and Christian religion.[38] The longest passage on the subject is in the entirely new fourth section. It is entitled "Du témoignage de l'Écriture et des Écrivains juifs sur Alexandre" ("On Scripture and the Jewish Writers' Account of Alexander") (pp. 523–576). Bossuet's authority is constantly called upon, with quotation and references on nearly every page. The argument opens with a sentence highly revealing of the author's state of mind: "No Society can exist without religion; and no religion, without the belief in a universal and special Providence." It is a striking change of direction on the part of the erudite writer. Asserted in 1775, Prideaux's authority is now rejected in favor of Bossuet's; cited in 1775, Newton's opinion is now considered "erroneous" and indicative of "systematic thinking"; ignored in 1775, Moyle's letters are now included in the notes for the sole purpose of being contested without real discussion. What had been seen as a relatively uninformed interpretation dictated by piety thirty years earlier is now presented as evidence of the erudite commentator's sensible impartiality: "All the objections to which Josephus's narrative has given rise regarding this Prince's journey to Jerusalem and his behavior toward that city's inhabitants must thus disappear in the eyes of a wise and impartial critic." The author plainly recognizes that in 1793 his English translator Sir Richard Clayton had been right to disagree with the opinion he himself had expressed in 1775. He also abandons any "Voltairian" irony and sarcasm: the king was able to read the inscription on the high priest's miter "either because he was able to guess based on the customs of the priests of a few Hellenic divinities or because he had learned it from the Samaritans and Phoenicians who accompanied him."[39]

With uncharacteristic carelessness, Sainte-Croix comes to affirm that even if there were still "errors and inaccuracies" in Flavius Josephus's narrative, "its content would not be any less true." Putting aside the need to organize sources according to a hierarchy, he compares two authors separated by seven centuries and the literary genres they respectively furthered: the prophet Haggai and the historian Josephus. Referring to a theological postulate borrowed from his model, he boldly confers the attributes of a historian on Haggai, even if it means infringing on the rules he himself had set for the use of erudition: "The prophecies are merely history written *ahead of time,* according to Bossuet's expression; they even supplement the Greek writers' account. . . . The Jews were saved by a special Providence. This fulfilled Haggai's prophecy, which implicitly confirms the content of Flavius's account." Religious conviction swept aside the methodological objection that Bayle had pointed out but not submitted to, namely that no "ancient historian of Alexander" ever refers to a visit to Jerusalem. Consumed by his faith and his desire to impose a Christian view of history, Sainte-Croix unduly turns Bayle into an ally and, possibly due to a mere slip, inaccurately quotes the *Dictionnaire,* distorting its meaning to suit his own.[40] As he himself underlines with a certain satisfaction, the support thus commandeered was important because "[Bayle] will certainly not be accused of prejudice or excessive credulity."

The undeniable abruptness of this change of opinion leads one to wonder about the author's reasons for attempting to breathe life into a historical vision that had continued to lose support over the previous thirty years. There is little doubt that the attempt was due to Sainte-Croix's own recent experience and his evolution toward a pious religiosity, which took him further away from any "philosophical" vision but also, as can be seen, made him wander far afield from his own critical standards. The Sainte-Croix of 1804 was no longer the Sainte-Croix of 1770–1775.

Like all the men of his generation, Sainte-Croix had had to contend with the revolution and its impact on individual and collective fates.[41] The erudite writer's family was caught in the middle of the specific troubles that shook the Comtat, a region whose inhabitants were not all in favor of unification with France. The turning point came in April 1791, when Sainte-Croix's oldest son was imprisoned by armed men calling themselves "the brave brigands of the army of the Vaucluse," and in the following September, when the farms of the Sainte-Croix estate were sacked.[42] In 1792, Sainte-Croix hurriedly left the Comtat-Venaissin for Paris, accompanied by his daughter. His wife would only be able to join them two years later, after narrowly escaping execution. Two of his sons perished during the revolution and his daughter died in 1806. All his assets were destroyed or sequestered and his library and papers burned or scattered. Then came what Dacier called "this sequence of marvelous events" (from the fall of Robespierre to the Directory), which in 1802 allowed him to rejoin what had become the *Institut de France's Classe d'Histoire et de Littérature ancienne.*[43]

It thus comes as no surprise that the terrible memory of the private trials the author faced in the midst of public upheavals left its mark on the preparation of the 1804 edition. In the funeral orations they delivered in 1809, his colleagues and friends in the institute emphasized his deep faith and unfailing confidence in Divine Providence. Sainte-Croix himself makes the connection between his biography and his thought in the preface to his book. He explains that he tried to overcome his memories of misfortune "by unreservedly and fervently giving [him]self over to [his] long-standing work." Sainte-Croix continues by rejecting his era's modernity, insisting on the defense of erudition threatened by the "philosophes and the *beaux-esprits,*" and pledging his intellectual and moral allegiance to the ancients, but first and foremost to Bossuet, who more than any other mastered "the true art of discussion." He denounces "most modern savants" as proponents of conjecture rather than facts, ready to "shake the yoke of authority," and attempting to discredit seventeenth-century savants by referring to them as *érudits.* Sainte-Croix sorrowfully and nostalgically notes that the seventeenth-century savants "had knowledge so vast that even their errors enlighten us and help us to discover the truth." Nearing the end of his life, Sainte-Croix chose this somewhat desperate but poignant manner to express his attachment to the ethic of the *grand siècle* and its most illustrious representatives.

Sainte-Croix and the Others

The attention I devote to Sainte-Croix's work is easily explained: the *Examen critique* is a milestone in the history of erudition and in the history of the history of Alexander. As we will see, the book was widely distributed and very well received outside of France.

However, neither the extent and persistence of the book's influence nor the highly selective nature of its author's references to historians and philologists of his time should suggest that the history of Alexander was neglected in Europe during this period. That is simply not the case. Only the Italian specialists appear not to have granted specific importance to the history of Alexander. With the exception of Paganino Gaudenzio's critical reflections on the sources as of 1646, of works on Alexander written in Italian by notables from the Germanic states (the Baron of Kossin in 1716 and Frederick Augustus of Brunswick-Oels in 1764),[44] and of a few isolated reflections by Vico,[45] only a single Italian manual of Greek history can be mentioned: the volume first published by the Abbé Carlo Denina (1731–1813) in 1782. The history of Macedon is addressed in volume 3, but is abruptly interrupted by the author when Alexander succeeds Philip to the throne. Nonetheless, Denina emphasizes Alexander's exceptional qualities: a "prodigy among human geniuses," who owed a great deal to the "lights of philosophy." The reader will learn no more, for the author, after mentioning that he had initially planned to cover the reigns of Alexander and his successors and epigones, claims he has stopped here due to the publication of John Gast's English volume (1782) covering Greek history up to the Roman conquest. Yet many books both good and bad had dealt with this period since Rollin and been published in France, England, and Germany. The real reason for volume 3's abrupt end was that the abbé had been called to the court of Frederick II and had decided to take the step that would lead him "from Greece to Germany, and from Macedon to Brandenburg and Prussia." The book therefore ends with an address to "the Great Frederick" brimming with sycophantic enthusiasm. The abbé made sure to display his new distinctions on the cover of the second edition (1784): "Accademico di Berlino e Storiografo di Sua Majesta Prussiana" ("Academician of Berlin and Historiographer of His Prussian Majesty"). After the move to Germany, he turned his attention to entirely different subjects, then became Napoleon's personal assistant librarian in 1804, working under the supervision of Antoine-Alexandre Barbier as of 1807.[46]

On the other hand, England, Scotland, and Germany made a major contribution to research and reflection on the Macedonian conquest and its short- and long-term consequences, both through manuals for a broad audience and specialized studies and sketches and in contexts and perspectives that varied significantly from one author or country to the other. The following pages will primarily deal with sources and scholarly method. The actual historical interpretations will be discussed later, in their national and contextual varieties and their often polemical contradictions.

Alexander in England and Scotland:
Manuals and Universal History

While the defeat at Chaeronea (338 BC) had long marked the end of Greek history, beginning in the 1770s British historians regularly included the history of Alexander in their histories of Greece (Oliver Goldsmith 1774; John Gillies 1786; William Mitford 1818). John Gast and John Gillies opened their books with Alexander the Great and delivered avant la lettre accounts of Hellenistic history, in a narrative form in Gast's case (1782) and a structural one in Gillies's (1802). Both authors had previously published works covering the earlier periods of Greek history: Gast's 1753 *Rudiments* ended with Philip's death; Gillies's 1786 *History of Ancient Greece* went from the origins of Greece to the dismemberment of Alexander's empire.[47]

By referring to all these authors as "historians of Greece," one runs the risk of causing confusion. It should therefore be noted that the genre's popularity also inspired polygraphs and booksellers to produce histories of Greece. A particularly noteworthy example is Oliver Goldsmith (1728–1774), better known for *The Vicar of Wakefield* and his poems, essays, and other plays. Living by his pen and gifted with an easy style and consummate art of organizing chapters and episodes, Goldsmith made a tremendous amount of money by writing histories of Rome, England, and Greece. His posthumously published *History of Greece* (1774) repeated an image of Alexander well established since Rollin and still unchanged in many circles: "In whatever light we view this monarch, we shall have little to admire, and less to imitate.... His intemperance, his cruelty, his vanity, his passion for useless conquests, were all his own" (2 [1821]: 224).

Another example deserves our attention. This is the *History of Ancient Greece* first published in Edinburgh in 1768 with no author credit, then reprinted in 1779 under the name of William Robertson. While the two have frequently been confused, including in recent historiographic studies, this writer has nothing to do with the illustrious Scottish philosopher-historian, who we shall soon discuss at length. Indeed, the two Robertsons' most lucid contemporaries—including Heyne, who published a highly unfavorable review of the German translation in 1779[48]—did not fall into the trap. The author of the *History of Ancient Greece* was the keeper of the records of Scotland, a purely Scottish title that was a far cry from the title of royal historiographer for Scotland bestowed upon the philosopher. Robertson admitted to his debt neither in his dedication "to His Royal Highness the Prince of Wales" nor in the preface; instead, he shamelessly tells the reader how original his book is compared to those by Rollin, Stanyan, and Goldsmith. In fact, his *History* was no more than an occasionally adapted translation of Alletz's manual (1763). Suffice it to say that the model selected was Rollin, and that one finds the same negative assessment of Alexander here as in Goldsmith. All these books met with considerable success, not only through their multiple English editions, but in many translations into French, German, and Italian.

Despite its special features, I will also mention the *Universal History,* which was launched in England in the late 1720s by George Sale (a translator of the Koran) and the mysterious George Psalmanazar (a specialist-impostor on the history of Formosa), who were soon joined by a cohort of English collaborators.[49] Though the publication was enormously successful on a European, then North American, scale, the results did not always live up to intention or expectations. Due to the significant editorial autonomy granted the various authors, the history of Alexander is discussed several times and in different contexts; as might be expected, it principally appears at the heart of the continuity and breaking points of the histories of Macedon and ancient Persia, but also in the context of the history of the Jews.[50] Here too, the image of Alexander does not differ much from the tradition inaugurated by Rollin. While favoring Arrian, "on account of his great impartiality" (8:496), the anonymous author of the history of Alexander cites and compares the other sources in often copious footnotes, "distinguishing, as far as we were able, the probable from the improbable, the certain from the doubtful.... And we have placed the evidence before our readers, that may decide for themselves" (8:660).

Due to extensive delays in the publication of the *Universal History*—and particularly its *Modern Part*—William Guthrie and John Gray, two polygraphs with mercenary pens, joined with the bookseller John Newberry to assemble a group of collaborators to prepare a complete *General History of the World* in a compact, concise form following the outline of the *Universal History*. The first volume appeared in 1764, as the sixty-first volume of Sale and Psalmanazar's *Universal History* was issued.[51] The British edition was followed by translations in all the European languages.

During the same period, Sainte-Croix's book circulated widely in erudite circles. The only known translation is the aforementioned 1793 version by Sir Richard Clayton based on the 1775 edition. The English translator justified his endeavor with the observation that the work had quickly become unavailable on the Continent and that "it was only in the hands of a few people of taste and erudition" in Great Britain. According to William Mitford, the *Examen critique* was well known to English savants, who always referred to it with great admiration—as confirmed by a survey of books featuring notes and references. The *Examen critique* was all the more noticed because William Vincent had reviewed the English version (1793), as we have just seen, and later made many references to it in his own book on Nearchus's journey.[52]

William Robertson, Alexander, and India

To understand the significance of the changes made to the history of Alexander, we must now turn to Scotland. As is well known, the Enlightenment movement in Scotland was extremely active. William Robertson is universally considered to have been its very soul and chief inspirer.[53] Born in 1721, Robertson studied at the University of Edinburgh before becoming a Presbyterian minister, then the "Principal of the College of Edinburgh" in 1762. London recognized his eminent position by bestowing him with the title of "His Majesty's Chaplain in Ordinary for Scotland" (1761), then the far more prestigious title of "King's Historiographer for Scotland" (1764). Heavily influenced by Voltaire and Montesquieu, he was also shaped by intellectual exchanges with close friends such as David Hume and Edward Gibbon. After the success of his *History of Scotland* in 1759, he hesitated in choosing the subject of his next book, wishing to avoid taking any chances in achieving his ardent desire to reach the largest audience possible. He asked his friends for advice. David Hume dissuaded him from turning to ancient history, telling him with a Voltairian turn of phrase that it was only frequented by a small number of scholars who already knew everything that could be written about the subject. Instead, he encouraged him to write *Modern Lives* in the manner of Plutarch, in which he could include "the remarkable popes, the kings of Sweden, the great discoverers and conquerors of the new Worlds, even the eminent men of letters. . . . The field is inexhaustible."[54] Finally, Robertson returned to his initial idea, which was to write a monograph on Charles V, Holy Roman Emperor. The book was published in 1769 (*History of Charles the Fifth*) and was followed by a monumental *History of America* (1777) and *An Historical Disquisition concerning Ancient India* (1791). These books all had an exceptional impact in Europe, both in their original language and in translation.[55]

The Macedonian king is included in book 1 of *History of America,* the first part of which is devoted to an outline of the progress of discoveries and navigation from antiquity to the modern era. The narrative moves from the Egyptians and Phoenicians to Greece, then to Alexander, "[whose] expedition into the East considerably enlarged the sphere of navigation and geographical knowledge" and whose genius made it possible to establish trade relations between India and the West. Robertson's argument is not original in and of itself, but the notes indicate that he knew the ancient sources and had carefully read the geographic literature (particularly d'Anville and, of course, Rennell). They also reveal that Robertson's highly positive view of Alexander comes directly from his reading of *The Spirit of the Laws.*[56] For the history of man is also the history of communication, in which Alexander would play a notable role.

Alexander is also an important presence in the first part of the *Historical Disquisition,* entitled "Intercourse with India, from the Earliest Times until the Conquest of Egypt by the Romans."[57] One could even say that he is its protagonist, playing a part he had previously held in *History of America,* but which was now considerably developed: that of the discoverer, trailblazer, and promoter of understanding and harmony between peoples. In the notes, Robertson conscientiously cites the ancient authors, notably Strabo, Diodorus, and especially Arrian (see note 6); the modern geographers are abundantly called upon, d'Anville again and even more so Rennell; at one point, Robertson heatedly polemicizes with Sainte-Croix (note 10). What is most surprising is that *The Spirit of the Laws'* chapters on commerce are cited only once, in reference to a relatively minor question of historical geography (the location of Zizer / Siger), while Robertson's "civilizing" theories about Alexander are directly borrowed from Montesquieu and / or entirely shared with him. Perhaps Robertson considered that the novelty of his approach was sufficiently established for him to take his distance from a model whom he never rejected but did not at the time want to acknowledge as his inspiration. Robertson could also rightly consider that, coming close to fifty years after the publication of *The Spirit of the Laws,* he had acquired his own knowledge of India, in part due to Scotland's special relationship with the subcontinent; several of his nephews and two of his sons were then serving with the British army in India.[58]

The *Historical Disquisition* was widely circulated in Europe. At least eight English-language editions are known to have been published from 1791 to 1821 in Great Britain, Ireland, and the United States, to which a much larger number of authorized and unauthorized printings must be added. It was immediately translated in France (1792), Germany (1792), Holland (1793), and Italy (1794). Reviews, references, and prefaces to the translations bear witness both to Robertson's well-established reputation and his discussion's significant impact in every European country. Writing in Holland in 1801, the translator of Feßler's German monograph (*Alexander der Eroberer,* 1797) justified his work by opening his preface with a quote from the Dutch version of Robertson's *Historical Disquisition* (published in 1793); in doing so, his avowed objective was to remind the Dutch reader that Alexander was not simply a "conqueror" (*Eroberer*) but also a true statesman.

John Gillies, Alexander, and Hellenistic History

Let's remain in Scotland. Following William Robertson's death in 1793, the office of king's historiographer for Scotland was passed on to John Gillies (1747–1836), who had a more direct relationship with the history of Alexander and his successors.[59] A brilliant student of the classics, Gillies initially built his reputation on his knowledge of ancient Greek, which he taught in Glasgow before becoming the "travelling tutor" to the count of Hopetown's sons. He also became known for several annotated translations of Greek classics, notably of the Attic orators and the works of Aristotle. As its subtitle clearly indicates, the first volume of translations (1778) was also an analysis of fourth-century Greek institutions and customs; as such, it led directly to the period of Macedonian domination. Later (1797), in his account of the life of Aristotle in the introduction to his translations, he did not fail to underline the importance of the role played by the philosopher in the young Macedonian prince's education. His work on the fourth-century Greek authors naturally prepared him for the book he was contemplating.

Gillies dedicated himself to preparing his *History of Ancient Greece* throughout his many stays on the Continent and in a more intensive manner once he settled in London in 1784. The book was published in 1786, met with great success, and was quickly translated into French (1788–1789), German (1797), and Italian (1796–1797). The French translation of the first part was begun by Benjamin Constant, who "gave up on this enterprise without any regrets, [as soon as he was] preempted by a Writer who better fulfilled this difficult task." Indeed, the future revolutionary Jean-Louis Carra had set to work on the translation and was to complete it in an extremely short time.[60] Carra did not hesitate to step in with his point of view. He himself specifies that the original preface (which is very short in the English edition) "has largely been blended into the translator's Preface." He tells the reader that "the philosophical spirit reigns over this work" and adds his personal commentary: "It is only through [this spirit] that History, Politics, Ethics, as well as all the Sciences, both natural and exact, can be analyzed in a manner consistent with real causes and real principles." There is therefore no comparison between this book and "so many enormous and vagabond compilations, with which we are inundated."

John Gillies was indisputably a philosopher-historian. In fact, he contributed to reflection on the philosopher-king by comparing Frederick of Prussia and Philip of Macedon (1789). Gillies was heavily influenced by Montesquieu, "who (Voltaire only excepted) is the most distinguished modern apologist of Alexander."[61] His express concern to avoid overwhelming the reader with narrative details considered useless was clearly inspired by Voltaire. The same is true of his ambition to avoid separating the history of politics and the history of the arts and "to combine with the external revolutions of war and government, the intellectual improvements of men, and the ever-varying picture of human opinions and manners."[62]

The history of Alexander takes up three of the *History of Ancient Greece's* forty-nine chapters. For the most part, it consists of a linear narrative, which does not contain any particular novelties with the exception that, like Robertson, Gillies fully embraces the positive view of Alexander earlier presented by Montesquieu. He introduces his final description of the Macedonian king by stating that "[such] was the reign of Alexander, whose character, being un-exampled and inimitable, can only be explained by relating his actions.... His natural humanity, enlightened by the philosophy of Greece, taught him to improve his conquests to the best interests of mankind" (2:669–670). Gillies's knowledge of Greek gives him a considerable advantage over most authors of manuals, a fact he does not hesitate to advertise by quoting the ancient authors in Greek and offering interpretations based on terminolog-ical research. He had also read numerous erudite writers and antiquarian scholars (Bayle, Sainte-Croix, de Guignes, Herbelot, Hancarville), philoso-phes (Montesquieu, Voltaire, Mably, Vico), travelers (Choiseul-Gouffier, the Baron de Tott), military historians (Guischardt), and geographers ("the ad-mirable d'Anville," Rennell).

In 1807, he published another book with a particularly ambitious title (*The History of the World*), to which Arnaldo Momigliano has briefly but rightly drawn attention. Let's look at the preface, in which the author clearly sets forth his objectives and methods. The book covers the vast period stretching from Alexander to Augustus, which is "considered by readers of reflection as leaving a sort of blank in history." This was the first historio-graphic endeavor of its type; in a way, it is a forerunner of all the books and manuals that have since appeared under the title *From Alexander to Actium*. Gillies states that he has worked on the subject for twenty years. He had certainly discussed it among his peers, given that an 1801 biographical sketch already announced the content and direction of the volume under preparation.[63] He himself presents the new book as a continuation of the previous one, but a continuation "[which] necessarily rises above the first in greatness and novelty of design." This time, he intended to go "beyond the chronology of kings, the intrigues of courts, the dry and often doubtful de-tails of negotiations and battles." Openly following the model of Herodotus, he aims to describe in detail the lives of peoples and countries, both in the Occident and the Orient. He explains that he wants to go against the ex-ample of Polybius and move away from a history exclusively of the victors to also consider the history of the defeated, the very ones who "gradually fell within the sphere of [Greece's] military exertion or of its commercial intercourse."

The title of the book's dense, five-section introductory section also serves as a subtitle to the entire book: *A Preliminary Survey of Alexander's Conquests, and an Estimate of His Plans for Their Consolidation and Improvements* (1:1–202).

After analyzing the factual reality of the king's projects (§1), Gillies surveys the various countries that made up the Achaemenid empire (§2); he follows this with a section on Egypt (§3), another on the Assyrian and Babylonian empires (§4), and finally a reassessment of Alexander's plans (§5). To this end, he states that he has collected every possible document, including the most paltry, as well as the information provided by modern travelers. Gillies completed his findings with a comparison of the various parts of the empire with the same countries at the beginning of the nineteenth century. Throughout these pages, the author supports his assertions and hypotheses with abundant footnotes (about eight hundred notes over the first five sections). These primarily include numerous citations of ancient authors (whose works Gillies has clearly consulted directly), then, among modern authors, travelers (Chardin, Bernier, Tavernier, Niebuhr, Volney, Bruce), commentators on Herodotus (Rennell, Larcher), geographers (d'Anville, Rennell), historians (Robertson, Vincent, Gibbon, Heeren), biblical exegetes (Bochart, Michaelis, Prideaux), and philosophes (Montesquieu, Voltaire, Diderot, Raynal). The quantity and diversity of the information collected enable the author to consider what characterizes the coherence and significance of this historical period, namely "the gradual transfer of dominion from the Greeks and Macedonians to the Romans and Parthians." In this overall context, Alexander's reign can and must be considered differently, no longer in the form of a military narrative, but as the political analysis of "the foundation of a new empire, destined steadily to dissolve into many separate monarchies, [so that] it is necessary to advert, not only to the exploits which he achieved, but to the extraordinary undertakings which he meditated" (p. 2). By comparing and contrasting him to other "Asiatic conquerors" (Assyrians, Egyptians, Scythes, Medes, Persians), Gillies also aims to determine and distinguish what was original about the Macedonian king's designs and what he borrowed from his predecessors.

The book's last lines forcefully acknowledge a failure extending across the three centuries the author has just analyzed. As Gillies melancholically concludes, the Macedonian conqueror's great plans were reduced to nothing by "the growing dishonesty of the Greeks, the proud tyranny of the Romans, the barbarous despotism of the Parthians and all succeeding Asiatic dynasties. . . . All conquerors admired Alexander; but none, perhaps, have ever had his power, and none, certainly, both the power and the will to imitate his example" (3:483).

The result shows the limitations of the questions asked and the methods used, as well as the gaps in the documentation, including those for which the author was personally responsible: though he knew the Latin and Greek texts well, he did not make use of the coins and inscriptions available in contemporary publications. Nonetheless, he remains notable and even praiseworthy. Within the *longue durée* of historiography, today's historian can see in Gillies's work a harbinger of the issues now commonly referred to as "continuity and change."

It must be noted that the book did not have the circulation or audience for which its author had hoped. While his *History of Ancient Greece* had been very favorably received in England and all the European countries, *The History of the World* met a dramatically different response. The book remained untranslated and was not even reviewed in the illustrious journal *Göttingische Anzeigen von gelehrten Sachen*, despite the fact that it published several hundred reviews a year. It is surprising that Heeren never cites it—was he mad at Gillies for borrowing so much from his most famous work (*Ideen zurr die Politik, den Verkehr und den Handel der vornehmsten Völker der alten Welt* [*Historical Researches into the Politics, Intercourse and Trade of the Principal Nations of Antiquity*]) without truly acknowledging the extent of his debt?[64] Even the reception in England was mixed, as shown by the long review published anonymously in 1807 in the *Edinburgh Review*. Aside from offering rhetorical congratulations to the author, the reviewer (who knew the subject well) criticized him on the essence of his theories, his knowledge of Greek, his deplorable style, his errors in evaluation (of the Rosetta Stone, for example), as well as the insufficient analysis of the sources. In short, Gillies was able to collect a certain amount of information, but was not able to use it as a historian; his book is limited to "a mere narrative of facts." While the reviewer stated that he considered Gillies a cut above Rollin and the *Universal History*, it was clear to all that the comparison was not particularly flattering.

James Rennell, Alexander's Conquest, and Establishing the Map of India

Robertson and Gillies inevitably bring us to a third figure who played a part in discussions of Alexander's conquests, at least regarding his expeditions in the Punjab and the Indus Valley. In the first lines of the *Historical Disquisition,* Robertson explained what had led to his research on India: "The perusal of Major Rennell's Memoir for illustrating his Map of Indostan, one of the most valuable geographical treatises that has appeared in any age or country, gave rise to the following work. It suggested to me the idea of examining more fully than I had done in the Introductory Book to my History of America, into the knowledge which the Ancients had of India, and of considering what is certain, what is obscure, and what is fabulous, in the accounts of that country which they have handed down to us."

This memoir on India so frequently quoted by Robertson, Gillies, and many of their contemporaries was published in three successive, constantly expanded editions in 1783, 1788, and 1793. It was entitled *Memoir of a Map of Hindoostan.* The first edition was translated into German (1787) and French (1788) by Jean Bernoulli (1744–1807), an astronomer for the king of Prussia and a member of the Berlin Academy's Class of Mathematics.[65]

Born in 1742, the young James Rennell embarked on a staggeringly successful career by leaping at the opportunities offered by India and the East India Company. He joined the navy in 1756 and fought off the coast of Brittany (at the same place and time that Sainte-Croix's uncle was a commander over the area from Morlaix to Saint-Brieuc). Then, like so many other Englishmen and Scotsmen eager for promotion and money, he decided to set sail for India, where he arrived a month after the taking of Pondicherry (1760). The Peace of Fontainebleau (1763) led him to leave the army and join the East India Company. Already passionate about mathematics and geography, he was appointed surveyor general for the territory administered by the company (at the age of twenty-one), then major in 1776. The following year, he returned to London at the age of thirty-five and remained there until his death in 1830 at the age of eighty-eight. He assembled a circle of savants and men of letters who met in his home and were nearly all members of the Royal Society, including its president, Sir Joseph Banks (to whom Rennell dedicated his *Memoir*). He also had great esteem for d'Anville, the French geographer who had himself produced several in-depth studies of the geography of India and the Persian Gulf. D'Anville was known as "the French Rennell," while Rennell was referred to as the "English d'Anville."[66]

An illustrious historian lived near Rennell: John Gillies was of the same generation (born in 1842, he lived to the age of eighty-nine) and became his close friend. Gillies gave Rennell valuable help when he referred to Greek authors whom he could not read in the original. This was the case when, after finishing his work on India, Rennell conceived the project of a vast study of the countries between the Indus and the Mediterranean. Published in 1800, his commentary on Herodotus was envisioned as one section of a much larger project, which was never completed. In it, Rennell heartily thanks Gillies for helping him to come to grips with Herodotus's Greek text.

Coming after his essay *The Bengal Atlas* (1782), the different versions of Rennell's *Memoir* aimed to take stock of new information on India's geography, while simultaneously explaining the documentary sources he had used. The author made good use of his experience in the field as surveyor general for Bengal. He also chose to extend his study far beyond Bengal and what he called Hindustan proper, to include the upper valley of the Ganges, the Indus Valley, the Deccan, and the eastern coast. It is absolutely clear—in this case as in so many others—that written reports of British military operations provided most of the new information. The geography under consideration is therefore a modern geography, as it could be determined at the time of the Mughal Kingdom and according to how its evolution could be tracked over the course of the British wars.

Though Rennell's focus was clearly on the present and future, he intended to use every resource at his disposal. He therefore introduced Greek and Roman sources, including in direct quotations. In fact, he noted that the name "India" itself came from antiquity, specifically from the Persians, who referred to the Indus Valley as "Hindush," a name passed on to the Greeks as "India." Rennell also makes the general observation that "India has in all ages excited the attention of the curious, in almost every walk of life, its rare products and manufactures, engaged that of the merchants; while the mild and inoffensive religion of Brama, and the manners inculcated by it, attracted the notice of philosophers" (1788, p. xxi); this also explains the repeated invasions. Some thirty pages on antiquity follow, in which Rennell's reflections are organized around Alexander: "India was but little known to the Greeks until Alexander's expedition. . . . [It] furnished the Greeks with a more extensive knowledge of India, although he traversed only the countries mentioned by Herodotus, that's the tract watered by the Indus and its various branches, and adjunct rivers. But the spirit of enquiry was now gone forth; and the long residence of Megasthenes, the ambassador of Seleucus at Palibothra, the capital of the Prasii, furnished the Grecians with the principal part of the accounts of India, that are to be found in Strabo, Pliny and Arrian" (p. xxv).

In Rennell, one once again encounters "Alexander the geographer," a figure that had been consistently studied in Europe at least since Cassini, and to whom d'Anville had himself devoted so much research and reflection. All this led Rennell to evaluate the hierarchy of historians of Alexander and, like his predecessors, to give preeminence to Arrian, based on considerations by this point widely accepted. Rennell's lines of argumentation essentially concern the identification of sites known to the ancient sources (Aornos, Bazeira, Alexandria on the Caucasus) and regional reconstruction based on reviewing the invasion routes followed by Alexander, Tamerlane, and Nader Shah.[67] Though they are not devoid of interest, one clearly cannot agree with all of the author's toponymic discussions or his digressions about individual stages of Alexander's armies' advances. One will simply observe that by comparing Punjab in his own time to Alexander's Punjab, Rennell devalues the scope of the Macedonian victories, which were won over divided and dispersed enemies: "The conquest of Punjab and Sind, would, with such an army [120,000 men and 200 elephants according to Arrian], be no very great matter in our times, although united; and yet this conquest is considered as a brilliant part of Alexander's history: the truth is, the romantic traveller is blended with the adventurous soldier; and the feelings of the reader are oftener applied to than his judgment" (1793, p. 130). Did Rennell intend to suggest that a future conquest of the Indus Valley would be far more difficult than the one carried out by the Macedonian armies? Possibly, for he himself was hostile to the then relatively prevalent idea that "the British might have extended their possessions in Hindoostan, *ad libitum*" (1793, p. cv).

The book contains few judgments about Alexander. One simply senses an admiration for the Macedonian conqueror and the certainty that he was not a madman merely guided by his own passions. Rennell manifestly likes leaders of this caliber, just as he admires the king of Mysore, Hyder Ali, who was ultimately defeated and killed by the English in 1782, but was able in little time "to improve both his revenues and his army to a degree beyond probability [and] to extend his territories: Such are the effects of firmness, perseverance and economy" (1793, p. xcix)—all virtues and qualities regularly attributed to Alexander by his ancient and modern admirers. Rennell even holds that the king of Mysore is an equal to Frederick the Great, with whom he compares him—with the exception of his cruelty—"but we are to consider that Hyder's ideas of mercy were regulated by an Asiatic standard" (1793, p. cii, note). Working as a geographer without being a specialist in the ancient sources or a historian, Rennell called on his friend Gillies to justify his positive evaluation of some of Alexander's enterprises. When alluding to the departure of Nearchus's fleet from the Indus Delta, he refers to it as *"the first European fleet which navigated the Indian Seas,"* adding, "according to Dr. Gillies, in his elegant History of Greece" (1788, p. 101; italics are Rennell's).[68]

Along with Robertson's book, Rennell's *Memoir* influenced many historians and savants. Gillies used it as a guide for the Indian chapters of his *History* (1786) and cited both Rennell and Robertson in his *History of the World* (1807). Some of his research on Arrian's *India* and Nearchus's voyage corresponded with those of a fourth British savant, William Vincent.

William Vincent and *The Voyage of Nearchus*

Nothing in William Vincent's background (1739–1815) suggested that he would become a specialist in the joint histories of Alexander the Great and the Persian Gulf—with the exception that his father's work as a commercial intermediary in Portugal had attracted his attention to the Lisbon-Goa route.[69] Having been admitted to Westminster School as a King's Scholar at the age of fourteen, he remained there until his death, with the exception of his classical studies at Cambridge (Trinity College) from 1757 to 1761. At Westminster, he moved upward (rather slowly) until he was appointed dean in 1802. Due to his heavy pedagogical and administrative responsibilities, his entrance into the circle of savants came late, in 1793, through his analysis of a much discussed passage by Livy. He then became more specifically known for reviewing the English translation (1793) of Sainte-Croix's *Examen critique* (1775) published by Richard Clayton.[70]

It is clear that Vincent was very familiar with the sources analyzed by Sainte-Croix. Most of his criticism relates to questions of scholarship. The review's interim conclusion suggests that Vincent was already at work on the book that would make his reputation across Europe: "But the subject is not yet exhausted, and we hope to see it yet pursued to a greater extent by some person who, with competent information, may have considered it without the prejudices of the Baron" (1793, p. 517).

In the *Voyage*, Vincent even states that he began his research "several years before the appearance of Major Rennell's *Maps and Memoirs*" (p. 24). While completing a study of the Greek language (1795), he prepared the

THE

VOYAGE OF NEARCHUS

FROM THE INDUS TO THE EUPHRATES,

COLLECTED FROM THE

ORIGINAL JOURNAL PRESERVED BY ARRIAN,

AND ILLUSTRATED BY

AUTHORITIES ANCIENT AND MODERN;

CONTAINING

AN ACCOUNT OF THE FIRST NAVIGATION ATTEMPTED BY EUROPEANS IN THE INDIAN OCEAN.

By WILLIAM VINCENT, D.D.

TO WHICH ARE ADDED

THREE DISSERTATIONS:

Two, on the ACRONYCHAL RISING of the PLEIADES,
By the Right Reverend Dr. SAMUEL HORSLEY, Lord Bishop of Rochester;
And by Mr. WILLIAM WALES, Master of the Royal Mathematical School in Christ's Hospital:
And One by Mr. DE LA ROCHETTE,
On the FIRST MERIDIAN of PTOLEMY.

Posteris an aliqua cura noſtrî, nefcio, nos certè meremur ut fit aliqua, non dico ingenio
(id enim ſuperbum) ſed ſtudio, ſed labore, et reverentiâ poſterorum.
PLINIUS, TACITO. Lib. ix. Ep. 14.

LONDON:
Printed for T. CADELL jun. and W. DAVIES (Succeſſors to Mr. CADELL) in the Strand.
MDCCXCVII.

9–10. Title pages of *The Voyage of Nearchus from the Indus to the Euphrates* by William Vincent (London, 1797) and of its French translation, *Voyage de Néarque, des bouches de l'Indus jusqu'à l'Euphrate* (Paris, 1800).

VOYAGE
DE NÉARQUE,

DES BOUCHES DE L'INDUS

JUSQU'À L'EUPHRATE,

O U

JOURNAL DE L'EXPÉDITION DE LA FLOTTE

D'ALEXANDRE,

Rédigé sur le Journal original de NÉARQUE conservé par ARRIEN,
à l'aide des éclaircissemens puisés dans les écrits et relations des
Auteurs, Géographes, ou Voyageurs, tant anciens que modernes ;

ET CONTENANT

L'Histoire de la première navigation que des Européens aient tentée
dans la Mer des Indes.

TRADUIT DE L'ANGLOIS DE WILLIAM VINCENT,
Par J. B. L. J. BILLECOCQ, Homme de loi.

A PARIS,

DE L'IMPRIMERIE DE LA RÉPUBLIQUE.
AN VIII.

publication of his major work, which was released in 1797 in the form of a quarto close to 550 pages long, with additional maps. At the same time, Vincent was also working on the *Periplus of the Erythean Sea,* which was long falsely attributed to Arrian.[71] Additionally, following a suggestion from his friend Robert Nares, the 1797 volume was supplemented in 1809 by the bilingual publication (in Greek and English) of the chapters on Nearchus sailing up the Persian Gulf. Two years earlier, in 1807, Vincent had published a second edition of his *Voyage,* which was not significantly different from the first edition; while he had added a critical discussion of a recent work by Rennell, he continued to quote Sainte-Croix from the 1775 edition of the *Examen critique.* Over the following years (about 1809 to 1815), he continued to collect notes for a new edition, but it was never published.[72] Already old and tired, the author never gave the reading public the book on Alexander's military campaigns that he had announced in 1797.

In the *Voyage,* Vincent clearly states that "[his] purpose is not to translate Arrian, but to make him intelligible to an English reader, and to investigate a variety of subjects, historical, geographical, and commercial" (p. xvi). As indicated by part of its title (*The Voyage of Nearchus from the Indus to the Euphrates Collected from the Original Journal Preserved by Arrian*), the book is like a long commentary on Arrian's *Indica,* which attempts to prove the authenticity of its primary source, *Nearchus's Journal;* Nearchus was at the head of Alexander's fleet (no matter his exact title). Vincent forcefully refutes the doubts that his compatriot Henry Dodwell (1664–1711) had expressed long before: "Notwithstanding its authenticity has been disputed . . . we may venture to assert that it presents to an unprejudiced mind every internal evidence of fidelity and truth. . . . As the writings of Arrian have become better known, the just standard of this illustrious character [Alexander] has been fixed" (pp. 2,4).

Fundamentally, *The Voyage of Nearchus* is an essay in geographical history, full of literary, geographical, chronological, and cartographic erudition. The reader is left to sort through sometimes interminable discussions and infinite digressions. Happily, the copious *Preliminary Disquisitions* (bk. 1) that come after the well-articulated preface provide the reader an advance account of most of the theories and conclusions that will be introduced over the subsequent chapters. Naturally, Vincent chose to structure his book according both to geography and chronology. He follows Alexander and Nearchus's marches and water voyages in minute detail. Book 2 (*From Nicaea to the Mouth of the Indus*) features long dissertations on the locations of Nicaea (from which Alexander left for India) and the Punjab and its rivers; book 3 (*Course from the Indus to the Cape Jask*) comes close to providing a day-by-day account of the first phase of Nearchus's journey up to his entrance into the Persian Gulf by individually studying and locating the thirty-three stops where the fleet docked; book 4 (*Gulph of Persia*) continues to follow in the wake of Nearchus's boats, based on the coasts and banks of the major regions known since antiquity (Carmania; Persia; Susiana; mouths of the Tigris and Euphrates). Vincent adds a chapter entitled "Sequel to the Voyage of Nearchus" (pp. 459–487), which the reader is asked to consider as "no uninteresting appendage to the work." It continues the narrative to the death of Alexander. The book's full title indicates that Vincent's research was based on "authorities ancient and modern." In the preface and throughout the following chapters, Vincent cites and thanks all those who helped him with their advice and/or their writing. He acknowledges his debt to "the modern writers and travellers." Among the travelers, he makes particular mention of his correspondent Carsten Niebuhr, "the best of modern travellers surviving" (p. iv). Among other things, Niebuhr provided Vincent with an interpretation of Arrian that would lead him to reluctantly voice a reservation about the beneficial nature of Alexander's policy, which is highly unusual coming from him.[73]

While d'Anville is naturally cited among the "Geographers" (pp. 21–26), it is in a critical manner, for according to Vincent "the *Antiquité géographique de l'Inde* is far from standing upon a level with the merits of his other works" (p. 22). On the other hand, Vincent states that he "consulted upon all occasions Major Rennell's *Memoirs.*" As a member of the circle of savants and friends who occasionally gathered in the illustrious major's home, Vincent was well acquainted with Rennell. But he is careful to specify that, while he constantly had Rennell's *Memoir* close at hand, he had "not profited by personal intercourse"; indeed, "[he] held it neither just or honourable to ask for information upon a subject that he had already occupied" (p. iv). These precautions did not prevent the spread of rumors attributing the concept and some of the chapters of *The Voyage of Nearchus* to Rennell.[74] In the second edition, Vincent made certain to distinguish himself from the (too) famous geographer (whom he suspected had not read the *Voyage*) and to criticize Rennell's commentary on Herodotus, which had been published in the meantime.

Either due to genuine apprehension or false modesty, Vincent stated that he feared his work was not properly appreciated. In order to show the novelty of his approach, he ably draws the reader's attention to the fact that "Major Rennell leaves Nearchus at the mouth of the Indus, and Mr. D'Anville takes him up at the entrance of the Persian Gulph; the intermediate space they have both abandoned, as too obscure or too uninteresting for investigation" (p. 3). Vincent thus devotes most of his book to navigation in the Gulf, a subject that had not been dealt with exhaustively by any of his predecessors.

In his obituary of Vincent (1816), Robert Nares observes that *The Voyage of Nearchus* did not sell well, or rather, to quote him more precisely, that "of profit it was never productive," for at least two reasons: its cumulative erudition and its price. Nonetheless, it was reissued ten years later (1807). It was also translated into French in 1800 and there was at least one plan for a German translation.[75] One should also emphasize that the book became widely known in different circles and countries through its numerous reviews, which were often very favorable, and to which we will return by placing them in the context of their development and publication.

Universal History and the History of Alexander in Germany

Any attempt at presenting an annotated list of German philosopher-historians and their works runs into a significant difficulty and a related paradox. On the one hand, the teaching and research environment in Germany was the most professionalized due to the large number of often generously endowed universities; the contributions of German history professors therefore had a major impact, particularly in the first third of the nineteenth century.[76] Yet there are relatively few German publications specifically devoted to Alexander—they are certainly far fewer and less immediately identifiable than those by the British authors discussed above. Despite the excellence of philological studies in Germany, there is no equivalent of Sainte-Croix, whose 1775 edition Friedrich August Wolf briefly considered translating into German.[77]

Of the great names that stand out to today's observer, many of whom taught at the University of Göttingen founded in 1737,[78] none devoted a sustained effort to working on the Macedonian conquest: Arnold Heeren (1760–1842) only mentioned it when a specific episode in Alexander's career overlapped with his field of choice, the organization of exchanges and commerce in antiquity, specifically in the great empires and kingdoms of the Near East; despite his numerous interests, Christian Gottlob Heyne (1729–1812) did not favor the history of Alexander, though he did deal with Alexander in a particularly interesting specialized essay in 1804—which will be given a detailed analysis in the proper context in Chapter 8)—and in reflections scattered in other publications (1763, 1796, 1804);[79] also in Göttingen, August L. Schlözer (1735–1809) only tackled the question of the Macedonian conquest through the history of Phoenicia and its commerce (1761). The list could be extended to include Johann Christoph Gatterer (1729–1799), Christian Daniel Beck (1757–1832), and a few others such as the specialists in the philosophy of history Johann Gottfried Herder (1744–1803) and Georg Wilhelm Friedrich Hegel (1770–1831). As for Barthold Georg Niebuhr (1776–1831), who is primarily known for his research on the history of Rome, he only dealt with Alexander in the classes he sporadically taught at the University of Bonn from 1825 to 1830. Those who came closest to Alexander were scholars specialized in the publication of ancient texts, such as Friedrich Schmieder, who published a noted bilingual edition of Arrian's Indian books in 1798, or specialists in geographical history, like Konrad Mannert (1756–1834) and Carl Ritter (1779–1859). One can also mention histories of commerce, in which Alexander always plays a notable part (aside from Schlözer 1761, see Schmidt 1765, Eichhorn 1775, Berghaus 1792, and of course Heeren).

Another aspect of this paradox is that one of the first monographs on the conquest was published in German in 1797 by Ignaz Aurelius Feßler (1756–1839), a polygraph of Hungarian background who led a wandering and tumultuous life. His *Alexander der Eroberer* was one of several volumes he devoted to "great men" such as Attila, Marcus Aurelius, Aristides, and Themistocles, etc. Curiously, he presents the book as a continuation of Abbé Barthélemy's *Anacharsis* (which ended with Philip's death). In his introduction, he asks the unoriginal question of whether Alexander was a benefactor or a scourge to humanity and proceeds to accept both interpretations over the course of chapters strictly organized according to chronology. The author has an adequate knowledge of the ancient sources (which he conscientiously cites in footnotes) and states that among the modern sources he has given priority to Sainte-Croix's *Examen critique* and John Gillies's *History of Ancient Greece*. The book was reissued several times, but aside from a Dutch translation (*Alexander de Veroveraar*, 1801), it did not have a noticeable impact in other European countries.

In his balanced review of the volume in the *Göttingische Anzeigen von gelehrten Sachen* (1797, pp. 1934–1937), Heyne aptly noted that until the

ALEXANDER
der Eroberer.

cui pro virtute *erat* felix temeritas.
Seneca de Benef. I. 13.

von DR. FESSLER.

Berlin,
bey F. T. Lagarde,
1797.

11. Title page of
Alexander der Eroberer
by Ignatius Aurelius
Feßler (Berlin:
Lagarde, 1797).

publication of Feßler's book, the history of Alexander had been treated
quite differently in the universal histories (*Universal-Geschichten*) and in
the abstracts (*Compendien*). The universal history was indeed extraordinarily cultivated in German universities (partly for pedagogical reasons), as
can be seen, for instance, in the inaugural lesson presented on the subject by
Friedrich von Schiller at the University of Iena in 1789,[80] as well as the articles published by Johann Christoph Gatterer in Göttingen in 1767. While

several universal histories were produced in Germany, all of which included a number of pages devoted to Alexander,[81] German savants also regularly participated in the translation/adaptation of universal histories originally published in England.[82] It was in these enormous volumes that Alexander found his place. The advantage was that by thinking about his outline and the consequent succession of major periods over which he divides material and describes respective significances, the author of the universal history is forced to express his perspective on the historical place of Alexander and his conquests in just a few words. Thus we have Gatterer (who is otherwise very hostile to the Macedonian conqueror) coining a phrase highly revealing of a silent dialogue between past and present: with Alexander, Europe gained ascendancy over Asia for the first time in history; according to the historian, power now rested in Europe.[83]

While they did not write books about Alexander, German scholars contributed in two valuable ways. One was the translation of foreign works (other than universal histories). A notable example is the translation of Goldsmith's *Grecian History* (1774) by the historian Beck (*Dr Goldsmith's Geschichte der Griechen*, 1806), in which the translator made many comments and additions, including a very up-to-date bibliography of Alexander (2:55–57). The numerous footnotes he added throughout the section on the Macedonian conquest (2:55–209) turned Goldsmith's popular history into a scholarly work. The other type of contribution favored by the Germans was the review: while the German scholars were not the only ones to engage in this kind of exercise, they had access to many journals, one of which had been considered throughout Europe since 1739 to be one of the essential places to establish a reputation.[84] Since 1763, the journal had been edited by Heyne, who was also director of the Göttingen library; Heyne was himself one of the journal's most active reviewers (more than 6,000 reviews), as were his two son-in-laws, Arnold Heeren and Georg Forster. For his part, Gatterer published many reviews in the journal he founded, also in Göttingen, the *Allgemeine historische Bibliothek* (1767–1781), which later became the *Historisches Journal* (1782–1799). Heeren reviewed for his own journal, the *Bibliothek der alten Litteratur und Kunst*. In analyzing this dual phenomenon of eighteenth-century translations and reviews of foreign works (particularly as practiced by Gatterer), Gérard Laudin recently wrote that "in terms of history, the Germans find themselves at the convergence point of European networks of circulation; they can take advantage of all the knowledge accumulated, write books and studies that compile and synthesize all of scholarly Europe's historical knowledge."[85] One should simply add that the German scholars were aware of this: in 1797, Friedrich Schmieder was pleased to note that translation was collecting "all the knowledge from all over the world" in Germany.[86]

The Conqueror-Philosopher

Chapter 3

War, Reason, and Civilization

Edward Bulwer-Lytton, Greek Antiquity, and the French Philosophers

In 1837, the English writer Edward Bulwer-Lytton published a book on the rise and fall of Athens.[1] The book was initially conceived to include the conflict between Philip and Athens and the consequences of the Macedonian conquests. For various reasons, the author did not go beyond the Peloponnesian War and therefore did not have reason to research the history of Philip and Alexander to discuss the "fall of Athens"—in any case we know nothing of his ideas on the subject.

The book we know today includes a chapter devoted to the presentation of Athens after the Greco-Persian Wars (4.1). Here, the author develops the idea (seen as a foregone conclusion) that without the Persians' victories, Athens would never have had the political and cultural impact that it had in the fifth century and that beyond that, Europe would not have enjoyed the incomparable Greek heritage that remained alive in the early nineteenth century. Bulwer-Lytton began his discussion by returning to the contribution of "the French philosophers of the last century." He strongly emphasized one of their admirable qualities—that of having condemned war and extolled peace: "Above all the earlier teachers of mankind, they advocated those profound and permanent interests of the human race which are inseparably connected with a love of PEACE; they stripped the image of WAR of the delusive glory which it took, in the primitive ages of society, from the passions of savages and the enthusiasm of poets, and turned out contemplation from the fame of the individual hero to the wrong of the butchered millions" (p. 363). Nonetheless, the author's fervor for the ideas of "those free and bold thinkers" was tempered by one regret. According to him, it was that "their zeal for that humanity . . . led them into partial and hasty views, too indiscriminately embraced by their disciples; and, in condemning the evils, they forgot the advantages of war." For, as he continues: "The misfortunes of one generation are often necessary for the prosperity of another. The stream of blood fertilizes the earth over which it flows, and war has been at once the scourge and the civilizer of the world; sometimes it enlightens the invader, sometimes the invaded, etc."

Edward Bulwer-Lytton (1803–1873) was a talented man. A successful novelist, convinced Philhellene, and supporter of democratic reforms in his country (he was in favor of the 1831 Reform Bill), he was fully aware of his era's scholarship on the subject of ancient Greece and Rome. The attention of today's observer is thus immediately drawn to his retrospective assessment of the eighteenth century. One must admit that his judgment is somewhat biased or, at the very least, simplistic.

Curiously, Bulwer-Lytton explicitly limits his study to the "French philosophers." It is true that Voltaire and Montesquieu—to name only two of the most influential philosophes—provided a decisive impetus, including through the many translations of their work in various European languages. Yet the debate on ancient Greece and Alexander was carried on in their wake by other philosopher-historians in Germany, Scotland, and England. Bulwer-Lytton also strips the French philosophers' reflections on love and war of their dialectic subtlety, perhaps because he wanted to take advantage of their prestige while establishing his own originality.

He was not the first to think about the reasons that Athens flourished in the decades that followed Xerxes's defeat and withdrawal. One need only read Linguet to be convinced of that. Linguet considers that "the magnificent remains" of which the Greeks took possession "became among the victors the prize of valor and the ornament of liberty." At this point, he compares Xerxes facing the Greeks to Philip II of Spain facing the Dutch: "By lavishing vast treasures against their enemies, both gave them the resources to defend themselves. They policed, they enriched the peoples whom they had wanted to dominate."[2] On several occasions (including in reference to Alexander), Linguet defended the theory that war produces progress, which was widespread at the time. For instance, it is accepted as self-evident in Schlözer and Schröckh's universal history for children. After stating that "no war is inevitable," the authors add that "it is often a necessary evil. . . . Despite its horrors, it can be accompanied by much good."[3]

From the Ancients to the Moderns

More significantly, it is both reductive and misleading to exclusively attribute the condemnation and disappearance of the "individual hero" to the "French philosophers." One could even say that there is no shortage of formal continuity from the ancients (Bossuet, Rollin, and their successors) to our philosopher-historians. In general, both groups pass hostile judgment on great conquerors as a matter of principle. Rollin repeats Seneca's violent condemnations of "the bandit and the destroyer of nations (*latro gentiumque vastator*)," in contrast to Hercules, "the pacifier of the entire earth and sea (*terrarum marisque pacator*)" (p. 375).[4] As an enthusiastic heir to this Roman movement extremely hostile to Alexander, Rollin expresses his horror at a conqueror who "does not scruple to sacrifice millions of men to his ambition or curiosity." His commentary is wholly in keeping with Christian history and shows no real compassion for the fate of the defeated caught up in a providential history beyond their understanding: "The conquerors are so many scourges sent by the wrath of heaven into the world to punish the sins of it." Rollin closes his assessment by suggesting to the reader that Alexander could well be considered "as one of the least valuable among [Plutarch's *Parallel Lives*]," especially in comparison to Epaminondas, Hannibal, and Scipio.

Rollin's use of the word "millions" does not imply that he carried out statistical evaluations. It is comparable to Montaigne's use of the word in his essay (3.6) denouncing the Spaniards' ravages in America: "So many cities levelled with the ground, so many nations exterminated, so many millions of people fallen by the edge of the sword, and the richest and most beautiful part of the world turned upside down for the traffic of pearl and pepper!"[5] Though Montaigne (a faithful reader of Plutarch) is contrasting Spanish policy and Alexander's policy, the figure used has no more documentary validity than the one put forward by Rollin. As for Bayle,[6] who does cite his sources on Caesar and comments on them at length, his use of the term "million" is supposed to mirror the Greek term "myriad." In fact, the term "myriad" can mean both "ten thousand" and a quantity so large that it is unquantifiable. The metaphor contains an undeniable performative strength reminiscent of Montaigne. As if it were necessary, its meaning is made explicit by Bayle, who mentions the execution of the Tyrians and relates it to the monarchic values of his time: "There is no prince in these days, but would be degraded from all his glory in a thousand volumes, should he do the twentieth part of what Alexander did."[7]

The unequivocal judgments passed by so many commentators do not only bespeak an attachment to the virtues of a "very Christian royalty," they also express contemporary concerns, born of the multiplication of murderous and ruinous wars in Europe and the yearning for "universal monarchy," a form of political hegemony in the Roman fashion, of which Montesquieu demonstrated the dangerousness and inanity in his *Reflexions sur la monarchie universelle en Europe* (*Reflection on the Universal Monarchy in Europe*) (1733–1734). The reflections of the Abbé Castel de Saint-Pierre (1658–1743) bear witness to the hope for a pacified Europe. Inspired by reading Plutarch's *Lives,* the abbé was a friend of Fontenelle who was elected to the Académie Française in 1695 and expelled in 1718 for harshly criticizing the reign of Louis XIV. Having attended the negotiations for the Treaty of Utrecht in 1712, he conceived a dream of perpetual peace. He proposed a very detailed *Projet pour rendre la paix perpétuelle en Europe* (*Project for Perpetual Peace*) in 1713, which was followed by the publication of an abridged version a few years later. In both volumes, he presented his arguments for the "immense advantages" of peace. "Advantage X" has a programmatic title devoid of any ambiguity: "Comparison of the Conqueror's Glory and the Pacifier's Glory". Here, Castel de Saint-Pierre contrasts conquests "little worthy of praise" with the "vast benefits a Prince can provide to his peoples and even to other neighboring peoples by solidifying the peace."

In Germany, Thomas Abbt's book on "merit" ranks the conqueror well below men of science and legislators, based on criteria previously detailed by the abbé de Saint-Pierre. Real good deeds are produced by the particular qualities of the mind (*Geist*), the soul (*Seele*), and the heart (*Herz*). The author successively considers the conqueror, the soldier, and the saint, then the great men, then the writer, the artist, and the preacher, by classifying them in relation to each other. A quote from Rousseau on "pitiless conquerors" and the "unbridled soldier" opens the chapter and leads the author to ask: "Thus speaks the poet; what does the historian think?" The subsequent discussion of conquerors makes no concessions. Abbt draws parallels between the "hotheads" (*Tollköpfe*) of Macedon and Sweden, condemning them for exclusively devoting themselves to dead-end adventures and vainglory. Both the Macedonians and the Swedes are categorized as "pure conquerors." Though they are not expressly named, Alexander and Charles XII are clearly the principal targets of his criticism.[8]

Based on similar considerations, Alexander was discredited in general history manuals published by two eminent professors at Göttingen and Leipzig—Johann Christoph Gatterer (1761) and Christian Daniel Beck (1788), respectively. While Beck admits that the Macedonian conquest had beneficial aspects, he also devalues the importance of Alexander's victories and marks an opposition between the conqueror and the true "positive hero," Scipio the African. Like many others before him, Gatterer asks whether the Macedonian king deserves to be called "the Great." He uses many of the same expressions as Rollin: "Additionally, if one considers his insatiable ambition, his fierce cruelty, his mad, blind audacity and his other vices, then one is rather inclined to consider this so-called hero a highwayman."[9]

On the other hand, these writers all followed in the wake of Bossuet in his *Politique tirée des propres paroles de l'Écriture sainte* (*Politics Drawn from the Very Words of Holy Scripture*) (1707) in lavishing praise on those kings who were protectors of the people, reigned justly, and promoted agriculture, navigation, and commerce.[10] This is exactly what Rollin recalled by referring to what he saw as Alexander's failure on the Euphrates: the regrettable failure (but willed by God and heralded by the prophets) of a plan that, according to Rollin, "merited the greatest applause"; indeed, "such works are truly worthy in great princes, and give immortal honour to their name, as not being the effect of a ridiculous vanity, but entirely calculated for the public good."[11]

Both "ancients" and "moderns" also distinguished between defensive war and war of conquest. Prideaux, for instance, was indignant that under the influence of his daily reading of Homer, Alexander "thought every thing said of Achilles in it [is] worthy of his imitation, and the readiest way to make him a hero also. . . . It was the main impulsive cause of all his undertakings." The author draws a radical opposition between "the actions of war, bloodshed and conquest of the most celebrated heroes" and what he calls "a righteous cause," which is defined as follows: "The just defence of a man's country, all actions of valour are indeed just reasons of praise; but in all other cases, victory and conquest are no more than murder and rapine; and everyone is to be detested as the greatest enemy to mankind, that is most active herein" (1799 [1715–1717], 1:302).

According to these criteria, Alexander certainly did not belong to the category of "true heroes, who most benefit the world by promoting the peace, welfare, and good of mankind." He did not defend the soil of his Homeland; on the contrary, like "Attila of [his] age," he dedicated himself to "the desolation of countries, burning of cities, and other calamities which attend war."

Similarly, in a book devoted to the Greek colonies in antiquity and particularly to the American colonists' war of independence, Sainte-Croix contrasts the shameful inaction of the ancient Ionians facing the Persians and the indestructible courage of the American colonists facing the English. His aim here is to show that training for war is absolutely indispensable to ensure the survival of a political community concerned with defending or claiming its independence. Sainte-Croix considers that in these situations war is necessary and even recommendable, given that it is waged to defend the community's territory against the aggression of a despotic power (whether Persian or British).[12] Praise of patriotic war can also be found in Diderot, among others: "One must make a great distinction between the hero who dyes the soil with his blood in defense of his homeland and intrepid bandits who find death on a foreign soil or inflict it upon its innocent and unfortunate inhabitants."[13]

While Montesquieu presents Alexander as the essence of the near-perfect conqueror in The Spirit of the Laws, he frequently denounced heroes in his other writings: "Since we have begun to weigh the value of the kings a little better, heroes have been covered with ridicule, so much so that whoever wanted to defend them would be even a thousand times more ridiculous" (My Thoughts, no. 575). Alexander is characterized by "his mania" and "his madness" for wanting to be adored (no. 1523). Making what was then a classic comparison his own, Montesquieu contrasts "the vainglory of Alexander" with "the glory of Epaminondas" (no. 810). One could also cite an occasional work written in 1751, Lysimaque, which is a sort of historical fiction that repeats the accusations traditionally leveled at the despot for his arbitrariness, particularly in unjustly condemning the advisor-philosopher Callisthenes, nephew to Aristotle.

While Montesquieu continues to mock conquerors and "heroes" elsewhere in the Pensées, he also refers to the founding of Alexandria as "the greatest project ever conceived" (no. 243), hails the opening of communica-

tions between the Orient and the Mediterranean (no. 1714), and is fascinated
by the intelligence of the design that guided the conqueror's decisions (no.
1731). These contradictions from one passage to the next are not unique to
Montesquieu. They attest to the development of interpretations, but also
to the persistent ambivalence surrounding the Macedonian king's image in
the face of eighteenth-century questions about the justification for land and
sea conquests and Europeans' relations with conquered peoples.

Even if we consider, as we must, certain nuances and evolutions, the novelty of the contribution made by the philosophes was not to be found in the
condemnation of warrior heroes or the exaltation of the king who puts his
people's happiness first, which were both principles previously developed
and illustrated by Bossuet, Rollin, and their epigones. It was in the way they
connected the two propositions through their interpretation of the figure
of Alexander the Great—whom they often compared and likened to contemporary kings and empire builders (Peter the Great, Frederick)—and their
overall assessment of his conquests. Rollin had recognized that posterity
benefited from the founding of cities by the conquering heroes, but—as he
immediately added—that this was at the cost of the "stream of blood they
spilled." Yet the philosophes argued that while the conquests may have
caused desolation, they led to substantial, even decisive progress. In the
final assessment, these positive transformations easily prevail, particularly
if the conqueror is a true philosopher-king and the war is declared legitimate; in this case, the progress observed can be considered the sign of a
successful conquest. For while it was regularly denounced, conquest was
not systematically condemned. To borrow the words of the "cosmopolitan-
philosopher" and future revolutionary Jean-Louis Carra in the introduction
to his "preventive" plan for the division of European Turkey, "a philosopher
can even justify conquest, [for] this conquest may deter other storms."[14] The
anonymous English reviewer of the Italian clergyman Denina's book on
Frederick of Prussia (1788) makes a similar argument. To justify the idea of
a philosopher-king's intense commitment to military activities, he refers
to the famous English philosopher and moralist Francis Bacon (1561–1626),
whose audience and circulation in Europe remained significant: "No body
can be healthful without Exercise, neither natural body, nor Politik; and
certainly to a Kingdom or Estate, a just and honourable war is the true
Exercise. . . . For in a slothful peace, both courage will effeminate and manners
corrupt."[15]

Here lie the originality and paradox of these philosophers, whose respective views on some of the kings of their time were often irreconcilable (Diderot was uncompromising in condemning Frederick as the "warrior-king").[16] While hostile to the warrior hero and devastating war, they could also exalt the memory of the conquerors whom they declared past or present bearers of a mission to benefit mankind. While their pens killed a classical hero whose reputation was already tarnished, in a sense they brought him back to life in another form, in the context of a Europe embarked on a vast endeavor to conquer and transform the world.

Alexander and the "Great Man": The Voltairian Model

Voltaire undoubtedly played a crucial role in this reflection on war and peace. Though he mocked the abbé de Saint-Pierre's proposals for Perpetual Peace in Europe, he borrowed some of his ideas regarding the notion one should have of the "great man."[17]

Voltaire also occasionally expressed harsh judgments of the Macedonian conqueror. In a letter to the Russian minister Shuvalov dated May 17, 1759, Voltaire claims to be safe from sycophancy and refers to the history of the Macedonian king to proudly tell his correspondent that "he who would deny or excuse the murder of Cleitus would bring contempt and indignation upon himself." But in another letter, he tries to persuade Shuvalov that the murder of Cleitus was largely offset by decisions more important in the history of mankind: revenge carried out in the name of Greece, the founding of Alexandria, love of the arts, etc. The same reversible arguments were used in exchanges with Frederick, who did not share the philosopher's indulgence: "Alexander was certainly not doing his duty by assassinating his friend after supper." In general, Voltaire abandons or qualifies his admiration for Alexander when he compares him to the Russian sovereigns of his time. In a letter dated March 16, 1737, he assures François Prévost d'Exiles that he is eager to see any document "on what Peter did that was useful for humankind," specifying that he "[prefers] an establishment advantageous to society to all of Alexander's victories." Similarly, in a letter to Shuvalov dated February 18, 1768, he knows no restraint in expressing his devotion to the tsarina ("I am an old madman in love with Catherine") and grants her a particularly eminent status: "She seems to me to be as superior to Alexander as the founder is to the destroyer."

While these occasional statements and courtier's impulses should not be given more importance than they deserve, one must recognize that Voltaire consistently expressed his preference for builder kings over destructive heroes. One sees this in a letter he sent on July 14, 1735, to his friend Thiérot, whom he had asked to provide him with documents on the reign of Louis XIV: "Nothing is left of those who led battalions and squadrons but their names. . . . You know that in my view the great men come first, and the heroes last. I call great men those who excelled in what is useful and pleasant. The ransackers of provinces are merely heroes." According to Voltaire, the question was regularly "debated in a very polite and learned Company, viz. Who was the greatest man, Caesar, Alexander, Tamerlane, Cromwell, &." Yet Voltaire decided this was a "trite and frivolous question" and focused on lending his support to the idea that only a man like Newton "is the truly great man [in front of] those politicians and conquerors (and all ages produce some) [who] were generally so many illustrious wicked men."[18] Throughout his writings, Voltaire puts the great thinkers of his time first, for "the light [coming] from Athens alone was probably not comparable to that which Newton and Locke spread over humankind in our day, etc." (*La Bible enfin expliquée*, 1776).

When he focuses on the category of kings and conquerors, the philosophe primarily tries to establish internal distinctions, for "there is a coarseness among princes, as there is among other men. . . . One must ignore the coarseness of kings, which would only be a burden to memory," and, on the contrary, "make known the great actions of sovereigns who changed the face of the earth and especially those who made their people better and happier" (*Nouveau Plan*, 1775). A similar statement is made in the *Discours sur l'histoire de Charles XII* (1731), in which Voltaire regrets that we "hold on to the memory of bad princes, like we remember floods, fires, and plagues." He goes on to condemn conquerors, whom he places "between the tyrants and the good kings" on his scale of values, and deplores once again that "men will more readily speak of the destroyer of an empire than of the one who founded it." However, while Alexander destroyed the Persian empire, he also built a new world, founding cities and developing commerce; he and his father Philip even inaugurated one of the four celebrated ages of history, "to which true glory is attached." He is therefore not a "conqueror destroyer."

Voltaire never wrote an entire book about Alexander (or Frederick). Curiously, he did write a great deal about Charles XII, whose qualities are not those he generally identifies to characterize the ideal statesman: on the contrary, Charles is "what the common man of all eras calls a hero, [one who] is hungry for carnage, [while the] legislating, founding, and warrior monarch is the true great man, and the great man is above the hero" (letter to Shuvalov, July 17, 1738). Instead, the image of Alexander as a "great man" emerges from the way Voltaire systematically draws an opposition between Charles XII and Peter: "Everything about Charles XII and Peter the Great is indifferent to me, with the exception of the good the latter did for mankind," he wrote in 1736 (*Conseils à un journaliste*). This is why Voltaire seeks to overcome Frederick's reticence in his correspondence with him. He recognizes that Peter certainly "has great flaws," but he pleads in his favor because his flaws "were compensated for by that creative spirit and that host of projects that were all imagined for the greatness of his country." The philosophe continues to list the development of the arts and the reduction in the number of monks, among other things, and compares Peter with Alexander. Like Alexander when he killed Cleitus, Peter displayed "vices and ferocity" and his qualities were infinitely superior to Charles's: "This tsar, born with little valor, fought battles, saw many a man killed at his side, personally vanquished the most powerful man on earth." Daring to be insolently ironic with Frederick, Voltaire adds: "I like a coward who wins battles" (letter to Frederick, January 1738). Then, implicitly including Peter and Alexander in his judgment, he elaborates on the well-established idea that private vices and public virtues can easily coexist in the great man: "I will not conceal his failings, but I will raise as high as I can not only what he did that was great and beautiful, but what he wanted to do. I wish that all the histories that only tell us of the kings' vices and furies were thrown to the bottom of the sea. What use do these registers of crimes and horrors serve other than to sometimes encourage a weak prince to excesses of which he would be ashamed had he not seen examples of them?"

When Peter came to power, Voltaire continues, "the Muscovites were less civilized than the Mexicans when they were discovered by Cortez." Peter "also wanted to be great through commerce, which leads both to the wealth of a state and the advantages of the entire world. He set about turning Russia into the commercial center for Asia and Europe; he wanted to connect the Dvina, the Volga, and the Don through canals, of which he had drawn up the plans, and open new paths from the Baltic Sea to the Black Sea and the Caspian Sea, and from these two seas to the northern ocean." Introduced in a most classic manner on the eve of the Swedish defeat at

Poltava (1709), the comparison between Charles and Peter turns to the latter's advantage, despite the fact that Peter "had not shed the coarseness of his education": "Charles had the title of 'Invincible', of which a single moment might deprive him; the neighboring nations had already given Peter Alexiowitz the name of 'Great', which, as he did not owe it to his victories, he could not forfeit by a defeat (*Histoire de Charles XII*, bk. 4).[19] Charles "brought all the hero's virtues to a point of excess at which they are as dangerous as the opposite vices." Elsewhere, Voltaire regrets that Charles was unable to make the peace that was offered to him by Peter: "If he had applied himself to making the arts and commerce flourish in his homeland, he would truly have been a great man; instead he was only a great warrior" (letter to Marshall Schulenburg, August 2, 1740). In the portrait of the king of Sweden that closes his *Histoire de Charles XII* (bk. 8), Voltaire makes explicit the lesson to be learned: "His life must teach kings to what extent a pacific and happy government is superior to so much glory."

In this, Voltaire was following an opinion by then well accepted in Europe. It is clearly apparent in Savary des Bruslons's *Dictionnaire du commerce*, first published in 1723. Here, the establishment of terrestrial, maritime, and naval commerce by Peter the Great is already recognized as a prodigious advance: "This Monarch always saw to the glory of his nation and the happiness of his Peoples."[20] Before Savary, Bishop Huet had not failed to announce the commercial development of Muscovy.[21]

Voltaire manifestly uses the same words and expressions to describe Peter's positive achievements and those of Alexander. The Macedonian king "is probably worthy of the name *Great* despite his vices" because "he founded more cities than he destroyed" (*Essai sur les mœurs*, chap. 141). This comparison had been made earlier by Fontenelle in the *Eloge funèbre* (*Eulogy*) delivered at the Académie Royale des Sciences in November 1725 in honor of the "conqueror-Academician" who had so thoroughly transformed Russia. Fontenelle emphasized the creation of a navy, the construction of bridges, the voyages of discovery and improvement of maps, and the construction of Petersburg, which immediately brought to mind the founding of Alexandria: "This city, to which he had given birth and his name, was to him what Alexandria was to Alexander its founder, and like Alexandria, it was so well situated that it changed the face of Commerce in its time, and replaced Tyre as its capital; similarly, Petersburg would change today's Routes and become the center of one of the largest Commercial activities in the

Universe" (pp. 120–121). Voltaire made the same comparison, several times juxtaposing the tsar's policies with Alexander's policy in Tartary: "In this respect I may venture to compare Peter the Great to Alexander; like him he was assiduous and indefatigable in his pursuits, a lover and friend of the useful arts; he surpassed him as a law-giver, and like him endeavored to change the tide of the commerce in the world, and built and repaired at least as many towns as that celebrated hero of antiquity" (*Histoire de Russie*, 2.16).[22] The comparison is primarily made through Voltaire's personal assessment of the relationship between Russians and Turks.[23] Nonetheless, the image constructed by comparing Alexander and Peter is of monarchs whose vices and excesses cannot obscure the debt they are owed by those they conquered: both rulers opened the world to advances of the human spirit.

Montesquieu and Alexander's Plans: "A Sally of Reason"

In one of the reflections collected in the *Spicilège* (no. 422), Montesquieu brings up the "miracle of the Universe" that was the Roman empire. He underlines the large number of "circumstances" that allowed for its advent, to the point that "such a thing may never happen again." Adding the examples of Alexander, Charlemagne, and Genghis Khan, he considers that "these conquerors of the universe never had a fully-formed plan to conquer the Universe. They only imagined the plan after the fact." He then develops the idea that Alexander expanded his initial plans as he chalked up victories: "He was not thinking of conquering Asia either, his plan was only to relieve the Greek colonies in Asia Minor, like Agesilaus and other Greek captains before him."

The contrast with the Alexander of *The Spirit of the Laws* is striking.[24] In the *Spirit*, prior Greek enterprises are not examples to be imitated, but precedents from which Alexander draws lessons for the future of his own plans (10.13). The conqueror is more generally presented as a man of reflection who sees far ahead and is subject neither to the uncontrollable happenstance of elusive circumstances nor the brutal power of irrepressible passions. In order to properly establish the man of intentions he wants to introduce to his readers, Montesquieu depicts him in contrast to other well-known historical figures.

The second to last paragraph of chapter 14 of book 10, entitled "Alexander," offers a kind of synoptic perspective on the Macedonian king's policy toward the Persians, which Montesquieu contrasts with Caesar's approach. The Roman general merely sought "to imitate the kings of Asia." In doing so, Caesar displayed "pure ostentation," which "drove the Romans to despair"—he was driven by a desire to be admired and to impose his power by resorting to artifice and subterfuge. For his part, Alexander did not allow himself to give in to impulses: "He did something that entered into the plan of his conquest"—a plan that called for a kind of association with the defeated, far removed from ostentatious and superficial imitation. Alexander made decisions based on preliminary rational analysis from which he elaborated a political project. Admittedly, Montesquieu acknowledges that Alexander did "two things that were bad [and] criminal actions." Yet even if the reader does not approve of Montesquieu's call to forgive and forget (by which he echoes Arrian), he understands that these impulsive actions never called into question or endangered the plan whose various aspects and successive stages Montesquieu has just detailed.

Looking at the parallel chapter (10.13) devoted to Charles XII, one finds the same balancing and line of reasoning. Just as chapter 14 shifts dramatically in its middle ("It is thus that he made his conquest; let us see how he preserved them"), chapter 13 is structured in two distinct justifying phases in which Alexander is favorably compared to Charles of Sweden.

While Charles certainly also had "designs," these were unrealistic, for "he was not ruled by the actual arrangements of things," while Alexander defined "a wise project [that] was wisely executed." Rather than being driven by "temerity" and the desire to display his "valour," Alexander showed wisdom. But what constitutes wisdom for a king leading his armies into a vast offensive far away from its bases (in Macedon or in Sweden)? It is simply to adapt his ends to his means and those of his adversary. This was exactly what Charles failed to do by launching into "a long war, one which his kingdom could not support." The more he advanced "in the inhabited regions of Poland," the more his lines of communication with the rear were rashly extended and the less his army could find supplies: "Sweden was like a river whose waters were cut off at the source while its course was being deflected." Charles also made the mistake of not analyzing the strengths and weaknesses of Peter the Great and his kingdom: Russia "was not a state in its decline . . . but a rising empire." Charles should have foreseen that his enemy would refuse to engage in combat with him until it felt ready to face the Swedish army and defeat it. The king of Sweden was his own victim—a victim of his recklessness and his inability to define a reasonable project and devote all his resources to carrying it out reasonably and wisely. Montesquieu expresses the conclusion to be drawn from his analysis as follows: "Charles was not ruled by the actual arrangements of things, but rather by a certain model he had chosen; even this he followed badly. He was not Alexander, but he would have been Alexander's best soldier." In other words, Charles allowed himself to become intoxicated with the heroic model he had dreamed up by reading Quintus Curtius. While he was a good soldier, he lacked the ability to be a great captain because he was unable to coolly analyze a situation that he had personally contributed to creating and that ran against his own best interests. The further he chased the Russian army into areas he did not control, because they were unknown to him, the more he put his army in jeopardy. His defeat can therefore be fundamentally explained "neither by nature or fortune," "but by the nature of things."

This double parallel with Caesar and Charles plays an essential part in constructing the historical figure of Alexander, who is posited to differ from these rulers in that he meticulously prepared his plans of conquest and carried them out without straying from the initial project. The opposition allows Montesquieu to skirt an apparently insurmountable obstacle, which is that aside from Alexander's desire to take revenge on the Persians in the name of the Greeks, the ancient sources say nothing of his war objectives and provide no description of his logistics preparations. Montesquieu fills in these gaps by showing the Macedonian as a rational man, a quality that the ancient historians always denied him, particularly "those who have wanted to make a romance of his story, those whose spirit was more spoiled than his." The Alexander of *The Spirit of the Laws* is entirely different: "Alexander, in the rapidity of his actions, even in the heat of his passions, was led by a vein of reason, if I dare use the term." Once the comparison has established his postulate, Montesquieu can confidently invite the reader to follow him: "Let us speak about him at length!"

Logistics and Strategy

According to Montesquieu, "Alexander left little to chance." Facing Darius, he developed a plan that heralded on a strategic level what he would implement on a political level. In both cases, reason prevails over passions or, to put it better, it controls them. The Macedonian king had analyzed the enemy he planned to attack. Using the knowledge thus accumulated, he prepared every aspect of his strategy down to the slightest detail.

Yet in essence Montesquieu knew no more about the Persian empire than his contemporaries; that is to say, practically nothing beyond the disastrous image of the empire disseminated by the Greek and Latin sources, which corresponded perfectly with contemporary ideas of the "despotic Orient." If Alexander's project was considered "sensible," it was because past and recent experiences of military conflict between the Greeks and Persians had shown that the Persians were far inferior in this area and that they were incapable of reforming themselves: "It was well known that the Persians were too great to correct themselves." This explanation had long been universally accepted. It is found in 1729, for instance, under the pen of D. Secousse, who explicitly follows in Bossuet's wake: "The expedition against the Persians was just, prudent, necessary, based on the most certain political maxims, and the fact that success was nearly infallible." Indeed, Darius's army was no more than "a gigantic body, but poorly proportioned, without strength, and as if overwhelmed by the weight of its mass. It cannot move and can barely hold itself up"; the image of the (Persian) idol with feet of clay was already well established.

Montesquieu credits Alexander for his foresight, which places the Macedonian offensive in a totally different context than Charles's war against Peter of Russia: Alexander knew that far from refusing to fight, the Great King, bloated with pride and arrogance, "would hasten [his] downfall by always giving battle." Montesquieu is clearly thinking of the famous debate that the ancient authors dramatized through the well-known royal court story of the king torn between the advice of good advisers and mere flatterers. Encouraged by his courtiers and a slave to his own passions, Darius allegedly put to death the Greek advisor Charidemus, who had warned him before the Battle of Issus of the danger of facing the Macedonian army in pitched battle. This convenient interpretation circulated in all the books. It can already be found in the work of the military practitioner and historian Folard, who sententiously remarked in 1727 that the "other misfortune of Sovereigns is that they find themselves unable to make a good choice among this crowd of effeminate and lost Courtiers, as is the case with the Kings of Persia, who always conceal the virtues that offend them."[25]

Folard also addressed the issue of supplies, recalling a maxim by Admiral de Coligny: "He said that an army was a monster that should always be formed first from the belly, and through the food with which it must be provided before one demands any further service from it." While he mentions the precedent of Alexander (whose victories he systematically devalues in comparison to those of Charles XII), Folard takes as an example Gustavus Adolphus's expedition and defeat in Poland, "a country where . . . the lack of supplies and warehouses made things impossible." The same had to be said of that hero he does admire, Charles XII, who was even more unfortunate than Gustavus Adolphus and lost his entire army "at the entrance to Muscovy" due to an utter lack of logistics.[26]

Did Montesquieu read Folard? It is possible, though his work is not included in the catalog of the library at La Brède. In any case, he stands out from the historians who preceded him due to the attention he devotes to Alexander's logistical preparations. While Alexander was confident in his strength and knew that he would be facing "a state in its decline," he was not surrendering his fate to "chance" in that—in contrast, once again, to Charles—he knew he could stray from his Macedonian bases without worrying about being cut off from his supply sources. Why? Because the Persian empire yielded its own resources to the invader. How? This was the explanation given by Montesquieu, who attributed it to Alexander, thereby crediting him with flawless lucidity: "As the empire was cultivated by a nation of the most industrious people in the world who plowed their lands on account of religious principle, a nation fertile and abundant in all things, it was very easy for an enemy to subsist there" (10.13).

To understand Montesquieu's reasoning, the reader must take a synoptic view of books 10 (*On the Laws in Their Relation with Offensive Force*) and 18 (*On the Laws in Their Relation with the Nature of the Terrain*). In chapters 7 and 8 of the latter, Montesquieu introduces countries where man's industry has brought waters forth and made the harvests thrive. Drawing on a famous passage in Polybius and Chardin's *Voyage en Perse*, Montesquieu posits that this was the case with the Persians under the Great Kings: "Today, one finds [water] in one's fields and gardens without knowing where it comes from" (18.7). Alexander therefore knew that he would be able to benefit from the measures which the Great Kings devoted to increasing their provinces' fertility and productivity. In Montesquieu's view, this is a resounding sign of Alexander's organizational abilities, which hinged on precise prior knowledge of the enemy he was coming to fight on its own turf; hence "he did not lack provisions" (10.14).[27]

Montesquieu has no trouble going on to show that the plan unfolded as intended: "Alexander owed his mastery of Greek colonies to the crossing of the Granicus; the battle of Issus gave him Tyre and Egypt; the battle of Arbela gave him the whole earth." Alexander chose to "[let] Darius flee after the battle of Issus" in order to focus on his primary objective of "consolidating and ruling his conquests." This carefully considered decision allowed him to easily take control of Egypt because "Darius had left [it] stripped of troops while he was collecting innumerable armies in another universe."

Based on a close reading of Arrian, Montesquieu's theory had previously been outlined by the Maréchal de Puységur, whose posthumous book on the art of war (Art de la guerre) was published the same year as the first edition of The Spirit of the Laws (1748). Puységur was another fervent admirer of the author of The Anabasis of Alexander who explicitly and firmly disagreed with those who accused Alexander of recklessness. He aimed first and foremost to underline the greatness of Alexander's strategic genius: "However great that hero may be shown to us in battle, in which we see that he is the one leading everything, I find him even far greater in his general plan for the conquest of Asia, and in the equally shrewd, prudent, and sustained manner of succeeding and remaining there.... To make the general plan for a war, to properly follow it, to properly execute it; undivided honor is due to the one who commands and undertook it" (p. 20). Puységur agrees that "there is nothing reckless or too hazardous in his enterprise to conquer Asia," and specifies that "based on my reading of Arrian, this is my understanding of Alexander's design to conquer Asia.... I discover the full depth of his project in the way that he speaks to his captains." Puységur is referring to the war council held by Alexander outside Tyre to defend his strategy to conquer the coasts up to Egypt (according to Arrian 2.17). Arrian concludes: "With these words Alexander easily won over his staff to the attack of Tyre." (2.18.1)

Project, design, plan, science, strategy: we find some of Montesquieu's key words here because both authors used Arrian to guide them toward Alexander, his conquests, and his thought. Due not only to the extraordinary influence of The Spirit of the Laws, but also to the specific global nature of his approach, it is Montesquieu who must be credited with the lasting and considerable innovation made to the history of Alexander at this stage. The image that imposes itself is that of a conquest made inevitable by the coherence of the strategic design and the intelligence of its tactical realization. The reader is quickly convinced that everything was planned from the start. Everything or *nearly* everything for, as we shall see, Montesquieu's Alexander was also able to adjust his plans and designs based on the obstacles and difficulties he encountered in the course of his progress through enemy territories.

Geography and Discovery: From Knowledge to Conquest

In one of his *Pensées* (no. 1731), Montesquieu vigorously emphasizes the coherence of Alexander's vision, from the death of Darius up to and including the conquest of India: "The valour that Alexander displayed in his conquest of the Indies has been praised. I would rather see people praise his conducts—how he linked together the Indies with Persia, with Greece; how he pursued Darius's murderers right into Bactria and the Indies themselves; how he had the skill to begin by subduing the territory north of the Indies and returning, so to speak, by the Indies; how he descended along the rivers so as not to be stopped at their crossings; how he thought to make his conquests relate to his conquests" (trans. H. C. Clark). The treatment is a little different in *The Spirit of the Laws,* which does not feature any uninterrupted narrative passages coming after Darius's final defeat (10.13–14). Jumping ahead to the Indian expedition in chapter 8 of book 21 on the history of commerce, one finds that the very idea of "design" is still present, but it is developed in a particular context.

Montesquieu states that "Alexander's design was to march to the East, but, upon finding the southern part full of great nations, towns, and rivers, he attempted to conquer it and did so" (21.8). Alexander changed his original plan. Why? Montesquieu does not reiterate the explanation traditionally accepted since antiquity; he does not say a word about or even allude to the "mutiny on the Hyphasis," by which Alexander's own soldiers allegedly forced him to turn back. The explanation provided is entirely different: due to new information received in the field, the king decided to go down the Indus, then reconnoiter and colonize the coast of the Persian Gulf. According to Montesquieu, he could not have thought of this earlier because no one knew anything about navigating the Indus and the Gulf. The example attests to Alexander's responsiveness and the close connection between his cognitive reflection and strategic elaboration: "At that time he formed the design of uniting the Indies with the west by a maritime commerce, as he had united them by the colonies he had established on the land."

Montesquieu explicitly contrasts this incident with the expedition launched by Darius close to two centuries earlier: "The voyage that Darius had the Persians make down the Indus and the Indian Sea was the fancy of a prince who wants to show his power rather than the orderly project of a monarch who wants to use it. This had no consequences, either for commerce, or for sailing, and if one departed from ignorance, it was only to return to it shortly." While the Great King was entirely dedicated to his egotistical passion for power and its trappings, Alexander remained guided by reason and sought to improve his knowledge in order to make a plan—not only a plan of conquest, but a plan that took into account all communication between the Indies and the Occident. Exploration was an indispensable prelude to conquest and to taking control of land and sea territories previously left in the dark of ignorance by the Persians. The decisions made next were a result of the geographic knowledge personally acquired by Alexander: "He went himself with some vessels to reconnoiter that sea, marked the places where he wanted ports, harbors and arsenals constructed.... He had wells dug and towns built."

By reconstructing the various stages of the conqueror's reflection, Montesquieu is logically led to deny that the king had already planned a passage to India and the Persian Gulf when he founded Alexandria.[28] Admittedly, he considers that Alexander "certainly had, in general, the project of establishing a commerce between the Indies and the western parts of his empire." But at that time he could not have considered realizing this commercial project through Egypt. Why? The answer never varies: "He had too little information to be able to form the project of carrying this commerce through Egypt.... He did not know about the Arabian Seas that are between the two." This explains the naval expeditions Alexander launched from Babylon and the Red Sea to circumvent the Arabian Peninsula. Though these missions ultimately failed, their captains brought back a great deal of precious information, including on the flora of the land of frankincense (whose coastline they had traveled along). Yet Montesquieu rejects the hypothesis that

Alexander had "the design of putting the seat of his empire in Arabia." Why? The explanation provided is always the same: "How could he have chosen a place unknown to him?"

The precisely calibrated image of Alexander in *The Spirit of the Laws* is formidably effective at proving a point. His successes on the battlefield are not due to his "temerity," but, on the contrary, to the "greatness of his genius." He is not a hero leading the charge at the head of his troops, but a king who thinks, reflects, and prepares, in keeping with the monarchic model of Montesquieu's time[29]—a king who only leaps into action after carefully taking stock of the available information on the countries and their people, then devising a plan and elaborating a strategy.

Alexander and Darius's Empire: From Voltaire to Linguet

Entirely absorbed by the logical and rational construction of his own reasoning and interpretations, Montesquieu does not openly or systematically court controversy with other commentators on Alexander's conquests—though explicit references can sometimes be found in his rough drafts.[30] Voltaire takes the opposite approach, exclusively revealing his views of Alexander's plans by disagreeing with his predecessors. We first see this in his systematic attack on Flavius Josephus and Rollin regarding the siege of Tyre. Voltaire steadfastly refutes the idea that Alexander decided to undertake such a difficult campaign merely to please the Jews, "who did not like the Tyrians," or even worse, that "the God of the universe only made Alexander march to conquer Asia to console a few Jews" (*La Bible enfin expliquée*). Alexander did not lack good reasons to march on Tyre, starting with strategic imperatives dictated by the necessity to seize the coasts, both to protect himself from sea attacks and the threat due to Darius's determination to raise a new army. As a close ally to the Great King with a formidable fleet and a port said to be impregnable, Tyre symbolically and literally posed both threats and therefore needed to be brought under Alexander's control. This is what Voltaire is getting at in a remark in the introduction to the *Essai sur les mœurs* (Introduction, §XLVI), which is repeated nearly word for word in his article on "Alexander" in *Questions* and the *Dictionnaire:* "He wanted to control Egypt before he crossed the Euphrates and the Tigris and deprive Darius of all the ports that could provide him with fleets. To carry out this design, which was that of a very great captain, it was necessary to besiege Tyre. This city was under the protection of the kings of Persia and ruled over the sea."

Referring to the ancient authors (Arrian, Quintus Curtius, Diodorus, Orosius), Voltaire considers that the decision to take control of the coasts was a wise one because "it was necessary, after having defeated Tyre, not to lose a moment before seizing the port of Pelusium. . . . He went from Tyre to Pelusium in seven days" (*Essai sur les mœurs*, Introduction, §XLVI). Here, Voltaire follows the same line as Montesquieu, who, without ever referring to the Jerusalem affair,[31] emphasized Alexander's successful strategy: "He maneuvered the Persians away from the seashore. . . . [As for] Tyre, it was attached to the Persians, who could not do without its commerce and its navy." This allowed Alexander to take control of Egypt while Darius was raising a new army (*Spirit of the Laws,* 10.14). The difference is that Montesquieu does not go to the trouble of responding to Rollin or Prideaux.

Voltaire never has occasion to discuss the later stages of the conquests in a comprehensive, exhaustive manner. He simply touches upon them in the course of his dispute with Quintus Curtius and the compilers, who considered that Alexander was behaving like a godless and lawless bandit in leading a campaign against the Scythians of Central Asia: "Quintus Curtius depicts these Scythians as peaceful, just men who are stunned to see a Greek robber come from so far away to subjugate peoples made indomitable by their virtues. He does not think of the fact that these invincible Scythians had been subjugated by the kings of Persia" (*Pyrrhonisme*). In the chapter of his *Histoire de Russie* entitled "On [Peter's] conquests in Persia," he notes as if it were self-evident that the reason Alexander led campaigns in these regions was simply that his enemy "the king of Persia [was] master of a large part of southern Scythia and the Indies." In the "History" entry in Diderot and d'Alembert's *Encyclopédie* (8,[1765], p. 222), he describes the full expanse of Xerxes's states and launches another attack on "the declaimers in verse and prose [who made the mistake] of accusing Alexander, the avenger of Greece, of being a madman for subjugating the empire of the Greeks' enemy." As the leader of a war of revenge, Alexander was duty-bound to roam across and subdue all the territories subject to the Great Kings: "He only went to Egypt, Tyre, and India because he had to, and because Tyre, Egypt, and India were under the dominion of those who had devastated Greece." In the *Dictionnaire:* "There can be no doubt that Alexander subdued that part of India which lies on this side of the Ganges and was tributary to the Persians." And in *La Bible enfin expliquée:* "[If he] went all the way to the Hydaspes in India, [it was] because that was where Darius's empire ended. In short, Voltaire's thesis—which is constantly directed against "the rhetoricians" (chief among whom one recognizes Rollin)—is simple: from the moment he landed, Alexander's stated plan was to conquer the Great Kings' entire empire, including its most remote regions (i.e., the land of the Uzbeks and the Scythians and India up to the Hyphasis). If the conquest continued after Issus and the death of Darius, it was not because of a perpetually unsatisfied conqueror's unbounded ambition, but because of the original design of a strategist dedicated to fulfilling the mission with which the Greeks had entrusted him: to wipe out Darius's empire and make it his own.

Voltaire's point of view was adopted by Linguet, who provided his scattered remarks with new discursive coherence. This is how he introduces the territorial objective Alexander set from the start: "It was not a small portion of Asia that he wanted to wrestle from the Persians. He was not simply thinking of building a kingdom more extensive than his own.... It was therefore predictable that the war would only end with the complete ruin of one of the two Kings" (1762, pp. 95–97; 1769, pp. 147–149). Linguet emphasizes the implacable nature of Alexander's plans in a statement clearly borrowed from Montesquieu (10.14): "The Battle of the Granicus had opened Asia to Alexander, that of Issus had won him Anatolia, Syria, Egypt, and that of Arbela gave him the rest of the Empire, Babylon, Susa, Persepolis etc." (1762, p. 132; 1769, p. 186).

Then, after Darius's death, "Alexander was able to see himself as the legitimate and peaceful possessor of the empire" (1762, p. 132; 1769, p. 186). To firmly respond to those who had always defended the opposite theory (most recently Mably),[32] Linguet clearly expresses his idea of Alexander's objective: "Moreover, one should not believe that he gave in to his bellicose ardor without having a well-determined, set goal. He did not indistinctly want to subjugate the world. He wanted the countries under the crown of Darius, whose every right he claimed to support. Despite the ridiculous ambition he is attributed, he only attacked the peoples whom he could consider the subjects of the throne that he had seized. If he fought the Scythians, it was because those savages had come to defy him with threats, and he settled for pushing them aside. If he penetrated the Indies, it was because they had belonged to the Persians since the first Darius had conquered them etc."[33] Linguet finds additional proof in Alexander's policy regarding the Indian

King Porus: "Alexander did not dethrone any of the Princes he defeated; he left them their rank and what power the Persians had not deprived them of, and this is more proof that he only wanted the Empire in the same form that Darius had possessed it" (1762, p.147; 1769, p. 201).

Alexander wisely never crossed the Hyphasis: "This river was to be the end of his empire, as it had been that of Darius's empire." And once his initial objective was achieved, he returned to Babylon. The conclusion is obvious: "[Despite] all the declamations to the contrary, Alexander was able to subject his ambition to rules and to only abide by laws, whether well or poorly founded.... He confined himself to subduing those peoples who could be subdued with an appearance of justice."[34] As an heir to Voltaire and Montesquieu, Linguet joined them in opposing "all the historians" who had imposed a false image of Alexander: "[They] limited themselves to praising his valor, which he pushed to temerity, and exaggerating the number of victims whom he sacrificed to ambition. They turn him into a kind of pirate, a determined bandit, who always walked straight ahead, with the vague design of knocking down everything that resisted him, without forming any plan to keep control of what he had seized. They developed neither his views nor his policy nor the art he put into making newly subjected peoples love his Empire" (1762, pp. 90–91; 1769, p. 20). This also explains why Linguet devoted a specific passage to Alexander's journey to consult with the oracle of Amon in Siwa Oasis. Going against Rollin and Mably, but also Prideaux, who had all emphasized Alexander's absurd ambition and the folly of the undertaking, Linguet attempts to show that the risks were limited and calculated: the Macedonian conqueror never sacrificed his carefully thought-out, vast designs to ambition or temerity.[35]

Alexander and the Image of the Strategist in Condorcet

An avowed admirer of the *Essai sur les mœurs,* Condorcet (1743–1794) touched on the history of Alexander in the various manuscripts and sketches known under the title of *Tableau historique des progrès de l'esprit humain* (1793–1794).[36] Here, the history of the progress of sciences and the mind is considered in successive stages, with a total of ten "periods." In the *Prospectus* of 1793, the fourth period is devoted to "the progress of the human mind in Greece up to the time of the division of the sciences around the age of Alexander." The

"Elements of the Fourth Period" in the *Tableau historique* are organized diachronically, though the narrative thread remains loose. Condorcet reviews the entire history of ancient Greece, naturally including—and even prioritizing—the history of the arts and sciences. His sources are often the ancient authors and possibly modern histories of Greece (which are not cited); he may have used *The History of Ancient Greece* by John Gillies, whose pertinent analyses he praised elsewhere.[37]

In any case, Condorcet discusses the history of Greece in the fourth century at some length, without forgetting to provide his own (rather commonplace) point of view on Persia's deplorable development up to the point when Philip significantly expanded the kingdom of Macedon. After his assassination, the crown was passed on to "a young son, without experience, who was only known for his spirited vigor." Condorcet has strong reservations about Alexander's personality, "pushing pride to the madness of wanting to pass himself off as a god, a prey to all the excesses of the most shameful debauchery, drunkenness, and anger." He is not far from considering Alexander's death justified, whether it was caused by his excesses (debauchery and drunkenness) or poison.

Yet he also states that he "admires [in him] the genius for war as well as for politics, the most expansive views of commerce, the zeal for the progress of enlightenment, etc." To this end, he repeats the major stages of an apparently irresistible conquest by paraphrasing statements also found in Montesquieu and Linguet: "A single victory makes Alexander the master of the shores of Asia Minor.... [Issus] opens the way to Asia for the Macedonians.... Having taken hold of the center of the Persian Empire, Alexander finished subduing the nations that composed it or rendering them harmless." Obsessed with what he saw as the importance of the Greek heritage, Condorcet has a specific explanation for the strategy that led Alexander to march against Tyre and Egypt after Issus. It stands out from his predecessors' interpretation in that it posits the danger posed by the Greek city states as one of Alexander's foremost strategic concerns: "It was necessary either to put an end to his conquests or to close the ports of Asia and Egypt to the Greeks."

Ultimately this did not matter much, given that Condorcet's primary purpose was not to make an "abridged account of the principal events of Greek history"; this only served to allow the reader "to appreciate the progress made by the human race and to identify its causes." One passage in particular draws attention. Of the advances then observable, Condorcet does not fail to underline those that relate to the expansion of commerce and changes to commercial routes (such as the loss of Athens' preeminence in favor of Tyre). Then comes a reflection on the appearance of a new type of political and military leader, which the author places between the Peloponnesian War and Alexander, that is to say—I emphasize in passing—during the period Linguet refers to as the "Age of Alexander" and Voltaire as the "Age of Philip and Alexander." This era saw the development of a "truly military art" and the use of "the kind of policy that consists in preventing the growth of a neighboring state … [not exclusively] through force … [but also] through the ruses of modern politics, that art of making treaties while holding back excuses to break them later." Was Condorcet thinking of Philip of Macedon in writing these sentences? It is highly possible, not to say perfectly likely.

What follows also concerns the definition of the new statesman, who is characterized by reason, a project, and perseverance in adapting the end to the means. The passage is worth quoting in its entirety: "[The policy] that consists in knowing the importance of possessing a port or a distant city for the power or wealth of a State, in forging in Thrace, Sicily, and Asia the chains that some wanted to put on Greece, acquired the same shrewdness and expanse. Ambition became well-reasoned and systematic. They are no longer those rapid conquerors of Asia who aimlessly march where they think they will find slaves and gold, they are warriors and politicians as clever as they are audacious, who calculate their enterprises, see that their marches are carried through, and look to the project they are executing for the means to succeed at the project they contemplate." It appears that what Condorcet has in mind are the Roman statesmen and their methods of conquest in the Eastern Mediterranean. Yet no matter which historical figures Condorcet was thinking of in writing and revising this unfinished manuscript, the vision is not unique to him. His conqueror-statesman with a design and a focus on the means to achieve it closely resembles the Alexander of Montesquieu, Voltaire, and Linguet.

Alexander in Scotland and England:
Plans, Designs, and the Arts of Peace

Interest in the French philosophes was particularly pronounced in a country that Voltaire, in exalting the light spread by Newton and Locke, described as "an island formerly ignored by the rest of the world"—in other words, England, to which we will append Scotland.

The image of Alexander as man of reason was fully embraced there. In 1755, before he "discovered" the figure of Alexander, William Robertson shared his opinion of the conqueror-civilizer in a review of a book on Peter the Great. Like his future two-tone portrayal of Alexander, Robertson's Peter combines "the vices of a man, the violence of a tyrant, and even, on some occasions, the fierceness of a barbarian." But he is first and foremost "a benefactor to mankind." In Robertson's view, there is no contradiction between the tsar's virtues and vices: "Perhaps even these defects in his character contributed towards the success of his undertaking; and with less impetuosity, and greater gentleness of disposition, with more refinement, and a nicer sense of decorum, he might have left his grand enterprise at a farther distance from perfection."[38]

Twenty years later, Robertson's reflections on the history of navigation and commerce in book 1 of his *History of America* (1777) led him to emphasize the importance of Alexander's conquests, which "considerably enlarged the sphere of navigation and of geographical knowledge among the Greeks." His remarks clearly indicate that he has weighed the pros and cons, evaluating what falls under operations of war and what belongs to the work of peace.

In the *Historical Disquisition* (1791) that would be his final publication, Robertson repeats some of these expressions to discuss Alexander's significant failings, but pays particular attention to "the grandeur and extent of his plans" and his desire to refine his knowledge of the land and use that to prepare vast rational plans to connect and consolidate the various regions of his empire ranging from India to the Mediterranean: "As amidst the hurry of war and the rage of conquest, he never lost sight of his pacific and commercial schemes."[39] Undoubtedly inspired by Volney's *Voyage en Syrie*, which he quotes several times, Robertson laments the disappearance of Palmyra, whose commercial strength had made it so useful and necessary to the development of exchanges with India. By contrast, his reflection fuels his notion of a beneficial conquest: "But it is a cruel mortification, in searching for what is instructive in the history of past times, to find that the exploits of conquerors who have desolated the earth, and the freaks of tyrants who have rendered the nations unhappy, are recorded with minute and often disgusting accuracy, while the discovery of useful arts, and the progress of the most beneficial branches of commerce, are passed over in silence, and suffered to sink into oblivion" (*Historical Disquisition,* p. 59).

This is why when Robertson discusses Alexander ("that extraordinary man") as he had discussed Peter the Great, he implores the reader not to dwell on "the violent passions which incited him, at some times, to the wildest actions, and the most extravagant enterprises," for Alexander "possessed talents which fitted him not only to conquer, but to govern the world" (*History of America,* 1812, 1:13). In a comparable fashion, when John Campbell introduces Nearchus's journey in John Harris's 1764 anthology of travel narratives, he condemns Alexander for "so many outrages on the rights of Mankind," but readily accepts that his plans were not driven by vanity alone, and that his true genius was expressed in his commercial projects.[40]

Though his *The Voyage of Nearchus* (1797) followed in the footsteps of Montesquieu, Rennell, Gillies, and Robertson (to name only the principal sources of inspiration), William Vincent was the first to so clearly declare his rejection of the good/bad alternative that had traditionally constructed historical discourse. He professes great admiration for the rational nature of the conqueror's thought. From the outset, he praises "the conception of design," but also his "prudence." At every moment, including at the beginning of operations apparently solely directed at conquest, the measures taken are "one evidence rather of a commercial than military tendency" (p. 146). Vincent holds that the time has come to invalidate the traditional image of the senseless warrior imposed by the rhetoricians and moralists: "The researches of modern historians and geographers have taught us to consider Alexander neither as an hero of chivalry on the one hand, nor as a destroying ravager on the other. We are no longer misled by the invectives of Seneca, or dazzled with the inflated declamation of Q. Curtius. As the writings of Arrian have become known, the just standard of this illustrious character has been fixed. . . . He never plundered a single province that submitted. . . . His conquests were attended with no oppression of the people, no violation of the temples, no insult to religion" (pp. 4–5). Vincent's Alexander shares the same priorities as Montesquieu's and Robertson's: "The geography of his empire and an accurate information concerning the several provinces formed one of the principal objects of his inquiries."

The review of the *Historical Disquisition* in the *Monthly Review* (September-November 1791, p. 2) noted that Robertson's views on Alexander "entirely coincide with those of Dr Gillies in his History of Ancient Greece." The remark is absolutely accurate in substance.[41] Explicitly referring to "Montesquieu, who (Voltaire only excepted) is the most distinguished modern apologist of Alexander" (*History of Ancient Greece,* 2:674 n. 49), Gillies is full of praise for a conqueror "animated by a zeal for public happiness": "Amidst the hardships of a military life, obstinate sieges, bloody battles, and dear-bought victories, he still respected the right of mankind, and practised the mild virtues of humanity. The conquered nations enjoyed their ancient laws and privileges; the rigours of despotism were softened, and the proudest Macedonian governors compelled by the authority and example of Alexander, to observe the rules of justice towards their meanest subjects" (2:630). Alexander knew how to adapt his goals to the means: "He was pre-eminent for his uniform and nice discrimination between difficulties and impossibilities. [One can see] how far his bare projects were warranted by reason and experience." So it went with his strategy to conquer the Mediterranean coasts. Those plans he did not have time to execute also bear witness to his desire to accumulate as much knowledge as possible about countries he intended to conquer. The words "wisdom," "sound policy," and "prudence" are repeated over and over.[42]

Far more than his talents for war, it is his admirable achievements that make him a true philosopher-king: "His natural humanity, enlightened by the philosophy of Greece, taught him to improve his conquests to the best interests of humanity." Gillies hails "the reign of Alexander, whose character, being unexampled and inimitable, can only be explained by relating his actions" (2:669–670). His negligible failings cannot outweigh his dazzling virtues, far less his achievements. A brave and generous warrior, he also improved and consolidated his conquests by founding cities, developing exchanges, seeking unity, and focusing on putting infertile land to good use. In 1807, Gillies would use comparable terms, but an even more enthusiastic tone—if that were possible—to once again exalt the Macedonian conquest's objectives and results throughout the first part of his *History of the World.*

John Gillies and the Philosopher-King

In what free time he allowed himself during the preparation of his history from Alexander to Augustus, Gillies wrote and published a book on

Frederick of Prussia, which drew a parallel between the Prussian king and Philip of Macedon. Seeking "to consider under similar points of views the genius of ancient and modern times" and to evaluate the two periods' respective merits in the fields of war and the arts, he decided that Philip was the ancient statesman best suited to be compared to Frederick.[43] The author greatly admired Prussia and its king, both of which were well known to him. Published as the Bastille fell, the book went largely unnoticed. What commentary it did elicit was fairly negative. This was the case with the review published by Heyne in 1790, as well as those by English critics, who considered that the comparison was not really suitable; one wrote that a proper equivalent for Philip's virtues could only be found "in the examples of Epaminondas, Trajan, or Aristides." The book was only translated into one language, German, and only partially at that. The Breslau philosopher Christian Garve (1742–1798), a friend and admirer of Frederick's (who had greatly appreciated Garve's translation of Cicero's *De Officiis*) who had little interest in Alexander, translated the first part of the book (the comparison of the two kings), but added relatively harsh critical remarks. He was particularly irritated by the suggestion that the two kings resembled each other. He considered that Frederick could only be compared to Marcus Aurelius, since both were philosopher-kings, which was certainly not the case with Philip.[44]

The book is surprising in that parallels involving Philip, particularly in contrast to his son, had otherwise practically vanished from philosophical history, though they were especially appreciated by advocates of moralizing history.[45] This is easily understandable given that from our philosopher-historians' perspective the unprecedented breadth of Alexander's objectives and achievements made the comparison relatively ineffective. For Voltaire, "the first age with which true glory is associated is that of Philip and Alexander," but it must be emphasized that Philip is primarily included because of the role that the age afforded to fourth-century Athenian artists and authors. For his part, Linguet only refers to the transition from father to son and to those instruments created by Philip and used by Alexander.[46] What followed (the victories over the Persians) falls under the history of the son and is exclusively credited to his merits. As for Montesquieu, he does not make the slightest allusion to Philip in his chapters on Alexander, despite the fact that he refers to the precedents set by Agesilaus and the Ten Thousand (*Spirit of the Laws*, 10.13). In fact, it can be said that the

theory that Philip's virtues and merits were infinitely superior to his son's,
which had traditionally been championed by thinkers from J. de Tourreil
(1697) to Rollin and Mably, had now entirely disappeared from philosophical history. Even when Philip's reign was given a positive evaluation by Gillies
or Mitford, for example, Alexander's achievements were never pushed into
his father's shadow.

One is also surprised that the comparison entailed a de facto devaluation
of Alexander's merits. Naturally, Gillies was perfectly aware of this and declared that he preferred Philip's work to "the unbending heroism of the son
[and] the tumultuous conflicts of Alexander and of Caesar." It would be a
mistake to see this either as a contradiction or a new development: from
1786 to 1807, Gillies remained steadfast in his laudatory evaluation of Alexander's achievement. In reality, the author was driven by his desire to explain what he saw as "an enlightened prince." Overall, the book is a work of
political philosophy rather than history—especially in that Gillies, like
other British historians (particularly Mitford) and his French translator
(Jean-Louis Carra), was fascinated with the similarities he believed he
had identified between the institutions of ancient Macedon, Prussia, and
England.[47]

The connecting thread of the parallel is defined as follows: "In all civilized nations, the most illustrious characters have fought distinction by the
pen or by the sword; because to excel in such pursuits requires the keenest
exertions of intellectual valour. The glory of Philip and of Frederick results
from combined excellence in arts, arms and letters" (p. 16). Gillies is not
afraid of exaggerating the analogy. He goes over the conditions of the two
kings' accession to the throne (among barbaric Macedonians and Prussians), their art of war (Frederick adopting and adapting Macedonian drills),
as well as their friendships with philosophers (Theopompus and Aristotle at
the Macedonian court prefigure Voltaire and d'Alembert with Frederick).

Yet Frederick is not absolutely worthy of "the regulated tameness of the
eighteenth century": like Philip before him, he frequently dedicated himself
to warfare. And Gillies aims to denounce "the demolition of cities, the desolation of provinces, thousands of men rendered miserable, or destroyed in
one day by the sword." He bemoans the admiration given to conquerors that
should be reserved for builder-kings: "I much fear that the military glory
of those renowned conquerors must not be examined too nicely, lest that
which at a distance shows an inestimable diamond prove on a nearer

survey but a sparkling bauble" (p. 50). He deems unacceptable the argument that "war, in fine, is the mother of arts, being indispensably necessary to awaken that energy and to excite those exertions, which alone can produce any extraordinary advancement towards national prosperity." On the contrary, the king must do all that is in his power to develop his country and make it prosperous and happy, that is: "To found cities, to build harbours, to drain marshes, to improve waste lands, to plant them with new colonies" (p. 31).

This is precisely the kind of policy with which Gillies credits Alexander in his other two books. Attributed here to Philip and Frederick—but only in the intervals between their wars—this policy allowed them "to convert the wilds of Thrace and the swamps of Pomerania into rich fields waving with yellow harvests. . . . Foreign nations admired their greatness and extolled their courage; the Prussians and Macedonians praised their goodness, and blessed their beneficence." Though in this case the author expresses doubts about the justification, Philip and Frederick could claim "that their industry repaired the evils that their ambition had occasioned." (p. 49)

Forgiveness and Atonement: Voltaire and Linguet's Perspective

If Gillies puts forward the argument of "reparation" (including to question its legitimacy in the example considered), it is because the notion is central to philosophical reflection on war and peace, conquest and postconquest.

To begin, let's return to Linguet's Alexander. The reason for this choice— were it necessary to repeat it—is not that the author of *Histoire du siècle d'Alexandre* should be considered the most original thinker of his generation. But he had a perfect grasp of the novelty Voltaire was first to introduce to the reflection on the Macedonian conquest. Linguet immediately incorporated it into his narrative and his discourse, which consequently acquired and expressed great coherence and powerful exemplarity.

Addressed to "His Majesty the King of Poland, duke of Lorraine and of Bar," Linguet's dedicatory epistle uses the most traditional style of flattering comparison, describing Stanislas "as brave as the first [Alexander], more constantly virtuous, but less fortunate." Linguet primarily wants to express "true reflections on the deplorable glory of conquerors," while also underlining the distinctive features of Alexander's policy. This is the thesis stated and tirelessly repeated throughout the introduction. To this end, Linguet uses the equally traditional rhetorical angle of contrasting the ruler with selected conquerors from Oriental history, including a Tartar (Genghis Khan), an Ottoman (Muhammad II), and a Persian (Thamas Kouli–Khan [Nadir Shah]). The author is all the more ready to recognize that they "covered themselves in the kind of glory that one can acquire in combat," given that he uses it as an argument against them. Their names have been passed on to posterity because they are "too famous in the history of the world's misfortunes; [they] were fierce men rather than admirable heroes." Indeed, if one follows the teachings of the "Sages," conquerors are not to be judged by their "success" but by their "motives." These princes only had "a bloodthirsty and cruel ambition. In oppressing unfortunate humanity with so many scourges, they never considered consoling it." Linguet is saddened that "the multitudes love their story [and] hear the tale of their exploits without shuddering."

Seen from this perspective, Alexander's wars are no exception to the rule. Linguet is even quick to recognize that there never was a "tyrant whose whims became more harmful to humanity than the valor of Alexander or Caesar was. . . . A single battle like Arbela or Pharsalus cost the world several thousand men and depopulated entire countries [and] Alexander's victories were a calamity for the unfortunates whom he put to death." In fact, if Alexander had done nothing but "ravage so many provinces, his name would be no higher than those of Tamerlane and Attila."

But war, "that destructive art, is as necessary as it is deplorable." It can also "produce changes advantageous to society, either when the tumult of war rouses spirits and pulls them out of the torpor into which rest had plunged them, or when mixing and commerce make nations more refined and industrious, or when the society's ideas are elevated by the victorious people's opulence, finding in the use of its riches the means to create new needs and new resources." This is particularly true of Alexander, who "offers the most important lessons." To learn from him, one must put aside "all circumstances unworthy of posterity, by only taking from the life of this Prince what can serve to characterize the Great Man. . . . The great advantage of his victories was enjoyed by the defeated, to whom they provided arts of which they were ignorant, and by posterity, to which the writers were able to pass on more certain and more useful knowledge." The Macedonian therefore stands out from other conquerors, which is exactly the sense of the book Linguet introduces to his readers: "It appears that the sciences and arts are a compensation, a salutary remedy prepared by nature for exhausted humankind. They are the spring flowers succeeding the winter ice. . . . It is from this perspective that I considered the age of Alexander" (*Siècle d'Alexandre* (1762), 5; (1769), 11–12).

By the time Linguet brought up the comparison with other conquerors of Asia, it had become a classic convention in discussions of the cruelties and benefits of military conquests throughout history. The parallel therefore came naturally to commentators. In his *Siècle d'Alexandre,* Linguet takes to task "an Academician [who] has nowadays made a long comparison between the conquest of the Indies by Alexander and that of the same country by Thamas Kouli-Khan."[48] The author targeted is Louis-Antoine de Bougainville, who had published a laborious comparison of the two conquerors ten years earlier (1752). Bougainville remained fundamentally hostile to Alexander and considered his Indian campaign unjust and illegitimate. But probably due to a desire to avoid getting on the philosophes' bad side and to conform to the spirit of the times, he also acknowledged that the campaign's ravages were not comparable to those caused by Nadir Shah during the expedition that led to the sacking of Delhi: "He was as generous as Nadir was barbaric, and only spilled the Indians' blood in combat. . . . On the contrary, Nadir brought swords and blood wherever he went; he did not subdue the Indies, he ravaged them. . . . His conduct was that of a bandit, a murderer, an arsonist, a scourge on the human race."[49]

Unlike Nadir, the Macedonian implemented policies based on decisions that were beneficial to the future of conquered countries: "[He wanted] to ensure his empire's rest or to make it more flourishing. At his orders, cities and fortresses sprang up everywhere, all placed in advantageous positions and intended to defend important passages, to keep the provinces at bay, to serve as barriers, as parade grounds, as warehouses for commerce. His views extended to everything etc." (p. 141). Bougainville concluded by refusing to grant Nadir the precedent he had used to promote his own glory: "Like Alexander, Nadir invaded the Indies, but he does not deserve the title he claims of second Alexander."

Voltaire also frequently engaged in this rhetorical exercise, though with infinitely more talent and verve. One example is found in chapter 88 of the *Essai sur les mœurs,* which is devoted to Tamerlane (1753). While recognizing that Tamerlane had certain qualities, Voltaire rejects those comparisons between the Tartar and the Macedonian frequently made "by the Orientals." The juxtaposition allows him to point out Alexander's unrivaled successes in developing the world's commerce and to assign the Macedonian a leading place in the continuum of Oriental history: "He is the only great man we have ever seen among the conquerors of Asia" (*Questions sur l'Encyclopédie*, s.v. "Alexandre" (§1),1771).

Yet Voltaire's admiration is not unreserved. He is well aware that war leads to atrocities and massacres and he knows that he has to take a position on a delicate question, which some of his contemporaries used to deny the Macedonian conqueror's glory. The editor of the *Journal de Trévoux* (1752, pp. 502–518) had recently drawn on the ancient sources and the *Universal History* to reproach Bougainville for failing to mention the unilateral and dishonorable violation of an agreement that Indian combatants had made with Alexander in good faith. He accused Alexander of "dark treason." Thus Voltaire pities "the nations so often prey to such horrible calamities." But compassion for victims is not the primary criterion of his judgment. According to him, many anecdotes highlighted by the denigrators need to be put into perspective, for they are "nearly always false and so often absurd." Should one join the denigrators in considering Alexander "a destroyer" or, on the contrary, should one forgive his failings in the name of the benefits he spread over the world he conquered? For Voltaire, there was no doubt: "Despite his vices, he was a man undoubtedly worthy of the title 'great'" (*Essai sur les mœurs,* chap. 141).

The thousands killed on the battlefield are not really a concern. Alexander was not required to "have more scruples about killing Persians at Arbela" than Frederick did "about sending a few impenitent Austrians to the next world" (letter to Frederick, August 1752). After all, as Frederick himself wrote Voltaire in January 1774, "we will be as unable to prevent [the scarlet fever] from wreaking havoc as to prevent [war] from disturbing nations. There have been wars since the world was the world, and there will be long after you and I have paid our toll to nature." In short, it was useless to constantly denounce the Macedonian conqueror for the massacres and ravages that necessarily come with any war.

Nonetheless, some of Alexander's actions appeared particularly horrible and condemnable. This was the case with the merciless punishment he ordered against the surviving Tyrians. Voltaire introduces the episode in a text entirely favorable to the memory of Alexander. He expresses his compassion for the victims: "If it were true that Alexander had two thousand Tyrians crucified after the taking of the city, I would tremble." That being said, such a decision might have been forced upon him by his enemies' inexpiable attitude—which in this case is exactly what the philosopher believes: "but I might excuse this atrocious vengeance against a people who had assassinated his heralds and ambassadors and thrown their bodies in the sea. I will recall that Caesar treated six hundred of the principal citizens of Vannes the same way, though they were far less guilty" (*La Bible enfin expliquée*).

Voltaire had previously mentioned this exemplum in a dialogue on the law of war. One of the speakers claims that strictly speaking there are no laws of war, as evidenced by the Romans who "made war like the Algerians who subjugate their slaves by regulation, but, when they fought to reduce nations to slavery, the sword was their law." To illustrate his point, the speaker uses the example of Caesar at Vannes: "Look at great Caesar, husband to so many wives, and wife to so many husbands. He crucified two thousand citizens from the Vannes area so that the rest would learn to be more pliant. Then, when the whole nation is well tamed, come the laws and the fine regulations. Circuses, amphitheatres are built, aqueducts are put up, public baths are constructed, and the subjugated peoples dance in their chains" (*L'ABC*, 1768, conversation 11).[50] The polemical tone used here is justified by the genre of the dialogue between two pleaders. Yet for all that, the lesson the reader takes away is almost the same: in discussing the measures that conquerors take against populations who resisted weapons in hand, one should consider the violence in relation to the advantages the defeated country drew from the conquest in the long term.

In 1769 (the year the second edition of his *Siècle d'Alexandre* was issued), Linguet published an entirely different type of volume, in which he pleaded for work to begin on digging new canals to improve trade routes in France. He included the Roman precedent by referring to the policy he claimed Rome had followed in Gaul after conquering it by force of arms. Here too, Linguet brings into play the war work/peace work categories. Whether dealing with Alexander or the Romans, both books use the same vocabulary and images: "What idea should we conceive of these conquerors who seemed only to take advantage of their superiority in a murderous art in order to introduce the defeated to all the resources of the beneficial arts! From one end of the earth to the other, they devoted themselves to atoning for the calamities of war that they brought there; they only tamed the barbarians to police them, only subdued the provinces to decorate them" (*Canaux navigables*, 1769, pp. 5–6).

An admirer of "all monuments of that type, with which the magnanimous people had covered the Gauls," Linguet even suggests in passing that he will inventory them and ensure that they are preserved: "It would be a beautiful book in which the history of all the monuments of this type were found ... monuments that we shamefully let waste away, for lack of simply having the courage or skill to maintain them" (p. 15). The author sees his idea through to its natural conclusion by suggesting that the authorities of his time use the army to dig the canals whose construction he promotes; this would allow it to "atone through useful work for its misfortune of being devoted by its state to ravaging the earth and exterminating men" (p. 30).

On the lookout for any precedent useful to his cause, he summons Tamerlane, despite the fact that he had recently followed Voltaire in contrasting the Tartar conqueror with his Alexander. Never mind being consistent from one book to the next! By nature and by definition, an *exemplum* can be used with equal talent by a pleader and his adversary—and even better when the two advocates are joined in one. Granted, Voltaire had already accepted that the Tartar conqueror, though inferior to Alexander, was not a mere destroyer. Linguet therefore offers his readers the following example to reflect upon: "The warriors [of Tamerlane] ... were not averse to working the soil they had so often bloodied. ... They used the hoe to open sources of population in the same deserts that they had made with the sword" (p. 40). It is worth noting the way the term "desert" is used here to exalt conquerors who revitalize soil and villages ravaged by their own weapons by digging canals: a perfect image of the atonement demanded of the guilty on the very spot of their devastations. Linguet used the same word in drawing an opposition between the Turks and Alexander. The former "ruined the cities to prevent revolts. They made a desert of their empire to ensure its protection."[51]

This also brings to mind the famous pages by Volney in his 1791 volume *Les Ruines*, which opens with a meditation on the ruins of Palmyra. Shortly before, Volney had published an account of his *Travels through Egypt and Syria* (1787), which was also a European success. In *Travels*, the philosopher-ideologist dedicates about twenty pages to a description of the ancient caravan city in the Syrian desert, which is borrowed from the English account published by Wood and Dawkins in London in 1753 and from which he reproduces an engraving. He reflects on the wealth of Palmyra, a city oriented toward the Persian Gulf and India. He concludes that its history is a tragic illustration of the destructive capacity of military conquests: "From that period, the perpetual wars of these countries, the devastations of the conquerors, and the oppressions of despots, by impoverishing the people, have diminished the commerce and destroyed the source which conveyed industry and opulence in the very heart of the Deserts: the feeble channels that have survived, proceeding from Aleppo and Damascus, serve only at this day to render her desertion more sensible and more complete" (*Travels*, 1798, 2:178).

Alexander had an entirely different policy, since far from creating or expanding fallow land and infertile steppes, "he repaired through truly laudable actions the bloodthirsty heroism that drove him to ravage so many provinces, [and he] took care to embellish Asia after having destroyed it."[52] In this, the Macedonian is true to the ideal of the philosophes, a king like Peter the Great who "embellished the desert."[53] As for Montesquieu, who was very hostile to the Russian monarch, he did not see why Peter wanted "to join the Black Sea to the Caspian Sea by a canal that goes from the Tanais to the Volga." Indeed, "what needs to be joined are nations to nations, not deserts to deserts."[54]

Debt and Reparation in *The Spirit of the Laws*

In chapter four of book 10 of *The Spirit of the Laws,* Montesquieu wrote: "It is for the conqueror to make amends for part of the evils he has done. I define the right of conquest thus: a necessary, legitimate, and unfortunate right, which always leaves an immense debt to be discharged if human nature is to be repaid." Bringing to a close a chapter entitled "Some Advantages for the Conquered Peoples," Montesquieu's opinion on the "debt to be discharged" does not contain any direct reference to Alexander. Yet given the context in which it is stated, one can undoubtedly affirm that it *also* concerns the Macedonian conquest.

Indeed, the facts and interpretations of which Alexander is subject and object foster a more comprehensive discussion, which in turn allows a better understanding of individual episodes or decisions taken by the conqueror. The two chapters on the conquest (10.13–14) should therefore not be considered outside of the overall discussion on war and war law, which determines their meaning and is found in book 9 (*On the Laws in Their Relation with Defensive Force*) and book 10 (*On the Laws in Their Relation with Offensive Force*). Book 9 must be kept in mind, since it is where the defensive force of despotic states is discussed (chapter 4), though it is difficult to detect in its pages even the slightest concrete allusion to the situation of the Persian empire facing Alexander. Instead, that situation is referred to implicitly in book 10, the volume most important to us. Its chapters are organized as follows:

Chapter 1   On Offensive Force
Chapter 2   On War
Chapter 3   On the Right of Conquest
Chapter 4   Some Advantages for the Conquered Peoples
Chapter 5   Gelon, King of Syracuse
Chapter 6   On a Republic That Conquers
Chapter 7   Continuation of the Same Subject
Chapter 8   Continuation of the Same Subject
Chapter 9   On a Monarchy That Conquers Its Neighbors
Chapter 10   On a Monarchy That Conquers Another Monarchy
Chapter 11   On the Mores of the Vanquished People
Chapter 12   On a Law of Cyrus
Chapter 13   Charles XII
Chapter 14   Alexander
Chapter 15   A New Means for Preserving the Conquest
Chapter 16   On a Despotic State That Conquers
Chapter 17   Continuation of the Same Subject

The chapters dealing with Alexander's conquest (which is compared with the offensives of Charles XII of Sweden) feature a particular development of the reflection on the "law of nations": this law regulates the "offensive force" and "is the political law of the nations considered in their relations with each other" (10.1). This discursive reasoning should be applied to interpreting the statement on "an immense debt to be discharged."[55]

In Montesquieu's view, a prince cannot allow ambition to be his only motive to decide on war, since his glory is not a legitimate right; if war is declared based on "arbitrary principles of glory, of propriety, of utility, tides of blood will inundate the earth" (10.2). Limitations to the law of conquest are set by a single principle, which allows some to attack and others to defend themselves—this is the principle of *preservation* (10.3): "Conquest is an acquisition; the spirit of acquisition carries with the spirit of preservation and use, and not that of destruction.... It is clear that, once the conquest is made, the conqueror no longer has the right to kill, because it is no longer for him a case of natural defense and of his own preservation.... The purpose of conquest is preservation." The principle of preservation must therefore remain in effect once the conquest has been accomplished. Montesquieu uses the principle to rank conquering powers. At the top of the scale, one finds the conquering power that "continues to govern its conquests according to its own laws and takes for itself only the exercise of political and civil government." Delighting in this observation, Montesquieu considers that "this first way conforms to the right of nations we follow at present." Rome is at the very bottom—this type of conquering power "exterminates all the citizens."

Bossuet's influence is in evidence here, including in Montesquieu's word choice. Indeed, the bishop of Meaux had directly addressed the problems of war and peace in his *Politics Drawn from the Very Words of Holy Scripture.*[56] In his view, a right of conquest was only "incontestable" by "the consent of peoples and by peaceable possession." This means that conquest must be accompanied and / or followed by "the tacit acquiescence of subject" because the conquering power has obtained "their obedience by honorable treatment or [by] some kind of agreement, like that which was reported between Simon the Maccabee and the Kings of Asia." The terminology "peaceable possession" fits quite closely with "preservation": force of arms cannot legitimize a conquest; war must immediately be succeeded by peace, but also by a form of active or passive adherence on the part of the vanquished to new masters who have done everything to obtain it.

Montesquieu goes further. The vanquished people can sometimes profit from the conquest (10.4). Since conquered states "ordinarily do not have force they had at their institution, corruption has entered them, their laws have ceased to be executed.... They can be relieved by the conqueror." In this context, the Roman practice is identified as the absolute opposite of Alexander's: "The Romans conquered all in order to destroy all; he wanted to conquer all in order to preserve all, and in every country he entered, his first ideas, his first designs, were always to do something to increase its prosperity and power" (10.14).

This is not the place for a detailed commentary on Montesquieu's analysis of Alexander's policy toward his peoples.[57] It will suffice to observe that in Montesquieu there is absolutely no doubt that the Macedonian fully "reimbursed" the "debt" constitutive of the "necessary, legitimate, and unfortunate right of conquest." This was certainly understood by "all the peoples he subjected" and who mourned him: "This aspect of his life, historians tell us, can be claimed by no other conqueror" (10.14).

With slight individual variations with regard to the scale of destruction and massacres brought by any war, Voltaire, Montesquieu, Linguet, Gillies, and a few others agree on the idea that military conquest is redeemed (or can be), as it were, by "benefits" dispensed to the conquered populations. The difference is that in Montesquieu the image of the debt is the outcome of a philosophical, legal, and political analysis of the right of conquest, and not simply an empirical appraisal of circumstantial military practices. For that matter, by closely following Arrian, Montesquieu (like Gillies after him) exonerates the king from the only two "bad deeds" he recognizes he committed: "He did two things that were bad: he burned Persepolis and killed Clitus. He made them famous by his repentance, so that one forgot his criminal actions and remembered his respect for virtue, so that these actions were considered misfortunes rather than things proper to him, so that posterity finds the beauty of his soul at virtually the same time as his ravings and weaknesses, so that one had to be sorry for him and it was no longer possible to hate him" (10.14). Thus Alexander does not have to "atone" for acts of violence and massacres that the philosopher's words have turned in his favor. However, the debt is an integral part of the conquest, so long as the conquest is legitimate. This was the case with Alexander's conquest of Darius's empire.

Chapter 4

A Successful Conquest

From the Work of War to the Work of Peace

In making a political assessment of the conquests, Linguet expressed his surprise and irritation that "the historians" (meaning the ancient authors) had said so little about Alexander's last year in Babylon. According to him, "they should not have left anything out regarding his occupations during this time of tranquility." One would have expected them to "reveal to us all the secrets of his policy, go into all the mysteries of the internal government, and depict Alexander surrounded by the arts of peace after so many years spent in the horror of combat." Indeed, it was during this short period (324–323 BC) that Alexander became a "Legislator and Founder of a new Empire. But the historians have left us next to nothing on these subjects."[1]

The same observation could be applied to the man who wrote it and made lofty promises to the reader in his book's introduction: "The toppling of this entire [Persian] empire under Alexander completed the task of making all its parts accessible. A prodigious revolution then took place in half the globe. Transported to Europe, the riches of Susa and Persepolis caused rapid change there. Interests and politics bound it to Asia, and once these ties were made, they were no longer broken" (1762, 6–9; 1769, 13–15). This auspicious start does not bear fruit. Linguet never provides a detailed explanation of what the "revolution" involved, nor does he develop the seductive idea he had suggested on the economic consequences of the transfer of Persian treasures.[2] While they were quick to salute Alexander as a builder-conqueror, even an educator-conqueror, many other historians and

philosophers of the time remained vague when it came to concretely analyzing the benefits of the Macedonian conquest. Voltaire himself was never
particularly explicit on the subject. In an essay published shortly before his
death, he was still quite emphatic in stating his admiration for Alexander: "I
would be amazed that a young hero, in the rapidity of his victories, had built
this multitude of cities, in Egypt, in Syria, among the Scythians, and all the
way to the Indies; that he facilitated the commerce of all nations, and
changed all its routes by founding the port of Alexandria. I would dare to
glorify him in the name of the human race" (*La Bible enfin expliquée,* 1776).
But he never truly developed what he meant by this beyond suggesting that
in founding commercial cities that have survived "to this day," the Macedonian conqueror displayed remarkable lucidity.

In his 1789 *A View of the Reign of Frederick II of Prussia,* John Gillies listed
the benefits and improvements the philosopher-kings brought to their
peoples and countries: "To found cities, to drain marshes, to improve waste
lands, to plant them with new colonies" (p. 31). In discussing Alexander's
positive endeavors, most modern authors generally say little about land en-
hancement outside of passing praise for the measures Alexander implemented in Babylon to ensure control of the Euphrates' waters or when some
of them deal with the function of the "weirs" built by the Persians across
the Babylonian rivers.[3] Far more emphasis is placed on the opening of large-
scale commerce between Europe and India.

To those eighteenth-century men who did not consider that Alexander
was exclusively driven by the spirit of conquest and personal ambition, it
seemed logical and indispensable for an intelligent conqueror to adopt
such a policy. In 1723, Savary des Bruslons wrote in the introduction to his
Dictionnaire du commerce that at the end of a war of conquest, a rapid resumption of production and exchanges was in the best interest of both parties.
Indeed, he wrote that "the victors would languish and soon perish with the
defeated, if, to quote Scriptures, they did not beat the iron of their swords
into plowshares, that is to say if they did not make use of the riches produced by land cultivation, manufactories, and commerce to preserve the
tranquil arts of peace, the advantages acquired in the horrors and tumult of
war." The objective of this chapter of my book is to determine which mod-
el(s) and context(s) led to the emergence and development of the view that
Alexander's enterprise and policy form a paradigm of the successful conquest. The idea was originally conceived by Montesquieu—though one must

acknowledge all that *The Spirit of the Laws* (1748) owes to Pierre-Daniel Huet's *Histoire du commerce* (1716).

In Montesquieu and his contemporaries, the debate is not restricted to the question of the opening of new commercial routes; the unity of an empire (any empire) is dependent on numerous other factors. The *Dictionnaire de l'Académie* offers the following definition of "commerce": "In a general sense, the word refers to *reciprocal communication*. More specifically, it applies to the communication between men of the production of their land and industry." In 1753, Véron de Forbonnais (who had read *The Spirit of the Laws*) was fully in step with his era when he opened his article on "Commerce" in Diderot and d'Alembert's *Encyclopédie* (3 [1753]: 690) in an equally ample manner: "Commerce, also means Communication and ordinary correspondence with someone, either merely for society, or also for some business."

Montesquieu, Alexander, and the Commerce of the World

Montesquieu held the same opinion. In book 21 of *The Spirit of the Laws* (*On the Laws in Their Relation to Commerce, Considered in the Revolutions It Has Had in the World*), he brings back Alexander, whom he had introduced in book 10 as a reasonable, perfectly organized conqueror driven by extremely well thought-out plans and designs.[4] In chapters 8 and 9 of book 21 (1757), Montesquieu also portrays (and praises) him as a thoughtful, wise statesman making all his decisions based on the knowledge he had acquired about the countries to which he directed his armies and efforts.

As has often been noted, book 21 is an exception in *The Spirit of the Laws* in that it is structured as a continuous narrative forming a genuine history of commerce from antiquity to the modern era. Montesquieu does make clear that there is a difference of scale between antiquity and his era, for "the commerce of the Greeks and Romans with the Indies was far less extensive than ours" (21.9). The history of commerce is punctuated and driven by successive "revolutions": "Commerce, sometimes destroyed by conquerors, sometimes hampered by monarchs, wanders across the earth, flees from where it is oppressed, and remains where it is left to breathe; it reigns today where one used to see only deserted places, seas, and rocks; there where it used to reign are now only deserted places" (21.5). A history of this type is therefore connected to the history of peoples and the history of conquests: "It is the history of communication among peoples. Its greatest events are formed by their various destructions and certain ebbs and flows of population and of devastations."

Two aspects take up most of Montesquieu's attention: ancient commerce and India's commerce.[5] This explains the pivotal role played by Alexander, which is even more important in the posthumous edition significantly expanded from the 1748 version. In the first edition, Alexander was included in a long chapter (7), "On the Commerce of the Greeks and That of Egypt after the Conquest of Alexander." In his revised edition, Montesquieu successively focuses "On the Commerce of the Greeks" (7); "On Alexander. His Conquest" (8); and "On the Commerce of the Greek Kings after Alexander" (9). The considerable reach of the Macedonian conqueror's vision and achievements also ensure that he appears in chapter 6 ("On the Commerce of the Ancients"): "The universal astonishment at Alexander's discovery of the Indian Ocean is sufficient proof of it." Here and elsewhere, Montesquieu's primary interest is in maritime commerce; in an initial draft, the title of book 21 (*On the Laws in Their Relation to Commerce and Navigation*) explicitly referred to a subject we have seen to be central to all of Montesquieu's contemporaries: commerce and navigation go hand in hand.[6]

The paragraph (1748) or chapter (1757) devoted to Alexander are introduced by the following sentence: "Four events occurred under Alexander that produced a great revolution in commerce: the capture of Tyre, the conquest of Egypt, that of the Indies, and the discovery of the sea to the south of that country." Consequently, "one cannot doubt that his design was to engage in commerce with the Indies through Babylon and the Persian Gulf." This was a radical upheaval for the Persians, who "were not sailors, and their religion itself barred them from any idea of maritime commerce." Montesquieu does mention that Darius had sent a fleet on the Indus and the Indian Sea, but according to him this initiative is a sign of his concern with prestige rather than "an orderly project. This had no consequences, either for commerce, or for sailing." The episode primarily bears witness to the improvements in navigation from Darius to Alexander. It fell to Alexander and his lieutenants to rediscover seas of which all knowledge had been lost. Thus the "Greeks [were] the first to bring commerce to the Indies from the South."

Montesquieu's Sources: Huet and His
Contemporaries (1667–1716)

The ancient sources, and singularly the works of Arrian and the relevant chapters by Strabo, are systematically cited in Montesquieu's footnotes. Yet there is no doubt that he had also read modern works. One such book was cited in the drafts of book 21 (in a highly critical manner, as it happens). This was the *Histoire du commerce et de la navigation des Anciens,* which was published in Paris in 1716 but actually dated back to the fall of 1667, when its author Pierre-Daniel Huet had submitted his report to its sponsor Colbert, the "Inspector and Superintendent-General of the Commerce and Navigation of this kingdom."[7]

The political context of the commission and realization of this report requires a few words of explanation. Impelled by relatively unfeigned scruples,[8] Huet suggests to the minister in his preface that it would have been preferable to appeal to the author of a recent publication on "the advantages which this State might draw from the Indian trade." Though the reference is anonymous, the author in question can easily be identified as the academician François Charpentier, who had published his *Discours d'un fidèle sujet du Roy touchant l'establissement d'une Compagnie françoise des Indes orientales, adressé à tous les François* in Paris in 1666.[9] The *Discours* opens as follows: "As it is a matter of great reputation and security to any State to have a people trained up in the knowledge and exercise of arms, so it is of great utility and convenience that they likewise addict themselves to Commerce, by which means the benefits of the whole world are brought home to their own doors. . . . Now, of all commerces whatsoever throughout the whole world, that of the East-Indies is one of the most rich and considerable" (pp. 1, 3).

Commissioning Charpentier was clearly part of Colbert's plan to found commercial companies that could compete with already powerful and prosperous foreign companies. The work and reflection that would lead to the incorporation of the Compagnie des Indes Orientales (French East India Company) began in 1664. To this end, reticent aristocrats and merchants had to be convinced to invest their money. After going over the reasons for various successes in these regions, particularly those achieved by the Dutch and English, Charpentier attempts to minimize the foreseeable risks of this kind of investment; he promises subscribers that in the event of war with competitors the king will do everything in his power to cover losses if the company is threatened. For that matter, he adds, this will be in the king's best interest, since he will buy shares in the company. The reputation of the ruler who is "the Arbitrator of all Europe . . . will carry good Fortune and Success to our Colonies." The appeal ends with a rousing call to contribute riding on promises of increased power and riches, both public and private: "Join yourselves then my Masters, Join yourselves my Generous countrymen in the pursuit of a glorious discovery, which has only been kept from you thus long, by our past disorders. A discovery that shall lead you to advantages not to be numbered, and which shall yet grow in the hands of our posterity. A discovery, *in fine,* that shall carry the fame and terror of your arms into the whole quarters of the world, where the French Nation itself was never heard of" (p. 38).

In the words of Daniel Dessert and Jean-Louis Journet, "Colbert set in motion a veritable advertising campaign" in order to collect the enormous sum of 15 million livres. It included "publication of a propaganda work by a zealous academician, sending of memoranda to those the minister thinks are likely or have the means to be interested, and even some more or less open pressure on the major provincial bodies."[10] Some foreign countries were also targeted, as indicated by the fact that the *Discours* was translated into German by Jean-Christophe Wagenseil,[11] as well as into English.

While Charpentier's pamphlet certainly fits into the category of "propaganda works," the report requested from Huet was a different matter—like other ministerial commissions, it was not intended to be published.[12] The publisher of the 1716 edition underlines the volume's originality and novelty, while for his part Huet acknowledges in the preface that he feels very isolated in carrying out the task assigned to him, "having no guide to show me the way, nor any to support me in the design." Though obviously self-aggrandizing, these statements are not totally unfounded, and his book can be considered the first in a long line. But it also fits into a contemporary movement of reflection in Europe about the relationship between navigation and commerce and financial and political power. Huet's analyses and arguments are developed through systematic recourse to history, including examples drawn from the most well-known events of antiquity.

It is hard to imagine what Colbert was expecting from Huet and to what extent the report guided his political choices (even modestly) or confirmed his convictions. The minister's engagement letter has not been preserved and we know nothing of his reaction (or that of his advisors). In any event, one must distinguish between the sponsor's possible hopes (which are unknown to us) and the extremely modest nature of the report submitted by Huet (which is recognized and patent). Though the *Histoire sommaire du commerce et de la navigation des Anciens, à Monsieur Colbert, Ministre d'Estat* (1667) fits into a "mercantilist" context, Huet is no thinker or theorist of economics. He has correctly been left out of the anthologies of economic thought in the eighteenth century, despite the fact that the period was so rich in economic debates.[13] The lack of any conclusion is evidence that Huet does not develop an actual theory. Nowhere does he state that he "intended to find in the Ancients, and particularly in Rome, the model for French policy in the Indies."[14]

Written on a purely empirical basis, the *Histoire sommaire du commerce* is supported by examples unmethodically collected from biblical and especially Greco-Roman sources. To quote an accurate description by one of Huet's biographers, "the author, accustomed by trade to dealing with the 'particular,' is ill at ease when it is necessary to discourse on the 'general.' The subject is vast, too vast.... Instead of the synthesis expected, one only finds separate notes, often disjointed, with unfortunate repetitions. While he did classify them, the author did not even go to the trouble of reworking them."[15] In fact, Huet would refer to the manuscript in his *Mémoires* as "a rude and unformed mass."[16]

The manuscript Huet gave Colbert in 1667 opens with several epigraphs (deleted from the 1716 volume). The first is taken from Jeremiah (1.14) and the second is a quote from Cicero (*Letters to Atticus,* 1.10) repeating a statement by Themistocles: "He who possesses the sea can have the need to dominate the whole of the world." These are accompanied by a reference to Thucydides (bk. 1), an excerpt from the Casaubon's commentary on Polybius, a reference to the *Histoire des Moluques,* and another to *Mare Clausum.* These citations explain how frequently the expression "dominion of the sea" comes up; picking up from his ancient sources (Thucydides, Castor of Rhodes), the author attempts to follow the notion's development through history. Alexander's choice to temporarily abandon "the empire of the sea" to the Persians in 334 BC indicates that his plans extended far beyond (17.1). From the founding of Alexandria, "his head is filled with vast designs for establishing an universal Monarchy." Later, he has "the desire of being the Master of all those countries, that is to say, of the rest of the world" (17.3, 6).[17]

This was a heavily discussed question in Europe at the time that Huet embarked on writing his report. Thirty years earlier, in 1635, the same texts had been commented upon by an author whom Huet is known to have read, since he quoted him in an epigraph to his manuscript. The writer was the Englishman John Selden (1584–1654) and the quote was taken from his *Mare clausum,* which was published in Latin in 1634, then in English in 1652 under the eloquent title *Of the Dominion of the Sea.* Here, the author develops the theory of the "closed sea" for the benefit of the king of England: he maintains that the example of the antique thalassocracies beginning with King Minos demonstrate that maritime spaces can be considered "a private Dominion, as a perpetual appendant of the British Empire." Also in 1652, Theodorus Graswinckel countered Selden's arguments by taking a position shared by his uncle the great Dutch jurist Hugo Grotius. In his 1609 *Mare liberum (Freedom of the Seas),* Grotius had taken sides in the dispute between the Dutch and Portuguese over the right to navigate freely on the Indian seas. Chapter 2 of *Mare liberum*[18] is entitled "The Portuguese Have No Right by Title of Discovery to Sovereignty over the East Indies to Which the Dutch Make Voyage." Here, Grotius responds point by point to the arguments of the Portuguese, who claimed that they could grant or deny Dutch ships from sailing on a sea of which they considered themselves to be the sole owners by right of discovery. But in fact, they had not discovered India, "a country which was famous centuries and centuries ago" (the author is referring to the Romans' voyages and conquests). The title of Chapter 5 is "Neither the Indian Ocean nor the Right of Navigation Thereon Belongs to the Portuguese by Title of Occupation." The chapter ends with the following observation: "And as for the assumption of the Portuguese that no one has sailed that ocean before themselves, that is anything but true. For a great part of that sea near Morocco, which is in dispute, had already been navigated long before, and the sea as far east as the Arabian gulf has been made famous by the victories of Alexander the Great, as both Pliny and Mela tell us."

The epigraph from Cicero (*Letters to Atticus* 1.10) was also featured on the title page of a book published in London in 1674 by a contemporary of Huet, the English aristocrat John Evelyn (1620–1706), who was known for his landscape gardening and related books. The subject of his *Navigation and Commerce* was similar to that of Huet's report: the relationship between dominion of the seas, navigation, and commerce. The discussion rests on the conviction that "Justice and the right of Nations are the objects of commerce: it maintains Society, disposes of action, and communicate the graces and riches which God has variously imparted" (p. 14). The book's subtitle (. . . *in Which Title to the Dominion of the Sea is Asserted* . . .) clearly indicates that the author is primarily focused on the interests of the king of England. Evelyn aims to show that the king's imprescriptible right to "Dominion of the sea" has always existed. He develops this argument in the last part of the book, going back to Caesar and citing Selden's conclusions in comparison to those of Grotius: "The sea is not only a distinct province, capable of propriety, limits and other just circumstances of peculiar dominion, as a bound, not bounding his Majesties Empire." It is a private property—a "private Dominion." Only "mercenary pens" could call such a self-evident fact into question.

Evelyn's historical study from the Flood, much shorter and far less detailed than Huet's, aims to illustrate the fact that there can be no powerful kingdom without navigation and commerce. On this subject, the author does not fail to refer to the example of the Netherlands, but also of the king of France: "witness the repair of his ports, building of ships, cutting new channels, instituting companies, planting of colonies, and universal encouragement of manufacture" (pp. 13–14). The same can be said of the king of England, for it is recognized that "whoever commands the Ocean commands the trade, and whoever commands the trade of the world commands the riches of the world, and whoever is master of that commands the world itself. . . . To pretend to Universal Monarchy without fleets [is nothing but] a politick Chymaera" (pp. 15–16).

Among the many examples taken from antiquity, the author makes particular mention of the Phoenicians (§14), "[who] were the first merchants in the world since the Deluge," and the Rhodians, "to whom some attribute even the invention of Navigation" (p. 52). Though he does not dwell on them, Evelyn makes certain to mention Philip and Alexander, who "were first masters at sea, and then of the world" (p. 30). The little space devoted to the Macedonians is due to the priorities of an author who considers the resources from sea fishing more important than the mines of Potosí or the riches acquired by Spain in the two Indies: in a sense, herring is more crucial than gold, silver, and spices![19] Given all the examples drawn from the past, it would probably have been incomprehensible for him not to mention Alexander the Great, but in such a European discursive context (the competition with the Netherlands for the "British seas") the Macedonian example did not do much to support an argument.[20] Similarly, Alexander is only briefly mentioned in John Locke's 1704 volume devoted to the history of navigation and, especially, to travel narratives.[21]

Huet's book is an entirely different thing—though admittedly it is restricted to antiquity. Chapter 17 is devoted to Alexander and opens with a clear, resounding statement: "While things were in this state, Alexander invaded the Persian empire, and by the conquest of it, changed (if I may so say) the face of the world: this made a great revolution in the affairs of commerce, we must esteem this conquest, and chiefly the taking of Tyre, with the foundation of Alexandria, as a new Epocha of commerce." The previous chapters (7–16) describe the state of the world in 334 BC from the perspective of commerce. Huet successively introduces all the peoples who were involved in commerce and launched maritime expeditions during this period succinctly defined by the words "Before Alexander."[22]

This overview prepares and reinforces the impact of chapter 17: none of the peoples introduced in the previous chapters escaped the Macedonian conqueror's control or the changes in commerce brought by his conquests. While Alexander's death caused a political disruption (the division of the empire into several antagonistic kingdoms), his initiatives in the realm of commercial exchanges were unaffected: "All his successors, however divided in their interests, did not differ in point of commerce, but followed those traces that were left them by Alexander" (18.1). This was the case with the Ptolemies and the exchanges they organized between Alexandria and India; it was to Alexander that the Hellenistic kings owed "the foundations of this correspondence, by the colonies of Greeks which he has established in India, and the cities he had built there" (18.2). In parallel with chapters 7–16, Huet studies the "Commerce of Rhodians after Alexander" (chap. 19) and the "Commerce of the Carthaginians after Alexander" (chap. 20). The latter chapter serves as an unfortunate complement to the author's earlier favorable assessment: "Never was Carthage more powerful than when Alexander besieged Tyre, its metropolis" (15.4).

Rome's clash with Carthage and the Hellenistic monarchies led to a new "revolution." Chapter 35 ("Sea Affairs after the Ruin of Carthage and Corinth") answers chapter 17 on Alexander's conquests: "The destruction of Carthage and Corinth changed the face of sea affairs" (35.1). Yet Alexander does not vanish from the historical stage. If only because of the immutable technical conditions of sea voyages (the coast must be kept within sight), Roman fleets often followed in the wake of Alexander and his successors' ships (17.6; 46.9). The Roman conquest of Egypt was full of the memory and legacy of the Macedonian king (chaps. 47–48), given that since Alexander, "Alexandria [had become] as it were a general staple between Egypt and Europe" (48.12), and that Alexander, according to Huet, "judged it necessary to make this country the principal seat of trade, and made choice of such a place as might be a mart for all parts of the world"; this was a positive contribution he bequeathed not only to "his century but also to the following centuries" (17.3). The same was true of the Indies, "little known in the West before Alexander. . . . That Prince's conquests made a farther discovery of the Indies to the Western World, but however very imperfectly. . . . The accounts that were written by Nearchus and Onesicritus inform us of the state of the Indian sea at that time" (52.1–2) and "this knowledge was not neglected by his successors" (52.3; chap. 54); indeed, "Nearchus left memorials of his expedition equally useful for war and for trade" (chap. 11).

Heretofore dominated by the Phoenicians in alliance with the Persians, the Mediterranean became a Greek sea; the destruction of Tyre wiped out the Phoenicians' former commercial domination and had devastating effects on Carthage's power. The situation's logical outcome was the founding of Alexandria, "a great and happy design"; Egypt became the hub of the new commercial relations between India and the West.

Though Huet occasionally denounces Alexander's ambition, the image his book conveys of him is extraordinarily positive. Alexander picks up where his father Philip left off. The latter "let no opportunity slip whereby he might increase his power . . . and he did not neglect any thing that might gain him the mastery of the sea. . . . We must not suppose that this prince, and all those people which I have mentioned, were so strenuously bent upon this Dominion of the Sea out of mere ambition only: no, commerce was the chief object of their desires; they were sensible how much their riches and power depended on it, and they had no less opinion of that maxim of Themistocles: That whoever was master of the sea was master of all things" (16.14).

From this perspective, Alexander's achievements are more dazzling than those of the Romans, whom the author chides several times for being less interested in the development of commerce than in pursuing military domination. Huet considers that unlike the Macedonian conquest of the Persian

empire, the Roman conquest of Carthage and Corinth did not have any beneficial consequences in the realm of exchanges. Rome's victory over Carthage changed the face of sea affairs, but not commercial affairs: "As they
were chiefly employed in war, commerce was much neglected" (35.1; see
also 37.1; 46.6, 9). The author therefore feels fully justified to emphasize the
vastness and depth of the changes brought by Alexander: "This change hap-
pening in the government of states and in the interests of the peoples,
having opened many ports and passages, gave a new turn to the conduct of
trade" (17.1). Huet's choice of words deserves to be underlined. He had clearly
understood that the fundamental novelty of Alexander's contribution was
the facilitation of communication and maritime exchanges thanks to the
opening of new "ports and passages." Formerly sealed off by the blindness
or incompetence of its masters, the Orient was now "open." It was open
not only because the Macedonian conquests led to its discovery by Europe,
but because Alexander removed the obstacles that the despots had created
to prevent communication. By stripping the Persians of their mastery over
navigation and ruining the Tyrians' commerce, the Macedonian king contributed to uniting the seas in a single empire. The founding of Alexandria
completed this first stage since, by a stark contrast, "in the time of their first
kings, the Egyptians despised all foreign commerce; there were not any considerable ports in the country, and they had even neglected the means
whereby they might have had them" (17.3).

The change was even more noticeable and abrupt in the heart of the
actual Persian empire, on the shores of the Persian Gulf and Indian Ocean.
In chapter 11, Huet discusses "the sea-commerce of the Ancient Persians."
His thesis is simple and clear: despite their country's advantageous location
"in the center of Asia," the Persians had neither fleets nor sailors aside from
those they levied from their tributaries (particularly the Phoenicians). They
completely withdrew from sea commerce, probably because they had to devote all their strength and revenue "to the preservation of their large fron-
tier. . . . Defending the entrance into their country on the sea-coasts," and
merely allowed trade by wagons along the Babylonian rivers (chap. 12). In a
way, the Persian kings were as unintelligent as the Muscovite princes of
modern times, who despite their country's exceptional position did not
have access to the sea: "The mistrustful and suspicious humours of their
princes do not permit them to go out of their country nor entertain any
commerce with strangers." This led Huet to hope for the arrival of "an enter-

prising prince who should civilize and reform the brutish spirit of this people, and who should make possible to gather riches by commerce" (42.3–4). Though he did not say it so plainly, could Huet have been hoping in 1667 that a tsar might one day realize in Russia the plans that Alexander had implemented in Persia?[23]

The fact remains that Alexander's policy made a dramatic break with the Great Kings' fears: "He applied himself to the knowledge of the Eastern seas. Several Phoenicians skilled in merchandize followed his army, and furnished themselves with the most valuable spices that grew in India. Alexander built several ports in the mouths of the Indus, and entered the Ocean by this river. At his return from India, he entered the Eulaeus, a river which crosses the country of Susiana, and sailed back by the Euphrates. . . . Before he left India, he sent his fleets under the conduct of Nearchus and Onesicritus to gain intelligence of the East and trace the coasts of Asia. They set out from the Indus and returned up the Euphrates" (17.4). In fact, his ultimate goal was "to renew the ancient course of trade to the Indies, and to re-establish their ancient correspondence with Egypt,[24] which the foundation of Alexandria was to help forward and render more useful by extending it to the extreme parts of the West."

In order to create "new ports and passages," he had had "to destroy the cataracts which the Persians had made in the mouth and other places of the Euphrates, to hinder the landing of strangers in their country"; thanks to Alexander, an uninterrupted connection was set up between India and Babylon (17.4), with a projected connection to Alexandria, "a mart for all parts of the world" (17.3).

In Huet's view, the cataracts reveal the extent to which "the Persians were unacquainted with sea-affairs" (chap. 11). Huet's information came from two ancient authors, Strabo and Arrian, who had both drawn from chroniclers witness to Alexander's era.[25] Since initially mentioning them in his 1667 report (p. 33), the bishop had said a word about the cataracts in his research on earthly paradise (1691): "The Persians, who did not understand navigation nor commerce or sea-fights, and being afraid that their country should be invaded by means of the Tigris and Euphrates, caused falls and cataracts to be made in many places of those rivers. Alexander restored them to their natural state so that ships could go up the Tigris as far as Opis and Seleuceia, and up the Euphrates as far as Babylon" (*A Treatise of the Situation of Paradise* [1694], pp. 61–62). The term "cataracts" is taken directly from the ancient texts (*katarraktai*). It has several translations in French and English: "sauts et cataractes" ("leaps and cataracts") (Huet); "ouvrages, fortification" ("structures, fortification") (Perrot d'Ablancourt 1646); "weirs, impediments" (Rooke 1729), etc. If we put aside an author who (boldly) imagined that the Persians "dug down into the bed of the Euphrates in a number of places, in order to stop the river being navigable,"[26] the contextual meaning is always the same, regardless of the term used. This is the meaning emphatically suggested by the ancient authors: the cataracts were artificial dams placed at regular intervals across the river, exclusively designed to prevent enemy fleets coming from the Persian Gulf traveling upriver and threatening the lands of the Great King.

However, Huet introduced very personal interpretations, which impart a new tone to the ancient texts on which he based his work. For one thing, the disastrous consequences of the cataracts in blocking the flow of commerce are neither mentioned nor even alluded to by Arrian and Strabo, who merely referred to military concerns; moreover, Arrian only mentions the Tigris. By overinterpreting a somewhat ambiguous expression by Strabo, Huet speculated that the Persians had also built cataracts on the Euphrates, consequently banning any fluvial-maritime exchanges between the Persian Gulf and Babylon. The reason for this interpretative leap is easily understood: it was absolutely indispensable to include the Euphrates (communications artery) and Babylon (center of commerce) in order to show the full significance of the history thus reconstructed. The proposed narrative of the discovery of India and its "opening" to the world credited Alexander the Great with the decisive impetus, while denouncing his Persian adversary's despotic immobilism.

Huet's entire argument was based on a close reading of the ancient texts and rested on what appears to be a misinterpretation of the function of the structures built on the Tigris.[27] Nonetheless, one cannot overstate the innovation Huet's book introduced to traditionally held images of the Macedonian conquest. For the first time, the discussion in Europe was not limited to a simple alternative between good and evil, between the positive and harmful effects of conquest, or to a blunt choice between warrior hero and conqueror-civilizer king. Though Huet did not realize it himself (he continued to denounce Alexander using a formulaic vocabulary),[28] he leads the reader to go beyond the moral debate and concretely perceive what the history of Alexander means in the context of a European continuum.

What historians today can in effect consider a major historiographic revolution is all the more notable for the fact that Huet was not a theorist and that he himself had no desire to establish one theory over another; he was a very traditional erudite writer and antiquarian scholar who applied his intimate knowledge of the ancient texts to the task with which he was (reluctantly) charged. If he prominently introduced a new Alexander concerned with opening new maritime commerce routes between East and West, it was only because he had been assigned a subject that was in the spirit of the times.[29] Born unpremeditated from Colbert's 1665–1667 commission on the general history of ancient commerce, this Alexander would fit harmoniously into the vision of his relationships with the countries and populations subject to his power and domination as it developed in Europe from the eighteenth to the twentieth century.

From the *Histoire du Commerce* to *The Spirit of the Laws* (1716–1748/57)

Huet's book was a major bestseller. The two French editions of 1716 were followed by a third edition published in Paris in 1727 and a fourth published in Lyon in 1764. The book's European circulation is eloquently attested to by the existence of five translations—in English (1717), Dutch (1722), Italian (1737), German (1763 and 1775), and Spanish (1793).

Huet's representation of Alexander was immediately adopted and disseminated in widely available volumes such as travel narratives; by 1719, Paul Lucas was shamelessly plagiarizing Huet in telling his readers that "the face of Egypt's commerce changed entirely after Alexander's conquest of this powerful kingdom."[30] In the "Préface historique" to his *Dictionnaire universel du commerce* (1723), Savary des Bruslons praised Huet and his book. He borrowed Huet's overview of the major stages of antique commerce, giving the founding of Alexandria a prominent place. Ten years later, one of the greatest popularizer-educators of the century—namely, Rollin—devoted chapter 2 of book 24 of his *Histoire ancienne* to commerce, "the most solid foundation of civil society, and the most necessary principle to unite men, of whatever country or condition they are." Article 2 ("Antiquity of Commerce. Countries and Cities Most Famed for It") draws both on Huet and Savary des Bruslons: "The taking of Tyre by Alexander the Great and the founding of Alexandria, which soon followed, occasioned a great revolution in the affairs of commerce."[31] In 1765, in the "India" entry of the *Encyclopédie* (8:661), Jaucourt wrote: "Though we know well enough that this commerce is not new, it is nonetheless a subject on which M. Huet deserves to be read, because he dealt with it learnedly & methodically, whether for ancient times or the middle ages." The following year, Huet was cited as a model and an example by one of the winners of the Académie Royale des Inscriptions et Belles-Lettres' competition, the Abbé Ameilhon, who in the preface to his book endeavors to convince the reader that despite "inevitable overlaps" with the materials used by his illustrious predecessor, he "tries to present them in a new light."

Huet was also well known to Voltaire, who mocked some of the interpretations in Huet's *Démonstration évangélique* in his *Essai sur les mœurs* and considered that, "of all his books, *Le Commerce et la Navigation des anciens* and the *Origine des Romans* are the most useful."[32] Voltaire certainly consulted Huet's history of commerce: in the critique of *The Spirit of the Laws* in his *Dictionnaire philosophique,* he sided with what he referred to as the *Traité sur le commerce des anciens* against Montesquieu in the discussion of Roman commerce. An expression in the *Essai sur les mœurs* (chap. 88) is reminiscent of Huet: "He changed the face of commerce in Asia, Europe, and Africa, of which Alexandria became the universal warehouse." In 1737, he hailed Alexander as a conqueror "forming colonies, establishing commerce, founding Alexandria and Iskenderun, which are today the center of trade in the Orient."[33] Contrary to established belief, Voltaire's statement here did not go against the prevailing views of his era. In fact, there is little doubt that Huet's book, which had been published twenty years earlier and was then very influential, left its mark on Voltaire.

Montesquieu had also read Huet. Scholars today can consult the notes that he wrote and dictated on the 1716 edition. These include the following summary of the beginning of chapter 17: "Alexander's conquests, especially the taking of Tyre and the founding of Alexandria, were a new era for commerce."[34] Montesquieu's word choice in *The Spirit of the Laws* ("great revolution in commerce") reveals the filiation with Huet. The diachronic structure of chapters 6–20 of book 21 closely follows the succession of chapters in Huet. As in the *Histoire du Commerce,* Alexander's policy is systematically contrasted with the Persians'. By explicitly referring to Arrian, Montesquieu also attributes a decisive importance to the destruction of the cataracts "that the Persians had put in these rivers [Euphrates, Tigris, Eulaeos]." But rather than explaining the erection of these dams by exogenous causes (danger from the exterior), he relies on a structural explanation of a religious nature, which is firmly in keeping with *The Spirit of the Laws*. This explanation is inferred from Persian sources, which Montesquieu only knew through their interpretation by the famous Hyde in his book on the religion of the Persians: "Further the Persians were not sailors, and their religion itself barred them from any idea of maritime commerce.... In order not to defile the elements, they did not navigate on the rivers. Still today, they have no maritime commerce and they call those who sail the seas atheists" (21.8, with the footnote).

Borrowing and continuity from Huet to Montesquieu should not be underestimated: Alexander's central role is already well established in Huet, as is the opposition drawn between the "passages" opened by the Macedonian king and the "closing" imposed by his Persian predecessors. At the same time, Montesquieu developed a line of thinking purely his own and in essence antagonistic to Huet's presentation. Without ever noting that his predecessor had already shown that Alexander was responsible for a veritable revolution in the history of commerce and navigation, Montesquieu did his best to underscore his divergences with him. These are sometimes expressed over secondary matters: for example, without citing Huet, he rejects the idea that Alexander ever considered establishing "the seat of his empire" in Arabia. The disagreement over the founding of Alexandria is more fundamental. Montesquieu does not believe that Alexander initially considered making the port city the hub of commerce with India, for his geographic knowledge was then insufficient "to be able to form such a project.... This thought could come to him only with the discovery of the Indian sea." At the actual time of its foundation, Alexandria was a purely Mediterranean concern: "This was a key for opening it in the very place where the kings, his predecessors, had locked it"—first and foremost from the Greeks, as Montesquieu explicitly states in a footnote. Even after the conquest of India, "it appears that he had no new views about Alexandria"; his objective remained the India-Babylon connection. It was only under the Ptolemies that "Egypt became the center of the universe."

"Must One Conquer a Country in Order to Trade with It?"

The exaltation of the figure of Alexander in Montesquieu can leave one somewhat perplexed. The lesson of empire that Montesquieu draws from the Macedonian experience seems to conflict with his consistently stated opposition to military conquests and great empires and his denunciation of conquering heroes—including Alexander—in writings predating and post-dating *The Spirit of the Laws*.

One could answer that by being identified as an exception, Montesquieu's image of Alexander was in a way confirming his principles, since the Macedonian king was stripped of the attributes of a conqueror, which were replaced by those of a sovereign guided by reason, exercising power based on knowledge, and able to introduce harmony and peace in a new world made up of exchanges and communications. Additionally, though he borrowed the diachronic framework of the *Histoire du Commerce,* Montesquieu distanced himself from Huet, whose Alexander dreamed of establishing a universal monarchy. This was the kind of hegemonic ambition leading to war and destruction whose erroneous principle and disastrous consequences Montesquieu had highlighted and vigorously contested in his *Réflexions sur la monarchie universelle en Europe* (1733–1734). One could say that his Alexander never succumbed to temptation.[35]

Yet that does not dispel the problem. On one occasion, the author of *The Spirit of the Laws* is himself confronted with a disturbing question in chapter 8 of book 21. Asking himself why "the Greeks were the first to bring commerce to the Indies from the South" thanks to Alexander's military enterprise, he points out the paradox in the following words: "But must one conquer a country in order to trade with it?" This is a legitimate question, given that a few chapters earlier Montesquieu had mentioned another example from antiquity, that of the Phoenicians, who "did not trade as a result of conquest; their frugality, their ability, their industry, their perils, and their hardships made them necessary to all nations in the world" (21.5). But Montesquieu identifies a fundamental difference between the Phoenicians and Alexander: the former "did not engage in a commerce of luxury," they engaged exclusively in "an economic commerce around the whole world," in which "traders, eyeing all the nations of the earth, take to one what they bring from another"; connected "to the government by one, the commerce founded on luxury [is intended] to serve its arrogance, its delights, and its fancies" (20.4). This kind of commerce is therefore linked to a form of domination.

Why is Alexander exempt from the implicit condemnation of commerce that only serves to enrich the dominant nation? First, because he was not an Asian despot obsessed with luxury: on the contrary, referring to the rousing panegyric in the last chapters of Arrian's *Anabasis*,[36] Montesquieu judges that the king's rule of life was "his own frugality and his own economy. His hand was closed for private expenditures; it opened for public expenditures" (10.14). His conquest is legitimated by his self-imposed objective: "To establish a commerce between the Indies and the western part of his empire" (21.8). When all is said and done, what remains are the advantages of a commercial system benefiting all involved. In books 9–10 to 20–21, Montesquieu suggests an image of Alexander without rough edges, which indisputably associates him with *"doux commerce"* and peace—it being understood that "the natural effect of commerce is to lead to peace, [and that] total absence of commerce produces the banditry" (20.2). Far from corrupting mores, "commerce cures destructive prejudices" (20.1). Alexander's way of thinking was not that of a trader or merchant; it was a comprehensive political notion uniting commerce, communication, and civilization. His historical role cannot be reduced to that of someone who opened new maritime routes. Beyond the purely economic aspects, "the history of commerce is that of communication among peoples" (21.5). This is what is truly at stake in Montesquieu's eyes: commerce contributes to establishing cooperation between the victors and the defeated, and therefore, *in fine*, to wiping out the impure signs of conquest, provided the conquest's primary objective was to institute the sound and equitable bases of a commerce that cannot be assimilated to predation.

How to Cement an Empire

"It is thus that he made his conquests; let us see how he preserved them": this sentence in the middle of chapter 14 of book 10 of *The Spirit of the Laws* introduces a discussion of the conception that Montesquieu's Alexander had of his empire as it was being built. Montesquieu closely follows the ancient sources throughout the chapter, citing them in footnotes. He particularly refers to Arrian, who had drawn a highly favorable portrait of Alexander and his policy. He also explicitly refers to a very famous opuscule by Plutarch, *On the Fortune or the Virtue of Alexander,* in which the Macedonian king is presented as a conqueror-philosopher entirely driven by a concern for unity, as expressed in the founding of a great number of Greek cities (seventy) and by the diffusion of Greek norms, which were held up as norms for humanity. Plutarch also stated that in this regard Alexander was in contradiction with Aristotle, who was said to have taught that the distinction between Greeks (the "masters") and barbarians (the "slaves") could not and should not be transgressed.

Driven by this concern for "preservation," the Alexander of *The Spirit of the Laws* forges alliances with the Persians: he does not settle for allowing them their civil laws; he also leaves them their mores, thus perfectly illustrating the principle of conquest that holds that "a people always knows, loves, and defends its mores better than its laws" (10.11). Additionally, "he rebuilt the temples of the Greeks, Babylonians, and Egyptians, that the kings of Persia had destroyed"—aligning himself once again with the image of the conqueror who "destroys harmful prejudices" (10.4). He does not judge peoples according to their mores, but to the loyalty they show him (10.14). Yet there is no question of leaving power in the hands of the Persians; as a faithful reader of Arrian, Montesquieu observes that, on the contrary, Alexander "put the Macedonians at the head of the troops and the people of the invaded country at the head of the government."

Montesquieu returns to this question in passing in book 30 (*The Theory of the Feudal Laws among the Franks in Their Relation with the Establishment of the Monarchy*). Here, he sharply attacks the theories developed by the Abbé Dubos on the conditions of the Franks' arrival in Gaul. In his *Histoire critique de l'établissement de la monarchie franque dans les Gaules* (1742),[37] the abbé affirmed that the Franks had penetrated Gaul peacefully, without any preliminary conquest: "According to him our kings, summoned by the peoples, did nothing but take the place and succeed to the rights of the Roman Emperors."[38] Montesquieu uses several arguments to take apart the abbé's book and offers a comparison intended to ironically comment on his adversary's theories. If one followed the Abbé Dubos's reasoning, Montesquieu teases, one could "prove, in the same way, that the Greeks did not conquer Persia." One would only have to consider the taking of Tyre as a particular exception, or else to take the ancient authors' word about the favorable oracles at Gordium and the oasis of Ammon or the high priest's enthusiastic welcome in Jerusalem: "See all the towns run out, so to speak, to meet him: see the satraps and the important men crowd forward, etc." But, Montesquieu continues, that would be an uncritical reading of authors like Quintus Curtius, Arrian, and Plutarch, who were not Alexander's contemporaries. Taking this devastating irony to its natural conclusion, he implies that such a method has not been conceivable since the invention of the printing press, which "has given us the enlightenment those authors lacked." How better to discredit his adversary's theories, including by resorting to a misleading analogy? (30.24)[39]

In other words, Montesquieu rejects all interpretations that tend to elude the phenomenon of military conquest by unilaterally insisting on the spontaneous compliance of the populations of the Persian empire. In his view, some of the Persians' attitudes (the princesses' grief after Alexander's death) and the king's decisions (dressing like the Persian kings) can only be understood in light of Alexander's victories and the Persians' defeats. It is only once he no longer has any armed opposition to face that the conqueror can take conciliatory measures "to cement all the parts of this new empire" in peace and cooperation.

While the context of the argument changes, there do not appear to be any flagrant contradictions in Montesquieu's thought between books 10 and 30. Indeed, the different methods by which Alexander was able to establish and maintain such an empire can also be attributed to realism. The first phase is military—a phase of frontal opposition against the Persians; in order to successfully complete it, Alexander united the Greeks against the Persians by using "the prejudice" (hostility toward the barbarians), a tactic he abandoned after the conquest in order to strengthen his hold (by bringing everyone together around him).[40] In the second phase thus defined, politics "entered into the plan of his conquest." The founding of Alexandria was also wisely conceived: "In order not to drain Greece and Macedonia, he sent a colony of Jews [there]." In a general manner, "the foundation of an infinite number of towns" was one of the components of a policy of territorial consolidation; they contributed "to cement all the parts of the new empire."[41]

Alexander was constantly focused on building his empire according to a principle of unity. Not only did he avoid imposing the Greeks' mores on the Persians, but he adopted theirs; this explains why "he showed so much respect for the wife and the mother of Darius and why he was so continent."

Alexander's desire to build an empire viable in the long term drove him to create a project that was practically revolutionary in Greek norms, "to unite the two nations and to wipe out the distinctions between the conquerors and the vanquished." As it happens, "nothing strengthens a conquest more than unions by marriage between two peoples"; this explains the marriages between Macedonian nobles and women of the Persian aristocracy (including Alexander's own marriage), which are described in great detail by Arrian and all the ancient authors and were chosen as a subject by so many painters of the modern era. All told, the policy's results were brilliant; the proof is "that he was mourned by all the peoples he subjected, [and that after his death] none of the Persians rebelled." Alexander was the only conqueror of his kind, one who was not considered "an usurper" by those he had subjected. He achieved the impossible—to unite the people around him as an individual: "It seemed he had conquered only to be the monarch of each nation and the first citizen of each town." In him, the contradictory principles of unity and diversity were reconciled.

Montesquieu's reflection follows a similar path in chapters 13–14 of book 10 and chapter 8 of book 21. The idea of commercial networks is never divorced from political will: Alexander carries out his objective to unite the Indies with the West by maritime commerce (21.8) and consolidates all the parts of this new empire through the founding of a large number of Greek colonies in Persia (10.14); a working parallel is drawn between the commercial union of India and the West and the founding of the colonies Alexander had established inland and those he plans to found on the Persian Gulf's Arabian coast (21.8).

Conquest and Civilization

By founding cities in the "savage" parts of the Persian Gulf, the king also displayed a civilizing perspective. Montesquieu's favored source Arrian describes populations living exclusively on fish: the Ichthyophagi (the Fish Eaters). From this, Montesquieu infers that Alexander "prohibited the Ichthyophagi from living on fish; he wanted the shores of this sea to be inhabited by civilized nations" (21.8).

However, he makes an important qualification in a footnote: "This cannot be understood of all the Ichthyophagi who inhabited a coast of ten thousand furlongs. How could Alexander have provided them their subsistence? How would he have made himself obeyed? Here it can be a question only of a few specific peoples. Nearchus in the book *Rerum Indicarum* says that at the extremity of this coast, near Persia, he had found some peoples whose diet was less dependent on fish. I would believe that this order of Alexander concerned this region or some other closer to Persia." Montesquieu is clearly introducing different degrees of the state of savagery. In doing so, he follows Arrian's model: based on environmental and climate conditions, Arrian defines different zones contrasted by the presence or absence of cultivated land, the presence or absence of crops comparable to those found in Greece, the raw and the cooked, etc.[42] Alexander's order (banning the consumption of fish) could only have had bearing on the Ichthyophagi who were already in contact with civilization; those who, according to Arrian, "did not live entirely like animals." In this sense, his decision was a reasonable one, because it was adapted to the level of development of the population in question; it represented a decisive advance both in terms of the mores of "savages" and those commonly accepted by civilized peoples, since it implicitly but unmistakably suggested a cultural leap toward sedentarization and agriculture.

This generally overlooked but remarkable passage by Montesquieu should be included in the long-standing discussion of the notion of *civilization* during the Enlightenment.[43] Even before the word first appeared (in the elder Mirabeau's *Ami des hommes* (1756), the term "civilized" (as opposed to "barbaric") was commonly used to refer to missionaries' evangelism; well-attested to in the political and "colonial" vocabulary of the seventeenth century, its use developed in a remarkable manner after 1750. Its significance is clear: "The verb *to civilize* is used to express savages' passage to a sedentary state. Reducing savages to a sedentary state was the fundamental activity of missionaries: it transforms savages into men" (G. Goggi). This slow, pacific work contrasts with the brutal destruction carried out by the Spanish conquistadors and others: "civilization is a relative state, the process of which implies an ideal of peace, education, and knowledge of a free state" (R. Monnier). This is the situation of dynamic transformation analyzed by Montesquieu in this passage.

The establishment of colonies on the shores of the Persian Gulf broke with the policy of the Great Kings, which "left the whole coast in the power of the Ichthyophagi. . . . It was accepted, before Alexander's expedition, that the southern part was uninhabitable" (21.8). Under these conditions, the ban against "living on fish" for some of the Ichthyophagi is not exclusively due to a decision to spread Greek norms—rather, the spread of these mores must contribute to securing in time and space the power born of the conquest. This is exactly how it was understood by Lacombe de Prézel, who was directly inspired by his reading of *The Spirit of the Laws* (though he does not cite it). De Prézel considers that in forbidding the Ichthyophagi from consuming fish, "Alexander [was] convinced that it is difficult to contain a people that is not itself held in place by its needs. His policy led him to direct toward Commerce all the ideas of the other Nations he had subjected to his rule, as the only means of keeping them conquered."[44]

It should be observed that there is no mention of "Alexander's order" in Arrian. It is Montesquieu himself who postulates that the cultural transformation of a half-savage population ("less Ichthyophagi") could only be achieved through the restriction imposed by the conqueror. Though he does not cite him on this point, Montesquieu may have been thinking of what Plutarch wrote in *On the Fortune or Virtue of Alexander* (1.5), with which he was very familiar. In discussing "Alexander's educational action," Plutarch states that the philosopher-king "trained the Hyrcanians in the practice of marriage, taught the Arachosians agriculture, convinced the Sogdians to feed their fathers rather than put them to death, the Persians to respect their mothers rather than take them as wives." The same method of presentation is found in chapter 5 of book 10 of *The Spirit of the Laws,* entitled "Gelon, King of Syracuse." In 1748, Montesquieu marveled at the humanity of the tyrant of Syracuse, who had included a most remarkable clause in the treaty with the Carthaginians: it required them to abandon "the custom of sacrificing their children. Remarkable thing! ... He exacted a condition useful only to the Carthaginians." In the version of the same chapter revised for the new edition Montesquieu was preparing at the time of his death, the title remains (temporarily?) unchanged, but the sentence has been completed as follows: "or rather, he stipulated one for mankind"—a formulation that gave the exemplum universal value. Additionally, between 1748 and 1755, Montesquieu added another example to the chapter, which was drawn from the history of Alexander: "The Bactrians had their elders eaten by large dogs. Alexander forbade them to do this, and this was a triumph he gained over superstition."[45] This behavior did not conflict with the policy later described by Montesquieu, which is based on the recognition and respect of the mores of the Greeks, Egyptians, and Babylonians (10.14). In every case referred to, Montesquieu develops the idea presented in chapter 4 of book 10, "Some Advantages for the Conquered Peoples." The conqueror can relieve the oppression suffered by a people under previous dominion, which was itself often marked by "corruption"; this was the case with the cultural traditions of the Greeks, Egyptians, and Babylonians under Persian rule. But also, "a conquest can destroy harmful prejudices, and, if I dare speak in this way, can put a nation under a better presiding genius"; this is exactly what Alexander did by fighting the Bactrians' "superstition" and "civilizing" some of the Ichthyophagi. The difference in treatment is due to differentiated cultural levels: Greeks, Egyptians, and Babylonians were people of civilized mores and the Bactrians and Ichthyophagi were not (according to Montesquieu). Alexander had no problem "sacrificing on [the former's] altars," but he could not allow the latter's "superstition" to remain as it was. In this, Alexander is indeed a man of the Enlightenment, one who not only explored a land reputed uninhabitable but incorporated it to the inhabited world and made its population a branch of mankind.

Chapter 5

Affirming and Contesting the Model

Navigation and Commerce

The model elaborated by Montesquieu met with considerable success in Europe. It is easily identified in the many histories of commerce that flourished in various European countries over the second half of the eighteenth century.[1] If these were generally presented under the rubric of "navigation and commerce," it was because that title best expressed the importance of large-scale maritime commerce and trading companies in European states and societies of the time. To quote Diderot and d'Alembert's *Encyclopédie*, "one can establish as a general dictum that the relations between, or if one can call it this, the union of Navigation and Commerce is so intimate that the ruin of one would necessarily lead to the ruin of the other, and that these two things must thus flourish or decline together."[2] These publications generally adopt the idea that Alexander brought about a commercial revolution. The similarity between certain expressions in Huet and in Montesquieu occasionally makes it difficult to determine whether their successors are favoring one or the other or combining the two without any concern for their differences.

In Germany, Montesquieu's wording and analysis were explicitly repeated by A. L. Schlözer in 1762, while *The Spirit of the Laws* was admiringly cited by F. S. Schmidt in 1766.[3] In France, the same expressions were closely emulated in several articles of the *Encyclopédie*. Both the entry on "Commerce" by Véron de Forbonnais (3:692) in 1753 and the entry on "Navigation" by d'Alembert|Mallet (11:54) in 1765 were heavily inspired by Huet and Montesquieu and participated in the propagation of the new image of Alexander. De Forbonnais writes that "[four] major events contributed to the revolution in *Commerce* under the reign of this prince" and follows *The Spirit of the Laws* in specifying that "Alexander appeared; he preferred being the leader of the Greeks rather than their master. . . . The discovery of the Indies and the sea to the south of this country opened their commerce." D'Alembert|Mallet recall that "the navigation and commerce [of Tyre] were transferred by the victor to Alexandria, the city this prince had built, admirably situated for maritime commerce, and which Alexander wanted to make into the capital of the empire of Asia which he contemplated."

Qualifications, even divergences, are sometimes introduced. Ameilhon, who was closer to Huet than to Montesquieu (whom he had read but did not cite), declared in 1766 that "this Prince regarded commerce as the strongest link that can unite all the peoples he proposed to subject to his dominion." Yet he differs from Montesquieu in considering that Darius's attempt to control the Persian Gulf and contact with Egypt were not mere "ostentation"; in doing so, the Great King had been a forerunner of Alexander, "for he liked commerce and felt naturally disposed to favor those who applied themselves to it, [and] was very curious to make discoveries in foreign countries." Ameilhon therefore considers "that Alexander did not have the honor of being the first to make recognized the coasts of the Ocean from the Indus to the Arabian Gulf" and does not repeat what Montesquieu wrote about the transformation of some of the Ichthyophagi into "civilized people." Alexander still plays an eminent role, but rather than making him the only one responsible for a revolution in commerce, Ameilhon situates him in a long line stretching from Darius to Ptolemy.[4]

One should also mention an enormous anthology devoted to the commerce of the ancients and published in 1809 by the distinguished amateur Jullien du Ruet, with the help of the young Letronne.[5] The book is based on a conviction shared by all those authors who in the same breath proclaim their admiration for Alexander's historical role and for the decisive influence of "commerce and industry" on societies. Du Ruet was an assiduous reader of Huet, Ameilhon, and Robertson and an admirer of Bossuet and Sainte-Croix (with whom he was close ideologically, but differed on questions of commerce). He celebrated Vincent's book, "full of new and profound views on the policy of Alexander, who was able not only to conquer" but also to develop spectacular ideas on global commerce.

This theory was illustrated with particular strength by the British historians.[6] The subtitle of Robertson's book on India (1791) makes clear its objectives: *And the Progress of Trade with That Country prior to the Discovery of the Passage to It by the Cape of Good Hope.* Robertson had already been full of praise for Alexander's conception of world commerce in his *History of America* (1777): "He was capable of framing those bold and original schemes of policy, which give a new form to human affairs. The revolution in commerce, brought about by the force of his genius, is hardly inferior to that revolution in empire, occasioned by the success of his arms. . . . As soon as he had accomplished the destruction of Tyre, and reduced Egypt to subjection, he formed the plan of rendering the empire, which he purposed to establish, the centre of commerce as well as the seat of dominion" (1.1.10).

Seized by the enthusiasm inherent to his subject, Robertson disagrees with Montesquieu's opinion (*Spirit of the Laws,* 21.8) and states that Alexander was already thinking of establishing a direct passage between the Red Sea and India when he founded Alexandria; his reason for believing this is that like the bishop of Avranches, he thinks the Phoenicians had a long tradition of commercial exchanges with the Persian Gulf. He also agrees with Huet in considering that "soon after his first successes in Asia, Alexander seems to have formed the idea of establishing an universal monarchy, and aspired to the dominion of the sea, as well as of the land" (*Historical Disquisition,* p. 13). For the rest, he draws on both *The Spirit of the Laws* and *Histoire du commerce et de la navigation des Anciens,* insisting on the connection between the Indus and the Euphrates and Alexander's order "to remove the cataracts or dams, with which the ancient monarchs of Persia, induced by a peculiar principle of their religion, which enjoined them to guard with the utmost care against defiling any of the elements, had constructed near the mouths of these rivers, in order to shut out their subjects from any access to the ocean. By opening the navigation in this manner, he proposed that the valuable commodities of India should be conveyed from the Persian Gulf into the interior parts of his Asiatic dominion, while by the Arabian Gulf they should be carried to Alexandria, and distributed to the rest of the world" (p. 28). This was a total reversal of the prevailing situation under Persian dominion, a period during which merchandise from India was transported by camel caravans to the Oxus, from where it was carried to the Caspian Sea, then to the Black Sea.[7]

In 1797, William Vincent's *Voyage of Nearchus* was published, punctuated with references to Huet and the great British authors who had opened the way to him (Rennell, Robertson, Gillies). Explicit or barely veiled allusions also attest to the influence of *The Spirit of the Laws*. This was clearly the understanding of a contemporary reviewer of the French translation: "It is only in our time that this great man has been properly known. His reputation was long in the grip of declaimers of morals. It was only fifty years ago that Montesquieu finally came along to say: 'We have said enough about his valor, let us speak of his prudence.'"[8]

Vincent is particularly striking for his insistence on affirming that Alexander was perfectly conscious of his historical role on the global stage. While taking position in favor of Montesquieu and against Robertson on the contextual reasons for the founding of Alexandria, he underlines the Macedonian conqueror's long-term insight: "He knew the value of this commerce, foresaw the consequences of it, and gave a direction to the course in which it flowed for eighteen centuries" (pp. 8–9). With this in mind, Vincent does not hesitate to suggest that all the goods associated with India in his time (rice, cotton, sugarcane, silk, etc.) were first purposefully imported by Alexander. From this he concludes that "[on] these articles, it is evident, Alexander depended for the foundation of the commerce he meditated, and for the introduction of these he was now planning the communication which was to perpetuate the intercourse between Europe and the East Indies" (p. 14). As we shall see, Vincent's theories had considerable success both in Great Britain and on the Continent; the French translation attests to that fact, as does the plan (albeit abortive) for a German translation.[9] The same was true of Robertson's *Historical Disquisition;* simultaneous German (1792), French (1792), Dutch (1793), and Italian (1794) translations speak to the Scottish historian's immense reputation throughout Europe.

The Peoples of the Empire

Montesquieu's civilizing of Alexander was no less influential in his own era. The extent of his impact can be assessed by turning again to the *Encyclopédie*. One article immediately stands out: it is the entry on the "Grecs" (1757), particularly in its first part ("Philosophie des—," 7:904–912).[10] The author provides a history of Greek philosophy and its various "sects" (Stoicism, Epicureanism, etc.) and connects the spread of philosophical doctrines to political history: "You will see that this philosophy also spread through the Greeks' victories and defeats." He concludes by stating that the best thing is to share with the reader a passage from Plutarch, "which shows the extent to which Alexander was his tutor's superior in political matters; praises the sound Philosophy; and can serve as a lesson to kings." The passage is an excerpt from the influential opuscule previously used by Montesquieu, *On the Fortune or the Virtue of Alexander,* which the author quotes in a dated translation by Amyot, though he does not credit the translator.[11]

Here, Plutarch develops the idea that unlike the philosophers, Alexander put his ideas into practice. He also went against his tutor Aristotle, who advised him "to treat the Greeks as if he were their leader, and other peoples as if he were their master (*despot*), and to have regard for the Greeks as for friends and kindred, but to conduct himself toward other peoples as though they were plants or animals; for to do so would have been to cumber his leadership with numerous battles and banishments and festering seditions." Alexander took the opposite approach, for "he believed that he came as a heaven-sent governor to all and as a mediator for the whole." In this capacity, he chose the path of friendship and communion: "Those whom he could not persuade to unite with him, he conquered by force of arms, and he brought together in a body all men everywhere, uniting and mixing in one great loving-cup, as it were, men's lives, their characters, their marriages, their very habits of life. He bade them all consider as their fatherland the whole inhabited earth, as their stronghold and protection his camp, as akin to them all good men, and as foreigners only the wicked" (329C). The author concludes: "This was Alexander's policy, by which he did not prove to be any less of a great statesman than if he had shown himself to be a great captain through his conquests." This statement was repeated nearly word for word in Jaucourt's article "Homme d'état" (1765, 8:279). Elsewhere, the chevalier expresses his keen admiration for a king who had made Greeks and foreigners "kin to each other."[12]

For his part, Linguet also insists on the novelty of Alexander's policy in dealing with conquered populations. He defends him against the accusations he had faced since antiquity for adopting the mores of the Persian kings: "Those who criticized him for the latter item did not think enough about the position in which he found himself. He was the master of vast and populated States, which contained more cities than he had soldiers. Wanting to perpetually contain them by force was an impossible thing.... This is what was felt by all the conquerors who sought to make their usurpations solid."[13] To illustrate his point, Linguet contrasts the policies of Alexander and the Turks, who built their empire "on fear. It was with blood that they cemented the union of their provinces. They ruined the cities to prevent revolts."[14]

In England, Robertson and Gillies enthusiastically adopted Montesquieu's theories. Also drawing on Plutarch, Robertson emphasizes the extent to which Alexander's policy "was repugnant to the ideas and prejudices of his countrymen" because it was based on the elimination "of all distinctions between the victors and the vanquished": the union between the Greeks and the Persians was both symbolized and made a reality by marriages and linguistic and cultural exchanges between Persians and Macedonians. On the same grounds, Gillies firmly believes in Alexander's desire "of uniting, by laws and manners, the subjects of his extensive monarchy"; to this end, "he built, or founded, no less than seventy cities, the situation of which being chosen with consummate wisdom, tended to facilitate communication, to promote commerce, and to diffuse civility through the greatest nations of the earth."[15]

As the primary subject of Vincent's study (1797), the creation of trade routes is closely connected with the setting up of a vast communication network between Europe and Asia. This is what radically differentiates Alexander's enterprises from previous Greek expeditions, which had no long-term ambitions and therefore no objectives other than pillage. Alexander was driven both by "a desire of knowing the coast as well as the interior of his empire, and a reasonable hope of uniting the whole by mutual communication and reciprocal interests" (p. 18). Hence the assessment offered by the author: "He considered every country he subdued as a portion of his future empire. He never plundered a single province that submitted, he raised no contribution by extortion.... His conquests were attended with no oppression of the people, no violence of the temples, no insult to religion. Order and regulation engaged his attention equally with the conduct of war" (p. 5). The king was not guided by "vanity," but by "utility." Founding cities was part of this vast plan as cultural as it was commercial. The author also acknowledges Alexander's civilizing efforts on the coasts of the Persian Gulf.

The reviewer for the *Bibliothèque germanique* is pleased that "Quintus Curtius's pompous praise" now has less influence on opinion than Vincent's analyses. Alexander's project was to "connect all known parts of the world, by penetrating to the sources of oriental wealth.... Thus he surrenders Europe, Asia, and Africa to the course of unexpected events of which his audacious genius would be the regulator." The reviewer then expresses his admiration for the Macedonian king's human achievement: "Many a man was able to conquer, but the centuries attest to the centuries how rare is this virtuous and sublime inspiration, which makes one conceive the desire, and predisposes the means to create great and beautiful political bonds, useful to the family of peoples" (vol. 1 [1800]: 89–90).

In his own review, Bourlet de Vauxcelles was careful to dissipate any ambiguity that might arise from overly emphasizing the opening of trade routes between India and the Mediterranean. To this end, he made clear to readers that even though the Macedonian enterprise brought India's riches to Europe, it was not dedicated to exclusive, one-way exploitation: "It was intended to create, administer, and fertilize a great empire that could link together all the parts of the universe."

The Weight of the Model: The Aborted Debate on Cataracts

Yet a contradiction was brought to light within this harmonious, logical structure. It relates to one of the key arguments, that of the destruction of the Babylonian cataracts, which, as we have seen, admirers of Alexander's commercial policy all saw as the indicator of the absolute break he imposed with the past. The history of this discussion shows that it quickly became difficult to cast even a partial doubt on an image apparently based on ancient documentation considered all the more unequivocal given that aside from Robertson no one had adopted the religious explanations Montesquieu had inferred from Persian traditions.[16]

Paradoxically, the element of doubt was instilled by one of the most uncompromising admirers of Alexander's positive accomplishments, William Vincent, although it was actually inspired by the Dane Carsten Niebuhr. In 1778, Niebuhr published an account of his travels in Arabia and surrounding countries (1774–1778). Like other travelers before him, he observed that Arabs living along the Tigris and Euphrates built dams and dikes for agricultural purposes, to prevent water from irrigating sown fields. An expert in the ancient texts, he did not fail to cite the pertinent passage from Arrian regarding cataracts and, using an empirical approach of an ethnographic type, openly suggested that the dikes built by Persians in antiquity were not intended to defend them from some outside maritime power, but were on the contrary used to protect and water the fields. His interpretation called into question the significance generally given to the destruction of the cataracts by Alexander; he had not torn down military structures due to the Persians' proverbial cowardice, but irrigation works, which were evidence of their interest in the development of Babylonian agriculture.[17]

Despite its author's prestige and renown, this passing remark could have remained buried in a travel narrative particularly rich in geographic and historical information. But this was not to be the case, for Niebuhr was in correspondence with Vincent, who considered his Danish colleague "the best of modern travellers surviving" (p. iv). Therefore, when he too tried to evaluate how long it took Alexander to sail to Opis (on the Tigris) in the appended chapter to his 1797 work, "Sequel to the Voyage of Nearchus," he had to include in his calculations the time taken by the Macedonians "to remove the dykes with which the Persian monarchs had obstructed the stream." He could not avoid referring to Niebuhr's observation, though he knew he risked tarnishing Alexander's reputation: "His historians delight in attributing these obstructions to the timidity of the Persians, and the removal of them to the magnanimity of the Conqueror; but Niebuhr, who found similar dykes both in the Euphrates and Tigris still existing, observes that they are constructed for the purpose of keeping up the waters to inundate the contiguous level; if so, the demolition is as derogatory from the policy and sagacity of the monarch, as it is flattering to his intrepidity" (pp. 463–464). Yet Vincent does not seem (or does not want?) to notice that doing this implies reconsidering his description of Alexander as one who opened fluvial and maritime routes; he prefers to define this episode as an exception, which he evades more than he comments upon.

None of Vincent's reviewers mentioned the issue. However, the inferences Vincent drew from Niebuhr were noted by other unconditional admirers of the Macedonian king's positive achievements and vigorously rejected. This was the case with John Gillies. He had previously praised Alexander's beneficial work in his 1786 *History of Ancient Greece:* "He removed the weirs, or dams, by which the timid ignorance of the Assyrian and Persian kings had obstructed the navigation of the great rivers. . . . By these and similar improvements, he expected to facilitate internal intercourse among his central provinces, while, by opening new channels of communication, he hoped to unite the wealthy countries of Egypt and the East, with the most remote regions of the earth." Returning to these questions in his 1809 volume, the

Scottish author emphatically challenged the suggestion made by Niebuhr and passed on by Vincent; while he paid homage to the Danish traveler's great reputation, he deemed it implausible that Alexander could have taken a position contrary to his constant policy of improvement of irrigation and navigation.[18]

Other authors attempted to formulate a reconciliatory synthesis. The German geographer Konrad Mannert used Niebuhr to conclude that, contrary to what the ancient sources stated, the dams in question had no military function: they were not permanent and were intended for irrigation; they created a temporary obstruction to navigation—hence Alexander's decision—but their destruction had no negative impact on fields and villages in the medium term. This line of reasoning provided a favorable outcome to the contradiction, since it safeguarded the memory of an Alexander who was eager to improve river traffic but not prepared to deal a fatal blow to rural prosperity.

Also in Germany, the evolution of Heeren's position is interesting. Heeren spoke several times on the question of India's commerce and the role played by Alexander during the sessions of the Göttingen Academy in the 1790s. Strongly influenced by Montesquieu's reflections but also those of Robertson and Vincent (on whose works he published detailed reviews), he tirelessly repeated that Alexander's objective was indeed to unite the peoples of the new empire through bonds of marriage and collaboration. Nonetheless, after having maintained over thirty years of research that the Persian-built dams were removed by Alexander to facilitate communications, he added a note of repentance to the final edition of his monumental *Historical Researches* (1828): "If I dared to oppose evidence so definite as that of Strabo, I should conjecture, with great probability, that these dams were made to restrain the river, and to prevent an inundation" (2:248 n. 1). He went on to admit that "the dams were no detriment to the navigation of the Euphrates; and although the maritime commerce of Babylon may have been much reduced under the Persian domination, it certainly was not to put a stop to altogether" (p. 249).

In other words, Mannert and Heeren were admitting that the cataracts were not barriers put up by the Persians to protect themselves from invaders from the sea. Heeren went so far as to make a passing challenge to a premise universally accepted since Huet: he stated that only the Tigris had cataracts; that the Euphrates had none; and that traffic between the sea and

Babylon was therefore not entirely blocked under the rule of the Persian kings. Yet neither scholar was prepared to present Alexander as anything other than an opener of maritime routes and promoter of large-scale commerce between India and Babylonia. They expressed significant qualifications and reservations, which cast doubt on the validity of the explanations provided by Arrian and Strabo—including in an awkward, even muddled form in Heeren's case—but they did not call into question the crux of the matter.[19]

It would have been extremely delicate to hypothesize that Alexander had permanently destroyed irrigation works useful to the Babylonian population; such a proposition would have cast serious doubt on the overall image of a conqueror who came to share his good deeds with conquered peoples and was, at the very least, supposed to repair and compensate for the destruction committed. The very idea was all the more unimaginable given that according to other information passed down by Arrian and Strabo, Alexander had received unanimous praise for completing major work near Babylon aimed at protecting the country both from serious flooding and catastrophic drought. The eighteenth-century authors considered this yet more evidence of the radical shift caused by Alexander—namely, the reclaiming of land left fallow by Persians imagined to have as little interest in developing agriculture as in promoting commerce. Like Strabo, who saw it as the mark of a "good king," John Gillies considered that by personally carrying out what he called "an agricultural survey" by river, Alexander had done an essential service to Babylonia.[20] Heeren was equally admiring in referring to the same episode: "He did not hesitate to entrust himself to a very small boat, and to redeem (*redimere*), at peril to his life, the resources accessible to the entire human race (*communia generis humani commoda*)."[21] Though fiercely hostile to conquest, Sainte-Croix was moved to admit that in this instance Alexander was guided by "wise views [and the] design to reestablish the channels and prepare the country's fertility by watering"; nearly eighty years earlier, Rollin, a fellow denouncer of Macedonian ravages, had characterized Alexander's Babylonian enterprise as "truly worthy in great princes, [which] are entirely calculated for the public good."[22] A *communis opinio* like this would have been seriously undermined if one simultaneously recognized that the destruction of the dams had led to the ruin of agricultural activity. At stake in this episode was Alexander's image: Was he a conqueror exclusively interested in war or a king concerned with the good of his peoples? And could the two images coexist, even partially, or were they mutually exclusive?

Fifteen years after Sainte-Croix, John Williams (1792–1858) resolutely took the opposite view to the dominant position. Primarily interested in questions of historical geography, he concluded that the dams in question, intended for irrigation, were built by the Babylonians ("Assyrians") with bricks and mortar and were therefore permanent. Operating according to purely military requirements, Alexander chose to destroy these structures despite the fact that he knew they were used for agriculture; indeed, his primary objective was "an enlarged commerce and the creation of a powerful fleet," even at the cost of hydraulic works essential to the peasants' lives. Francis R. Chesney (1789–1872) was certainly reading Williams when he wrote in his (belated) account of his Euphrates mission of 1834–1836 that "the removal of these walls would have been favourable to navigation; but in other respects it was detrimental, and particularly so by diminishing the productions of the country."[23]

Historians of Alexander did not take into account Williams's writings and Chesney's report. Moreover, even such determined critics of Alexander as Rollin and Sainte-Croix in France and later George Grote in England gave up on using the episode to support their arguments—at least in the last two cases this was most likely because they did not see how to go against Arrian and Strabo; unnerved, they simply chose not to discuss it.[24] This explains how Carsten Niebuhr's initial suggestion sank into oblivion and remained there until the middle of the twentieth century.[25]

An Inexpiable Debt?

Despite the success with which it met, the image of a conqueror from Europe opening the way to commerce and civilization was not imposed without opposition, or—more accurately—was never imposed in an incontestable and uncontested ideological hegemony. As mentioned above,[26] one reason for this is that a great number of works inspired by the tradition of the ancients and published in France,[27] Germany,[28] and England continued to denounce the conqueror's vices and the harmful effects of his conquest. The exaltation of Alexander found in British writers inspired by Voltaire and Montesquieu,[29] for example, did not apply to every author and reach every audience. John Gast's criticisms remained very influential. One need only turn for evidence to the entry on "Alexander the Great" in the *Encyclopædia Britannica* (1790 Dublin ed., 385–386). Its author methodically attacks the conqueror's failings: "His ambition [never] satisfied, which rose even to madness; his excesses with regard to wine." He refuses to weigh Alexander's qualities against his vices since to his mind "one good legislator is worth all the heroes that ever did or will exist." You would think you were reading Rollin.

Criticism and reservations did not only come from a circle of scholars and writers who had by assumption developed a principled hostility to the philosophes. Even Linguet, who often praised the positive consequences of Alexander's conquests, admitted that there was much left to be accomplished. Because Alexander died too young, most of his reign was dedicated to military operations. If he had remained on the throne longer, he could have more intensely devoted himself to works of peace. Such enterprises "could have won him in the eyes of the sages entire forgiveness for all the blood that his youth had spilled." Alexander did not entirely make amends for the devastation of conquered countries; he is only half forgiven. This reservation is all the more notable given that it is found in the conclusion to Linguet's positive assessment of the Macedonian king's conquests.[30]

In fact, the praise lavished on Alexander and his policy by several of the philosophes, as well as their admiration for Peter the Great and Frederick of Prussia, were not free of contradiction. Depending on whether the philosopher-analyst emphasizes a king's constructive activities or his war enterprises, the same ruler can be praised by some as a "father" and denounced by others as "an oppressor"; to mention only one example, Frederick of Prussia was not universally considered a philosopher-king, even less a "citizen-king."[31]

Coming after the Abbé de Saint-Pierre's book (1713), Immanuel Kant's essay *Zum ewigen Frieden: Ein philosophischer Entwurf* (*Perpetual Peace: A Philosophical Sketch*) (1795) shows that the abhorrence of war and the aspiration to "general peace in Europe" powerfully endured throughout the century. In a collection of apologues (allegedly) addressed to young princes, the curious author Pierre-Sylvain Maréchal includes Alexander in his battle between kings and tyrants; he writes that Alexander was "the great troublemaker of the human race." For his part, Baron d'Holbach, who aimed to establish and proclaim the moral foundations of the relationship between people and

populations, condemns every conqueror, describing them as "shrunken geniuses." Alexander does not escape his attack on the ambition of anyone
"who is pretentious enough to believe that he will better govern the new
[subjects] he will subjugate." One could possibly have "forgiven him for his
conquests in Asia, [if he] had brought happiness to the states he had inherited from his fathers." But this was not the case, since he disappeared "without
having given the universe the slightest mark of wisdom, enlightenment, or
virtue, without which there is no honor or glory."[32]

Unless they resolutely supported one of the two images suggested and
disseminated by the ancient authors, historians and philosophers often
had difficulty choosing between the two. They often shared the resulting
moral torment with their readers. Even those moved to admire Alexander's
achievements could not always avoid carefully weighing them out against
his vices. Consider the example of the Scottish judge and historian Lord
Woodhouselee (1747–1813), who taught Universal History at the University
of Edinburgh from 1780 to 1800 under the name of Alexander Fraser Tytler.
In 1782, he published a summary of the course, which expanded considerably with subsequent editions and was widely circulated in England and
the United States (the 135th edition was published in Concord, New Hampshire, in 1849; the book was translated into Japanese in 1870). Not particularly favorable to Montesquieu's political analyses (particularly to book 2 of
The Spirit of the Laws), the author hides neither the difficulty of his task nor
his inclination when it comes time to make an assessment of Alexander's
accomplishments. Like many of his contemporaries, he addresses the question by asking whether positive decisions had "redeemed" the disasters of
conquest: "Twenty other cities of the same name [Alexandria] were built by
him in the course of his conquests. It is such works as these that justly en-
title the Macedonian to the epithet of Great. But rearing in the midst of deserts those nurseries of population and of industry, he repaired the waste
and havoc of his conquests. Except for those monuments of his glory, he
would have merited no other epithet than that assigned by the barbarians
of India, *The Mighty Murderer*" (*Elements of General History, Ancient and Modern*
1818, p. 44).

These problems were also tackled in Germany by the philosopher Christian Garve, a close friend of Kant, particularly in his 1788 book on morality
in politics. Garve, who was also a fervent admirer of Frederick, examines at
length the reasons that could be used to justify starting a war or a conquest

throughout the course of history. For instance, he considers that the war Gustavus Adolphus waged in Germany was a just one, because the king of Sweden was the savior "of a party howling under oppression" (the Protestants), and one that returned Germany to "the freedom of conscience." Following a model well established at least since Voltaire, he also contrasts Charles XII and Peter the Great: "The latter provided his vast states, which extended into Asia, all they principally needed for the progress of industry, commerce, and civilization."

The philosopher's discussions of the intentions of the heads of armies lead him to introduce the case of the "hero-adventurer," who "would join the fray without the slightest provocation." Should he be excused? To reply, the author makes the striking and unprecedented leap of comparing the legendary Inca Manco Cápac and Alexander the Great.[33] Supposing that Manco Cápac annexed countries to make them "more civilized" (*gesitterer*) and that the Macedonian king "only fought Darius to deliver Asia from the yoke of despotism, and to introduce it to the arts, the enlightenment (*Aufklärung*), and the freedom of Greece," one could agree that "posterity had justly applauded them." Admittedly, he writes, "the enterprise would be bloody, but it could have an advantage in sight . . . at least for all the nations involved." The author remains guarded, because the hypothesis requires one to imagine that these conquerors had "purity of intent and probability of success"—which remains to be proved. Hence he concludes that "it is rare to be able to chart these kinds of plans and equally rare to find pretexts of this type. The cases to be categorized under this rubric are so infrequent that they cannot be taken into consideration in establishing a general rule."[34] In short, it is far from certain that Alexander should be placed in the category Garve defines as that of the "just princes."

A paper presented to the Académie Royal des Inscriptions et Belles-Lettres on November 29, 1782, by Abraham-Hyacinthe Anquetil Duperron (1731–1805) expresses firm but still qualified opposition.[35] This self-described "voyager in the Great Indies" had discovered and first published the *Avesta*, the sacred book of the ancient Persians, which he had collected from the Parsis in India. Over his many voyages, he developed the conviction that one must know "the naturals" from the inside, rather than assuming from the outset that they were barbaric and inferior—which explains his hostility to Montesquieu's positions on Asian despotism and the relations between metropolis and colony. Anquetil puts on an emphatic performance in addresses "to the nations that possess the original text of the books of Zoroaster" (1771) and "the people of Hindustan" (1778) and his biographers have tended to idealize the man and his ideas, presenting him as an energetic defender of the rights of peoples against contemptuous and destructive European colonization. Yet several of his books (*Plan d'administration*, 1788; *Dignité du Commerce*, 1789; *L'Inde en rapport avec l'Europe*, 1798) show that he was actually in favor of the establishment of commercial ties between Europe and India, so long as the European ventures were led by France.

On one occasion, Alexander and "his incendiary races" are subjected to the condemnations Anquetil hurled at those he called "conquerors by profession" and compared to "overgrown children." To this end, he adopted as his own the common observation (previously made by Rollin and Mably) that the Macedonian conquest was even more illegitimate when it was directed against "a free people, independent of the Persian kings, and who were therefore in no way involved in the dispute the Macedonian king could have had with these monarchs." This people were the Mards, who were described by the ancient authors as a population living in a state of barbarism, even savagery. Though hostile in principle to the violent conquest carried out by the Macedonian army, the author qualifies his judgment after making a specific remark. Anquetil interprets a text by Polybus[36] to suggest that the conqueror had taken measures to turn a nomadic population into an agricultural people. According to the anthropological criteria of the time (which endured long after, supposing that they ever vanished), this is a positive assessment in that the royal decision entailed progress from barbarism to civilization and from war (linked to nomadism) to peace (characteristic of peasants).[37] Anquetil uses words we have previously encountered: "This was to repair, as much as he could, the damage of an invasion guided by the spirit of conquest, carried out by violence."[38] For all that, Anquetil maintains his disapproval: the measure taken for the Mards was only partial reparation, which does not absolve Alexander of his unjustified aggression.

Pierre-Charles Levesque (1736–1822) later faced a similar predicament. Called to the court of Saint Petersburg in 1773 on Diderot's recommendation, he had become a specialist on Russia and its "savage" peoples.[39] He was also a distinguished Hellenist, a translator of the Greek classics (Thucydides, Plutarch, etc.), and an established historian: he held the Collège de France's chair in *History and Ethics* from 1791 to 1812; in 1793, his course was entitled "Political, Philosophical, and Literary History of Greece."[40] In 1811, he published the third volume of his ancient history, devoting about one hundred pages to Alexander.[41] His assessment shows his admiration for the man. Nonetheless, his opinion is accompanied by a noteworthy reservation: "His establishments, useful to humanity, expiate the evils that accompanied his conquests; if he allowed himself to bloody the earth, and if he destroyed a part of mankind, it was in the alas! deceptive hope of making that which remained more flourishing and wealthier." The interpolation "alas! deceptive" clearly tells the reader that the devastation due to Alexander's conquests was at best only partially "expiated." The author's position seems to be in keeping with the reservations he had firmly expressed earlier in disagreeing with Voltaire on the civilizing role of Peter the Great.[42] While the connection he proposed here is well-founded, it must be noted that Levesque was not the first to turn the philosopher of Ferney's parallel between Peter and Alexander against them. Mably had earlier compared the Macedonian and the Russian in a joint negative appraisal, going against Voltaire in strongly denying that they had achieved anything as legislators and civilizers.[43] In including a reservation in his otherwise favorable portrait of the "conqueror-teacher," Levesque may have been influenced by the theories of Sainte-Croix (who was himself frequently in agreement with the abbé) and/or directly by reading Mably, whom he had enthusiastically praised in 1787.[44]

Alexander and Tyre: The Phoenician Mirage

Of the Macedonian king's various enemies, the Phoenician people posed a serious problem for commentators due to the general admiration for their historic role in the development of commerce, exchanges, and civilization. Montesquieu emphasized that the Phoenicians, who "did not trade as a result of conquest, [were indispensable] to all nations of the world" (*Spirit of the Laws*, 21.5), a position on which he was followed and warmly approved by Jaucourt.[45] The author of *The Spirit of the Laws* was also in at least partial agreement with Huet on this point (and with Bochart, his principal source). Huet did not hesitate to credit the Phoenicians with the first circumnavigation of Africa and had emphasized the scale and importance of their commerce—particularly that of Tyre. As for Montesquieu, he had included in chapter 11 of book 21 a long discussion of the *Periplus* of Hanno, which "seems to be the journal of our own sailors." Huet underlined the contrast between the limited extent of the Phoenicians' continental territory and the expanse of their maritime and commercial influence. In explaining this, he became one of the first to make an analogy with the Dutch of his own time. The parallel with the Netherlands can also be found in Montesquieu, as well as in Linguet—in Montesquieu to point out its virtues (he also includes Venice in the comparison) and in Linguet to reiterate his contempt for merchants and his rejection of luxury trade.[46] While Huet did criticize Alexander for the way he treated Tyre, he primarily recognized that the destruction of Tyre and the founding of Alexandria were the bases on which the king "made a great revolution in the affairs of commerce";[47] as we have seen, this expression was repeated nearly word for word by Montesquieu, then by many other authors in Europe. In the introduction to book 1 of the 1780 edition of Raynal's *Histoire philosophique et politique des établissements et du commerce des Européens dans les deux Indes* (*A Philosophical and Political History of the Settlements and Trade of the Europeans in the East and West Indies;* commonly known as *Histoire des deux Indes*), Diderot famously praises commerce and exchanges, illustrating his statement with the example of the Phoenicians, whom he refers to as "the first in the history of nations"; this people "lives on through its reputation: it was a navigating people. . . . Fortunately situated for the commerce of the Universe . . . the Phoenicians could, if not connect the earth's inhabitants to each other, at least be the intermediaries of their exchanges."[48]

It is therefore easy to understand that the Tyre episode encouraged a few observers to express or confirm their doubts regarding Alexander and his policy. Harshly condemned by Bayle and the authors in line with Rollin-Mably, the destruction of the Phoenician city aroused much controversy and polemics, which are echoed in Voltaire's *L'ABC* conversations.[49] Even when it was not made explicit, the question raised by the wording used—should Tyre have been destroyed?—left no doubt as to the (negative) answer suggested.

The pioneering role of the Phoenicians was elaborated on by several authors in Germany, who simultaneously expressed reservations and even condemnations regarding Alexander. A student of the famous Göttingen Orientalist Michaelis, August Ludwig von Schlözer (1735–1809), published his general history of the ancients' commerce and navigation in 1758 in

Sweden. It was translated into German three years later.[50] Schlözer, a reader of Huet (whom he followed with reservations) and Montesquieu (whom he profoundly admired), paints a rather mitigated picture of the Macedonian conquest. Admittedly, he attempts to avoid openly taking sides with Alexander or Tyre. But his great admiration for the Phoenicians qualifies his appreciation of the destroyer of Tyre. He repeats and adopts as his own *The Spirit of the Laws*' laudatory statement regarding Alexander's decisive influence on the direction of commerce;[51] he admits that "Greece then spread a great light on the knowledge of the world"; he also applauds the conqueror's lucidity in choosing the site of Alexandria. Yet he devotes most of his book to the Phoenicians, and fervently analyzes "the services they did to the human race with their commerce" (pp. 66–102); he must note that compared to Alexander, "they discovered more lands than all the other peoples were able to" (p. 81). While it may have heralded Alexandria's future prosperity, the destruction of Tyre first marked the end of the initial phase of antique commerce (p. 350).

The Phoenicians were also very present in the book Johann Isaac Berghaus published on the history of navigation in 1792. Berghaus was saddened that a people as remarkable as those of Tyre had disappeared beneath the conqueror's blows.[52] Johann Gottfried Herder, another adherent to the Phoenicians-Dutch analogy, unequivocally sided with the Tyrians against Alexander. In a passage violently hostile to the civilizations and empires of the ancient (and modern) Orient and the colonial enterprises of modern Europe, he extols "the industrious, flourishing towns [which] rendered the wealth, industry and science of a certain part of the world common to all, and [which] thus could not avoid promoting humanity, perhaps without the design." Given his strong reservations about Carthage, Herder underlines the importance of the Phoenicians' contributions: "This they did, not in the character of conquerors, but in that of merchants, and founders of colonies." Alexander is therefore condemned, like every other conqueror, since "no conqueror disturbs the course of nature so much as he who destroys flourishing commercial towns . . . unless some neighbouring place quickly succeed them." This was the case in Alexander's era: "When the Macedonian conqueror destroyed Tyre, Alexandria flourished."[53] Christian Gottlob Heyne would make a very similar argument in Göttingen in 1805.[54]

Daniel Defoe, Scipio, and Alexander: The Interpretation of a Politically Committed Journalist (1725)

Alexander's policy concerning the Phoenicians brings us to an author whom one would not expect to encounter in a book on images of Alexander in modern Europe: Daniel Defoe (1683–1731). Aside from being a renowned novelist, Defoe was a highly productive publicist and journalist who eagerly engaged in the debates of his time, generally without a hint of subtlety or restraint when he presented himself as a herald and defender of Great Britain's interests. His most famous books, which remain very popular to this day, frequently consist of a fictional narrative relating assorted voyages and discoveries; they are also vigorous defenses of emigration and (British) colonies. The emphasis is placed on commerce rather than conquest itself: new markets must be found for British industry.[55] Outside of the fictional context, he tirelessly repeated these themes in more overtly political works such as *A Plan for the English Commerce* (1728) and *A General History of Discoveries and Improvements,* which was initially published in article form in 1725–1726. The latter work's full title meaningfully associates the three elements constitutive of power: *Commerce, Navigation, and Plantation.* It is here that we find Alexander introduced in a surprising historical role. Never subsequently cited, this essay by a publicist and journalist probably did not have many readers outside the regular audience of the London periodicals. Yet it should not be overlooked in an examination of European public opinions and the images then circulating.

Defoe states that he wants to use an enjoyable form to tell his readers of "the most flourishing Arts, the most useful discoveries, and the most advantageous improvements ... [made] for the good of Mankind." First among these discoveries and improvements are commerce and navigation. To discuss them, the present must be connected to the past in such a way that one becomes aware of discoveries made in antiquity and since lost. The author highlights countries that were once "peopled, cultivated and improved" before being subjected to devastation and returning to a primitive state. Defoe believes that these countries deserve to be rediscovered and restored to their initial state, "especially as the commerce of the world is now established." It falls to the European countries to tackle this rediscovery and restoration, for if God created such great riches it was obviously not for them to remain unexploited. Thus the book ends with a call to the Christian powers of Europe to unite and reconquer North Africa, from Utica to Fez, and "to clear the coasts of Africa from this bloody race of Infidels which now possesses it." This would be for the ultimate good of commerce, "which is a certain communication of Nations occasioned by the necessities and for the good of Mankind; the enemies of trade are enemies to all men: pirates and sea-robbers are wild beasts" (pp. 142–143).

If the countries in question had returned to a wild state, it was because they had been devastated by conquering enemies of work and commerce. As one can imagine, Defoe places the Moors and Turks first among these enemies of humanity, for their conquests ruined the wealth of countries where milk and honey once ran and where millions of industrious people lived. But there are at least two other culprits: Alexander, for destroying Tyre, and Scipio, for annihilating Carthage. In the long term, they can be said to have paved the way for the Muhammadans' conquest.

As can be seen, Defoe cleverly subverts the image of the irreproachable conqueror based on the incredible virtues attributed both to Alexander and Scipio (including their shared "continence" in dealing with captive princesses). This tactic also draws on the (widely held) conviction that the Phoenicians served as trailblazers in the history of commerce and navigation and therefore of civilization. From this perspective, Alexander's conquest was a catastrophe. Despite his inclination for men of science, the king did not hesitate to ravage Tyre and put to death no less than 26,000 citizens after a cold-blooded massacre. Defoe sadly asks: "How many philosophers, astronomers, and men of genius for all sorts of virtuous improvements did Alexander destroy in the ruin of that one City?" and postulates that all the wisdom and knowledge there accumulated was wiped out at once and for all time (p. 95). If one adds the subsequent destruction of Carthage, the final judgment is beyond appeal: "What a loss then to the commerce of Europe have those two actions been, which men in those days called glorious; and how have we reason to blast the memory of Alexander the Great and Scipio Africanus with a mark of infamy never to be wiped out, for destroying the only two governments in the world, which were qualified to make all the rest of mankind great and happy?" (p. 99)

Naturally, Defoe is aware of the subsequent founding of Alexandria. But in his view it does make up for what he deems the irreparable loss of Tyre. While Alexandria became prosperous, this was long after Alexander's day, and its relations were limited to Greece and Italy, "whereas the Tyrian merchants had established a commerce through the whole Mediterranean up to the mouth of the Straits; had planted colonies at Carthage, at Cadiz, at Palermo, and several other places, which Alexander never had any interest in, or influence over; nor did the knowledge and study of Arts and Sciences ever come to any extraordinary height at Alexandria as it had done at Tyre" (p. 95). Possibly inspired by Alexander's remorse for his bloodthirsty behavior, the founding of Alexandria only resulted in failure: the blow dealt to global commerce was indeed a mortal one (pp. 126–127).

The only reference cited by Defoe is Walter Raleigh's *Historie of the World* (1652). Defoe certainly found an uncompromising depiction of Alexander the Great in chapter 2 of book 4 of that work, as well as a violent attack on the Romans in book 6, which is devoted to the Punic Wars.[56] But as far as can be seen, he did not have a particular interest in this period in history; he did not write as a historian but as an avowed polemicist seeking to create an opinion. Alexander is turned into a metaphorical precedent for the considerable ravages that can be caused by a conqueror assaulting a thriving commercial city, for any conquest is antithetical to commerce: "War, Tyranny and Ambition, those enemies to all peaceable dispositions have continual persecuted trade; often the industrious trading part of the world has been beggared and impoverished by the violence and industry of arms. As trade enriches the world, and industry settles and establishes people and nations, so war, victory and conquest have been the destroyers of every good thing; the soldier has always been the plunderer of the industrious merchant" (*General History,* p. 123). The only justifiable and even desirable wars and conquests are those waged against populations of bandits and pirates, such as the war Defoe would like to see carried out against the infidels, the Moors and the Turks. The positive outcome of such a war would be recultivation, population growth, and the return of the commerce and arts that had flourished before the fatal destruction Alexander inflicted on Tyre and Scipio later inflicted on Carthage. The Moors then settled in the area, followed by the Turks. Both peoples were too accustomed to cruelty and robbery to cultivate the land (beyond their immediate consumption) or promote commerce.

There is little doubt of the direct connection between the Carthaginians and the English. In fact, it is expressed by Defoe, who considers that Hanno "is the Sir Walter Raleigh of the Carthaginian empire," and later refers to Sir Walter Raleigh as "the English Hanno" (pp. 106, 125). In Defoe's eyes, the breadth of Tyrian commerce was never equaled in later times; the only possible comparison would be with commerce conducted by the British.[57] It therefore comes as no surprise that in the same breath Defoe pleads for recapturing and revitalizing these countries, which would allow the natives to wear civilized clothing and thereby open a new market for British manufacturers.

Even though British authors continued to see Carthage as a precedent from which it was suitable both to take inspiration and distance,[58] and even though French authors also used the Carthage-England parallel to polemical ends (most often anti-British),[59] one can rightly consider that Defoe's argument belongs to such a specific political context and discursive logic that it loses heuristic pertinence. It nonetheless illustrates the common eighteenth-century idea which emphasized the supreme excellence of trading peoples unfortunately destroyed by conquering peoples. The idea was particularly forcefully defended by Melon in his *Political Essay upon Commerce* (1734, 1736; chap. 4: "Of Colonies"):[60] "The spirit of conquest and the spirit of commerce mutually exclude each other in a nation," he wrote, using the conquests of Alexander, Genghis Khan, and Tamerlane as reprehensible examples (chap. 7: "Of Military Government").

The Hesitations of the Chevalier de Jaucourt (1753–1765)

Diderot and D'Alembert's *Encyclopédie* was by far the best known and most widely circulated of the great eighteenth-century publishing endeavors to combine erudition and philosophy, popularization and compilation. Due to the absence of biographical entries (according to d'Alembert's wishes), the *Encyclopédie* did not feature an article specifically dedicated to Alexander the Great. Additionally, one cannot really speak of an "Alexander of the *Encyclopédie*," despite the fact that there are hundreds of references to the Macedonian king throughout its volumes.

Several authors of *Encyclopédie* entries are unsparing with the Macedonian conqueror. To be convinced of it, one need only turn to the entries on "Gloire" and "Grandeur," both by Marmontel; "Héroïsme" by Diderot; and "Héros" and "Homme d'État," both by Jaucourt.[61] The same expressions are repeated from one entry to the next. Highly critical of Alexander's beneficial accomplishments, Marmontel rails against "those who celebrate conquerors," and carefully distinguishes between "the vulgar man [who] admires and bows low" and "the wise man [who] is not impressed, [for] he sees that what is called the light is nothing but a reflected glare, superficial and temporary." Or, as Marmontel writes elsewhere: "It is false that in the opinion of the common man the idea of personal greatness is reduced to its philosophical purity.—The minds of the multitude [love] the marvelous." He continues: "Left to the people, the truth changes and is obscured by tradition. . . . Will there not be at least one class of men far enough above the vulgar, sufficiently wise, courageous, and eloquent to arouse the world against its oppressors and make it see that a barbaric glory is odious?"

The author of the entry on "Heroism" is equally brutal: "But the people is always the people; and since it has no idea of true greatness, it often sees as a hero he who, when reduced to his true value, is the shame and scourge of the human race." The same is true of the article on the "Statesman," in which Jaucourt denounces "the common man [who] always supposes that statesmen who governed happily had a prodigiously expansive mind and nearly divine genius; but often all that is needed to succeed at it is a sound mind, solid views, diligence, follow-through, prudence, and favorable conditions"—as evidenced by Alexander the Great, Jaucourt underlines. Elsewhere, the same author contrasts "the wise and foolish opinions of the common man" when it comes to "evaluating" men.[62]

Let us dwell a little longer on the Chevalier Louis de Jaucourt, who is particularly interesting from this perspective. Born in 1704, this intriguing character received a thorough education in Geneva, Cambridge, and Leiden before returning to France at the age of thirty-two. With a background both in literature and the sciences (he was qualified as a doctor), he was invited by d'Alembert to write articles for the *Encyclopédie*. The tireless compiler made a gargantuan contribution ranging across every field of knowledge, from medicine to geography and from botany to ancient and modern history. In total, he wrote 17,266 articles, or about 25–30 percent of volumes 8–13 and close to 50 percent of volumes 14–18, to the point that these volumes can accurately be described as the *Encyclopédie* of Diderot, d'Alembert, and Jaucourt. The author of the entry on Jaucourt in the 1842 edition of Michaud's *Biographie universelle ancienne et moderne* (*Universal Ancient and Modern Biography*) takes care to point out that the chevalier always remained moderate in his opinions: "He was able to guard against the lapses [of the philosophes] and the passages from his pen may be those in which we find the fewest reprehensible things!" Jaucourt described himself as a philosophe without passion. This did not stop him from steadfastly fighting the positions of the Roman church and many of his articles "implicitly defy the Bourbons' ideology of absolutism."[63]

Steeped in Greek and Latin culture, Jaucourt wrote numerous articles between 1753 and 1765 in which he had occasion to evoke the memory of the Macedonian king or simply to allude to it.[64] In the entry on "Grecs" (*Encyclopédie,* 7[1757]:912–915), in which he deals with history and literature, he mentions the "third age of Greece," which marks the Age of Alexander—also referred to by him as "Ages, the four—" (15[1765]:172). It should be noted, however, that the figure of Alexander is absent from the entries on "Cruauté" (4[1754]:517–519) and "Vies" (17[1765]:256–257). Of the many ancient examples of cruelty, Jaucourt mentions Philip and several Roman emperors, but not Alexander. The conqueror's absence from the entry on "Lives" is less gratifying. Clearly, *Lives* are exclusively written for those "illustrious men" of antiquity who are "examples of virtues dedicated to the human race." Jaucourt considered that neither Alexander nor Caesar fit in this category. However, the Macedonian king is honored in the "Statesman" entry ("Alexander showed himself to be a great statesman, after proving he was a great captain"). Jaucourt did not have a perfectly homogenous image of Alexander, which he could tirelessly repeat in every article requiring a reference to the conqueror.

Borrowing R. Schwab's expression, Jean Ehrard recently observed that "Jaucourt must have known *The Spirit of the Laws* by heart." Indeed, it is rare that Jaucourt does not quote Montesquieu's book and its "excellent reflections." Failing that, the paraphrase is so obvious that it could not escape the reader's practiced eye.[65] The direct influence of Montesquieu is particularly significant in the entries relating to politics and the law, where Jaucourt "openly makes himself the voice of the Baron de Montesquieu . . . like an appeal for Enlightenment justice."[66] Naturally, in the article on "Conquête" (3[1753]:899–901), Montesquieu is first among "the enlightened guides known by all, who have newly and attentively traveled these thorny roads." The first part on the "right of conquest" is a paraphrase of the pertinent chapters of book 10 of *The Spirit of the Laws.* Jaucourt then refers his reader to the source: "I am omitting the rules of conduct that must be observed by the various conquering states for the good and preservation of their *conquests;* they will be found in the illustrious author of *The Spirit of the Laws.*" Does this elision mean that Jaucourt shares Montesquieu's views on the benefits of the Macedonian conquest? One might think so, particularly since his opening quotes the famous sentence from *The Spirit of the Laws* about "the immense debt" tied to "the right of conquest." But one might also begin to doubt it upon reading the second part of the entry, which collects Jaucourt's own remarks "on conquest considered as a means of acquiring sovereignty." Remark 2 includes a reflection by Montesquieu (*Spirit of the Laws*, 10.2) but does not cite its author: "Do not speak of the glory of the prince for making conquests, his glory would be pride; it is a passion, not a legitimate right."

The conclusion Jaucourt comes to is the absolute opposite of his model's. He (mistakenly) sees the above as a direct reference to Alexander and consequently likens his conquests to no more than a form of banditry: "Thus when Alexander brought war to the most distant peoples, who had never heard of him, certainly such a *conquest* was no more a just title to acquire sovereignty than banditry is a legitimate means to enrich one's self. The quality & the number of people do not change the nature of the action; the injury is the same, the crime is equal." Though it does not explicitly refer to Alexander, the conclusion is equally unsettling: "It is the fate of heroes to ruin themselves in conquering countries they then lose." The entry "Héros (*Gramm.*)" leaves no doubt as to the position taken by Jaucourt, who draws an opposition between the "hero" and the "great man": "[The latter] joins to talents & genius most of the moral virtues; he only has beautiful & noble motives in his conduct; he only listens to the public good, the glory of his prince, the prosperity of the state, & happiness of the peoples. . . . The title of *hero* depends on success, that of the great man does not always depend on it. His principle is virtue, which is unshakeable in prosperity as in misfortune."

While Jaucourt does not reject the designation "hero," in his eyes "the perfect *hero* is the one who joins to all the ability & valor of a great captain a sincere love and desire for public felicity" (8[1765]:182). Nowhere does he suggest that Alexander deserved such a distinction. One comes to think that if Jaucourt did not discuss all of Montesquieu's views on the beneficial results of Alexander's conquests, it was because he disagreed with some of the arguments developed in *The Spirit of the Laws*.

To illustrate his argument, Montesquieu referred to a law decreed by Gelo, which forbade defeated Carthaginians from carrying out human sacrifices (10.5). Long before Sainte-Croix stepped into the debate without citing

Jaucourt,[67] the chevalier wrote a personal commentary seriously qualifying his agreement with the remark in *The Spirit of the Laws*.[68] Additionally, his reservations regarding Alexander's excessive territorial ambitions are frequently attested to. In the entry "Temple de la gloire" (16[1775]:87), he regrets that Alexander did not devote all his energy to ensuring the freedom "of all the states and all the cities of Greece" and that he did not create "legitimate bounds to his empire; he would have put all his joy into making it fortunate, to bringing it prosperity, to making laws and justice flourish there as well as he made the arts and sciences flourish; he would have exercised the most lasting influence on every heart, he would have acquired sublime glory, he would have become in every regard the admiration of the universe!"

The article on "Guerre" (7[1757]: 996–998) reveals that Jaucourt was viscerally attached to peace. Here too, the example of Alexander illustrates a negative statement on a war started for hidden and illegitimate motives: "The offenses the Greeks had received from the Persians" were only alleged pretexts—"the real motives for his enterprise were the ambition to make himself known, supported by the hope for success." Citing Grotius, Jaucourt denounces the ever-disastrous consequences of war: "War stifles the voice of nature, of justice, of religion, and of humanity. It only brings banditry and crimes into the world; with it marches dread, famine, and desolation . . . ; it ravages the countryside, depopulates the provinces, and reduces the cities to dust. It exhausts states flourishing amidst the greatest successes etc." (7.998).

When he advocates for peace over war, it is not as a scholar but as a philosopher distressed to see Europe ravaged again: "The gazettes currently [1757] only echo the sorrows it inflicts on land and on sea, in the ancient and the new worlds, upon peoples who should strengthen the bonds of a benevolence that is already too weak, rather than sever them" (7.998). In this context, any declared exception in favor of Alexander's wars would diminish the strength of the argument. Similarly, Jaucourt concludes that the endeavor ended in failure and that this would have been the case even if Alexander had had a son worthy of succeeding him.[69]

Nonetheless, during the same period and in the same pages, the chevalier continues to express his admiration for a king "who never showed himself to be more worthy of the name of *great*, than when he decreed an edict that all good people are kin to one another & that only bad people were those to be known as *foreigners.*" He even considers that the king has become an example: "Now that commerce is linked to the entire universe, that politics is enlightened about its interests, that humanity extends to all the peoples, there is no sovereign in Europe who does not think like Alexander."[70]

Jaucourt is highly characteristic of that category of author-readers who maintain and disseminate a shared opinion of Alexander, according to their principles but also to an internal discursive logic, which can noticeably vary depending on the articles they were asked to write over quite a long period. This creates a composite image, which can also be found in the articles of the dictionaries.[71] Like most of his contemporaries, Jaucourt condemns Alexander's private vices, on one occasion opposing him to Muhammad: the latter "had Alexander's intrepidness," but also "the liberality and sobriety which Alexander would have needed to be a great man in everything."[72] At the same time—and without ever falling into sycophantic praise—Jaucourt credits Alexander with many political virtues, including in articles not focused on the Macedonian king. This is the case with the article on "Éphèse": "The day of Alexander's birth, the city's soothsayers began to cry out that the destroyer of Asia had come into the world." The author ironically comments on this traditional tale: "One does not forget that this destroyer traveled to Ephesus after the Battle of the Granicus and restored democracy there" (5[1756]:773). His principles of political morality led him to condemn Alexander's actual wars, but not necessarily his conquests, inasmuch as the king took measures favorable to the human race, particularly his policy on "foreigners."

Diderot, the *Histoire des deux Indes,* and Alexander's Conquests

This difficulty in harmoniously fitting Alexander's conquests into Enlightenment thought is also found in one of the great bestsellers of the last third of the eighteenth century, the aforementioned *Histoire des deux Indes* credited to Guillaume-Thomas Raynal (1713–1796). First published in 1770, the book was at the forefront of the fight against slavery in the colonies.[73] As Raynal so clearly expresses in his introductory paragraph, his project deals exclusively with the history opened by "the discovery of the New World and the route to India by the Cape of Good Hope." Following in Voltaire's wake, Raynal considers that this opening was the most interesting event "to mankind in general." Adopting a method regularly employed in the many histories of commerce then available (though the *Histoire des deux Indes* is more than that), Raynal provides a synoptic overview ranging from the Phoenicians—the first trading and navigating people—the Greeks, and the Romans (but not Alexander) to the modern era: "Such was the state of Europe, when the Portuguese monarch, at the head of an active, generous and intelligent people, surrounded by neighbours who still preyed upon each other, formed a plan of extending his dominions by sea and land" (bk. 1, intro., see also 19.6). Aside from these reminders, ancient history is not systematically mentioned as a precedent. Needless to say, references to Alexander are isolated and rare and do not play a central part in Raynal's exposition or reasoning. Nonetheless, they remain of interest because they reveal the selective view of Alexander held by some brilliant popularizers of the time, as well as the qualifications and changes these popularizers made from one edition to the next. A single edition can also contain different, even contradictory opinions, since authors' contributions were not necessarily standardized or coordinated.

Generally speaking, the book's tone is set by the introductory paragraphs to books 12 and 13, which contrast the points of view of Europeans in the eighteenth century and at the beginning of the seventeenth century. In the seventeenth century, "the thoughts of all men were generally turned towards the concerns of the New World, and the French appeared as impatient as other nations to take a share in them" (13.1). But by the time of the book's writing, people questioned and criticized the colonies' very existence. To be clear about the consequences of European conquest and colonization, one had to examine the connection between the benefits derived and the miseries created in the colonies. This is why the glory of the discovery generally attributed to the Spaniards could only be confirmed if it was to the Antilles' advantage. Inspired by the homonymous article in the *Encyclopédie*, the *Histoire des deux Indes* states that true glory "is the lot of virtue, and not of genius; of useful, great, beneficent, splendid, and heroic virtue." It is the lot of Regulus, Cato, or Henri IV, but not that of Caesar or Pompey—for "the conquerors, as well ancient as modern, are now put upon a level with the most abhorred class of mankind." And "though an enterprise be in itself a good one, can it be laudable, if the motive of it be vicious?" (12.1). Implicit in the very question, the suggested answer destroys the argument of "redemption of the debt" and "reparation."

For the first time, Alexander appears here in the context of ancient commercial contacts between Egypt and the Indian Sea, "the true channel of wealth" (1.11). Considering the delta's position at the gates of the Orient and Occident, "Alexander formed the design of fixing the seat of his empire in Egypt, and of making it the centre of trade to the whole world." The author (whoever he might be) continues in glowing terms about "this prince who had more discernment than any other conqueror . . . [and who was] the greatest commander that history and fable have held up to the admiration of mankind." The wording is reminiscent of Voltaire. It is more guarded in the 1770 edition: here, Alexander was declared an "ambitious prince," eager "to subjugate" every country, and his merits were expressed in a less enthusiastic manner; he was simply "more enlightened than conquerors commonly are." Referring to the routes between the Red Sea and the Valley of the Nile, Raynal (if it was truly him) states that he is basing himself on "a writer who has entered deeply into this subject"—the reference is certainly to Ameilhon, though Huet was probably also consulted.[74]

Admiration for Alexander's positive role is also clearly expressed in the discussion that the 1770 edition (4.21) devoted to Hindustan at the time that Dupleix was attempting to bolster the French presence there. The author offers a quick flashback to the ancient conquests, stating that if surviving accounts are to be trusted, "the conquerors of the most distant times, Bacchus, Semiramis, Senusret, Darius crossed [the region] like torrents and left macabre traces of their passage everywhere they went." Alexander's conduct is said to be entirely different: he "followed in their footsteps without imitating their conduct." Possibly inspired by Montesquieu, Raynal underlines the tremendous respect the Macedonian showed for "the laws, customs, and religion of the country" and the resulting veneration of his name in India. In the author's view, the consequences of the Macedonian conquest were indisputably seen "as a good thing, because they gave rise to the rich commerce that the Macedonians, Greeks, and Syrians subsequently carried out there." Moreover, the conquest began a long period of peace and tranquility, which lasted until the invasion of Genghis Khan and his "hordes of Tartars."

The same issues are presented in a singularly different light in the 1780 edition (4.21). The Indian travels of Bacchus, Hercules (rather than Semiramis), Senusret, and Darius, "weapons in hand," are judged uncertain, and there is no more mention of the destruction they caused. This removes the discursive foundations for contrasting their misdeeds with beneficial policies exclusively implemented by Alexander. By contrast, the 1780 edition insists on the Indians' traditional virtues and their country's prosperity: "When Alexander entered these regions, he found very few kings and many free cities." Republican aspirations to the purity of mores incited inhabitants to overthrow corrupt kings. The analysis clearly condemns a conqueror who "would have subdued the whole country, had not death overtaken him in the midst of his triumphs."

By Raynal's own admission, he called "into [his] assistance men of information from all nations" to prepare his book. Diderot stands out among his collaborators for having written or rewritten many pages and even chapters, particularly in the 1780 edition. Like others before me, I am tempted to attribute chapter 21 of book 4 in the 1780 edition to Diderot. It is indeed well known that Diderot was a leader of the battle against conquests and the colonies in what can be called his anticolonialist phase.[75] In those fragments now definitively attributed to him, Diderot treats Alexander harshly, contrasting ancient history and the history of his time: "One must no longer expect . . . expeditions in which we see a handful of men led by an ambitious leader roaming a part of the globe, subjugating, devastating, slaughtering everything that stood in his way. This man in whose presence the stunned earth kept silent, will not be seen again. . . . The fanaticism of religion and the spirit of conquest, these two causes disturbing the globe, have ceased. . . . It has passed, the time of the founding and toppling of empires!" In other words, Alexander cannot and should not be considered a happy precedent to European conquests that would themselves be imagined beneficial. Diderot thrusts him back into a world forever vanished, full of that spirit of conquest, which carries away everything in its path like a torrent, to the great misfortune of the human race.

Introduced by Diderot in the 1780 edition, the true hero of the story is the Indian Sandracottus, who "by following the conqueror in his expeditions, had learned the art of war. . . . He collected a numerous army, and drove the Macedonians out of the provinces they had invaded. [He was] the deliverer of his country. . . . How long he reigned, or what was the duration of the empire he had founded, is not known."[76] Interestingly, Diderot was not the first to honor the memory of Sandracottus as the leader of a revolt against the conquerors. Ten years earlier (1770), the Indian ruler had already been the hero of the "Discours sur l'histoire ancienne des Indes" presented by Abbé

Roubaud in his *Histoire générale de l'Asie, de l'Afrique et de l'Amérique* (1:601–659): "This man [Sandracottus], who acquired less celebrity by doing great things than the Greek Hero did in his country, first exhorted his compatriots to shake off the yoke of foreign domination, [and] he chased the Macedonians out of the provinces they had invaded," thus becoming the "Deliverer of his country." There is no doubt that Diderot borrowed this passage from Roubaud nearly word for word. The difference is that in Roubaud, Alexander is among those ancient conquerors "driven by the goad of curiosity, perhaps even by a feeling of beneficence"; in fact, in paraphrasing Montesquieu without naming him, the abbé credits the Macedonian king with great commercial designs between "the Indies and the Occident." But, he continues, his stay in India (which he scoured rather than conquered) did not have lasting effects on the country: "The succession of its princes was not even interrupted; it was only a momentary disruption without a revolution. The moment the Hero of Macedonia closed his eyes, India was entirely free. By following him in his expeditions, the Indian Sandracottus had learned the art of war." The end of the story suggests some disenchantment about Sandracottus, who "used the title of Deliverer of his country to make himself master of it. . . . All the peoples were equally subjugated. . . . We do not know the duration of the Empire he founded." Diderot's wording ("Deliverer of his country to make himself master of it") is once again taken from Roubaud, but rather than subjugating all the peoples of India, Sandracottus "united the whole Hindustan under his laws."[77] One suspects that this phrasing (a lawgiver vs. a conqueror) was a better fit for Diderot's image of a liberator.

It is revealing that the figure of Sandracottus is far different in William Robertson, who on the contrary believed that Alexander's conquest had lasting effects and that it was successfully continued by his successor Seleucus: "Even India, the most remote of Alexander's conquests, quietly submitted to Pytho the son of Agenor, and afterwards to Seleucus, who successively obtained dominion over that part of Asia. Porus and Taxiles, notwithstanding the death of their benefactor, neither declined submission to the authority of the Macedonians, nor made any attempt to recover independence." Personally convinced of the advantages he stood to gain from Indian commerce, "Seleucus, in order to curb Sandracottus . . . advanced considerably beyond the utmost boundary of Alexander's progress in India." Without giving any further details, Robertson refers to the treaty between

Seleucus and Sandracottus, "in consequence of which that monarch quietly retained the kingdom he had acquired" (*Historical Disquisition,* pp. 27–38). Any hint of an Indian revolt against the Macedonian invaders is removed from the narrative; the harmony and concord desired by Alexander continue to reign.

1. Drawing of a mausoleum in Mashhad-i-Madar-i-Suleiman (Persia) by Johann Albrecht von Mandelslo (in *Voyage en Perse et en Inde,* 1637–1640); mausoleum later identified by British diplomat James Morier (1809–1810) as being that of Cyrus the Great at Pasargadae.

2. François Laurent, posthumous portrait of the Baron de Sainte-Croix, holding a copy of his book in his right hand (1838), Musée Calvet, Avignon.

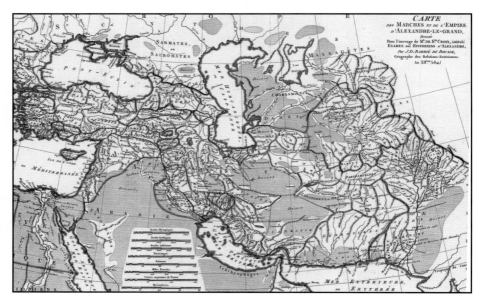

3. Map of Alexander's empire by Jean-Denis Barbié du Bocage, in *Examen critique des anciens historiens d'Alexandre* by the Baron de Sainte-Croix, 1804 edition.

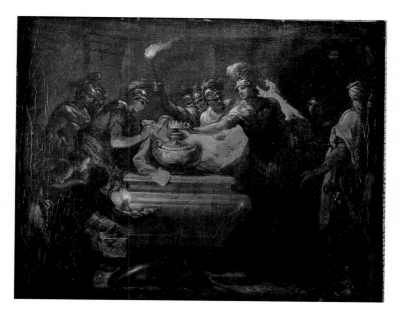

4. Hyacinthe Collin de Vermont, *Alexander Victorious over the Persians Has a Gold Crown Placed on Darius's Tomb* (1735), Musée Lambinet, Versailles.

5. Johannes Glauber (1646–1726, attributed to), *Alexander Visiting the Tomb of Darius,* Musée des Beaux-Arts, Nantes (canvas awaiting restoration).

6. Pierre-Henri de Valenciennes, *Mount Athos Carved as a Monument to Alexander the Great* (1796). Restricted gift of Mrs. Harold T. Martin 1983.36, The Art Institute of Chicago.

7. Pierre-Henri de Valenciennes, *Alexander at the Tomb of Cyrus the Great* (1796). Restricted gift of Mrs. Harold T. Martin 1983.36, The Art Institute of Chicago.

8. Pierre-Henri de Valenciennes, *Cicero Discovering the Tomb of Archimedes* (1787), Musée des Augustins, Toulouse.

9. Giovanni Benedetto Castiglione, *Alexander at the Tomb of Cyrus* (c. 1645–1650). Pepita Milmore Memorial Fund and Edward E. MacCrone Fund, 1981.10.1, Courtesy National Gallery of Art, Washington, DC.

10. Hubert Robert, *Alexander the Great before the Tomb of Achilles* (c. 1755–1757), Musée Lambinet, Versailles.

11. *The Triumphal Entry of Alexander the Great into Babylon after the Conquest of Persia,* English caricature mocking King George III (1793), British Museum, London. Photo © The Trustees of the British Museum.

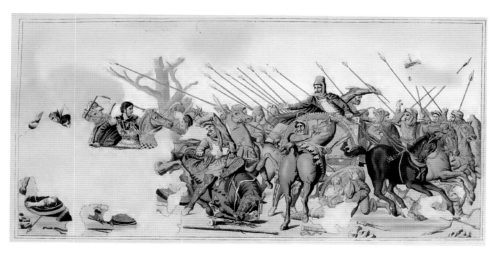

12. Drawing of the mosaic in the House of the Faun discovered at Pompeii on October 24, 1831, and depicting a battle between Alexander and Darius. Drawing by Antonio Niccolini (in *Quadro in musaico scoperto in Pompei,* 1832).

Christ: Gottl: Heynè Gul.mo Vincent

Vir D. C.

Cum et antea Doctrinam tuam et ingenii acumen admirarer, nunc vero inspecto Nearcho tuo, ea nominis tui existimatio et claritas inter nos invaluit, ut habearis nobis inter populares tuos unus ex paucissimis, qui verae eruditionis non modo in verborum et litterarum apicibus haerentis, sed in ipsis quoque rebus ac factis antiquitatis, eorumque caussis et rationibus positae, notionem justam et certam habent. Geographiae antiquae partem eximiam quae in notitia Indiae & Persiae illustratis versatur, tam praeclarè illustrasti, ut magnum in litteras beneficium attulisse videaris. Libri tui encomium factum videbis in Recensibus nostris litterariis, cujus exemplum appono, si forte adsunt tibi qui Teutonice interpretari possint. Bene tecum actum erit si inter populares tuos tantas ex opera tua laudes consequutus fueris, quam inter extraneos, in quibus me habeto vel maxime colentem Te, et amantem.

C. G. Heynè

Script: Gottingae d: XXX. Maii 1797.

13. Unpublished letter from Christian Gottlob Heyne to William Vincent, dated May 30, 1797, inserted in the copy of Vincent's book *Voyage of Nearchus from the Indus to the Euphrates* (1797) given and inscribed by the author to his French translator Jean-Baptiste-Louis-Joseph Billecocq, Bibliothèque Nationale de France, Paris.

III

Empires and Nations

Chapter 6

Lessons of Empire, from the Thames to the Indus

From Nearchus to the East India Company

The importance of British books in the previous chapters should come as no surprise. At a time when Great Britain was being forced to abandon part of the territory it had conquered (the American colonies) but continued to build a global empire in the face of French competition (royal, revolutionary, then Napoleonic), the history of Alexander was no longer solely the prerogative of classicists and Hellenists, nor the exclusive domain of the moralist historians: it was incorporated into imperial thought in the shape of a dialogue between the present of British-dominated India and a past that included Alexander, a figure often evoked and / or invoked as a precedent in which one could or must seek inspiration.

There was a long tradition of seeing Alexander as the first European to open India to European curiosity and enterprises. Beginning in antiquity, his admirers stated that he had been the only one (aside from Dionysus) "to have brought war to the Indians" and to have succeeded where Semiramis and Cyrus had failed; Montesquieu made certain to refer to this tradition in order to better establish Alexander's role as a discoverer (*Spirit of the Laws*, 21.8). In the modern era, the filiation between Alexander and the Portuguese was celebrated in book 7 of *Os Lusiadas* (1572)—Montesquieu wrote that reading "[its] poetry, one feels something of the charms of the *Odyssey* and the magnificence of the *Aeneid*" (21.21). The great Camões had not failed to make use of the figures of the ancient conquerors of India, including the mythical Semiramis and Ninyas, but also of Alexander, "the young prince crowned with the palms of victory," and to depict his own contemporaries

as the direct heirs to these glorious forebears.[1] The same filiation had already
been claimed by Lopez de Castanheda in his 1552 history of the conquest of
the Indies, to the sole benefit of the king of Portugal, since "Alexander's conquests were carried out on land by him in person against nations that were
little trained in or used to feats of arms, while the Portuguese conquest of
India was achieved by royal captains after a sea voyage of one year and eight
months; after having overcome hunger and thirst . . . they had to face men
armed not with bows and spears as in the time of Alexander, but men . . .
whose power was far greater than that of King Porus."[2] Half a century later,
Grotius brings a shift from an epic tone to legal diagnosis. Grotius assures
the reader that the Portuguese had no particular right to forbid their Dutch
competitors from sailing in the Indian Sea; they could not claim to have
discovered it since Alexander's ships had preceded them.[3] Finally, with the
first attempts at critical readings of the Greek and Latin texts, the ancient
narratives were synoptically compared with the accounts of Portuguese
travelers on the ocean and the Gulf.[4]

In 1797, the subtitle of William Vincent's *Voyage of Nearchus* left nothing
to the imagination; the reader knows from the outset that the volume will
consist of "an account of the first navigation attempted by Europeans in the
Indian Ocean."[5] By choosing to focus his research and thought on Nearchus's account and on navigation between the Indus and the Euphrates,
Vincent made "the voyage of Nearchus the first event of general importance
to mankind, in the history of navigation." In order to illustrate the connection between past and present, the author follows Voltaire in noting that
"the Paropamisian Alexandria and that on the Iaxartes continue to this day
[to be] cities of importance" (p. 7). And by emphasizing that William Robertson had already perfectly demonstrated "the advantages derived to
every country which has participated in the commerce of the East Indies,"
Vincent adds a commentary that enhances Alexander's merits as a precedent: "It is a glory which even the more important discoveries of modern
Europe cannot obliterate" (p. 9). Vincent returns to the charge: the effect of
the navigation planned by Alexander was "to perpetuate the intercourse
between Europe and the East Indies" (p. 17). He goes even further, postulating
a cause-and-effect relationship between the Macedonian conquest and
the European conquests: "At a later period, [the voyage of Nearchus] was the
source and origin of the Portuguese discoveries, the foundation of the
greatest commercial system ever introduced in the world, and conse-

quently the primary cause, however remote, of the British establishments in India" (p. 2).

Vincent dedicates his edition of the *Periplus of the Erythrean Sea* (1800) to the British monarch ("To the King"), in hopes that his reflections on the origins of navigation might attract the attention of a sovereign who had given Great Britain "a pre-eminence unexampled in the annals of mankind" (p. v). He highly praises this king who launched vast voyages of discovery, "not for the purpose of navigation, but for the interchange of mutual benefits, and for promoting the general intercourse of mankind." The author offers the book "as a tribute to the patron of every science, in which the interests of navigation and geography are concerned"; it will therefore certainly be agreeable for the British king "to trace navigation to its source, and discovery to its commencement." Vincent also expresses the wish that "officers, both naval and military, in the service of Government, or the Company, as well as commercial men and men of letters, may feel an interest in recurring to the original intercourse opened between India and Europe."

Well received in France and Germany,[6] Vincent's book elicited many reactions in Great Britain. Some English critics expressed reservations. One informed his readers that only lovers of erudition would get anything out of the book, adding that the last word would not be said until Major Rennell published his research on India; the comparison was obviously not flattering for the dean of Westminster.[7] Another made numerous remarks about Vincent's manifest lack of knowledge of Indian languages.[8] Nonetheless, the reviews were generally written in a descriptive form, closely related to current events, and predominantly positive. The critic for the *Gentleman's Magazine* (September 1797, p. 766) underlined that from now on no one would be able to claim that Alexander was a madman: on the contrary, he was a king with wise and reasonable commercial designs. A similar assessment was printed in the *Scots Magazine* (Vol. LIX, 1797, p. 331). The critic for the 1797 *Annual Register* went so far as to say that the commercial consequences of Nearchus's voyage were comparable to those of Christopher Columbus's discoveries, but that Alexander's officer was superior to Columbus and Vasco de Gama because he was responsible for the Portuguese discoveries and the circumnavigation of Africa: "[The voyage of Nearchus] is the principal link in the future chain of communication with Europe.... This is the first voyage of general importance to mankind;... it is still the first of which any certain record is preserved."[9] As for the editor of the

London Review 1797, he admits that Alexander's achievement was "to bring the wealth and commerce of the Indies within the reach of his European subjects."[10]

The reviewer for the *British Critique*—a journal with close ties to Vincent— devoted no less than twenty-seven pages of the June 1797 issue to analyzing the *Voyage*.[11] He stresses the long-term positive consequences of Alexander's projects: "the Alexandrian Greeks, the Romans, the Arabians, the Portuguese, the Britons, have successively crowded into the ports which he opened, and the rivers which he made navigable." He places particular emphasis on the book's interest to "a nation so deeply engaged as we are, in the commerce of the East and in the navigation of the shores described; no subject could have been found more worthy of the attention thus bestowed upon it than the Voyage of Nearchus." He notes that recollections of navigating such inhospitable shores are probably responsible for the terror that regularly seizes the minds of navigators who have followed in the wake of Nearchus's ships and "have, by successfully exploring the whole coast, left little to be added by the researches of others." For these reasons, he continues, the book will be most significant to "the geographer and the historian"; additionally, "the richest commercial company in the world will certainly pay attention to a work, so honourably connected with that country, in which their power and influence are continually exerted, in promoting every branch of useful knowledge."

The author had clearly not forgotten what William Vincent had written about the help he received from the East India Company thanks to some of its employees. One of these was James Rennell, who had taken advantage of his post as surveyor general to gather a great deal of information about the geography of ancient and modern India.[12] The major had in fact expressed his emphatic thanks and compliments to the East India Company at a time (1788) when it was the subject of controversy in London: "Whatever charges may be imputable to the Managers of the Company, the neglect of useful science, however, is not among the number. The employing of Geographers and Surveying Pilots in India, and the providing of astronomical instruments, and the holding out of encouragement to such as should use them, indicate, at least, a spirit somewhat above the mere consideration of gain; . . . [all that] ought to convince us that in a free country, a body of subjects can accomplish what the State itself despairs ever to attempt, etc." (*Memoir of a Map of Hindoostan,* 1788, p. vii n.; 1793, p. v n.).[13]

Vincent also salutes "the Gentlemen in the service of the East India Company." He even affirms that "if the Journal of Nearchus can now be presented to the Public with any degree of perspicuity or any hope of affording pleasure, it is due to the liberal spirit of the East India Company, to the Presidency at Bombay, to the ability of the officers employed upon the service" (*Voyage of Nearchus,* p. vii).

Among his sources, Vincent (like Rennell before him) makes particular note of Alexander Dalrymple (1737–1808), who had provided him with "a variety of charts with observations of his own" (p. 286). Born to an old Scottish family, Dalrymple had had a precocious and fast-moving career comparable to Rennell's.[14] He was hired by the company at fifteen and appointed to a writership. By dint of studying and traveling, he obtained a higher position in Madras but was eventually dismissed. He conducted widely noticed research in geography and hydrography and was later given the title of "Hydrographer to the Admiralty." Though he also took a keen interest in navigation in the Pacific Ocean, he published many maps and documents concerning the Indian Ocean and the Persian Gulf and had a trove of unpublished material. At the time Vincent wrote about him, his work had previously been noted by Robertson in his *History of America* and Rennell in his *Memoir.* Dalrymple shared "his whole collection published and unpublished" with Vincent. The map he sent him had been drawn based on the account of the leaders of a small squadron sent from Bombay in 1774 under Captain Blair, "for the purpose of exploring the coast between the Indus and the Gulph of Persia."[15] Dalrymple prefaced the expedition's report by writing that the "coasts here described are so little known that every particular must be acceptable, *as we have scarcely any account of them* since the time of Alexander the Great" (p. vi, Vincent's italics). The author later reiterated the importance of the information gathered thanks to the company's patronage: "If the English India Company had not directed a survey of this coast to be made, the expedition of Nearchus could not have been properly illustrated, nor the narrative of Arrian so fully vindicated, as it may be now, from the charge of imposture" (p. 46, see also pp. 286–287).

The East India Company's interest in studies of this type was as old as the company itself. After being published in Paris in 1716, Huet's history of commerce had immediately been translated in England. Interestingly, the anonymous English translator dedicated his work "to the Honourable sir Gregory Page, Chairman, Henry Well, Deputy-Chairman, and to the other Directors

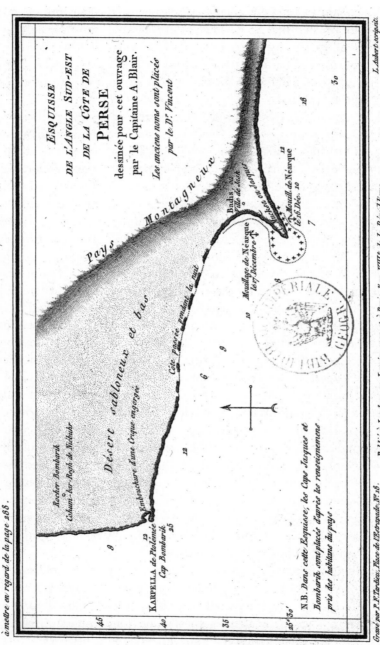

à mettre en regard de la page 288.

ESQUISSE
DE L'ANGLE SUD-EST
DE LA CÔTE DE
PERSE
dessinée pour cet ouvrage
par le Capitaine A. Blair.
Les anciens noms sont placés
par le Dr. Vincent.

Pays Montagneux

Rocher Bombarik
Cohum-bar-Regh de Niebuhr

Désert sabloneux et bas

Embouchure d'une Crique engorgée

Côte passée pendant la nuit

Badis ou
Ville de Briz
Muchao ou Jasques
Mouillage de Néarque
le 16. Déc. 10

Mouillage de Néarque
le 17. Décembre.

KARPELLA de Ptolémée
Cap Bombarik

N.B. Dans cette Esquisse, les Caps Jasques et
Bombarik sont placés d'après les renseignemens
pris des habitans du pays.

Gravé par P.F.Tardieu, Place de l'Estrapade. N.º 18.   Publié à Londres en Janvier 1797. et à Paris l'an VIII.e de la République.

L. Aubert scripsit.

12. Map of the Persian Gulf by A. Blair, published in William Vincent, *Voyage of Nearchus*, 1797, later reprinted and adapted in French in the translation by Billecocq (*Voyage de Néarque*, 1800, opposite p. 288). Département des cartes et plans GE E-183. Bibliothèque Nationale de France, Paris.

of the *East India Company*" (a list of twenty-two names follows). The reasons for the dedication deserve to be heard: "I could not think a treatise of this kind could properly be published under any other patronage but Yours, who are, as far as can be gathered from the best accounts, the most glorious and important Society for trade that ever flourished in any Nation. You are certainly the best judges of the subject the author has treated of, and will look back with pleasure on the various efforts of all Monarchs and states to raise commerce to that pitch, which was reserved for the honour of Great-Britain, for You only to effect, and maintain" (*History of Commerce and Navigation of the Ancients* 1717, pp. iii–v). Possibly directly inspired and financed by its dedicatees, the translation had allowed Pierre-Daniel Huet's body of knowledge to be nearly immediately shared with the heads of the company and every Briton who had an interest in commerce in general, and Indian commerce in particular.

The History of Alexander: Franco-British Translations and Confrontations

The pattern was repeated in the opposite direction when William Vincent's body of knowledge was shared with the French-speaking public. At the time that his book was published in London in the first months of 1797, England feared a French landing. However, when the Directory's fleet did prepare to cast off, it was to take control of Egypt. As we know, Bonaparte's initial victories soon paled by comparison to the disaster at Aboukir (1798). Perhaps the French government believed that an analysis of the Indian successes of the "first European" might contribute, however modestly, to restoring commerce and navigation? In any case, this was the firm conviction Citizen Billecocq expressed to readers of his "Translator's Preface." The firsthand information he provides on the question calls for a few comments.

The essential point is that the translation was the result of an official commission and that it was published "under the auspices of the French government." Billecocq salutes "the daily efforts by which [the government] supports the progress of the sciences, amidst the important concerns with which it is occupied, and the inevitable expenses that exhaust its resources." As he asserts in his opening, it is the state's duty to finance useful research because "the government of a free people is the natural protector of all work whose object is to expand or perfect human knowledge." Billecocq suggests that, in his estimation, the government's interest is probably also political. He shares this observation with the reserve of one "who has been honored with the Government's confidence on this occasion": "Perhaps that in ordering the translation of *The Voyage of Nearchus* it thought that another means for us to successfully fight the most implacable of our enemies was to bring into our language the useful works composed by the English and thus to appropriate the most precious of their national riches" (p. xvi.). The statement is reminiscent of the one included by Louis-Mathieu Langlès in his foreword to the 1801 translation of English travel accounts "by different officers for the East India Company": "The surest means of bringing down this terrifying colossus weighing over the seas is to attack the English possessions in the East Indies. This is where our blows must be directed; and it is quite amusing to owe the most important notions for the execution of this great project to their own travelers." He particularly emphasizes the account by Franklin, an "estimable traveler" who makes a passing mention of highly credible information regarding "the forces the English keep [in Bombay]."[16]

The competition with a "rival nation" is also on display in Billecocq's introduction. In Africa, England "took credit for discoveries made by the French"; Billecocq pays tribute to Citizen Fleurieu, who had corrected the situation, at least in writing.[17] Indeed, the translator had made sure to supplement and even rectify his information by "naturalizing" it with what he had read by French authors including "the famous d'Anville and the respectable Rollin," as well as the "modest" Gosselin, who had sent him notes on what he considered Vincent's unfounded hypotheses. Gosselin had published a study in which "he identifies several errors made by these scholars; he compares Doctor Vincent's account with those of the ancient authors and the work of d'Anville and the modern geographers, and sheds light on what navigation in the Persian Gulf once was and is today."[18] Billecocq also acknowledges Barbié du Bocage, "whose reputation as a geographer has long been established" and who is also known to have vigorously contested Vincent's geographic and cartographic notions; he judged his dissertation "generally muddled and verbose; [it] serves only to decide on very few facts," concluding that, all in all, "it does not teach us much or let us know where we stand." Nonetheless, Barbié added that one "must admit that it occasionally provides enlightening ideas, of which I took advantage."[19] Whatever it took to reestablish the balance between French knowledge and English knowledge! For his part, Sainte-Croix vigorously asserted his anteriority and that of several French scholars (such as d'Anville and de la Barre) by reminding readers that he had himself devoted a detailed discussion to the question in his previous edition.[20]

The attacks become extremely violent in *Tableau chronologique et moral de l'histoire universelle du commerce des Anciens* (1809) by Jullien du Ruet, an avowed admirer of Napoleon and his expansionist policy.[21] Referring to Vincent, whose book and theories he otherwise quotes and borrows from abundantly, his tone turns openly hostile, even insulting: "One is sorry to too often perceive that exclusive national spirit which never dies in an Englishman, and which drove [Vincent] more than any other to many paradoxes concerning Commerce and Navigation of peoples whose superiority he thought necessary to disguise. ... It is especially in the English authors that one finds such strange sophistries, which their imperturbable disdain uses to disparage all that preceded them, as well as all of which they are not the authors" (pp. ii; xxiv; 293–294).

It is true that at this moment when historians, geographers, and philosophers tended to think of Alexander's commercial enterprises side by side with those of their own era in the Mediterranean and India, Franco-British relations were particularly tense. Scholars did not hesitate to wade into the debate and polemics alongside politicians and the military. The Baron de Sainte-Croix denounced the Treaty of 1763 and announced his support for the American insurgents against the unbearable demands of a colonial power whose authority they rejected. In London, William Vincent leant his voice and pen to the "anti-leveller" offensive by denouncing the "Voltairian *philosophes*," among whom he had the audacity to include the unfortunate Baron de Sainte-Croix.[22] And what of Anquetil Duperron's impassioned attacks on "audacious, cruel, and deceitful Albion," which had "usurped" power in India, and those English governors who had scandalously accumulated wealth at the cost of "a thousand families decimated, cities and villages left in ashes, provinces and kingdoms devastated"?[23] In *L'Inde en rapport avec l'Europe* (1798), Duperron's subtitle makes explicit that he is "also presenting a detailed, accurate, and frightening picture of English Machiavellianism" in India; this is why the book is dedicated to "the manes of Dupleix and Le Bourdonnais." Indeed, the English "had brought ... a spirit of avidity, an odious and cruel inquisition that eventually devastated the country after having ruined the individuals." Clearly, the French erudite writers did not live outside society.

For that matter, neither did the English—witness James Rennell, who highlighted the contemporary resonance of his research on Herodotus.[24] At the very beginning of his preface, he explained that the part of the world from India to Europe had been "the great theatre of ancient history in Asia, as well as of European commerce and communication in modern times." In the epistolary dedication addressed to George-John Earl Spencer, "First Lord and Commissioner of the Admiralty," he plainly expressed his profound detestation of "the desperate projects of the inveterate enemy of mankind against the safety and the interests of THIS EMPIRE." Vincent also crossed swords with the enemies of Great Britain. In the preliminary remarks to book 1 of his *Periplus* (1800), he again underlines the extent to which research on ancient commerce was useful for "a nation now mistress of those Indian territories which were known to Alexander only by report" and rages against foreigners such as Duperron and Bernoulli who claimed to denounce the injustice of British domination: "But who ever asserted that conquest was founded upon justice?," he exclaims (pp. 6–7), judging that it is simply founded on necessity, the necessity that consists of forcing distant nations to open to European commerce. Following in Vincent's wake, the critic for the *Gentleman's Magazine* (1800, p. 857) even described the *Periplus* as a paean to Great Britain and expressed his hope that a former governor-general of India would use Vincent's book to present a defense of his own conduct; readers could easily grasp this barely veiled allusion to Warren Hastings. Three years earlier, the same critic had contrasted the wisdom of Alexander's commercial plans with the folly of the enterprises undertaken by the "French republicans" (*Gentleman's Magazine* 1797, p. 766). This was a far cry from the declaration of principle articulated by the founders of the *Bibliothèque germanique* in 1720: "Nations' reciprocal prejudices must be banished from the republic of letters." It is also true that Rennell's profound hostility to the French Revolution and Napoleon did not prevent him from loudly declaring his esteem and admiration for his French colleague Bourguignon d'Anville—in the same way that Vincent and his French translator engaged in a thoroughly courteous correspondence.

In an article published upon Vincent's death sixteen years after the appearance of Billecocq's translation, Robert Nares claimed that Vincent had written and printed a letter (which Nares had apparently never seen) in response to the French geographer Barbié du Bocage, "who had very unhand-somely attacked his voyage of Nearchus, but this was never published." Nares also provided his own explanation for the conditions that, according to him, led to the creation of the French version: "[It] had been made under the express authority of Bonaparte. At that period of inveterate enmity on his part, it would not have been safe, perhaps, to translate an English work, on any subject, without that sanction."[25] Regardless of the actual scope of the plans for an offensive against India often (too) generously attributed to Napoleon (particularly by the English) from the Egyptian campaign and beyond,[26] there is no doubt that on both sides of the Channel propaganda from Bombay as well as London regularly associated these plans with the memory of Alexander.

British Travelers and Spies in Alexander's Footsteps

In 1828, the Dutch researcher Pieter Otto Van der Chys published a thesis consisting of a geographic commentary on Arrian's *Anabasis of Alexander.* Though his sources naturally included scholars such as Vincent, Sainte-Croix, and Heeren, many others were travelers, some of whom were already distant memories like Chardin and de Bruyn (Le Brun), while others such as the Englishmen John Malcolm, William Ouseley, James Morier, and Robert Ker Porter were more recent. Van der Chys lucidly notes that these were generally speaking voyages of exploration sparked by the fears that Napoleonic ambitions provoked in London, Bombay, and Calcutta regarding the stability of the British dominion in India; he adds that it was especially important to provide a new commentary on Arrian given that Alexander's exploits took place "in the very regions that were revealed to Europeans in our own time." Even after the French threat had vanished, he continues, the British relentlessly pursued exploration between Persia and India and sent numerous diplomatic missions to Persia to secure the shah's alliance against the Russians.[27]

This reality was also fully acknowledged by John Williams, the author of one of the first monographs on Alexander and of another book on the historical geography of Xenophon's *Anabasis* and Alexander's campaigns: "The course of events rapidly tends to make the geographical positions of Modern Persia an object of deep interest to every patriotic Briton." The "course of events" did not refer so much to the French threat as to a potential Russian push against the Persians, then the English (*in Persas atque Britannos*).[28] To a certain extent, studying Alexander's marches and itineraries was supposed to allow the British to define a modern strategy in the regions roamed by the Macedonian.

Broadly speaking, the British serving in India had fairly accurate knowledge of the ancient sources on the history of Alexander, and specifically on the conquest of India. The subject's popularity was illustrated by a remark made by the reviewer of Vincent's *Periplus* (1800) in the *Anti-Jacobin Review and Magazine* (1802, p. 349): he observed that people in England were currently infinitely more interested in any of the expeditions carried out by Alexander's generals than by ventures launched during the Roman era.

Christopher Hagerman has looked at this aspect of the question in an extremely well-informed recent study.[29] Not only did lives and histories of Alexander hold an enviable place in British society's book culture, Hagerman explains, but the archives show that classical education was prized at Haileybury College, where the future officers and employees of the Indian Civil Service were trained from 1806 to 1858. Some exam subjects based on passages from the classical authors (Plutarch, Quintus Curtius) reveal that the history of Alexander was a well-studied field, particularly when it came to reflections on his objectives and policies for India and its inhabitants. The same was true at the East India Company's military academy at Addiscombe, which operated from 1809 to 1860. Due to the easily postulated homology between the Macedonians' situation and their own, young Britons serving in India had a veritable fascination for Alexander; they enjoyed seeing themselves reflected in the positive image of the conqueror, while glorifying the results of the British dominion in India.

Among his sources of information, Vincent cites "Mr. Jones, Resident for the Company at Busheer and Basra"; born in 1764, Jones had spent some twenty years working for the company in Basra. His account was considered all the more important because he had made "frequent visits to the interior part of the country, [and] is better qualified to decide points of doubt than almost any European who has been in Persia" (*Voyage of Nearchus*, p. 287). Many of the (unpublished) marginal notes that Vincent handwrote in the copy of his book sent to Billecocq quoted Hartford Jones. We will soon encounter him again.

There were few European travelers in Persia to whom Vincent could refer. In the east, none of them—whether Tavernier, Otter, Pietro della Valle, Thévenot, or Carsten Niebuhr—had traveled by land beyond Persepolis; they knew nothing of the Persian coast beyond the port of Bushehr, where travelers to or from India embarked and disembarked. As several reviewers observed, the regions lying between the Indus Delta and Persia and described by Vincent were visited by very few travelers.[30] Hence the decisive importance of the ancient sources, and particularly of Arrian, for descriptions and reconstructions.

Yet fifteen years later, the ancient sources had apparently lost some of their crucial importance to British travelers and geographers, if one is to judge by the epistolary dedication John MacDonald Kinneir addressed to Sir John Malcolm in the opening to his *Geographical Memoir of the Persian Empire* (1813): "The great provinces of Mekran and Seistan, which intervene between Persia and India, and a knowledge of which it was of so much importance to acquire, were, before you projected and carried into effect the plan for exploring them, only known to Europeans from the indistinct accounts of ignorant natives or the obscure page of the historians of Alexander the Great" (pp. iii–iv). Born to a large Scottish family in 1769, John Malcolm had embarked very early on a career with the East India Company—by 1783, he was in its service in Madras. The next year, he participated in the campaign against Seringapatam, the capital of the king of Mysore, Haider Ali. He then learned Persian with a view to pursuing a diplomatic career, which he began under the protection of Lord Wellesley. In 1799–1800, his protector sent him as an envoy to Persia to fight French influence and restore commerce. After landing in Bushehr, he traveled to Tehran, then Kashan, and finally succeeded in reaching an agreement with the Persian government before sailing down the Tigris to Basra and reembarking for Bombay in Bushehr (1801). He would carry out a second mission to Persia in 1810 on behalf of the Indian government. His mission was complicated by the fact that London had simultaneously sent an official ambassador, Hartford Jones, who conducted negotiations with the Persian government.

Meanwhile, France and Russia had considerably expanded their influence; Napoleon had signed the Treaty of Finkelstein with the shah on May 4, 1807, then sent the Gardane mission to Tehran to reform the Persian army and ensure the treaty was applied, but also to identify itineraries to India. Signed on July 7 of the same year, the Franco-Russian Treaty of Tilsit severely threatened British positions—or in any case, this is how it was perceived in London and Bombay. By contrasting the Franco-Russian offensive that was supposed to set off from Astarabad with the "injustice" of Alexander's campaigns, French pamphlets of the period defined its objectives as follows: "To chase the English out of Hindustan once and for all, deliver beautiful and rich lands from the British yoke, open new routes to the civilized industries of Europe, and of France in particular."[31] Overall the Gardane mission was a failure; Hartford Jones arrived in Tehran in February 1809 just as Gardane was leaving.

Malcolm was accompanied by a group of young East India Company officers whom he entrusted with reconnoitering regions and itineraries which were poorly known and had never been marked out. Two of the officers (Grant and Fotheringham) were murdered on the Ottoman border. Earlier, Grant, Lieutenant Christie, and Ensign Pottinger had been charged with thoroughly exploring the provinces of Makran, Balochistan, and Sistan. Pottinger's account is full of reminiscences of Alexander's expedition and Nearchus's naval journey (of which Pottinger compares his own observations with Vincent's analyses). For this very reason, it was used by historians seeking a better understanding of the ancient texts, particularly those dealing with the route Alexander followed from the Indus to Carmania.[32] Two other officers had been sent to Basra and charged with gathering geographic and strategic information about other regions on their way to rejoining Malcolm in Tehran. These two officers were Captain John MacDonald Kinneir and Lieutenant William Monteith.[33]

Born in 1782 of the alliance between two illustrious Scottish families, John MacDonald Kinneir (known as Kinneir) had been driven by financial necessity to apply for a position as a cadet with the East India Company; he arrived in Madras in 1803. Distinguished for his valor, he accompanied Malcolm to Persia. After reconnoitering a highly dangerous route from Hamadan to Saneh, he was charged by Malcolm to join Monteith in measuring the stages of the route from Shiraz to Shuster; traces of this mission can be found in the book Kinneir published in 1813 on the geography of the Persian empire—and which he dedicated to Sir John Malcolm, as we have seen. Each section was meticulously described thanks to a young assistant-surveyor who was born and trained in India and had accompanied Kinneir.[34] The Scotsman therefore felt he was in a position to conclude that following Malcolm's reconnaissance plan, the ancient historians of Alexander were no longer as

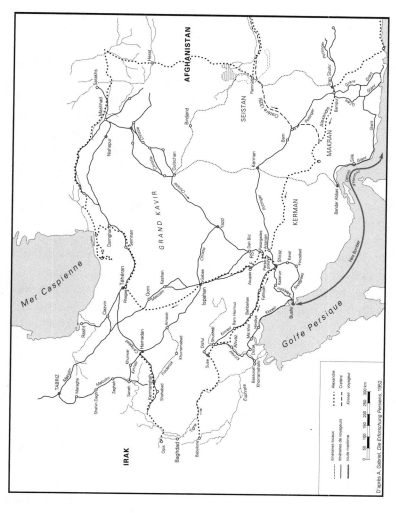

13. Routes followed by British travelers in Persia (early nineteenth century), from A. Gabriel, *Die Erforschung Persiens: Die Entwicklung der abendländlichen Kenntnis der Geographie Persiens* (Vienna: Verlag A. Holzhauens, 1952), opposite p. 136.

important as they once had been. For his part, Pottinger emphasized (p. 263) that the Greek authors knew very little about the countries located on India's western borders and that in these circumstances, progress could only be made through well-organized journeys such as the one he had undertaken with Christie. Additionally, the findings from the company's ships' military explorations and expeditions in the Gulf diminished the significance of Nearchus's account.[35]

In 1813, Kinneir completed a mission "to visit all the countries through which a European army might attempt the invasion of India" (p. viii). Published in 1818, his report takes the reader from Constantinople to Baghdad. As the title itself makes clear (. . . *with Remarks on the Marches of Alexander and the Retreat of the Ten Thousand*), it is full of reminders of Alexander's expedition, which is often associated here with the marches of Xenophon's Ten Thousand—for Xenophon was another source closely studied by strategists who then lacked knowledge of the Ottoman empire's interior regions. The author carefully examines the stages of Alexander's journey from Cappadocia to Issus, and compares the ancient narratives with his own data from the battlefield where Alexander faced Darius. Though the Napoleonic threat had evaporated by the time the book was published, the author justified his inclusion of a *Dissertation on the Invasion of India* (pp. 512–539) by stating that this was the very reason for his mission and, furthermore, that the French threat had been replaced by the Russian threat.[36] Unequivocally rejecting the idea that Egypt was a potential starting point for an expedition to India, the author asks whether a modern army could follow Alexander the Great's route through Asia Minor and Persia, or Nadir Shah's itinerary through Russia and Bukhara. Kinneir did not think so, and supported his analysis with two complementary arguments: modern day Persians were far more redoubtable soldiers than those in Darius's time and "Alexander, after all, did not conquer India; the banks of the Hyphasis were the limits of his progress." In short, the precedent set by Alexander tended to lead to the conclusion that it was highly improbable for a European army to successfully invade India.[37]

In a way, Kinneir was dissipating the concerns relayed by David Hopkins some years earlier based on the same comparison of the Macedonian expedition and the one that Hopkins believed "the modern Alexander" was about to launch through Asia Minor and the Cilician Gates. According to Hopkins, the two plans had significant similarities, with the exception that "the Cor-

sican usurper" would not have to face the "formidable Scythians," given that
their descendants (i.e. the Russians) would instead come to his assistance.
Additionally, Napoleon had more experience than Alexander. To make his
demonstration even more plausible, Hopkins followed every step of Alexander's campaigns through Central Asia up to the invasion of India (even if it
meant sometimes contradicting Rennell); he explained that "being the first
in time, and the only one recorded with minuteness, [they] deserve our very
serious consideration". There was also no doubt in his mind that Napoleon
would adopt Alexander's policy of taking advantage of his enemies' internal
divisions and playing on the hostile rivalry between several Indian kingdoms.[38] Clearly, individual authors plundered the ancient sources in very
selective ways determined by the political context that justified the examination of past and present.

From one end of the former Achaemenid empire to the other, British travelers encountered reminders of Alexander and / or evoked them with a
degree of complacency. Witness Elphinstone and his troop, who crossed
the Hydaspes in 1809: "So precisely does Quintus Curtius' description of
the scene of Porus' battle correspond with the part of the Hydaspes
where we crossed, that several gentlemen of the mission who read the passage on the spot, were persuaded that it referred to the very place before
their eyes!"[39] The example of Alexander Burnes is equally fascinating.
Burnes was another young Scottish cadet (born in 1805) who joined the East
India Company at sixteen. On the recommendation of Sir John Malcolm,
then governor of Bombay (and to whose memory Burnes would dedicate the
third volume of his travel narrative), he was charged in 1830–1831 with delivering five horses sent to the maharajah of Lahore as a gift from the king
of England. With the approval of the governor-general, he then continued
his journey, seeking to walk from India to the Caspian. He devoted himself
to this new mission with an enthusiasm that he described as increased ten-
fold by his lifelong desire "to visit Alexander's conquests." His reconnaissance trip took him to Bukhara via Kabul (where he would meet a tragic
death a decade later), after which he left from the Caspian Sea to cross Persia
from north to south and finally embarked at Bushehr on the Persian Gulf to
return to India.

He wrote about his travels in a three-volume book entitled *Travels into
Bokhara,* which includes both his often colorful travel narrative and the official reports he submitted to the authorities. The book was a great success.

The memory of the Macedonian expedition constantly runs through its pages. Throughout his entire journey, Burnes examines the relationship between the current topography and the landscape described in the ancient sources. He inquires into locating the altars Alexander erected to mark the end of his march. He reflects on the course of the rivers crossed by Alexander and described by Arrian; on the site of Alexander's victory over Porus; on the cities founded by the Macedonian king; on the people of Kafiristan's claim that they are descended from Alexander's soldiers; on Alexander's marches in Sogdiana, etc. He is so obsessed and inhabited by the image of Alexander that he turns it to his advantage in writing to a local prince; he tells him the British king is "mighty in rank, terrible as the planet Mars, a monarch great and magnificent, of the rank of Jemshid, of the dignity of Alexander, unequalled by Darius, just as Nousherwan, etc." (3:61).

The mission on the Indus was justified by gaps in the documentary record; throughout his narrative, Burnes regularly summons Arrian and Quintus Curtius.[40] He explains this tendency by stating that "it is difficult to describe the enthusiasm one feels on first beholding the scenes which have exercised the genius of Alexander. That hero has reaped the immortality which he so much desired, and transmitted the history of his conquest, allied with his name, to posterity. A town, a river, which lies on his route, has acquired a celebrity that time serves only to increase; and while we gaze on the Indus, we connect ourselves, at least in association, with the ages of his distant glory. Nor can I pass over such feelings without observing that they are productive of the most solid advantages to history and science. . . . The descent of the Indus by Alexander of Macedon is, perhaps, the most authentic and best attested event of profane history" (3:15–16).

Upon landing in Bombay after sailing from Bushehr, Burnes had to delight in the fact that he had just followed the routes once taken by the Macedonian king and visited the cities "from which Greek monarchs, far removed from the academies of Corinth and Athens, had once disseminated among mankind a knowledge of the arts and sciences, of their own history, and the world." He continues with this simultaneously enthusiastic and nostalgic meditation as follows: "In the journey to the coast, we had marched on the very line of route by which Alexander had pursued Darius; while the voyage to India took us on the coast of Mekran and the track of his admiral Nearchus" (2:141–142).

A few years earlier, in January 1828, his brother James Burnes had gone down the Indus, also thinking of himself as following on from the "Macedonian hero." Like his brother, he looked to the ancient sources because "after all, the ancients, I believe, had a better idea of the Delta of the Indus than the writers of our time." To carry out his own comparisons and reflections, he did not fail to refer to Vincent's book.[41]

A later reconnaissance mission also deserves to be mentioned. This was the 1835–1837 Euphrates mission headed by Francis Rawdon Chesney (1789–1872). Its objective was to determine the feasibility of using the Euphrates as a waterway to India as compared to the route via Egypt and the Red Sea, on which Chesney had previously reported. Though there is no need to go into the details of these operations here, it should be noted that Chesney frequently found himself in Alexander's footsteps and that he made certain to emphasize the fact. The deployment of a flotilla on the Euphrates is strikingly reminiscent of the period 324–323 BC: the two steamships built in England were transported to Syria in separate parts, then by caravan to the Euphrates, where they were reassembled, following exactly the same process that Alexander ordered when he had ships built in Phoenicia, transported on the Euphrates in separate parts, then sailed to Babylon by river.

Chesney's second volume includes a sort of general history of the Orient from the Flood to the beginning of the nineteenth century, followed by extensive reflections on the history of commerce and exchanges (chap. 58). After devoting two chapters to Persian history, Chesney dedicates no less than three to a detailed account of Alexander's conquest (2:251–378). Written by a distinguished amateur, the book is valuable because it provides us with the image of the Macedonian conquest as it was seen by most leading British colonial officers. The discussions of the return from India and the voyage of Nearchus primarily repeat Robertson's and Vincent's theses (though neither author is cited), crediting Alexander with grandiose plans to develop commerce and exchanges between India and Babylon and beyond that toward the Mediterranean.[42] It would not be exaggerating to consider that Chesney saw Alexander's expedition as a precedent for potential plans of the British government.

It should nonetheless be noted that some of Vincent's theses were contested—perhaps as an aftereffect of the discoveries made by British travelers in Persia, Central Asia, and India. Vincent's ideas came in for particular criticism in the April–July 1821 issue of the *Quarterly Review,* which

featured a review of volume 5 of William Mitford's *History of Greece,* published three years earlier in 1818. The latest manifestation of a long series
inaugurated by Temple Sanyan a century earlier, Mitford's book borrowed
Vincent's interpretations nearly verbatim. The reviewer for the *Quarterly
Review* was very critical both of the book in general and of the author's method,
which he considered the very antithesis of the approach of a philosopher-
historian like Gibbon. He particularly targeted chapter 60 of *The Voyage of
Nearchus,* which Mitford had openly admitted was lifted from the book of a
"very capable commentator, at once scholarly and full of talent and intelligence."[43] The critic responded in a similar vein, developing a particularly
thorough argument against the instrumental view of the history of Alexander
and Nearchus as it had been put forward by Vincent.[44]

Citing Vincent, he contests the idea that Alexander's campaign can be
seen as "the primary cause of the British establishments in India."[45] He considers such an assertion "rather extravagant," since if one were to follow
Vincent, "there would be no end of assigning causes" (p. 167). This remark is
noteworthy in that it clearly fits into a discussion important to the eighteenth-
century philosopher-historians, as can be seen, for instance, in the interest
expressed by Vincent and some of his contemporaries for "unintended consequences."[46] The critic manifestly wants to communicate that Vincent is far
removed from reflections of this kind, despite the fact that they affect one's
assessment of Alexander's modernity. Indeed, he notes, Nearchus's voyage
was certainly remarkable in the context of its period, but aside from a collection of names and the idea that such a voyage was in the realm of possibility,
its results were meager: "Science was too much in its infancy to enable the
navigator to add facts of real importance to the knowledge of maritime
affairs" (p. 167). To say this was to banish Alexander to a glorious but distant
past.

Upholding Local Customs or Assimilation? Plutarch and Alexander in British Imperial Debates

The memory and precedent of Alexander did not simply serve as fodder for
discussions of the conquests and geographic knowledge of India and the
routes leading there. In the final two decades of the eighteenth century,
they were also included in heated debates in England and Scotland re-

garding the relations to be established with defeated peoples subject to the British domination exercised by the East India Company and its managers and agents.

Published six years before *The Voyage of Nearchus*, the *Historical Disquisition on India* (1791) was to be the last work by the famous Edinburgh historian William Robertson (he died two years later). As I have had opportunity to underline in previous chapters, the author, heavily inspired by some of Montesquieu's reflections and analyses, here gives prominence to Alexander as the opener of new trade routes to India and the promoter of an innovative imperial policy. If Alexander and the Macedonian conquests play such an important part in several of Robertson's works, it is because Robertson primarily organized his thinking to address the questions of colonial conquests and empire and specifically the relations and contact (real and/or desired) between European peoples and conquered and colonized peoples (no matter the form of "colonization"). Though characterized by distinctive stages of evolution, past and present were tightly intertwined within Robertson's overall vision of European expansion.[47] In this sense, the *Historical Disquisition* brought to a close the reflection begun by *The History of America* (1777), in which Robertson had already included Alexander in the history of discoveries made by European expeditions to America and the Orient. The earlier book also very clearly raised the question of relations between Spanish conquerors and indigenous communities. The same issues were at the heart of the *Historical Disquisition,* but were now explicitly articulated in terms of British policy in India.

Robertson was certainly not the first to evoke Alexander's policy in the context of philosophical, moral, and political reflection. In condemning the actions of the Spanish, Montaigne (who did not always take a laudatory view of the Macedonian conqueror) had already expressed his regret that these countries had not fallen under the control of Alexander or the Romans, who would have brought them civilization in a gentle manner, mixing the Greek and Roman virtues with the indigenous people's own qualities.[48] The dialogue between past and present was also explicit in Montesquieu, whose Alexander was shown in direct opposition not only with the ancient Romans, but also the modern-day Spaniards. Alexander eradicated superstition among conquered peoples; on the contrary, the Spaniards "brought [to the Mexicans] a raging superstition" (*Spirit of the Laws,* 10.4). In the article "Étranger" in the *Encyclopédie* (VI[1756]: 51), the Chevalier de Jaucourt even made Alexander into an example for his time: "Today that commerce has connected the entire universe, that politics are enlightened regarding its interests, and that humanity extends to every people, there is no sovereign in Europe who does not think like Alexander."

While it participates in the colonial reflection that took place on a European scale, Robertson's position retains an acute specificity. Both his 1791 book and the reactions it provoked fit into a typically British political context. In the preface to the *Historical Disquisition,* Robertson locates the book's genesis in his reading of James Rennell's *Memoir* on Hindustan, "one of the most valuable treatises that has appeared in any age or country." Robertson then introduces the first part of the *Historical Disquisition,* namely the different stages of the discovery of India from antiquity to the modern era, as well as what was known of India's geography at the time of writing; hence the emphasis on Alexander's role in the development of geographic knowledge of India and its commerce. While it is the most developed, this first part remains indissociable from what the author himself referred to as an "Appendix" devoted to "some observations upon the genius, the manners, and institutions of the people of India." A follower of the then-common theory of "the permanence of the institutions, and the immutability in the manners of its inhabitants," Robertson drew on information in accounts from Alexander's time, making the assumption that India had not been lastingly changed by its various conquerors. While the strictly geographic part is intended to be "amusing and instructive," the appendix deals with more crucial problems relevant to the present and future of European dominion. Robertson explains his approach in the following terms: "If the account which I have given of the early and high civilization of India . . . shall be received as just and well established, it may have some influence upon the behaviour of Europeans towards that people" (pp. 331–332).

Having condemned the general conduct of European conquerors, "proud of their own superior attainments in policy, science and arts," he concludes his book on a particularly solemn note, fully aware that he is writing his last message to his contemporaries: "If I might presume to hope that the description which I have given of the manners and institutions of the people of India could contribute in the smallest degree, and with the most remote influence, to render their character more respectable, and their condition more happy, I shall finally close my literary labours with the satisfaction of thinking that I have not lived or written in vain" (p. 334).

Though Rennell, long an employee of the East India Company, occasionally gives indications of his position on British dominion,[49] his *Memoir* could not in itself have inspired the writing of the *Historical Disquisition*'s appendix. Robertson's appeal for a policy respectful of the Indian civilization should instead be seen in the context of the impeachment proceedings against Warren Hastings, which had opened in 1788.[50] The prosecution's arguments, which had been extensively developed by Edmund Burke, denounced the governor-general's fraudulent practices and misappropriations. But in a more general sense, it was the entire East India Company and British policy in India that were being called into question. On December 1, 1783, in a speech made before the Hastings case, Burke had stated that, contrary to those conquerors who left behind structures and projects aimed at improving the fate of vanquished populations, the British had built neither roads nor bridges nor canals nor hospitals—in short, nothing that would serve the common good. Through its inability to "redeem" its conquest, British dominion in India had lost all moral and political justification.[51] Burke shared with Robertson and a few others the conviction that Indian society and civilization deserved infinitely better than the blind and predatory domination mercilessly exercised by the company and its agents.

It is eminently clear that in Robertson's eyes Alexander was a model the British should reflect upon. A reader of Plutarch and Montesquieu, he was convinced of the soundness of Alexander's policy toward the Persians and more generally toward defeated populations now included in a great empire, which its founder sought "to establish in the affection of the nations he had subdued," through abandoning "all distinctions between the victors and the vanquished" (p. 24). In doing so, Alexander had met a challenge faced by all conquerors: how to maintain an empire's obedience and loyalty in the face of enormous distances and a limited number of victorious troops. To this end, Alexander created a new army drawing on the manpower of the dominated countries. Hence the importance of the measures taken in Susa, on the return from India, which Robertson had learned of from the ancient sources: here, Alexander combined the Macedonian contingents and the indigenous contingents. In the unlikely event that his readers had not already made the connection, Robertson explains the extent to which today's political concerns are like those of yesterday, and consequently how important an example Alexander's policy is for the present day: "He appointed that every officer in [the army] entrusted with command, either superior or subaltern, should be European. As the ingenuity of mankind naturally has recourse in similar situations to the same expedients, the European powers, who now in their Indian territories, employ numerous bodies of natives in their service, have, in forming the establishment of these troops, adopted the same maxims, and probably without knowing it, have modelled their battalions of Sepoys upon the same principles as Alexander did his phalanx of Persians" (p. 32).

The parallel between the Persian contingents created by Alexander and the Indian sepoys is extremely enlightening; as can be seen by the reactions to news of the Vellore Mutiny of 1806, the British had until then been convinced of the sepoys' absolute loyalty.[52] Some twenty years later, the German historian Barthold Georg Niebuhr used the same comparison, but in an entirely different sense: firmly opposed to Alexander's Iranian policy, Niebuhr considered that establishing Persian regiments would have been ruinous for Macedonian dominion—as proven by the sepoys, whose effectiveness and loyalty were only due to the fact that they were supervised by British officers.[53]

Robertson gives his remarks even more strength of conviction by preemptively responding to two arguments he expects to hear: that of Alexander's relative failure, and that of the difference of scale (Alexander only conquered a negligible part of what was known of India at the end of the eighteenth century). The historian proclaims that in fact the events that followed Alexander's death "illustrate and confirm the justness of [our] speculations and conjectures by evidence the most striking and satisfactory." As for the second objection, he answers it in an original, unprecedented manner, with a confidence that could only be grounded in personal conviction. Relying on the indigenous armies he had raised and the network of colonies he could use as supply stations, Alexander firmly intended to launch a new Indian campaign, which would have taken him much further than his previous ventures: "Alexander must have made rapid progress in a country where every invader, from his time to the present age, has proved successful" (pp. 35–36).

Robertson's positions on Indian civilization were vigorously contested by proponents of the assimilation of India's populations and the forced spread of European cultural values. In their counterattack, Robertson's opponents reclaimed the precedent of Alexander from him, inverting its meaning to serve their own argument. If both interpretations could be up-held, it was because they shared two lines of argument—which they used in opposite ways. Both factions considered that Indian society had retained its values and had not fundamentally changed since the earliest antiquity; one saw this as evidence that its wisdom and balance should be preserved, while the other believed it was essential to transform and modernize it by introducing it to European values and ways of life. *On the Fortune or the Virtue of Alexander* could be used to support both interpretations. Plutarch's dis-courses could be seen as evidence of Alexander's "liberal" policy toward vanquished peoples whose customs and religions he respected and whose elites he appointed to the new empire's government. But Plutarch added that the Macedonian king "established more than seventy cities among savage tribes, and sowed all Asia with Grecian magistracies, and thus overcame its uncivilized and brutish manner of living. . . . Those who were vanquished by Alexander are happier than those who escaped his hand" (1.5). His praise of the spread of Greek norms and their acceptance by subjected peoples could easily be exploited by those who believed it was necessary to Europe-anize the territories subject to British rule.

This was the case with Charles Grant. Born in 1746 to a poor Scottish family of which one member had already become a nabob, Charles Grant served nearly uninterruptedly with the East India Company from 1772 to 1790, rising to an eminent position on its Board of Trade. After returning to London as a rich and powerful man, he continued his ascent and became a member of the Court of Directors. During the process of renewing the East India Company's charter (1792–1793), he wrote his *Observations on the State of Society among the Asiatic Subjects of Great-Britain, Particularly with Respect to Morals, and on the Means of Improving It;* a few copies of the manuscript were printed on the occasion of Grant's presentation to the Court of Directors in 1797. In 1792, Grant's proposal to officially authorize Christian missions to India under the aegis of the company had been rejected; he now reiterated it as an epistolary introduction addressed to his peers and pertaining to "the communication of Christianity to the natives of our possessions in the East" (pp. i–iv). A few years later (1805), his fellow Scotsman John Mitchell made similar arguments in his *Essay on the Best Means of Civilising the Subjects of the British Empire in India and of Diffusing the Light of the Christian Religion throughout the Eastern World.* I will not give a detailed analysis of these es-says' relatively simple arguments (imperial challenges and the deplorable state of Indian society and civilization required a policy of assimilation, including by spreading the Gospel); I only wish to indicate the context in which both men introduced Alexander and Plutarch into a very contemporary debate, without failing to refer to Montesquieu and, even more so, to Robertson.[54]

Grant and Mitchell declare that their reflections are intended to contribute to elevating the mental, moral, and economic standards of British subjects in India. Given Indian society's extreme state of degradation, it is Great Britain's duty not to leave in place deplorable superstitions (which are compared to the human sacrifices the Spanish had found in Mexico); it must introduce both "the Gospel and the European light."[55] Grant also develops the idea that such a process takes place by spreading the conqueror's language among the population.

In view of the external danger posed by French ambitions, it was necessary to consider the means to be implemented to preserve the empire; the mere announcement of an enemy army approaching India's borders could put an end to the sepoys' loyalty. The only solution for Grant was "to establish in their minds such an affectionate participation in our lot, such an union with our interests" that could only be created "[through] a principle of assimilation, a *common-bond*." Grant considers this conclusion is amply confirmed by the precedent of Alexander. He had learned of the precedent through his critical reading of the *Historical Disquisition,* of which he admiringly quotes a passage,[56] and which he uses as follows: "[This principle] directed, according to [Robertson], the policy of the Grecian conqueror of that country, in securing his Eastern acquisitions. However different, in other respects, the circumstances of that celebrated personage may be from ours, in this we agree with him, that we have an Asiatic empire to maintain.... That leading idea is plainly the principle of *assimilation*" (p. 205). Grant is simply pointing out the limits of the analogy. It is no longer possible to proceed in as universal a manner as Alexander did. It is not desirable to erase the distinctions between the two races, nor to impose laws devised for England in Asia; instead one must build bonds of affection and interest with the subjects through religion and language. As in Alexander's case, such a policy would have the dual advantage of increasing the subjects' "happiness," and, by winning them over to the Christian religion, attaching them to the masters through affection and interest, rendering British authority "permanent and secure."

Though John Mitchell was less dogmatic than the "born again" Grant, his arguments were not fundamentally different. While he defends the British from the ramifications of the comparison with Rome and Carthage often used against them, he follows Burke in admitting that they have much to make amends for and should therefore "compensate to an inoffensive people these acknowledged injuries." A new policy is necessary to defend "the honour, the interests, and the security of the British empire" and must closely combine "civilising and enlightening Hindostan and the East"; civilization and Christianity are two inseparable aspects of the same process, since "without civilisation, Christianity could not be so successfully propagated." A few months before the Vellore Mutiny (July 1806) caused by the prohibition against Hindu soldiers wearing certain distinctive signs of their culture (including facial hair), Mitchell also emphasizes the potential danger posed by the sepoys. It would therefore be advisable to create "a close and cordial union and co-operation among the members of the empire . . . in order to cement it." One of the primary means for achieving the union must be to establish settlers on fertile land; in exchange for the parcel of land, they would provide military service. Referring to *The Spirit of the Laws* (10.10), Mitchell states that this is a favored method for protecting imperial territory from attacks and insurrections. He then refers to Robertson to observe that this was Alexander's colonial policy in Persia and India; in the face of external ambitions (on France's part), it was time once again to "follow the example of the Great Macedonian." It was also necessary to mix populations in colonial settlements, as Alexander had done, "in order to consolidate his empire, and control or conciliate his new subjects"; as Robertson had shown (he is cited again), this policy was a foundation of "the wonderful permanency of his conquests, amid the subsequent concussions of his empire."[57]

Other Britons criticized proposals of this kind not out of idealism, but solid realism driven by a concern that "under the able but unprincipled despotism of Buonaparte, France would conquer England on the banks of the Ganges." In a book structured around the parallel between Alexander and Napoleon, David Hopkins admits that it is certainly Britain's responsibility to elevate the Hindus' moral and philosophical standards, but he does not hide that in his view Christianization is likely to have negative effects: indeed, it would be easy for the French conqueror to repeat what he had done in Egypt, namely to appear as the Hindus' liberator from "the civil tyranny" to which they were subjected. Hopkins argues that rather than Christianizing the Hindus, it would be better for the empire's security to ship thousands of British soldiers to Egypt, then to India, and to send twenty thousand sepoys to Egypt in exchange; this would be an excellent means "to secure the fidelity of our Asiatic soldiers serving in Egypt, for we shall possess their families as hostages for their good conduct."[58] This was a far cry from Robertson's generous views.

Chapter 7

Alexander in France from
the Revolution to the Restoration

Alexander and the Revolution: The Pen and the Paintbrush

Political discourse during the revolutionary period in France was marked by incessant references to Greco-Roman antiquity; this accounted for the fame of the Abbé Mably, the champion of Sparta's frugality and civic virtues.[1] Mably violently denounced Alexander in the successive editions of his *Observations sur les Grecs*, which were circulated throughout Europe. While Mably followed directly from Bossuet and Rollin and his epigones, he went beyond them in that his primary objective was to systematically and openly take apart the theories Montesquieu elaborated in *The Spirit of the Laws*.[2] This negative image was dominant among the revolutionaries.

The pedagogical conception of history as "teacher of life" was still alive and well. To take one example, consider the famous philosopher, traveler, and politician Volney (1757–1820). In 1795, he was invited to lecture on history and historical method before the students of the École Normale, which had recently been founded by the Convention Nationale.[3] During his sixth and last lesson, Volney sought to examine "the influence that history books generally exercise on the following generations, and on the conduct of peoples and their governments." According to him, assiduous reading of the *Iliad* had aroused "Alexander's bellicose furies." He added: "It is not absurd to suppose that the conquest of Asia was due to this simple fact." The professor continued by taking on Quintus Curtius, whose work "has become the principal driving force behind the terrible wars that have shaken the entire north of Europe over the end of the last century and the beginning of the current one." Volney's audience clearly understood that he was referring to the famous war between Charles XII of Sweden and Peter the Great. Using the type of induction he had applied to Homer ("by going back from the effects to the causes"), Volney considered that Quintus Curtius's influence on Charles XII of Sweden had led to the "shaking then strengthening [of] the Russian empire, and in a sense to its transplantation into Europe, through the founding of Saint Petersburg and the departure from Moscow, where Tsar Peter I would probably have stayed had it not been for this crisis."

By the time Volney was preparing his lessons, this idea was already common. It had been clearly expressed one century earlier in *Jugement sur le caractère d'Alexandre*, which is included in the posthumous edition of Vaugelas's translation of Quintus Curtius and opens with the following statement: "It has always appeared to me that the History of Alexander is one of those things that we should only let young people read with tremendous precautions." In 1757, Jean-François Marmontel (1723–1799) wrote in his article on "Gloire" in Diderot and D'Alembert's *Encyclopédie* (7[1757]:717) that "Quintus Curtius's novel may have been Sweden's undoing; Homer's poem, India's undoing." The ex-revolutionary Publicola, alias Jean-Baptiste Chaussard, himself inspired by Volney, held a similar opinion. In the preface to his annotated translation of Arrian (1802), he vigorously denounced the vanity of the conquests of Alexander, a ruler who "limited himself to destroying." He describes Arrian as the polar opposite of Quintus Curtius, whom he considers responsible for Alexander's usurped reputation. He laments the fact that his *Histories* "are included among the classics used by the secondary schools of the French Prytaneion." A book of this sort "should not be put in the hands of youth, [for] its subject is dangerous to present in an era when passions are brewing" (pp. x–xi).

This negative image of Alexander is also found in a little-known text by the young Bonaparte. During his studies in Brienne (1779–1884), Bonaparte devoured every book in the library.[4] Unable to read Greek and Latin, he tackled the ancient authors in translation. His favorite reading was Plutarch's *Lives,* which happened to be recommended by the military authorities. During this period of his life, Bonaparte did not admire Alexander so much as the Spartan leaders, particularly Leonidas and the men who sacrificed themselves at Thermopylae. Though he would later say how little regard he had for Rollin, he wrote summaries of some of the historian's texts (on the government of the Persians, ancient Egypt, the Peloponnesian War, Carthage, etc.). He certainly also read Bossuet, whose *Discours* was excerpted in manuals specially prepared for students of military schools in 1777; the authorities considered that "the lessons given by a bishop to a Dauphin of France should not be overlooked in the course of study intended for French noble youth."[5] During the years he served in Valence, Bonaparte expanded the scope of his reading even further, taking full advantage of the resources of the bookseller Aurel. A great admirer of Rousseau, Mably, and Raynal, he also read Montesquieu.

In 1780, the Abbé Raynal, then at the height of his glory, was admitted to the Lyon Academy, where he created a competition whose subject was the positive and/or negative consequences of the conquest of America. Given the absence of submissions, the subject was modified in 1791 to ask, "Which truths and opinions are most important to impart to men for their happiness?" The young lieutenant from Corsica participated. The academy ruled that none of the fifteen texts submitted deserved to win the prize. The reviewers were particularly hard on Bonaparte's submission. No matter: as Edouard Driault has rightly noted, it serves as an "interesting record of Bonaparte's intellectual development." Antiquity figures prominently in the piece, mostly in a rather awkward, redundant form. Bonaparte expresses his boundless admiration for Sparta and the Spartans, a perfectly happy people who proved their heroism at Thermopylae, like the Athenians at Marathon; his legislator-heroes were Lycurgus the Lacedaemonian and the Corsican Pasquale Paoli, "who for a time brought the golden age of Athens and Sparta back to life in the heart of the Mediterranean."[6] A kind of panegyric on Reason, the third part of the text denounces those conquerors driven by their fateful passions. In discussing this group, Bonaparte does not forget to include his opinion on the Macedonian king, who was characterized by insatiable ambition and pride, "which made him conquer and ravage the world" and present himself as a god. Just like Cromwell and Louis XIV, Alexander is judged in a harsh light; Richelieu fares no better, for he was seized "with the same folly that altered Alexander's brain!"[7] Situated in a particularly pronounced revolutionary context, the young Bonaparte's Alexander is clearly borrowed from judgments and images popularized by Rollin and Mably and established as standards. One can also easily identify residual traces of Bonaparte's reading of Boileau and his condemnation of the ruler he refers to as "the madman who reduced Asia to ashes" (*Satire* 8).

Yet it must also be noted that this negative image coexists with an entirely different image, which is in keeping with a dual appreciation found throughout the ages; as we have seen, Alexander is both an example and a counterexample. In particular, painters continued to represent manifestations of the Macedonian king's public and private virtues. My first example will be that of a rather obscure provincial painter who probably typifies a certain kind of ordinary career path. Born in 1738 in Carcassonne, where he would die in 1803, Jacques Gamelin was a member of the Académie Royale de Peinture, Sculpture et Architecture de Toulouse, but his stay in Paris apparently did not yield any particular distinctions. Disappointed, he returned to Toulouse, then traveled to Rome in 1765 thanks to the generosity of a patron of the arts. There, he obtained the official title of "Painter of Battles" before eventually returning to his native Languedoc in 1774.[8] Totally devoted to the revolution and the return to antiquity, in 1792 he produced a series of about twenty drawings inspired by stories from ancient times. Four of these illustrate moralizing little tales showing Alexander the Great's virtues: his trust in the doctor Philip (one of the scenes most often depicted in drawings and vignettes); his continence and nobility in dealing with the Persian princesses; his generosity and absolute devotion toward the soldiers dying of thirst; his conduct with the priestess of Delphi. On the back of each of these "antique" drawings, Gamelin mentioned the source he consulted; as with many other contemporary painters, it is always Rollin, whom he cites with accuracy. Gamelin only turned to Rollin for images favorable to the Macedonian hero, all of which date (according to Rollin) from the period when Alexander behaved as a king admirable for his magnanimity and virtue.[9]

Gamelin's choices appear to follow the recommendations for the pictorial decoration of the Château de Choisy made by Charles-Nicolas Cochin, director general since 1755 of the Bâtiments du Roi, the administration for royal buildings and other public works, in a letter addressed to the Marquis de Marigny on October 14, 1764. Cochin's ideas are completely in keeping with the times: he suggests that rather than concentrating on the warlike virtues, painters should take an interest in the "generous, deeply humane actions of good kings."[10] Consequently, Cochin proposes that they choose edifying scenes from the lives of Augustus, Trajan, Titus, and Marcus Aurelius. Among the other famous kings of antiquity mentioned in his correspondence, one finds Cyrus (for his generosity and moderation), but also Alexander: Cochin refers to one of his "acts of feeling and humanity" (with his soldiers dying of thirst) and his "veneration for heroes," revealed when he visited the tomb of Cyrus.

Until the beginning of the nineteenth century, the location of the tomb at Pasargadae had not been identified. The only existing drawing of it, which had been drafted on site by the German traveler Mandelslo on his trip from Esfahan to Bandar Abbas (on the Persian Gulf) early in 1639, was little known and was not referred to as a representation of Cyrus's tomb. The tomb therefore remained unidentified, without any associated visual depiction, throughout the eighteenth century. However, anyone could read about Alexander's visit in the ancient authors. Several even provided a description of the monument borrowed from narrators who were present in the king's entourage. The most famous episode took place during Alexander's second visit to Pasargadae, on the return from India (325 BC). The tomb had been looted and completely emptied, which was profoundly upsetting to Alexander, who had planned to pay tribute to Cyrus as a resounding symbol of his policy of mutual understanding with the Persians. Consequently, "Alexander seized the Magians who were the guardians of the tombs and tortured them that they might reveal the perpetrators. [But they did not accuse anyone], and so Alexander let them go."[11] Alexander then had the tomb and sarcophagus restored.

Of the scenes from the history of Alexander, this one was only rarely painted from c. 1650 to c. 1750.[12] The subject was depicted in a particularly grandiose manner in 1796 by Pierre-Henri de Valenciennes (1750–1819). The perspective is not from inside the tomb looking at the sarcophagus, but from outside, toward the structure in its environment, in a manner more directly inspired by the ancient texts [photo]. The scene is enlivened by a narrative element reproducing some of the facts passed down by Arrian. Alexander is at the center of the painting, followed by his bodyguards, looking toward Cyrus's tomb; between the tomb and what appears to be a temple, one sees a group consisting of two mages (identifiable by their white robes, beards, long hair, and headbands) and armed men leading the mages to Alexander to be interrogated by the soldiers behind him, whom Alexander points to with his right hand. On the left is the Macedonian camp, with the royal tent clearly visible in the foreground.

But was Valenciennes's objective truly to celebrate Alexander's policy? There are reasons to believe it was not. Valenciennes was primarily a painter of ruins and landscapes, a specialization he had cultivated through his friendship with Hubert Robert and his many trips to Italy. He had worked in the same vein when he painted *Le Mont Athos dans la Thrace taillé en statue d'Alexandre* (*Mount Athos in Thrace Carved into a Statue of Alexander*), which was inspired by a project attributed to Alexander in antiquity; the scene is also set in a seaside landscape of mountains and forests.[13] A parallel can be established between this picture and another canvas by the same painter: *Cicéron découvrant le tombeau d'Archimède* (*Cicero Discovering the Tomb of Archimedes*). In both paintings, Valenciennes includes famous figures from antiquity discovering and honoring the tombs of other ancient personages. Both scenes are set in landscapes combining the sea, mountains, lush vegetation, and ruins. In the same way that he painted *Alexandre au tombeau de Cyrus* (*Alexander at the Tomb of Cyrus*) by using narrative details found in Arrian, Valenciennes here drew inspiration from Cicero and his letter to his brother Quintus.

The ancient texts emphasized the beauty and tree-filled luxuriance of the site of Cyrus's tomb: "It was in the royal park (*paradeisos*); round it had been planted a grove of all sorts of trees; the grove was irrigated, and deep grass had grown in the meadow" (*Anabasis of Alexander*, 6.29.4). Valenciennes lays it on thick, importing landscape settings taken out of their context, but particularly common in his painting. They include a marine landscape that would be completely inappropriate if the painter were required to be faithful to geography. The scene fascinates by its combination of reality and unreality. The landscape of sea, mountains, and exuberant vegetation is entirely imagined by the artist, who manifestly did not go to the trouble of doing any research in one of the many travel narratives about Persia. In the midst of this gentle "Italian" setting, one discovers obelisks in the distance, a temple by all appearances Egyptian, and "a tomb of Cyrus" also very Egyptian in its construction and its plated and carved decoration. The broken door lying on the ground even bears an inscription supposed to represent the one that Arrian and other authors had written was "in Persian characters"; here, it is clearly "rendered" in symbols supposed to evoke hieroglyphic writing. These multiple borrowings from an Egypt solely known through travelers' drawings certainly make this painting a fine example of French and European Egyptomania.[14] However, it would be most imprudent to extrapolate any political significance from the picture (relating to the Egyptian expedition launched from Toulon two years later). Egyptomania did not necessarily have a political hue expressive of current events.

These observations on the subjects of academic painting undoubtedly deserve to be expanded upon and nuanced. We should at least note that it was easier and more rewarding to follow aesthetic and social norms and conventions and paint a compassionate and generous Alexander rather than an Alexander launching vast plans to develop peace, commerce, and prosperity. It is therefore no surprise that visual representations of Alexander do not include the equivalent of the vignette illustrating the grandeur of Great Britain's pacific achievements in India, as seen in an "allegorical cartouche" in James Rennell's *Memoir of a Map of Hindoostan* (1783) and explained by the author in the following terms: "Brittania receiving into her protection the sacred Books of the Hindoos, presented by the Pundits, or LEARNED BRAHMIN: in allusion to the humane interposition of the British Legislature in favor of the Natives of Bengal, in the Year 1781. BRITANNIA is supported by a pedestal, on which are engraven the Victories, by means of which the British Nation obtained, and has hitherto upheld, its influence in India: among which the two recent one of PORTO NOVO and SHOLINGUR, gained by GENERAL COOTE, are particularly pointed out by a SEPOY to his comrade" (p. xii). This does not necessarily imply that the "public at large" only knew Alexander through the codes of academic painting. One could, like Linguet, exalt the "revolution" produced by Alexander and be fascinated by the *Reines de Perse;*[15] one could enjoy Le Brun's paintings and be a reader of *The Spirit of the Laws;* one could denounce the horrors of war, admire Alexander's pacific plans, and have an aesthetic appreciation for a battle painter's talents.

Sainte-Croix and the Alexander of *The Spirit of the Laws*

This bipolarity of Alexander's image can also be found in the works of historians, antiquarian scholars, and erudite writers. The views held by Montesquieu and his British epigones were vigorously and consistently contested by the Baron de Sainte-Croix, most particularly in the 1804 edition of his *Examen critique des anciens historiens d'Alexandre-le-Grand,* which features a notable evolution in some of his positions.[16] While he expressed respect for Montesquieu, Sainte-Croix often questioned his methods of reasoning and his conclusions. With one exception,[17] references to *The Spirit of the Laws* are opportunities Sainte-Croix created to highlight a factual error on Montesquieu's part[18] and, especially, to pick apart his interpretations or at least to qualify or correct them, sometimes accentuating the criticism he carried

14. *Brittannia [sic] receiving into her protection the sacred Books of the Hindoos, presented by the Pundits, or learned Brahmin,* in James Rennell, *Memoir of a Map of Hindoostan or the Mogul's Empire . . . ,* 1783, frontispiece (caption p. xii, quoted p. 227 [chap. 7]).

over from one edition to the next.[19] None of Montesquieu's theories escaped the baron's censure, whether he was discussing the policy toward the Persians, the founding of colonies, or his interest in the development of commercial networks. Sainte-Croix refused to believe that Alexander could be absolved of his crimes (particularly the murder of Cleitus) or to admit that he had achieved anything at all as a builder.

The baron simultaneously rejected the scale and historic significance of the founding of cities by Alexander. He considered that the king certainly did not have time to concern himself with this, given the speed of his marches; besides, many cities named "Alexandria" were founded later; and finally—still according to the author of the *Examen critique*—the Greeks surely had no desire to settle in a hostile environment so far from their homeland and could not devote themselves to agricultural labor because "in a state of continual apprehensions or hostilities, where the whole force was required for its defence, few hands could have been spared for the cultivation of the ground or the labours of agriculture." As for these colonies' commercial and business function, Sainte-Croix aims to make definitive statements to sweep aside an argument found throughout the works of Voltaire, *The Spirit of the Laws*, and the books of their partisans: "Commerce depends on the easy and secure conveyance of merchandise, and a proper medium of barter and exchange. Mutual wants will likewise often form an intercourse between distant nations, but if the inhabitants of the cities imagined to have been founded by the Conqueror, were only furnished with the common productions of the country from their own settlements, they were not likely to be possessed of many articles of traffic, that could have been an object to their neighbours, and as to their own country, every hope of a safe and regular communication between Greece and the Paropamisus or the banks of Iaxartes was totally cut off."[20]

The author observes that the colonies had a mixed population of army veterans, disloyal soldiers, indigenous people, and even prisoners; lacking a common spirit and shared interests, they were fated to disappear. Elsewhere, Sainte-Croix emphasizes the profound difference with earlier Greek colonies "founded under the auspices of liberty and without any self-interest or ambition on the part of the colonizing country." For his part, Alexander only sought to "guarantee the loyalty of the vanquished peoples." Sainte-Croix adds: "Pride also played its part. This prince imagined that these cities would be so many monuments to his conquests, the memory of which they would pass down to the most distant posterity."[21] This statement is reminiscent of one made in 1775, and again in 1804: "All the cities that this prince founded in the different regions that he roamed should still be seen as trophies of his victories."[22] While Sainte-Croix does not bother to mention it, the term is directly borrowed from Mably, who had methodically attacked the Alexander of *The Spirit of the Laws* in the second edition of his

Observations (1776), including with regard to the urbanization policy Montesquieu attributed to him.[23]

In the 1804 version, Sainte-Croix also criticized the positions of British historians who had fallen in with Montesquieu's opinion. Going beyond *The Spirit of the Laws*' suggestions, William Robertson underlined the strategic importance of the network of cities and strongholds founded by Alexander. On the contrary, Sainte-Croix considered that "most of these cities were too isolated and too far from each other to form such a chain."[24] By saying this, Sainte-Croix also rejected Montesquieu's conviction regarding the success of the founding "of a great number of Greek colonies [and] an infinity of cities," which would explain Persia's calm and imperial loyalty amidst the civil wars that broke out between the victors after Alexander's death (10.14).

The only exception that Sainte-Croix recognizes is Alexandria, which, as its founder had hoped, is a testament to his lasting glory. By referring to Huet and Robertson, Sainte-Croix underlines that Alexander "wanted to announce his new conquest by establishing something worthy of him. The long and astonishing resistance of the Tyrians, lacking any assistance, gave him a powerful idea of the resources that could be provided by commerce.... The nations of the Occident and the Orient were thus brought together by a common interest; the fruit of an enterprise admitted by humanity."[25] This rare praise for one of the conqueror's founding acts also had its contextual reasons. Going against an entire current of thought (well represented by Mably in the *Entretiens de Phocion* that exalted the traditional values of Egypt and the Egyptians, Sainte-Croix for once agreed with Linguet and Voltaire (though he did not cite them)[26] in contrasting "the enterprise admitted by humanity [Alexandria]" with the construction of the pyramids, "wonders of labor and eternal monuments to the tyranny of the princes"—who happened to be suspicious of foreign navigators, particularly Greek ones. Yet it must be noted that in 1779 Sainte-Croix had seriously qualified his endorsement. In a book openly presented as a defense and picture of the American insurgents, he drew abundantly on the precedent of antique colonization and returned to the attack by writing: "Its founding would have deserved the gratitude of the human race, which it united by the ties of commerce, had the project not been suggested to him by the idea of making it the capital of a vast empire cemented by blood and established on the ruin of so many nations" (*De l'état et du sort des colonies, des anciens peoples*, pp. 293–294). Sainte-Croix's choice of words clearly expressed his opposition to Montesquieu, who was convinced that Alexander's many colonies allowed him "to so effectively cement all the parts of his new empire" (10.14). Here too, Sainte-Croix came closer to Mably, who had relentlessly denounced the fragility of an imperial structure based on fear rather than laws.[27]

Additionally, Mably never hid his aversion for what he saw as the harmful consequences of the voyages of discovery and the expansion of commerce, which are at the very root of the decadence of empires.[28] This is one of the poor choices made by Peter the Great, whose failure Mably compares to Alexander's: "Nothing was impossible for Alexander, and he could even have given the Persians the taste for freedom, had he been able to conceive of that design. One can reproach Tsar Peter the First for not taking advantage of his successes and victories to establish a new government in his country. It is because he did not at least attempt to do so that he will be mixed up with princes who have a glorious reign; but he will never be ranked among the legislators and benefactors of their nation" (*Observations*, 1766, pp. 288–289). Sainte-Croix carries out his demonstrations based on identical or very similar presuppositions: "Throughout time these regrettable interests of commerce have thus spilled torrents of human blood," he exclaims.[29] Elsewhere, he feigns to be surprised that the Tyrians, "a trading people that had so long neglected the profession of war," could have put up such resistance to Alexander.[30]

In a particularly firm passage in the 1804 edition, Sainte-Croix is ironic about the commercial policy that Robertson and Vincent followed Montesquieu in crediting to the Macedonian conqueror and questions the validity of the documentary basis for such a theory. He begins by criticizing *The Spirit of the Laws* (21.8): "Could it be in order to associate oneself with the glory of famous men that one sometimes credits them with views that could only have been the fruit of time and experience? This is the case with the idea that one supposes drove the Macedonian conqueror to penetrate so far into Asia to unite the Indies with the Occident through maritime commerce, like he had united them through colonies he established inland" (p. 415). Then comes the turn of William Vincent, worthy heir to Montesquieu: "One then attempted to demonstrate that in the voyage of Nearchus, which began at the mouth of the Indus, Alexander did not have as his objective the vanity of executing what no one before him had dared to attempt; but that the plan for his voyage was, in his genius, the fruit of a system based on the presumption of the advantages that could be drawn from it, on the desire to know the coast as well as the interior of his empire; and on the certain hope of uniting all of this through bonds of mutual communication and a fortunate reciprocity of interests" (pp. 415–416).

Sainte-Croix goes on to vehemently criticize Robertson, who had disagreed with Montesquieu in his writing about Alexandria and credited Alexander with the glory of having foreseen all the long-term commercial consequences of the conquest of India. In this case, Sainte-Croix gleefully contrasts Vincent and his compatriot, citing a note from *The Voyage of Nearchus:* "It is perhaps imputing too much to the foresight of this extraordinary man to assert that he had preconceived this comprehensive scheme of commerce from the first foundation of Alexandria."[31] Sainte-Croix continues his attack on Robertson in the following terms: "Such insight would be all the more admirable in that, according to a famous writer, it led Alexander to found the city bearing his name in Egypt; and that, despite all his military operations, he did not give up on attracting to it the lucrative commerce that the Tyrians had had with India. If this had truly been the prince's design, why during the years of these same operations did he not allow the restoration of Tyre, which had kept its commercial relations and would naturally become Alexandria's rival? ... Why did he favor the traffic of the Phoenicians who accompanied him in India?" (pp. 414–415). He then deals the death blow to Vincent: "Without any regard for these or other observations it is useless to mention, he goes further. If Nearchus's account mentions rice, sugar, silk, or sugarcane, he immediately affirms that Alexander pursued his exploration of the Indies in view of introducing to Europe these objects previously unknown" (p. 415). At the end of the polemic, Sainte-Croix denounces his predecessors' tendency to turn "the man who defeated Darius and Porus into an armed merchant" and to "give the emulator of Hercules the ideas of a trading post chief!" This sentence is an interesting expression of the aristocrat's contempt for the trading professions, which paradoxically leads Sainte-Croix to recognize in Alexander the virtues of a passionate classical hero, which he otherwise strives to denounce.

The author suggests that his readers should instead return to the sources. To this end, he refers to Alexander's speech to his troops on the Hyphasis and to the king's prayer by the ocean.[32] He concludes that "certainly such a prayer does not herald the design we assume on the part of the Macedonian conqueror to expand geographic knowledge and multiply commercial relations that could unite the different parts of the world! ... Doesn't one formally deny history by subscribing to this wild idea of crediting Alexander with grand views of commerce?" (p. 416). If Alexander went to India and traveled along the coast of the Persian Gulf on the return journey, it was for entirely different reasons: an exacerbated desire to go further than any of his predecessors, including Cyrus and Semiramis, and the thirst for glory and immortality—in short, because of his passions, not his reason. This interpretation is in keeping with Mably's negative judgment of an Alexander driven by "temerity" and totally lacking "wisdom." This is exactly why Sainte-Croix also refuses to agree with Montesquieu in believing that Alexander was able to manage his finances with moderation. The erudite writer has no trouble finding support in ancient texts full of observations and downright condemnations of Alexander's taste for luxury, "which was an insult to the mores of his homeland and the misfortune of the vanquished."[33]

Still going against *The Spirit of the Laws,* Sainte-Croix asserts that it would have been better to maintain the distinction between the victors and the vanquished because "it was still needed to secure his conquests or ensure new ones. The distinction conveyed enthusiasm, which the Macedonians could not convey to the Medes or the Persians; it was too powerful an incentive to dare to destroy it so soon."[34] Consequently, Sainte-Croix also aims to shatter the validity of the principal source used by Montesquieu and his partisans: Plutarch's *On the Fortune or the Virtue of Alexander,* the two discourses that had long been a standard reference in noncritical works in praise of Alexander.[35]

As a translator of Plutarch's works, the canon D. Ricard had already expressed serious doubts regarding their credibility; referring to Rousseau's *Ode à la Fortune* and Rollin's authority, the translator refuses to believe that "the subjected nations were happy to be under the yoke of the king of Macedon," that the idea of mixed marriages came to Alexander through philosophical reflection, or that the conqueror truly thought about "establishing among [all men] a universal peace and harmony."[36] During the same period, La Harpe (1739–1803) stated in his literature classes that the discourses were no more than "a jeu d'esprit that Plutarch could only have allowed himself as a youthful amusement." For that matter, he was "too good a philosopher" to believe that a conqueror could have thought "to put all the governments in the world at the same level." La Harpe further refines his idea through a diagnosis that does not exclusively apply to antiquity: "On the contrary, all [the conquerors] had enough common sense to leave to each people what could never be taken from it by force—its mores, its customs, its opinions, which can never be changed other than by the imperceptible power of time, which changes everything."[37] Sainte-Croix held a similar position, declaring that one could not "settle on the puerile declamations of Plutarch's discourse ... in favor of the change of mores introduced by this Prince." On a more general level, he rejected the idea that Alexander had implemented a policy comparable to that of Augustus, "who united all the nations, from the pillars of Hercules to the banks of the Euphrates, [to the point that they] formed a single nation, as it were."[38]

This statement shows that the opposition to Montesquieu's Alexander is articulated in a broader, more "philosophical" denunciation, expressed with an emphasis that can be reminiscent of the tone of *Histoire des deux Indes*.[39] Sainte-Croix shares with Robertson (who is cited in this regard) the conviction that Indian civilization was already in full bloom and had no need to be dominated by an invader from Europe. "Happy was this people by the immutability of its mores and its inalterable gentleness," he proclaimed, adding, "had it only remained unknown to a class of men who are enemies of joy and humanity!" His commentary makes a close connection between past and present: "These expressions by an English author are only too true. And Camões, rather than being satisfied with making his giant predict storms and shipwrecks, should have, in penetrating the future, announced the long sequence of moral and political calamities that the Portuguese would cause by rounding the Cape of Good Hope" (p. 738). Alexander is not treated any more indulgently, he whose "hands [are] stained with the blood of nearly all the peoples of Asia" and whose death was welcomed by Sainte-Croix because it allowed "rest for the human race."[40]

Now we turn to the last page of the 1804 *Examen critique*. Having reached the end of his analysis of the conquest of India and the voyage of Nearchus, Sainte-Croix evokes the journeys of George Vancouver, whose travel account had just been published in London by his brother.[41] In the introduction, Vancouver marvels at the positive consequences of the European conquests in the light of Enlightenment progress: "In contemplating the rapid progress of improvement in the sciences, and the general diffusion of knowledge since the commencement of the XVIIIth century, we are unavoidably led to observe, with admiration, the active spirit of discovery, by means of which the remotest regions of the earth have been explored; a friendly communication opened with their inhabitants, and various commodities, of a most valuable nature, introduced among the less-enlightened part of our species. A mutual intercourse has also been established, in many instances, on the solid basis of a reciprocity of benefits; and the productive labour of the civilized world has found new markets for the disposal of its manufactures" (p. i).

Sainte-Croix examined the English traveler's idea that "a bridge has been established, thanks to which we can carry to the most unknown beaches, to every one of nature's children, the benefits of civil society." He immediately indicated his skepticism about what he manifestly considered an expression of excessive optimism. The terms he uses are very similar to those used ten pages earlier, in his commentary on the consequences of various conquests on India and its civilization: "Happy they will doubtless be if they do not at the same time receive the pestilential germ of our vices and if they can escape from the tyranny of our false needs, a scourge no less redoubtable for them than our mercantile cupidity, the enemy of the little innocence and happiness that still remain on this earth, in a few deserts or in the middle of the Pacific Ocean" (p. 750). Among these deserts, Sainte-Croix certainly included those of Scythia, which were peopled by those noble savages who, according to Quintus Curtius, had come to lecture Alexander: "We seek after places that are desert and free from human cultivation rather than cities and rich fields," they told the Macedonian conqueror, accusing him of being "the robber of all the nations."[42] In Sainte-Croix's view, the nobility of the "Scythian savage" could only be rivaled by that of the Iroquois chief who was said by the Chevalier de Crèvecœur ("an adoptive member of the Oneida nation") to have warned his peers gathered to discuss relations with the Europeans that by "living like Whites, we will stop being what we are, the children of our god, who made us hunters and warriors."

The parallel between the ancient Scythians and the modern Iroquois (which had previously been suggested by the Abbé Guyon in 1736) was all the more evident in that it was made explicit by Crèvecœur's publisher, who may himself have been influenced by the famous book by Père Lafitau, a proponent and frequent user of these kinds of comparisons.[43] An explanatory footnote states: "This speech, whose masculine and savage eloquence is truly admirable, is reminiscent of the beautiful harangue on the part of the Scythian ambassadors sent to Alexander, as reported by Quintus Curtius. . . . There is a language for men of nature, and a language for civilized men." If Sainte-Croix, who is otherwise critical of Quintus Curtius, accepts the heuristic validity of the speech attributed to the Scythians, it is because the "testimony" supports his general hostility toward conquerors, and in this case Alexander. In a more general manner, as his commentary on Vancouver reveals, Sainte-Croix did not believe in the virtues nor even in the principle of pacific rapprochements between the victors and the vanquished, or in other words, between the conquering Europeans and the "savages" of the ancient and new worlds; according to him, the latter could only lose through contacts that threatened to destroy their identity. Voltaire, on the contrary, had judged that such "savages" had no nobility and that they should be brought down by the power and intelligence of a civilizing conqueror, namely Peter the Great, whom he explicitly compared to Alexander.[44]

The Bossuet / Rollin / Mably / Sainte-Croix Current's Influence in France

In the postrevolutionary era (from the empire to the Restoration), the opinions expressed in France on the history of Alexander were unequivocal. Many adopted an interpretation close to that of Sainte-Croix (who was himself influenced by Mably), even if it meant turning Rollin into their guide and master through a marked return to tradition, which was similar to Sainte-Croix's return to Bossuet in 1804. It should also be noted that it was under the Restoration, in 1821, that the academician Antoine-Jean Letronne decided to publish a new edition of the complete works of Rollin, whom he believed had been unfairly attacked "by pedants jealous of his success" and whose authority had suffered due to "Voltaire's sarcastic remarks, repeated by one thousand echoes." Saint-Albin Berville, the author of *Éloge de Rollin*, added that the attention of professors and students should be drawn back to "the splendors of Antiquity, which were a repository of salutary instructions for [Rollin]."[45]

Dictionary entries bear witness to the trend. Take the example of the successive editions of the *Dictionnaire Chaudon-Delandine*. While the 1769–1779 editions tended to pass on the opinion of the philosophes,[46] the author of the entry on "Alexander the Great" in the 1810–1821 editions borrowed expressions from Rollin and the Abbé Guyon, but did not cite them. Though he repeated Montesquieu's laudatory arguments, he qualified them with serious criticism communicated in formulaic language: "Who would dare to argue that good outweighed evil in Alexander's actions; that his existence was more useful than damaging to humanity? . . . His glory, if it is glory to wreak havoc in the world and cause the loss and desolation of one million men; his grandeur, if it is grandeur to be the originator of great sorrows, gave license to the ambitious who took him as a model" (1810, pp. 206; 1821, pp. 288–289). The 1810 and 1821 entries end with a parallel between Philip and Alexander. Highly unfavorable to the conqueror of Asia, the piece is manifestly inherited from the moralizing tradition constructed by Rollin and others based on the model created by Jacques de Tourreil in 1691. The author's leanings are revealed in the bibliography, which includes works widely varied in terms of their nature and importance but all hostile to the memory of the Macedonian king: Boileau's *Satire* 8, Frederick Augustus's and Sainte-Croix's books, as well as the passage from Bayle's *Dictionnaire historique et critique* on Alexander's "superstition." Boileau's text and de Tourreil's portrait of Alexander had already served as references for a very hostile article in the *Dictionnaire de Trévoux* edited by the Jesuits.[47]

The very year in which the first volume of the ninth edition of Chaudon's *Nouveau dictionnaire historique* was published (1810), Joseph-François and Louis-Gabriel Michaud were preparing the launch of an even more ambitious enterprise, the *Biographie universelle*, the first volume of which would be printed in 1811 in direct and open competition with Chaudon.[48] Written by Louis-Gabriel Michaud himself, with the assistance of Etienne Clavier (1762–1817),[49] the entry on "Alexander the Great" covers more than twenty-four densely set columns. As was customary, it combines narrative and judgment. The author's point of view is expressed under the obvious influence of the movement originally distinguished by Rollin's *Histoire ancienne*. Far from being different from common conquerors, "Alexander seems to come closer to the commonness of men, by giving in to every last excess of intemperance." To express the expansive arrogance of Alexander's pride, the author calls on Bossuet. The actual assessment opens with a well-oiled sentence: "Of the historians of the victor of Asia, some placed him up among the gods, for his virtues, and the others brought him down among ordinary men, for his vices." Michaud does not hide his preference. Having quoted *The Spirit of the Laws* (10.14), he comments: "These considerations on the Macedonian conqueror did not appear to his detractors to be worthy of the sagaciousness of Montesquieu, and the opinion of M. de Sainte-Croix, who treated him more severely, has found quite a large number of supporters." The dictionary articles reveal that the conflicting theses found in *The Spirit of the Laws* and the *Examen critique* dominated discussion of Alexander the Great, his history, and his influence on the history of the world.[50]

Confrontations between these two points of view are found in many other anthologies and popularizing works of the period. Known by the antique name of Publicola during the revolution, Pierre-Jean-Baptiste Chaussard (1766–1823) published a translation with commentary of Arrian's *Anabasis of Alexander* in 1802. The book was given a harsh reception both by historians like Christian Gottlob Heyne and literary critics like Jean-François Boissonade.[51] His sources include what he calls "the wild imaginings of Doctor Vincent on the voyage of Nearchus from the mouths of the Indus to the Euphrates."[52] But he does not repeat any of Vincent's conclusions on trade routes and the founding of cities. Similarly, in the anthology of texts on Alexander that he assembled in his third volume, he quotes all of chapters 13 and 14 of book 10 of *The Spirit of the Laws* (3:105–112), but omits chapter 8 of book 21. In the category of "Historiens" ["Historians"] only Bossuet, Rollin, Barthélemy, and Bougainville are cited (without cuts; 3:75–102); for even though he rejects the excessive importance given to the history of the Jews by "the virtuous Rollin" (and by Bossuet), the author appreciates the moral code that dictated Rollin's "judgment of Alexander" (1:xxiii). The anthology also includes long excerpts from Mably and de Tourreil, both of whom are included in the "parallels" category (3:159–177). An uncompromising and not particularly subtle critic of Voltaire and, especially, Montesquieu (whom he opposes to Mably and Sainte-Croix), he is a passionate devotee of the 1775 *Examen critique,* which he praises unreservedly (1:xii, n. 1) and paraphrases and cites abundantly, quoting the entirety of the baron's attacks on Montesquieu's theories (1:xxxvii–xl, 2:420–422). All told, the author considers that as a sign of Greece's decadence, Alexander's conquest was "raised on the tomb of liberty, and on the ruins of civilization's progress" (2:8). As for himself, he writes that he is "the champion of the conquests of liberty, inveigh[ing] against the conquests of despotism [that] aim to destroy the empire of the enlightenment" (3:307).

It should nonetheless be noted that Chaussard's thought is not monolithic. He follows Sainte-Croix without fully subscribing to his prejudices. He states that he prefers "the moral conquests of a Confucius, who enlightened Asia," to an Alexander who "devastated" it; he also praises the achievements of Cook and La Pérouse, who "brought to savage peoples our arts and their benefits, becoming forever respectable victims of their love for the sciences and humanity" (1: viiii). As can be seen, the former revolutionary differs from his avowed model in that he believes in progress and Europe's civilizing mission. His reasoning is grounded in the profound difference between ancient and modern wars. Indeed, in his view, when one studies "the motives for wars, the way of making war, the things, the men, everything is different between the ancients and the moderns." This explains why the Macedonian king is an antimodel, because "by reducing heroism to personal designs, he made a mistake . . . not only regarding the foundations but also the duration of the universality of his glory" (1: vii). Like Diderot before him in the *Histoire des deux Indes* (1780) and Constant after him in 1813, Chaussard refuses to grant Alexander the benefit of modernity; the conqueror was certainly not a predecessor, however distant, of the Enlightenment, for, as he writes, "it is a generous view and one that belongs to the principles of the current constitutions to link happiness and the improvement of the fate of the human race to conquest" (1: v). Waged for essentially commercial reasons, modern wars lead one to "preserve" rather than devastate; declaring Alexander a destroyer, Chaussard relegates him to a past that cannot be assimilated.

One also finds a profound detestation for Alexander in the letters that Paul-Louis Courier wrote to Sainte-Croix while he was a soldier stationed in Italy. Courier is particularly aggressive in a letter dated November 27, 1807, in which he also encourages Sainte-Croix to finish his revision of the 1804 *Examen critique*: "Do not praise your hero to me; he owed his glory to the century in which he appeared. Without that, what more did he have than Genghis Khan or Tamerlane? A good soldier, a good captain, but his virtues were common. . . . As for him, he did nothing that would not have been done without him. Long before he was born, it had been decided that Greece would take Asia. But especially, I ask you not to compare him to Caesar, who was something other than a starter of battles. Yours founded nothing. . . . Fortune brought him the world, what was he able to make of it?" (*Œuvres complètes*, 1855, p. 276).[53]

Jean-Claude-François Daunou (1761–1840), a former revolutionary like Chaussard and a former associate then opponent of Napoleon, held the chair in History and Ethics at the Collège de France from 1820 to 1830.[54] As the college's candidate, he was selected by Élie Decazes, the new president of the Conseil des Ministres (1817), over the Académie Royal des Inscriptions et Belles-Lettres' candidate, Désiré-Raoul Rochette, whose views on the

Macedonian conquest I will discuss below. Daunou succeeded two famous Hellenists in the History and Ethics chair: Pierre-Charles Levesque, who had written about Alexander in his *Études de l'histoire ancienne* (1811), and Étienne Clavier, who had contributed to the article on "Alexander the Great" in the 1811 *Dictionnaire Michaud*.

Daunou's eighth and ninth lessons at the Collège de France were devoted to Diodorus of Sicily's *Library of History*. In opening his comments on book 18 (*History of the Successors of Alexander*), Daunou expresses a point of view on the conqueror nearly identical to Rollin's. Instead of "governing by wise laws; provoking and favoring progress in agriculture, commerce, and the arts; maintaining harmony between the orders of the State; finally reigning through justice and beneficence," Alexander "sacrificed millions of men to his ambition, to his vain glory. . . . He bathed in the blood of the peoples. . . . Conquerors such as Alexander are horrible scourges for the human race," Daunou states, rejecting the opinion of those who had claimed that the conqueror "had changed the world's commerce." Seeing "the praise lavished [on conquerors] after their death as an even more deplorable calamity," he continues his acerbic critique of Voltaire and Montesquieu, but also of John Gillies "and other moderns," who had all found certainties in Plutarch's *On the Fortune of Alexander* discourses, despite the fact that these were "not worthy of the slightest confidence, [and were] the miserable productions of a declaimer, as M. Clavier has said." It was therefore better to follow "the opinion of Seneca and Boileau, the only one reconcilable with sound morals and actual history." Imitating Rollin and Sainte-Croix (who is never named), Daunou concludes his demonstration-declamation by quoting Bossuet and the *Discours sur l'histoire universelle*.[55]

In his laudatory note on Daunou, B. Guérard states that he admires his attention "to mixing the lessons of history with those of ethics and with defending civilization against barbarism and peoples against their tyrants." Guérard also suggests that the condemnation of the Macedonian conqueror could also be a projection onto the present, aimed at another target, or in other words "another Alexander, whom he had known well but whose name he does not pronounce, [but who] was present in his thought and gave even more vigor to his quill" (p. 154).

Other authors overtly courted controversy by openly using "their" Alexander against the "usurper." Among them was Benjamin Constant. He had acquired an impressive classical and erudite education over his stays at

German and Scottish universities (Erlangen in 1781–1783; Edinburgh in 1783–1785; Göttingen in 1811–1814); he had a lasting friendship with Thérèse, one of Heyne's daughters and long the (unhappy) wife of Georg Forster (who died in 1794). He had already tackled Greek history and begun a translation of Gillies's *History of Ancient Greece*.[56] He also knew some of Sainte-Croix's work. As far as can be told, he consistently expressed serious reservations regarding the historical role played by Alexander, whom he considered partially responsible for the decadence of the polytheistic religion.[57] For reasons he explains elsewhere, he also did not believe that the Macedonian conqueror's alleged efforts to civilize the "Fish Eaters" had the slightest effect—differing in this from the eighteenth-century philosophers whose theories he claimed to fight. Referring to Vincent and various travel accounts, but without citing the relevant passage in Montesquieu (though he had read him extensively), Constant expresses a judgment that cannot be challenged: "The inhabitants of the coast visited by Nearchus remain today as they were two thousand years ago. Today, as then, these hordes wrest from the sea an uncertain subsistence.... Need did not instruct them; poverty did not enlighten them; and modern travelers found them as they were observed by Alexander's admiral twenty centuries ago" (*De la religion*, 1824, 1:155).

At once hostile to the ideals of the Great Nation and in favor of restoring some form of monarchy, he published his anti-Napoleonic broadside *L'Esprit de Conquête* (*Spirit of Conquest*) in 1813. The polemic deals with war and peace in the context of the death throes of the Napoleonic regime and opens with a reflection (on the utility of wars) which is paradoxical only in appearance, for Constant intends to limit this example to antiquity and the Middle Ages, as opposed to "the present situation of the Europeans." War ("a savage impulse") retreats in direct proportion to the advance of commerce ("civilized calculation"; *L'Esprit de conquête*, I.2); this implies that Carthage (England) would now defeat Rome (the French empire). He does not fail to discuss some of the ideas developed in book 10 of *The Spirit of the Laws*. Without noting the atypical nature of Montesquieu's Alexander, he judges that unlike modern conquerors (read: Napoleon), ancient conquerors did not seek to impose their political rules or mores on conquered nations (*L'Esprit de conquête*, XII). Constant's hope is expressed through what he presents as an indisputable conclusion: war had now been supplanted by commerce as an arbiter of power and prestige. Neither the spirit of conquest nor conquerors

had a place in today's world. Alexander the Great was therefore relegated to
a sealed past: "Philip's son would no longer dare to suggest the invasion of
the universe to his subjects" (II) and contemporary populations would refuse to sacrifice themselves to satisfy "the ambition of one of these men who
want to repeat Cambyses, Alexander, or Attila." If they were consulted, they
would answer: "Learn civilization! Learn peace!" (XV). In this prime example
of the manipulation of history, Alexander is introduced side by side with the
"mad" Cambyses and Attila only to serve as a veiled representation of another
conqueror still so close and so differently detested.

One must also include Chateaubriand among the critics of Alexander-
Napoleon. He frequently condemned Alexander as a bloodthirsty conqueror
who, like Napoleon, did not hesitate to sacrifice the lives of thousands of
soldiers to acquire and / or expand a power considered despotic.[58] If we leap
thirty years forward, we can say that, to a certain extent, the Alexander of
Adolphe Thiers's *Histoire du Consulat et de l'empire* is the extreme culmination of an iconic construct elaborated within the liberal movement that
began and developed as of the 1810s.[59] Making a merciless assessment of
Napoleon's reign, Thiers places him "among the captains of all time" and
compares him to Alexander, whose strategic merits he tends to devaluate
(thus going against Montesquieu). He then undertakes a long comparative
analysis "under the more general revelation of talents and destiny," referring to Alexander, Hannibal, Caesar, Charlemagne, and Frederick. The
Macedonian is characterized as he was in the Rollin-Mably tradition, concerned exclusively with his glory rather than the good of his homeland: "No
life could be more tumultuously useless than his. . . . Though he changed
the whole aspect of the then civilised universe . . . he did not carry Grecian
civilization beyond Ionia and Syria, where it had been already planted, and
he left Greece in a state of anarchy, which only prepared it for the conquest
of the Romans." Compared to "Hannibal, on whom God bestowed the greatest
gifts of intellect and character," Alexander does not amount to much, including in comparison to Napoleon.

Alexander, Promoter of Commerce

Neither the impressive knowledge of Sainte-Croix—whose authority continued to cast a long shadow—neither the renown of the authors associated

with the rejection of Alexander's positive image should lead one to believe that they carried the day. As shown by the debates at the Institut de France over the 1810 Decennial prize,[60] the principles and methods defended by Sainte-Croix were subjected to intense criticism, while in the same period the current born of *The Spirit of the Laws* and its British epigones did not run dry.

At the end of the revolutionary period (1800), the current was fueled by the French translation Vincent's *The Voyage of Nearchus* (1797). Unpublished archives on the translation can be found on a copy of the *Voyage* in the collection of the Bibliothèque Nationale de France.[61] A handwritten dedication on the flyleaf reveals that this was the (English) copy that the translator Jean-Baptiste-Louis-Joseph Billecocq[62] received in thanks from the author. Sent from London and dated December 10, 1800, Vincent's autograph letter (written in excellent French) is evidence of his great courtesy toward his translator (who had undoubtedly recently sent him a copy of his translation): "Doctor Vincent presents this volume to M. Billecocq as an expression of his gratitude, for the excellence of the French translation will carry the reputation of this work everywhere where the French language is spoken; his confidence, for he entrusts M. Billecocq with the additions and corrections he was not himself able to publish; and that M. Billecocq is perfectly free to adopt or reject according to his own judgment and discretion."

The copy in question is indeed full of often copious marginalia in English, which remains unpublished (though Vincent incorporated some in the second edition). Four years later, Billecocq gave his copy to the Bibliothèque Nationale, adding his own dedication bearing witness to the studious hours he had spent in its reading room: "Citizen Billecocq, French translator of the Voyage of Nearchus, considered himself lucky, though he placed infinite importance on the present with which Doctor Vincent had honored him, to use it to pay homage to the Bibliothèque Nationale, by leaving it as a monument of his gratitude for the help he found there in the course of his literary work" (Paris, Plûviose 6, Year 12, January 28, 1804. Signed: Joseph Billecocq).

The translator did not fail to underline the importance of the "present of great value to its age" which he was bringing to the attention of the French public, since it could interest "navigators, geographers, astronomers, chronologists, philosophers, lovers of history and voyages. Every class of savant and reader will find in this book clarifications of facts likely to rectify their ideas, stabilize their doubts, increase their knowledge, and interest their hearts." This explains why the release of the English edition in 1797 had been announced in *Connaissance des temps à l'usage des astronomes et des navigateurs* (Year 8, Paris, February 1798, p. 394), a periodical published by the Bureau des Longitudes. In order to facilitate the book's distribution, the bookseller Maradan chose to publish it in one octavo (three volumes) at a more reasonable price than the Imprimerie de la République quarto (15 francs rather than 21 francs).

A comment by the reviewer for the *Spectateur du Nord* (July 1800) ("this book was lacking from the general history of voyages") offers an interesting key. Since Ramusio in 1563 and Harris and Campbell in 1764, Arrian's *Indica* had been classified in one of the most popular categories of books: the travel narrative.[63] Though Nearchus's sea journey was not even mentioned in the Chevalier de Jaucourt's article on "Périple" in the *Encyclopédie* (13[1765]:374–377), lovers of this literary genre—who were often also geography enthusiasts—were prepared to welcome Vincent's book. It is therefore easy to understand why Gilles Boucher de la Richarderie included a critical summary of it in his *Bibliothèque universelle des voyages*. De la Richarderie devoted some fifteen pages to "Navigation and voyages among the ancients," in which he discussed two volumes by Vincent, *The Periplus of the Erythræan Sea* and *The Voyage of Nearchus,* and acknowledged that he had borrowed a great deal from the writings of the geographers Mentelle and Malte-Brun. The paradoxical Delisle de Sales was practically alone in considering (before Vincent's book) that Nearchus's journey "was not in and of itself of great importance" and that its author illustrated "the credulousness of the ages of barbarity."[64]

The Abbé de Vauxcelles was full of extraordinary praise. Explicitly recalling the role played by Montesquieu in reevaluating the figure of Alexander, he underlined the originality and importance of the Macedonian king's designs and associated him with the praise he had just lavished on the French translation of George Vancouver's *Voyages* (1800). De Vauxcelles joined Vancouver in applauding the "great bridge of communication established, thanks to which we can carry to the most unknown beaches . . . the benefits of civil society," then mixed past and present in enthusiastic formulations: "This idea is true and sublime, and it must be recommended to the approaching century. But the greatest idea after this one is undoubtedly that conceived by Alexander, of bringing Europe to share in the felicities of

Asia; of making the riches of the Indian Ocean flow back to the Mediterranean. To penetrate by ship to the sources of Oriental riches. This was the goal of a voyage he ordered Nearchus to embark on" (*Paris pendant l'année 1801*, p. 121).

He added that the government's initiative had concurrently spread "the most beautiful conception of Antiquity and one of the noblest enterprises of modern times." As we have seen, three years later Sainte-Croix took the exact opposite view to de Vauxcelles—though he did not cite him—and referred to both notions as interpretative "lunacy" and illusions created by an expansionist European model that he rejected.

The violent opposition expressed here only had a limited impact. In France, political conditions encouraged both a general peace among European nations and expansion overseas. In 1802, for instance, Joseph Eschassériaux, a member of the Tribunat and firm believer in the ideals of the Great Nation, seized upon the Proclamation of the Consuls on 18 Brumaire ("to bring this great European family closer together through solid and lasting ties") to plead for peace; he invokes the great figures of Las Casas, Henri IV, L'Hôpital, the Abbé de Saint-Pierre, and Rousseau to support his argument. At the same time, he regrets the failure of the Egyptian expedition, which forced that nation "to go back into the night of superstition and barbarism." One must distinguish, Eschassériaux argues, between the destructive conquerors that must be condemned (Attila, Genghis Khan, Muhammad) and those "few conquerors [whose] genius saved twenty peoples from servitude [and] created, reformed, and civilized nations." The author includes Alexander among the benefactor-conquerors: "Antiquity mourned the death of Alexander and regretted that the captains who inherited his vast Empire did not inherit his genius, and of ambition only had worry and weakness; the revolutions that travel the world would not have immediately plunged the countries he subjected to his laws into barbarism" (p. 68). Essentially, Alexander's objectives heralded the current ambition "to reopen to Europeans a less perilous route to the heart of vast and populous Asia and to use the products of their arts to ask again to receive from Indian avidity the gold it had absorbed since the discovery of the New World; this route was shown to all seafaring peoples by the conquest of Egypt."[65]

Though he does not cite him, Eschassériaux is not far from sharing de Vauxcelles's opinion (1801) of Alexander's premonitory lucidity and

modernity. Similarly, in an analysis presented to the Classe de Sciences Morales et Politiques in Year 9 (1801), the famous geographer Gosselin showed
great critical acuity in discussing and casting doubt on the identification of
various ancient sites, but in substance repeated Vincent's thesis of Alexander as "the first in Europe to conceive the project of commerce that would
encompass the entire known world at that time . . . and the project of making
Alexandria the warehouse for merchandise from the Orient and the Occident."[66] In the *Journal de l'Empire* dated January 2, 1807, E. Jondot shared his
opinion: "It was Alexander who had the glory of linking the Mediterranean
and the Indian Ocean by commerce . . . and one can say that he lay the foundations of the immense commerce that in the following ages enriched
Rome, Constantinople, Venice, and Genoa." In the *Spectateur du Nord,* one of
the French émigré organs in Germany,[67] the reviewer describes the Macedonian past as one of the components of the European present. Nonetheless,
his interest in the voyage of Nearchus is not only due to the circumstances
"that have in recent times attracted our attention to various parts of Africa
and Asia." If Vincent's book is worth reflecting upon, it is because it fits into
the history "of the relations that nature has organized between Europe and
these two other parts of the world, relations so important that they were a
part of all the great revolutions of which history has retained the memory."
The author then observes that from his point of view (which is directly inherited from the source volume) the encounter between past and present
gives the ancient sources additional credibility: "The south of Asia has always made the rest of the world dependent on its industry. . . . Due to the
wealth [of these regions] and their position on the globe, they influence all
commercial relations. This consideration adds to the importance of the
book we are announcing, but also gives new motives for the interest it in-
spires. Alexander's name mixed with those of our European navigators, the
picture of the ancient customs compared to the habits and mores that our
modern religions and invasions have created in the same places, spread over
these narratives a charm, a kind of truth that most of the other accounts do
not have" (July 1800, pp. 81–82).

Few were those who did not make any concessions to the positive image
of Alexander. Even Chateaubriand allowed himself a surprising burst of
praise by comparing the French and Macedonian armies: "our armies like
Alexander's spread light among the peoples where our flag wanders: Europe
became French under Napoleon's footsteps, like Asia became Greek in Alex-

ander's course."[68] We see here that the manipulation of Alexander's image varied not only depending on the political context of the day, but on the immediate necessities of a specific argument.

Any mention of commerce with the Indies generally leads to the introduction of Alexander in the role attributed to him by Vincent. Consider Joseph-François Michaud, the elder of the two brothers who launched the renowned *Biographie Universelle* in 1811. In 1801, he published a history of the empire of Mysore, which was no more than a translation-paraphrase-compilation of English texts. "Today, as our eyes begin to look to India," he writes, one must see in the history of Hindustan, "a terrible lesson to the leaders of nations who want to conquer more countries than they can govern." Given Michaud's known opposition to Bonaparte, one could think that the warning was aimed at him, but the rest of the text is more or less in his favor. Michaud refers to "the companies of merchants who [followed] in Alexander's footsteps after a fashion" and Bonaparte's expedition in Egypt at the head of "thirty thousand Europeans armed for the cause of liberty." In a "Historical Table of the Relations Established by Commerce," he goes back to Darius and the sea explorations of Scylax, regarding which he transcribes the opinion of "the most enlightened writers"; the terms used show that he is carefully lifting from chapter 8, book 21, of *The Spirit of the Laws*. While noting that "the scholars do not agree about Alexander's projects," he shows quite clearly which side he is on by explicitly relying on William Vincent's authority:[69] "His conquests opened a new route, and the commerce with India, now being carried out through Egypt and Syria, was opened to the nations of the Occident. . . . Alexandria became one of the most flourishing cities in the Orient" (2:430).[70]

The case of the compiler Jullien du Ruet is also revealing. In 1809, he published an enormous volume devoted to the history of ancient commerce, but also to its relationship with the present era. Its extensive foreword makes it abundantly clear that du Ruet is in the ideological circle of the "incomparable Bossuet" (p. xx) and Sainte-Croix. He praises Sainte-Croix's book, admirable for its "erudition and insight . . . one of the most beautiful historical, critical, and philological monuments of which modern science can boast" (p. xxii). The editor also points out that "after so many misleading theories," the book allows one "to return to the practical truth." But how does one reconcile a return to tradition and the exaltation of commerce? The author feels compelled to apologize for having a quote from the *Histoire des deux Indes* as an epigraph to "an elementary work, which must every-where carry the stamp of wisdom and the austere truth."[71] Unaware that the citation's author is actually Diderot, he exonerates himself by reminding the reader that Raynal "had the noble courage of retraction!" Also in the foreword, the author denounces "a few ancient and modern Aristarchuses too prompt to blame Commerce for the corruption of peoples, as if the arts and industry were not, in their nature as much as their object, under the immediate influence of public mores and under the absolute direction of rulers" (p. xvi). He includes Huet and Ameilhon among his sources, but also "Robertson's too-short work on ancient India" and Vincent's book, "full of new and profound views on Alexander's policy and this extraordinary prince's commercial outlook" (pp. xx–xxii). Du Ruet also has occasion to express reservations about Bossuet, in whose work commerce has a "fleeting place," and, more pointedly, about Sainte-Croix, who is "perhaps overly in-clined by his principles to work himself up against Commerce and those who opened the most ambitious roads; [he] may not have given Alexander's conceptions enough credit, both in terms of navigation and of actual trade" (pp. xxiii–xxiv). He deems Sainte-Croix's accusations that Vincent turned "Alexander into *a trading post chief*" unfounded.

One of the book's leitmotifs is the present era's debt to the navigators and traders of antiquity: "Upon seeing by what miracles, despite navigation that lacked everything down to the compass and the telescope, the traders of the ancient World earned the right to enter into the councils of Senusret, Sol-omon, Alexander, and Augustus; modern commerce will no longer be able to doubt that it is on the traces of Hanno, Pytheas, and Nearchus that it must set off toward elevated destinies" (p. xxx). Alexander is the most notable of all the precedents, which explains why he plays a central part in the book.[72] Du Ruet adorns him with all the attributes of modernity. A small selection of quotes will suffice to illustrate his argument: "His genius surmised a part of the great schemes that modern commerce would one day rise to.... By founding Alexandria, he himself set down the first ring of this magical chain, which in the succession of centuries was to connect Europe to the Commerce of the entire world, and connect on its shore the peoples of the two poles. He is first to enter India, and finally delivers this magnificent country to the rest of the world's knowledge" (pp. xii–xiii).

Alexander and Napoleon

But while Alexander's policy was constantly praised, the praise was also a function of the connections that the author established with the politics of his time. Du Ruet thanks Napoleon for having restored mores and morality, but simultaneously warmly approves his desire to establish a "national industry" and compete with British commerce and traders. Moving between past and present, Du Ruet manifests acute irritation with the English, including those scholars whom he cites favorably (such as Vincent) but whose "imperturbable arrogance" he denounces. European policy is in keeping with that of Alexander, who is referred to as "the Napoleon of the Ancient World, [who] cleared the path to a universal commerce for Europe" (p. xxiii; see also p. 426). In Egypt, Persia, and on the route to India, Napoleon is walking (or would walk) in Alexander's footsteps. Indeed, India needs to be seized from the "monopolistic people" who exploit it: "This is where French commerce must go to repair its debts: the imperial eagle may already be showing it the path!" (p. 186). In doing so, "the Peacemaker of the modern universe" would follow the path opened and marked out by Alexander and Nearchus (p. xxx).

The preceding examples illustrate the link made between the image of Alexander as promoter of commerce and that of an emperor who was imagined to have set off on the footsteps of his model both on the Egyptian expedition and in his supposed plans to conquer India. I will only provide a limited selection of examples of a literary genre worthy of an exhaustive study.[73] In announcing the republication of a translation of Quintus Curtius in the March 1807 issue of the *Mercure de France* (p. 555), a critic offered a comparison flattering to his emperor: "Reading this story acquires a new degree of interest today that a hero formed from this great model is executing before our eyes projects no less vast and more reasonable than those of the Greek hero, without abandoning like he did the heart of his own state" (p. 555). Two years later, in the same periodical, Pierre-Louis Guingené, a friend of Daunou, reviewed the performance at La Scala in Milan of a play written by Lamberti "for the return of the Italian army after the German war." The story is set in Harmozia, on the Persian Gulf, while Alexander impatiently and anxiously awaits the arrival of his friend Nearchus. "It was difficult in general to collect more connections between the subject chosen in history and the subject to be treated," Guingené notes, struck by the obviousness of the allusions: "While waiting for Nearchus, Alexander sees to the needs of his vast empire. He remembers that he is not only the master and general of his army, but the friend and father of the peoples." The triumphal cortege includes numerous Cretan soldiers (read: Italian), as well as mixed contingents of Macedonians and Persians. Alexander comes at the end of the cortege, "standing on a shining, very tall chariot, crowned with laurels and holding an olive branch; the chariot is pulled by eight white horses, magnificently equipped and led by hand by Indian slaves." Lamberti's play ends with the arrival of ambassadors sent by all the peoples to give thanks and pay homage to Alexander. Only the Arabs have refused to come to meet him. The Arab pirates living off "their mercantile operations that impoverish the earth," who "alone deprive the world of the sweetness of peace," are easily recognizable as the English, both sailors and traders;[74] the metaphor is richly ironic, given that the British navy was then trying to fight those referred to as the "Arab pirates" of the Gulf.[75]

But what of the emperor himself, who, as we have seen, had developed a fairly negative idea of Alexander in his youth?[76] There is nothing to indicate that the memory of Alexander was particularly on Napoleon's mind during his years in power—despite the fact that his courtiers and admirers always sought to make analogies between the two conquerors and that certain official artists deliberately chose to represent Napoleon charging on horseback in the manner of Alexander or, more accurately, in the manner of the modern artists like Le Brun who had depicted Alexander's charge at the Granicus and Arbela. *The Triumphal Entry of Alexander into Babylon* sculpted by Thorvaldsen at the Quirinal Palace on order of the emperor could well be an allegorical representation of the triumph of Napoleon as imagined by the sculptor based on a servile reading of Quintus Curtius.[77]

Yet on several occasions Napoleon did choose to depict himself in the Macedonian's footsteps in the Orient, whether it was upon arriving in Corfu, with "Alexander's kingdom before his eyes," or landing in Egypt and writing to his brother Joseph that "this land so fertile can witness the rebirth of the centuries of Alexander and Ptolemy," or announcing to his soldiers that "the first city [they would] encounter had been built by Alexander ["who did everything in a day"] and [that they would find] at each footstep great memories worthy of exciting the imagination of the French."[78]

15. *Alexander the Great in This Triumphal Chariot Greeted by the Goddess of Peace.* Relief by Bertel Thorvaldsen, currently in the Quirinal Palace, Rome. Thorvaldsen Museum, Copenhagen. Photo by Ole Woldbye.

One also recalls the opening of *The Charterhouse of Parma* (1839): "On 15 May 1796, General Bonaparte made his entry into Milan at the head of the youthful army which had just crossed the bridge at Lodi and let the world know that after all these centuries, Caesar and Alexander had a successor."[79] The following year, Flaubert used the same comparison during his travels.[80] The analogy persisted in that it seemed to pertain to the evident nature of mythical memory, but it should be noted that in looking for a model for reorganizing and remodeling Europe under his authority, Napoleon favored the Roman empire rather than Alexander's exploits. Additionally, the comparison with Alexander (and Charlemagne) was not a particularly happy one from the perspective of dynastic history, as Talleyrand reminded the Senate in an 1805 speech delivered in the presence of the emperor: "Frivolous and deceitful analogies! ... Charlemagne was a conqueror and not a founder.... By constantly pushing back the limits of his conquests, Alexander only prepared bloody funeral rites for himself: the great, heroic thought of succession never entered his mind; Charlemagne and Alexander left their Empire to anarchy."[81] Talleyrand's statement fits neatly with an evaluation of Alexander's reign found among both the admirers and detractors of the Macedonian of his time:[82] the minister was a diligent reader!

During his exile, Napoleon "read about Alexander's expedition in Rollin, he had several maps open before him; he complained of a narrative told without taste, without intention, which he said left no idea of Alexander's large views; he occasionally had the urge to rewrite a piece etc."[83] He also liked to read Arrian, certainly due to his primary interest in strategic and military affairs.[84] Napoleon was quite critical of Alexander's abilities in this area; he considered that he had infinitely less merit than the Spartans Leonidas and Agesilaus, given that by comparison the Macedonian conqueror had far fewer obstacles to overcome: "With him, one does not find any beautiful maneuver worthy of a great general."[85] Napoleon always criticized Alexander for having continued toward Egypt after the victory at Issus, rather than taking advantage of it to finish off Darius; here too, one has the impression of reading Rollin and Mably. Moralizing history always had a powerful influence on Napoleon. He turned to it to borrow the image of an abrupt change in Alexander: "When Alexander reached the peak of glory and success, his head started to spin or his heart went bad. He had begun with the soul of a Trajan, he ended with the heart of Nero and the mores of Elagabalus."

What impressed Napoleon about Alexander was not the military victories, but his political reflections. He disagreed with those who spoke of the "good luck" of great leaders, for in reality "when one wants to study the reasons for their success, one is surprised to see that they had done everything to obtain it." Similarly, Napoleon considered that Alexander's enterprise was not "a mere irruption, a kind of deluge. No; everything was calculated in depth, executed with audacity, led with wisdom. He proved to be at once a great warrior, a great politician, and a great legislator." Here, the emperor sounds just like Montesquieu. For that matter, he continued, all the great captains of antiquity are remarkable "for the precision of the schemes and the well thought-out relationship between the means and their consequences, the efforts and the obstacles. They succeeded only by conforming to this, no matter the audacity of their enterprises or the extent of their success. They always continued to make war into a science. It is in this single respect that they are our models, and it is only by imitating them that we can hope to approach them."[86] Napoleon claimed to have particular admiration for Alexander's Oriental policy: "He had the art of making defeated peoples love him. He was right to have Parmenion killed, he who foolishly thought it was wrong that he had left Greek mores behind. It was highly politic of him to go to Ammon; this is how he conquered Egypt. If I had stayed in the Orient, I would probably have founded an empire like Alexander, by going on a pilgrimage to Mecca, where I would have prayed and genuflected."[87]

The deposed emperor added that he agreed with Alexander "in all his discussions with the Macedonians," referring to the objections certain Macedonian leaders (Parmenion, Cleitus) raised to Alexander's projected Iranian policy. Napoleon may also have been thinking of the Macedonian when he regretted that he had not been able "to make each of the [European] peoples into a single body of nations."[88] It was also Napoleon's alleged ability to adopt local customs that led some among the English to worry that he would be able to rally Indian populations behind the same principles that he had proclaimed in Egypt (following Alexander's example).[89] While they affirmed that in such a case local populations and their mores, religions, and women would be protected, other commentators considered that on the contrary this "projected" expedition in collaboration with the Russians was "as just a cause as Alexander's, who wanted to conquer the entire world."[90] This only goes to show the extent to which memory is pliable and its uses variable.

Naturally, these scattered fragments of disjointed conversations and monologues in distant exile have no other objective than to provide an after-the-fact illustration of the strategic abilities and in-depth political reflection of the deposed ruler who uttered them—or to whom they are generously attributed. What is notable is that Napoleon continued to think about the two contemporary images of Alexander and made use of both. He never let go of the image of an overambitious man unable to resist the vapors of glory, whose character withered once he came in contact with the Orient (from Trajan to Elagabalus); but as the head of an empire, Napoleon favored the image of the political leader who could define a rational policy toward the defeated elites and intended to implement it despite the opposition of leaders in his entourage (there had been no shortage of Parmenions in Napoleon's own general staff). Alexander was well placed in Napoleon's gallery of reasonable conquerors, but the prestige of the Spartans Leonidas and Agesilaus remained unrivaled in his gallery of heroes.

Commerce, Colonization, and Civilization

We now come back to Jullien du Ruet. Du Ruet shows that one could combine respect for Sainte-Croix's ethics and agreement with Vincent's commercial theories; one could support a return to tradition and admire Alexander as a promoter of European commerce. One could also be a follower of the Enlightenment, guarded about the idea of conquest, but nonetheless convinced of the positive consequences of the Macedonian enterprise. Pierre-Charles Levesque is a good example of this position; as we have seen, his *Études de l'Histoire ancienne* expressed his doubts that Alexander's achievements could have "expiated" the devastation he was responsible for in the countries crossed by his armies.[91] For all that, as a writer who states in the preface to his book that he is "a European proud of the progress of modern Europe" (1:xii), Levesque is not indifferent to Alexander's accomplishments. On the contrary: in Levesque, the conqueror removes the cataracts erected by the Persians to block the Babylonian rivers, thus "[calling] into his empire the fleets of all nations"; as opposed to the Asian despots, "his genius tended to bring men and nations closer together and to make one single people of all the peoples who recognized his empire"; he organizes great feasts in Ecbatana with performances of "the masterpieces by which Aeschylus, Sophocles, and Euripides had portrayed the city of Athens." Levesque contrasts his hero with other conquerors, using phrases bearing the influence of the current started by *The Spirit of the Laws:* "The others brought barbarism to the immense expanse of their conquests, and Alexander conquered a considerable part of the globe to civilize it; they were devastators and only he was a teacher.... Alexandria became the ornament of Egypt and the trading post of the commercial Universe. [The cities he founded] contributed to facilitating communication between the peoples, to expanding their commerce, to defending them from the barbarians, and to the rise of civilization among the vagabond nations" (1811, 3:468–469).

Published as a response to an English book, Sainte-Croix's 1779 volume *De l'état et du sort des colonies* dealt with a related issue, which was considered crucial at the end of the eighteenth century: Should colonies be founded and if so what should be their status? To this end, while criticizing the dissertation Bougainville had written on the subject in 1745, Sainte-Croix establishes parallels between ancient and modern colonization (the English colonies in America serve as the modern example). This debate, already very present in Montesquieu,[92] had never died down, as seen for example by the launch of a *Journal des Colonies* in 1791 and the publication of Talleyrand's *Essai sur les avantages à retirer des colonies nouvelles* in 1797. This probably explains why the Institut's Classe d'Histoire et de Littérature Ancienne chose colonization as the subject of its competition: "To search for everything the ancient authors and monuments can teach us on the History of the establishment of the Greek colonies etc." The prize was awarded in 1814 to Désiré-Raoul Rochette, who was born in 1790 and had been appointed to the History chair of the Lycée Impériale at the age of twenty.[93] In 1815, he published a final version of his award-winning essay in four volumes. Though he underlines that the colonies founded under Alexander and after have very specific characteristics that differentiate them from previous Greek colonies (1:4–6), the author includes a long discussion of them in volume 4 (bk. 7).

Rochette draws heavily on Montesquieu and Huet to carry out his analysis; like Huet, he sees Alexander as "the first who conceived a plan for a monarchy and at the same time a universal commerce." Aside from *The Spirit of the Laws,* the author frequently refers to the works of Robertson and Vincent. He is following in their footsteps and calling on their authority when he launches an attack on Sainte-Croix, "a respectable scholar ... blinded by the prejudices expressed on every page of his *Examen critique,*" a book that he fears "engulfed the great statesman in the hate he directed at the conqueror." Rochette affirms that the king's goal "was to defend his nascent and still poorly consolidated empire against the invasions of the barbarian peoples, often defeated and never tamed, which he had recently added to his states."

This image of Alexander would find its way into the Ministry of Education's history handbooks. One of the best known and most widely circulated French manuals was by Poirson and Cayx. It was first published in 1827 and had reached its twelfth edition by 1853. On the title page of each successive edition, the publishers specified that this *Précis de l'Histoire ancienne* was "adopted by the Royal Council of the University of France and prescribed for the teaching of ancient history in royal middle schools and other public education establishments."[94] When dealing with Alexander the Great, the authors systematically cite *The Spirit of the Laws* and Sainte-Croix in footnotes (pp. 358, 366); they also refer to Gillies, Volney, and Levesque (on Persepolis). In the 1831 edition, the author discussing the changes brought by Alexander adds a reference to the king's decision to prohibit "the barbarian custom [in Bactria] by which the Bactrians left their fathers who had reached a decrepit old age to the dogs"; though he does not credit Montesquieu, he has obviously borrowed the exemplum from *The Spirit of the Laws* (10.5), whose 1757 edition he could have discovered late in the day. In this Alexander, one recognizes all the qualities underlined by Montesquieu and other "philosophes": "The passion for conquests, mixed with great projects for discoveries, navigation, commerce.... Measures to attract India's commerce into the central provinces.... All beliefs respected and protected.... The many colonies that tended at once to maintain the Persians in obedience, to regenerate them through contact with Europeans, to finally unite the two peoples, etc." The final verdict firmly takes position against "the declaimers who called him a madman" and follows the opinion of "the great minds, since Condé, Bossuet, and Montesquieu, who were struck with the loftiness of his ideas and his schemes." The rest of the text leaves no doubt as to the identity of its primary inspirer: "His conquest was just; it delivered Greece from the dangers and humiliations that the kings of Persia had meted out to it for two hundred years. Additionally, he made it salutary to the vanquished, and thus settled the immense debt that any conqueror owes to humanity" (p. 372). In introducing a passage from Diodorus, the authors then unreservedly praise "the projects conceived to bring the scattered members of the great human family closer together through the ties of religion and commerce."

If we return to another category of the popularizing literature, it is particularly interesting to note that the article on "Alexander the Great" in the *Dictionnaire Michaud* is among those that were heavily revised for the 1842 edition. The revision was carried out by Vincent Parisot (c. 1805–1861), a second-rate author who was prolific in the realms of literature and antiquity. While the text of the 1811 *Michaud* is unchanged and the bibliography has not been supplemented, Parisot added no less that eighty-six copious footnotes. Though the footnotes are supposed to complete Michaud's text, they systematically take the opposing view. Even a partial synoptic comparison of two propositions quickly reveals that Parisot had chosen *The Spirit of the Laws* over the *Examen critique*:

Michaud 1811

"These considerations on the Macedonian conqueror did not appear worthy of Montesquieu's sagaciousness to his detractors, and the opinion of M. de Sainte-Croix, who treated him more severely, has found quite a large number of partisans."

"The narratives by all these historians have been discussed with much insight and depth in the volume entitled: *Examen critique des anciens historiens d'Alexandre* by M. de Ste-Croix."

Michaud 1842

N. 83- "The dominant opinion on Alexander today is that which we have just voiced. One should rather add to Montesquieu's praise than take away from it.... In our eyes, he still combines the triple glory of always having had lofty, human, and civilizing views, despite the narrow prejudices of the Macedonians; of never having slumbered or slumped with success (notes 48, 57, 79); and finally, as it seems to us, to have been on the verge of adding to his glory, his good deeds, and the civilization of the world at the time he died. His death was certainly one of the greatest calamities that a vast territory ever had cause to wail about."

N. 86- "Ste-Croix's volume is certainly the fruit of much study, and can serve as an endless source. But he did not see his hero with enough loftiness and independence. He has no fixed opinion of him. An honest and ingenuous soul, he wants to blame Alexander for his vices on principle, which explains his indulgence with Quintus Curtius.... Nonetheless, Ste-Croix is to date the most worthy man of those who want to study the life of Alexander. To fully reap the fruits of it, one must merely consider the facts from a slightly higher plane."

In Parisot's view, the conclusion was obvious: it was undoubtedly "to expand the limits of civilization that Alexander endeavored to upset all the barriers that nature seemed to have put between Europe and Asia."

It would be neither useful nor reasonable to postulate that the compiler Parisot had become aware of Johann Gustav Droysen's *Geschichte Alexanders des Grossen* (1833) between the two editions of the *Michaud*, given that he does not cite Droysen's book and that it was not available in French. Far more simply, his stance fits neatly into a debate whose terms were perfectly known and identified because it had been going on for many years. One could make the same observation regarding later manuals, which sometimes used the authority of Poirson and Cayx to present the same image of Alexander, citing Sainte-Croix and Montesquieu but primarily finding inspiration in *The Spirit of the Laws*.[95] Finally, how could one overlook the *Vie de Alexandre le Grand* (1852), written by Lamartine when he was reduced to producing commercial "subsistence" literature? He claims to have drawn heavily from Sainte-Croix's *Examen critique,* a book "too little known by the average reader, but the work of a philosopher and a politician. It is not only history restored, but history reasoned" (1:ii). Lamartine ingenuously proposes an unlikely synthesis: "M. de Sainte-Croix is Alexander's Montesquieu!"

Chapter 8

German Alexanders

Christian Gottlob Heyne: From European Wars to Alexander's Campaigns

A few months after the French publication of the *Examen critique des anciens historiens d'Alexandre-le-Grand*—the date was June 4, 1805—the University of Göttingen hosted its annual ceremony to announce the winners of the university prizes. On this occasion, Christian Gottlob Heyne, "professor of eloquence and poetry" since 1763, revealed the curriculum for his courses. He aimed to combat "the paradoxical opinion according to which wars have contributed to spreading the arts and sciences and perfecting the human race." Evoking "the crusades, the destruction of the Caribbean, the Inquisition, the Dragonnades, and the wars of religion," he affirmed that "history makes no mention of wars undertaken with the stated design of extending civilization and propagating the arts and sciences." He refused to believe that Alexander ever planned "to civilize the entire world, to unite all peoples with each other, and to make the Greek language and civilization rule everywhere." If one were to analyze what Alexander actually did during his life or what is known of his plans, one would see that there is no factual basis for "such a reverie" or "these beautiful commercial speculations." In reality, these interpretations were imagined "based on the political and commercial ideas of our time, but they are without foundation; they cannot be presented as historical truths." Alexander's only ambition was to conquer the world.[1]

Upon final publication, Heyne added a long essay (also in Latin) entitled *On Alexander and His Plans for Putting All the Parts of the Universe in Mutual*

Communication. It was intended to expand on the remarks and observations made in Heyne's preliminary presentation, repeating its principal points: in and of themselves, wars do not have invigorating virtues; their positive effects are illusory; and while "savage and barbarian peoples" can sometimes make progress thanks to their more cultured victors, this does not preclude negative consequences—defeated peoples lose their traditions and, in any case, the improvements in question are only actual benefits if they are passed on in respect for life (*incolumitas*), peace (*pax*), and mutual communication (*societas*). As for the development of the taste for literature occasionally observed, it does not justify the loss of happiness and dignity; indeed, it is better "to grow old far from the corruption of letters, in rough honesty and the traditional customs of illiterate ancestors." For that matter, no one can claim—and far less prove—that Alexander was thinking of the spread of literature on his expeditions to Asia. Only the most common individual could believe such nonsense, which was often also used to justify the Europeans' arrival on foreign soil under the false pretext of progress, when the true causes were "the desire to dominate (*dominandi libido*), the wish to put lands to pillage, and the avidity of merchants."

One can also have doubts regarding the idea that Alexander's ambition was "to roam the entire world and to join all the people by mutual ties and lead them to a single way of life (*ad unum vitae cultum*)." Alexander's relations with other peoples were based on the outcome of war and not "on persuasion, contracts, or philosophical reflections. . . . If any commerce was established, it was that of merchandise and not of men," and it was only carried out in the interest of the victor, not to promote peace. Heyne repeats the arguments in favor of the Phoenicians, which we have seen in the works of other German authors (Schlözer, Berghaus, Herder)[2]: "Indeed, what a remarkable design to want to destroy Tyre, a city long devoted to the practice of commerce, in order to prepare by force of arms a new domination of Asia!" Similarly, the only objective of the projected expedition against Carthage was to serve the avidity of merchants "and not to spread belles-lettres and the arts." Moreover, the conqueror "never dreamed of turning Alexandria into the center of global commerce: that was the product of chance and circumstances"; the new city was actually founded to be thrust against Carthage. Ultimately, the results of the conquest were damning: Greece was impoverished and Macedonia was ruined and depopulated to the point that it later became an easy target for Rome. Heyne reflects on the relationship between sources and interpretations to come to the conclusion that the image of Alexander imposed by his eighteenth- and nineteenth-century contemporaries was a product of historians forcing their representations and analysis of the present onto the past. This was a noteworthy observation coming from an author who had spent his entire career drawing comparisons and analogies between antiquity and his own era and engaging in debates on European politics and the French Revolution, even if it meant openly disagreeing with his son-in-law Georg Forster, who had joined the "Society of German Friends of Liberty and Equality" in Mainz.[3]

Until 1804–1805, Heyne had only dealt with Alexander in passing, in reviews of scholarly works such as Feßler's biography published in 1797 and Chaussard's commentary on Arrian in 1802.[4] In 1784, he had also reviewed a curious, dense volume by the English writer Thomas Pownall (1722–1805), a specialist and participant in the relationship between (the British) metropolis and (American) colonies. His book sang the praises of Alexander, "the first statesman who ... combined the interests and power of commerce with the operations of polity"; to achieve this, Alexander put an end to Tyre's influence, thus rendering Persia's power inoperative; he founded Alexandria with the objective of turning it into the greatest center of commerce, connected to the Orient by a series of settlements and factories. At this stage, Heyne had begun to express serious doubts about the feasibility of the plans attributed to Alexander and to question their moral justifications.[5]

It is somewhat surprising that in 1805 Heyne singled out Pownall rather than targeting more prestigious authors. But he could hardly get involved in controversy with his other son-in-law, A. Heeren, who argued for a positive image of Alexander, or William Vincent, with whom he maintained cordial relations. Heyne therefore chose to refer to his (real or imagined) opponents by the collective and anonymous term of "scholars" (*viri docti*). Aside from Pownall, the only author named is the Baron de Sainte-Croix, about whom Heyne had just published a highly positive review.[6] Heyne drew many arguments and demonstrations from Sainte-Croix to support his own vision of war and Alexander, explicitly repeating his declaration on the relief of the "human race" at the news of the Macedonian conqueror's death.

Inspired by his close reading of the *Examen critique,* Heyne's papers in 1805 were primarily a function of a particular political context. French troops had occupied Hanover in 1803. As a correspondent member of the Institut National de Paris, Heyne had been one of several people charged with intervening with the French authorities to ensure they respected the city and the University of Göttingen. French minister of war Berthier had acceded to the demand in the name of the first consul, announcing his decision in a letter dated 21 Prairial, Year 11: "The sound of weapons must not interrupt the activities [of the members of the university]; the French nation honors the men of letters and scholars of every country." Heyne also received a letter guaranteeing the inviolability of the university and its members.[7] This explains the beginning of the June 4, 1805, text, in which Heyne refers to the harshness of the times, then pays tribute to "the empire of the French, [which] tempers the asperity of war by its humanity," while regretting that "the savagery integral to the human race (*ingenita humano generi feritas*) makes it impossible to think that the violence of war will ever disappear."

Other historians and philosophers had preceded Heyne on this path in Germany, including in Göttingen. There had been much discussion and reflection on the theme of war and conquest by scholars in moral and political philosophy (Thomas Abbt; Christian Garve; Johann Gottfried Herder), but also by historians such as Johann Christoph Gatterer in Göttingen in 1761 and Christian Daniel Beck in Leipzig in 1788. Though thinkers such as Beck acknowledged that conquest had had advantages in terms of communication and commerce "between the most remote states in the world," the general trend was to put Alexander back in the camp of "hero conquerors" who left more desolation than benefits in their wake. In his comments on Gatterer's and Beck's passages, Gérard Laudin considers it possible that "the model of the war of conquest, with references to Caesar and Alexander, [could] revive the opposition to Louis XIV's war of conquest, which had been very poorly received in Germany, and to which Herder was still referring in 1774."[8] The memory of Louis XIV certainly remained detestable given that in 1792, Georg Forster compared "the monstrous character of [his] enterprises as a vain sovereign avid for glory" with that of Xerxes',[9] who epitomized the despot in the realm of the *exempla*. But it must be emphasized that Herder was including Alexander's adventure in a more global vision of colonial history. His denunciation of the destruction of Tyre is related to the European expansionist enterprises of the modern era in a tone closely resembling that of the *Histoire des deux Indes* by Raynal (and Diderot), which was probably an important source for him: "How do the ancient Phoenicians put to shame the Europeans for their senseless conduct, when, in so much later ages, and with much more skill in the arts, they discovered the two Indies! These made slaves, preached the cross, and exterminated the natives: those, in the proper sense of the term, conquered nothing; they planted colonies, they built towns, and roused the industry of the nations, which, after all the deceptions of the Phoenicians, learned at length how to know and profit by their own treasures."[10]

Another severe critic of Alexander was Johann Isaac Berghaus, the author of a history of navigation published in 1792. Alexander and Alexandria are discussed in book 3, which is devoted to commerce in Egypt from the beginning of the fourth century BC to Ptolemy (1:518ff.). Though he notes the importance of *The Spirit of the Laws* among his sources and borrows a well-known expression from Montesquieu about the new course of commerce encouraged by Alexander (1:40), Berghaus also expresses substantive differences of opinion with Montesquieu and often chooses to follow Mably. In adopting Mably's point of view, he articulates serious doubts about Alexander's colonial foundations; he nonetheless makes an exception for Alexandria since "the founder himself had chosen this site to be his residence." Yet Berghaus is primarily driven by a conviction that associates him with an entire current that was favorable to the Enlightenment and as such aimed to exclude Alexander from the modernity that it implied and delivered: "The term *Aufklärung* is too often perverted, and the spirit of commerce appears under the euphemistic mask of the right of humanity" (1:xi). Consequently, he refuses to credit the Macedonian king with a central role in the history of the progress of maritime routes and commerce, for in truth he brought "more bad than good"; he goes so far as to refer to Alexander as a "scourge of humanity (*Geissel der Menscheit*)."[11]

The context in which Heyne expressed his views in 1805 was clearly shaped in Germany by the rejection of wars and conquests. For his part, it was not the first time he denounced war and its perils.[12] Born to a very poor family, he had personally suffered from the ravages of the Seven Years' War (1756–1763) by losing his position as a secretary-librarian during the bombing of Dresden by Prussian troops. His first academic lecture was delivered on September 17, 1763, on a memorable double occasion: it was the twenty-sixth anniversary of the Georgia Augusta and the celebration of the recently signed peace. The lecture praised the Ptolemaic dynasty, and particularly Ptolemy I, for turning Alexandria into a haven for all scholars and the sciences and literature in the midst of the disasters that followed

Alexander's death—just as the electors of Hanover, true lovers of peace, had turned Göttingen into a great metropolis of the sciences and arts. At the time, Heyne's vision of Alexander was still moderate: he devoted his introduction to imagining the progress in the arts and literature if Alexander had lived another thirty or forty years and he underlined the conqueror's geographic curiosity, the work of his surveyors Diognetus and Beton, and the importance of Nearchus's *Periplus*.

Thirty years later, Heyne provided a kind of overview of Macedonian history in which he singled out for praise the benefits of Philip's policy, which favored agriculture, navigation, and commerce, but did not condemn Alexander, contrary to more traditional parallels; he even recognized that we owe the spread of the belles-lettres and philosophy to Alexander's "temerity." However, he also made clear that Macedon drew little advantage from all this (*Opum regni Macedonici auctarum*, 1792). In another lecture (*Repentina auri argentique affluentia*, 1804), he denounced the pillaging committed during the wars waged in antiquity and the modern era, including by Alexander. Heyne underlined that the riches thus accumulated had never been used to improve the fate of populations.[13] The learned professor was therefore following on from his own reflections on war and peace when, in 1805, he was led to discuss the misfortunes of populations at the hands of Alexander, which current events in Hanover contrasted with the "civilized" behavior of the French authorities.

Greek History, the History of Alexander, and German Identity: Barthold Georg Niebuhr and His Contemporaries

A few months after Heyne's 1804 lecture, another German scholar and historian of antiquity took an attitude markedly different from the spirit of negotiation with which Heyne and his colleagues approached the French occupation authorities in Hanover. Born of Danish origin in a region heavily contested by Denmark and Prussia (Schleswig-Holstein), Barthold Georg Niebuhr (1776–1831) was the son of the famous Carsten Niebuhr, a Prussophile who sided with Frederick William's Prussia and became a high-ranking officer in its administration. After the disaster at Ulm (November 1805), Barthold translated Demosthenes's *First Philippic* and dedicated it to Tsar Alexander. He was preparing to publish the translation when the defeat at

Austerlitz in December limited its circulation to word of mouth. It would be reprinted and widely circulated shortly after his death in January 1831. Here, Niebuhr explained in clear terms that the Macedonian despot represented Napoleon, the former crushing republican Greece at Chaeronea, the latter occupying the German states after his military victories. In both cases, defeat was due to the collaboration between cities and states (Greek; German) and the victor (considered a liberator from the oligarchies) and to the absence of moral resistance; in a way, the German Demosthenes had been as little heard as the original Athenian. The analogy was carried to its logical conclusion by a striking sentence that closed the 1831 foreword: "Greece bears the responsibility for its disappearance; it is the Germany of antiquity (*das Deutschland des Alterthums*)."[14] At the time, German unity was no more real than Greek unity had ever been.

Niebuhr's remarks take on their full meaning in the context of a divided Prussia devastated by the defeat at Jena and the harsh political and financial conditions imposed by Napoleon. This foreign occupation by a country heretofore respected and even admired by many for its revolution caused real trauma. The *Reden an die deutsche Nation* (*Addresses to the German Nation*) publicly delivered by Fichte in Berlin in 1807 give an evocative account of this German distress. At the time, Wilhelm von Humboldt (1767–1835), a former student of Heyne's in Göttingen who had developed a passion for ancient Greece, was writing a dissertation on the fall of the free Greek city states to "the Macedonian barbarians" (1807–1808). He too saw an analogy with what Germany was experiencing in his own time. He considers that "one should take the end of Greek independence as the center of global history"; this is where the Germans, who have intimate and specific connections to ancient Greece, can find "a living energy" to build a national identity, through a new "educational training for man" (*Bildung*) whose development must be encouraged.[15] The following year (1809), he was appointed head of the Ministry of the Interior's "Section for Worship and Public Instruction" in Berlin under the authority of the Baron von Stein (1757–1831), who had served the Prussian monarchy following its losses at the hands of Napoleon and who had been instrumental in instituting reforms intended to lift up Prussia and increase its power. In 1810, he founded a new university (which now bears his name and that of his brother), organized according to entirely new pedagogical and political rules, in which antiquity was an essential component. He hired his friend Friedrich August Wolf, a fellow former student at Göttingen who had been chased out of his professorship in Halle when Bernadotte had ordered the university closed. Shortly after his arrival in Berlin, Wolf published a report on the sciences of antiquity (*Alterthumswissenschaft*),[16] which he dedicated to Goethe. Here, he argued for a radical transformation of research and reflection on Greek and Roman antiquity by establishing a dynamic link with the construction of a national identity. Indeed, Wolf affirmed, the Germans were the only moderns to have such a close spiritual, linguistic, and cultural relationship with the ancient Greeks; Wolf "is counting on Goethe to prevent the heritage of knowledge about antiquity 'to be torn from the homeland by foreign hands.'" Positioned on the border between science and politics, a nationalist claim of this type was aggressive in that it "served to affirm the superiority of German classical studies over those of other nations, and more specifically to devalue the French philological tradition that had been the primary means of accessing the antique world throughout the eighteenth century."[17]

This context provides a better understanding of a surprising statement made by Barthold Georg Niebuhr. The Bonn historian did not hesitate to present Sainte-Croix's *Examen critique* as "a work very unsatisfactory to a German scholar, and [it] must be treated by us as if it did not exist. The whole work must be done over again. As regards the facts in the life of Alexander, we need not hesitate to follow Arrian."[18] Such remarks were clearly inspired by the assumed certainty of German erudition's intrinsic superiority to French philology (thus relegating the latter to the obscurity of a sealed past). Niebuhr was admittedly not the only one to contest the methods of Sainte-Croix and other French erudite writers; Benjamin Constant, who knew Germany well and appreciated German erudition in the history of religions, did not have any qualms about writing that "Greece and the Orient resemble dried-up mummies in the writings of Fréret, Dupuis, and Sainte-Croix," in contrast to the studies of Creutzer and Görres, in which "these arid memories become elegant and admirable statues, worthy of the chisel of Praxiteles and Phidias."[19] What is specific to Niebuhr's categorical affirmations is the emphasis on nationalism. Niebuhr's condemnation of Sainte-Croix's *Examen critique* remains isolated; on the contrary, many German historians of the time showed their admiration and deference for the baron's work, no matter the reservations they may have otherwise expressed regarding individual aspects of his methods and conclusions.[20] Wolf even considered translating the *Examen critique* for a time.

After the double humiliation of the rout at Jena and Napoleon's entry into Berlin (October 1806), Niebuhr followed the Prussian government into exile, then accepted various ministerial duties before receiving the title of royal historiographer and being appointed a professor at the University of Berlin; it was here that he presented, then published the *Römische Geschichte* that made his international reputation. He also wrote a considerable number of studies of Greek and Latin texts. Of these, his 1812 reflections on the Pseudo-Aristotle's *Economics* is particularly noteworthy as a text that would henceforth be taken into account by historians of Alexander—or at least those interested in anything beyond narrating the campaigns.[21]

In 1823, Niebuhr settled in Bonn, where he would die eight years later. In the summers of 1825 and 1826 and the winter of 1829/1830, he lectured on ancient history from the origins to the Roman era.[22] These lectures include many chapters devoted to Sparta and Athens, but also to Philip's Macedon and Alexander's conquests. Here, contemporary Germany is not only always close at hand, it is constantly on Niebuhr's mind. In fact, he deals with late fourth-century BC Athens and Macedon in parallel with early nineteenth-century Germany. In referring to the destruction of Thebes in his discussion of the beginnings of Alexander's reign, Niebuhr comments that it "produced great consternation throughout Greece, similar to that which followed a decidedly lost battle against the French in our own days" (Lecture 75). The same is true in the chapters in which Niebuhr discusses Philip and Demosthenes. Though Niebuhr denounced Philip in 1806 through a devastating comparison with Napoleon as oppressor of Germany, he constantly praised him in his ancient history lectures. Philip is repeatedly considered an "unquestionably uncommon and extraordinary man" due to the decisive part he played in creating a real Macedonian state which resulted from the union of several peoples into the same nation (Lecture 69); one would not be mistaken to suggest that Niebuhr was thinking of the role he hoped to see the kingdom of Prussia play both in the present and the future. A little further (Lecture 72), Niebuhr is able to draw a parallel with Demosthenes, admiring him without contradiction and comparing him to a man heroically struggling against fate. The demoralization of the Greek city states had taken root at the end of the Peloponnesian War and materialized with clashes between city states and violent internal revolutions: "Athens was in a state of indolence and weariness until Demosthenes appeared. . . . The condition of Athens had been in a manner jejune, though with much more elegance than that of Germany during the period from the thirty years' war until the middle of the eighteenth century" (trans. Schmitz, 2:387).

No other Athenian political figure can be compared to Demosthenes, not even Lycurgus. He can also not be compared to Phocion, who accepted the principle of Macedonian domination. Niebuhr explains that Demosthenes's aversion for Phocion "is intelligible to those who have observed the conduct of men at the time of the confederacy of the Rhine, among them some (whom I have known) were very far to have been dishonest, but who were incapable of any enthusiasm, sacrifice and confidence, and who imagined that misery did not really consist in being enslaved by a foreign ruler, but in the evils which follow the train of war and in personal sufferings.... Phocion belongs to that class of people, to whom in modern times no honest man would erect a monument." Niebuhr concludes even more emphatically by depicting himself as a young Athenian forced to choose sides: "From my early youth, I have felt a healthy aversion to Phocion; and this aversion in the course of years has only increased.... I should have joined Demosthenes unconditionally. (*Vorträge*, 2:446–447 = *Lectures*, 2:424–425)

By praising Philip and Demosthenes in the same breath, the politically committed historian could speak highly of two statesmen who had admittedly faced off in antiquity but to whose modern avatars he gave complementary roles. Now free of any analogy with Napoleon but taking on the garb of the king of Prussia, Philip is primarily concerned with the unification of Macedon (Prussia) and Greece (the German states); as for the modern Demosthenes (who could be Niebuhr himself), he is a monument to resistance against the enemy (namely, the French) and at variance with those who played a political game similar to Phocion's (the shameful collaboration with the enemy); while an implacable adversary of the Macedonian Philip, Niebuhr's Demosthenes was thus an ally to the German Philip in spirit.

Due to his focus on European and German issues and his radical hostility to anything relating to the "Orient," Niebuhr was infinitely less prone to admire Alexander, who had adopted oriental customs and made Greece Persian rather than making the Orient Greek.[23] In fact, the only thing he admired about the Macedonian conqueror was that he was the first European to enslave Asia to Europe (Lecture 74). As for the rest, Niebuhr was far more guarded, including in the comparison he made with Philip, which followed an approach well known since antiquity and, in Europe, the early seventeenth century:[24] if Alexander was more cultivated than his father and boasted higher moral qualities (though his proven drunkenness tarnishes the picture), it was because Philip, who "had spent his youth in a half-barbarian court," summoned Aristotle to educate his son. Additionally, Philip forged the military instruments (armies and generals) that allowed Alexander to carry his conquests to victory.

Of course, Niebuhr does recognize and admire the conqueror's fame: "Very few men have acquired such an immense celebrity, both in Asia and Europe, as Alexander; and among all the great men of history, if we except Charlemagne, and, in a less degree, Constantine, he is the only one that has become a poetical being (*zu einem poetischen Wesen*). Alexander is for the East what Charlemagne is for the West" (trans. Schmitz, 2:398–399). Yet he expresses his reservations on every page. Regarding Alexander's character, Niebuhr "unhesitatingly declare[s] that he [has] formed a very unfavourable opinion of him." Enumerating the assassinations and executions perpetrated after his accession to the throne, Niebuhr considers that Alexander displayed "a cruelty like that of the house of the Medici in the sixteenth century." Admittedly, "he was attached to Aristotle; but even lions and tigers show a certain kindness to those who have fed and nursed them in their youth, until the beast of prey awakens in them in all its ferocity!" As for his generosity toward the Persian princesses, it was hardly extraordinary.

While Niebuhr has to acknowledge Alexander's gifts as a strategist, he also repeats models created by the previous century's moralizing history: by attacking the Persian empire without plans or preparations, the Macedonian king had acted "with a spirit of an adventurer and of a gambler," staking everything on an uncertain success. He also considers that Alexander never truly took an interest in the organization of the empire because he was obsessed with a single idea: to amalgamate the Greeks and Macedonians with the Orientals. Niebuhr tirelessly denounces this policy in the most vigorous terms: "He ought to have had the Orientals constantly kept distinct, and subordinate to the Hellenic races," he proclaims, adding that the colonization was a failure in that the cities Alexander founded did not lead to the spread of Hellenism. The situations of Egypt and Asia Minor improved, but this was not the case with Phoenicia, Babylon, and the Oriental satrapies, which were devastated by the conquests, and even less so with Greece and Macedon, which became impoverished, depopulated, and degraded. Alexander's only beneficial and lasting achievements were the

founding of Alexandria and the voyages of Nearchus, which "did great service to geography."

It is difficult to avoid thinking that behind Alexander, Niebuhr is referring to Napoleon. The French emperor's name is mentioned several times in
the discussion of the Macedonian conquests. Niebuhr compares the two
leaders' exceptional strategic eye (an observation that soon became banal
in the literature). Parallels are drawn between a few episodes from the conquests: the suffering endured by Alexander's soldiers during the march
through Baluchistan is comparable to the hardships of the Grande Armée
during the retreat from Russia; at a time when diplomatic missions were
arriving from all over the world, Babylon was to Alexander what Dresden
was to Napoleon before his Russian campaign—"the scene of the most brilliant period of his life, on account of the homage which he there received."
None of these analogies are really gratifying, not even the joined triumphs
of Babylon and Dresden which, according to the author's contextual logic,
primarily herald (and not without satisfaction) the disappearance of the
conquerors and the splitting up of their empires. The same is true of the
comparison by which Niebuhr affirms that Alexander "has also become
the national hero of the Greeks, although he was as foreign to them as Napoleon was to the French."

Geography, Voyages, and Alexander's Conquests:
Translations and Original Studies

Often accompanied by staunch condemnations, the many reservations
about Alexander's adventure found in the German literature from the Enlightenment to Romanticism were also based on the objective situation of
a pluralist, divided Germany which, unlike France, the Netherlands, and
Great Britain (not to mention Spain and Portugal), had never been in a position to build a colonial empire. To a certain extent, this is what Fichte cele-
brates in his *Reden an die deutsche Nation* (1807): "Just as foreign to the
German is the freedom of the seas, which is so frequently preached in our
days—whether what is intended be real freedom or merely the power to
exclude everyone else from it. Throughout the course of centuries, while
all other nations were in rivalry, the German showed little desire to participate in this freedom to any great extent, and he will never do so."[25] He con-

tinues that Germany has all the intellectual and material resources to do without these alleged advantages; as for what is "the only true advantage that world-trade brings in its train, viz. the increase in scientific knowledge of the earth and its inhabitants, [the German's] own scientific spirit will not let him lack a means of exchange." Yet Fichte remains a realist and regretfully observes that to satisfy their own needs, the Germans nonetheless had an "indirect participation in the booty of other worlds . . . [and had] drawn profit from the sweat and blood of a poor slave across the seas."

As the product of a peculiar political and ideological context, Fichte's insistence on the specific way (*Sonderweg*) of German history and science should not be allowed to create misleading illusions. German scholars did not remain entrenched in their national restraints. Many also took a lively interest in the history of navigation and commerce from the perspective of an overall history of Europe's relations with Asian countries and populations; they contributed significantly to establishing "the great map of the world."[26] In doing so, they included reflections and discussions on Alexander's conquest considered as a precursory segment of this history. As an introduction to the idea, recall what Arnold Heeren wrote in his *Ideen zur die Politik, den Verkehr und den Handel der vornehmsten Völker der alten Welt* (*Historical Researches into the Politics, Intercourse and Trade of the Principal Nations of Antiquity*) in 1793, manifesting a kind of national pride: "Never has the knowledge of the globe and its inhabitants been so generally studied; and never has a people been so zealous in searching for everything that could relate to it as ours is in the present day" (*Idées sur les relations* [French trans.], 1[1800]:ix).

Among the sedentary scholars, Matthias Sprengel (1746–1803) is a case in point of Heeren's observation. A former student of Schlözer in Göttingen, he was a "professor of history" at the University of Halle in 1783 when he published the initial version of his history of geographic discoveries, an eloquent example of German erudition's investment in extra-European worlds. He took a particular interest in the history of British establishments in India, including in the sense of what we call "immediate history" (in his 1786 *Geschichte der Maratten* [*History of the Marathas*]). He also spoke out against the East India Company's excesses. In the heavily revised 1792 version, Sprengel, who had read Schmidt (1765), Sainte-Croix (1775), and Rennell (1788) and admired Robertson and Heeren, devoted a specific discussion to Alexander, who "opened a great part of the Asian territories on which we only disposed of fragmentary information that was for the most part fabulous"—the author is referring to the countries of the Iranian plateau, Central Asia, and the Indus Valley (pp. 84–92).[27] The same year (1792), the German edition of Robertson's *Historical Disquisition* was published in a translation by Georg Forster (1754–1794), who was both a son-in-law to Heyne and a brother-in-law to Sprengel. Lacking a university position worthy of his reputation (he was the librarian at Mainz), Forster published a great number of reviews in the journal edited by his father-in-law in Göttingen. A cosmopolitan spirit who maintained close ties with England (his forbears had left Yorkshire to settle in Prussia in 1642) and was a fervent partisan of revolutionary ideas from Paris, Forster was focused on the open sea. He had sailed on Cook's second voyage with his father Johann Reinhold Forster, who played an important part in his education and had himself extensively discussed Robertson's *History of America*. In a way, the two Forsters were forerunners of the more brilliant W. von Humboldt, who combined his travel experience with reflections on the awakening of "savages" to civilization under the influence of traditions inherited by the Europeans from Greece and Rome. Von Humboldt would also later develop highly favorable views on Alexander the Great's civilizing enterprises.[28]

Father and son were among the multitude of translators who played such an important part as cultural intermediaries between Scottish and English authors and the German public.[29] Following on from and/or in parallel with his father, Georg frequently took a critical approach to the question of British colonial policy in India. As he assured in his translator's preface, he was very careful to accurately translate Robertson's thought into German, aided in this by his perfect English. While he bitterly regretted (p. ix) that Robertson did not take into account important German publications, despite their contribution "to the history of commercial exchanges between the inhabitants of various parts of the world" (he explicitly deplores the lack of references to Sprengel's 1783 book), Georg remained a great admirer of the *Historical Disquisition* and more generally of Scottish historiography of the Enlightenment. He did not hide this fact in the introduction to his translation or in his review of the original in *Göttingische Anzeigen* in 1791.[30] Heyne had also expressed his great esteem for Robertson's volume.[31]

Heyne also praised Vincent's *Voyage of Nearchus*. Shortly after receiving the book in Göttingen, he sent its author a courteous letter written in Latin and dated May 30, 1797; he offered his congratulations, wished Vincent as much success in his country (*inter populares tuos*) as he had received abroad (*inter extraneos*), and included with the letter a very favorable review (*encomium*) published on April 29 of the same year in *Gottingische Anzeigen* (marginal note).[32] In the second edition of his *Voyage* (1807, p. xxiii), Vincent would congratulate himself on the "favourable report of Professor Heyne in the *Gottingen Journal*." In fact, the anonymous review was not by Heyne but by Arnold Heeren.[33] Vincent would also express his satisfaction at the praise he received from Friedrich Schmieder. In his bilingual edition (Greek, Latin) of Arrian's *Indica* (1798), Schmieder stated his admiration for the *Voyage* (pp. iii–xiii; primarily paraphrased). The same volume featured Latin translations of Dodwell's dissertation and Vincent's refutation (pp. 233–264), which were included to provide the reader with all the pertinent information, though Schmieder did not hide that he agreed with Vincent (and Sainte-Croix). In 1696, Dodwell had called into question the authenticity of Nearchus's memoirs used by Arrian. Vincent, on the contrary, showed throughout his book (1797) that Nearchus's memoirs were an excellent firsthand account. Schmieder referred to the *Voyage* as "a very famous book of which no one in Germany is unaware" and noted that a translation had been announced in public catalogs (*in indicibus publicis*). Vincent also mentioned a possible translation: in an unpublished handwritten note in the volume now in the Bibliothèque Nationale collection, he mentions that the corrections he had written into the copy given to Billecocq in December 1800 were also sent to his German translator, Dr. Simon of Lüneburg.

The story does not end there. According to the *Intelligenzblatt der Allgemeine Literatur-Zeitung* dated March 1, 1797, Johann Reinhold Forster had received a copy of the *Voyage* from the author and had "begun translating it as a continuation of and counterpart to Dr. Robertson's *Alten Indien*, which had been translated by his memorable son" [Georg Forster, who had died on January 10, 1794] (p. 236). The paper added that a "bookseller well known in Germany will publish it. It has been announced to prevent any competition (*zur Verhütung der Concurrenz*)." On June 17 of the same year, the *Intelligenzblatt* announced the imminent publication of a "German translation of this very important and interesting book" by a bookseller in Magdeburg (*der Keilschen Buchhandlung*) (p. 663). One must therefore assume that Johann Reinhold Forster had been contacted by this bookseller to translate Vincent's book, but that the project was dashed by his death on December 9, 1798. This interpretation is all the more probable given that in his preface dated December 16, 1797, Schmieder, scholarly commenter on Arrian and professor at the Magdeburg Gymnasium Lutheranum, had told his readers about an upcoming German translation and thanked Johann Reinhold Forster for having liberally offered his advice and opinion, as well as access to his library in Magdeburg (p. xiv). He added that, in his opinion, "it was entirely to Germany's credit (*laus est Germaniae*)" to have eminent scholars in this field while simultaneously encouraging translations, which allowed these scholars to see "all the knowledge from all over the world (*ex universo orbe*) converge in Germany" and to take advantage of it (pp. xi–xii).

For reasons unknown to us, Dr. Simon—the second translator mentioned by Vincent in December 1800 (working for "the competition"?)—was manifestly not any more successful.[34] However, the translator Gabriel Gottfried Bredow, a well-known specialist in antiquity and the author of a manual on ancient history widely distributed in Germany, did publish a partial German version of the first volume (1800) of the *Periplus of the Erythrean Sea*,[35] accompanied by an equally partial translation of Rennell's *Herodotus* (1800), and a full translation of Gosselin's *Géographie des Grecs* (1790). This is yet more evidence of German scholars' and the general public's extraordinary appetite for books about travel, geography, and commerce from antiquity to the contemporary period.

Alexander the Great in Heeren and Schlosser

Voyages of discovery, historical and economic geography, commerce and colonization in antiquity and the modern and contemporary periods, and the organization of states—in short, everything the Göttingen School called *Staatistik*—were at the heart of the research and thought of one of the most prolific but also most forgotten historians of his generation, Arnold Heeren.[36] Born in 1760, he studied in Göttingen from 1779 to 1784, where he was primarily influenced by Christian Gottlob Heyne, to the point that he became Heyne's friend, son-in-law, and, to top it all off, his first biographer. He led his entire university career in Göttingen, where most of his courses were on ancient geography and commerce.

Heeren is one of the many champions of peace and its pacific activities, first among which he ranked commerce. This is the recurrent theme in the introduction to the first edition (1793) of the major book Heeren would constantly revise until 1828.[37] He intends to serve as a positive alternative to all those who devote their energy to describing battles and conquerors: "We are told about peoples' wars and expeditions, but rarely do we learn of the ideas that made them act and the goal they wanted to attain." He praises the progressive role of communications and commercial relations, "one of the surest ways for the communication of ideas and the Enlightenment," and ends with an invocation both powerful and emphatic: "May the warrior peoples that were at the forefront [of the great stage of universal history] move away to make room for those more modest ones who stand in the distance! May the march of the peaceful caravans hide from us the spectacle of devastating armies, and the nascent walls of the new colonies shield us from the sad sight of ransacked cities!" (*Idées sur les relations,* 1:7). While he glorifies the role played by trading peoples in world history, Heeren also chooses to resolutely support a positive view of Alexander's conquests. In the same introduction, he points out that one of the major revolutions was due to Alexander, who was inhabited "by the passion for peaceful arts, which so singularly distinguishes him."

In keeping with the project set forth in his preface to the *Ideen* (to study "the period previous to Alexander the Great"), Heeren does not deal with the Macedonian conquest other than where it touches on the history of the people of Asia (Phoenicians, Egyptians, Persians, Indians). The first volume of this overview published in 1793 had been preceded by erudite studies on the history of commerce between India and the Persian Gulf, which were by necessity more directly concerned with the history of Alexander. In 1791, Heeren presented and published two papers to the Academy of Göttingen on the Greeks' potential knowledge of India and their commerce there. Following Montesquieu and Robertson, the papers developed an interpretation of the major transformations brought by an Alexander who established mutual communication between his peoples and destroyed the dams the Persians had built on the Tigris and Euphrates, thus reopening the way to sea and river exchanges between the Persian Gulf and Babylonia.[38] The first part of the study opened with a laudatory reference to Robertson's *Historical Disquisition,* which Heeren would review at length the following year (1792) in the journal he edited; his review did not fail to underline that, though totally independent from one another, he and Robertson had presented nearly identical ideas in the *Ideen* and *Historical Disquisition* respectively—the former was then still unpublished, but its premises had been discussed in his university courses.[39]

Early in 1797, his father-in-law asked him to review *The Voyage of Nearchus,* which had been sent to him by the author. His review in the April 1797 issue of the *Göttingische Anzeigen* was certainly laudatory, but it was scattered with reservations, his own work on the subject making him competitive with the dean of Westminster. In order to establish that he had formed his own opinion before even reading *The Voyage of Nearchus,* he made certain to refer to a study of Nearchus's seafaring that he had presented before the Göttingen Academy in September 1796 and which was then waiting to go to press.[40] This allowed him to observe that he shared Vincent's view of an Alexander driven by grandiose political and commercial plans. He stated that he too unequivocally rejected "the declamations of modern historians hostile to the Macedonian king," who was actually a "rebuilder" (*Wiederaufbauer*) and a "genius" (p. 667). In his *Handbuch der Geschichte des Alterthums* (*Manual of Ancient History*), Heeren also referred to Vincent's book, introducing it as having the "most learned researches and illustrated with excellent charts."[41] Yet he did not cite Vincent much in his *Ideen,* including in the more recent editions; he prefers to refer the reader to his own study on Nearchus, published in 1799.[42] Clearly, he considered that he enjoyed a chronological priority over Vincent, which in his mind entailed scientific precedence. In Heeren (as in Forster, Robertson's translator), one senses a certain irritation with British authors' unfamiliarity with German publications. The only original contribution with which Heeren credits a British historian is that Vincent had access to the East India Company's archives (*die Archive der Ostindischen Compagnie*) and Dalrymple's papers and maps and "was therefore able to make a comparison between the Macedonians' relations and those of the British navigators" (pp. 669–670). A few years later, Heeren also had an opportunity to comment on Vincent's other book, *The Periplus of the Erythrean Sea.*[43]

Despite the sharp criticism it received from Barthold Georg Niebuhr, *Ideen* became in its various editions one of the most well-known books in Europe and the United States in the first half of the nineteenth century; its translations in French, English, and Dutch were greeted with occasionally enthusiastic reviews.[44] It was heavily referenced in works published from 1840 to 1860, including textbooks.[45] The same was true of his *Handbuch,* which was first published in 1799 and constantly reprinted until 1828, with corrections and additions, then translated into French, English, and Italian.[46] The volume's priorities were clearly indicated in its extended title: *Particularly with Regard to the Constitutions, the Commerce and the Colonies of the States of Antiquity.* Of the sources he used, Heeren singles out for praise the *Examen critique,* which he describes as the "principal work on the history of Alexander, and important in more respects than one," adding that it "contains more than the title implies, though [it is] by no means a strictly impartial estimate of that prince's character" (p. 173). Indeed, the author aims to popularize the positive image that was then dominant (in Europe, if not in Germany). It had been passed on from Montesquieu and his British epigones and Heeren had himself contributed to reinforcing it through his own research: "The reign of Alexander the Great, in the eyes of the historical inquirer, derives its great interest, not only from the extent, but from the permanence of the revolution which he effected in the world. To appreciate properly the character of this prince, who died just as he was about to carry his mighty projects into execution, is no easy task; but it is totally repugnant to common sense to suppose that the pupil of Aristotle was nothing more than a wild and reckless conqueror, unguided by any plan.... The union of the east and the west was to be brought about by the amalgamation of the dominant races by intermarriages, by education, and, more than all, by the ties of commerce, the importance of which much ruder conquerors, in Asia itself, soon learnt to appreciate" (pp. 173, 177). Heeren stated that he particularly admired Alexander's policy on the elites of vanquished countries, and saw it as the best proof of his genius.

Friedrich Christoph Schlosser (1776–1861), who was twenty years Heeren's junior and a fellow former student at Göttingen (in theology), cannot be considered a scholar of the caliber of Wolf, Niebuhr, Boeckh, and Droysen. He published many works of broad popularization, which were nonetheless well informed and made him one of the most widely read authors both in Germany and abroad. Alexander the Great is very present in volumes 2 and 3 of his history of antiquity (*Universalhistorische Übersicht der Geschichte der alten Welt und ihrer Kultur*), which were published in 1826 and translated into French in 1828. According to his French translator Marie-Philippe-Aimé de Golbéry's amiable pronouncement, "Mr. Schlosser's universal history is more suitable than any other work to judge of the state of the historical sciences in Germany because it is entirely composed of results. There is nothing the author has not read, nothing of which he has not made good use" (*Histoire universelle de l'Antiquité,* 1:vi): this was an elegant way of describing an intelligent compilation. Yet Schlosser's undertaking goes beyond mere passive quotations; he has a particular predilection for commenting on Sainte-Croix's *Examen critique,* to the point that one gets the impression it never strayed from his writing desk; he has acquainted himself with the accounts of British travelers and makes full use of them; he knows the sources and occasionally contributes perspectives either original in content or in the way they are articulated, some of which would later be borrowed by Droysen.[47] It appears that he was the first to repeatedly and lucidly use a previously little-known text, the *Economics* by the Pseudo-Aristotle (*Histoire universelle,* III:13–18), the date and content of which had been commented upon by Niebuhr in 1812. In doing so, he provided a most interesting analysis of the empire's financial administration. Schlosser is among the few authors cited (late) by Droysen, who referred to him as "actually a historian of great style." Yet this remark is not necessarily laudatory, nor is the explicit comparison to Gillies, given that Droysen had reservations about the British historian.[48]

Schlosser's book provides a relatively flat description of the conquest (2:405–485) and, more significantly, a very interesting section in volume 3 (pp. 1–46) entitled "Alexander in Relation to His Century," which presents a synthetic account of the ways and means by which Alexander organized and administered his empire. The image of Alexander on which it sheds light is close to the one found in Heeren: a king "who personally ran the administration of his vast empire and undertook the work required to return Assyria and Babylon to their former splendor and to make communications by river and canal more active than ever before" (2:484) and "to bring to life the agriculture of those regions [Bactria-Sogdia]" (3:19). Schlosser disagrees with those who "claimed that Alexander's conquests spread luxury and idleness" because "the arts could only spread through greater luxury and a more magnificent court" (3:1, 26); this was an empirical but noteworthy contribution to the discussion of luxury that had taken place throughout the eighteenth century and been revived in Germany in 1781 by a competition held by the Academy of Hesse-Kassel and won by an anthropologist-philosopher from Göttingen, Christoph Meiners (1747–1810).[49] The book also includes the predictable passage on geographic discoveries, since "Alexander had a general staff absolutely in keeping with our ideas, and this general staff consisted of a geography section and another section in charge of maps, measurements, and encampments" (3:31).

Geography and the History of Alexander at the University of Berlin (1820–1833)

In closing, let us return to the recently founded University of Berlin. In 1820, Carl Ritter (1779–1859) was appointed to its newly created chair in geography. Johann Gustav Droysen, then barely twenty, was among those who attended Ritter's seminars in the winter semester of 1827 and the summer semester of 1828.[50] Here, Ritter presented his research and reflections on ancient geography and on the ethnography and geography of Asia. Released in book form after his death, as was the custom, under the title *Geschichte der Erdkunde und der Entdeckungen* (*History of Geography and Discoveries*), the professor's lectures include a section solely devoted to Alexander the Great and to the opening of the Oriental world, specifically India (pp. 65–74); he quotes Sainte-Croix and Vincent's *Periplus* (in Bredow's translation). The lectures from after 1833 include Ritter's praise for Droysen's history of Alexander, in which Ritter applauds his ability (partially acquired in his own classes) to analyze the geography of Alexander's campaigns. Droysen was also considered an excellent specialist in historical geography by Alexander von Humboldt, Carl Ritter's mentor.

The young scholar's profound interest in this discipline can be seen in the many references to travelers' accounts and geographers' studies in the footnotes to his *Geschichte Alexanders des Großen* (1833). In fact, one of his first scholarly publications was the review in March 1833 (nine months before his own book was issued) of a geographic commentary of Arrian published by the Dutch researcher P. O. Van der Chys in 1828. From the outset, he affirms that "ancient geography does not really have any task more difficult and more interesting than that of explaining the campaigns and plans of conquest of Alexander the Great" since "the history of Alexander, more than that of any other conqueror, goes hand in hand with geography. . . . The nature of countries and peoples was his guide (*Die Natur der Länder und Völker war seine Führerin*)."[51] While he acknowledges that Van der Chuys could not have had access to it, he refers to a study on Alexander's campaign in the Punjab presented by his mentor Ritter at the Berlin Academy on June 18, 1829.[52] Van der Chys also could not have known about the book the Norwegian-born, Bonn-based scholar of Indian studies Christian Lassen (1800–1876) had just devoted to Punjab (*Pentapotamia indica*). Lassen used Greco-Roman sources on Alexander's expedition in Punjab in parallel with Sanskrit and Arabic sources, as well as reflections and commentaries on the expedition by modern historians and geographers (Rennell, Heeren, Vincent, Sainte-Croix, etc.).[53]

I will add that another professor at the University of Berlin, the famous philosopher Georg Wilhelm Friedrich Hegel (who died in 1831 and whose seminars Droysen attended in 1827–1829) also liked to refer to the image of the great discoverer, who was "the first to open the Oriental world to Europeans," as well as the image of the ruler passionate about sciences and "the most generous protector of the arts";[54] these representations had formed very early and still haunted the European historical and geographical literature at the time that Hegel was preparing and delivering his lectures.

IV

The Sense of History

Chapter 9

After Alexander?

The "Age of Alexander"

While supporters of the diverse and conflicting theories on the Macedonian conquest clung to their individual convictions, all those in the field had serious doubts about the recognized, clearly defined existence of a specific historical period said to begin with the Macedonian king's conquests and included in the *longue durée*.

Scholars will recall Voltaire's declaration in the introduction to his *Siècle de Louis XIV*. Driven by a methodical concern to avoid basing history on a mere accumulation of "facts," and on the contrary to "set before posterity . . . the spirit of mankind," Voltaire considers that "[whosoever] thinks, or, what is still more rare, whosoever has taste, will find but four ages in the history of the world," which stand out without question and range from antiquity to the era that came before his own generation: "These four happy ages are those in which the arts were carried to perfection, and which, by serving as the era of the greatness of the human mind, are examples for posterity. The first of these ages to which true glory is annexed is that of Philip and Alexander. . . . The second age is that of Cæsar and Augustus. . . . The third is that which followed the taking of Constantinople by Mahomet II. . . . Lastly, the fourth age is that known by the name of the age of Louis XIV, and is perhaps that which approaches the nearest to perfection of all the four" (*Age of Lewis XIV,* intro.).[1]

As can be seen, the first of the great ages identified by Voltaire is not strictly speaking the "age of Alexander." The son is associated with the father and the names of the artists and thinkers mentioned as the age's

principal treasures primarily refer to the period before Alexander and symbolized by great figures: "Pericles, Demosthenes, Aristotle, Plato, Apelles,
Phidias, and Praxiteles; and this honor has been confined within the limits
of ancient Greece." With the exception of the painter Apelles and the philosopher Aristotle (who both worked by Alexander's side and even at his service),
the individuals cited refer to what we call the "classical" Greek world, that of
the triumphant or dying Greek city state, between Pericles and Demosthenes.
According to this definition, Alexander closes the age that bears his and his
father's name rather than inaugurating one defined by original, specific
characteristics. The next part of Voltaire's proposal leaves no doubt as to his
position: "The rest of the known world was then in a state of barbarism." We
shall soon see that Voltaire further elaborated on these reflections in his
La Bible enfin expliquée (1776), but that his contemporaries did not take these
developments into account.[2]

In referring to Voltaire, the Chevalier de Jaucourt provides some clarifications of his own. He also identifies four ages "that are primarily called the
four famous ages, whose productions were admired by posterity." With the
precision of a notary, he specifies that "the word 'age' is here understood in a
vague manner to mean a span of 60 to 80 years, more or less." The first of
these ages, which he studiously avoids calling the age of Alexander, "began
ten years before the reign of Philip, Alexander the Great's father." Though
Jaucourt does not indicate when it ended, the reader is led to believe it includes the reign of Alexander but does not go beyond it.[3] Jaucourt had been
even clearer in his "Greeks" entry: Alexander's reign brings to a close "the
third age of Greece" or "age of Alexander" in which "one must admire the
number of great men" in every field: this is followed by a nonexhaustive list
of twenty-five figures classified by category (poets, orators, philosophers,
historians), "who flourished in the third age of Greece, an incomparable age
that made this nation's glory fly to the end of the world, and will carry it to
the end of time." Jaucourt continues with the "fourth age of Greece," characterized by the empire's long-expected breakup.[4]

Linguet's statements are of the same tenor.[5] If Linguet decided to consider history by studying the "age of Alexander," it is because he chose to
focus on the "sciences and letters" and that from this perspective Alexander's reign "is in the study of Antiquity the fixed point from which one can
begin to measure the progress of the human spirit." As with his model Voltaire, the term "age" is extendable in Linguet. It is in accord with the chrono-

logical term defined by Jaucourt, as we can see when Linguet notes that "for sixty years, Greece had been populated with all types of great men who contributed to the glory of their homeland." The origins of this "age" even extend further back in time, to the aftermath of the Greco-Persian Wars, which "flooded Greece with gold and silver [that] facilitated the perfection of the arts." For this very reason, Linguet states that "this illustrious age could have been designated by other names." If he chose the title-designation known to us, it was because "it was especially in the time of Alexander that its fruits became more perceptible. . . . We can [therefore] see the glory days of Greece as belonging to his age."

Unlike Voltaire, Linguet not only refers to the Greek past for his definitions, he includes Alexander's achievements in Asia and their consequences in Europe. He presents these changes in grandiose phrases: "Then half the globe was witness to a prodigious revolution. . . . The Age of Alexander is therefore the first interesting period in the history of the human spirit." To ensure "the happiness of his new subjects," Alexander relied on the Greeks, "an enlightened people . . . [who sought] to dispel ignorance through their conquests. Their skill successfully assisted this Prince's great views." Thus Alexander was able "to provide the defeated with the arts they did not know, [and] his conquests and his taste for the arts having made Asia and nations heretofore disgraced by the name of 'barbarian' share in the knowledge held in Greece, it was thought necessary to attribute the honor of this revolution to him."

The reader would like to find proof and illustration of the author's introductory statements in the body of the text. But neither chapters 17–24 (1762) nor books 3–4 (1769) satisfy the curiosity so cleverly aroused by Linguet. He never develops his intuitive statement about "the rapid change" caused by the transfer of "Susa and Persepolis's riches" to Europe.[6] The fact that he constantly denounced "external commerce" for developing a luxury in no way "necessary to mankind's subsistence" but potentially harmful to society and certainly destructive to "the so-called savages" may explain why he was not inclined to analyze the commercial transformations attributed to the conquest by some of his illustrious predecessors.[7] In any case, this was not the most important thing in his eyes: "If Alexander enlightened [mankind]," he stated, "it was by encouraging, by magnificently rewarding, those who worked to provide [man] with Enlightenment; and this is the kind of glory that suffices for kings. The Marcus Aureliuses and Fredericks are rare in the history of the world." With this statement, Linguet intends to reject Plutarch's image of a conqueror-philosopher coming to spread Greek laws and mores in Asia[8]—a surprising stance for an author who claimed to be convinced of the beneficial effects that the conquest had on "nations heretofore disgraced by the name of 'barbarian.'" In reducing the figure of Alexander to a patron of existing glory, Linguet enumerates the Greek artists and creators, but primarily focuses on Homer and the artists and writers of the classical era; he lists Pythagoras, Thales, Phidias, Aeschylus, Aristophanes, Plato, Socrates, Herodotus, Thucydides, Xenophon, etc. The contemporaries of Alexander mentioned by Linguet include Aristotle, Diogenes, and Apelles. Yet the author never refers to the prodigious new period that he claims was started by the Macedonian conquest, to the point that it vanishes behind the ghost of an "age of Alexander" reduced to shining in the refracted glory of classical Greece. Linguet also does not explain how "Alexander's new subjects" were able to enjoy "the arts they did not know" or how these nations were able to "share in the knowledge held in Greece" once they were "debarbarized" (as we would call it).

Forty years later, Moutonnet de Clairfons (1740–1813)[9] carried the contradiction through to its conclusion. After recalling the existence of "four brilliant eras for the Sciences, Arts, and Letters," he evokes the age of Alexander by offering a very quick overview of Greek literature since Homer and the Archaic period in the form of a dry enumeration. Naturally, he comes to question the legitimacy of the designation: "According to this so varied nomenclature, one clearly sees that the age of Alexander cannot be called Greece's golden age. . . . I admit that it was a brilliant period, but it cannot exclusively be called the golden age. Homer alone should prevent it. Indeed, how can we call a golden age one that did not bring forth the most elevated and surprising genius?" (p. 7). Homer's incomparable brilliance, which was already dazzling in classical Greece and even at the court of Alexander, rendered any idea of artistic innovation and cultural renewal obsolete, including in the new states of Asia.

Greek History and the History of Alexander

The difficulty of conceiving a new historical periodization spared no one. It was most clearly expressed by those who, in praising the greatness of

Athens and the momentum of freedom, passed harsh judgment on Alexander and the Macedonian conquests and were tempted to answer in the negative to the question they asked of themselves but did not always formulate: "Is Alexander part of the history of Ancient Greece?" Or even: "Should he be considered a part of Greek history?"

In 1739, in the preface to volume 2 of his *Grecian History,* Temple Stanyan explained that he was ending his narrative with the defeat of Athens and the death of Philip not only because others had already given detailed accounts of the history of Alexander, but also and especially because, in his opinion, "the affairs of Alexander are not, strictly speaking, to be looked upon as a continuation of the Grecian story, since they relate almost entirely to Macedonia and Persia. . . . The Grecians still subsisted, but in so low and lifeless condition that from the time of Alexander's captains . . . there were very few among them, who were distinguished for arms and counsels, and not many for Arts and Learning."[10]

A century later, the British historian George Grote (1794–1871) also asked himself whether he should include the history of Alexander in the Greek history he had begun conceiving and organizing in the early 1820s and was now in the process of writing.[11] The question was largely rhetorical, given that Grote devotes three dense chapters and close to three hundred pages to the conquest. Yet the reader quickly understands what the author means. From the beginning, one reads that "the Asiatic conquests of Alexander do not belong directly and literally to the province of an historian of Greece" (12:67–71). According to the author, this assessment is particularly true of the last seven years of the campaign, which "can hardly be regarded as included within the range of this subject" (12:243–244). But in a more general manner, Grote follows Niebuhr (whom he quotes several times) in considering that the status of the Greeks in Alexander's Macedonian army was comparable to that of the contingents of the Confederation of the Rhine in Napoleon's 1812 army (12:69–70). In other words, Alexander's enterprise was not truly a Greek one. It is therefore easy to understand that Grote deals with the affairs of Greece during the Asian expedition in a separate chapter (94) in order to clearly show that the two histories follow parallel but separate courses. While he recognizes that the expedition had "real consequences beneficial for humanity,—a great increase of communication, extension of commercial dealing and enlarged facilities for the acquisition of geographical knowledge" (12:368), he denies that it provided the impetus for a Hellenization of the Orient; on the contrary, it caused a form of Orientalization of Greece. Finally, he accepts the idea that Alexander's appearance "forms a sort of historical epoch," but only from the perspective of the protagonist's personality and military and strategic abilities, which made him a general "above the level of his contemporaries" (12:71–72). In other words, the man had exceptional talents, but the overall results of his conquests were far from positive, particularly in terms of purely Greek interests.

Admittedly, Grote was responding to and contesting the views Johann Gustav Droysen had presented in his successive works of 1833, 1836, and 1843. But the positions he expresses also fit into a line of thought purely his own, which other historians of the second half of the eighteenth century and the early nineteenth century set out and/or heralded in their own ways.[12]

For an example of Alexander's detractors, I will consider John Gast and his *History of Greece* (1782), which ended with the Roman conquest. As his previous book *Rudiments* (1753) had already promised, this new volume focused on the ideas of decadence and decline. As a proponent of providential history, Gast considers that the conquests had harmful effects on Greece and Macedonia; the history of the region was now marked "by depopulation, a disputed throne, and repeated inroads of enemies"; as for Greece in the century that followed Alexander's adventure, it was beset by "intestine divisions, and a general decay of virtue, [which] reduced [it] to a condition the most contemptible."[13] Therefore, while Alexander is included in Greek history, the fourth period he opens (and which the author defines as 124 years long) is the negation of all the values that had led to the greatness of Greece in the first three periods (though the third period, which lasted 114 years, had already seen the appearance of "ostentation, luxury and insolence"). In his inspiration and approach, Gast is a direct heir to Rollin, who emphasized the extent of the disasters caused by Alexander, a ruler responsible for the ruin of his country, while his successors opened a period that proved even worse.

Niebuhr, who had nothing but antipathy for Alexander, later introduced a preliminary reflection on "the late period of Greek history," meaning the history after the defeat of the Greeks by Philip of Macedon at Chaeronea in 338 BC. He asks if "the Greeks are at all worthy of being made the object of serious historical studies." The answer is decisively positive: "Their national history still presents much that is attractive, and deserves to be known, and Greece still continued to manifest herself in the characters of individual men. They still remained a people that was great even in its fallen state, and radiant, with the reflex of lofty genius of the extraordinary men who adorn its earlier history."[14] Niebuhr's word choice clearly indicates that the Greece of the so-called late periods primarily lived on through the memory of a glorious past, the course of which was interrupted by the Macedonian enterprises.

There were also historians who looked positively on the Macedonian conquest but asked themselves whether it should be included in Greek history, and if so, how they could justify that choice. I will look at two examples, Pierre-Charles Levesque and Désiré-Raoul Rochette, whose views on Alexander's policy were discussed earlier.[15] Levesque opens his section on the conquest by providing his readers an explanation for its inclusion: "Alexander's fame invites us to give an account of his exploits more expansive than it should be in a history of Greece; they are partly foreign to it, but they are precious, because they belong to the history of the world."[16] A few years later (1815), Rochette followed suit in his book on the colonies, explaining that he would end "the *Histoire des colonies grecques* with the Battle of Chaeronea, a fatal period during which Greece lost its freedom and all the rights that went with it." Yet he also aims to deal with the colonies founded by Alexander and his successors. This apparent contradiction explains his awkward position in the opening to book 7, the last in the volume, which he had not originally intended to devote to the colonies. In his eyes, this is "the most difficult, thorny part." Indeed, he has to introduce "establishments erected by the hands of despotism, in imitation of these ancient colonies, in countries until then foreign or even unknown to the Greeks, most of which could not be considered real colonies." Rochette's pompous justification is not so different from the one offered by Levesque: the enlargement of the world and the unprecedented development of commerce under Alexander mean that a work on the colonies cannot exclude the period that began with the Macedonian conquest—which Rochette also refers to as "the age of Alexander."[17] This development allowed him to take a firm stance in the ongoing dispute between the partisans of Montesquieu and those of Sainte-Croix.

The End of History?

Montesquieu's partisans (who included Rochette) were faced with the apparently insurmountable difficulty of explaining the empire's rapid breakup when they had all provided such richly detailed accounts of the intelligence and effectiveness of a policy Alexander conceived for the long term. Montesquieu had not left them many keys to understand and explain a historical phase that was outside the compass of books 9 and 10 of *The Spirit of the Laws*. In following the logic of his argument, Montesquieu did emphasize the stunning successes of the Persian policy implemented by Alexander, a conqueror "mourned by all the peoples he subjected" and who "cemented all the parts of this new empire so well that after his death . . . none of the Persian provinces rebelled" (10.14). It was by using this idea as a foundation that William Robertson created his image of an empire victoriously surviving the death of its founder, particularly in India. Not only did the Scottish historian go beyond what Montesquieu wrote, but he ignored the stark contrast expressed in *The Spirit of the Laws* with "trouble and confusion of the most horrible civil wars, after the Greeks had annihilated themselves." While Montesquieu said no more than that, one of his *Pensées* (no. 99) introduced a very explicit reflection on the fragility of the imperial construction: "This great machine, deprived of its intelligence, came apart" because it was only "kept faithful" by the king's charisma.

An opponent of Montesquieu's Alexander like Mably would not find it difficult to reply that the aftermath of the conquest was absolutely in keeping with an insane venture: "Conquests so rapid, expansive, and disproportionate to the Macedonian forces could not be maintained," particularly since "Alexander had not had time to pass laws because he was always in a rush to make new conquests." As for the Persians' reaction to Alexander's death, there was no cause to be surprised or pleased about it, given that "the Persians were accustomed to grovel under despotism and were made to be slaves." Mably legitimized his conclusion by drawing on the authority of a "famous politician," namely Machiavelli, who had entitled the fourth chapter of *The Prince*, "Why the Kingdom of Darius, Conquered by Alexander, Did Not Rebel against His Successors after His Death." According to Machiavelli, the answer was in the very nature of despotic government: it is difficult to take control of a kingdom, "but once it is conquered, it is very easy to maintain oneself there." Mably concluded that the Persians' alleged love for Alexander had nothing to do with the discussion: "It was the ambition of the Macedonian generals and not the indocility of the Persians that produced a succession of revolutions under Alexander's successors."[18]

While far more moderate and often in agreement with *The Spirit of the Laws,* Jaucourt had an absolute loathing for war and conquerors[19] and had no illusions about the aftermath of the conquests. Inaugurated by the death of Alexander, "the fourth age of Greece" was characterized by the empire's predictable breakup: indeed, "these states . . . were anything but solidly conquered; they had given in to the forces, the courage, the skill, or if you like the fortune of Alexander, but it was not possible for such a new & so rapidly imposed yoke to be long-lasting." Jaucourt went on to affirm that the disaster was not only due to the lack of an indisputable heir: "Had this monarch had a son able to succeed him, there is reason to believe he would not have been able to long contain so many peoples, so different in their mores, languages & religion."[20] He is manifestly trying to rank the causes of the empire's breakup by importance, pointing to structural reasons (the fragility of a heterogeneous empire) as a determining factor rather than dwelling on contextual reasons (the absence of an heir). In doing so, he expressed in simple terms an analysis shared by Montesquieu and Mably and which has bearing beyond the particular case of Alexander, namely that excessively large empires were unmanageable and were fated to collapse "under their own weight."

Isaac Iselin also subscribed to the common view of the decadence of Greece but remained convinced of the theory of humanity's progress. He judged that Alexander's conquests had positive consequences not for the city states, but in the territories of the princes and kings. He believed that the effect of the arrival of the one he called "a young hero" (*ein junger Held*) was to "unite under his sovereignty all the civilized parts of the earth, all the virtues, all the human talents of active Greece, all the treasures, all the advantages of the Orient." This combination of the hero and the wise man should have led to decisive progress: "The sciences, the arts, commerce, abundance, well-being, peace, and in their wake humanity and order, all the European and Asian peoples made happy . . . and all of that would have had happy consequences until our time. The world would have escaped the barbarian yoke of Rome, and would have been protected from the iron scepter of the North! But the hero died too young, and he was the only one who could have carried out 'such a marvelous revolution' and made good on its great hopes!" Yet despite his death, the world was changed because several of his successors inherited his courage and love of science and the arts and sowed many precious branches of admirable Greece's virtues and qualities in the territories that fell under their power.[21] One finds a comparably optimistic vision in Heeren, who considers that two of Alexander's successors, Ptolemy and Seleucus, were able like him to foster commerce and the arts in their kingdoms. Robertson was of the same opinion. While he emphasized that Alexander's death was a catastrophe, he remained convinced that thanks to Seleucus's intelligent policy it did not spell the end of harmonious relations between the Macedonians and India.[22]

Nonetheless, due to Montesquieu's omissions and their own contradictions, the position of those who admired Alexander's work was generally uncomfortable and difficult. Turning back to John Gillies's *History of Ancient Greece* (1786), we find that Gillies was an enthusiastic reader of Voltaire and Montesquieu, who (as we have seen) amply praised the Macedonian king's virtues and achievements. Yet the end of the story is infinitely darker and more discouraging. Emphasizing that the conqueror was both "unexampled and inimitable" amounts to telling the reader that Alexander was such an exceptional man that he had neither past nor future: only "his genius might have changed and improved the state of the ancient world." True, "in Egypt, the first successors of Alexander accomplished the commercial improvements planned by that prince; and the kings both of Egypt and of Syria affected, in their magnificent courts, to join the arts and elegance of Greece to the pomp and luxury of the East. But their orientation was greater than their taste; their liberal characters were effaced by the continual contact of servitude; they sunk into the softness and insignificance of hereditary despots, whose reigns are neither busy nor instructive; nor could the intrigues of women and eunuchs, or ministers equally effeminate, form a subject sufficiently interesting to succeed the memorable transactions of the Grecian republics" (2:678–680).

Gillies's rejection also extended to Greece itself, which was characterized by the decadence of the arts and thought. After the blossoming of literature, philosophy, and the fine arts "in the latter years of Alexander," the following period saw an entirely different situation because "the source of that health and vigour, from which the beauty flowed, had already begun to fail." According to Gillies, "Under the Macedonian government, Greece produced not any original genius in the serious kinds of poetry.... Soon, after the death of Alexander, painting and the kindred arts ceased.... Soon after the age of Alexander, genius disappeared; literature and the arts alike degenerated (2:683–686). Only "the science of geography" experienced lasting progress, thanks to Alexander's surveyors Beton and Diognetus, whom Gillies mentions by referring to the studies of Cassini published close to a century earlier.[23] The historian also includes Aristotle's reflections and studies in the moral sciences, presenting them with the care one would expect from such an expert on the works of the philosopher of Stagira.

Consequently, Gillies joins those who restrict the sense of the term "age of Alexander" to the era encompassing the reigns of Philip and his son and which Voltaire described as the time when "the arts of drawing, painting, sculpture, and architecture appeared in their most beautiful light." For the rest, the medium- and long-term assessment is largely negative, given that Gillies considers that the colonies founded by Alexander (which he had earlier praised) did not have the effect their founder expected: "The feeble mixture of Grecian colonization diffused through the East, was sufficient, indeed, to tinge, but too inconsiderable to alter and assimilate, the vast mass of barbarism. But as the principle of degeneracy is often stronger than that of improvement, the sloth and servility of Asia gradually crept into Greece."[24] As Gillies points out in a footnote,[25] the only lasting result was the propagation of the Greek language, at least "among the higher ranks of men," which endured until the taking of Constantinople by the Turks, "so that, from the time of Homer, it subsisted with little variation, as a living tongue, for two thousand and four hundred years."

Literary production after Alexander was often said to be distressingly mediocre, whether in discussions of poetry, history, or theater. This had already been Temple Stanyan's stated reason for not dealing with Alexander and his successors in his *Grecian History* of 1743. For his part, Jaucourt added that "the loss of eloquence" went hand in hand with "the ruin of the Republic."[26] By adopting an opinion already unanimously shared, Gillies found himself defending the same position as a determined opponent of the Macedonian expedition: the Baron de Sainte-Croix. The baron relentlessly denounced the "decadence of letters" in the name of principles and observations expounded as follows in the 1775 edition of the *Examen critique des anciens historiens d'Alexandre-le-Grand*: "The state of letters depends in every country upon its political constitution. Public liberty gives birth and animation to talents of every denomination; despotism strangles them at once.... The death of Alexander in its turn produced another revolution, which was attended with effects equally melancholy and fatal to the general repose and to the progress of science and literature.... The reign of Alexander may be reckoned the second stage of the decline of history.... The total extinction of the democratic form of government involved in it the fall of literature, and more particularly of history, which admits of no cultivation with success under arbitrary power."[27] Like Gillies when he followed in the footsteps of Strabo, Sainte-Croix expressed his dismay that "Hegesias, the Magnesian, first introduced to Greece, as Strabo informs us, the Asiatic style of eloquence which wastes, like a courtezan, every artifice to enliven the passions that habitude hath palled!" This was Sainte-Croix's way of denouncing the decadence of the art of oration under the influence of "Asiatization" and the attendant perversion of the traditional rules of composition and elocution in classical Greece.[28] It is easy to understand how such a widely shared point of view smoothly passed into educational manuals, in which the death of Alexander marks a caesura that cannot be crossed.[29]

Thirty years after his *History of Ancient Greece,* Gillies published a book of post-Alexandrian history covering a far more extensive period of time, ranging from Alexander to Augustus.[30] In the introduction's first lines, the author opportunely notes that Alexander "may be viewed under two distinct aspects: either as the termination of republican Greece ... or as the commencement of a Grecian dynasty in the East." In this new book, Gillies chooses to adopt the second perspective, namely "the foundation of a new empire destined speedily to dissolve into many separate monarchies." This is why he considers it necessary to return to examining those projects the king had conceived at the time of his death. His stated enthusiasm for these projects is in stark contrast to his closing remarks, which do not leave the reader in any doubt about the immediately devastating nature of the conqueror's death.

The calamity was not only felt by the vanquished, "who had experienced his protection and clemency" and who now "must lie at the mercy of insolent foreigners." It also had immediate consequences for the victors in that it led to the abandoning of the king's projects, which extended toward Arabia as well as Carthage and Spain, "the Peru and Mexico in antiquity." Had these projects come to fruition, "the unstrained intercourse of the ancient world would have nearly accorded with what the discovery of America realized, on a still larger scale, in the modern." But, as the great Italian antiquarian scholar Visconti wrote during the same period, "death made these great projects vanish and prevented the world's happiness!"[31] Gillies recalls "the improvements of his fleet and army, his discoveries by sea and land, the productive and commercial industry which he had made to flourish, and that happy intercourse of sentiment and affection in which he had laboured to unite the great nations of the East." In short, "after his controlling mind had withdrawn, the system he had formed and actuated fell in pieces, and instead of consentient members, exhibited rather jarring elements." While "many great events deserve commemoration and many splendid characters solicit regard" in the twenty years that followed his death, one must admit that the period was primarily characterized by "a wild maze of crimes and calamities." In fact, it was in this capacity and only in this capacity that the period could interest "the statesman, the general, above all the philosopher," since it is not the description of virtuous conduct but the just denunciation of shameful attitudes that puts man back on the straight and narrow. A similar assessment is found soon after in Désiré-Raoul Rochette, who considers that "Alexander's premature death at once destroyed the work of the present and the hopes of the future. The seeds that he had sown with such a liberal hand were stifled as they were born; his empire . . . collapsed from all quarters. . . . The fruit of his designs disappeared with him."[32]

While Herder was hostile to empires both ancient and modern and a critic of a Persian empire founded on conquest and plunder, he feigned to believe in the purity and grandeur of Alexander's unifying projects: "How vast was the idea to make of all this country a Greece in language, manners, arts, trade and colonization, and to render Bactra, Susa, Alexandria, and many other cities, each a new Athens!" But this was only to better decry its predictable failure, since "the dominions of Alexander were in no respect united: they were scarcely consolidated into a whole even in the mind of the conqueror himself. . . . This has been the case with every state formed by such extensive and speedy conquest, and supported only by the mind of the conqueror." Indeed, in Herder's eyes, such a project could not be reconciled with the just aspirations of "various nations and countries [that] soon reclaim their rights." Herder adds that Seleucus's successors might have found a solution by making "Babylon their residence. . . . They would probably have retained more power toward the east." Nonetheless, the contradiction was insurmountable because "then, it may be presumed, they would sooner have sunk into enervating luxury, [because], in all this, the invariably recurring natural laws of political history are conspicuous."[33]

Faced with an outcome they themselves judged disastrous, the Macedonian conqueror's admirers were reduced to a defensive position and left with a single recourse to defend their argument: to embark on a fictional history supposed to confirm their analysis of the reality of the past by sharing

with the reader their vision of the world's marvelous development had Alexander lived longer. Devoting himself to the task with nervous fervor, Rochette does not fear grandiloquence:

> The Greek institutions and mores propagated in these distant regions, the
> useful alliances contracted between the two peoples, the riches of commerce
> spread by the good deeds of the prince, the roads and canals opened, the cities
> and fortresses built inland, the ports, the arsenals, the warehouses built on
> the coasts, so many means of civilization and rapprochement [would have]
> ensured a lasting existence to these colonies, and combined under the same
> name of 'subjects' the vanquished and the victors.... The face of the world
> would probably have changed.... Subjected to the influence of this active
> and enterprising genius, all the parts of this vast empire would soon have
> opened communications between each other of which he had first conceived
> the idea and facilitated the means.... The circulation of commerce favored
> that of enlightenment; everywhere defenses were erected against barbarism,
> and sanctuaries opened to the sciences; these would have been the results of
> a reign entirely devoted to the great interests of humanity, had it continued to
> the ordinary length of our destinies.[34]

Conversely, it is easy to understand how a critic of the conqueror like
Paul-Louis Courier could write a fervent entreaty such as the one he sent to
Sainte-Croix on November 27, 1807: "Do not say to me, *if he had lived!* For
every day he became more ferocious and more of a drunk.... If he had not
died, he would still be ravaging!"[35] Though he probably did not know it,
Courier was repeating one of the accusations made by Heyne in his 1805
thesis: had Alexander lived longer, "he would have commanded over deserted lands and men reduced to solitude."[36]

Since the uses of rhetoric are infinitely flexible, it comes as no surprise
that a detractor of Alexander such as Grote uses "had he lived" to acknowledge that the king would undoubtedly have pursued his efforts (as attested
to in his lifetime) to open roads and promote communications and commerce (12:367–368), only to more forcefully deny that there was any truth to
the "intentions highly favourable to the improvements of mankind" attributed to Alexander by those whom Grote refers to as the "eulogists of
Alexander," and among whom he places Droysen first (12:352, 357, n. 2). A
critic who did a comparative reading of Droysen and Grote some years later

was not mistaken to judge that for Grote, "Alexander ended the past instead of opening up the future."[37] The British historian's interpretation represents a kind of culmination of eighteenth- and early nineteenth-century reflection, but is also a specific response to an alternative proposition presented as of the early 1830s by Droysen, who held that on the contrary, far from being the end of history, Alexander's conquest had opened up the future. As proof of his theory, Droysen pointed to "the prosperity of such a great number of flourishing cities, the magnificence of the products of art, the thousand new pleasures that charmed and embellished life, and, in large numbers, those more elevated needs met by the daily more active circulation of a literature equally remarkable for its taste and variety."[38] Unfortunately, Droysen never wrote the works in which he had announced that he would analyze these developments in detail.

From Alexander to Christ

Alexander did not represent the end of history for subscribers to providential history, which postulates that Alexander's entire career was foretold in the prophecies of Isaiah, Haggai, and Daniel. As we have seen, this position was endorsed and defended by Sainte-Croix in 1804 when he drastically revised his passages on Alexander's visit to Jerusalem.[39] As Rollin wrote, "God breaks at every interval his silence, and disperses the clouds which hide him, and condescends to discover to us the secret springs of his providence, by causing his prophets to foretell, a long series of years before the event, the fate he has prepared for the different nations of the earth."[40] Following on from Bossuet with more insistence than his model, he sees Divine Providence behind every particularly noteworthy episode of Alexander's career, including the fall of Tyre, his visit to Jerusalem, and the interruption of work on the Euphrates a few months before his death.[41]

Rollin returns to the subject at the end of book 15, at the point where he describes the transition to the period of the Diadochi, whom he will discuss in detail in the following chapters.[42] He aims to explain to his readers how so many massacres and so much devastation could have been perpetrated: "One must not believe . . . that Providence abandoned these events at random"; in reality, "it was preparing everything for the coming of the Messiah." Alexander's conquest and its aftermath were an essential stage in the realization of a preliminary, essential condition, namely "the uniting of all the nations that were to be the first enlightened by the Gospel, through the bond of a single language that was Greek." It was appropriate for these nations to be subjected to masters who did not speak the same language as they did: "Through the commerce of this language, which had become the most common and the most general, God made the apostles' preaching more prompt, easier, and more uniform." But the Greeks who came with Alexander unknowingly fulfilled another mission, which was also in keeping with the "divine secrets": "It has also been noted that God's aim in extending the Greeks' conquests exactly to the regions to be converted by the Gospel, was to spread the Greeks' philosophy there beforehand, in order to humanize the barbarian peoples." Reading between the lines, Rollin is inferring that the spread of Greek philosophy would allow the barbarians of Asia to begin to have a true inner life ("to go into themselves through serious reflection"), but also to establish a distinction between the body and the mind, and "to awaken in them the idea of the immortality of the soul and the last end of man; to call back the first principles of natural law; to provide rules for the duties of life, and to establish the most essential ties of the society of which individuals are members." For Rollin, "Christianity took advantage of all these preparations, and collected the fruits of all the seeds that Providence had long sown in minds and which the grace of Jesus Christ had made sprout in the time decreed by the divine secrets from the beginning of time."

In the *Discours sur l'histoire universelle* (1681), Bossuet already considered that the union of land and sea under the same empire had facilitated "the commerce of many different people, otherwise strangers to each other," and had thus offered "the most powerful and effectual means that Providence made use of for the spreading of the Gospel."[43] But in Bossuet, this unity is only fully realized under the Roman empire. The mission entrusted to Alexander and his successors was certainly important but much more limited: "To Protect the People of God." In writing a continuous history of Alexander and his Diadochi, Rollin does not explicitly contradict his master and inspirer but presents this period as an essential component of the *evangelical preparation* through the spread of the Greek language and philosophy. To some extent, though Rollin does not cite Plutarch, he offers a Christian and providentialist reading of his *On the Fortune or the Virtue of Alexander,* which presents Alexander as a philosopher come to civilize the barbarians, initiate them to the masterpieces of Greek literature, spread Greek laws and peace among them, and prepare the unity of the world. But Rollin is careful to avoid inducing a positive image of Alexander the conqueror, which would contradict the condemnations he expresses throughout book 15 and particularly in his assessment of Alexander's reign. God knows how to recognize his own: though they were unwittingly enlisted in a divine mission beyond their ken, the Greeks remained guilty of inexpiable crimes. In this regard, Rollin comments that it is "very remarkable that nearly all those close to Alexander and all his officers perished miserably. God punished every one of these usurpers."

Voltaire and the "Hellenists" of Jerusalem

In what would be his final treatise (*La Bible enfin expliquée*, 1776), Voltaire wrote a most interesting commentary on the Books of the Maccabees. The date and style of the volume impelled him to include a long discussion of Alexander and the state of Judea under his government, emphasizing the calm and peace the country's inhabitants then enjoyed: "For ten years under Alexander the Jews were able to breathe. . . . It was a time of rest for them." To justify his remarks, he strikes out at "compilers" such as Rollin and Prideaux and reiterates how highly he thinks of Alexander and his reign, "a young hero who built this multitude of cities in Egypt, in Syria, among the Scythians, and all the way to the Indies, and who facilitated the commerce of every nation and changed all its routes by founding the port of Alexandria." He concludes on this point, exclaiming that he "would dare to pardon him in the name of the human race." None of this was particularly new coming from Voltaire, nor was what immediately follows regarding what he elsewhere called the age of Alexander. While he does not use that terminology here, the general sense is the same: "It has not been enough noted that the time of Alexander created a revolution in the human spirit as great as the empires of the earth.[44] A new light, though mixed with dense shadows, came to enlighten Europe, Asia, and a part of northern Africa. This light came from Athens alone . . . [and] had begun to enlighten spirits of every kind." This is followed by a statement on Aristotle, who had passed on to Alexander all his spiritual riches from Athens: "No man had more spirit, more grace and taste, more love for the sciences than this conqueror."

Voltaire then explains that the same was true of his generals, "who cultivated the fine arts all the way into the tumult of war and the horrors of the factions." This is where the first novelty lies: by attributing the same qualities to the general-successors as to their leader, Voltaire extends his vision beyond the reign of Alexander.

According to Voltaire, this period brought mankind more reason and less superstition: "The Jews themselves got rid of [their] pompous style." The origin of these transformations of the mind and spirituality was what we would call Hellenization, which spread the knowledge of Greek philosophy to the countries of the Orient: "Plato's sublime ideas on the existence of the soul, its distinction from the animal machine, its immortality, the sorrows and rewards after death, first penetrated among the Jewish Hellenists established with great privileges in Alexandria, and from there to the Pharisees of Jerusalem. Until then, everything had been temporal, material, and mortal in the eyes of this people both vulgar and fanatical. Everything changed after Alexander, under the Ptolemaic and the Seleucid dynasties." By this, Voltaire meant to say that it was in this period that the transformations brought by Greco-Macedonian rule were most visible: "The Books of the Maccabees prove as much."

The novelty introduced by Voltaire is easily apparent, even intuitively: it is the conviction that the transformation of the modes of thought and belief in Judea took place through the introduction and diffusion of Greek philosophy (symbolized by Plato) by those he called the "Jewish Hellenists"—a term which, by opposition to *Hebraioi* (Hebrews), refers to those Jews who "spoke in the Greek way" (*ellenizein*), including in synagogue. The passage reveals that in his final reflections on the Macedonian conquest and its long-term effects, the philosopher went beyond the chronological caesura he himself had associated with the "age of Alexander." At least in this case, Alexander's conquest does not simply mean the end of Athenian classicism: it opens up the way to a future whose outlines are hinted at by Voltaire.

But while the role of the diffusion of the Greek language in the birth of Christianity was also noted by Heyne and Herder and, in his way, by Gillies,[45] one does not find a single late eighteenth- or early nineteenth-century historian of Alexander who has read, let alone meditated on this chapter of *La Bible enfin expliquée*. In a 1943 article, Elias Bickerman, for whom the Enlightenment held no secrets, became the first and only scholar to reintroduce Voltaire into the discussion of Droysen's idea of *Hellenismus*.[46] On this occasion, he recalled that "the overarching idea which drew [Droysen] to this forgotten period, [was] that Hellenism was a preparation for Christianity." Arnaldo Momigliano later contributed to the discussion of this point, underlining that Droysen had drawn on the definitions of the *Hellenistai* in the Acts of the Apostles and in Scaliger to come up with the term *Hellenismus* "to designate the civilization of the Greek-speaking world after Alexander." As Momigliano also aptly stated, Droysen's attraction to this period in history was primarily due to a personal process related to his deep faith. Even the choice of the term *Hellenismus* reveals Droysen's "aim of making Christianity intelligible in historical terms.... Religion mattered for him. He always felt that Providence had been at work in sending Alexander and in making East and West meet in the kingdom of his successors.... He claimed that Hellenism was an avenue (or rather *the* avenue) to Christianity."[47]

As surprising as it may seem and despite the fact that Bickerman had made an original contribution, Momigliano does not appear to have been aware of his study. Obsessed by contemporary political concerns (the fear that Nazi Germany would prevail), Bickerman considers the Hellenistic period as a mirror of the present. This is another reason that he tends to argue against some of the positions supported in "the Germanic universities," among which he includes what he saw as the undue preeminence and precedence given Droysen. This is why he refers to Voltaire "as ever in advance of others" and that he alludes to his text on Maccabees, regretting that Voltaire's commentary has never been noted: "His observation was buried in the casuistry of his 'the Bible finally explained'; it has had no influence. Seventy years later, a German scholar, Johann Gustav Droysen, in developing the same, but this time Hegelian, thesis, published the first '*History of Hellenism*', giving this rather inappropriate name to the period following Alexander." Naturally, Bickerman does not suggest that Droysen was directly inspired by Voltaire. He simply provides a reminder that half a century before Droysen, the philosopher of Ferney was the first to consider the period that began with Alexander's conquest from this angle.

Théodore Jouffroy and His Contemporaries

This delicate question of influences, legacies, and borrowings brings us to an adapted translation of John Gillies's *History of Ancient Greece* published in 1841 by Émile Ruelle with the assistance of Alphonse Huillard-Brihales.[48]

In the authors' final depiction of Alexander, one easily recognizes a phrase taken directly from Gillies ("An extraordinary man, who had no model and still has no equal"), while others are clearly of their own invention: "Each of his victories was a triumph for the divine idea. . . . Thus was the immortal role of Alexander in humanity's destinies accomplished: he was neither a conqueror nor a great man, he was the missionary of Providence, and the angel who came to announce to the world the reign of Jesus Christ." Alexander, first bearer of the Good News to a humanity in need of redemption? The authors put forward this surprising assertion under the authority of a certain Jouffroy, who has undoubtedly remained completely unknown to historians of Alexander (as he long was to me). Jouffroy's words are allegedly quoted to the letter, as indicated by the use of quotation marks.[49] We will soon see that Ruelle had in fact put in his two cents. His claim of intellectual kinship is not entirely unwarranted, but it is in spirit rather than to the letter. Ruelle returns to the question further along, in the part of the translation that is no longer that of *The History of Ancient Greece* (and also not strictly that of *The History of the World*), but what he calls the *Précis de l'histoire des successeurs d'Alexandre jusqu'à la réduction des différents États en provinces romaines* (see 2:273–467). Here too, he interprets Jouffroy's thought without citing him: "Alexander appeared to have been personally entrusted with the mission of spreading to the Ganges the Greek civilization that was to encompass both the Orient and the Occident, this harmonious and expressive language that was to be that of Christianity and the new law."

As was usually the case in manuals, the reference was not indicated by anything other than the author's name ("says M. Jouffroy"); the reader was left to do a background check for himself, if he had the opportunity. Théodore Jouffroy (1796–1842) is a now long-forgotten philosopher who had something of a reputation in his lifetime and the half century that followed his death. A recent biographer even calls him "one of the leading thinkers of his generation."[50] A specialist in philosophy and moral psychology, he taught at the university of Paris and the École Normale Supérieure, and became a professor at the Collège de France with a chair in Greek and Latin Philosophy in late 1832. He resigned due to illness in a letter dated December 30, 1837; that year, his course had been devoted to "the systems of Greek philosophy before Socrates."[51] After 1830, he became more directly involved in political life and was deputy for the Doubs from 1831 to 1842, taking part in the major debates of the period.

A quick investigation reveals that after the closing of the École Normale Supérieure in 1822, Jouffroy went through a difficult time during which he wrote a great deal for newspapers, particularly for *Le Globe,* the liberal paper of which he was a founder in September 1824. The first volume of his *Mélanges philosophiques* (1841) contains an article published in *Le Globe* on June 16, 1827. This article which the author personally categorized in the section on "Philosophy of History" is entitled "Du rôle de la Grèce dans le développement de l'humanité" ["On Greece's Role in the Development of Humanity"]. His argument is closely connected to the contemporary world, which the author considers to be dominated by "the third world, the American-European world … today a giant that has no rival on earth." But, Jouffroy asks himself, what does that world make of Greece, "its glorious homeland," Greece, which "was the first to defeat the barbarians? And yet Greece is in Europe and yet Europe is Christian." This inaction is scandalous: "If ever a people was predestined by the heavens to a special fate and deserved the name of people of God, it was that one." Alexander played a particular role in this confrontation between Europe and Asia: "After the Greco-Persian Wars, Alexander's expedition was the greatest event that history has remembered. The Greco-Persian Wars had saved civilization in the cradle; Alexander's expedition was the first act of its youth. This expedition was something new in this world: instead of conquering by force, Alexander conquered by art; instead of destroying, he founded; instead of stupefying, he enlightened. … It was less a conquest than a mission." Note Jouffroy's wording: it was not an exhausted and decadent Greece that launched the assault on Asia, but a Greece full of strength and in the prime of youth. As for the term "mission," it is justified by the direct link Jouffroy establishes between the Macedonian conquest, intellectual and spiritual renewal, the elimination of old religions, and the advent of Christianity. Here is the entirety of the pertinent passage from the philosopher's article:

> Alexander's expedition put in contact, mixed, and threw into the same system all the nations of the Orient. Through it, the ideas of every nation became acquainted; they understood each other, controlled each other, rallied to the torch of the Greek spirit, and of this intellectual union was born the first civilized world, the Greek or Oriental world, out of which came Christianity. Christianity, like philosophy, was the popular summary of all that the wisdom

of this first world had found to be true about man's fate. The previous religions, daughters of the senses and the imagination, had been no more than children's and barbarians' religions. They all predated civilization. Christianity was the first rational religion, the first religion of men. It was the product, the expression, and the crowning achievement of the first age of civilization, and by that itself the principle and soul of the second. Thus was accomplished the immortal role of Greece in the destinies of mankind. (1827, pp. 68–69)

Like his contemporaries who admired Aeschylus's *Persians*,[52] Jouffroy sees Marathon and Salamis as the first victories of European civilization, a civilization of whose inevitable superiority he is convinced. While he admits that "conquest is unjust in and of itself," it "leads to great good when it is carried out by a superior civilization." This is the context for his remarks on Alexander's "mission."[53] It would be easy to establish connections between Jouffroy's expressions and some of Droysen's wording and views; one could also attempt a comparison with Hegel's lesson on "the passage to the Greek world (*Übergang zur griechischen Welt*),"[54] which Droysen may have heard while he was a regular at the philosopher's seminars in the years 1827–1829. Yet it is best to avoid a facile path that would most likely lead one down the wrong track. Instead, this text "discovered" by chance (in the course of step-by-step research) suggests that during the first third of the nineteenth century, a common idea was circulating in different formulations in Paris, Berlin, and other capitals of European (or even "American-European") thought. This was that Alexander's conquest was not the end of history; on the contrary, it heralded Christianity and prepared a new phase of universal history in which glorious Christian Europe, heiress to Greece and Alexander, played a dominant role, one which made it duty-bound to return Greece to its greatness and freedom.

Chapter 10

Alexander, Europe, and the Immobile Orient

The First European

Aside from the providentialist Christians, who came to the conclusion that the Macedonian adventure was a stage on the way to the heralded birth of Christianity, and the erudite Christian Droysen, who knew that it had prepared the conditions for Christianity's appearance, historians and commentators had to admit that the adventure had come to a dead end: they either judged that disaster was part and parcel of the vices inherent to an unjust and bloody conquest or regretfully recognized that the death of its genius organizer had left the world bereft of his grandiose projects for positive change. Both camps were left to ask whether the history of Alexander deserved a chapter in Greek history. Pierre-Charles Levesque, who was inclined to answer in the negative, intuited that it was necessary to break out of the confines that the question entailed. He therefore chose to address the history of Alexander as a chapter in "the history of the world."[1]

Like others, Théodore Jouffroy followed a line of thought directed toward the present and the future. He did not adopt the point of view of the historian—for he was not a historian—but that of his own calling as a politically committed philosopher; from the outset, he considered the history of Alexander as a chapter in the history of Europe. He stated that this history had been shaped by a millennial conflict with the Orient. The Orient was the original source of "the seeds of civilization," which were only able to take root and develop in the "safe shelter" of Greece—the base from which "the apostle Alexander" led his "mission" to rally every nation to "the torch of the Greek spirit." This was the advent of the "first world" to which Europe was heir. Alexander therefore belongs to a living history, whose continuation found Europe faced with a new mission: to break the Metternich system and "send the unworthy masters of Greece back to Asia with the flick of a finger." The "unworthy masters" were the Ottoman Turks.

The image associating the Athenian memory of Salamis with a victory over the Orient had already frequently been used by Roman authors faced with the Parthian threat;[2] it was also evoked at the end of the Byzantine period, when several authors referred to the Turks who were at the gates of Constantinople as "Persians." The memory of Greece was also cultivated in the other camp, where the new master of Constantinople / Istanbul, Mehmed the Conqueror (1451–1481), listened to readings from Arrian and admired Alexander's exploits.[3] In the modern era, the Ottoman fleet's defeat at Lepanto (1571) was celebrated in Zakynthos (then under Venetian rule) by a performance of Aeschylus's *Persians* in Venetian.[4] Voltaire also hailed "this superiority of a generous & free small people over all of enslaved Asia, [which] may be what is most glorious in man." While specifying that the analogy was about all "that one can get from our knowledge of these distant times," he added that "[one] also learns by this event that the peoples of the Occident have always been better sailors than the Asian peoples. When one reads modern history, the victory at Lepanto is reminiscent of that at Salamis."[5]

Compared to the image of Themistocles (who was known as the triumphant hero of Salamis), Alexander's image had the singular quality of no longer bringing to mind a heroic defense against an army or fleet from the East, but a whole series of victories won by a European army as it advanced deeper and deeper into the heart of Asia. In this sense, research and publications on Alexander and his historical role were regularly included in Europe's reflection both on its own history and the progress due to its territorial ambitions and advances in Oriental countries. The Macedonian conquest was generally analyzed as an in vivo experiment on what the Europeans could accomplish in an Orient whose fundamental characteristics were thought to have remained immutable since the Achaemenid empire. In this context, Alexander is no longer a mere precedent: he is the first actor of the history of European expansion.

The joint reference to Alexander and the crusade against the infidels was noted at the court of Burgundy as early as the fifteenth century[6] and continued into the seventeenth century. In 1645, Gaudenzio asked whether the

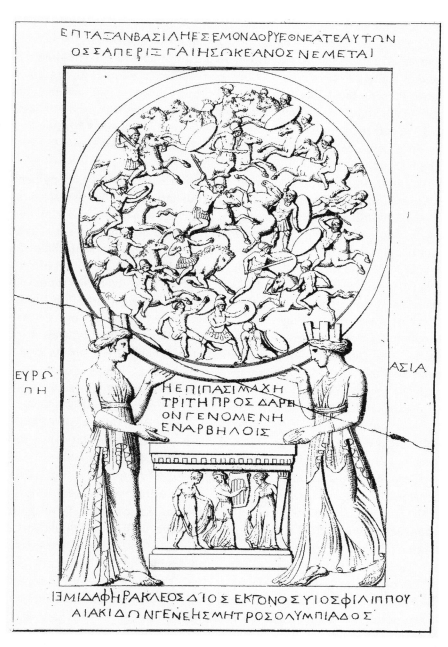

16. Europe and Asia in a Roman-era bas-relief in honor of Alexander the Great, drawing published by E. Q. Visconti in *Examen critique des anciens historiens d'Alexandre le Grand* by the Baron de Sainte-Croix, 1804, pp. 777–790.

Macedonian experience could serve to inform the mounting of an expedition that would "expel the barbarous Ottoman from Europe and Asia."[7] He answered in the negative, explaining that Alexander had had the good fortune of facing the Persian king Darius, an opponent without any military merit. Present-day Turks, however, had proved that they had astute quartermasters and great commanders such as Selim, Suleyman, and Mehmed II. To defeat them, one would have to create several excellent armies that would coordinate their marches in order to disperse the enemy forces—which Alexander had not had to do to fight Darius.

The following year, the dedication to "His Lordship the Duke of Enghien" at the beginning of Perrot d'Ablancourt's translation of Arrian's *Anabasis of Alexander* confirmed that Alexander, or the image one had of him, could be used as an invigorating precedent for a projected or imagined expedition into the countries he had victoriously roamed. In his address to the dedicatee Condé (the duke of Enghien), Perrot d'Ablancourt entreated him to "read the achievements of the Duke of Enghien who lived two thousand years ago. Until such time as restless Europe puts its weapons in the hands of the new Alexander, to avenge it a second time of the Tyrant of Asia that threatens its freedom. These are the wishes of all of Christianity." Ten years earlier, Yves Duchat had dedicated a bilingual French-Greek *Hymne d'Alexandre le Grand* to the king of France. He enjoined the king to make peace with the other European princes in order "to turn his weapons against the Ottomans, and destroy the barbarous and cruel dominance of the Turks." His vision of a future victory is directly borrowed from the history of Alexander as it was learned from Plutarch; he hopes to see the day when the king of France is seated on Constantine's throne, just as Demaratus had seen Alexander seated on Darius's throne in Susa.[8] Around 1675, the young Fénelon also began dreaming of a Christian recapture of Greece, a uniting of the Orient and the Occident, and an "Asia that would see the dawn again after such a long night." He conjures up the image "of the blood of the Turks mixing with that of the Persians on the plains of Marathon" and the image of a "Greece free to practice its religion, philosophy, and the fine arts."[9]

It does not much matter whether or not a Crusade was planned around the middle of the seventeenth century and if so at what date; the Turkish threat or the European idea of it was felt deeply enough for the example of Alexander's expedition to be seen as a hope for a potential victory over an (Ottoman) enemy that was feared but that one sought to belittle by identifying it with another (Persian) enemy, itself well known to the ancient writers devoted to the memory of the man who had come from Europe to defeat it.[10]

That Alexander's defeat of Darius was seen as a decisive victory in the history of Europe and its relationship with the Orient in the latter half of the eighteenth century and beyond is strikingly illustrated by the words Johann Christoph Gatterer uses to refer to Darius's defeat and situate it in the *longue durée*. It would be an understatement to say that this professor at the University of Göttingen was no admirer of the Macedonian conqueror, given that to his mind introducing "the marvels of Phoenicia and India" amounted to dealing with the "principal episodes of this bandit's life." His portraits of Alexander are very negative in the *Handbuch der Universalhistorie* (*Handbook of Universal History*) (1765) and simply vitriolic in his *Abriß dere Universalhistorie* (*Abstract of Universal History*) (1773).[11] In 1767, he published his plan for a universal history (he was one of the specialists in the genre). Following the volume's strictly chronological approach, he also includes Alexander in the span of the Persian empire, eloquently drawing attention to Darius's defeat: "Darius Codomannus allowed the passage to the Greco-Macedonian system. For the first time, the seat of domination is in Europe." In his *Weltgeschichte* (*History of the World*) (1787) he dealt with the Persians and the Greeks, using similar and equally powerful wording: "And thus thanks to Alexander [who took full control of territories that had previously belonged to the Persian monarchy], for the first time global domination moved away from the Asians and into European hands."[12]

While lecturing at the University of Bonn about forty years later, the German historian Barthold Georg Niebuhr, who was even more contemptuous of the Asians than he was hostile to Alexander,[13] also considered that the conquests spelled a radical shift in the world's equilibrium, which could not be compared to the disruptions brought by Constantine and Charlemagne: "To us also, Alexander is a man of extraordinary importance, inasmuch as he gave a new appearance to the whole world. He began what will now be completed in spite of all obstacles—the dominion of Europe over Asia; he was the first that led the victorious Europeans to the East. Asia had played its part in history, and was destined to become the slave of Europe."[14] At the dawn of the nineteenth century, Arnold Heeren also turned to the memory of the exploits of Alexander the European and the weakness of Darius the Asian to make a connection with the state of the Ottoman empire, finding a sign of Europe's coming victory in the analogy: "We behold, in the present day, a similar empire, which possibly may not even require the reverses of three defeats, to afford on the banks of the Hellespont, the same spectacle which followed the success of Alexander on the Granicus, at Issus, and at Arbela."[15]

At practically the same time, the English writer John Williams (1792–1858) opened his biography of Alexander the Great with considerations on Greece's millennial place in "the principal scene of the great struggle between the eastern and the western worlds." He explained that this clash was both unavoidable and permanent because it was due to "system[s] of education transmitted down from the remotest ages," which had created insurmountable differences in mores, feelings, ways of life, etc. The Orient and the Occident had always been in a state of war wherever they bordered on each other—in other words, everywhere, given that "the Europeans are on the banks of the Ganges and on the shores of the Caspian, and the Asiatics on the banks of the Danube and the shores of Adriatic. Yet there appears no sign of an approaching termination."[16] Considered as Europe's "first" assumption of power over Asia by Gatterer, then Niebuhr, the events of Alexander's period heralded the imminent second assumption of power dreamed of by Heeren and Niebuhr.

These very firm stances dating from 1767 to 1830 are undoubtedly connected to what would be called the "Eastern question," and particularly to the results of the European-Russian-Turkish wars of 1768–1774, 1787–1792, and 1821–1830, which led to Turkey's loss of territory on the Black Sea (withdrawal from Crimea) and in the Balkans. The Greek revolt of 1821, the "massacre at Chios" in 1822, and the siege of Messolonghi in 1826 were major shocks to European public opinion, which acclaimed the English-French-Russian fleet's victory in Navarino Bay, then Greek independence (1829–1830). Europe and Russia had shifted from the defensive position they held a century earlier and gone on the offensive on the Black Sea, in Egypt, the Balkans, and all the way to Algeria (1830); some were even devising plans for the agrarian colonization of Syria.[17]

It was also during this period that Pierre David published the two parts of his heavy-handed poem *Alexandréide* (1826 and 1829), one of the many "philhellenic" statements then flourishing in Europe and particularly in France. Quoting a speech made before the French Chamber of Peers, the author stated that "the times have come to pass, the Turks must break camp or the Greeks bury themselves in the sacred ground" (part I, lines 32–33). If France helped the Greeks, it would be in "the interest of humanity and religion." It was Europe's responsibility "to spread the Enlightenment there, to stabilize public prosperity" (II, vii). David seized on the memory of Alexander because "by recalling a great example, one can awaken great ideas." He also saw "many analogies between the modern situation and the antique situation: Alexander repelling the barbarians to the depths of Asia, avenging Greece for Xerxes's attacks, by protecting its future from the great king's insults and irons."[18]

Jouffroy was therefore clearly not an isolated voice in the spring of 1827 when he declared in a liberal paper entirely committed to the Greek insurrection that he saw Alexander's "mission" as a first victorious march, which offered a glimpse of a second one. To a certain extent, one could then move between past, present, and future to connect three points on the map of Europe's territorial advances and its resistance through collective memory: Salamis, Persepolis, and Istanbul. The hope was that the third city would soon also be the site of a victory, which many considered as inevitable as the fall of Darius and the triumph of Alexander had once been.[19]

The First of the Hellenes?

In their zeal for the Greek cause, French philhellenes exemplified a combative vision probably contemplated by certain leaders of the revolt of the 1820s, but which was not that of the Greek representatives of the Enlightenment, whose ambition was then to free themselves of the Ottoman yoke but not necessarily to chase the Turks into Asia or "get back" Constantinople through a military campaign. The most famous of these Greek thinkers was Adamantios Korais.[20] Born in Smyrna in 1748 to a family of notables and scholars, he studied ancient Greek and the antique authors, first in the Netherlands, then in the French city of Montpellier (where he studied medicine). He spent the revolution years in Paris, tirelessly defending the cause of Greek independence. In 1803, he presented a *Mémoire sur l'état actuel de la civilisation dans la Grèce* before the Société des Observateurs de l'Homme. He intended to counter the opinions of poorly informed Europeans by showing "the growth of the Enlightenment" in his country, including (but not only) through the distribution of Greek translations of famous works which were published in Venice and included Rollin's *Histoire ancienne,* Fénelon's *Télémaque,* and Montesquieu's *Considérations.*

Two years earlier, there had been numerous reminders of the past in *Appel aux Grecs* (1801), a French translation of a Greek nationalist pamphlet by Adamantios Korais, but these primarily concerned the heroes of Thermopylae, Marathon, and Salamis, "who resisted the prodigious armies of Persia, the vastest, most powerful, most formidable monarchy that then existed on the globe" and forced Xerxes to a shameful retreat. Yet the Thessalonians and Macedonians of his time had their place in the *Appel:* he reminded them that their forefathers "defeated Darius, a monarch far more formidable than the effeminate despot who reigns today." Nonetheless, Alexander is never cited. The reason was simple and was agreed upon by several late eighteenth-century historiographers: Korais considered the Macedonian defeat of the Greeks the first step in their gradual loss of freedom. This also explains his criticism of those Greeks who had "allowed themselves to be corrupted by the gold of the Macedonians."[21] The Greeks' subjection "to Alexander's successors" was their "first enslavement," followed by those that successively chained them to the Romans, the Byzantines, and the Turks. At the same time, Korais carefully distinguishes the Ottoman yoke from the others, because it is the work of "a people three times barbarous, a bandit people, a people different in language and religion." By comparison, the Byzantine yoke was "nearly tolerable" and the Romans before them had "honored the Greeks as more learned than they were"; as for the Greeks' fate after Alexander's death, it was not desperate, in that "the successors were also Greeks." The text continues to show that, among the Diadochi, the Ptolemaic rulers turned Egypt into a land of exile and shelter for the arts and letters chased out by the fall of Athens.

Others presented a more favorable image of Alexander the Great.[22] This was true of Daniel Philippides and Gregory Constantas in their *Geographia Neôterikè* (*Modern Geography*) (1791) and, especially, of Rigas Velestinlis (1757–1798). The former dreamed of a future Hellenic state, which would also include the Aegean Islands and Asia Minor. They wrote that "the nation of the Greeks spread a great deal in the time of Alexander the Great" and rejected Demosthenes's attacks on the "barbarian" character he attributed to the Macedonians. This is still a long way from the irredentist doctrine of the "Great Idea" expressed by mid-nineteenth-century historians (particularly Konstantinos Paparrigopoulos) who used Droysen's works to suit their purposes. It was only in this context that Alexander would be fully integrated into a combative vision of the Hellenic nation, which intends "to govern the Orient."[23]

The case of Rigas Velestinlis is particularly interesting.[24] As a partisan and admirer of the Enlightenment, he spread the new ideas in Greek by translating passages from the *Encyclopédie*,[25] but also the Abbé Barthélemy's *Jeune Anarcharsis* (in collaboration). He also started a translation of *The Spirit of the Laws*.[26] Yet Rigas, who was involved with other conspirators in a plot to revolt against the Ottomans, also wanted to spread his ideas through images. He took refuge in Vienna, home to a powerful Greek diaspora, and published his *Karta tès Hellados* (*Map of Hellas*).[27] Inspired by the work of Delisle and Barbié du Bocage, the map was explicitly intended to "aid in understanding the voyage of the young Anarcharsis" and to be "for Hellenes and Philhellenes." As such, it was not limited to the Balkan territories; it also encompassed "a part of [Greece's] many colonies (*apoikiai*) in Europe and Asia Minor," therefore including the part of Asia Minor located west of the line Rigas drew from the city of Myra in Lycia in the south to Bithynia in the north. Considered as a group both European and Asian, "the people descending from the Hellenes" include "the inhabitants of Rumelia, Asia Minor, the Mediterranean islands, Moldavia and Wallachia." The map's several sheets are covered in the author's commentary, as well as drawings of coins and plans (of Thermopylae, Athens, Constantinople). Rigas tells the reader that everything he has shown is "Hellas, the places where the Hellenes our fathers lived, where they fought, which they made immortal through their genius and their weapons." Yet despite the fact that he extolled the universal value of Greek culture, Rigas was not promoting a type of imperialism. On the contrary, he sought to organize a new Hellas based on Jacobin ideas. He imagined a "Hellene republic" that was both multiethnic and multicultural, in which the Turks would also have a place.[28]

What is noteworthy is that from Rigas's perspective Alexander the Great is an integral part of the heritage of antiquity and that he must serve as a reference to modern Greeks; this was why his name was on the map in capital letters. Indeed, while the map's commentaries primarily served to illustrate the glorious history of the city-states, they did not overlook the Macedonian king. Several of Alexander's coins were reproduced; Macedon was referred to as his "homeland"; and the Granicus was described as the site of one of his exploits. "Alexander and the fourteen Ptolemies, the last of which was

Cleopatra," are also included in the list of sovereigns who "actually ruled over Greece." In his *Thourios* [*Patriotic Hymn*], Rigas even calls on Alexander to "come out of his tomb" and look upon the still remarkable courage of present-day Macedonians.[29]

What is even more interesting is that the same year (1797), Rigas had a portrait of Alexander engraved in copper and printed in Vienna. He intended the portrait as an item of revolutionary propaganda for the Greeks (like his map, his constitutional proposals, and his "Thourios" ("War Song"). According to his own statement to the judge who interrogated him following his arrest, 1,200 copies of the *Portrait* were printed on the Müller printing shop's presses to be distributed to Greeks in Vienna, Bucharest, and elsewhere.[30] What we are looking at is both a history lesson through text and (especially) image and a real political program expressed through various illustrations, which take on their full significance through a carefully calculated layout.

The engraving sits in a 43 cm × 27 cm (16.9 × 10.6 inches) frame. The texts and images all illustrate the joint themes of war and peace, though the emphasis does appear to be on peaceful activities. The central image of Alexander in profile (left > right), his long curly hair coming out from beneath a helmet with a richly detailed visor, is surrounded in all four corners by miniature portraits of each of the four generals who were his principal successors: Seleucus, Antigonus, Cassander, and Ptolemy. The portraits are assembled in two pairs: to the left, Seleucus (top) and Ptolemy (bottom) wear the diadem associated with their position as kings and founders of dynasties (the Seleucids and the Lagids); to the right, Antigonus (top) and Cassander (bottom) wear helmets, which highlight their role as war chiefs. In the spaces delimited on all four sides, one recognizes representations of four of Alexander's exploits: two victorious battles are on the left (the Granicus) and right (Arbela), while at top and bottom, two peaceful scenes are given pride of place on the same vertical axis as the portrait of Alexander; at top, a resounding demonstration of royal virtues (the families of Alexander and Darius); at bottom, Alexander's triumphal entry into Babylon as he is cheered by the population. Below the illustrations, a bilingual text (Greek on the left, French on the right) lists the major events of Alexander's life (his birth; learning philosophy from Aristotle; cutting his teeth in Chaeronea "under the command of his father, whom he succeeded on the throne of Macedon at the age of 21"; the destruction of the Persian empire "in Asia

17. *Portrait of Alexander* by Rigas Velestinlis, copper engraving, Vienna, 1797.

and Africa"; the founding of cities; his death "at the age of 32"). The text ends with the following words, which are reminiscent of those on the *Karta:* "Published by Rigas Velestinlis the Thessalian, for the Greeks and the friends of Greece (*philhellenes*)."

According to another text printed above the illustrations, the image of Alexander was itself allegedly copied from an original piece, which is reproduced life-size in the upper left corner of the handbill: "This engraving depicts the busts of Alexander and his generals based on an Oriental red agate in the Imperial cabinet in Vienna; the four pictures along the borders represent, first, his triumphal entry into Babylon, 2nd, the routing of the Persians at the Granicus, 3rd, the total defeat of Darius, and 4th, that king's family at Alexander's feet." One can legitimately have questions about the identity of the engraved stone alleged as a source by Rigas, as well as the composition itself, which features Alexander and four Diadochi. The drawings of Alexander's exploits are clearly replicas of paintings by Le Brun, which are known to have widely circulated in this form in France and Europe. In fact, the drawing itself is not by Rigas, but is a replica of a drawing made by the famous engraver Salomon Kleiner from an engraved stone then in a private collection in Vienna. Rigas could not have seen this stone because it had been purchased by Catherine II of Russia by this time (1796–1797). Instead, he copied Kleiner's drawing and added his own Greco-French caption.[31]

In any case, the choice of subject and composition shows that Alexander was one of the major figures of the history of the Hellenes whom Rigas wanted to offer as models to his contemporaries in order to incite them to rebel against the Ottoman yoke and revive Greece's bygone glory. As the author's own commentaries so strongly suggest, the figure praised by Rigas is certainly not the destroyer of the Greeks' freedom (in fact, Chaeronea is not included on the *Karta* and the *Portrait*'s commentary makes no reference to the Greeks' defeat, merely mentioning the "courage and military talents" Philip's son had shown on this occasion). This Alexander is also not the conqueror condemned by Rollin for being solely driven by his own ambition (the part of the expedition after the victory at Gaugamela is not mentioned) or the adventurer whose fragile accomplishments were wiped out after his death (on the contrary, the four kings and generals imply a succession over a long time span, but also across space, since Asia, Egypt, Greece, and Macedon are gathered around the founder). No, the historical figure that Rigas wants to provide as an example to the people of his nation is the compassionate king who welcomed his adversaries and, in Rigas's own words, the young king who "was recognized as the leader of the Greeks [and whose] entire forces he directed against the Persians"—that is to say, the one recognized by the ancient texts as the chief of a war of liberation of the Greeks of Asia (Minor). By underlining (in language inherited from Voltaire) that "several considerable cities, even to this day, owe their existence to him," Rigas better established the connection between past, present, and future. His dream was not to re-create some empire of Alexander's; instead, he saw the Macedonian as the protector of the city-states and the hero / herald of Greek freedoms in the face of the Asian oppressor whom he had defeated in battles depicted to the right and left of the *Portrait*.[32] Naturally, his political vision implied that Constantinople and western Asia Minor be torn from the Ottoman yoke. But it is equally clear that this possibility was not to be realized through a war of conquest, but as a consequence of a war of independence launched and carried out by the Hellenes and other subjugated populations whom Rigas situated west of a line drawn from Lycia to Bithynia. While Rigas held up the image of Alexander as hero-liberator of the Greeks, his political program and territorial vision were closer to those of the Athenian rhetorician Isocrates, who had pleaded under Philip II for the Greeks to settle in large numbers in an "Asia" west of a line that he drew "from Cilicia to Sinope."

At the same time, for fairly obvious reasons, Greek historiographers and political thinkers of the late eighteenth century shared an opinion found throughout European historical and polemic literature: that the Ottoman empire was infinitely less dangerous since its defeat at the hands of the Russians. Korais writes that beginning in 1769, the Greeks noticed "that the statue they worshipped rested on feet of clay."[33] Korais suggests analogies with the past to illustrate the deplorable state of the empire: the Ottoman empire is undermined by the revolts of the "modern satraps" and "the new Ashurbanipal, surrounded by women and eunuchs, irritated in body and spirit by an excess of sensuality, will not dare even to set foot beyond the threshold of his palace to show his enemies the shadow of a general!"[34] For his part, as a preamble to his *Nouveau statut politique*, Rigas affirmed that "Christians and Turks consider that the tyrant named sultan is prey to his senile instincts, that he is surrounded by eunuchs and uneducated and bloodthirsty courtiers, that he has forgotten and been contemptuous of humanity, that even innocence has not found favor with his heart, and that the most beautiful kingdom in the world, which scholars in all parts have praised, has fallen into an appalling state of anarchy." Another analogy is introduced on his *Karta,* through the symbols used to represent the armies engaged and printed next to the names of the battles: Hercules's club for the Greeks and the spear for the Persians *and* the Turks. As Georges Tolias has noted, "the association of Turks and ancient Persians is common in Greek writings since the sixteenth century, if not earlier."[35] We will now see that the same was true in European historical literature between the Enlightenment and Romanticism.

The Sick Man of Asia

In a letter to Leopold (von) Ranke dated February 27, 1842, the historian and economist Wilhelm Roscher congratulated himself for the education he had received from Arnold Heeren and Gervinus (Heeren's former student and biographer) and more specifically for their recommendation to use the method of analogy. Roscher specified that when used as a means rather than a goal, this method was the best one to describe the comparable development of certain peoples; among the most striking examples of well-founded analogies, he mentioned the comparison between "the contemporary situation of Turkey and the final days of the ancient Persian empire."[36]

Heeren often explained that he found it necessary to make past and present intersect, because, as he wrote in the preface to his *Handbuch,* "the transactions of our times have thrown a light upon ancient history, and given it an interest which it could not formerly possess." The study of history thus made it possible to obtain "a clear and unprejudiced view of the great drama now performing around us." For that matter, he asked, "of what use is the study of history if it do not make us wiser and better? unless the knowledge of the past teach us to judge more correctly the present?"[37] The recourse to analogy was also a product of the objective conditions for historians of ancient Persia in the late eighteenth century and the first third of the nineteenth century. At the time, their research could not rely on Achaemenid written sources; while Persepolis became increasingly well known over the first third of the nineteenth century (Heeren had a fairly heated polemic with Herder on the subject), the royal inscriptions were not deciphered (despite the fact that so-called Persepolitan writing had already led to important scholarly works) and with the exception of a fragmentary stele discovered in 1799 during the Egyptian Expedition and a few small objects gathered by passionate antiquarian scholars, researchers were not aware of any Achaemenid epigraphic documents from the countries formerly subject to the Great King.[38] Writing with exaggeration determined by his own prejudices, Herder stated: "Even the ancient languages of Persia are dead: and the sole monuments of its magnificence, the ruins of Persepolis, remain, with their elegant letters and colossal figures, hitherto inexplicable."[39]

To write his major work on the organization of the Persian empire, Heeren therefore had to rely on travel narratives and the ancient Greek writers (whom he often cites, referring to Brisson's 1590 volume). He is particularly fond of citing Brisson and Chardin in support of each other.[40] This method starts from an assumption, which it turns into a cognitive process: that in Europe, the social, political, and religious institutions of the great Asian states were thought to have generally remained in place from antiquity to the eighteenth century. Around the same time, James Mill said much the same thing in his own evocative way: "By conversing with the Hindus of the present day, we, in some measure, converse with the Chaldeans of the time of Cyrus; with the Persians and Egyptians of the time of Alexander." A century earlier, Benoist de Maillet had already pointed out that the many changes of dynasty had in no way modified the "inclinations and customs" specific to the Egyptians: "Nature and the climate had shaped them and nature easily reasserts itself. Thus do we still find in today's Egyptians more or less the same genius, nearly all the same customs as in the past."[41]

This belief in the overwhelming burden of secular continuity was based on the conviction that all the "Asian" states were of a single type: the despotic state. In fact, Heeren, who had read Montesquieu, voices the question that obsessed him and which, in his words, "is of the highest interest with reference to the general history of mankind, namely, how it came to pass that the system of absolute despotism, which has always characterized the Asiatic governments, should have been so constantly maintained, and, under every political revolution, uniformly?"[42] For all of these reasons, the analogy between the Persian empire and the Ottoman empire quickly imposed itself, even before Heeren had theorized its conclusions and purpose.

These analogies could be comparisons of limited scope, suggested by the fact that the ancient Persian empire "in Asia comprehended all that now belongs to the Persians and Turks," and that inside their empire "there were several nations which were only tributary, and not properly subjects of Persia, as it is the case at this day with respect to the Turkish empire."[43] But the analogies more frequently developed were comprehensive. In the early sixteenth century, Machiavelli had already used the history of Darius and Alexander to attempt to explain the specificity "of a state governed by a sole Prince and by his servants," of which the Ottoman empire served as a full-fledged example.[44] Over the course of the eighteenth century, analogies were made by those who drew a parallel between the decline of the Achaemenid empire under the reign of the last Darius and the terminal illness eating away at the Ottoman empire in their own time. Assimilated to each other through homology, the two empires come to represent the "Sick Man" of immobile Asia.

The weakness of the Ottoman empire was evaluated in different manners by seventeenth- and eighteenth-century authors. In 1645, Gaudenzio considered it infinitely stronger facing Europe than Darius's empire had been facing Alexander. Yet thirty years later Michel Febvre pressed the king of France to launch an offensive against "Turkey, which has always considered your majesty as the future conqueror of its territory." He argued that Turkey found itself in a state far inferior to what it had once been: "The provinces are depopulated, the cities deserted, the people ruined, the land, which was once the most fertile and most delicious in the world, now lies fallow and abandoned. . . . In a word, it is a vast, desolate empire," comparable to the statue of Nebuchadnezzar—in other words, a giant with clay feet.[45] A century later, the Englishman Paul Ricaut's *History of the Present State of the Ottoman Empire* had a lasting influence in Europe, particularly on Montesquieu; Jaucourt speaks of it as an "admirable history." Ricaut agrees that the countryside is becoming depopulated and the sultan's revenue is diminishing, adding that "the Militia is now becoming degenerate, soft and effeminate."[46] Nonetheless—and not without an aggressive irony—Ricaut also judges that by following principles of government contrary to those of the Romans (who favored commerce, industry, and the development of the peoples of their empire), the Turks were achieving good results (1.15). They had taken measures (transferring populations) to populate the countries under their authority so that "they could lose many men at war and their land would still be cultivated." He acknowledges that "it is true that Alexander did, with an army for the most part composed of Macedonians, make a conquest of the best part of the Eastern world; but this empire, like a ship that had much sail and no ballast, or like a fair tree overcharged with boughs too heavy for its stem, became a windfall on a sudden." In other words, the Turkish empire is far stronger than the Macedonian's ephemeral empire![47]

Like the "giant with clay feet" from the prophecy of Daniel, the tree would commonly be used as a metaphor to illustrate the intrinsic weakness of excessively large empires, whose branches stretched too far and roots were superficial, leaving them unable to withstand the slightest headwind, as had been the case with the Persian empire and now the Ottoman empire.[48]

The theory of the Achaemenid empire's structural weakness and accelerated decline after Cyrus's death had already been put forward by the Greek authors of antiquity. The modern authors only had to copy them, paraphrase them, and dress them in their own rhetoric to accentuate their effects, without adding anything new other than the Ottoman analogy.[49] In 1748, Montesquieu wrote that the Greek victories "had made known just how superior the Greek manner of doing battle and their sort of weapons were; and it was well known that the Persians were too great to correct themselves" (*Spirit of the Laws,* 10.13). There was nothing original about this statement. Bossuet and Rollin had said it all before, through their uncontextualized readings of book 3 of Plato's *Laws,* book 8 of the *Cyropaedia,* and the authors who dealt with Alexander's adversary.

Rollin takes stock of the Persian empire through regular, repetitive assessments: "The Cause of the Declension of the Persian Empire and the Change That Happened in Their Manners" (*Ancient History,* 4.4 §5: after Cyrus's reign); "Causes of the Frequent Insurrections and Revolts in the Persian Empire" (12.1 §12: upon the death of Artaxerxes II, c. 356); "Vices Which First Caused the Declension, and at Last the Ruin of the Persian Empire" (15 §11: upon the death of Darius III). The third assessment is introduced the way the first one ended, with a statement that as soon as Cyrus died (in 530 BC), the empire was sapped by the same structural problems that would lead to its collapse before Alexander two centuries later (330). The primary reason for its decline was moral decadence. After Cyrus, "the luxury and extravagance rose in time to such an excess as was little better than downright madness. . . . The only care [of Cyrus's successors] was to support the pomp of sovereignty, [but] the subjects neither obeyed nor marched but with unwillingness and reluctance." At the same time, the king "left the care of education entirely to women, that is, to princesses, brought up in a country where vanity, luxury and voluptuousness reigned in the highest degree, [so that] Cyrus did not, at least, take them along with him, in order to draw them out of that soft and effeminate course of life." As for posts as governors and superior officers, "they were generally bestowed upon people without either service or merit," and the empire was nothing "but a forced assemblage of different nations, without any common tie or relation among them"; this led to many revolts. Rollin thus makes clear that Alexander's plans were facilitated by the state of the empire upon his arrival; the decline of Persian education (which Plato and Xenophanes had highly praised in referring to Cyrus's era) made the Persian army ineffective and weak, commanded by "princes who gave themselves up a prey to idleness and effeminacy and who grew careless of military discipline."

With the exception of Bayle, who saw the display of wealth as an illustration of the power of the Great Kings, Alexander, and the sultans,[50] and Linguet, who insisted on breaking with the commonly held opinion and proposing a historical-anthropological explanation,[51] the modern writers and historians considered that the luxury associated with the campaigns of the Great King and the sultan symbolized their military impotence and easily explained their defeats by armies that were low in numbers and poor, but courageous. Rollin writes: "Would not the reader believe that he had been reading the description of a tournament, not the march of an army? Could he imagine that princes of the least reason would have been so stupid as to incorporate with their forces so cumbersome a train of women, princesses, concubines, eunuchs and domestics of both sexes?" (*Ancient History*, 15.4). Hence Rollin's conclusion, which was the commonly shared assumption: "The dazzling splendour of the Persian monarchy concealed a real weakness; and this unwieldy power, heightened by so much pomp and pride, was abhorred by the people; so that this colossus, at the very first blow, fell to the ground"[52] (15.11).

That the Persians were militarily incapable was one of the foregone conclusions about the empire of the Great Kings. This was so obvious that Folard (following so many others) was led to devaluate Alexander's victories over "a multitude of men and very few soldiers." In a more specific manner, Folard took advantage of the opportunity to provoke the Turks of his own time, drawing inspiration from Livy, who had strived to show that Alexander could not have won in Italy the victories he won in Asia because he would have had to face courageous soldiers and greatly talented generals: "Now we have the Turks conquering Persia today, are there any resources they do not encounter? Let them come to the West, they will meet their match with their innumerable forces. For what can the greatest numbers achieve against a greater art and advantageous weapons, which will make up for the lack in numbers?" (Folard, *Histoire de Polybe*, Commentaire, 1[1721]:254)

A comparison of Mably's two books quickly reveals that the author uses the same images and sometimes the same words to describe the Persian and Ottoman empires during the reigns that followed their hero-founders' exploits:

> Mably, *Le droit public de l'Europe*, 1748
>
> Corrupted by the education of the seraglio, Suleiman's successors wielded the sword of the heroes who had founded and expanded the empire like imbeciles. Revolutions became even more frequent; sultans incapable of ruling were the playthings of the indocility and avarice of the Janissaries.... In the palace of the Great Lord, all is mystery. Invisible women and slaves, these are the forces that drive everything and that the Grand Vizier often does not know. (pp. 225, 235)

> Mably, *Observations on the Greeks*, 1786 [French 1749]
>
> The declension of that empire had been apparent since the reign of Xerxes.... The calm blessings of peace degenerated into sloth and voluptuousness: the pressure of the crown was too heavy a burden for a monarch sinking into the lassitude of pleasure. Imprisoned in their palaces, the Eastern princes delegated their authority to rapacious, cruel, ignorant and treacherous ministers.... If one wicked, weak, or luxurious prince is frequently sufficient to overturn a monarchy established on solid and equitable principles, how was it possible the empire of Cyrus resist the united vices of his successors. (pp. 184, 191)

The Persian empire also suffered from another problem diagnosed by many observers of the Ottoman empire: the absence of rules of succession and the recurrence of dynastic struggles and assassinations. This is what Montesquieu explained about the "prince hidden in his palace" under despotic regimes: "It happens that the one who ascends the throne immediately has his brother strangled, as in Turkey, or blinded, as in Persia." To carry through his analogical demonstration, Montesquieu refers in a note to Ricaut's book on the Ottoman empire and to Justin on "comparable" practices in Achaemenid Persia. Finally, he completes his selection of despotic exempla by introducing Prince Darius's plot against his father, the Great King Artaxerxes II. He rejects the explanation provided by his source[53] and gives his own, turning to one of the most well-established Orientalizing representations in the European literature: "It is simpler to believe that this was some intrigue in these seraglios of the East, those places where artifice, wickedness, and deceit reign in silence and are covered by the darkness of night, where an old prince who becomes more imbecilic every day is the first prisoner of the palace."[54] All the authors clearly agreed that the Persian kings' seraglio was as corrupt as that of the sultans. This can be seen in the way the Abbé Guyon uses the word in denouncing the palace of the kings of Babylon, but also Alexander's palace, which after the death of Darius "became a seraglio similar to those of the kings of Persia, where he kept 360 concubines" (Histoire des Empires et des Républiques, 4:377).[55]

In the late eighteenth and early nineteenth centuries, following the Russian defeats of the sultan's armies, the weakness of the Ottomans was unreservedly recognized by analysts and historians regardless of whether they supported a European (or Russian) intervention. One of the arguments remained the analogy between the Persian and Ottoman empires. Witness Herder, explaining in 1787–1789 that Darius's empire was ripe for conquest: "Corruptions, revolts, conspiracies, assassinations, unsuccessful enterprises, and the like, are almost the most remarkable occurrences that the latter history of Persia affords... The throne tottered even under the best princes, till Alexander burst into Asia, and in a few battles put an end to the internally unsettled empire." Disaster was inscribed in the history "of such a senseless empire and so inimical to mankind," which the philosopher characterizes through a terminological comparison with the Ottomans: "Fate has taken vengeance of these sultans: they are swept away from the face of the Earth, as if by the pestilent simoon."[56]

During the same period (1788), Volney (1759–1820) tirelessly repeated the judgments and vocabulary found throughout the literature in his Considerations on the Wars with the Turks. He agrees with the theory that "this mighty Colossus, decayed in all parts, waited only for a shock to dissolve it." One of the most major causes and symptoms of decline was that the sultans were confined in the palaces rather than with their army: "When they began to shut themselves in their seraglios, benumbed by indolence, satiated even to apathy, and depraved by the flattery of a slavish court, their minds contracted with their enjoyments... and their government grew as vicious as themselves." And things could not change: "The sultan will continue to vegetate in his palace, while his wives and eunuchs nominate to employments; his Viziers put up to auction governments and places; the Pachas to pillage the subjects and impoverish the provinces."

Hostile to a European military enterprise but in favor of a Russian offensive against the Turks, Volney defends his proposition by comparing the Russians with the Macedonians, explaining that "it is precisely those barbarians who are the fittest for the conquest we speak of. It was not the most polished of the Greeks who conquered Asia, but the rude mountaineers of Macedonia." The Turks that the Russians would have to battle are implicitly but transparently likened to the Persians who faced Alexander. Here, Volney is contesting the idea that to make war, a people needs to be rich. This is only the case if one wants "to make war according to the custom of rich nations, who require in their camps all the gratifications and indulgencies which cities afford" (pp. 36–37). While the sentence is certainly borrowed from Rollin's discussion of Darius's Persian army before the Battle of Issus, Volney was probably not unaware that the image he used to attack the Ottoman army came from the *Anabasis of Alexander,* which Rollin quietly emulated: Arrian reports that before the Battle of Issus, Darius had sent to Damascus "everything else a great king takes with him on campaign for his extravagant way of living."[57]

Volney was not the first to establish a bridge between Alexander and the Russians. Voltaire had been even more explicit in doing so. After long years of preparation, Voltaire had published his *Histoire de l'empire de Russie sous Pierre le Grand* in 1763. Here, he develops the idea of the creation of an entirely new Russia instigated by the great conqueror-legislator tsar. He recounts that in 1722, the tsar had made certain to answer the shah of Persia's call for help because "he had for considerable time formed a project to make himself master of the Caspian Sea, by means of a powerful naval force, and to turn the tide of commerce from Persia and a part of India through his own dominions."[58] Voltaire sees the arrival of the Russian army in Derbent as a suggestion to link Peter and Alexander through the danger posed by the barbarians, which had been a constant since antiquity. Indeed, "according to the Persian tradition, the city of Derbent was partly repaired and fortified by Alexander the Great."

In referring to barbarians past and present, Voltaire is irked by the "good savages" discourse that Quintus Curtius attributes to the Scythian ambassador who was introduced to Alexander: "Other rhetoricians, thinking to imitate Quintus Curtius, have studied to make us look upon those savages of Caucasus and its dreary deserts, who lived wholly upon rapine and bloodshed, as the people in the world most remarkable for austere virtue and justice." This is far from the case, given that, on the one hand, the Scythians "were never other than destroyers" and, on the other, Alexander, by obvious contrast, "built towns in the very country which they inhabited." On this point, Voltaire compares Tsar Peter to King Alexander: "Like him, he was assiduous and indefatigable in his pursuits, a lover and friend of the useful arts; he surpassed him as a lawgiver, and like him endeavoured to change the tide of commerce in the world, and built and repaired at least as many towns as that celebrated hero of antiquity."[59]

In the first third of the nineteenth century, Barthold Georg Niebuhr was certainly the historian who made the most systematic use of the Ottoman and, more generally, "Asian" analogy. Over the summer semester of 1830, he devoted several lessons to the final days of the Persian empire, by which he meant the period from the reign of Artaxerxes II to the reign of Darius III (c. 400–330 BC).[60] While he claims that he does not understand why Plutarch had devoted one of his *Lives* to King Artaxerxes, he uses this text as a connecting thread, because "it is remarkable on account of the description of the customs, manners, and mode of acting in the East." One does not need to be a specialist in Oriental affairs to grasp its significance; one only needs to have some knowledge of the history of the Persian and Mongol kings, for the same characteristics are found in Plutarch. The Persian court functioned exactly as the courts of the Hindus and the Marathas did in the present day "and the despotism of a sultan is altogether opposed to the European type, such as it was established by the Greeks." Niebuhr goes on to state that the *Life of Artaxerxes* "is particularly important because it reveals to us the state of dissolution of the Persian empire, which greatly resembles the condition of Turkey at the end of the eighteenth century (*in dem Zustande wie die Türkei am Ende des 18. Jahrhunderts*)." Among the characteristics shared, or which Niebuhr assumes to be shared, he lists "the greatest cruelties of the Eastern despot"; the power of the royal princesses who controlled a particularly weak king; central power's inability to impose its rule in the provinces and nations of the empire (exactly as in Turkey, where Egypt joined many nomadic peoples in refusing to recognize the sultan's power); the great autonomy of the satraps (like the Turkish pashas in the late eighteenth century).

The reigns of his successors were made even worse by a development common to the "Asiatic states, [where] the princes sink into voluptuousness and to the most perfect indolence." Thus there is no reason to consider that Darius III was a ruler of any distinctive quality. Admittedly, the empire appeared tranquil, but "from the condition in which Alexander found it, it is manifest that this was only the stillness of death: the empire was an old, decrepit, and decayed body, with absolutely no strength." Alexander's battles were won over cowardly soldiers fighting in a disorganized army.

Heeren, who had recognized that the first Darius's territories were firmly under control, also paints a disastrous picture of the empire under the last Darius, which he uses as a prototype of the Asian empires and their inevitable decline. Here, one finds the same words and analysis applied to the government and to scheming in the seraglio by the queen mother and eunuchs.[61] The decline "resembled, in this respect, other great despotic dynasties"—from ancient Persia to modern Turkey—"which, at first, collapse in their internal structures, and on an impulse from without, are shaken to pieces." The shock was made all the more unbearable by the fact that despite the reforms introduced, the Persian army did not measure up to the European armies: "The military institutions never attained the perfection which marks those of Europe." Once again, Heeren uses an analogy: "The example of the Turkish empire continues to show with what difficulty an Asiatic, who is always half a nomad, can be inured to discipline. As this is an offspring of a sense of honour and love of country, so on the other hand, despotism is the parent of license and brutality, which may indeed display their energies in furious onsets, but not in deeds of cool daring like those of Europeans. . . . The straits of Thermopylae first presented to the astonished Asiatics a sight completely novel to them."[62]

Historians of Alexander and the Diadochi continued to use the analogy.[63] Droysen repeats his predecessors' assessment: "The inevitability of the fall of Darius's empire was a function of its expanse, its relationship with vanquished peoples, and defective military and administrative organization."[64] Droysen also makes a comparison with the Ottoman empire, but introduces a different causality than that suggested by his precursors: the cause of the Persian defeat "was not the corruption of the mores of the court,

of the dominant race, or of the subjugated peoples; this corruption, a perpetual companion to despotism, is never detrimental to despotic power. The
greatest empire of modern times is the proof of it; in it, we see a power that,
despite the licentious disorders of the court and the harem, amidst the ca-
bals and turpitudes of the greats, the changes of sovereign obtained through
violence, the cruelties against nature exercised on parties still all-powerful
the day before, manages to increasingly expand its military and diplomatic
successes in every direction. What led to Persia's misfortune was that it was
in the hands of a succession of rulers who were too weak."[65] Forty years
later (1877), his opinion of the Ottoman empire is in the past tense ("the Ottoman empire was long enough the proof of this"),[66] but his analysis of the
Achaemenids remains the same.

The Regeneration of the Orient

According to Volney, the Russian plan "to reign at once over Byzantium and
Babylon, over Athens and Ecbatana, over Jerusalem, Tyre and Palmyra" was
inspiring because its stated objectives were "to emancipate so many nations
from the odious yoke of fanaticism and tyranny; to restore the arts and sciences into their native soil; to open a new career to legislation, to commerce
and industry; to efface, if possible, the glory of the ancient East by that of
the new."[67] This quote combines two of the most widely held convictions of
the last part of the eighteenth century, which were that Europe owed the
beginning of civilized life to Asia and that to make good on this debt contracted in antiquity, European interventions should aim to restore the
Orient to its past glory.

A 1798 article in the French newspaper *La Décade philosophique* sheds
light on this perspective.[68] Basing his argument on Volney, the author considers that the objective of the republic's enterprises must be both "to open
new sources of opulence accessible to every nation without putting a yoke
on any of them, and [to] gratefully [return] the Sciences and Arts to those
lands which passed them on to us, but where their torch has gone out." He
continues: "Whoever feels the value of civilization and the Enlightenment
must ardently desire that Europe settle its debt with the ancient world.
Whoever is sensitive to the marvels of the Arts and industry must cry out to
see the nations that gave us the most important models entirely disappear

under the domination of barbarians who glory in the destruction they carry out and in their aversion for all that is most amazing in the creations of human intelligence. The misfortunes of the benefactor peoples should at least move those peoples who prosper by their good deeds."

These same justifications were used by admirers of Alexander's achievements. As Bourlet de Vauxcelles emphasized,[69] the Macedonian conqueror's historical role was both "to make Europe share in the felicities of Asia and to make the riches of the Indian Ocean flow back to the Mediterranean" and to restore Asia's prosperity and wealth, which had been jeopardized by disgraceful tyrants. Starting with Huet's first writings, this was exactly the sense that the erudite writers and scholars had nearly unanimously given to the episode of the cataracts built by the Persians on the Babylonian rivers; by destroying the cataracts, Alexander opened a country to large-scale commerce with India after its development had been blocked and its wealth dried up by the Great Kings' pusillanimous policy.[70]

Heeren, who was convinced that the period of Persian domination had reduced Babylonia's agricultural and commercial prosperity to nothing, called Alexander's initiatives "beneficial" (*als wohlthätigen Entwürfe*) and referred to him both as a "genius" and a "restorer" (*Wiederaufbauer*).[71] The same was true of Gillies, who credited the Macedonian conqueror with the will to reopen river and sea routes and to develop agriculture through maintaining canals and draining farmland. It was assumed that these obligations characteristic of good government had been totally neglected by the Persians: "The barbarous policy of the Persians had ruined the foreign traffic of Assyria. Under the same odious tyranny, agriculture and manufactures had also fallen to decay. Alexander . . . examined and improved the reservoirs of water and canals indispensable to a country where all is desert, that cannot be duly supplied with moisture, and where all is of exuberant fertility, that can be flooded and drained at the proper seasons, etc." (*History of the World*, 1[1809]:193). Elsewhere Gillies wrote that he did not attribute the decline of the Persians "to their effeminacy and luxury"; instead he considered that "without acquiring any of those arts and improvements which usually attend peace and opulence . . . the Persians were prepared for destruction rather by their ignorance of the arts of peace and war."[72] The superiority of Alexander—in other words of Europe—was therefore on the order of knowledge (today one would speak of scientific and technological superiority).

While the reviewer for the *Edinburgh Review* of October 1807 expressed strong misgivings about Gillies's book and stated his skepticism regarding its glorified image of Alexander, he resituated Alexander in a vast historical perspective that extended to the modern era: "The countries of Western Asia afford no very flattering precedent to those who, confident in the perfectibility of mankind, see nothing but prospects of brilliancy before them, and anticipate ages of progressive improvement, with no danger of backward steps, and no boundary but the dissolution of the world. It is in the desolate plains, and among degraded inhabitants of those regions, that we must look for the source of our arts, our letters, our religion, our population itself" (p. 40). Not without "melancholy," he considers that throughout history "a sort of compensation" had played a part in the state of human society: as Asia gradually declined, the European kingdoms' prosperity and civilization increased, to the point that "they have supplied the place of Egypt and Ionia, rather than they have added to the permanent mass of civilized life." He writes that there is no doubt that "relatively to the state of society in those countries, a more important epoch is fixed by the subsequent conquests of Alexander. . . . Asia became, for a period of 900 years, the seat of regular military discipline, of diffused opulence, of legal government and of philosophy."

The Awakening of Egypt

Of all the countries conquered by Alexander, Egypt was best suited to the parallels frequently made between past and present (particularly in France). Despite the polemics started by Voltaire and Linguet, who saw nothing great in the country's history or monuments, the most widespread opinion held Egypt to be the source of ancient Greece's knowledge and arts; as Pierre-Charles Levesque recalls in an introduction to his reflections on the history of Greek sculpture, the Greeks "must be seen as a new people, or at least as a newly civilized people, in comparison to the Egyptians and the great nations of Asia."[73] In this regard, Egypt is a country to which Alexander and the modern conquerors owe a debt; the moderns had to repair the harm done by the Ottoman administration.

This idea was glorified by those Greeks who had taken sides with the French and saw the Egyptian Expedition as the promise of or prelude to the freeing of their country from the same Ottoman yoke, through the creation of what a pamphlet published in 1801 called "the Gallo-Greek nation."[74] The pamphlet was published by the famous Adamantios Korais, whom we have previously encountered, under the pseudonym Atromète de Marathon. Initially published in 1801 under the warlike title of *Military Fanfare* (*Salpisma polemistērion*), this text addressed to Korais's compatriots was translated into French in 1821 under the title of *Appel aux Grecs*. Here, Korais presses the Greeks to join the French armies "composed of heroes, as were those of Marathon, Thermopylae, and Salamis." Indeed, these Frenchmen "have invaded the empire of the tyrant of Greece, and taken Egypt out of his bloody hands, . . . and restored enlightenment and liberty to the Egyptians." In this, the expedition was reminiscent of the Ptolemies, "who advanced civilization in this wealthy land." Korais continues: "Egypt is a second Greece; it is here that upon the decline of the splendor of Athens, the sciences took refuge; it is here that our compatriots restored them to glory, forming academies, collecting those admirable libraries that have since been burned by the enemies of the Greek name, by the coreligionists of our current tyrants. Let the lights be rekindled in Egypt and let them start from there to go awaken Greece!" (*Appel aux Grecs,* p. 37).

With this text, Korais was adapting for the Greeks a vision that had been widely circulated through other channels. The dialogue between past and present was facilitated by Alexandria and the Suez Canal, two aspects of Egyptian history recorded in the landscape (as a landscape-relic in the latter case). The former had been founded by Alexander, while a discovery made in the Isthmus of Suez (published by François-Michel de Rozière in 1809) suggested that the latter dated back to a distant Egyptian and Persian antiquity and had then been reopened by the Ptolemies.

All the European travelers and residents in Egypt mention these monuments. Founded by "a famous conqueror, as cautious as he was brave," as Maillet noted,[75] Alexandria served as a reminder of the glory of its founder and the splendor of the time of the Ptolemies. "The face of Egypt's commerce entirely changed upon Alexander's conquest of this powerful kingdom," wrote Paul Lucas, who had undoubtedly read Huet; unfortunately, he added, the Turks (of whom Maillet said "they prefer the egg of today than the chicken of tomorrow") "nearly entirely ruined commerce, according to the genius of their nations and the maxims of their policy."[76] During the same period, Jacques Savary called for the opening of a canal between the

Nile and the Red Sea.[77] Leibniz had earlier enjoined Louis XIV to conquer Egypt, "which would ensure him immortal glory once [he] had dared to make a path for [himself] or his descendants toward the exploits of Alexander,"[78] and in 1703 the Académie Royal des Sciences in Paris offered to dig a new canal, thanks to which "the face of the world would change; China and France, for example, would become neighbors, and one would pity the fate of the barbarous centuries when the Europeans had to go around Africa to get to Asia."[79]

The Macedonian conqueror was also praised by the Baron de Tott, who defended him against the accusation inherited from Boileau that he was a madman who had roamed the entire universe fearing neither God nor man; on the contrary, the Macedonian king built Alexandria "to give a center to the universe and to unite two hemispheres of the globe." Tott evokes the memory of "the elevated genius" to plead for the city's resurgence through a European conquest, which he calls for by clearly situating it in Alexander's footsteps: "To what pitch of splendor did he not raise Alexandria, in its origin? He joined it to the Nile by a canal at once navigable, and useful for cultivation. It became the city of all nations, the metropolis of commerce. He is honored even by its ashes, piled up by the barbarity of ages, and which wait only for some beneficent hand to expand them, and cement the reconstruction of the most stupendous edifice hitherto conceived by the human."[80]

Gillies would later quote Tott's *Memoirs* word for word in expressing his desire to see Alexandria rise from its ashes.[81] For his part, calling himself a "real philosopher," Linguet stated his aspiration in 1784 to see "an enlightened prince [awaken] these languishing lands right away." As he compares Alexander's expedition to the one against "those Turkish dogs" that was said to be under preparation "from Crimea to Hungary," his opposition to the war gradually disappears as his wish grows for "a revolution that would restore the throne of the Ptolemies" and reopen the Suez Canal—"that useful monument [that] has disappeared, [while] the useless pyramids have remained." He strongly hopes that the Nile, the Isthmus of Suez, and the Red Sea "recover their ancient and natural prerogative to be the link, the shared warehouse of the three parts of the ancient world."[82]

Clearly, what was wanted and sometimes planned for was the end of the Turkish-Muhammadan interlude, the rebirth of the city of Alexandria, and the reopening of the canal that had allowed for direct connection between the Mediterranean and the Red Sea and that would "today" allow ships to reach India without having to take a detour around the Cape of Good Hope.

While the memory of Alexander was used to political ends by William Vincent, who made the connection with British rule in India,[83] it is easy to understand why it was simultaneously so present on the Egyptian Expedition and in books recounting and analyzing it.[84] The April 1, 1798, issue of *Le Moniteur* already referred to the well-guarded secret in wondering whether the French "are destined to repeat an expedition even more brilliant than Alexander's."[85] In 1809, in the historical introduction to the *Description de l'Égypte*, Jean-Baptiste-Joseph Fourier justifies the Egyptian campaign by evoking the "homeland of the arts ... that has passed on its knowledge to so many nations, [and that] is today plunged into barbarism." He makes certain to include Alexander among the precedents: "No less remarkable for his political views than for the success of his arms, [Alexander] endeavored to give common interests to the most distant nations and to found cities all the way to the ends of the earth. He discovered, so to speak, the Indian Ocean, recognized the importance of navigation and commerce, and chose Alexandria to be the center for the communications he wanted to establish between peoples."

Alexander is also very present in an article in *La Décade égyptienne,* in which Citizen Girard aims "to propose the methods *to restore* to this region its former fertility and to establish communications there that would once again make it the warehouse of India's riches." Here, the work of the Ptolemies is presented as a return to the arts "of Greece in Egypt, their first homeland." The author cites Huet and Robertson and provides the reader a summarized history of commerce in Egypt.[86]

One also finds Alexander in J.-M. Le Père's report on communications between the Indian Ocean and the Mediterranean, published in the *Description de l'Égypte* in the wake of Le Père's research in Egypt over the winter of 1799/1800. The author, who was well acquainted with the literature of his time (including Montesquieu and Robertson) but does not cite it, introduces the Persians and "their religious prejudices, which led them to close the mouths of the Tigris and Euphrates with dikes," as well as Alexander, who not only destroyed the dikes but surpassed the Persians "by the extent of his projects: making Indian commerce flow into the heart of these vast states [and] by building Alexandria ... bringing the riches of India into this new Mediterranean port."[87] (The same historical references would be tirelessly repeated up to and including the writings of Ferdinand de Lesseps.)[88]

Upon reading the objectives attributed to Bonaparte by Jean-Baptiste-Joseph Fourier, one cannot help but think of the praise lavished upon

Alexander in nearly identical terms by his eighteenth- and early nineteenth-century admirers: "[Bonaparte] intended ... to expand on irrigation and cultivation, to open a constant connection between the Mediterranean and the Arabian Gulf, to found commercial establishments, to offer the Orient the useful example of European industry, in order to make the inhabitants' condition more pleasant, and to provide them all the advantages of a sophisticated civilization. One could not reach this goal without the continual application of the arts and sciences" (*Description de l'Égypte*, 1[1809]:viii–ix).

We know that in his order of the day for June 22, 1798, Bonaparte evoked the memory of the builder of Alexandria. A synoptic reading of Fourier and historians of Alexander in the period 1760–1800 creates the impression that Alexander's program in the Orient was an advance version of the one prepared by the Ideologues for Egypt. It is easy to understand the enthusiasm of Jullien du Ruet, who constantly combines and identifies the image of Alexander ("the Napoleon of the ancient world") with that of the emperor he admired: "To him fell the honor of avenging Egypt dishonored by the despicable masters who had kept it under the brutal yoke of ignorance since Cambyses: Alexander put his glory to creating men and cities on a land sufficiently overwhelmed by temples and Pyramids. In founding Alexandria, he himself put in place the first ring of this magic chain, which was in the succession of centuries to link Europe to the entire world's Commerce and link on its shore the peoples of the two poles" (*Tableau de l'histoire universelle*, 1:xii, 497).

The comparison was all the more evident given that since the late sixteenth-century Alexander's expedition had also been regularly presented as a voyage of discovery undertaken by geographer-surveyors and "Aristotelian" scholars charged by the king with studying the flora, the rivers, the mores of the peoples, and Babylonian astronomy.[89] In these conditions, the homothety attains a kind of formal and contextual perfection. From one civilizing hero to the next, by "uniting force and science,"[90] soldiers and scholars of Europe together organized the inventory and appropriation of a world to which they brought the assistance of the Enlightenment.

Oriental Hoarding and European Circulation

Let us return once more to Linguet. Recall the enthusiastic declarations in the introduction to his *Siècle d'Alexandre,* particularly this one: "A prodigious revolution then took place in half the globe. Transported to Europe, the riches of Susa and Persepolis caused rapid change there. Interests and politics bound it to Asia, and once these ties were made, they were no longer broken" (1762 ed., pp. 6–9; 1769 ed., pp. 13–15). Unfortunately, in this case as in many others, Linguet does not explain by what ways and means Alexander brought this revolution to Europe and Asia. What he wants to say is clear enough: he is alluding to the vast treasures of the Great Kings, which Alexander seized from Babylon, Susa, Persepolis, and Pasargadae. The Macedonian conqueror had a detailed inventory made of the treasures, of which we find traces in Greco-Roman texts. The ancient authors affirmed that the Persian treasures were stored in the royal palaces and that the gold and silver were kept in large jars, to be used only on express order from the king; most of it remained untouched in the treasuries. These texts were well known (particularly the one by Herodotus) since they had been compiled by Brisson in 1590, then by John Potter in the first half of the eighteenth century; they were again compiled by August Boeckh in 1818.[91]

John Gillies raised the same question, adopting a wishful tone as he contemplated the potential great prosperity that was shattered by the king's death: "Had Alexander lived to consolidate his conquests ... the unrestrained intercourse of the ancient world would have nearly accorded with what the discovery of America realized, on a still larger scale, in the modern. The precious metals of Spain (for it abounded in both sorts) would have been freely and securely exchanged for the spices of India, the perfumes of Arabia, and the manufactures of many industrious intermediate countries" (*History of the World,* 1:191).

These all-too-brief allusions fit into a general reflection that can be followed throughout the eighteenth century. On several occasions, Christian Gottlob Heyne asked how victors throughout history had used the gargantuan plunder they had gathered by the end of their campaigns. On January 2, 1790, in a conference addressed to the "new prorector" Christoph Gatterer, Heyne examined the resources of the kingdom of Macedon and their successive increase, decrease, and collapse over the ages. In keeping with his numerous public interventions in favor of peace, he praises Philip II for using his resources to improve agriculture, navigation, and commerce. He is less admiring of Alexander, whose conquests claimed many lives without bringing prosperity to Macedon itself.[92] Ten years later, Heyne spoke on the same subject again, but expanded the scope of his remarks to include contemporary examples (the pillage of Delhi by Nader Shah; the plunder collected by the British in 1799 in Seringapatam, capital of the last king of Mysore, Tipu Sahib, who was killed during the siege;[93] the gold and silver accumulated by the Spanish in Peru). He asks whether the yield from this war loot had served to increase the prosperity of the countries and their populations, to launch public works, to transform agricultural practices, or to reinforce commerce and exchanges. He does not fail to mention the Persian treasures and their capture by Alexander. Noting that none of the kings of Asia made their riches bear fruit, choosing instead to hoard them, he concludes that the "great empires are one of the plagues of the human race." Like the kings of Asia (*omnes Orientis reges*), the Great Kings gave in to their "avidity" (Cambyses), their "weak minds" (Darius), or their "vain luxury" (Xerxes); they thought neither of the development of the arts nor the flourishing of commerce. The Persian empire was therefore an easy target for Alexander, who seized its treasures; all the riches accumulated since Croesus and Darius were squandered during the civil wars that followed the king's death. Heyne observes that despite the admiration expressed for Philip and Alexander in antiquity, they actually only used their riches to display their military virtues, their glory, and their royal splendor. The Romans had acted no differently. Finally, Heyne concludes, it must be recognized that the capture of these Asian treasures did not serve the good of the populations—quite the opposite, in fact.[94]

As for Pierre-Charles Levesque, he does not take the perspective of redistribution, but of circulation. By examining the policies carried out by "the kings of Asia," he deduces a general rule. He judges that "the Persians had no idea of the art of finances," from which he concludes (or postulates) that the rules of money-hoarding observed by Herodotus among the Great Kings "appear to be that of all the Oriental governments," which he contrasts with "modern [i.e., European] governments, [of which] the most spendthrift have a far less negative conduct for the public interest, since even when they wildly squander riches, they are putting them into circulation."[95]

These reflections are in accordance with those earlier presented by another author, André de Claustre, in discussing one of the episodes most famous in Europe (which was also mentioned by Heyne): the pillaging of the treasures of the Great Mogul by Nader Shah. De Claustre provides an inventory of the treasures and explains that "one hundred workmen were kept busy for fifteen days melting & making into bars the gold & silver not in coined money, in order to make transportation easier." He then asks a most interesting question, in keeping with Linguet's remarks, which is "whether this revolution of riches . . . is an event entirely indifferent to the rest of the world." Like his contemporaries, who had all read François Bernier's *Mémoires* and his *Lettre à Colbert*, Claustre reminds the reader that the gold and silver of America "ended up in the Mughal empire never to leave it again." The answer to the author's own question about what became of these treasures comes as no surprise: they are accumulated in underground treasuries, "from which they are nearly never removed, other than when there is the most urgent necessity," just as in Persepolis, where, according to Barthélémy, there were "subterranean passages, in which are deposited immense sums." In his dissertation *On the Immense Treasures in Bullion and Coined Money of the Ancient Sovereigns of Asia* (1808), Thomas Maurice also deplores "the pernicious practice of burying money in vast quantities," and denounces the overwhelming responsibility of India, an "avaricious glutton, whose rapacious jaws, from the first of time, have swallowed the gold and silver of the world, [so that], in comparison, the riches of Xerxes and Darius were trifling." All things considered, Claustre concludes, the transfer of treasure cannot "do much harm" to the Moghuls for "there is so little difference between not using your riches and not having any." However, "it would do much good to the rest of the world, where the circulation of money takes place, that is if it is true that a great wealth of money is a good thing."[96] This is obviously the same idea expressed in Linguet in 1762, but also in Levesque in 1811.

The same image is found in all these authors: in the Orient, money is locked in royal treasuries, and therefore remains inert; in Europe, it circulates, therefore creating wealth. Indeed, the necessity for circulation between economic agents had been a favored line of thought for seventeenth- and eighteenth-century economists attempting to define the optimal conditions for production, exchanges, and ultimately general prosperity.[97] It is therefore a philosopher-king's duty to adopt the appropriate policy, favorable to his kingdom. Diderot reminded Frederick of this in an uncompromising remonstrance. He articulates the opposition between two ways of using public money through a differential analysis of political regimes. The philosopher does not mince words in reminding the king of Prussia that if he wants to shed his "warrior king" garb and turn into a "citizen king," he must abide by the following precept (among others): "That those innumerable metals buried in your coffers, by returning into circulation, give life to the body politic; that your personal riches, which can be lost through a setback, henceforth only have as their basis the national wealth, which will never dry up!" (*Histoire des deux Indes,* 1780, 5.10).[98]

According to Montesquieu, this was actually the policy followed by Alexander, whose "hand was closed for private expenditures, [and] opened for public expenditures." His economy was characterized by "his own frugality," while he showed "his immense prodigality for great things." The reason for this choice belongs to the ethics of a power put at the service of the people: "In every country he entered, his first ideas, his first designs, were always to do something to increase its prosperity and power" (*Spirit of the Laws,* 10.14). From Montesquieu to Diderot and from Alexander to Frederick, philosophical reflection pleads in favor of circulation, which is a guarantee of public prosperity, as opposed to private hoarding, which enriches the despot and impoverishes the kingdom's population.

In studying Athens' silver and gold resources after the Second Greco-Persian War, August Boeckh made a comparative digression on the vast reserves of the Persian kings, which were not put in circulation (*nicht im Umlauf*). Following the same model as his predecessors who had asked themselves about the capture of the Great Mogul's treasures by Nader Shah, he did not fail to refer to the large quantity of precious metals that "flowed back to the Occident" once seized by Alexander, but also the use they were put to. At the end of his analysis, he comes to the conclusion that they were partially put into circulation through royal expenses, but also the wars of Alexander's successors. A significant part also "slept in the treasuries," while another amount "was worked" (as it had been by the Persians), in both cases due to economic constraints; indeed, if all these precious metals had been thrown into circulation at once, "their price in relation to other merchandise would have fallen far below what it was in reality."[99]

In 1833, Droysen picked up from his mentor Boeckh (whose seminars he had attended) and developed an idea with which many agreed. In his view, one of the most considerable revolutions introduced by Alexander was the putting into circulation of the Persian treasures: in a limited number of years, the treasures were all pushed into the economic circuit, "like the heart pumps out blood. It is easy to understand that work and commerce began to spread them, by an ever increasing speed of circulation, through the longtime tired limbs of the empire. One can see how, by these means, the economic life of peoples, which the Persian domination had sucked out their strengths like a vampire, renewed and prospered."[100] Droysen did not deny the short-term negative consequences, particularly the drop in the value of money, but he implied that in the long term the positive consequences would largely outweigh the negative, particularly given that Alexander reinjected his treasures into economic life, including through major irrigation and drainage projects in Babylonia and Greece, which contributed to increasing farmable surfaces and production.

In a culmination of a collective reflection that endured throughout the eighteenth century and was explicitly revived by Linguet in 1762, Droysen borrowed the mercantilists' metaphor of blood circulation, by which currency irrigates the body of the nation the way blood irrigates the human body (he uses the French term *circulation* rather than the German term *Umlauf*). More or less the same image was found in Jullien du Ruet, who explained the agony of the Persian empire as follows: "Commerce is to the political life of empires as blood is to the animal economy.... Deprived of its subsistence, the empire with the most phalanxes, the most glorious in conquests, slumps under its own weight. (*Tableau de l'histoire universelle,* 1:8). Hence the role played by a great genius who restores circulation: "Some repairing genius (can) fly to its assistance and prevent its certain decline by restoring its commerce and industry to circulation." In this case, the "repairing genius" is Alexander. Following the European model, the Macedonian conqueror awakens an empire crushed by the predatory rule of an "Asiatic" king who, by diverting riches to his coffers and tunnels, had lost interest in commerce and navigation to the point of blocking the circulation of currency and merchandise and dooming the different nations that made up his empire to thrombosis and asphyxia.

Conclusion

The historiography of the long eighteenth century did not limit its scope to observing the Greek city-states of the classical period to the exclusion of the period that followed the city-states' defeat at the hands of Philip of Macedon. Instead, it developed increasingly well-argued reflections on the history of Alexander the Great, whose protagonist continued to arouse the most contradictory judgments and to feed the opposition between ancients and moderns. Booksellers, writers, and readers' shared interest in Alexander is evidenced by the publication in a wide variety of languages of numerous Greek history manuals in which his adventure holds an increasingly notable place, and that of several biographical monographs issued in France, Germany, and England from 1665 to 1829.[1] This sustained interest is also marked by specific interventions by erudite writers and philosopher-historians, particularly in France and England, as well as Alexander's topical presence in publications in a wide range of fields of knowledge (history, geography, commerce, political science, philosophy, etc.). Succeeding both the young man on a voyage of initiation of the *Alexander Romance* and its various iterations in vernacular languages and the later ideal-type of the fighter-hero now denounced in all quarters, the Alexander of the Enlightenment was elevated by some into a guardian of European memory and identity—though not without debates and polemics. Others, on the contrary, tried to make Alexander into a foil or at least a counterexample.

When seeking to explain the development of an autonomous historiography of Alexander, one is initially tempted to point to the success of research and publications on antiquity beginning in the sixteenth and seventeenth centuries. There is certainly some truth here, given that the interest in ancient history long went hand in hand with an effort to better publish, translate, and comment on the Greek and Roman authors from which exegeses and interpretations were developed. It was also through scholarly editions of the "ancient historians" that the history of Alexander was approached, as evidenced by the title of the competition announced by the Académie Royale des Inscriptions et Belles Lettres in 1769.

Yet this explanation falls short in that it fails to take into account the specificity of the historiography. If the history of Alexander was frequently alluded to in the Europe of the long eighteenth century, it was primarily due to the existence of a second figure. Though this second figure may have been in Alexander's shadow, its role was nonetheless considered inseparable from that of the protagonist on whom it conferred a prestige made even greater by a historical mission deemed grandiose.

In a preliminary statement to an article on the Europeanization of the classical Orient written in 1944–1945, Elias Bickerman stated: "Twice in the course of time European civilisation has extended beyond its borders and imposed itself on the immobile East: in our time and in the wake of Alexander the Great's conquest."[2] Bickerman wrote in a particular political context, two centuries after *The Spirit of the Laws* and Voltaire's *Essai sur les Mœurs*, but expressed a Eurocentric view previously held by eighteenth-century observers. It can be summarized in three propositions: first, that Alexander was the first European to gain control of the Orient and establish settlers from Europe there; second, that this Orient was "immobile," meaning that it was not only stagnant but also incapable of transforming itself by its own means—which is exactly what European observers in 1750–1830 thought of the Ottoman empire, which was itself regularly likened by analogy to the Persian empire of the last Great King. Hence the third proposition, which was that the study of Alexander's empire also nurtured reflection on the history of European expansion, or, more accurately, that they nurtured each other.

This is the underlying meaning of the debates surrounding Alexander's modernity. It is denied by those who oppose the very principle of military conquest and the creation of vast empires in the name of their own conception of modernity; by those who express an unwavering opposition to modern colonial conquests; by those who consider that Alexander was not driven by generous ideals proper to the Great Nation; and by those in Europe who directly suffered the ravages of Napoleonic expansionism. On the other hand and despite the fact that he was so critical of an antiquity he constantly relegated to the distant past, Voltaire considered the Macedonian's founding of cities as the groundwork that heralded European commerce in Asia in his own time. By saying this, he included Alexander in the continuity of the European history of Great Discoveries, if only as a distant precedent. Similarly, identifying an "age of Alexander" in the *longue durée* signifies that to some extent the Macedonian king heralded the European modernity symbolized by the thriving "age of Louis XIV." But this reversal of perspectives is primarily due to Montesquieu. Not that the great philosopher was ever a champion of European imperialism—on the contrary. But the admirably coherent image of Alexander he created seemed to reconcile the empire, commerce, peace, and the unity of humankind. This character subsequently escaped his creator's control and was used in service of authentically expansionist ends, with which Montesquieu would have disagreed.

The creation and reception of the image of a "regenerative" Alexander are intimately connected with the history of modern Europe as conqueror and to the definition of its identity in relation to the Orient as it subjects it to its own rules. By identifying the Macedonian king as a "precedent" and even a full-fledged "participant," one establishes and increasingly perfects a homology between an ancient conquest whose excesses were "redeemed" by its benefits and a modern conquest that "returns" to the Orient the advantages it had delivered to Europe at its beginnings. Official and unofficial explanations for the Egyptian Expedition leave no doubt as to the development of these concepts: if considered on the order of representation, Aristotle's prestigious support and the fact that Alexander was accompanied by "geographers" and "men of science" herald the "expedition of scholars" to the Valley of the Nile in 1798. The same is true in England and Scotland of the direct relationship established between the Macedonian and British conquests in India. In this sense, both the image of Alexander as it takes shape at that time and the context of its genesis are integral elements of Orientalism which escaped Edward Said's analysis; admittedly, Said began his analysis with Bonaparte's Egyptian campaign and took little interest in the previous phase, which, following the logic of his own approach, can be referred to as *proto-Orientalism* or, better yet, *Enlightenment Orientalism*. This phase deserves to be studied in and of itself and to be reintegrated in the *longue durée*.[3]

Historical reflection on the Macedonian conquest has fed questions and debates about European expansion toward the Orient and the East Indies.

One particular issue holds an absolutely central place in this line of inquiry, in direct relation with the accounts and interpretations previously offered by the ancient authors. This is the question of how conquerors should behave toward conquered populations, and particularly toward the elites of countries now subject to a European power. Montesquieu addressed this very problem under the title "How to Cement an Empire." His decisive interest in this aspect of conquest was attuned to his favored sources—the writings of Arrian and Plutarch on the subject—but also to the violent debates that had raged in the Roman era, with some accusing Alexander of having yielded to Oriental mores and customs rather than imposing those of Greece. The same clash is found among the erudite writers and philosophes, some of whom followed Montesquieu in praising the Macedonian king for his policy of understanding and collaboration with the Persian elites, while the others followed Rollin, Mably, and Sainte-Croix in denouncing him for having caused the Orientalization of Greece. As seen in Great Britain from about 1785 to 1820, the debate did not exclusively concern scholars and exegetes; it resonated deeply with contemporary politics and saw Plutarchian theories being put to use both by partisans of the Europeanization and Christianization of India's populations and those who relentlessly opposed such a policy of assimilation.

Even among those who had followed Montesquieu in crediting Alexander with a policy that was both intelligent and humane, some recognized that the policy thus defined entailed a danger whose gravity became plainly apparent under his disgraceful or at best incapable successors. For a revealing example of a major interpretive trend, one need go no further than John Gillies's disillusioned comments: "The feeble mixture of Grecian colonization diffused through the East was sufficient, indeed, to tinge, but too inconsiderable, to alter and assimilate, the vast mass of barbarism. But as the principle of degeneration is often stronger than that of improvement, the sloth and servility of Asia gradually crept into Greece" (*History of Ancient Greece* 2:680).

This diagnosis resonates with the image of the Orient analyzed by the same author in previous chapters[4]: "The hardy and intrepid Persian warriors were themselves subdued by the vices of the luxurious city [of Babylon]." Therefore, like its predecessors, the Persian empire was dominated by the system of "Asiatic despotism," which is "more favourable to the extension than to the permanence of empire. The different members of the unwieldy body were so feebly connected with each other, that to secure their common submission required almost as much genius as to achieve their conquest."

Forty years later, the positions Barthold Georg Niebuhr put forward in his public classes (1829–1830) are expressed with all the force of a historian profoundly hostile to the Orient and the Orientals and thus having strong reservations about Alexander's Iranian policy. He judges that Alexander should exclusively have sought support from the Greco-Macedonians referred to as the "dominant nation" (*zur herrschende Nation*), in which he reluctantly agrees to include the populations of Asia Minor that were already partially Hellenized. As for colonization, he adds, it had perverse effects, as proved by the example of Seleucia (on the Tigris), which was nothing but "an island in the midst of a barbarous country."[5] Borrowed from Roman texts, this image of the island lost in the midst of an Asian sea and threatened with indigenous submersion was exceptionally powerful throughout the nineteenth and twentieth centuries. In a terrifying form, it established the idea of the clash of civilizations, by which it was unreasonable to promote a policy of collaboration between Europeans and Orientals, whether in Alexander's time or "now," due to the great risk that the West would in return experience the deplorable consequences of a wave of Orientalization.[6]

Niebuhr's fellow early nineteenth-century German historian Arnold Heeren took the opposite position and underlined Alexander's successes in this domain. As early as 1799, he believed that in "nothing probably is the superiority of his genius more brilliantly displayed than in his exemption of national prejudice."[7] This is nonetheless an ambiguous, if not critical compliment, for like many analysts and thinkers before him (Montesquieu, Mably), Heeren was in favor of "mediocre states," by which one meant small states (*Kleinstaaten*) as opposed to big empires. In later editions of his *Handbuch*, he stated that he was sorry that the success of Alexander's policy ("the forced amalgamation of races") had as a corollary "the obliteration of national character" of the different elements that made up the empire: populations lost the cultural specificities particular to "nations" and "their own languages sunk into mere provincial dialects" (*Volksdialekten*).[8] Conceived on the basis of the history of Alexander and its developments under the successors, this last statement evokes an observation made by Heeren around the same time regarding contemporary history. In analyzing Europe's political situation after the Congress of Vienna, Heeren elaborated on Germany's situation, noting "the necessity of forming the German states into a political union, as far as it was possible. It was loudly demanded by the public voice and never was the national spirit of Germany (*Deutsche Nationalgeist*) so much excited." The question remained how this could be accomplished. Heeren immediately rejected the possibility of "the transformation into one state (*Umformung zu einem Staat*)," because, as he clearly specified, "that would have been the grave of German improvement and European freedom." To his mind, it could only be through "a union of the existing states of Germany."[9] Looking at these arguments side by side strongly suggests (at the very least) that Heeren's view of Alexander's empire developed at the same pace as his very conservative thinking about Germany in his time.

About twenty years later (1843), Droysen, who was a great admirer of Alexander and an active campaigner for a united Germany, devoted a special study to Alexander's founding of colonial cities, drawing his unattributed inspiration both from Plutarch and Montesquieu, which he supplemented with all the scholarship since accumulated on the location and organization of these cities. Droysen violently condemned "the appalling monstrosities due to the systems of colonization attempted by the Christian nations of Europe for the last three centuries," contrasting them with Alexander and his "truly grandiose system [that] was based on the suppression of any distinction between victors and vanquished, and the principle of equalization and of actual fusion."[10] It is easy to see why the author emphasized his research's contemporary relevance: "The events of the Hellenistic period hold more than an inspiration for the laborious pastimes of erudition," he wrote, clarifying that this kind of research made it possible to carry out "one of the most grandiose tasks of the present time." Through comparative approaches ("Was the Hellenistic world a colonial world?"), the conviction that the era opened by Alexander was a modern one remains central to the thinking of historians of the Hellenistic world in the postcolonial phase—but that's another story.

In the long term, Europe turned to "the first European conqueror of the Orient" for the inspiration to carry out its own imperial history and/or to give meaning to various national histories (the debates surrounding German unity and on the future of liberated Greece), approaching Alexander in a manner sometimes arrogant, sometimes anxious, but always fascinated.

Throughout the nineteenth century and into the first part of the twentieth century, many of those who analyzed and participated in empires looked to the history of Alexander to discover "lessons of colonization";[11] they searched the distant Macedonian past for the principles and methods that could help them to resolve the contradictions between unity and diversity, between empire and nations, and between the affirmed history of Europe and the subordinate histories of the subjects of empire.

BIBLIOGRAPHY

NOTES

ACKNOWLEDGMENTS

INDEX

Bibliography

Primary Sources

A.J.D.B. Review of Sainte-Croix, "Des anciens gouvernemens fédératifs." *Magasin Encyclopédique,* (1799): 7–26.

Anonymous. "Sur une ancienne communication de la Méditerranée avec la Mer Rouge." Paris: *Histoire de l'Académie des Sciences,* 1703: 83–86.

———. *Grand trésor historique et politique des Hollandais dans tous les états et empires du monde.* Rouen: Chez Ruault, 1712 = *Memoirs on the Dutch trade in all the states, empires, and kingdoms of the world,* translated from the French by Mr. Samber, 2nd ed. London: C. Rivington, 1719.

———. Review of Bougainville, *Parallèle* (1752). *Journal de Trévoux* (1752), 502–518.

———. Review of *Allgemeine Weltgeschichte,* vols. 1–2 (1765). *Allgemeine Historische Bibliothek* 3 (1767): 233–242; all volumes. *Historisches Journal von Mitgliedern des Königlichen Historischen Instituts zu Göttingen* 3 (1774): 255–283.

———. Review of Sainte-Croix, *Examen critique* (1775). *L'esprit des Journaux* 5 (1776): 59–71.

———. *Histoire Universelle depuis le commencement du monde jusqu'à présent, composée en Anglais par une Société de Gens de Lettres, nouvellement traduite en François par une Société de Gens de Lettres.* Vol. 7: *Contenant la suite de l'histoire des Babyloniens, celle des Mèdes et celle des Perses jusqu'à la mort de Darius Codoman, d'après les auteurs grecs et latins.* Paris: Moutard, 1780.

———. *Histoire Universelle . . .* Vol. 12: *Contenant l'Histoire de Crète, de Cypre, de Samos et des autres îles grecques, et partie de celle des Macédoniens.* Paris: Moutard, 1780.

———. *Histoire Universelle . . .* Vol. 13: *Contenant la suite de l'Histoire des Macédoniens jusqu'au temps où les Romains firent la conquête du Royaume de Macédoine.* Paris: Moutard, 1780.

———. *Histoire Universelle . . .* Vol. 16: *Contenant l'Histoire des Juifs depuis leur retour jusqu'à la mission de Jésus-Christ.* Paris: Moutard, 1780.

———. *Entretiens des notables de l'autre monde ou dialogue entre Alexandre le Grand, Constantin le Grand, Henri le Grand, Pierre le Grand, Frédéric le Grand, Louis le Grand, Vergennes le Grand.* n.p., 1787.

———. Review of Gillies, *View on the Reign of Frederick II* (1789). *Critical Review, or, Annals of Literature* (1789): 524–527.

———. Review of Gillies, *View on the Reign of Frederick II* (1789). *Monthly Review, or, Literary Journal* (1789): 230–239.

———. Review of Robertson, *Historical Disquisition* (1791). *Monthly Review, or, Literary Journal* 6 (1791): 1–11.

———. Review of Heeren, *Ideen* (1796). *British Critique* 10 (1798): 455–459.

———. Review of Vincent, *Voyage of Nearchus* (1797). *European Magazine, and London Review* 31 (March 1797): 169–172.

———. *Observations on the expedition of General Buonaparte to the East and the probability of his success considered, to which is added a brief sketch of the present state of Egypt ; and historical account of Alexandria . . . with some remarks on its local importance should it become the Mart of the East . . .* London: Cawthorn, 1798.

———. Review of Vincent, *Voyage of Nearchus* (1797). *British Critic* 10 (1798): 1–12 and 170–185.

———. Review of Vincent, *Voyage of Nearchus* (1797). *Monthly Review, or, Literary Journal* 26 (1798): 254–265.

———. *Correspondance de l'armée françoise en Égypte interceptée par l'escadre de Nelson publiée à Londres.* London: P. F. Fauche et Compagnie, 1799.

———. Review of Vincent, *Voyage de Néarque* (1800). *Bibliothèque germanique* 1 (Year 9 [1800]): 89–90.

———. Review of Vincent, *Voyage de Néarque* (1800). *Le Spectateur du Nord* (July 1800): 71–82.

———. *Public Characters of 1800–1801.* Dublin: J. Moore, 1801.

———. "Projet d'une expédition dans l'Inde, par terre," *Paris pendant l'année 1801,* vol. XXXI. London (1801):195–202.

———. *Notice des ouvrages de M. D'Anville.* Paris: Fuchs et Demanne, 1802.

———. *Public Characters of 1803–1804.* London, 1804.

———. Review of Sainte-Croix, *Examen critique* (1804). *Journal de l'Empire* (August 27, 1805): 1–4 (in notes); (July 22, 1806): 3–4.

———. *Catalogue des livres de feu M. d'Ansse de Villoison.* Paris: Debure père et fils and Tilliard, 1806.

———. Review of Vincent, *Voyage of Nearchus* (1797). In Edmund Burke (ed.), *The Annual Register, or a View of the History, Politics and Literature for the Year 1797.* 2nd ed., 431–435. London, 1807.

———. Review of Gillies, *History of the World* (1807). *Edinburgh Review, or, Critical Journal* (October 1807): 40–61.

———. *Catalogue des livres de feu M. Guilhem de Clermont Lodève de Sainte-Croix.* Paris: Debure père et fils, 1809.

———. *Rapport du Jury institué par S. M. l'Empereur et Roi pour le jugement des Prix décennaux, en vertu des décrets des 24 Fructidor an 12 et 28 novembre 1809*. Paris: Imprimerie impériale, 1810.

———. *Rapports et discussions de toutes les Classes de l'Institut de France sur les ouvrages admis au Concours pour les Prix décennaux*. Paris: Baudoin et Garnery, 1810.

———. "Biographical Memoir of Alexander Dalrymple Esq." *Naval Chronicle* 35 (1816): 174–204

———. "Remarks on Mr Mitford's View of the Constitution of Macedonia, Contained in the New Volume of His History of Greece," review of Mitford, *History of Greece*, vol. 5 (1818). *Blackwood's Edinburgh Magazine* 5 (April–September 1819): 443–451.

———. Review of Mitford, *History of Greece*, vol. 5 (1818). *Quarterly Review* 25 (April–July 1821): 154–174.

———. "Notice historique sur la vie et les ouvrages M. Niebuhr," *Histoire et mémoires de l'Institut royal de France. Académie des Inscriptions et Belles-Lettres*, VII (1824): 160–174.

———. *Encyclopédie des gens du monde, répertoire universel des sciences, des lettres et des arts, avec des notices sur les principales familles historiques, et sur les personnages célèbres, morts et vivants, par une Société de savans, de littérateurs et d'artistes, français et étrangers*. Vol. 1. Paris: Librairie de Treuttel et Würtz, 1833.

———. Review of Heeren, *Historical Researches*, vols. 1–2 (1833). *Edinburgh Review, or, Critical Journal* (1834): 87–123.

Ablancourt, Nicolas Perrot d'. *Les guerres d'Alexandre par Arrian, de la traduction de Nicolas Perrot, sieur d'Ablancourt. Sa Vie, tirée du grec de Plutarque, et ses apophtegmes de la mesme traduction*. Paris: Louis Billaine, 1646, 1664.

———. *Lettres et Préfaces critiques publiées avec une introduction, des notices et un lexique par Roger Zuber*. Paris: Librairie Marcel Didier, 1972.

Abbt, Thomas. *Vom Verdienste* (1765). In *Vermische Werke*. Vol. 1. Berlin: Fr. Nicolai, 1772.

Adams, John. *The Flowers of Ancient History Comprehending, on a New Plan, the Most Remarkable and Interesting Events, as Well as Characters, of Antiquity Designed for the Improvement and Entertainment of Youth*. 3rd ed. London: G. Kearsley, 1796.

Allegmeine Weltgeschichte von der Schöpfung an bis auf gegenwärtige Zeit . . . ausfertiget von Wilhelm Guthrie, Johann Gray und anderen Gelehrten. Aus dem Englischen übersefst: aus den Originalschriftstellern berichtiget, und mit einer fortlausenden Zeitrechnung und verschiedenen Anmerkungen versehen von herrn Christian Gottlob Heyne . . . Vol. 2. Leipzig: M. G. Weidemanns Erben und Reich, 1765.

Allgemeine Weltgeschichte im Englischen herausgegeben von Wihl. Guthrie und Joh. Gray, übersefst und verbessert von Christian Gottlob Heyne. Vol. 8. Troppau: J. G. Trafsler, 1785.

[Die] Allgemeine Welthistorie die in England durch eine Gesellschaft von Gelehrten ausfertiget worden. In einem wollständigen und pragmatischen Auszuge von Friedrich

Eberhard Boysen, mit einer Vorrede Johann Christoph Gatterers. Halle: J. J. Gebauer, 1767 (vols. 1–3), 1768 (vol. 4), 1769 (vol. 5).

Alletz, Pons-Augustin. *Abrégé de l'histoire grecque depuis les temps héroïques jusqu'à la réduction de la Grèce en province romaine, dans lequel on voit les guerres les plus célèbres de cette nation, son esprit, ses mœurs; les Grands hommes qu'elle porta dans son sein: les Législateurs, capitaines, philosophes, orateurs, poètes, historiens, et artistes.* Paris: chez Nyon, 1763, 1764; new ed. Paris: chez Bailly, 1774.

Alverdy, Charles de l'. *Tableau général raisonné et méthodique des ouvrages contenus dans le recueil des Mémoires de l'Académie royale des Inscriptions et Belles-Lettres, depuis sa naissance jusques et y compris l'année 1788, servant de supplément aux tables de ce recueil.* Paris: Didot l'aîné, 1791.

Ameilhon, Abbé Hubert-Pascal. *Histoire du commerce et de la navigation sous le règne des Ptolémées. (Ouvrage qui a remporté le Prix de l'Académie Royale des Inscriptions et Belles Lettres.)* Paris: Saillant, 1766.

Amyot, Jacques. *Les oeuvres morales et meslées de Plutarque, translatées du Grec en François par Messire Jacques Amyot* . . . Paris: Imprimerie de Michel de Vascosan, 1572.

Anderson, Adam. *An Historical and Chronological Deduction of the Origin of Commerce from the Earliest Accounts Containing an History of the Great Commercial Interests of the British Empire to Which is Prefixed an Introduction Exhibiting a View of the Antient and Modern State of Europe and of the Foreign and Colonial Commerce, Shipping, Manufactures, Fisheries, etc., of Great Britain and Ireland.* 4 vols. London, 1801.

Anquetil Duperron, Abraham-Hyacinthe. *Zend-Avesta. Ouvrage de Zoroastre, contenant les idées théologiques, physiques et morales de ce Législateur, les cérémonies du culte religieux qu'il a établi et plusieurs traits importants de l'ancienne histoire des Perses. Traduit en français sur l'original Zend, avec des remarques, et accompagné de plusieurs Traités propres à éclairer les matières qui en font l'objet.* 3 vols. Paris: N. M. Tillard, 1771.

——. *Législation Orientale, ouvrage dans lequel [on montre] quels sont en Turquie, en Perse et dans l'Indoustan les principes fondamentaux du gouvernement* . . . Amsterdam: Michel Rey, 1778.

——. "Recherches sur les migrations des Mardes." *Mémoires de l'Académie Royale des Inscriptions et Belles-Lettres* 45 (1782): 87–150 and 50 (1787): 4–47.

——. *Recherches historiques et géographiques sur l'Inde* . . . *enrichies de cartes et de plans particuliers, précédées d'une lettre sur les Antiquités de l'Inde.* In J. Bernoulli (ed.), *Description historique et géographique de l'Inde.* Vol. 2. Berlin: Bourdeaux, 1786.

——. "Plan d'administration pour l'Inde." In J. Bernoulli (ed.), *Description historique et géographique de l'Inde.* Vol. 3, part I, ix–lvi. Berlin 1788.

——. *Dignité du commerce et de l'état de commerçant.* Paris: chez la Veuve Tilliard, 1789.

——. *L'Inde en rapport avec l'Europe. Ouvrage divisé en deux parties; la première sur les intérêts politique de l'Inde; la seconde sur le commerce de cette contrée; dont les dif-*

férentes portions renferment des vues utiles à toutes les nations qui ont des colonies . . .
et qui présente en plus un tableau détaillé, exact et effrayant du Machiavélisme anglais
dans cette dernière contrée . . . 2 vols. Paris: Lesguilliez frères, Year 6 (1798).

———. *Considérations philosophiques, historiques et géographiques sur les Deux Mondes*
(1780–1804). Edited by G. Abbbatista. Pisa, 1993.

Anville, Jean-Baptiste Bourguignon, d. *Éclaircissements géographiques sur la carte de*
l'Inde. Paris: Imprimerie royale, 1763.

———. "Recherches géographiques sur le Golfe persique et sur les bouches de l'Euphrate et du Tigre." *Mémoires de l'Académie Royale des Inscriptions et Belles-Lettres*
30 (1764): 132–197.

———. *Antiquité géographique de l'Inde et de plusieurs autres contrées de la Haute Asie.*
Paris: Imprimerie royale, 1775.

———. *Traité des mesures itinéraires anciennes et modernes.* Paris: Imprimerie royale,
1779.

———. "Mémoire de géographie ancienne." In *Œuvres de M. D'Anville,* 2:1–13. Paris,
1834.

Argens, Jean-Baptiste de Boyer, Marquis d'. *Histoire de l'esprit humain ou mémoires*
secrets et universels de la République des Lettres. Vol. 12. Berlin: Haude and Spener,
1768.

Arc de Sainte-Foix, Philippe-Auguste. *Histoire du commerce et de la navigation des peu-*
ples anciens et modernes. 2 vols. Amsterdam, 1758.

Bacon, Francis. *The Essays or Councils, Civil and Royal.* London: T. Childe, 1701.

———. *The Advancement of Learning.* Edited by W. A. Wright. Oxford: Clarendon Press,
1869 [1605].

Baillet, Adrien. *Des enfans devenus célèbres par leurs études ou par leurs écrits. Traité*
historique. Paris: A. Dezallier, 1688.

Barbier, Antoine Alexandre. "Notice sur la vie et les principaux ouvrages de M.
l'abbé Denina." *Magasin Encyclopédique* (January 1814): 113–128.

Barre, Louis François Joseph de la. "Essai sur les mesures géographiques des Anciens." *Mémoires de l'Académie des Inscriptions et Belles-Lettres* 32 (1770): 51–170.

Barthélemy, Abbé. *Travels of Anacharsis the Younger in Greece during the Middle of the*
Fourth Century before the Christian Era. Vol. 7. London: G. G. J. Robinson, 1791
[French 1787].

Baudelot de Dairval, Charles-César. *De l'utilité des voyages et de l'avantage que la Re-*
cherche des Antiquitez procure aux Sçavants. 2 vols. Paris: Pierre Auboüin et Pierre
Emery, 1686.

[Baumgarten, Sigmund Jacob]. *Uebersetzung der Allgemeinen Welthistorie die in En-*
geland durch eine Gesellschaft von Gelehrten ausgefertiget worden. Vol. 7: *Nebst den*
Anmerkungen der hollandischen Uebersetzung auch vielen neuen Kupfern und Karte.
Genau durchgesehen und mit häufigen Anmerkungen vermeret von Sigmund Jacob
Baumgarten. Halle: J. J. Gebauers, 1748.

Bayle, P. *Dictionnaire historique et critique,* Rotterdam : Reinier Leers, 1697.

———. *The Dictionary Historical and Critical: The Second Edition Carefully Collated with the Several Versions of the Original by Mr Des Maizeaux.* Vol. 4 [1697]. London, 1737.

Beauzée, Nicolas. *Histoire d'Alexandre le Grand par Quinte-Curce* (1782). 4th rev. ed. 2 vols. Paris: Barbou et Le Normand, 1806.

Beck, Christian Daniel. *Anleitung zur Kenntniss der allgemeine Welt- und Völker-Geschichte für Studirende.* Part II: *Bis auf die Theilung der Carolingischen Monarchie.* Leipzig: Weidmann, 1788.

———. *Anleitung zur genauer Kenntniss der allgemeine Welt- und Völker-Geschichte vorzüglich für Studirende.* Part I: *Einleitung. Urgeschichte bis zu der Regierung Alexanders des Maced.* 2nd rev. and enlarged ed. Leipzig: Weidmann, 1813.

———. *Dr. Goldsmiths Geschichte der Griechen:* see Goldsmith, Oliver.

Berghaus, Johann Isaac. *Geschichte der Schifffahrtskunde bey den vornehmsten Völker des Alterthums.* 2 vols. Leipzig: in der Gräffeschen Buchhandlung, 1792.

Bernegger, Michael. *Alexander Magnus idemque se ipso minor, i.e. dissertatio historico-politica, in qua ex. Q. Curtio artes et instrumenta magnitudinis Alexandrae eruntur, proponuntur ac illustrantur, vitiaque breviter etiam ostenduntur, quibus degenerans jam et minor priorem gloriam fœdavit.* Strasbourg, 1634.

Bernier, François. *Voyages de de Fr. Bernier, contenant la description des Etats du Grand Mogol, où il est traité des richesses, des forces, de la justice et des causes principales de la décadence des Etats de l'Asie, et de plusieurs événemens considérables, et où l'on voit comment l'or et l'argent, après avoir circulé dans le Monde, passent dans l'Hindoustan d'où ils ne reviennent plus.* Rev. and corrected ed. 2 vols. Amsterdam: Paul Marret, 1724.

———. *Travels in the Mogul Empire* A.D. *1656–1668.* Rev. and improved ed. Westminster: A. Constable, 1891.

Biedma, Don Fernando de. *Vida de Alexandro Magno . . . dirigela a la Magestad de Phelipe IV. Rey de las Españas.* Madrid: Imprenta del Reyno, 1634.

Blair, John. *History of the Rise and Progress of Geography.* London: T. Cadell and W. Ginger, 1784.

Blanc, Antoine [Le Blanc de Guillet]. *Manco-Capac, premier Ynca du Pérou, tragédie représentée pour la première fois par les Comédiens François ordinaires du Roi, le 12 juin 1763.* Paris: Belin, 1782.

Blanchard [Blancardus], Nicolas. *Arriani de expeditione Alexandri Magni Historiarum Libri VII.* Amsterdam: J. Janssonium, 1668.

Boeckh, August. *Die Staatshaltung der Athener, vier Bücher, mit einundzwanzig Inschriften.* Vol. 1. Berlin: Realschulbuchhandlung, 1817.

Boismêslé, Jean-Baptiste Torchet de. *Histoire générale de la marine contenant son origine chez tous les peuples du monde, ses progrès, son état actuel et les expéditions maritimes anciennes et modernes.* Vol. 1. Paris: P. Prault et A. Boudet, 1744.

Boissonade, Jean-François. "Histoire des expéditions d'Alexandre par Arrien de Nicomédie à l'occasion de la traduction de M. P. Chaussard." *Journal des Débats*

(December 15 and 18, 1802). Reprinted in M. Naudet (ed.), *J.-F. Boissonade critique littéraire sous le premier empire*, 1:172–184. Paris: Didier et Compagnie, 1853.

———. "Sur l'Examen critique des anciens historiens d'Alexandre le Grand." *Le Mercure de France* (1805): 160–177. Reprinted in M. Naudet (ed.), *J.-F. Boissonade critique littéraire sous le premier empire*, 1:185–200. Paris: Didier et Compagnie, 1853.

———. "De Sainte-Croix." *Journal de l'Empire* (April 6, 1809). Reprinted in M. Naudet (ed.), *J.-F. Boissonade critique littéraire sous le premier empire*, 1:474–475. Paris: Didier et Compagnie, 1853.

Boissy d'Anglas, François-Antoine. *Discours prononcé le 13 mars 1809 aux funérailles de M. de Sainte-Croix, Membre de l'Institut de France*. Paris: Baudoin, 1809.

Bonamy, Pierre-Nicolas. "Réflexions générales sur les cartes géographiques des Anciens, et sur les erreurs que les historiens d'Alexandre le Grand ont occasionnées dans la Géographie." *Histoire de l'Académie des Inscriptions et Belles Lettres* 25 (1753): 40–53.

Bonaparte, Napoléon. *Le discours de Lyon*. Introduction by Édouard Driault. Éd. Morancé: Paris, 1929 [1791].

Bonucci, Carlo. *Gran musaico di Pompei, descritto da Carlo Bonucci architetto*. Naples, 1832.

Borheck, Christian. *Arrians Feldzüge Alexanders des Grossen, aus dem griechischen übersetz*. 2 vols. Frankfurt am Main: Hermann, 1790–1792.

Bossuet, Jean-Bénigne. *A Discourse on the History of the Whole World Dedicated to His Royal Highness the Dauphin, and Explicating the Continuance of Religion with the Changes of States and Empires, from the Creation till the Reign of Charles the Great*. London: M. Turner, 1686 [French 1681].

———. *Politics Drawn from the Very Words of Holy Scripture*. Translated and edited by Patrick Riley. Cambridge: Cambridge University Press, 1990 [French 1707].

[Bossuet]. *Extraits de l'Histoire Universelle de M. Bossuet, évêque de Meaux, à l'usage des élèves de l'Ecole Royale militaire* (Cours d'études à l'usage des élèves de l'Ecole Royale militaire. Ve Division. Abrégés d'Histoire, VIe Partie). Paris: Nyon l'aîné, 1777; Paris: A. Delalain, 1818.

Boucher de la Richarderie, Gilles. *Bibliothèque universelle des voyages, ou Notice complète et raisonnée de tous les voyages anciens et modernes dans les différentes parties du monde, publiés tant en langue française qu'en langues étrangères, classés par ordre de pays dans leur série chronologique, avec des extraits plus ou moins rapides des Voyages les plus estimés de chaque pays, et des jugemens motivés sur les Relations anciennes qui ont le plus de célébrité*. Vol. 1. Paris: Treutell et Würtz, 1808.

Bougainville, Antoine de. *Dissertation qui a remporté le prix de l'Académie des Inscriptions et Belles Lettres en l'année 1745*. Paris: Desaint and Saillant, 1745.

———. *Parallèle de l'expédition d'Alexandre dans les Indes avec la conquête des mêmes contrées par Tahmas-Kouli-Khan*. Paris, 1752.

———. "Examen d'un passage de la vie d'Alexandre, où Plutarque rapporte la mort de Statira, femme de Darius." *Mémoires de l'Académie* 25 (1753): 32–39.

Boulanger, Nicolas-Antoine. *Histoire d'Alexandre*. In *Œuvres de Boullanger* [sic], vol. 8. Paris: Jean Servières et Jean-François Bastien, 1793.

Bourlet de Vauxcelles, Simon Jérôme. Review of Vincent, *Voyage de Néarque* (1800). In M. Peltier, ed., *Paris pendant l'année* 32 (1801): 121–126.

Bredow, Gabriel G. *Handbuch der alten Geschichte, Geographie und Chronologie*. 3rd rev. ed. Altona: J.-F. Hammarich, 1816 [1799].

——(ed.). Untersuchungen über einzelne Gegenstände der alten Geschichte, Geographie und Chronologie. Altona: Fr. Hammerich, 1800.

Brisson, Barnabé, De Regio Persarum principatu libri tres, Paris: Chez Prevosteau,1590.

Brunswick, Friedrich-August, Prince of. Critical Reflections on the Character and Actions of Alexander the Great, Written Originally in Italian. London: T. Becket-P.A de Hondt, 1768 [French 1765].

Buache, Philippe. "Recherches géographiques sur l'étendue de l'empire d'Alexandre, et sur les routes parcourues par ce Prince dans ses différentes expéditions. Pour servir à la carte de cet Empire, dressée par M. Delisle pour l'usage du Roi." *Mémoires de l'Académie royale des Sciences* (1731): 110–123.

Buchanan, Claudius. *Memoir on the Expediency of an Ecclesiastical Establishment for British India, Both as the Means of Perpetuating the Christian Religion among Our Own Countrymen, and as Foundation for the Ultimate Civilization of the Natives*. 2nd ed. Cambridge: Hilliard and Metcalf, 1811.

Bulwer-Lytton, Edward. *Athens: Its Rise and Fall: With Views of the Literature, Philosophy, and Social Life of the Athenian People*. Paris, 1837.

——. *Athens: Its Rise and Fall: Bicentenary Edition*. Edited by Oswyn Murray. London: Routledge, 2004 [1837].

Burke, Edmund. *Reflections on the Revolution in France and on the Proceedings in Certain Societies in London Relative to This Event, in a Letter Intended to Have Been Sent to a Gentleman in Paris*. 2nd ed. London: Dodsley, 1790.

——. *The Speeches of the Right Honourable Edmund Burke in the House of Commons and in Westminster-Hall*. 4 vols. London: Longman, Hurst, Rees, Orme, and Brown, 1816.

——. *The Writings and Speeches of Edmund Burke*. Vol. 7: *India: The Hastings Trial, 1788–1795*. Edited by Peter Marshall. Oxford: Oxford University Press, 2000.

Burnes, Alexander. *Travels to Bokhara, Being an Account of a Journey from India to Cabool, Tartary and Persia, from the Sea to Lahore, with Presents from the King of Great-Britain, Performed under the Orders of the Supreme Government of India in the Years 1831, 1832 and 1833*. 3 vols. London: John Murray, 1834.

Burnes, James. *A Narrative of a Visit to the Court of Sinde, a Sketch of the History of Cutch, from its First Connexion with the British Government in India till the Conclusion of the Treaty of 1819, and Some Remarks on the Medical Topography of Bhooj*. Bombay: Summachar Press, 1831.

Bury, Richard de. *Histoire de Philippe et d'Alexandre*. Paris: De De Bury, D'Houry, and Debure l'Aîné, 1760.

Calmet, Antoine. *Histoire universelle sacrée et profane depuis le commencement du monde jusqu'à nos jours*. Vol. 2. Strasbourg: J.-R. Doulssecker, 1736.

Camoens, Luis de. *Os Lusiadas*. Lisbon: Antonio Gôçalves, 1572.

Capper, James. *Observations on the Passage to India through Egypt, also by Vienna and Constantinople to Aleppo and from Thence by Bagdad, and Directly across the Great Desert to Bassora, with Occasional Remarks on the Adjacent Countries, an Account of the Different Stages, and Sketches of the Several Routes on Four Plates*. London: W. Fanden and J. Robson, 1775.

Carlyle, Thomas. "The Life of Heyne" (1828). In *Critical and Miscellaneous Essays Collected and Pepublished*, 2nd ed., 1:1–46. London: James Fraser, 1840.

Carra, Jean-Louis. *Essai particulier de politique dans lequel on propose un partage de la Turquie européenne*. Constantinople, 1777.

Carra, Jean-Louis. See Gillies, J. 1788–89.

Cassini, Jean-Dominique. "De l'origine et du progrès de l'Astronomie et de son usage dans la géographie et la navigation." In *Œuvres diverses de M. I. D. Cassini, de l'Académie royale des Sciences=Mémoires de l'Académie Royale des Sciences depuis 1666 jusqu'en 1699* 8 (1730): 1–54.

Castanheda, Fernao Lopez, de. *Histoire de Portugal, contenant les entreprises, navigations et gestes mémorables des Portugallois, tant en la conqueste des Indes Orientales par eux découvertes qu'ès guerres d'Afrique et autres exploits*. Paris: J. Houzé, 1587.

———. *Historia do descobrimento e conquista de India*, [1552], nova edição, Lisbon: Typographia Rollandiana, 1833.

Castel de Saint-Pierre, Abbé Charles-Irénée. *Ouvrages de politique*. Vol. 1: *Contenant l'abrégé du projet de paix perpétuelle*. 2nd rev. and expanded ed. Rotterdam: Jean-Daniel Deman, 1738.

———. *Projet pour perfectionner l'éducation avec un discours sur la grandeur et la sainteté des hommes*. Paris: Briasson, 1738.

———. *Projet pour rendre la paix perpétuelle en Europe*. Utrecht: Antoine Schouten. Paris: Fayard, 1986 [1713].

Caylus, Anne-Claude de. *Recueil d'Antiquités*. Vol. 5. Paris: Chez N.M. Tilliard, 1763.

Cayx, Rémy Jean-Baptiste-Charles, and Poirson, Auguste Simon Jean-Chrysostome. *Précis de l'Histoire ancienne*. Paris: Louis Colas et L. Hachette, 1827.

Chalmers, Alexander. *The General Biographical Dictionary Containing an Historical and Critical Account of the Lives and Writings of the Most Eminent Persons in Every Nation, particularly the British and Irish, from the Earliest Accounts to the Present Time*. Vol. 30. London, 1816 (entry for William Vincent pp. 371–387).

Charpentier, François. *A Treatise Touching the East-Indian Trade or a Discourse (Turned out of French into English) concerning the Establishment of a French Company for the Commerce of East-Indies*. Edinburgh: A. Anderson, 1695 [French 1666].

Chateaubriand, François René, Vicomte de. *Essai historique sur les révolutions* (London, 1797). In *Œuvres complètes de M. le vicomte de Chateaubriand,* vol. 1. Paris: Pourrat fils éditeurs, 1835.

———. *Analyse raisonnée de l'Histoire de France.* Paris: F. Didot, 1853 [1836].

Chaudon, Louis Maïeul. *Nouveau dictionnaire historique-portatif ou Histoire abrégée de tous les hommes qui se font fait un nom par des Talens, des Vertus, des Forfaits, des Erreurs etc. etc., depuis le commencement du monde jusqu'à nos jours . . . par une Société de Gens de Lettres.* Rev., corrected, and expanded ed. Vol. 1. Amsterdam: M.-M. Rey, 1769; Caen: G. Le Roy, 1779.

———, and Antoine-François Delandine. *Dictionnaire historique, critique et bibliographique, contenant les vies des hommes illustres, célèbres ou fameux de tous les pays et de tous les siècles, suivi d'un dictionnaire abrégé des mythologies et d'un tableau chronologique.* Vol. 1. Paris: Ménard et Desenne, 1821.

Chaussard, Pierre Jean-Baptiste. *Histoire des expéditions d'Alexandre, rédigée sur les mémoires de Ptolémée et d'Aristobule ses lieutenants, par Flave Arrien, de Nicomédie, surnommé le nouveau Xénophon, consul et général romain, disciple d'Epictète.* Vols. 1–4. Paris: Genets, Year 11 (1802).

Chénier, Marie-Joseph. "Rapport sur le grand prix de littérature 1810." In *Œuvres de M.-J. Chénier, revues, corrigées et augmentées,* 4:171–175. Paris: Guillaume, 1824.

———. *Tableau historique de l'état et des progrès de la littérature française depuis 1789.* Paris: Ledentu, 1835.

Chesney, Francis Rawdon. *The Expedition for the Survey of the Rivers Euphrates and Tigris Carried on by Order of the British Government in the Years 1835, 1836 and 1837, Preceded by Geographical and Historical Notices of the Regions Situated between the Rivers Nile and Indus.* 2 vols. Longman: London, 1850; repr. 2 vols. New York: Greenwood Press, 1969.

———. *Narrative of the Euphrates Expedition Carried on by Order of the British Government during the Years 1835, 1836, and 1837.* London: Longmans, Green, 1868.

Christina of Sweden. *The Works of Christina Queen of Sweden. Containing Maxims and Sentences, in Twelve Centuries; and Reflections on the Life and Actions of Alexander the Great. Now First Translated from the Original French. To Which Is Prefix'd an Account of Her Life, Character and Writings, by the Translator.* London, 1753 [French 1751].

Clarke, Edward Daniel. *The Tomb of Alexander: A Dissertation on the Sarcophagus Brought from Alexandria and Now in the British Museum.* Cambridge, 1805.

Clarke, Samuel. *The Life and Death of Alexander the Great, the First Founder of the Grecian Empire . . . as also, struggle Life and Death of Charles the Great, King of France and Emperor of Germany.* London, 1665.

Claustre, André de. *Histoire de Thamas Kouli-Kan, roi de Perse.* New ed. Paris: Briasson, 1743.

Colbert, Jean-Baptiste. *Lettres, instructions et mémoires de Colbert publiés d'après les ordres de l'empereur.* P. Clément (ed.). Paris: Imprimerie nationale, I-VII, 1861–1873.

Collective. *Dictionnaire universel françois et latin.* Commonly know as Dictionnaire de Trévoux. Paris: Compagnie des Libraires, 1771.

Condillac, Étienne Bonnot de. *Cours d'étude pour l'instruction du Prince de Parme.* Vol. 5. Parma: Imprimerie royale, 1775.

Condorcet, Marie Jean Antoine Nicolas de Caritat, Marquis de. *Tableau historique des progrès de l'esprit humain. Projets, esquisse, fragments et notes (1772–1794).* Edited under the direction of J.-P. Schandeler and P. Crépel. Paris: INED, 2003.

Constant, Benjamin. *Essai sur les mœurs des temps héroïques de la Grèce, tiré de l'histoire grecque de M. Gillies.* London, 1787.

———. *De l'esprit de conquête* (1813). In Kurt Klooke and Béatrice Fink (eds.), *Œuvres complètes,* series 1, 8:527–598. Tübingen: Max Niemeyer Verlag, 2005.

———. *De la religion considérée dans sa source et ses développements.* Vol. 1. Paris: Bossange père, Bossange frères, Treutel et Wurtz, Rey et Gravier, Renouard, Ponthieu, 1824.

———. *Du polythéisme romain considéré dans ses rappors avec la philosophie grecque et la religion chrétienne.* Vol. 1. Introduction by M. J. Matter. Paris: chez Béchet Aîné, 1833.

Courier, Paul-Louis. *Œuvres complètes.* Expanded by A. Carrel. Paris: Firmin Didot, 1855.

Crèvecoeur, Michel Guillaume Jean de. *Voyage dans la Haute-Pennsylvanie, et dans l'état de New-York.* Paris: Chez Maradan, I–II, 1801.

Dacier, Bon-Joseph. *Éloge de M. d'Anville.* In *Notice des ouvrages de M. D'Anville,* 1–42. Paris: chez Fuchs et Demanne, 1802.

———. *Rapport historique sur les progrès de l'Histoire et de la Littérature ancienne depuis 1789 et sur leur état actuel.* Paris: Imprimerie impériale, 1810.

———. "Notice sur M. de Sainte-Croix." *Le Moniteur* no. 188 (1811).

———. "Notice historique sur la vie et les ouvrages de M. de Sainte-Croix." *Magasin Encyclopédique* (July 1811): 109–140.

Daunou, Jean-Claude-François. *Œuvres complètes de Boileau Despréaux avec des preliminaries et un commentaire revus et augmentés,* I. Paris: Chez Peytieux, 1825.

———. *Cours d'études historiques,* volume XII. Paris: Chez Firmin Didot frères, 1846.

David, Pierre: see Phalantée, Sylvain.

Defoe, Daniel. *A General History of Discoveries and Improvements in Useful Arts, Particularly in the Great Branches of Commerce, Navigation, and Plantation, in All Parts of the Known World. A Work Which May Entertain the Curious with the View of Their Present State, Prompt the Indolent to Retrieve Those Inventions That Are Neglected, and Animate the Diligent to Advance and Perfect What May Be Thought Wanting.* London: J. Roberts, 1725–1726.

Delalleau de Bailliencourt, Alphonse-Marie-Florimond. *Cours normal d'Histoire grecque. Livre-Atlas renfermant: 1° Un traité de l'histoire grecque depuis les temps les plus reculés jusqu'à la réduction de la Grèce en province romaine; 2° Un Atlas historique spécial de géographie grecque, composé de dix cartes coloriées, avec texte en regard par Jean-Louis Sanis, à l'usage des Institutions de tous les degrés.* Paris: Henri Plon, 1862.

Delambre, Jean-Baptiste Joseph. *Rapport historique sur les progrès des sciences mathématiques depuis 1789 et sur leur état actuel.* Paris: Imprimerie impériale, 1810.

Delambre, C., "Notice sur la vie et les ouvrages du Comte de Fleurieu." In *Mémoires de l'Académie Royale des Sciences de l'Institut de France,* volume I (1816): 73–90.

Delandine, Antoine-François. *Couronnes académiques ou Recueil des prix proposés par les Sociétés Savantes, avec les noms de ceux qui les ont obtenus, des Concurrens distingués, des Auteurs qui ont écrit sur les mêmes sujets, le titre et le lieu d'impression de leur s ouvrages; Précédé de l'Histoire abrégée des Académies de France.* 2 vols. Paris: chez Cuchet, 1787.

Delisle, Guillaume. "Détermination géographique de la situation et de l'étendue des pays traversés par le jeune Cyrus dans son expédition contre son frère Artaxerxès et par les dix mille Grecs dans leur retraite." *Histoire et Mémoires de l'Académie royale des Sciences* (1721): 56–68.

———. "Remarques sur la carte de la mer Caspienne envoyée à l'Académie par Sa Majesté Czarienne." *Histoire et Mémoires de l'Académie royale des Sciences* (1721): 245–254.

Delisle de Sales, Jean-Baptiste-Claude [Jean-Baptiste Isoard de Lisle]. *Histoire complète de l'ancienne Grèce.* 3rd ed. Vol. 10. Paris: Bureau de l'Histoire des Hommes, 1786.

———. *Histoire philosophique du monde primitif.* 4th rev. and expanded ed. Vol. 6. Paris, 1793.

Denina, Carlo. *Istoria politica et letteraria della Grecia libera.* Vol. 3. Venice: Stamp. Graziozi, 1784 [1782].

Desclaisons, Nicolas. *Précis des histoires d'Alexandre le Grand et de Jules César, et de leurs faits militaires, soit comparés, soit opposés entre eux, suivi de différens points de comparaison ou d'opposition entre ces deux guerriers.* 2 vols. Paris: Méquignon le Jeune, 1784.

Diderot, Denis. "Contributions à l'histoire des Deux Indes." In L. Versini (ed.), *Diderot. Œuvres,* 3:579–759. Paris: Coll. Bouquins, 1995.

Diderot, Denis, and Jean Le Rond d'Alembert (eds.). *Encyclopédie, ou dictionnaire raisonné des sciences, des arts et des métiers.* ARTFL Encyclopédie Project, University of Chicago. http://encyclopedie.uchicago.edu/.

Droysen, Johann Gustav. *Geschichte Alexanders des Grossen.* Hamburg: Perthes, 1833.

———. Review of Van der Chys, *Commentarius* (1828). *Jahrbücher für wissenschaftliche Kritik* (March 1833): 471–480.

———. *Geschichte des Hellenismus.* Vol. 1: *Geschichte der Nachfolger Alexanders.* Hamburg: Perthes, 1836.

———. *Geschichte des Hellenismus.* Vol. 2: *Geschichte der Bildung des hellenistischen Staatensystem.* Hamburg: Perthes, 1843.

———. *Städtegrundungen Alexanders und seiner Nachfolger.* n.p., 1843.

———. *Histoire de l'hellénisme*. Translated by Auguste Bouché-Leclercq. 3 vols. Paris: Ernest Leroux, 1883–1885.

———. *History of Alexander the Great*. Translated by Flora Kimmich. Philadelphia: American Philosophical Society, 2012.

Dubos, Abbé Jean-Baptiste. *Critical Reflections on Poetry, Painting and Music, etc.* Translated by Thomas Nugent, 3 vols. London: J. Nourse, 1748.

Duchat, Yves. *Hymne d'Alexandre le Grand, avec les parallèles de luy & de Philippe et des Roys tres-chrestiens Louys XIII, heureusement régnant & Henry le Grand. Dédiez au Roy.* Paris: Imprimerie de Jean Ibert, 1624.

Du Verdier, Gilbert Saunier. *L'histoire entière d'Alexandre le Grand, tirée d'Arrien, Plutarque, Justin, Joseph, Quin te-Curce et Frensheimius.* Paris: Théodore Girard, 1671.

Eichhorn, Johann Gottfried. *Geschichte des ostindischen Handels vor Mohammed.* Gotha: C.-W. Ettinger, 1775.

Elphinstone, Monstuart. *An Account of the Kingdom of Caubul and Its Dependencies in Persia, Tartary and India, Comprising a View of the Afghaun Nation, and a History of the Dorаunee Monarchy.* London: Longman, Hurst, Rees, Orme, Brown, and Murray, 1815.

Eschassériaux, Joseph (the Elder). *Tableau politique de l'Europe au commencement du XIXᵉ siècle et moyens d'assurer la d urée de la paix générale.* Paris: chez Baudoin, Pluviôse Year 10 (1802).

Evelyn, John. *Navigation and Commerce. Their Original and Progress. Containing a Succinct Account of Traffick in General; Its Benefits and Improvements; of Discoveries, Wars and Conflicts at Sea, from the Original of Navigation to This Day; with Special Regard to the English Nation; Their Several Voyages and Expeditions to the Beginning of Our Differences with Holland; in Which His Majesties Title to the Dominion of the Sea is Asserted, against the Novel and Later Pretenders.* London: Benj. Tooke, 1674.

Fauriel, Claude. *Chants populaires de la Grèce moderne recueillis et publiés avec une traduction française, des éclaircis sements et des notes. Vol. 2: Chants historiques, ro manesques et domestiques.* Paris: Didot, 1825.

Febvre, Michel. *L'état présent de la Turquie où il est traité des vies, mœurs et coûtumes des Ottomans & autres peuples De leur Empire divisés par 14. nations qui l'habitent, toutes opposées à la Puissance qui les gouverne et & les unes aux autres, sept desquelles sont Infide lles et sept Chrétiennes.* Paris: chez Edme Couterot, 1575.

Félibien, André. *Les reines de Perse aux pieds d'Alexandre.* In *The Tent of Darius or the Queens of Persia at the Feet of Alexander* [bilingual edition]. London, 1704.

Feßler, Ignatius Aurelius. *Alexander der Eroberer.* Berlin: Lagarde, 1797.

———. *Alexander de Veroveraar.* Translated by M. Stuart. Amsterdam: Johannes Allart, 1801.

Fichte, Johann Gottlieb. *Addresses to the German Nation.* Translated by R. F. Jones and G. H. Turnbull. Chicago, 1922 [German 1808].

Flathe, Ludwig. *Geschichte Makedoniens und der Reiche, welche von macedonischen Königen beherrscht wurden. Vol. 1: Von der Urzeit bis zum Untergang des persisch-macedonisch*

Reiches; vol. 2: *Von Untergang des persisch-macedonisch Reiches biz eum Ausgange des Reiches der Ptolemäer.* Leipzig: J. A. Barthe, 1832–1834.

Folard, Jean-Charles de. *Histoire de Polybe nouvellement traduite du grec par Dom Vincent Thuillier, avec un commentaire ou corps de science militaire enrichi de notes critiques et historiques par M. de Folard.* Paris: Gandouen, Gilfrit et Armand, 1727 (vols. 1–2), 1728 (vols. 3–4); 1729 (vol. 5), 1730 (vol. 6).

Fontenelle, Bernard Le Bovier de. "Éloge du Czar Pierre I." *Histoire et Mémoires de l'Académie Royale des Sciences* (1725): 105–128.

Forster, Georg. "Vorrede zur Uebersetzung." In William Robertson, *Historische Untersuchung über die Kenntisse der Alten von Indien.* Berlin, 1792.

Fourier, Jean-Baptiste-Joseph. "Préface historique." In Edme François Jomard (ed.), *Description de l'Égypte: ou recueil des observations et des recherches qui ont été faites en Égypte pendant l'expédition de l'armée française, publié par les ordres de Sa Majesté l'Empereur Napoléon le Grand.* Vol. 2.2.1, text 1, i–xcii. Paris: Antiquités, 1809.

Franklin, William. *Observations Made on a Tour from Bengal to Persia in the Years 1786–7, with a Short Account of the Remains of the Celebrated Palace of Persepolis and Other Interesting Events.* London: Cadell, 1790.

Fraser, James. *The History of Nadir Shah, Formerly Called Thamas Kuli Khan, the Present Emperor of Persia, to Which Is Prefixed a Short History of the Moghol Emperors.* London: W. Strahan, 1742.

Frederick of Prussia (the Great). *L'Esprit du Chevalier Folard tiré de ses Commentaires de Polybe pour l'usage d'un officier. De main de maître.* Leipzig, 1761.

———. *Œuvres de Frédéric le Grand - Werke Friedrichs des Großen.* Library of Trier University (Germany). http://friedrich.uni-trier.de/

Gamelin, Jacques: see Musée de Carcassonne.

Garve, Christian. *Abhandlungen über die Verbindung der Moral mit der Politik, oder einige Betrachtungen über die Frage: in wiesern es möglich sey, die Moral des Privatlebens bey der Regierung der Staaten zu beobachten.* Breslau: Korn, 1788.

———. *Sur l'accord de la morale avec la politique, ou quelques considérations sur la question: Jusqu'à quel point est-il possible de réaliser la morale de la vie privée, dans le gouvernement d'un état.* Berlin: Imprimerie royale, 1789.

———. *Fragmente zur Schilderung des Geistes, des Charakters und der Regierung Friedrich des zweyten.* Vol. 1. Breslau: Korn, 1798.

Gast, John. *The Rudiments of the Grecian History from the First Establishment of the States of Greece to the Overthrow of Their Liberties in the Days of Philip the Macedonian.* London: John and James Rivington, 1753.

———. *The History of Greece from the Accession of Alexander of Macedon till Its Final Subjection to the Roman Power, in Eight Books.* 2 vols. London: Basil, 1782, 1797.

Gatterer, Johann Christoph. *Handbuch der Universalhistorie nach ihrem gesamte Umfange von Erschaffung der Welt bis zum Ursprung der moisten heutigen Reiche und Staaten.* Vol. 1. 2nd exanded ed. Göttingen: Widow Vandenhöck, 1765 [1761].

———. "Von historischen Plan und der darauf sich gründenden Zusammenfüfung der Erzählungen." *Allgemeine historische Bibliothek* 1 (1767): 15–89.

———. "Von der Kunst zu übersetzen, besonders in Absicht auf historische Schriften." *Allgemeine historische Bibliothek* 2 (1767): 5–22.

———. "Zufällige Gedanken über die Verdienste der Teutschen um die Historie." *Allgemeine historische Bibliothek* 2 (1767): 33–64.

———. "Räsonnement über die jetzige Verfassung der Geschichtkunde in Teutschland." *Historisches Journal von Mitgliedern des Königlichen historischen Instituts zu Göttingen* 1 (1772): 255–290.

———. *Abriß dere Universalhistorie in ihrem ganzen Umfange, Zw. Aufl. völlig ungearbeitet und bis auf unsere Zeiten fortgesetz.* Göttingen: Widow Vandenhöck, 1773.

———. *Weltgeschichte in ihrem ganzen Umfange.* Part II: *Von Cyrus bis zu und mit Völkerwanderung.*Volume 1: *Perser und Griecher.* Göttingen: Vandendoeck und Ruprecht, 1787.

———. *Versuch einer allgemeinen Weltgeschichte bis zu Entdeckung Amerikens.* Göttingen: Vandendoeck und Ruprecht, 1792.

Gaudenzio, Paganino. *I fatti d'Alessandro il Grande, spiegati e suppliti con non pochi avvenimenti de' nostril tempi, massime quelli delle Alemaniche Guerre.* Pisa: Stamperia A. Maffi e L. Landi, 1645.

Gibbon, Edward. *The Decline and Fall of the Roman Empire.* 6 vols. London, 1776–1789.

Gillies, John. *The Orations of Lysias and Isocrates Translated from the Greek with Some Accounts of Their Lives, and a Discourse on the History, Manners and Character of the Greeks, from the Conclusion of the Peloponnesian War to the Battle of Chæronea.* London: J. Murray, 1778.

———. *The History of Ancient Greece, Its Colonies and Conquests, from the Earliest Accounts till the Division of the Macedonian Empire in the East, including the History of Literature, Philosophy and the Fine Arts.* 2 vols. London: A. Strahan, 1786.

———. *Histoire de l'ancienne Grèce. de ses colonies et de ses conquêtes. depuis les premiers temps jusqu'à la division de l'empire macédonien dans l'Orient. On y a joint l'Histoire de la Littérature. de la Philosophie & des Beaux-Arts.* Translated by M. Carra. 6 vols. Paris: chez Buisson, 1787–1788.

———. *A View of the Reign of Frederick II of Prussia, with a Parallel between That Prince and Philipp II of Macedon.* London: Strahan and Cadell, 1789.

———. *Vergleichung zwischen Friedrich dem Zweiten und Philipp, dem Könige von Macedonien.* Translated by Christian Garve. Breslau: G. Löwe, 1791.

———. *Aristotle's Ethics and Politics, Comprising His Practical Philosophy, Translated from the Greek.* 2 vols. London, 1797; new ed. London: Cadell, 1813.

———. *The History of the World from the Reign of Alexander to That of Augustus, Comprehending the Latter Ages of Greece, and the History of the Greek Kingdoms in Asia and Africa, from Their Foundation to Their Destruction, with a Preliminary Survey of Alexander's Conquests, and an Estimate of His Plans for Their Consolidation and Improvements.* 2 vols. London: Strahan, 1807; 3 vols. Philadelphia: Hopkins and Earle, 1809.

Girard, Pierre-Simon. "Mémoire sur l'agriculture et le commerce de la haute Égypte." *La décade égyptienne. Journal littéraire et d'économie politique* 3 (Year 8 [1799–1800]): 27–96.

Gleig, George. "The Life of Dr Robertson." In *The Historical Works of William Robertson,* 1:vi–lxxiv. Edinburgh, 1813.

Goldsmith, Oliver. *The Grecian History, from the Earliest State to the Death of Alexander the Great.* 2 vols. London: J. and F. Rivington, 1774.

———. *Geschichte der Griechen von frühesten Zeiten bis auf den Tod Alexanders des Großen. Nebst einem kurzen Abriß der Geschichte Griechenlands von dieser Periode an, bis auf die Eroberung Constantinopels durch die Osmanen. Aus dem Englischen nach der neueste Ausgabe übersetzt, berichtig, und mit vielen Anmerkungen und Zusätzen versehen von Ch.D. Beck.* Part II. 2nd rev. ed. Leipzig: im Schwickertschen Verlage, 1807 [1792].

———. Preface to W. Guthrie-J. Gray, *A General History of the World.* Repr. in A. Friedman (ed.), *Collected Works of Oliver Goldsmith,* 5: 277–289. Oxford: Clarendon Press, 1966 [1764].

Gosselin, Pascal-François-Joseph. *Géographie des Grecs analysée, ou les systèmes d'Eratosthènes, de Strabon et de Ptolémée comparés entre eux et avec nos connaissances modernes.* Paris: Imprimerie Didot l'Aîné, 1790.

———. "Recherches sur les connaissances géographiques des anciens relativement à cette mer [Golfe persique]." Summary of a presentation in *Mémoires de l'Institut National des Sciences été des Arts: Sciences Morales et Politiques* 4 (Year 11 [1802]): 69–70.

Grant, Charles. *Observations on the State of Society among the Asiatic Subjects of Great-Britain, Particularly with Respect to Morals and on the Means of Improving It, Written Chiefly in the Year 1792.* [London, 1797]

Graswinckel, Theodorus. *Maris liberi vindiciae adversus Petrum Baptistam Burgum, ligustici maritimi dominii assertorem.* The Hague, 1652.

Gronovius, Abrahamus. *Polybii Historiarum libri qui supersunt, interprete I. Casaubono, J. Gronovius recensuit.* 3 vols. Amsterdam, 1670.

———. (ed.). *Justinii Historiae Philippicae culm integris commentariis.* Leiden: Th. Haak, 1719.

Grote, George, *History of Greece.* Vol. 4. Reprinted from the 2nd London ed. New York: Harper and Brothers, 1853.

———. *History of Greece.* Vol. 12. Reprinted from the 2nd London ed. New York: Harper and Brothers, 1856.

Grotius, Hugo. *De jure belli ac pacis libri tres=Le droit de la guerre et de la paix.* Paris, 1625; new translation by Jean Barbeyrac. 2 vols. Amsterdam: chez Pierre de Cour, 1724.

———. *The Freedom of the Seas or the Right Which Belongs to the Dutch to Take Part in the East Indian Trade.* Translated by R. Van Deman Magoffin; edited with an introductory note by J. B. Scott. New York, 1916 [Latin 1609].

Guérard, B. *Notice sur M. Daunou suivi d'une notice sur M. Guérard par N.N. de Wailly.* Paris: Librairie de Dumoulin, 1853: 1–187.

Guingené, Pierre-Louis. Review of Lamberti, *Alessandro in Armozia* (1808). *Mercure de France* 37 (1809): 292–295.

Guischardt, Charles. *Mémoires militaires sur les Grecs et les Romains, où l'on a fidèlement rétabli, sur le texte de Polybe et des tacticiens grecs et latins, la plupart des ordres de bataille & et des grandes opérations de la guerre, en les expliquant selon les principes et la pratique constante des Anciens, & en relevant les erreurs du Chevalier de Folard et des autres commentateurs . . .* 2 vols. The Hague: Pierre de Hondt, 1758.

Guthrie, William Esq., John Gray Esq., and Others Eminent in This Branch of Literature. *A General History of the World from the Creation to the Present Times, including All the Empires, Kingdoms and States; Their Revolutions, Forms of Government, Laws, Religions, Customs and Manners; the Progress of Their Learning, Arts, Sciences, Commerce and Trade, together with Their Chronology, Antiquities, Public Buildings, and Curiosities of Nature and Art.* London: J. Newberry, R. Baldwin, S. Crowder, J. Coote, R. Withy, J. Wilkie, J. Wilson and J. Fell, W. Nicoll, B. Collins, and R. Raikes, 1763 (vol. 1), 1764 (vol. 2).

[Guthrie, William, and John Gray]. *Allgemeine Weltgeschichte von der Schöpfung an bis auf gegenwärtige Zeit . . . ausfertiget von Wilhelm Guthrie, Johann Gray und anderen Gelehrten. Aus dem Englischen übersetzt: aus den Originalschriftstellern berichtiget, und mit einer fortlausenden Zeitrechnung und verschiedenen Anmerkungen versehen von herrn Christian Gottlob Heyne . . .* Vol. 2. Leipzig: M. G. Weidemanns Erben und Reich, 1765.

———. *Die Allegmeine Welthistorie die in England durch eine Gesellschaft von Gelehrten ausgefertiget worden. In einem wollständigen und pragmatischen Auszuge von Friedrich Eberhard Boysen.* Preface by Johann Christoph Gatterer. Halle: J. J. Gebauer, 1767 (vols. 1–3), 1768 (vol. 4), 1769 (vol. 5).

———. *Allgemeine Weltgeschichte im Englischen herausgegeben von Wihl. Guthrie und Joh. Gray, übersetzt und verbessert von Christian Gottlob Heyne.* Vol. 8. Troppau: J. G. Traßler, 1785.

Guyon, Abbé Claude-Marie. *Histoire des empires et des républiques depuis le Déluge jusqu'à Jésus-Christ. Où l'on voit dans celle d'Egypte et d'Asie la liaison de l'Histoire Sainte avec la profane; et, dans celle de la Grèce, le raport de la Fable avec l'Histoire.* Paris: Simart, Jean Rouan and Jean Nully. Vol. 1: *Egyptiens* (1733); vol. 2: *Assyriens, Babiloniens, Mèdes* (1738); vol. 3: *Perses* (1736); vol. 4: *Les Macédoniens* (1736); vol. 5: *Les Macédoniens, Seconde partie* (1740); vol. 6: *Les Ptolémées* (1740).

Harris, John. *Navigantium atque itinerantium Bibliotheca, or a complete Collection of Voyages and Travels consisting above six hundred of the most authentic writers . . . originally published in two volumes in folio by John Harris . . . now carefully revised with large additions and continued to the present time.* Edited by John Campbell. Vol. 1. London: T. Osborne et al., 1764 [1705].

Heeren, Arnold-Herman-Ludwig. "Commentatio de Graecorum de India notitia et cum Indis commerciis. Pars Prior: De India Graecis cognita." *Commentationes Societatis Regiae Scientiarum Gottingensis recentiores* (1791): 121–156.

———. Review of Robertson, *Historical Disquisition* (1791). *Bibliothek der alten Litteratur und Kunst* 9 (1792): 105–121.

———. "Commentatio de Graecorum de India notitia et cum Indis commerciis. Commentatio altera De mercaturae Indicae ratione et viis." *Commentationes Societatis Regiae Scientiarum Gottingensis recentiores* (1793): 63–90.

———. "Commentatio de Romanorum de India notitia et cum Indis commerciis. Pars Prior: De India Romanis cognita." *Commentationes Societatis Regiae Scientiarum Gottingensis recentiores* (1793): 91–111.

———. *Ideen zur Politik, den Verkehr und der Handel der vornehmsten Völker der Alten Welt.* Vol. 1: *Afrikanische Völker* (1793); vol. 2: *Asiatische Völker* (1796). Göttingen: Vandenhoek & Ruprecht.

———. "Commentatio de prisca Sinus persici facie maxime secundum Nearchi, classis Alexandri ducis, descriptionem." *Commentationes Societatis Regiae Scientiarum Gottingensis recentiores* (1799): 138–158.

———. *Handbuch der Geschichte des Alterthums, mit besondere Rücksicht auf ihre Verfassungen, ihren Handel und ihre Colonien.* Göttingen: Widow Rosenbusch, 1799; 5th improved ed. Göttingen: J. F. Röwer, 1828.

———. *Idées sur les relations politiques et commerciales des anciens peuples de l'Afrique.* Translated from the German. Vol. 1. Paris: chez Buisson, Pougens et Dugour, Year 8 (1800).

———. *Ideen über die Politik, den Verkehr und den Handel der vornehmsten Völker der alten Welt.* Vol. 1, part I. Vienna: Franz Härter'schen Buchhandlung, 1817.

———. *Handbuch der Geschichte des Europäischen Staatensystems und seine Colonien von seiner Bildung seit der Entdeckung beiden Indien bis zu seiner Wiederherstellung nach dem Fall des Französischen Kaiserthrons, und der Freiwerdung von Amerika.* Part II. In *Historische Werke,* vol. 9. Göttingen: J. F. Röwer, 1822.

———. *Historical Researches into the Politics, Intercourse and Trade of the Principal Nations of Antiquity.* Translated from the German. 2 vols. Oxford: Talboys, 1833.

———. *A Manual of Ancient History Particularly with Regard to the Constitutions, the Commerce and the Colonies of the States of Antiquity.* Translated from the German. 6th ed. London: H. G. Bohn, 1854.

[Heeren, Arnold-Herman-Ludwig]. Review of Vincent, *Voyage of Nearchus* (1797). *Göttingische Anzeigen von gelehrten Sachen* (April 29, 1797): 665–675.

———. Review of Vincent, *Periplus,* vol. 1 (1800). *Göttingische Anzeigen von gelehrten Sachen,* 18 (April 1801), Volume 63: 617–624.

———. Review of Vincent, *Periplus,* vol. 2 (1805). *Göttingische gelehrte Anzeigen* (1806): 702–711.

Hegel, Georg Wilhelm Friedrich. *Vorlesungen über die Philosophie der Geschichte* (introduction by Dr. E. Gans), Third Volume (Dr. K. Hegel, ed.). Berlin: Duncker und Humblot, 1848.

——. *Lectures on the Philosophy of History.* Translated by J. Sibree. London: H. G. Bohn, 1861 [German 1848].

Hennings, W. (ed.). *Deutscher Ehren-Temple.* (Bearbeitet von einer Gesellschaft Gelehrten) 6. Gotha: Henning, 1824.

Henry, Pierre-François. *Route de l'Inde ou description géographique de l'Égypte, la Syrie, l'Arabie, la Perse et l'Inde, ouvrage dans lequel on a renfermé un précis de l'histoire, et le tableau des mœurs et coutumes des peuples anciens et modernes, qui ont habité ces différentes contrées, depuis les temps les plus reculés jusqu'à nos jours.* Partially translated and adapted from the English. Paris: Carteret et Dentu, Year 7 (1799).

Herbelot, Barthélémi d'. *Bibliothèque orientale ou dictionnaire universel contenant généralement tout ce qui concerne la connaissance des Peuples de l'Orient, leurs histoires véritables ou fabuleuses . . .* Paris, 1697.

Herder, Johann Gottfried. *Persepolis, eine Muthmassung.* Gotha: C. W. Ettinger, 1787.

——. *Outlines of a Philosophy of the History of Man.* Translated from the German by T. Churchill. New York: Bergman, 1800 [German 4 vols., 1784–1791].

Heyne, Christian Gottlob. *Sammlung antiquarischer Aussäge.* Volume 1. Leipzig: Weidmanns Erben und Reich, 1778.

——. Review of Robertson, *Geschichte von AltGriechenland* (1779). *Göttingische Anzeigen von gelehrten Sachen* (August 1779): 773–776.

——. *Éloge de Winkelmann.* Translated from the German. Göttingen: I. C. Dieterich, 1783.

——. Review of Pownall, *Treatise* (1782). *Göttingische Anzeigen von gelehrten Sachen* (January 17, 1784): 97–109.

——. *Allgemeine Weltgeschichte im Englischen herausgegeben von Wilh. Guthrie und Joh. Gray, übersezt und verbessert . . .* Vol. 8. Troppau: J. G. Traßler, 1785.

——. "De genio Saeculi Ptolemaeorum" (1763). *Opuscula Academica* 1 (1785): 76–134.

——. *Opuscula Academica collecta et animadversionibus locupletata.* 6 vols. Göttingen: H. Dietrich, 1785–1812.

——. Review of Gillies, *View on the Reign of Frederick II* (1789). *Göttingische Anzeigen von gelehrten Sachen* (May 1790): 834–838.

——. Untitled note. *Göttingische Anzeigen von gelehrten Sachen* (June 1792): 1032

——. "Opum regni Macedonici auctarum, attritarum et eversarum, caussae probabiles." *Neues Magazin für Schullehrer* 1, no. 2 (1792): 281–300 = *Opuscula Academica* 4 (1796): 159–177.

——. Review of Feßler, *Alexander* (1797). *Göttingische Anzeigen von gelehrten Sachen* (1797): 1934–1936.

——. Review of Chaussard (1802). *Göttingische gelehrte Anzeigen* (1803): 740–743.

——. "Repentina auri argentique affluentia quasnam rerum vicissitudines attulerit, ex historiarum antiquarum fide disputatur." *Commentationes Societatis Regiae Scientiarum Gottingensis recentiores* 15 (1804): 246–259.

——. Review of Sainte-Croix, *Examen critique* (1804). *Göttingische gelehrte Anzeigen* (1805): 809–815 and 817–820.

——. "De Alexandro M. id agente, ut omnem terrarum orbem commerciis mutuis jungeret (Adjecta Commentatio)" (1805)=*Opuscula Academica* 6 (1812): 346–362.

Heyne, Christian Gottlob: see [Guthrie, William, and John Gray], *Allgemeine Weltgeschichte*.

Hoffmann, Samuel Friedrich Wilhelm. *Die Alterthumswissenschaft. Ein Lehr- und Handbuch für Schüler höherer Gymnasialclassen und für Studirende.* Leipzig: J. C. Heinrichs, 1835.

——. *Bibliographisches Lexicon der gesammte Literatur der Griechen.* 2nd expanded ed. 3 vols. Leipzig: Böhme, 1838 (vol. 1), 1839 (vol. 2), 1845 (vol. 3).

Holbach, Paul-Henri Thiry, Baron d'. *La morale universelle ou les devoirs de l'homme fondés sur sa nature.* Vol. 3. *Des devoirs de la vie privée.* Amsterdam: Michel Rey, 1776.

Hopkins, David. *The Dangers of British India from French Invasion and Missionary Establishments. To Which Are Added Some Account of the Countries between the Caspian Sea and the Ganges, a Narrative of the Revolutions Which They Have Experienced, Subsequent to the Expedition of Alexander the Great, and a Few Hints Respecting the Defence of the British Frontiers in Hindostan.* London, 1808; 2nd ed. 1809.

Huet, Pierre-Daniel. *Histoire sommaire du commerce et de la navigation des Anciens. à Monsieur Colbert. Ministre d'Estat.* 1667, MS, Bibliothèque nationale de France, Suppl. fr. 5307.

——. *A Treatise of the Situation of Paradise.* Translated from the French. London: J. Knapton, 1694.

——. *Histoire du commerce et de la navigation des anciens.* Paris: Fr. Fournier and A.-U. Coustelier, 1716 [anonymous]; Paris: A.-U. Coustelier, 1716.

——. *The History of the Commerce and Navigation of the Ancients, Written in French by Monsieur Huet, Bishop of Avranches, Made English from the Paris Edition.* London: B. Lintot, 1717.

——. *Historie van den Koophandel en zeevart de aloude volkeren op bevel van den Heer Colbert, Minister van Vrankryk.* Delft, 1722.

——. *Huetania ou Pensées diverses de M. Huet, evesque d'Avranches.* Paris: Jacques Estienne, 1722.

——. *Commentarius de navigationibus Salomonis.* Amsterdam, 1692=*Commentaire sur les navigations de Salomon.* In *Traitez géographiques et historiques pour faciliter l'intelligence de l'Ecriture Sainte par divers auteurs célèbres,* 2:1–277. The Hague: G. Van der Poel, 1730.

——. *Storia del commerzio et della navigazione degli antichi di monsignore Huet.* Translated from the 2nd French ed. by A. Belloni. Venice: F. Pitterri, 1737.

———. *Geschichte der Handlung und Schiffahrt der Alten, aus dem Franzosichen überseßt.* n.p. 1763; Vienna, 1775.

———. *Historia del comercio y de la navigacion de los Antiguos, escrita en Frances por el Ilustrisimo Señor Pedro Daniel Huet.* Madrid: Ramon Ruiz, 1793.

———. *Memoirs of the Life of Peter Daniel Huet Written by Himself.* Translated from the Latin by John Aikin. 2 vols. London, 1810 [French 1718].

Humboldt, Alexander von. *Cosmos: A Sketch of a Physical Description of the Universe.* Translated from the German. Vol. 2. London: H. G. Bohn, 1849.

Humboldt, Wilhelm von. "Ueber die Aufgabe des Geschichtschreiber" (1821)="On the Historian's Task." *History and Theory* 6 (1967): 57–71.

Iselin, Isaac. *Ueber die Geschichte der Menscheit.* New and improved ed. 2 vols. Zurich: Füeßtin und Comp., 1770 [1764].

Jondot, Etienne. Review of Vincent, *Voyage de Néarque* (1800). *Journal des débats* (January 2, 1807): 2–4.

Jördens, K.H. (ed.). *Lexicon deutscher Dichter und Prosaisten, II.* Leipzig: Weidmann, 1807.

Jouffroy, Théodore. "Du rôle de la Grèce dans le développement de l'humanité," *Le Globe,* 1827. In *Mélanges philosophiques.* 7th ed., 64–72. Paris: Hachette, 1901 [1833].

Jullien du Ruet, Denis. *Tableau chronologique et moral de l'histoire universelle du commerce des Anciens, ou aperçus politiques de l'histoire ancienne rapportée au commerce, pour en démontrer l'origine, l'utilité et l'influence, dès les premiers âges du monde jusqu'à la naissance de la monarchie française.* Paris: Garnery, Le Normant et Nicolle, 1809.

Kinneir, John Macdonald. *A Geographical Memoir of the Persian Empire Accompanied by a Map.* London: John Murray, 1813.

Kinneir, John Macdonald. *Journey through Asia Minor, Armenia and Koordistan in the Years 1813 and 1814, with Remarks on the Marches of Alexander and Retreat of the Ten Thousand.* London: John Murray, 1818.

Korais, Adamantios. *Chant de guerre des Grecs qui combattent en Égypte pour la cause de la liberté.* Imprimerie grecque d'Égypte, 1801.

———. Mémoire sur l'état actuel de la civilisation dans la Grèce, lu à la Société des Observateurs de l'Homme, le 16 Nivôse, an XI (6 janvier 1805) par Coray. Paris, 1803.

———. ΣΑΛΠΙΣΜΑ ΠΟΛΕΜΙΣΤΗΡΙΟΝ (1801). Translated as Appel aux Grecs, traduit du grec moderne d'Atromète, natif de Marathon, avec la proclamation d'Ypsilanti aux Français. Paris: Baudoin frères, 1821.

Kossin, Dionisio, Barone di. *L'Eroismo ponderato nella vita di Alessandro il Grande, illustrata con discorsi istorici, politici e morali.* 2 vols. Parma: P. Monti, 1716.

Lacombe de Prezel, Honoré. *Les progrès du commerce.* Amsterdam, 1761.

Ladvocat, Abbé Jean-Baptiste. *Dictionnaire historique-portatif contenant l'histoire des patriarches, des princes hébreux, des empereurs, des rois et des grands capitaines; de dieux et des héros de l'Antiquité payenne; des Papes, des Saints-Pères, des évêques et cardinaux célèbres*... New corrected and expanded ed. Vol. 1. Paris: Veuve Didot, 1760.

Lafitau, Père Jean-François. *Mœurs des Sauvages amériquains, comparées aux mœurs des premiers temps*. 2 vols. Paris: Saugrain l'Aîné and Charles Estienne Hochereau, 1724.

La Dixmerie, Nicola-Bricaire de. *Les deux âges du goût et du génie français sous Louis XIV et sous Louis XV, ou: parallèle des efforts du génie et du goût dans les sciences, dans les arts, et dans les lettres, sous ces deux règnes*. Paris: chez Lacombe, 1769.

La Harpe, Jean-François de. *Lycée ou cours de littérature ancienne et moderne*. Vol. 4: *Anciens.-Histoire, philosophie et littérature mêlée*. Paris: chez Depelafol, 1825.

Lamartine, Alphonse de. *Vie de Alexandre le Grand*. 2 vols. Paris: Firmin Didot frères, 1859.

Lamberti, Luigi. *Alessandro in Armozia: Azione scenica, scritta per ritorno dell'armata italiana dalla guerra germanica*. Milan: Giovani Silvestri, 1808.

Langlès, Louis-Mathieu. *Voyages dans l'Inde, en Perse etc., avec la description de l'île Poulo-Pinang, nouvel établissement anglais près de la côte de Coromandel, par différents officiers au service de la Compagnie des Indes orientales*. Translated from the English. Paris: Lavillette et Cie, 1801.

Las Cases, le Comte de. *Le Mémorial de Sainte-Hélène*. Edited by G. Walter. 2 vols. Paris: Gallimard, 1956.

Lassen, Christian. *Commentatio geographica. atque historica de Pentapotamica Indica*. Bonn: E. Weber, 1827.

Leibniz, Georg Wilhelm. *Projet d'expédition d'Égypte présenté à Louis XIV*. In *Leibniz. Œuvres, publiées pour la première fois d'après les manuscrits originaux avec notes et introductions par Louis Alexandre Foucher de Careil*. Vol. 5. Paris: Didot Frères, 1864; repr. Georges Olm Verlag: Hildesheim, 1969.

Le Vayer, François de la Mothe. *Jugements sur les anciens et principaux historiens grecs et latins dont il nous reste quelques ouvrages* (1646). In *Œuvres de François de la Mothe Le Vayer*. New rev. and expanded ed. Vol. 4, part I. Dresden: Michel Groell, 1761.

Leland, Thomas. *All the Orations of Demosthenes, Pronounced to Excite Athenians against Philipp of Macedon. Translated into English, Digested and Connected, So as to Form a Regular History of the Progress of the Macedonian Power, with Notes Historical and Critical*. Dublin: W. Sleater, 1756; 2nd ed. London: W. Johnston, 1757.

———. *The History of the Life and Reign of Philip, King of Macedon, the Father of Alexander*. 2 vols. London, 1758.

Lemercier, Louis. *Alexandre*. In *Homère, Alexandre, Poèmes*, 103–200. Paris: Renouard, 1800.

Lenglet-Dufresnoy, Abbé Pierre Nicolas. *Méthode pour étudier l'histoire avec un catalogue des principaux historiens, et des remarques sur la bonté de leurs ouvrages et sur le choix des meilleures éditions*. New ed. Vol. 1. Paris: Pierre Gandoin, 1735.

————. *Supplément de la méthode pour étudier l'histoire avec un supplément au catalogue des Historiens et des remarques sur la bonté, et le choix de leurs éditions.* Part II. Paris: Rollin et De Bure, 1741.

————. *Méthode pour étudier la géographie, dans laquelle on donne une description exacte de l'Univers . . . avec un discours préliminaire sur l'étude de cette science et un catalogue des cartes et descriptions les plus nécessaires.* 3rd ed. 8 vols. Paris: Rollin fils, 1741–1742.

————. *Méthode pour étudier l'histoire, avec un catalogue des principaux Historiens, accompagné de remarques sur la bonté de leurs ouvrages et sur le choix des meilleures éditions.* Rev., corrected and considerably expanded by M. Drouet. Vol. 4. Paris: Debure and N. M. Tillard, 1772.

————. *Tablettes chronologiques de l'Histoire universelle, sacrée et profane, écclésiastique et civile, depuis la création du monde jusqu'à l'an 1775, avec des réflexions sur l'ordre qu'on doit tenir et sur les ouvrages nécessaires à l'étude de l'Histoire. Tome Premier contenant l'Histoire Ancienne.* Rev., corrected and expanded by J. L. Barreau de la Bruyère. Paris: De Bure et Delaguette, 1778.

Le Père, Jacques-Marie. "Mémoire sur la communication des mers des Indes à la Méditerranée par la mer Rouge et le golfe de Soueys." In E. Jomard (ed.), *Description de l'Égypte: ou recueil des observations et des recherches qui ont été faites en Égypte pendant l'expédition de l'armée française, publié par les ordres de Sa Majesté l'Empereur Napoléon le Grand,* 4:7–370. Paris: Etat moderne, 1809.

Letronne, Jean-Antoine. Review of Kinnear, *Journey through Asia Minor* (1818). *Journal des Savants* (January 1819): 106–116.

————. *Œuvres complètes de Rollin. Nouvelle édition, accompagnée d'observations et d'éclaircissements historiques par M. Letronne.* Paris: Firmin Didot, 1821.

Levesque, Pierre-Charles. *Histoire de Russie,* I–V. Yverdon, 1782.

————. *Histoire des différents peuples soumis à la domination des Russes ou suite de l'histoire de Russie.* 2 vols. Paris: de Bure l'aîné, 1783.

————. *Éloge historique de M. l'abbé de Mably, qui a partagé le Prix extraordinaire proposé par l'Académie royale des Inscriptions et Belles-Lettres, pour l'année 1787, à la prière d'une personne qui ne veut point être connue.* Paris: Guillot, 1787.

————. "Recherches chronologiques sur la sculpture chez les Grecs jusqu'au temps de Phidias." *Journal des Savants* (1792): 198–210.

————. *Études de l'histoire ancienne et de celle de la Grèce; de la constitution de la république d'Athènes et de celle de Lacédémone; de la législation, des tribunaux, des mœurs et usages des Athéniens; de la poésie, de la philosophie et des arts chez les Grecs.* 3 vols. Paris: Fournier Frères, 1811.

Linguet, Simon-Nicolas-Henri. *Histoire du siècle d'Alexandre, avec quelques réflexions sur ceux qui l'ont précédé.* Amsterdam, 1762.

————. *Histoire des révolutions de l'empire romain, pour servir de suite à celle des Révolutions de la République.* Vol. 1. Paris: Desaint, 1766.

————. *Théorie des Lois civiles ou principes fondamentaux de la société.* London, 1767; Paris: Fayard, 1984.

——. *Canaux navigables ou développement des avantages qui résulteraient de l'exécution de plusieurs projets en ce genre pour la Picardie, l'Artois, la Bourgogne, la Bretagne, et toute la France en général, avec l'examen de quelques-unes des raisons qui s'y opposent . . .* Amsterdam: Cellot, 1769.

——. *Histoire du siècle d'Alexandre.* 2nd corrected and expanded ed. Amsterdam: Cellot, 1769.

——. *Du plus heureux gouvernement ou parallèle des constitutions politiques de l'Asie avec celles de l'Europe.* London, 1775.

——. "Préparatifs de la guerre contre les Turcs. Réflexions sur les effets qui peuvent en résulter." In *Annales politiques, civiles et littéraires du XVIIIe siècle,* 11: 232–246. [London,] 1784.

Locke, John. *The Whole History of Navigation from Its Original to This Time* (1704). In *The Works of John Locke,* 11th ed. Vol. 10. London, 1812.

Lowth, Robert. *Isaiah. A New Translation with a Preliminary Dissertation and Notes Critical, Philological and Explanatory.* 2nd ed. London: J. Dodsley and T. Cadell, 1779.

Lucas, Paul. *Voyages de Paul Lucas fait en MDCCXIV etc. par ordre de Louis XIV dans la Turquie, l'Asie, Sourie, Palestine, Haute et Basse-Egypte.* New edition, vol. 3. Rouen: Chez Robert Machuel, 1724.

——. *Troisième Voyage du Sieur Paul Lucas dans le Levant, mai 1714–novembre 1717, présenté par Henri Duranton.* Saint-Etienne: Publications de l'Université de Saint-Etienne, 2004.

Mably, Gabriel Bonnot de. *Le droit public de l'Europe fondé sur les traitez conclus jusqu'en l'année 1740.* Rev. and expanded with historical remarks by J. Rousset. Amsterdam, 1748 [1746].

——. *Observations sur les Grecs.* Geneva: Compagnie des Libraires, 1749.

——. *Observations sur les Romains.* Geneva, 1751.

——. *Observations sur l'histoire de la Grèce ou des causes de la prospérité et des malheurs de la Grèce.* 2nd ed. Geneva: Compagnie des Libraires, 1766.

——. *Observations on the Manners, Government, and Policy of the Greeks.* Translated from the French by Mr Chamberland. Oxford, 1784 [French 1749].

——. *De l'étude de l'histoire, à Monseigneur le duc de Parme.* Rev. and corrected ed. Maastricht: Cavalier Libraire, 1778 = *Œuvres complètes de l'abbé Mably,* 12:1–318. Lyon: chez Veuve de J. B. Delamollière et Falque, 1796.

——. *De la manière d'écrire l'histoire.* Paris, 1783 = *Oeuvres complètes de l'abbé de Mably,* 12:321–500. Lyon: Veuve de J. B. Delamollière et Falque, 1796.

——. *Observations sur l'histoire de France* (1765). Rev. edition by M. Guizot. Paris: Brière, 1823.

Machiavelli, Niccolo. *The Prince.* Harvard Classics Edition. Translated by N.H. Thomson. New York: P.F. Collier & Son Company, 1909–1914.

MacPherson, David. *Annals of Commerce, Manufactures, Fisheries and Navigation, with Brief Notices of the Arts and Sciences Connected with Them, Containing the Commercial Transactions of the British Empire and Other Countries.* 4 vols. London, 1801.

———. *The History of the European Commerce with India to Which Is Subjoined a Review of the Arguments for and against the Trade with India, and the Management of It by a Chartered Company with an Appendix of Authentic Accounts.* London: Longman, Hurst, Rees, Orme, and Brown, 1812.

McCluer, John. *An Account of the Navigation between India and the Gulph of Persia at All Seasons with Nautical Instructions for That Gulph, Published at the Charge of the East India Company by Alexander Dalrymple* [nautical memoirs and journals published by Dalrymple before June 1, 1789]. London: G. Bigg, 1786.

Maillet, Benoist de. *Description de l'Égypte contenant plusieurs remarques curieuses sur la géographie anciene et moderne de ce païs, sur les monuments anciens, sur les mœurs, les coutumes, et la religion des habitants, sur le gouvernement et le commerce, sur les animaux, les arbres, les plantes etc . . . composée sur les mémoires de M. de Maillet, ancien consul de France au Caire, par M. L'Abbé Le Mascrier, enrichi de cartes et de figures.* 2 vols. Paris: Louis Genneau and Jacques Rollin, 1735.

Malcolm, John. *The History of Persia from the most early period to the present time,* a new edition, I. London: John Murray, 1829.

Malouet, Pierre Victor. *Considérations historiques sur l'empire de la mer chez les Anciens et et les Modernes.* Antwerp: LePoittevin Delacroix, 1810.

Malte-Brun, Conrad. *Précis de géographie universelle ou description de toutes les parties du monde sur un plan nouveau, d'après les grandes divisions du globe; précédée de l'Histoire de la géographie chez les peuples anciens et modernes, et d'une théorie générale de la géographie mathématique, physique et politique.* Vol. 1: *Histoire de la géographie.* Paris: Fr. Buisson, 1810.

Mannert, Konrad. *Geschichte der unmittelbaren Nachfolger Alexanders.* Leipzig: Dyksche Buchhandlung, 1787.

———. *Geographie der Griechen und Römer.* Vol. 5: *Indien und die persische Monarchie bis zum Euphrat.* Nuremberg: E. C. Grattenauer, 1797.

Maréchal, Pierre-Sylvain. *Apologues modernes à l'usage du Dauphin, premières leçons du fils aîné du roi.* Brussels, 1788.

Mascardi, Antonio. *Dell'arte istorica trattati cinque.* Venice: Paolo Baglioni, 1674.

Maurice, Thomas. *A Dissertation on the Quantity of Bullion and Coined Money in the Ancient World, Comprising a Short History of the Gold and Silver Mines of Asia, and a Survey of the Immense Treasures Possessed by the Ancient Sovereigns of India.* In *Indian Antiquities,* vol. 8. London: Bulmer, 1806.

Meiners, Christoph. *Geschichte des Luxus der Athenienser von den ältesten Zeiten an bis auf den Tod Philipps von Makedonien.* Kassel: Ph. O. Hampe, 1782.

Melon, Jean-François. *A Political Essay upon Commerce.* Translated from the French by D. Blindon. Dublin, 1738 [French 1734, 1736].

Menou, Jacques. *Troisième rapport sur Avignon et le Comtat Venaissin, fait à l'Assemblée nationale dans la séance du 12 septembre 1791 . . . au nom des Comités de constitution, diplomatique et d'Avignon.* Paris: Imprimerie nationale, 1791.

Mentelle, Edme. *Géographie ancienne*. In *Encyclopédie méthodique*, vol. 1. Paris: Panckoucke, 1787.

Mentelle, Edme, and Conrad Malte-Brun. *Géographie mathématique, physique et politique de toutes les parties du monde, rédigée d'après tout ce qui a été publié d'exact et de nouveau par les géographes, les naturalistes, les voyageurs et les auteurs de statistique des nations les plus éclairées*. Vol. 1. Paris: Tardieu and Laporte, 1803.

Michaud, Joseph-François. *Histoire des progrès et de la chûte de l'empire de Mysore sous les règnes d'Hyder-Aly et Tipoo-Saïb*. 2 vols. Paris: Giguet, 1801.

Michaud, Louis-Gabriel. "Alexandre le Grand." In *Biographie universelle ancienne et moderne*, 1:495–506. Paris: Michaud Frères, 1811.

———. "Alexandre le Grand." In *Biographie universelle ancienne et moderne*, 1:397–410. New ed. with an additional 86 footnotes by V. Parisot. Paris: A. Thoisnier Desplaces, 1842.

Mill, James. *The History of British India*. 3 vols. London: Balwin, Cradock, and Jow, 1817.

Millin, Aubin-Louis. Review of Sainte-Croix, *Examen critique* (1804). *Magasin Encyclopédique* (1805): 26–31, 344–357.

Mitchell, John. *An Essay on the Best Means of Civilising the Subjects of the British Empire in India and of Diffusing the Light of the Christian Religion throughout the Eastern World*. Edinburgh: James Ballantyne for W. Blackwood, 1805.

Mitford, William. *The History of Greece*. Vol. 5. London: Cadell and Davies, 1818.

Modonese, Pietro Lauro. *Arriano di Nicomedia chiamato nuovo Xenofonte dei fatti del Magno Alessandro re di Macedonia, nuovamente di Greco tradotta in Italiano*. Venice, 1543; repr. Verona, 1730.

Montaigne, Michel Eyquem de. *Essays*. Translated by C. Cotton and edited by W. C. Hazlitt. 3 vols. London: Treves and Turner, 1877.

———. *Les Essais*. Updated to modern French and introduced by Claude Pinganaud. Paris: Arléa, 2002.

Montesquieu, Charles-Louis de Secondat, Baron de La Brède et de. *Oeuvres complètes*. Presentation and notes by Daniel Oster; preface by Georges Vedel. Paris: Éditions du Seuil, 1964.

———. *The Spirit of the Laws*. Translated and edited by A. M. Cohler, B. S. Miller, and H. S. Stone. Cambridge: Cambridge University Press, 1989.

———. *Pensées. Le Spicilège*. Edited by Louis Desgraves. Paris: Robert Laffont, Collection Bouquins, 1991.

———. *Lettres Persanes*. Edited under the direction of Jean Ehrard and Catherine Volpilhac-Auger. In *Œuvres complètes de Montesquieu*, vol. 1. Oxford: Voltaire Foundation, 2004.

———. *Persian Letters*. Translated with an introduction and notes by C. J. Betts. London: Penguin, 2004.

———. *Œuvres complètes de Montesquieu*. Oxford: Voltaire Foundation, 2000–.

———. *My Thoughts*. Translated and edited with an introduction by H. C. Clark. Indianapolis: Liberty Fund, 2012.

Moréri, Louis. *Le Grand Dictionnaire historique ou le mélange curieux de l'Histoire Sainte et Profane*... Lyon: Jean Girin et Barthélemy Rivière, 1674.

Moutonnet de Clairfons, Julien-Jacques. *Réflexions sur les siècles d'Alexandre, d'Auguste, de Léon X et de Louis XIV*, n.p., 1806.

Moyle, Walter. *The Works of Walter Moyle*. Vol. 2. London, 1726.

Nares, Robert. "Life of Dr. Vincent." *Classical Journal* 13, no. 26: 221–226; no. 27: 190–215.

Niccolini, Antonio. *Quadro in musaico in Pompei scoperto in Pompei a di 24 ottobre 1831 descritto ed esposto in alcune tavole dimostrative*... Naples: Stamperia reale, 1832.

Niebuhr, Barthold Georg. *Demosthenis erste Philippische Rede, im Auszug überseßt.* New ed. with a preface. Hamburg: Fr. Perthes, 1831.

———. *Vorträge über alte Geschichte, and die Universität zu Bonn gehalten.* Edited by M. Niebuhr. Vol. 2. Berlin: Reimer, 1848.

———. *Lectures on Ancient History from the Earliest Times to the Taking of Alexandria by Ocyavian, Translated from the German Edition by Dr. L. Schmitz.* 3 vols. Philadelphia: Blanchard and Lea, 1852.

Niebuhr, Carsten. *Reisenbeschreibung nach Arabien und andern umliegenden Länder.* Vol. 2. Copenhagen, 1778.

———. *Voyage de M. Niebuhr en Arabie et en d'autres pays de l'Orient, avec l'extrait de sa description de l'Arabie et des observations de M. Forskal,* I-II. French translation. Switzerland: Chez les Libraires associés, 1780.

Olivier, Claude-Mathieu. *Histoire de Philippe, roi de Macédoine et père d'Alexandre.* 2 vols. Paris: de Bure l'Aîné, 1740.

Ouseley, Sir William. *Travels in Various Countries of the East, More Particularly Persia. A Work Wherein the Author Has Described, as Far as His Own Observations Extended, the State of These Countries in 1810, 1811 and 1812, and Has Endeavoured to Illustrate Many Subjects of Antiquarian Research, History, Geography, Philology and Miscellaneous Literature with Extracts from Rare and Valuable Oriental Manuscripts.* Vol. 1. London: Rodwell and Martin, 1819.

Parisot, Valentin: see Michaud, Louis-Gabriel.

Pelisseri, M. de. *Histoire royale de Philippe, roy de Macédoine, tirée exactement des plus rares thrésors de l'antiquité.* Toulouse: R. Bosc, 1669.

Pfizer, Gustav. *Geschichte Alexanders des Grossen für die Jugend, mit zwei Thorwaldsens Alexanderszug und einer Karte der Heerzüge Alexanders.* Stuttgart: Sam. Gott. Liesching, 1846.

Phalantée, Sylvain [David, Pierre]. *L'Alexandréide, ou la Grèce vengée, poème en vingt-quatre chants.* 2 vols. Paris: Didot, 1826–1829.

———. *Athènes assiégée, poème.* Paris, Didot, 1827.

Piron, Alexis. *Callisthène (Tragédie).* Paris: Veuve Merge, Le Gras, Veuve Pissot, 1730.

Poirson, Auguste Simon Jean-Chrysostome, and Rémy Jean-Baptiste Charles Cayx. *Commission de l'Instruction Publique. Programme pour l'enseignement de l'histoire ancienne dans les collèges royaux.* Paris: Colas, 1820.

———. *Précis de l'Histoire ancienne.* Paris: Louis Colas and L. Hachette, 1827.

Potter, Johann. *Griechische Archäologie, oder Altertümer Griechenlandes.* Part III, with treatises by Johann Jacob Raumbach. Halle: Johann Jacb Gebauer, 1778.

Pottinger, Sir Henry. *Travels in Beloochistan and Sinde Accompanied by a Geographical and Historical Account of These Countries.* London: Longman, Hurst, Rees, Orme, and Brown, 1816.

———. *Travels in Beloochistan and Sinde,* with an introduction by Rosie Vaughan. Karachi: Oxford University Press, 2002 [1816].

Pownall, Thomas. *A Treatise on the Study of Antiquities as the Commentary to Historical Learning, Sketching Out a General Line of Research: Also Marking and Explaining Some of the Desiderata.* London: J. Dodsley, 1782.

Prideaux, Humphrey. *The True Nature of Imposture Fully Displayed in the Life of Mahomet.* London: W. Rogers, 1697.

———. *The Old and New Testament Connected in the History of the Jews and Neighbouring Nations, from the Declension of the Kingdoms of Israel and Judah to the Time of Christ.* London, 1715–1717; Edinburgh: S. Schaw, 1799.

Pufendorf, Samuel von. *De rebus gestis Philippi Amyntae Filii* (Diss. Acad. Selectiones). Lund, 1675.

Puységur, Jacques François de Chastenet, Marquis de. *Art de la guerre par principes et par règles.* Paris: Charles-Antoine Jombert, 1748.

Raleigh, Sir Walter. *The Historie of the World in Five Bookes . . . from the Creation . . . untill the Romans (Prevailing over All) Made Conquest of Asia and Macedon.* London, 1652 [1614].

Ramusio, Giovani Battista. *Navigationi et Viaggi.* 3rd ed. Vol. 1: Venice: Stamp. dei Giunti, 1563.

Raphelius, Georgius. *Arriani Indica, das ist die Indianische Geschichte oder Reisebeschreibung der Flotten Alexanders des Grossen, aus d. Griech. ins Deusche überstezzet.* Hamburg: Ch. Liebezeit, 1710.

Raynal, Guillaume-Thomas. *A Philosophical History of Settlements and Trade of the Europeans in the East and West Indies.* Translated from the French by J. Justamond. 3rd ed. London: Cadell, 1777 [1770].

———. *Histoire philosophique et politique des établissements et du commerce des Européens dans les deux Indes.* 4 vols. + atlas. Geneva: chez Jean-Léonard Pellet, 1780 [1770]; Paris: Bibliothèque des Introuvables, 2006 (10 vols.).

———. *A Philosophical History of Settlements and Trade of the Europeans in the East and West Indies.* Edinburgh, 1804.

———. *Histoire philosophique et politique des établissements et du commerce des Européens dans les deux Indes.* Vol. 1 (bks. 1–5). Ferney-Voltaire: Centre international d'études sur le XVIIIᵉ Siècle, 2010 [1770].

Redesdale, Lord. "A Short Account of the Author and of Pursuits of His [Mitford's] Life with an Apology for Some Parts of His Work." In *History of Greece by W. Mitford, with His Final Additions and Corrections, Carefully Revised by William King*, 1:ix–xliv. London: T. Cadell and W. Blackwood, 1838.

Remers, Julius August. *Handbuch der ältern-Geschichte, von Schöpfung der Welt bis auf die große Volkërwanderung*. 3rd ed. Braunschweig: Schulbuchhandlung, 1794 [1783].

Rennell, James. *A Bengal Atlas: Containing Maps of the Theatre of War and Commerce on That Side of Hindoostan: Compiled from the Original Surveys, and Published by the Order of the Honourable Court of Directors for the Affairs of the East India Company*. London, 1781.

———. *Memoir of a Map of Hindoostan or the Mogul's Empire, with an Examination of Some Positions in the Former System of Indian Geography, and Some Illustrations of the Present One, and a Complete Index of Names to the Map*. London: Printed by M. Brown for the author, 1783.

———. *Memoir of a Map of Hindoostan or the Mogul's Empire, with an Introduction Illustrative of the Geography and Present Division of That Country, and a Map of the Countries Situated between the Head of the Indus and the Caspian Sea, to Which Is Added an Appendix Containing an Account of the Ganges and Burrampooter Rivers*. London: Printed by M. Brown for the author, 1788.

———. *Memoir of a Map of Hindoostan or the Mogul Empire with an Introduction Illustrative of the Geography and Present Division of That Country, and a Map of the Countries Situated between the Head of the Indus and the Caspian Sea: Also a Supplementary Map Containing the Improved Geography of the Countries Contiguous to the Heads of Indus, to Which Is Added an Appendix Containing an Account of the Ganges and Burrampooter Rivers, The Third Edition with a Supplementary Map Containing the New Geography of the Peninsula of India and an Explanatory Memoir*. London: Printed by W. Bulmer for the author, 1793.

———. *The Geographical System of Herodotus Examined and Explained by a Comparison with Those of Other Ancient Authors and with Modern Geography*. 2 vols. London, 1800; London: Rivington, 1830.

Ricard, Dominique. *Oeuvres morales de Plutarque traduites en françois*. Vol. 4. Paris: Veuve Dessaint, 1785.

Ricaut, Paul. *The Present State of the Ottoman Empire, Containing the Maxims of the Turkish Politie, the Most Material Points of the Mahometan Religion, Their Sects and Heresies, Their Convents and Religious Votaries, Their Military Discipline, in Three Books*. 3rd ed. London: J. Starkey and H. Brome, 1670.

Rigas, Véléstinlis. "Thourios (Chant de guerre)" (1797). In Claude Fauriel, *Chants populaires de la Grèce moderne*, 2:15–27. Paris: Firmin Didot, 1825.

———. *Karta tès Hellados* (1797). Map of Greece drawn by Rigas, discussed in online journal *E-perimetron* Vol. 3, No. 3, 2008 and Vol. 5, No. 2, 2010. http://www.e-peri metron.org.

———. *Nea politikè diokèsis* (1796). Greek text and French translation, *La Nouvelle administratrion politique*. In A. Dascalakis, *Rhigas Velestinlis*, 75–91. Paris, 1937.

Ritter, Carl. "Alexander des Großen Feldzug am Indischen Kaukasus" (1829). *Abhandlungen der Koniglichen Akademie der Wissenschaten zu Berlin* (1832): 137–174.

———. *Geschichte der Erdkunde und der Entdeckungen. Vorlesungen an der Universität zu Berlin gehalten, herausgegeben von H. U. Daniel*. Berlin: Georg Reimer, 1861.

Robertson, William. Review of A. Gordon, *The History of Peter the Great*, I-II. *Edinburgh Review* (1755): 1–8.

———. *The History of Ancient Greece, from the Earliest Times, till It Became a Roman Province*. Edinburgh, 1768 [anonymous], 1778, 1786; carefully corrected ed. Edinburgh: W. Creech, 1812.

———. *History of America*. 1st American ed. from the 10th London ed. 2 vols. Philadelphia: Johnson and Warner, 1812 [1777].

———. *Historical Disquisition concerning the Knowledge Which the Ancients Had of India and the Progress of Trade with the Country, Prior to the Discovery of the Passage to It by the Cape of Good Hope, with an Appendix on the Civil Policy, the Laws and Judicial Proceedings, the Arts, the Sciences, and Religious Institutions of the Indians*. London: Basil, 1792 [1791].

———. *Historische Untersuchung über die Kenntisse der Alten von Indien une die Fortschritte des Handels mit diesem Lande vor der Entdeckung des Weges dahin um das Vorgebirge der guten Hoffnung*. Translated from the English with a preface by Georg Forster. Berlin: Voss, 1792.

———. *Recherches historiques sur la connaissance que les Anciens avaient de l'Inde et sur le progrès du commerce avec cette partie du monde avant la découverte du passage par le Cap de Bonne Espérance, suivies d'un appendix contenant des observations sur l'état civil, les loix et les formalités judiciaires, les arts, les sciences et les institutions religieuses des Indiens* [Anonymous French translation]. 2 vols. Paris: Buisson, 1792; Maastricht: Jean-Paul Roux et Compagnie, 1792 = *Recherches historiques sur l'Inde ancienne*. In J. A. C Buchon (ed.), *Œuvres complètes de W. Robertson*, 1:505–626. Paris: A. Desrez, 1837.

———. *Ricerche storiche su l'India antica, su la cognizione che gli Antichi ni avevano, et su i progressi del commercio con queste paese avanti la scoperta del passagio pel capo di Buona Speranza*. Translated from the English by Guglielmo Romagnosi. 2 vols. 1794; Milan: Vincenzo Ferrario, 1827.

Rochette, Désiré-Raoul [Raoul-Rochette]. *Histoire critique de l'établissement des colonies grecques*. Vol. 4. Paris: Treuttel et Wûrtz, 1815.

———. Reviews of Niccolini, *Quadro in musaico in Pompei* (1832) and Bonucci, *Gran musaico di Pompei* (1832). *Journal des Savants* (May 1833): 286–298.

Roget, Philippe. "Historiens allemands contemporains. Jean-Gustave Droysen, Histoire de l'Hellénisme." *Revue germanique et française* 29 (1864): 228–245; 32 (1867): 87–100

Rollin, Charles. *Histoire ancienne des Égyptiens, des Carthaginois, des Assyriens, des Mèdes et des Perses, des Macédoniens, des Grecs*. 13 vols. Paris: Estienne, 1731–1738.

———. *The Ancient History in Eight Volumes.* 8th ed. Edinburgh, 1787–1790.

———. *The History of Arts and Sciences of the Ancients.* Translated from the French. Vols. 1–4. London: J. and P. Knapton, 1737–1739.

———. *The History and Travels of Alexander the Great.* Translated from the French. Berwick: R. Taylor, 1770.

———. *The Life of Alexander the Great, King of Macedon, Compiled from Ancient History.* Philadelphia, 1796.

———. *Histoire ancienne.* In *Œuvres complètes.* New ed. with observations and historical clarifications by M. Letronne. Vol. 5:366–484 (*Histoire de Philippe*); vol. 6:5–379 (*Histoire d'Alexandre*). Paris: F. Didot, 1821.

Rooke, John. *Arrian's History of Alexander's Expedition, Translated from the Greek, with Notes Historical, Geographical and Critical, to Which Is Prefixed Mr Le Clerc's Criticism upon Quintus Curtius and Some Remarks upon Mr Perizonius's Vindication of That Author.* London, 1729, 1814 (2 vols.).

Roubaud, Pierre Joseph André, Abbé de. *Histoire générale de l'Asie, de l'Afrique et de l'Amérique, contenant des discours sur l'histoire ancienne des peuples de ces contrées, leur histoire moderne et la description des lieux, avec des remarques sur leur histoire naturelle & des observations sur les religions, les gouvernements, les sciences, les arts, le commerce, les coutumes, les mœurs, les caractères, etc. des nations.* 2 vols. Paris: Des Ventes de la Doué, 1770.

Rousseau, Jean-Jacques. "Economie ou Oeconomie." In D. Diderot & d'Alembert (eds.), *Encyclopédie ou Dictionnaire raisonné des sciences, des arts et des métiers,* 5 (1755): 337–349.

Rozière, François-Michel de. "Notice sur les ruines d'un monument persépolitain découvert dans l'isthme de Suez." In Edme François Jomard (ed.), *Description de l'Égypte: ou recueil des observations et des recherches qui ont été faites en Égypte pendant l'expédition de l'armée française, publié par les ordres de Sa Majesté l'Empereur Napoléon le Grand.* Vol. 3.1.1, text 1, 265–275. Paris: Antiquités, 1809.

Ruelle, Emile, and Alphonse Huillard-Brihales. *Histoire résumée des temps anciens comprenant l'Histoire de la Grèce de Gillies, abrégée et modifiée . . .* 2nd corrected and expanded ed. 2 vols. Paris: Pourchet Libraire, 1845 [1841].

Sabbathier, François. *Dictionnaire pour l'intelligence des auteurs classiques grecs et latins, tant sacrés que profanes, contenant la géographie, l'histoire, la fable, et les antiquités, dédiés à Monseigneur le duc de Choiseul.* Vol. 2. Châlons-sur-Marne: Seneuze, Delalain, Barbou, and Hérissant, 1767.

———. *Le manuel des enfans ou les maximes des vies des hommes illustres de Plutarque, ouvrage dédié à Monseigneur le Dauphin.* Châlons-sur-Marne: Seneuze, Delalain, Barbou, and Hérissant, 1769.

Sainte-Croix, Guillaume-Emmanuel-Joseph Guilhem de Clermont-Lodève, Baron de. *Examen critique des anciens historiens d'Alexandre le Grand* (manuscript prepared for the Prix de Pâques 1772), 1771.

——. "Observations sur les ruines de Persépolis" (1773). Manuscript published by Maria-Stefania Montecalvo in *Quaderni di Storia* 50 (2004): 5–57.

——. *Examen critique des anciens historiens d'Alexandre le Grand.* Paris: Dessain Junior, 1775.

——. *De l'état et du sort des colonies des anciens peuples, ouvrage dans lequel on traite du gouvernement des anciennes républiques, de leur droit public etc. avec des observations sur les colonies des nations modernes, et la conduite des Anglais en Amérique.* Philadelphia [Yverdon], 1779.

——. *Observations sur le traité de paix conclu à Paris, le 10 février 1763, entre la France, l'Espagne et l'Angleterre, relativement aux intérêts de ces Puissances dans la guerre présente.* Amsterdam, 1780.

——. *Histoire des progrès de la puissance navale d'Angleterre,* I–II. Yverdon, 1782.

——. *Remontrances des États du Comté Venaissin [au Pape, pour demander la permission d'imprimer les cahiers des délibérations des communautés].* In *Recueil de pièces fugitives concernant la révolution du Comtat-Venaissin et de la ville d'Avignon,* vol. 1, item no. 9. Avignon, 1791.

——. *A Critical Enquiry into the Life of Alexander the Great by the Ancient Historians, from the French of the Baron de St. Croix, with Notes and Observations by Sir Richard Clayton.* 2 vols. Bath: G. G. and J. Robinson, 1793.

——. "Notice sur la vie et les ouvrages de Jean-Jacques Barthélemy." *Magazin Encyclopédique* 1, no. 2 (Year 3 [1795]): 72–93, 237–242.

——. *Mémoire sur le cours de l'Araxe et du Cyrus.* Paris, Year 5 (1797).

——. *Examen critique des anciens historiens d'Alexandre le Grand.* 2nd considerably expanded ed. Paris: Imprimerie de Delance et Lesueur, Year 12 (1804).

——. *Examen critique des anciens historiens d'Alexandre le Grand.* 2nd considerably expanded ed. with eight intaglio plates. Paris: Henri Grand et Bachelier, 1810.

——. *Eloge historique de J. J. Barthélemy.* n.p., n.d.

Sainte-Croix, Théophile-Guillaume Guilhem de. *Déclaration de M. de Sainte-Croix, officier au régiment de Beauvaisis, concernant sa détention au quartier général des brigands sortis d'Avignon.* In *Recueil de pièces fugitives concernant la révolution du Comtat-Venaissin et de la ville d'Avignon.* Vol. 4, item no. 120. Avignon, 1791.

Savary, Claude-Etienne. *Lettres sur l'Égypte, où l'on offre le parallèle des mœurs anciennes et modernes de ses habitans, où l'on décrit l'état, le commerce, l'agriculture, le gouvernement, l'ancienne religion du pays, la descente de S. Louis à Damiette, tirée de Joinville et des auteurs arabes, avec des cartes géographiques.* 2nd rev. and corrected ed. 3 vols. Paris: Onfroi, 1786.

Savary, Jacques. *Le parfait négociant ou instruction générale pour ce qui concerne le Commerce de toute sorte de marchandises, tant de France que des pays étrangers . . .* Paris: Jean Guignard, 1675.

Savary des Brulons, Jacques. *Dictionnaire universel du commerce . . . continué sur les mémoires de l'auteur et donné au public par Ph-L. Savary (son frère).* 3 vols. Paris: Jacques Estienne, 1723.

Schiller, Friedrich von. "The Nature and Value of Universal History: An Inaugural Lecture [1789]." *History and Theory* 11 (1972): 321–334.

Schlosser, Friedrich Christoph. *Histoire universelle de l'Antiquité [Universalhistorische Uebersicht der Geschichte der alten Welt und ihre Cultur.* Frankfurt am Main: F. Varrentrapp, 1826–1834]. Translated from the German by M. P. A. de Golbéry. Vols. 2 and 3. Paris: F. G. Levrault, 1828.

Schlözer, August Ludwig von. *Versuch einer allgemeinen Geschichte der Handlung und Seefahrt in den ältesten Zeiten.* Rostock: Kopp, 1761 [Swedish 1758].

——. *Vorstellung seiner Universal-historie.* Göttingen und Gotta: J.-Ch. Dieterich, 1772.

——, and Johann Mathias Schröckh. *Histoire universelle continuée jusqu'à notre temps, et précédée d'un discours pour y préparer les enfans; deux ouvrages traduits de l'allemand de Mrs Schloetzer [sic] et Schroeck.* Tubingen: Jean-George Cotta, 1781.

Schmieder, Friedrich. *Arriani Historia Indica, cum Bonav. Vulcanii Interpretatione Latina per multis locis emendatore.* Halle: Jac. Gebauer, 1798.

Schmidt von Rossan, Friedrich Samuel. *De commerciis et navigationibus Ptolemaerum.* In *Opuscula, quibus res antiquae praecipue Aegyptiacae explanantur,* 125–379. Karlsruhe: Maklott, 1765.

Schmidt, Karl. *Die Feldzüge Alexanders des Grossen nebst Indischer Geschichte in sieben Büchern, nebst Heinrich Dodwelles Prüfung der Seereise des Nearch und von Bougainville Abdhlandlung von der Seereise des Hanno, und den carthaginensischen Handelsplätzen die er an den Küsten von Africa angelegt hat. Mit Landcharten, etc.* Braunschweig, Wölgenbuttel, and Meissner, 1764.

Schnitzler, Jean-Henri. "Alexandre-le-Grand." In *Encyclopédie des gens du monde,* 1:379–385. Paris: Treuttel and Würtz, 1833.

Schröckh, Johann Mathias. *Allgemeine Weltgeschichte für Kinder.* Part I: *Alte Geschichte.* 2nd improved and enlarged ed. Leipzig: Weidmanns Erben und Reich, 1786.

Secousse, Denis. "Dissertation sur l'expédition d'Alexandre contre les Perses" (presented April 6, 1723). *Mémoires de littérature de l'Académie des Inscriptions et Belles-Lettres* 5 (1729): 415–430.

Séguier de Saint-Brisson, Nicolas-Maximilien-Sidoine. "Tableau systématique de la science de l'antiquité, traduit de l'allemand de M. Wolf." *Magasin Encyclopédique* no. 5 (1812): 78–116, 349–383; no. 6: 112–145.

Selden, John. *Mare clausum seu de dominio Maris libri duo.* London, 1635 = *Of the Dominion of the Sea.* London: William Du Gand, 1652.

Séran de la Tour. *Parallèle de la conduite des Carthaginois à l'égard des Romains dans la seconde guerre punique avec la conduite de l'Angleterre à l'égard de la France dans la guerre déclarée par ces deux puissances en 1756.* Paris, 1757.

Sevin, Abbé François. "Recherches sur la vie et les ouvrages de Callisthène." *Mémoires de littérature de l'Académie des Inscriptions et Belles-Lettres* 8 (1727): 126–143.

Shuckford, Samuel. *The Sacred and Prophane History of the World Connected, from the Creation of the World to the Dissolution of the Assyrian Empire at the Death of*

Sardanapalus, and to the Declension of the Kingdoms of Judah and Israel under the Reigns of Ahaz and Pekah. 2nd ed. Vol. 3. London: H. Knaplock and J. and R. Tonson, 1740 [1726–1730].

Silvestre de Sacy, Antoine-Isaac. *Notice sur M. Guilhem de Clermont Lodève de Sainte-Croix insérée dans le Catalogue des livres de sa Bibliothèque.* Paris, 1809.

———. "Sainte-Croix, Guillaume-Emmanuel-Joseph-Guilhem de Clermont-Lodève, baron de." *Dictionnaire de biographie Michaud,* 283–286.

Sonnini de Manoncourt, Charles-Nicolas-Sigisbert. *Travels in Greece and Turkey Undertaken by Order of Louis XVI and with the Authority of the Ottoman Court.* 2 vols. Translated from the French. London: Longman and Rees, 1801.

Sprengel, Mathias Christian. *Geschichte der Maratten bis auf den letzen Frieden mit England den 17. May 1782.* Halle: Johann Jacob Gebauer, 1786.

———. *Geschichte der wichtigsten geographischen Entdeckungen bis zur Ankunft der Portugiesen in Japan 1542.* Berlin 1786; 2nd enlarged ed. Halle: Hemmerde und Schwetschke, 1792.

Stanyan, Temple. *The Grecian History, from the Original of Greece to the Death of Philipp of Macedon.* Vol. 2. London, 1739, 1752 (2 vols.).

———. *The Grecian History, from the Original of Greece to the Death of Philip of Macedon.* 2 vols. London: J. and R. Tonson, 1751.

Struvé, Burkard, Christian Gottlieb Buder, and Johann Georg Meusel. *Bibliotheca Historica.* Vol. 3, part II. Leipzig: Weidmann, 1788.

Tailhié, Abbé Jacques. *Histoire d'Alexandre.* In *Abrégé de l'Histoire ancienne de Monsieur Rollin.* 2nd rev., corrected, and expanded, 3:258–433. Lausanne: M.-M. Bousquet, 1754.

Talleyrand, Citoyen [Charles-Maurice de Talleyrand-Périgord]. *Essai sur les avantages à retirer des colonies nouvelles dans les circonstances présentes.* Read at the public session of the Institut National on 15 messidor Year 5 (1796). Paris, 1797.

Tilladet, Abbé de. *Dissertations sur différens sujets composées par Mr. Huet, ancien évêque d'Avranches et quelques autres savants.* Vol. 1. Florence: P.-C. Viviani, 1714.

Tooke, William. *Observations on the Expedition of General Buonaparte to the East, and Probability of Its Success Considered, to Which Is Added a Brief Sketch of the Present State of Egypt, and Historical Account of Alexandria, the Two Harbours of That City Accurately Delineated, Its Former Splendor and Present State Contrasted, with Some Remarks on Its Local Importance Should It Become the Mart of the East, Together with a Few Particulars relating to the Navigation of the Red Sea.* London: George Cawthorne and Messrs. Richardson, 1798.

Tott, Andras. *Memoirs of the Baron de Tott on the Turks and the Tartars.* Translated from the French. 3 vols. Dublin, 1785.

Tourreil, Jacques de. *Introduction à la traduction des Philippiques de Démosthène* (1691). In *Œuvres de Mr de Tourreil de l'Académie royale et l'un des Quarante de l'Académie françoise.* Vol. 1. Paris: Brunet, 1721.

Ubicini, Jean-Henri Abdolonyme. "La Grande Carte de la Grèce." In *Revue de Géographie*. April 1881, 241–253; July–December 1881, 9–25.

Vancouver, George. *A Voyage of Discovery to the North Pacific Ocean and round the World in Which the Coast of North-West America Has Been Carefully Examined and Accurately Surveyed, Undertaken by His Majesty's Command, Principally with a View to Ascertain the Existence of Any Navigable Communication between the North Pacific and North Atlantic Oceans, and Performed in the Years 1790, 1791, 1792, 1793, 1794 and 1795*. 3 vols. London: Robinson and Edwards, 1798.

———. *Voyages de découvertes à l'océan pacifique du Nord et autour du monde*. Translated from the English. 3 vols. Paris: De l'imprimerie de la République, 1799–1800.

Van der Chys, Pieter Otto. *Commentarius geographicus in Arrianum de expeditione Alexandri*. Leiden: J. C. Cyfveer, 1828.

Van Limburg Brouwer, Petrus. *Histoire de la civilisation morale et religieuse des Grecs*. Vol. 5, part II: *Depuis le retour des Héraclides jusqu'à la domination des Romains*. Groningen: W. van Boekeren, 1839.

Vaugondy, Robert de. *Essai sur l'histoire de la Géographie ou sur son origine, son progrès et son état actuel*. Paris: Antoine Boudet, 1750.

Velestinlis, Rhigas. *Œuvres Révolutionnaires*. Translated by D. Panélodimos. D. Karabéropoulos (ed.). Athens: Société des études sur Phères-Vélestino-Rhigas, 2002.

Vico, T. *The New Science*. Translated from the 3rd ed. (1744) by T. G. Bergin and M. H. Fisch. Ithaca, NY: Cornell University Press, 1948.

Vincent, William. *A Sermon Preached May 13, 1792, in the Parish Church of St. Margaret's, Westminster*. London: T. Cadell, 1792.

———. Review of Clayton, *A Critical Inquiry* (translation of Sainte-Croix, *Examen critique* [1775]). *British Critic* 3 (1793): 510–517, 620–629.

———. *The Voyage of Nearchus from the Indus to the Euphrates, Collected from the Original Journal Preserved by Arrian and Illustrated by Authorities Ancient and Modern, Containing an Account of the First Navigation Attempted by Europeans in the Indian Ocean*. London: Cadell and Davies, 1797.

———. *Le Voyage de Néarque, des bouches de l'Indus jusqu'à l'Euphrate ou Journal de l'expédition de la flotte d'Alexandre, rédigé sur le Journal original de Néarque conservé par Arrien, à l'aide des éclaircissements puisés dans les écrits et relations des auteurs, géographes ou voyageurs, tant anciens que modernes, et contenant l'histoire de la première navigation que les Européens aient tentée dans la mer des Indes, traduit de l'Anglois par J. B. L. J. Billecocq, homme de loi*. Paris: Imprimerie de la République, Year 8 (1800); Paris: Maradan, 1800 (3 vols.).

———. *Periplus des rothen Meeres oder Nachricht von der Schiffahrt der Alten und der Ostküste Afrikas*. In G. G. Bredow (ed.), *Untersuchungen über einzelne Gegenstände der alten Geschichte, Geographie und Chronologie*, 715–797. Altona: Fr. Hammerich, 1800.

———. *The Periplus of the Erythrean Sea*. Part I: *Containing an Account of the Navigation of the Ancients from the Sea of Suez to the Coast of Zanguebar, with Dissertations*.

London: T. Cadell and W. Davies, 1800; Part II: *Containing an Account of the Naviga-tion of the Ancients from the Gulph of Elana in the Red Sea to the Island of Ceylon, with Dissertations.* London: T. Cadell and W. Davies, 1805.

———. *The Commerce and Navigation of the Ancients in the Indian Ocean.* Vol. 1: *The Voyage of Nearchus from the Indus to the Euphrates;* vol. 2: *The Periplus of the Eryth-rean Sea.* London: T. Cadell and W. Davies, 1807.

———. *The Voyage of Nearchus and the Periplus of the Erythean Sea, Translated from the Greek.* Oxford: Oxford University Press, 1809.

Volney, Constantin-François Chassebœuf de La Giraudais, Comte. *Considerations on the War with the Turks.* Translated from the French. London: J. Debrett, 1788 [French 1788].

———. *Les Ruines. Méditation sur les révolutions des empires.* n.p., 1791.

———. *Travels through Egypt and Syria in the Years 1783, 1784 & 1785 Containing the Present State of Those Countries, Their Productions, Arts, Manufactures & Commerce with Observations on the Manners, Customs and Government of the Turks & Arabs.* Translated from the French. 2 vols. New York: Duyckinck, 1798 [French 1787].

———. *Leçons d'Histoire prononcées à l'Ecole Normale en l'an III de la République française (1795).* Paris, 1800.

Voltaire [François Marie Arouet]. *Letters concerning the English Nation.* London, 1733.

———. *The Works of Voltaire: A Contemporary Version.* 43 vols. Paris: E. R. DuMont, 1901.

———. *Œuvres complètes en ligne.* http://www.voltaire-integral.com/

———. *Œuvres historiques.* Introduced, established, and annotated by René Pomeau, Gallimard: Paris, 1957.

———. *Mélanges.* Text established by Jacques Van den Heuvel; preface by Emmanuel Berl. Paris: Gallimard, 1961.

———. *Correspondance.* Edited by Théodore Besterman; index by Yves Gibeau. Vol. 1: *1704–1738;* vol. 2: *1739–1748.* Paris: Collection Bibliothèque de la Pléiade, Galli-mard, 1963–1964.

———. *Essais sur les mœurs et l'esprit des nations et sur les principaux faits de l'histoire depuis Charlemagne jusqu'à Louis XIII.* Introduction, bibliography, list of variants, notes and index by René Pomeau. 2 vols. Paris: Classiques Garnier, Éditions Bordas, 1990.

———. *Political Writings.* Translated and edited by D. Williams. Cambridge: Cam-bridge University Press, 1994.

———. *Anecdotes sur le czar Pierre le Grand. Histoire de l'empire de Russie sous Pierre le Grand.* Edited by Michel Mervaud. In *Les œuvres complètes de Voltaire,* vols. 46–47. Oxford: Voltaire Foundation, 1999.

Vuitard, Claude. *Les faicts et conquestes d'Alexandre le Grand, Roy des Macédoniens, descripts en grec, en huict livres, par Arrian de Nicomédie surnommé le nouveau Xéno-phon: traduicts nouvellement de grec en françoys.* Paris: Imprimerie de F. Morel, 1581.

Williams, John. *The Life and Actions of Alexander the Great*. London: John Murray, 1829.

——. *Two Essays on the Geography of Ancient Asia Intended Partly to Illustrate the Campaigns of Alexander and the Anabasis of Xenophon*. London: John Murray, 1829.

Wolf, Friedrich August. "Darstellung der Alterthums-Wissenschaft nach Begriff, Umfang, Zweck und Werth." *Museum der Alterthums-Wissenschaft* 1 (1807): 1–145. In S. F. W Hoffmann (ed.), *Fr. Aug. Wolf, Darstellung der Alterthumswissenschaft; nebst einer Auswahl seiner kleinen Schriften und literarischen Zugaben zu dessen Vorlesungen über die Alterthumswissenschaft*, 5–76. Leipzig: August Lehnhold, 1833.

——. "Darstellung der Alterthums-Wissenschaft": see Séguier de Saint-Brisson, Nicolas-Maximilien-Sidoine.

Woodhouselee, Alexander Fraser Tytler, Lord. *Plan and Outlines of a Course of Lectures on Universal History, Ancient and Modern Delivered in the University of Edinburgh by Alexander Tytler, Illustrated with Maps of Ancient and Modern Geography, and a Chronological Table*. Edinburgh: William Creech, 1782.

Wyttenbach, Daniel. Review of Sainte-Croix, *Examen critique* (1775). *Bibliotheca Critica* 2, no. 1 (1778): 129–140.

——. Review of Sainte-Croix, *Examen critique* (1804). *Bibliotheca Critica* 3, no. 3 (1805): 138–143.

Modern Studies

Abbatista, Guido. *James Mill e il problema indiano: Gli intellettuali britannici e la conquista dell'India*. Milan: Giufrè, 1979.

——. "The Literary Mill": per una storia editoriale della *Universal History* (1736–1765)." *Studi Settecenteschi* 2 (1981): 91–133.

——. "Un dibattito settecentesco sulla Storia Universale (Ricerche sulle traduzioni e sulla circolazione della *Universal History*)." *Rivista Storica Italiana* 111, no. 3 (1989): 614–695.

——. "The English *Universal History*: Publishing Autorship and Historiography in an European Project." *Storia della Storiografia* 39 (2001): 103–108.

——. "'Barbarie' et 'sauvagerie' in un contributo di Anquetil-Duperron al dibattito settecentesco sulle varietà del genre humano." In *Abraham-Hyacinthe Anquetil-Duperron, Considérations philosophiques, historiques et géographiques sur les deux mondes (1780–1804). Edizione, Introduzione e Note*, xix–civ. Pisa, 1993.

Allen, Calvin H., Jr. "The State of Masqat in the Gulf and East Africa 1785–1829." *International Journal of Middle East Studies* 14 (1982): 177–227.

Alvarez Lopera, José. "Philipp V of Spain and Juvarra at the Palace of La Granja: The Difficulty of Being Alexander." In N. Hadjinicolaou (ed.), *Alexander the Great in European Art (20 September 1997–11 January 1998)*, 37–46. Thessaloniki: Institute for Mediterranean Studies, 1997.

——. "Las vitudes del Rey. Las historias de Alejandro Magno para el palacio de La Granja." In José Miguel Morán Turina (ed.), *El Arte en la corte de Felipe V,* 141–156. Madrid: Museo National del Prado, 2002.

Amini, Iradj. *Napoleon and Persia: Franco-Persian Relations under the First Empire.* Washington, DC: Mage, 1999.

Andrae, Bernard. *Das Alexandermosaïk aus Pompeji, mit einem Vorwort des Verlegers une einem Anhang: Goethes Interpretation des Alexandermosaiks.* Recklinghausen: Verlag Aurel Bongers, 1977.

Angelomatis-Tsougarakis, Helen. *The Eve of the Greek Revival: British Travellers' Perceptions of Early Nineteenth-Century Greece.* London: Routledge, 1990.

Apostolopoulos, Dimitris. "La fortune de Montesquieu en Grèce dans la seconde moitié du XVIIIᵉ siècle." *Cahiers Montesquieu 5 (Montesquieu du Nord au Sud)* (2000): 81–88.

Argyropoulos, Roxane D. "Présence de Montesquieu en Grèce de la Révolution française à l'indépendance grecque." *Cahiers Montesquieu 5 (Montesquieu du Nord au Sud)* (2000): 89–96.

Assali, Jean-Charles. *Napoléon et l'antiquité.* PhD diss., Faculté de Droit et de Science politique d'Aix-Marseille, 1982 (typewritten).

Ataç, Akça. "Imperial Lessons from Athens and Sparta: Eighteenth-Century British Histories of Ancient Greece." *History of Political Thought* 27 (2006): 642–660.

Athanassou-Kallmyer, Nina M. *French Images from the Greek War of Independence, 1821–1830.* New Haven, CT: Yale University Press, 1989.

Avlami, Chryssanthi, Jaime Alvar, and Mirella Romero Recio (eds.). *Historiographie de l'antiquité et transferts culturels: les histoires anciennes dans l'Europe des XVIIIᵉ et XIXᵉ siècles.* Amsterdam: Rodopi, 2010.

Baack, Lawrence J. *Undying curiosity: Carsten Niebuhr and the Royal Danish Expedition to Arabia (1761–1767).* Stuttgart: Oriens et Occidens 22, 2014.

Bancarel, Gilles. "L'Histoire des Deux Indes au XXIᵉ siècle." In *G.-T. Raynal, Histoire philosophique et politique,* 1:9–38. Paris: Bibliothèque des Introuvables, 2006 [1780].

Barletta, Vincent. *Death in Babylon: Alexander the Great and Iberian Empire in the Muslim Orient.* Chicago: University of Chicago Press, 2010.

Barrell, John. *The Spirit of Despotism: Invasions of Privacy in the 1790s.* Oxford: Oxford University Press, 2006.

Barthold, Vassili Vladimirovitch. *La découverte de l'Asie. Histoire de l'orientalisme en Europe et en Russie.* Translated by Boris Nikitine. Paris: Payot, 1947.

Baruch, Daniel. *Linguet ou l'irrécupérable.* Paris: François Bourin, 1991.

Basch, Sophie, and Henry Laurens. *Lamartine, la Question d'Orient: Discours et articles politiques.* Brussels: André Versaille, 2011.

Bayliss, Andrew. "Greek, but Not Grecian? Macedonians in Enlightenment Histories." In James Moore, Ian MacGregor Morris, and Andrew Bayliss (eds.), *Reinventing History: The Enlightenment Origins of Ancient History,* 219–246. London: Center for Metropolitan History, 2008.

Baumgarten, Albert I. *Elias Bickerman as a Historian of the Jews*. Tübingen: Mohr Siebeck, 2010.

Beaton, Roderick, and David Ricks (eds.). *The Making of Modern Greece: Nationalism, Romanticism and the Uses of the Past (1797–1896)*. Farnham, Surrey: Ashgate, 2009.

Becker-Schaum, Christoph. *Arnold Herrmann Ludwig Heeren. Ein Beitrag zur Geschichte der Geschichswissenschaft zwischen Aufklärung und Historismus*. Frankfurt am Main: Peter Lang, 1993.

Benot, Yves. *Les Lumières, l'esclavage, la colonisation*. Collated and introduced by R. Desné and M. Dorigny. Paris: La Découverte, 2005.

Berchtold, Jacques. *Les Prisons du roman (XVIIᵉ–XVIIIᵉ siècle)*. Geneva: Droz, 2000.

Berghaus, Johann Isaac. *Geschichte der Schifffahrtskunde bey den vornehmsten Völker des Alterthums*, I–II. Leipzig: in der Gräffeschen Buchhandlung, 1792

Berman, Russel, A. *Enlightenment or Empire: Colonial Discourse in German Culture*. Lincoln, NE: University of Nebraska Press, 1998.

Biancaforte, Elio. *Visions of Persia: Mapping the Travels of Adam Olearius*. Cambridge, MA: Harvard University Press, 2003.

Biasutti, Franco. "Alessandro Magno nella Philosophiegeschichte di Hegel." In Franco Biasutti and Alessandra Coppola (eds.), *Alessandro Magno in età moderna*, 272–284. Padova: CLEUP, 2009.

Biasutti, Franco, and Alessandra Coppola (eds.). *Alessandro Magno in età moderna*. Padova: CLEUP, 2009.

Bichler, Reinhold. *"Hellenismus." Geschichte und Problematik eines Epochenbegriffs*. Darmstadt: Wissenschaftliche Buchgesellschaft, 1983.

Bickerman, Elias. "L'européanisation de l'Orient classique. À propos du livre de Michel Rostovtzeff." *Renaissance* 2–3 (1944–1945).

———. "The Europeanisation of the Classical East: À propos of the book by Michel Rostovtzeff." Translated by A. Kuhrt. In J.G. Manning (ed.), *Writing History in Time of War*, 33–43. Stuttgart: F. Steiner, 2015.

Binoche, Bertrand. "Civilisation, le mot, le schème et le maître-mot." In Bertrand Binoche (ed.), *Les équivoques de la civilisation*, 10–30. Seyssel: Champ Vallon, 2005.

———(ed.). *Les équivoques de la civilisation*. Seyssel: Champ Vallon, 2005.

Blanke, Horst Walter. "Die Kritik der Alexanderhistoriker bei Heyne, Heeren, Niebuhr und Droysen. Eine Fallstudie zur Entwicklung der historisch-philologischen Methode in der Aufklärung und im Historismus." *Histoire de l'Historiographie* 13 (1988): 106–127.

Boedeker, Hans-Eric, Philippe Büttgen, and Michel Espagne (eds.). *Göttingen vers 1800: l'Europe des Sciences de l'Homme*. Paris: Cerf, 2010.

Boistel, Guy. *L'astronomie nautique au XVIIIe siècle en France: tables de la lune et longitudes en mer*. Lille: Atelier National de reproduction des thèses, 2003.

Bondi, Sandro Filippo. "A. H. L. Heeren, politica et commercio: qualche riflessione." *Rivista storia italiana*, n.s., 3 (1999): 774–797.

Bonnet, Jean-Claude (ed.). *L'empire des Muses. Napoléon, les Arts et les Lettres*. Paris: Belin, 2004.

Bosworth, Albert, Brian, "Droysen: Alexander the Great." Foreword to *J.-G. Droysen, History of Alexander the Great*. Eng. translation 2010: 15–21.

Boulad-Ayoub, Josiane. "L'Institut d'Égypte et *La Décade égyptienne*." In J. Boulad-Ayoub and G.-M. Cazzaniga (eds.), *Traces de l'Autre. Mythes de l'antiquité et Peuples du livre dans la construction des nations méditerranéennes (Bibliotheca Alexandrina 19–21 avril 2003)*, 41–66. Pisa: Edizioni ETS, 2004.

Bourke, Richard. "Edmund Burke and the Politics of Conquest." *Modern Intellectual History* 4, no. 3 (2007): 403–432.

Bourra, Olivier. "Trompettes de Jéricho." In Simon-Nicolas-Henri Linguet, *Mémoires de la Bastille*, presented and annotated by Olivier Bourra, 7–57. Paris: Arléa, 2006.

Bouyssy, Maïté. "Le *Mémorial des Grecs*, miroir du philhellénisme des années 1820." *Revue germanique internationale* 1–2 (2005): 45–59.

Bowden, Hugh, "Review Article: Recent travels in Alexanderland." *Journal of Hellenic Studies* 134 (January 2014): 136–148

Bradley, Mark (ed.). *Classics and Imperialism in the British Empire*. Oxford: Oxford University Press, 2010.

Brahimi, Denise. *Arabes des Lumières et Bédouins romantiques*. Paris: Éd. Le Sycomore, 1982.

Brauer, George C., Jr. "Alexander in England: The Conqueror's Reputation in the Late Seventeenth and Eighteenth Centuries." *Classical Journal* 76, no. 1 (1980): 34–47.

Bravo, Benedetto. *Philologie, histoire, philosophie de l'histoire. Étude sur J. G. Droysen, historien de l'Antiquité*. Wroclaw, 1968.

Briant, Pierre. "Impérialisme antique et idéologie coloniale dans la France contemporaine: Alexandre modèle colonial." *Dialogues d'histoire ancienne* 5 (1979): 283–292 (=Briant, *Rois, tributs et paysans*: 283–291).

———. "Des Achéménides aux rois hellénistiques: continuités et ruptures", 1979 (=Briant, *Rois, tributs et paysans*, 291–330).

———. "Colonisation hellénistique et populations indigènes. II: Renforts grecs dans les cités hellénistiques d'Orient." *Klio* 64, no. 1 (1982): 83–98 (=Briant, *Rois, tributs et paysans*, 263–279).

———. *États et pasteurs au Moyen-Orient ancien*. Paris: Éditions de la Maison des Sciences de l'Homme and Cambridge University Press, 1982.

———. *Rois, tributs et paysans. Études sur les formations tributaires du Moyen-Orient ancien*. Paris: Les Belles Lettres, 1982.

———. "Histoire et idéologie: les Grecs et la 'décadence perse.'" In M.-M. Mactoux and E. Geny (eds.), *Mélanges Pierre Lévêque*, 3:33–47. Paris: Les Belles Lettres, 1989. English translation, "History and Ideology: the Greeks and Persian Decadence." In Th. Harrison (ed.), *Greeks and Barbarians* (Edinburgh Readings of the Ancient World), Edinburgh University Press (2002):193–210.

———. "Guerre et succession dynastique chez les Achéménides: entre coutume perse' et violence armée." In A. Chianotis and P. Ducrey (eds.), *Army and Power in the Ancient World*, 39–49. Stuttgart: F. Steiner, 2002.

———. "La tradition gréco-romaine sur Alexandre le Grand dans l'Europe moderne et contemporaine." In M. Hagsma et al. (eds.), *The Impact of Classical Greece on European and National Identities*, 161–180. Amsterdam, 2003.

———. "Alexandre 'grand économiste': mythe, histoire, historiographie." *Annuaire du Collège de France* (2004–2005): 585–599.

———. "Alexander the Great and the Enlightenment: William Robertson (1721–1793), the Empire and the Road to India." *Cromohs* 10 (2005): 1–9.

———. "Alexandre et 'l'hellénisation de l'Asie': l'histoire au passé et au présent." *Studi Ellenistici* 16 (2005): 9–69.

———. "Alexandre sans le commerce de l'Inde." In "Montesquieu, Mably et Alexandre le Grand : aux sources de l'histoire hellénistique," *Revue Montesquieu* (2005–2006): 151–185.

———. "Montesquieu, Mably et Alexandre le Grand." *Revue Montesquieu* 8 (2005–2008): 151–185.

———. "Montesquieu et ses sources: Alexandre, l'empire perse, les Guèbres et l'irrigation (EL X.13–14; XVIII.7)." *Studies on Voltaire and the Eighteenth Century* 5 (2006): 243–262. (English translation in *Kings, Ccountries and Peoples*, forthcoming.)

———. "Retour sur Alexandre et les katarraktes du Tigre: l'histoire d'un dossier" [Part I]. *Studi Ellenistici* 19 (2006): 9–75. (Partial English translation in *Kings, Countries and Peoples*, forthcoming.)

———. "Alexandre le Grand aujourd'hui (v): Histoire du *Siècle d'Alexandre* de Linguet." *Annuaire du Collège de France* (2006–2007): 613–634.

———. "De Thémistocle à Lamartine. Remarques sur les concessions de terres et de villages en Asie mineure occidentale de l'époque achéménide à l'époque ottomane." In P. Brun (ed.), *Scripta Anatolica. Hommages à Pierre Debord*, 165–191 (Ausonius, Études 18). Paris: de Boccard, 2007.

———. "Alexandre dans l'œuvre de Voltaire." *Annuaire du Collège de France* (2007–2008): 681–689.

———. "Retour sur Alexandre et les katarraktes du Tigre: l'histoire d'un dossier (suite et fin)" [Part II]. *Studi Ellenistici* 20 (2008): 155–218.

———. "Alexander and the Persian Empire, between 'Decline'and 'Renovation.'" In W. Heckel and L.-A. Tritle (eds.), *Alexander the Great: A New History*, 171–188. Oxford: Wiley-Blackwell, 2009.

———. "Alexander the Great." In G. Boy-Stones, B. Graziosi, and P. Vasunia (eds.), *The Oxford Handbook of Hellenic Studies*, 77–85. Oxford: Oxford University Press, 2009.

———. "Le thème de la 'décadence perse' dans l'historiographie européenne du XVIIIᵉ siècle: remarques préliminaires sur la genèse d'un mythe." In L. Bodiou et al. (eds.), *Chemin faisant. Mélanges en l'honneur de Pierre Brulé*, 19–38. Presses Universitaires de Rennes, 2009. English translation, "The Theme of 'Persian

Cecadence' in Eighteenth-Century European Historiography: Remarks on the Genesis of a Myth." In John Curtis and St John Simpson (eds.), *The World of Achaemenid Persia,* 3–15. London: Tauris, 2010.

———. *Alexander the Great and His Empire.* Princeton, NJ: Princeton University Press, 2011.

———. *Alexandre le Grand.* 7th rev. and corrected ed. Paris: PUF, 2011.

———. "Orientaliser l'Orient, ou: d'un orientalisme à l'autre." In J. Wiesehöfer, R. Rollinger, and G. Lanfranchi (eds.), *Ktesias' Welt/Ctesias World,* 507–513. Wiesbaden: Harrassowitz Verlag, 2011.

———. "Des Scythes aux Tartares, et d'Alexandre de Macédoine à Pierre de Russie: l'histoire de l'Europe au passé et au présent." In S. Karp and C. Volpilhac-Auger (eds.), *Le Siècle des Lumières. IV: L'héritage de l'Antiquité dans la culture européenne du XVIIIe siècle,* 33–46. Moscow, 2012.

———. "Les débats sur la royauté macédonienne dans l'Europe du XVIIIe siècle: quelques jalons anglais." In K. Konuk (ed.), *Stephanephoros. De l'économie antique à l'Asie Mineure. Mélanges en l'honneur de Raymond Descat,* 221–227. Bordeaux, 2012.

———. "Philipp II. von Makedonien und Friedrich der Große in den Überlegungen des 18. Jahrhunderts in Europa." In R. Rollinger et al. (eds.), *Altertum und Gegenwart. 125 Jahre Alte Geschichte in Innsbruck,* 1–20. Innsbruck, 2012.

———. "Grote on Alexander." In K. Demetriou (ed.), *Brill's Companion to George Grote and the Classical Tradition,* 329–365. Leiden: Brill, 2014.

———. "La figure de Néarque dans l'historiographie européenne (XVIIe–XVIIIe siècles). In D. Marcotte (ed.), *D'Arrien à William Vincent: le Périple de Néarque et sa postérité=Geographia Antiqua* 22 (2013): 15–20.

———. *Darius in the Shadow of Alexander.* Translated by Jane Marie Todd. Cambridge, MA: Harvard University Press, 2015.

———. "Michael Rostovtzeff, Elias Bickermann and the "Hellenization of Asia." In J. Manning (ed.), *Writing History in Time of War,* 13–31. Stuttgart: F. Steiner, 2015.

———. *Kings, Countries and Peoples: Selected Studies on the Achaemenid Empire.* Leiden: Brill, forthcoming.

Bridges, Emma, Edith Hall, and P. J. Rhodes (eds.). *Cultural Responses to the Persian Wars: Antiquity to the Third Millenium.* Oxford: Oxford University Press, 2007.

Broc, Numa. *La géographie des philosophes. Géographes et voyageurs français au XVIIIe siècle.* Paris: Éditions Ophrys, 1975.

Brot, Muriel. "La bibliothèque idéale d'Antoine-Alexandre Barbier." In J.-C. Bonnet (ed.), *L'empire des Muses,* 91–111. Paris: Belin, 2004.

Brown, Stuart J. "William Robertson (1721–1793) and the Scottish Enlightenment." In Stuart Brown (ed.), *William Robertson and the Expansion of the Empire,* 7–35. Cambridge: Cambridge University Press, 1997.

———. "William Robertson, Early Orientalism and the *Historical Disquisition* on India of 1791." *Scottish Historical Review* 88, no. 2 (2009): 289–312.

———. (ed.). *William Robertson and the Expansion of the Empire*. Cambridge: Cambridge University Press, 1997.

Bryant, George J. "Scots in India in the Eighteenth Century." *Scottish Historical Review* 64, no. 177 (1985): 22–41.

Bucciantini, V. "Le annotazioni manoscritte del Decano William Vincent al volume The Voyage of Nearchus conservato nella Westminster Abbey Library." In D. Marcotte (ed.), *D'Arrien à William Vincent: le Périple de Néarque et sa postérité =Geographia Antiqua* 22 (2013): 75–88.

Buchon, Jean-Alexandre C. (ed.). *Œuvres complètes de W. Robertson*. 2 vols. Paris: A. Desrez, 1837.

Buraselis, K., "The roman world of Polyainos: aspects of a Macedonian career between Classical Greece and provincial present." *Archaiognosia* 8 (1993–1994):121–140.

Burger, Jean-François. "La *Biographie universelle* des frères Michaud." In J.-C. Bonnet (ed.), *L'empire des Muses*, 275–290. Paris: Belin, 2004.

Büttgen, Philippe: see Boedeker, Hans-Eric.

Callard, Cécile. *Le Prince et la République. Histoire, pouvoir et société dans la Florence des Médicis au XVIIe siècle*. Paris: PUPS, 2007.

Cambiano, Giuseppe. "Herder et la jeunesse de l'Antiquité." In C. Avlami, J. Alvar, and M. Recio (eds.), *Historiographie de l'antiquité et transferts culturels: les histoires anciennes dans l'Europe des XVIIIᵉ et XIXᵉ siècles*, 67–83. Amsterdam: Rodopi, 2010.

Carey, Daniel. "Reading Contrapuntally: *Robinson Crusoe*, Slavery and Postcolonial Theory." In D. Carey and L. Festa (eds.), *The Postcolonial Enlightenment: Eighteenth-Century Colonialism and Postcolonial Theory*, 105–136. Oxford: Oxford University Press, 2009.

Carnall, Geoffrey. "Robertson and Contemporary Images of India." In Stuart J. Brown (ed.), *William Robertson and the Expansion of the Empire*, 210–230. Cambridge: Cambridge University Press, 1997.

Carré, Jean-Marie. *Voyageurs et écrivains français en Égypte*. 2nd rev. and corrected ed. 2 vols. Cairo, 1956.

Cassirer, Ernst. *The Philosophy of the Enlightenment*. Princeton, NJ: Princeton University Press, 1951 [1932].

Catalog: L'Histoire d'Alexandre le Grand dans les tapisseries au xvᵉ siècle. Fortune iconographique dans les tapisseries et les manuscrits conservés. Brepols, 2013.

Catalog: Oeuvres d'art du Musée du Louvre à Thessalonique. De Platon à Voltaire et Koraïs: la philosophie grecque ancienne et les Lumières. Thessaloniki Museum of Archeology, 2012.

Cavalier, Odile (ed.), with the collaboration of Maria-Stefania Montecalvo. *La Grèce des Provençaux au XVIIIᵉ siècle. Collectionneurs et érudits*. Avignon: Ville d'Avignon et Fondation Calvet, Imprimerie Laffont, 2007.

Centanni, Monica. "Alexander the Great." In A. Grafton, G. W. Most, and S. Setttis (eds.), *The Classical Tradition*, 25–32. Cambridge, MA: Harvard University Press, 2010.

Cerasuolo, Salvatore. "*La Esposizione della Scienza dell' Antichità* di Friedrich August Wolf." In S. Cerasuolo (ed.), *Friedrich August Wolf e la Scienza dell'Antichità,* 17–51. Naples, 1997.

———. (ed.). *Friedrich August Wolf e la Scienza dell'Antichità.* Naples, 1997.

Ceserani, Giovanna. "Narrative, Interpretation and Plagiarism in Mr. Robertson's *History of Ancient Greece." Journal of History of Ideas* 66, no. 3 (2005): 413–436.

———. "Modern Histories of Ancient Greece: Genealogies, Contexts and Eighteenth-Century Narrative Historiography." In A. Lianeri (ed.), *The Western Time of Ancient History,* 138–155. Cambridge: Cambridge University Press, 2011.

Charle, Christophe. "Peut-on écrire une histoire de la culture européenne à l'époque contemporaine?" *Annales. Histoire, Sciences Sociales* no. 3 (2010): 1207–1221.

Charles-Roux, François. *Bonaparte gouverneur d'Égypte.* Paris: Plon, 1935.

Chartier, Roger, and Henri-Jean Martin (eds.). *Histoire de l'édition française.* Vol. 2: *Le livre triomphant.* Paris: Fayard / Le Cercle de la Librairie, 1984.

Chiesa, Francesca, Paola Stirpe, and Andrea Paribeni (eds.). *Images of Legend: Iconography of Alexander the Great in Italy.* Rome: Gangemi, 2006.

Christodoulou, Kyriaki, E. "Alexandre le Grand chez Voltaire." In U. Kolving and C. Mervaud (eds.), *Voltaire et ses combats,* 1423–1434. Oxford: Voltaire Foundation, 1997.

Clarke, Martin L. *Greek Studies in England.* Cambridge: Cambridge University Press, 1945.

Claval, Paul. "Playing with Mirrors: The British Empire according to Albert Demangeon." In A. Godlewska and N. Smith (eds.), *Geography and Empire,* 228–243. Oxford: Blackwell, 1994.

Clavié, Lucien. "Références antiques et conscience nationale allemande de la fin du XVIIIe siècle aux années 1830." In D. Foucault and P. Payen (eds.), *Les autorités. Dynamique et mutations d'une figure de référence à l'Antiquité,* 107–113. Grenoble: Éd. Million, 2007.

Clogg, Richard. "The Classics and the Movement for Greek Independence." In M. Hagsma et al. (eds.), *The Impact of Classical Greece on European and National identities,* 25–46. Amsterdam, 2003.

Collective. *La tenture de l'histoire d'Alexandre le Grand.* Collections du Mobilier National, Catalog for the exhibition "Alexandre et Louis XIV: tissages de gloire" (Galerie des Gobelins, September 21, 2008–March 1, 2009). Paris: RMN, 2008.

Curtis, Vesta, and Elizabeth Errington (eds.). *From Persepolis to the Punjab: Exploring Ancient Iran, Afghanistan and Pakistan.* London: British Museum Press, 2007.

Dalrymple, William. *The Return of a King: The Battle for Afghanistan.* London, 2013.

Dascalakis, Apostolides. *Rhigas Velestinlis. La révolution française et les préludes de l'indépendance hellénique.* Paris, 1937.

———. *Les œuvres de Rhigas Vélestinlis. Étude bibliographique suivie d'une réédition critique avec traduction française de la brochure révolutionnaire confisquée à Vienne en 1797.* Paris, 1937.

Delia, Luigi. "Crime et châtiment dans l'*Encyclopédie*. Les enjeux de l'interprétation de Montesquieu par de Jaucourt." *Dix-Huitième Siècle* 41 (2009): 469–486.

Delinière, Jean. *Weimar à l'époque de Goethe*. Paris: L'Harmattan, 2004.

Delon, Michel. "Alexandre conquérant et séducteur." In Franco Biasutti and Alessandra Coppola (eds.), *Alessandro Magno in età moderna*, 187–200. Padova: CLEUP, 2009.

Deloche, Jean, Mannonmani Filliozat, and Pierre-Sylvain Filliozat. *Voyage en Inde, 1754–1762. Anquetil-Duperron, Relation de voyage en préliminaire à la traduction du Zend-Avesta. Présentation, notes et bibliographie*... Paris: Maisonneuve et Larose, 1997.

Demangeon, Albert. *The British Empire: A Study in Colonial Geography*. London, 1925 [French 1923].

Demetriou, Kyriacos N. *George Grote on Plato and Athenian Democracy*. Frankfurt am Main: Peter Lang, 1999.

Desgraves, Louis, and Catherine Volpilhac-Auger. *Catalogue de la Bibliothèque de Montesquieu à la Brède*. Naples, 1999.

Desné, Robert. *Histoire de Grèce, traduit de l'anglais de Temple Stanyan, texte établi par*... In *Diderot. Le modèle anglais*, 42–151. Paris: Hermann, 1975.

Dessert, Daniel, and, Jean-Louis Journet. "Le lobby Colbert: un royaume ou une affaire de famille?" *Annales. Histoire, Sciences Sociales* 30, no. 6 (1975): 1303–1336.

Devine, Thomas Martin. *Scotland's Empire 1600–1815*. London: Penguin, 2003.

Dezemeiris, Reinhold. "Annotations inédites de Montaigne sur le *De rebus Gesti Alexandri Magni* de Quinte-Curce." *Revue d'histoire littéraire de la France* (1916: 399–494 ; 1917: 605–636; 1918: 592–622; 1919: 577–600).

Dharampal-Frick, Gita. "Entre orientalisme des Lumières et idéalisme révolutionnaire: Georg Forster et Mathias Sprengel face au colonialisme." *Revue germanique internationale* 7 (2008): 9–20.

Dirks, Nicholas D. *The Scandal of Empire: India and the Creation of Imperial Britain*. Cambridge, MA: Harvard University Press, 2006.

Dosson, Simon-Noël. *Étude sur Quinte-Curce*. Paris: Hachette, 1887.

Downie, John Alexander. "Defoe, Imperialism and the Travel Books Reconsidered." In R. D. Lund (ed.), *Critical Essays on Daniel Defoe*, 78–96. New York: G. K. Hall, 1997.

Driault, Edouard. *La politique orientale de Napoléon. Sébastiani et Gardane, 1806–1808*. Paris: Felix Alcan, 1904.

———. *La question d'Orient depuis ses origines jusqu'à la paix de Sèvres*. 8th rev. ed. Paris: Felix Alcan, 1921.

———(ed.). *Napoléon Bonaparte: Le discours de Lyon* (1791). Paris: Éd. Morancé, 1929.

Droulia, Loukia et al. "Mélanges. Deux siècles après: le projet révolutionnaire de Rigas Velestinlis et son impact dans le Sud-est européen." In *Annales historiques de la Révolution française* no. 319 (2000): 127–140

Ehrard, Jean. *Lumières et esclavage. L'esclavage colonial et l'opinion publique en France au XVIIIe siècle*. Brussels, 2008.

Errington, Elizabeth, and Vesta Curtis (eds.). *From Persepolis to the Pundjab: Exploring Ancient Iran, Afghanistan and Pakistan*. London: British Museum Press, 2007.

Escudier, Alexandre. "De Chladenius à Droysen. Théorie et méthodologie de l'histoire de langue allemande (1750–1860)." *Annales. Histoire, Sciences Sociales* 58, no. 4 (2003): 743–777.

Espagne, Michel: see Boedeker, Hans-Eric.

Euanggelatos, S.A. *Istoria tou theatrou en Kephallènia (1600–1900)*. Athens, 1970.

Famerie, Étienne. *Jean-Baptiste-Gaspard d'Ansse de Villoison. De l'Hellade à la Grèce. Voyage en Grèce et au Levant (1784–1786)*. Hidelsheim: Olms, 2006.

Fernandez Talaya, Teresa. "Las pinturas encargadas por Juvarra para la galeria del palacio de La Granja." *Reales Sitios* 119 (1964): 41–48.

Ferreyrolles, Gérard, Béatrice Guion, and Jean-Louis Quantin. *Bossuet*. Paris: PUPS, 2008.

Fornaro, Sotera. "Lo 'Studio degli Antichi.' 1793–1907." *Quaderni di Storia* (1975): 109–155.

———. "I Greci Barbari di Ch.-G. Heyne." In C. Pandolfi, S. Fornaro, and G. Cerri (eds.), *Christian Gottlob Heyne, Greci Barbari*, 9–41. Lecce: Argo, 2004.

———. *I Greci senza lumi. L'antropologia della Grecia antica in Christian Gottlob Heyne (1729–1812) e nel suo tempo*. Göttingen: Vanderhoeck und Ruprecht, 2004.

———. "Christian Gottlob Heyne dans l'histoire des études classiques." *Revue Germanique Internationale* 14 (2011): 15–26.

Francesconi, Daniele. "William Robertson on Historical Causation and Unintended Consequences." *Cromohs* 4 (1999): 1–18.

Frankfort, Enriqueta Harris. "The Alexander Mountain." In N. Hadjinicolaou (ed.), *Alexander the Great in European Art*, 248–251. Thessaloniki: Institute for Mediterranean Studies, 1997.

Freeman, Edward Augustus. "Alexander the Great. (*History of Greece* by G. Grote, vol. XII, London, 1856)." *Edinburgh Review* (April 1857)=*Historical Essays*, 161–206. London: Macmillan, 1873.

Fuhrmann, Manfred. "Wilhelm von Humboldt e l'università di Berlino." In S. Cerasuolo (ed.), *Friedrich August Wolf e la Scienza dell'Antichità*, 69–86. Naples, 1997.

Furcy-Raynaud, Marc. *Correspondance de M. de Marigny avec Coypel, Lépicié et Cochin. Nouvelles archives de l'art français* 3rd ser. 19 (1903).

Gabba, Emilio. "Colonie antiche et moderne" (1991). In *Cultura classica e storiografia moderna*. 41–61. Bologna: Il Mulino, 1995.

Gabriel, Alfons. *Die Erforschung Persiens. Die Entwicklung der abendländlichen Kenntnis der Geographie Persiens*. Vienna: Verlag A. Holzhausens, 1952.

Gallo, Daniela. "Pouvoirs de l'antique." In J.-C. Bonnet (ed.), *L'empire des Muses*, 317–329. Paris: Belin, 2004.

Gallo, Luigi. "Pierre-Henri de Valenciennes et la tradition du paysage historique." In Daniel Rabreau (ed.), *Annales du Centre Ledoux*. Vol. 2: *Imaginaire et création artis-*

tique à Paris sous l'Ancien régime (XVIIe–XVIIIe siècles). Art, politique, trompe-l'œil, voyages, spectacles et jardins, 185–207. Paris: William Blake and Arts et Arts, 1998.

Garner, Guillaume. "Économie politique et statistique à l'université de Göttingen (1770–1820)." In H. E. Boedeker, P. Büttgen, and M. Espagne (eds.), Göttingen vers 1800: l'Europe des Sciences de l'Homme, 457–482. Paris: Cerf, 2010.

Gaullier-Bougassas, C. "Alexandre et l'Europe des Lumières: le premier Européen conquérant de l'Orient. Lecture de l'ouvrage de P. Briant, Alexandre des Lumières." In Les Grandes Figures historiques dans les lettres et les arts (July 2015). http://figures-historiques.revue.univ-lille3.fr/wp-content/uploads/2015/07/Alexandre-et-lEurope-des-Lumi%C3%A8res.pdf.

Gaulmier, Jean. "Volney et ses Leçons d'histoire" (1962). In Autour du Romantisme. De Volney à J-.P. Sartre, 61–77. Paris: Éditions Ophrys, 1977.

———. L'idéologue Volney (1757–1820). Contribution à l'Histoire de l'Orientalisme en France (1951). Paris, 1980.

Gierl, Martin. "Christoph Meiners: histoire de l'humanité et histoire universelle à Göttingen. Race et nation comme outils de politisation des Lumières allemandes." In H. E. Boedeker, P. Büttgen, and M. Espagne (eds.), Göttingen vers 1800: l'Europe des Sciences de l'Homme, 515–534, Paris: Cerf, 2010.

Gilli, Marita (ed. and trans.). Un révolutionnaire allemand, Georg Forster (1754–1794). Paris: Édition du Comité des travaux historiques et scientifiques, 2005.

Gleigg, George (ed.). The Historical Works of William Robertson. 6 vols., Edinburgh, 1813.

Goblot, Jean-Jacques. Documents pour servir à l'histoire de la presse littéraire. Le Globe 1824–1830. Paris: H. Champion, 1993.

———. La jeune France libérale. Le Globe et son groupe littéraire 1824–1831. Paris: Plon, 1995.

Godlewska, Anne, and Neil Smith (eds.). Geography and Empire. Oxford: Blackwell, 1994.

Goff, Barbara E. (ed.). Classics and Colonialism. London: Duckworth, 2005.

Goggi, Gianluigi. "Le mot civilisation et ses domaines d'application, 1757 à 1770." Studies in Voltaire and the Eighteenth Century 246 (1996): 363–377.

———. "Les contributions de Diderot aux Livres I–IV . . ." In Anthony Struggel et al. (ed.), Guillaume-Thomas Raynal, Histoire philosophique et politique des établissements et du commerce des deux Indes, Édition critique, 1:749–766. Ferney-Voltaire: Centre international d'études du XVIIIe siècle, 2010.

———. "La collaboration de Diderot à l'Histoire des Deux Indes: l'édition de ses contributions." Diderot Studies 33 (2013): 167–212.

———(ed.). Diderot. Fragments politiques échappés du portefeuille d'un philosophe. Paris, 2011.

Gorshenina, Svetlana "Alexander the Great and the Russians: a look at the Conqueror from Central Asia", in C. Antonetti (ed.), Proceedings of the International conference "Anabasi. Sulle orme di Alessandro dalla morte di Dario," forthcoming.

Goulemot, Jean-Marie. "Alexandre à la lumière du XVIIIe siècle." *La Quinzaine Littéraire* (April 2013): 20.

Grafton, Anthony. *The Footnote: A Curious History.* Cambridge, MA: Harvard University Press, 1998.

Grange, Henri. "Les réactions d'un adversaire des philosophes: Linguet." *Revue d'histoire littéraire de la France* (1979): 208–221.

Gratziou, Olga. "To monophyllo tou Riga tou 1797. Paratēreseis stē neoellenikē eikonographia tou Megalou Alexandrou." *Mnémon* 8 (1982): 130–149.

Grell, Chantal. *L'histoire entre érudition et philosophie. Étude sur la connaissance historique à l'âge des Lumières.* Paris, 1993.

———. *Le Dix-huitième Siècle et l'antiquité en France 1680–1789.* 2 vols. Oxford: Voltaire Foundation, 1995.

———. "Télémaque et Alexandre. L'image du conquérant dans l'éducation des ducs de Bourgogne et d'Anjou." In P. Barniche, J. P. Poussou, and A. Tallon (ed.), *Pouvoirs, contestations et comportements dans l'Europe moderne. Mélanges en l'honneur de J. M. Bercé,* 341–360. Paris, 2005.

———, and Christian Michel. *L'École des Princes ou Alexandre disgrâcié.* Paris: Les Belles Lettres, 1988.

Grémy-Deprez, Sandra. "Une source privilégiée du *Télémaque:* les *Vies des Hommes Illustres* de Plutarque." *Littératures classiques* 70 (2010): 225–242.

Grosrichard, Alain. *The Sultan's Court: European Fantasies of Asiatic Despotism (Wo Es War).* Translated by L. Heron. London: Verso, 1998 [French 1979].

Guerci, Luciano. "Linguet storico della Grecia e di Roma." *Rivista Storica Italiana* 93 (1981): 615–679.

Guiomar, Jean-Yves, and Marie-Thérèse Lorain. "La carte de Grèce de Rigas et le nom de la Grèce." *Annales Historiques de la Révolution Française* 319 (2000): 101–125.

Hackel, Christiane (ed.). *Philologe. Historiker. Politischer. Johann Gustav Droysen (1808–1884).* Berlin: G. H. Verlag, 2008.

Haechler, Jean. *L'Encyclopédie de Diderot et de . . . Jaucourt. Essai biographique sur le chevalier Louis de Jaucourt.* Paris: Champion, 1995.

Hagerman, Christopher. "In the Footsteps of the 'Macedonian Conqueror': Alexander the Great and British India." *International Journal of the Classical Tradition* 16, nos. 3–4 (2009): 344–392.

———. *Britain's Imperial Muse. The Classics, Imperialism and the Indian Empire, 1784–1914,* New York: Palgrave Macmillan, 2013.

Hall, Edith. "Aeschylus' *Persians* via the Ottoman Empire to Saddam Hussein." In E. Bridges, E. Hall, and P. J. Rhodes (eds.), *Cultural Responses to the Persian Wars: Antiquity to the Third Millenium,* 167–199. Oxford: Oxford University Press, 2007.

Hall, Edith, and Phiroze Vasunia (eds.). *India, Greece, and Rome, 1757 to 2007.* Bulletin of the Institute of Classical Studies: Supplement. London: Institute of Classical Studies, 2010.

Hamilakis, Yannis. *The Nation and Its Ruins: Antiquity, Archaeology and National Imagination in Greece*. Oxford: Oxford University Press, 2007.

Harbsmeier, Michael. "World Histories before Domestication: The Writing of Universal Histories, Histories of Mankind and World Histories in Late Eighteenth Century Germany." *Culture and History* 5 (1989): 93–131.

Hadjinicolaou, Nicos (ed.). *Alexander the Great in European Art (20 September 1997–11 January 1998)*. Thessaloniki: Institute for Mediterranean Studies, 1997.

Hardwick, Lorna, and Carol Gillespie (eds.). *Classics in Post-Colonial Worlds*. Oxford: Oxford University Press, 2007.

Hartog, François. *Anciens, Modernes, Sauvages*. Paris: Éd. Galaade, 2005.

Havard, Gilles. "'Les forcer à devenir Cytoyens.' État, sauvages et citoyenneté en Nouvelle-France (XVIIᵉ–XVIIIᵉ siècles)." *Annales. Histoire, Sciences Sociales* 64, no. 5 (2009): 985–1018.

Hazard, Paul. "Le Spectateur du Nord." *Revue d'histoire littéraire* 13 (1906): 26–50.

———. *La crise de la conscience européenne (1650–1715)*. Paris, 1935.

Heidenreich, Marianne. *Christian Gottlob Heyne und die alte Geschichte*. Munich: K. G. Saur, 2006.

Hentsch, Thierry. *L'Orient imaginaire: La vision occidentale de l'Est méditerranéen*. Paris: Éditions de Minuit, 1988.

Hopkirk, Peter. *The Great Game: On Secret Service in High Asia*. London : John Murray, 1990.

Imbruglia, Girolamo. Review of Briant, *Alexandre des Lumières*. *Cromohs* 18 (2013): 149–157.

Irmscher, Johannes. "Friedrich August Wolf e Goethe." In S. Cerasuolo (ed.), *Friedrich August Wolf e la Scienza dell'Antichità*, 171–176. Naples, 1997.

Israel, Jonathan. *A Revolution of the Mind: Radical Enlightenment and the Intellectual Origins of Modern Democracy*. Princeton, NJ: Princeton University Press, 2010.

Iverson, John R. "La guerre, le grand homme et l'histoire selon Voltaire: le cas de l'Histoire de l'empire de Russie sous Pierre le Grand." In U. Kolving and C. Mervaud (eds.)., *Voltaire et ses combats*, 1413–1422. Oxford: Voltaire Foundation, 1997.

Jasanoff, Maya. "Collectors of Empire: Objects, Conquests and Imperial Self-Fashioning." *Past and Present* 184 (2004): 109–135.

Jurien de la Gravière, Jean-Pierre-Edmond. *Les campagnes d'Alexandre. L'Asie sans maître*. Paris: Plon, 1883.

———. *Les campagnes d'Alexandre. L'héritage de Darius*. Paris: Plon, 1883.

———. *Les campagnes d'Alexandre. La conquête de l'Inde et le voyage de Néarque*. Paris: Plon, 1884.

Karabéropoulos, Démétrios. *O Mégas Alexandros tou Règa Belestinlè* [The Alexander the Great of Rigas Vélestinlis]. Athens, 2006. Available at http://www.karaberopoulos .gr/karaberopoulos/pdf/Megas_Alexandros_fylla.pdf.

Karp, Sergueï, and LarryWolffarry (eds.). *Le mirage russe au XVIIIe siècle*. Ferney-Voltaire: Centre international d'études du XVIIIe siècle, 2001.

Kaye, John William. *The Life and Correspondence of Major-General Sir John Malcolm, Late Envoy to Persia and Governor of Bombay, from Unpublished Letters and Journals.* 2 vols. London: Smith, Elder, 1856.

Kirchner, Thomas. *Les Reines de Perse aux pieds d'Alexandre' de Charles Le Brun, tableau manifeste de l'art français du XVIIIe siècle.* Translated by A. Virey-Wallon. Paris: Éditions de la Maison des Sciences de l'Homme, 2013.

Kitromilidès, Paschalis M. "On the Intellectual Content of Greek Nationalism: Paparrigopoulos, Byzantium and the Great Idea." In D. Ricks and P. Magdalino (eds.), *Byzantium and the Modern Greek Identity,* 25–33. Aldershot, Hampshire: Ashgate, 1998.

———. "The Enlightenment and European Identity." In E. Chrysos, P. M. Kitromilidès, and C. Svolopoulos (eds.), *The Idea of European Community in History,* 1:191–198. Athens: National and Capodistrian University of Athens, 2003.

———. "An Enlightenment Perspective on Balkan Cultural Pluralism. The Republican Vision of Rhigas Velestinlis. *History of Political Thought* 24, no. 3 (2003): 465–479.

———. "Adamantios Korais and the Dilemnas of Liberal Nationalism." In Paschalis M. Kitromilidès (ed.), *Adamantios Korais and the European Enlightenment,* 213–223. Oxford: Voltaire Foundation, 2010.

———. *Enlightenment and Revolution: The Making of Modern Greece.* Cambridge, MA: Harvard University Press, 2013.

———(ed.). *Adamantios Korais and the European Enlightenment.* Oxford: Voltaire Foundation, 2010.

Klooke, Kurt. *Benjamin Constant: Une biographie intellectuelle.* Geneva: Librairie Droz, 1984.

Klooke, Kurt, and Beatrice Fink (eds.). *Benjamin Constant. L'esprit de conquête.* in *Œuvres complètes* VIII, 1: 527–598. Tübingen: Max Niemeyer Verlag, 2005.

Kontler, Lázló. "William Robertson and His German Audience on European and Non-European Civilisations." *Scottish Historical Review* 80, no. 1 (2001): 63–89.

———. "Translation and Comparison: Early-Modern and Current Perspectives." *Contributions to the History of Concepts* 3 (2007): 71–102.

———. "Translation and Comparison II: A Methological Inquiry into Reception in the History of Ideas." *Contributions to the History of Concepts* 4 (2008): 27–56.

———. "Mankind and Its Histories: William Robertson, Georg Forster and a Late Eighteenth-Century German Debate." *Intellectual History Review* (2012): 1–19.

Koubourlis, Ioannis. *La formation de l'histoire nationale grecque. L'apport de Spyridon Zambélios (1815–1881).* Athens: Institut de recherches néo-helléniques, 2005.

———. "European Historiographical Influences upon the Young Konstantinos Paparrigopoulos." In R. Beaton and D. Ricks (eds.), *The Making of Modern Greece: Nationalism, Romanticism and the Uses of the Past (1797–1896),* 53–63. Farnham, Surrey: Ashgate, 2009.

———. "Les péripéties de l'intégration des anciens Macédoniens dans une 'histoire de la nation grecque'. Un aspect de l'histoire du nationalisme grec à partir des

Lumières grecques et jusqu'à la formation de l'école historique nationale." In C. Avlami, J. Alvar, and M. Recio (eds.), *Historiographie de l'antiquité et transferts culturels: les histoires anciennes dans l'Europe des XVIIIᵉ et XIXᵉ siècles*, 149–167. Amsterdam: Rodopi, 2010.

Kupisz, Kazimierz. "Alexandre le Grand dans les *Essais* de Montaigne." In K. Kristodolou (ed.), *Montaigne et la Grèce 1588–1988*, 179–193. Paris: Aux Amateurs de Livres, 1990.

Lanfranchi, Thibaud. "Vies multiples d'Alexandre le Grand." *Acta Fabula* 15, no. 6 (2014). http://www.fabula.org/revue/document8815.php

Larrère, Catherine. *L'invention de l'économie au XVIIIe siècle. Du droit naturel à la physiocratie*. Paris: PUF, 1992.

———. "Montesquieu et l'histoire du commerce." In M. Porret and C. Volpilhac-Auger (eds.), *Le temps de Montesquieu*, 319–335. Geneva: Lib. Droz, 2002.

Lassus, Yves. *L'Égypte, une aventure savante: Avec Bonaparte, Kléber, Menou, 1798–1801*. Paris: Fayard, 1998.

Laudin, Gérard. "Les grands hommes de l'Antiquité et la réflexion sur le génie en Allemagne de 1760 à 1790." *Dix-Huitième Siècle* 27 (1995): 213–222.

———. "Les enjeux allemands de la réception des ouvrages historiques français dans les revues de Gatterer, 1767–1781." In Pierre-André Blois, Roland Krebs, and Jean Moes (eds.), *Les Lettres françaises dans les revues allemandes du XVIIIᵉ siècle*, 177–189. Bern: Peter Lang, 1997.

———. "De la *magistra vitae* au tribunal de l'Histoire: la mémoire de l'humanité dans les histoires universelles allemandes des XVIIᵉ et XVIIIᵉ siècles." In Jean-Charles Margotton and Marie-Hélène Pérennec (eds.), *La Mémoire*, 149–158. Lyon: Presses Universitaires de Lyon, 2003.

———. "De la bourgade à la métropole. Sociabilité érudite, politique et artistique, politique de représentations." In G. Laudin (ed.), *Berlin 1700–1929*, 13–46. Paris, 2009.

———. "Christoph Meiners lecteur de Montesquieu et son traducteur dans la France révolutionnaire." In C. Avlami, J. Alvar, and M. Recio (eds.), *Historiographie de l'antiquité et transferts culturels: les histoires anciennes dans l'Europe des XVIIIᵉ et XIXᵉ siècles*, 223–237. Amsterdam: Rodopi, 2010.

———. "L'histoire comme science de l'homme chez Gatterer et chez Schlözer." In H. E. Boedeker, P. Büttgen, and M. Espagne (eds.), *Göttingen vers 1800: l'Europe des Sciences de l'Homme*, 483–514. Paris: Cerf, 2010.

———(ed.). *Berlin 1700–1929. Sociabilités et espace urbain*. Paris: L'Harmattan, 2009.

Laurens, Henry. *Aux sources de l'orientalisme: La Bibliothèque Orientale de Barthélémi d'Herbelot*. Paris: Maisonneuve et Larose, 1978.

———. *Les origines intellectuelles de l'expédition d'Égypte*. Istanbul, 1987.

Laurens, Henry: see Basch, Sophie.

———, Charles G. Gillispie, Jean-Claude Golvin, and Claude Traunecker. *L'expédition d'Égypte, 1798–1801*. Paris: Armand Colin, 1989.

Lawson, Philip. *The East India Company: A History*. New York: Longman, 1993.

Leghissa, Giovani. "L'Antiquité grecque comme miroir de la *Deutschtum*." In Didier Foucault and Pascal Payen (eds.), *Les autorités. Dynamiques et mutations d'une figure de référence à l'Antiquité,* 213–221. Grenoble: J. Million, 2007.

——. *Incorporare l'antico. Filologia classica e invenzione della modernità.* Milan: Mimèsis Edizioni, 2007.

Lemny, Stefan. *Jean-Louis Carra (1742–1793): Parcours d'un révolutionnaire.* Paris: L'Harmattan, 2000.

Lesseps, Ferdinand de. *Percement de l'Isthme de Suez: Exposé et documents officiels.* Paris: Plon, 1855.

Levillain, Charles-Edouard. *Vaincre Louis XIV. Angleterre-Hollande-France: Histoire d'une révolution triangulaire.* Seyssel: Champ Vallon, 2010.

Lianeri, Alessandra (ed.). *The Western Time of Ancient History: Historiographical Encounters with the Greek and Roman Pasts.* Cambridge: Cambridge University Press, 2011.

Lichtenberger, André. *Le socialisme au XVIIIᵉ siècle.* Paris, 1895.

——. *Le socialisme utopique. Études sur quelques précurseurs inconnus du socialisme.* Paris, 1898.

Lilti, Antoine. "Comment écrit-on l'histoire intellectuelle des Lumières? Spinozisme, radicalisme et philosophie." *Annales. Histoire, Sciences Sociales* 64, no. 1 (2009): 171–206.

Livingstone, David N., and Charles W. J. Withers (eds.). *Geography and Enlightenment.* Chicago: University of Chicago Press, 1999.

Lombard, Nicole. "Vieillesse de l'écrivain, jeunesse du conquérant: Montaigne et Alexandre le Grand." In C. Jouanno (ed.), *Figures d'Alexandre à la Renaissance,* 263–286. Turnhout, Belgium: Brepols, 2012.

Losurdo, Domenico. "Fichte et la question nationale allemande." *Revue française d'histoire des idées politiques* 13, no. 1 (2001): 297–319.

Lux, David S. *Patronage and Royal Science in Seventeenth-Century France.* Ithaca, NY: Cornell University Press, 1989.

MacGregor Morris, Ian. "Navigating the Grotesque, or, Rethinking Greek Historiography." In James Moore, Ian MacGregor Morris, and Andrew Bayliss (eds.), *Reinventing History: The Enlightenment Origins of Ancient History,* 247–290. London: Center for Metropolitan History, 2008.

Maindron, Ernest. *Les fondations de Prix à l'Académie des Sciences: Les lauréats de l'Académie 1714–1880.* Paris, 1881.

Mantran, Robert. "Les débuts de la Question d'Orient (1774–1839)." In Robert Mantran (ed.), *Histoire de l'empire ottoman,* 421–458. Paris: Fayard, 1989.

Marchand, Suzanne. *Down from Olympus: Archaeology and Philhellenism in Germany, 1750–1970.* Princeton, NJ: Princeton University Press, 1996.

——. "Philhellénisme et orientalisme en Allemagne." *Revue germanique internationale* 1–2 (2005): 9–22.

——. *German Orientalism in the Age of Empire: Religion, Race and Scholarship.* Cambridge: Cambridge University Press, 2009.

Marcone, Arnaldo. "La polemica di Niebuhr verso Heeren." *Rivista storia italiana*, n.s., 3 (1999): 809–830.

Marino, Luigi. *I maestri della Germania: Göttingen 1770–1820.* Turin: Einaudi, 1975.

———. *Praeceptores Germaniae: Göttingen 1770–1820.* Göttingen: Vandenhoeck und Ruprecht, 1993 [Italian 1975].

Markham, Clements-Robert. *Major James Rennel and the Rise of Modern English Geography.* London, 1901.

Markner, Reinhard, and Giuseppe Veltri (eds.). *Friedrich August Wolf: Studien, Dokumente, Bibliographie.* Stuttgart: F. Steiner, 1999.

Marshall, Peter (ed.). *The Writings and Speeches of Edmund Burke.* Vol. 7: *India: The Hastings Trial, 1788–1795.* Oxford: Oxford University Press, 2000.

Massimi, Jean-Robert. "Montrer et démontrer: autour du Traité de la situation du paradis terrestre de P. D. Huet (1691)." In Alain Desreumaux and Francis Schmidt (eds.), *Moïse géographe*, 203–225. Paris: Vrin, 1988.

Maufroy, Sandrine. "Friedrich August Wolf, un modèle philologique et ses incidences européennes." *Revue Germanique Internationale* 14 (2011): 27–39.

Meinecke, Friedrich. *Historism: The Rise of a New Historical Outlook.* New York: Herder and Herder, 1972 [German 1959].

Menant, Sylvain, and Robert Morrissey (eds.) with the collaboration of Julie Meyers. *Héroïsme et Lumières.* Paris: Champion, 2010.

Méricam-Bourdet, Myrtille. "'Les registres des exportations peuvent l'apprendre': Voltaire entre investigations historiques et polémique." *Dix-Huitième Siècle* 40 (2008): 431–445.

Mervaud, Christiane, and Mervaud, Michel. "Le Pierre le Grand et la Russie de Voltaire: histoire ou mirage?" In S. Karp and L. Wolff (eds.), *Le mirage russe au XVIIIe siècle,* 12–35. Ferney-Voltaire: Centre international d'études du XVIIIe siècle, 2001.

Mervaud, Michel (ed.). *Voltaire. Anecdotes sur le czar Pierre le Grand. Histoire de l'empire de Russie sous Pierre le Grand.* 2 vols. In *Les œuvres complètes de Voltaire,* vols. 46–47. Oxford: Voltaire Foundation, 1999.

Meyssonier, Simone. *La balance et l'horloge. La genèse de la pensée libérale en France au XVIIIᵉ siècle.* Montreuil: Éditions de la passion, 1989.

McGilvary, George K. "The Scottish Connection with India 1725–1833." *Études écossaises* 14 (2011): 13–31.

Michel, Christian. "La permanence du héros." In C. Grell and C Michel (eds.), *L'école des princes ou Alexandre disgrâcié,* 97–137. Paris: Les Belles Lettres, 1988.

Miliori, Margarita. "Europe, the Classical Polis and the Greek Nation: Philhellenism and Hellenism in Nineteenth-Century Britain." In R. Beaton and D. Ricks (eds.), *The Making of Modern Greece: Nationalism, Romanticism and the Uses of the Past (1797–1896),* 65–77. Farnham, Surrey: Ashgate, 2009.

Miller, Frederick P., with Agnes F. Vandome and John McBrewster. *Rigas.* Mauritius: VDM Publishing House, 2010.

Minuti, Rolando. "Mito e realtà del dispotismo ottomano: note in margine ad una discussione settecentesca." *Studi Settecentesci* 1, no. 1 (1981): 35–59.

———. *Oriente barbarico e storiografia settecentesca: rappresentazioni della storia dei Tartari nella cultura francese del XVIII secolo.* Venice: Marsilio, 1994.

———. "Gibbon and the Asiatic Barbarians: Notes on the French Sources of the *Decline and Fall.*" *Studies on Voltaire and the Eighteenth Century* 335 (1997): 21–44.

———. "L'Inde dans l'oeuvre de Montesquieu." In M. Fourcade and I. G. Zupanov (eds.), *L'Inde des Lumières: Discours, histoires, savoirs: XVIIè–XIXès siècles,* 79–107. Paris, 2013.

Momigliano, Arnaldo. "Ancient History and the Antiquarian." *Journal of the Warburg and Courtauld Institutes* 13 (1950): 283–315=*Problèmes d'historiographie,* 244–293. Paris: Gallimard, 1982.

———. *George Grote and the Study of Greek History.* London, 1952=*Problèmes d'historiographie,* 361–382. Paris: Gallimard, 1982.

———. "Gibbon's Contribution to Historical Method." *Historia* 2 (1954): 450–463=*Problèmes d'historiographie,* 321–339. Paris: Gallimard, 1982.

———. "J. G. Droysen between Greeks and Jews." *History and Theory* 9 (1970): 139–153=*Problèmes d'historiographie,* 383–401. Paris: Gallimard, 1982.

———. *Polybius between the English and the Turks: The Seventh J. L. Myres Memorial Lecture.* Oxford, 1974.

———. "Flavius Josephus and Alexander's Visit to Jerusalem." *Athenaeum* 57, nos. 3–4 (1979): 442–448=*Settimo contribuo alla storia degli studi classici e del mondo antico,* 319–328. Roma, 1984.

Monnier, Raymonde. "Usage d'un couple d'antonymes au 18e siècle. La civilisation et son revers, la barbarie." *Dix-Huitième Siècle* 40 (2008): 523–542.

Montecalvo, Maria-Stefania. "Il progetto di viaggio 'au Levant' di G.-E.-J. de Sainte-Croix." *Quaderni di Storia* 55 (2002): 219–232.

———. "[Sainte-Croix], *Observations sur les ruines de Persépolis.*" *Quaderni di Storia* 59 (2004): 5–57.

———. "Les relations intellectuelles entre Séguier et le baron de Sainte-Croix." In Gabriel Audisio and François Prugnière (eds.), *Jean-François Séguier: Un Nîmois dans l'Europe des Lumières,* 165–190. Aix-en-Provence: Édisud, 2005.

———. "Sainte-Croix et les sources pour l'étude du monde grec." In O. Cavalier (ed.) with the collaboration of M.-S. Montecalvo, *La Grèce des Provençaux,* 38–45. Avignon: Ville d'Avignon et Fondation Calvet, Imprimerie Laffont, 2007.

———. *Guillaume-Emmanuel-Joseph Guilhem de Clermont-Lodève, Baron de Sainte-Croix (1746–1809). Carteggio e bibliografia.* 2 vols. Florence, 2014.

Moore, James, Ian MacGregor Morris, and Andrew Bayliss (eds.). *Reinventing History: The Enlightenment Origins of Ancient History.* London: Center for Metropolitan History, 2008.

Moore, James, and Ian MacGregor Morris. "History in Revolution? Approaches to the Ancient World in the Long Eighteenth Century." In James Moore, Ian MacGregor

Morris, and Andrew Bayliss (eds.), *Reinventing History: The Enlightenment Origins of Ancient History*, 3–29. London: Center for Metropolitan History, 2008.

Morris, Henry. *The Life of Charles Grant, Sometime Member of Parliament for Inverness-Shire and Director of the East India Company*. London: John Murray, 1904.

Morrissey, Robert. *L'empereur à la barbe fleurie: Charlemagne dans la mythologie et l'histoire de France*. Paris: Gallimard, 1997.

——. "Charlemagne et la légende impériale." In Jean-Claude Bonnet (ed.), *L'empire des Muses: Napoléon, les Arts et les Lettres*, 331–347. Paris: Belin, 2004.

——(ed.). ARTFL Encyclopédie Project, University of Chicago. http://encyclopedie .uchicago.edu/.

Mullack, Ulrich. "De la philologie à l'histoire politique de la culture. Le cheminement intellectuel de Hermann Ludwig Heeren vers une science historique de l'homme." In H. E. Boedeker, P. Büttgen, and M. Espagne (eds.), *Göttingen vers 1800: l'Europe des Sciences de l'Homme*, 559–579. Paris: Cerf, 2010.

Murray, Oswyn. "Introduction." In Edward Bulwer-Lytton, *Athens: Its Rise and Fall: Bicentenary Edition*. Edited by Oswyn Murray, 1–35, 527–532. London: Routledge, 2004.

——. "L'invention d'une Athènes romantique et radicale: *Bulwer Lytton, Athènes, Grandeur et décadence*", *Métis*, n.s., 3 (2005): 351–364.

——. "Ireland Invents Greek History: The Lost Historian John Gast." *Hermathena* 185 (2008): 22–106.

——. "Ancient History in the Eighteenth Century." In A. Lianeri (ed.), *The Western Time of Ancient History*, 301–306. Cambridge: Cambridge University Press, 2011.

Musée de Carcassonne, *Jacques Gamelin, 1736–1803*. Les collections du Musée des Beaux-Arts de Carcassonne 2. Carcassonne, 1990.

Muthu, Sankar. *Enlightenment against Empire*. Princeton, NJ: Princeton University Press, 2003.

Nicolet, Claude. *La fabrique d'une nation. La France entre Rome et les Germains*. Paris: Perrin, 2003.

Nippel, Wilfried. *Johann Gustav Droysen: Ein Leben zwischen Wissenschaft und Politik*. Munich: C. H. Beck, 2008.

O'Brien, Karen. *Narratives of Enlightment: Cosmopolitan History from Voltaire to Gibbon*. Cambridge: Cambridge University Press, 1997.

Osterhammel, Jürgen. *Die Entzauberung Asiens: Europa und die asiatischen Reiche im 18. Jahrhundert*. 2nd ed. Munich: C. H. Beck, 2010 [1998].

Pagden, Anthony. *European Encounters with the New World, from Renaissance to Romanticism*. New Haven, CT: Yale University Press, 1993.

——. *Lords of the World: Ideologies of Empire in Spain, Britain and France (c. 1500–1800)*. New Haven, CT: Yale University Press, 1995.

——. *Peoples and Empires: Europeans and the Rest of the World from Antiquity to the Present*. London: Phoenix Press, 2001.

———. *Worlds at War: The 2500-Year Struggle between East and West.* Oxford: Oxford University Press, 2008.

Pandolfi, Claudia, Sotera Fornaro, and Giovanni Cerri (eds.). *Christian Gottlob Heyne, Greci Barbari.* Lecce: Argo, 2004.

Paoletti, Giovanni. *Benjamin Constant et les Anciens: Politique, religion, histoire.* Paris: Champion, 2006.

Pasley, Rodney. *'Send Malcolm!': The Life of Major-General Sir John Malcolm.* London: BACSA, 1982.

Paviot, Jacques. *Les ducs de Bourgogne, la croisade et l'Orient (fin XIVᵉ siècle-XVᵉ siècle).* Paris: Presses de l'Université de Paris-Sorbonne, 2003.

Payen, Pascal. Review of Briant, *Alexandre des Lumières. Revue des Études Anciennes* 115, no. 2 (2013): 225–231.

Pericolo, Luigi. "Le Roi et le favori. Essai d'interprétation sur *Les Reines de Perse* de Charles Le Brun." *Annali della Scuola Normale Superiore di Pisa* 6, no. 1 (2001): 125–148.

Perrot, Jean-Claude. *Une histoire intellectuelle de l'économie politique (XVIIᵉ–XVIIIᵉ siècles).* Paris: EPHE, 1992.

Peters, Martin. *Altes Reich und Europa. Der Historiker, Statistiker und Publizist August Ludwig (v.) Schlözer (1735–1809).* Münster: Lit Verlag, 2005.

Philippson, Nicholas. "Providence and Progress: An Introduction to the Historical Thought of William Robertson." In Stuart J. Brown (ed.), *William Robertson and the Expansion of the Empire,* 55–73. Cambridge: Cambridge University Press, 1997.

Piemontese, Angelo Michele. "The Heroic Deeds of Alexander as Portrayed in Rome." In Francesca Chiesa, Paola Stirpe, and Andrea Paribeni (eds.), *Images of Legend: Iconography of Alexander the Great in Italy,* 43–68. Rome: Gangemi, 2006.

Pintard, René. *Le Libertinage érudit dans la première moitié du XVIIᵉ siècle.* Geneva: Slatkine, 2000 [1983].

Pitts, Jennifer. *A Turn to Empire: The Rise of Imperial Liberalism in Britain and France.* Princeton, NJ: Princeton University Press, 2005.

Platania, Marco. "Dynamiques des empires et dynamiques du commerce: inflexions de la pensée de Montesquieu (1734–1802)." *Revue Montesquieu* 8 (2005–2006): 43–66.

———. "Relire l'histoire colonial au XVIIIe siècle. L'édition critique de l'Histoire des deux Indes." *Cromohs* 18 (2013): 23–35.

Plet, François (ed.). *Une géographie de l'Amérique du Nord à la fin du XVIIIe siècle. Saint-John de Crèvecoeur, Voyage dans la haute-Pensylvanie et dans l'État de New York depuis l'année 1785 jusqu'en 1798. Édition sélective et critique.* Paris, 2002.

Pottinger, George. *Sir Henry Pottinger, First Governor of Hong Kong.* New York: St. Martins Press, 1997.

Poumarède, Gérard. *Pour en finir avec la Croisade. Mythes et réalités de la lutte contre les Turcs aux XVIᵉ et XVIIᵉ siècles.* Paris: Presses Universitaires de France, 2004.

Promies, Wolfgang. "Georg Forster: citoyen du monde ou individu apatride?" *Revue Germanique Internationale* (1995): 71–81.

Psilakis, Catherine. Review of Briant, *Alexandre des Lumières. Histara, les comptes rendus,* 2014. http://histara.sorbonne.fr/cr.php?cr=1767.

Quillien, Jean. *G. de Humboldt et la Grèce. Modèle et histoire.* Lillle: Presses Universitaires de Lille, 1983. English translation, "On the Historian's Task," *History and Theory* 6 (1967).

Raby, Julian. "Mehmed the Conqueror's Greek Scriptorium., *Dumbarton Oaks Papers* 37 (1983): 15–34.

Ranum, Orest. *Artisans of Glory: Writers and Historical Thought in Seventeenth-Century France.* Chapell Hill: University of North Carolina Press, 1980.

Raskolnikoff, Mouza. *Histoire romaine et critique historique dans l'Europe des Lumières: la naissance de l'hypercritique dans l'historiographie de la Rome antique.* Strasbourg, 1992.

Reill, Peter, Hans. *The German Enlightenment and the Rise of Historicism.* Berkeley: University of California Press, 1975.

Rendall, Jane. "Scottisch Orientalism: From Robertson to Mill. *Historical Journal* 25, no. 1 (1982): 43–69.

Retat, Pierre. "L'âge des dictionnaires." In R. Chartier and H. J. Martin (eds.), *Histoire de l'édition française,* 2:232–241. Paris: Promodis, 1984.

Reynaud, Commandant. "Alexandre le Grand colonisateur." *Revue Hebdomadaire* (April 11, 1914): 195–212.

Ricks, David: see Beaton, Roderick.

Ricuperati, Giuseppe. "*Universal History:* storia di un progetto europeo. Impostori, storici ed editori nella *Ancient part.*" *Studi Settecenteschi* 2 (1981): 7–90.

———. "Jacques-Bénigne Bossuet et l'histoire universelle." In *Storia della storiografia* 35 (1999): 27–61.

Rihs, Charles. *Voltaire. Recherches sur les origines du matérialisme historique.* Geneva, 1977.

Roberto, Umberto. ""Del Commercio del romani": politica e storia antica nelle riflessioni del Settecento." In Carlo Zaccagnini (ed.), *Mercanti e politica nel mondo antico,* 327–361. Rome: l'Erma di Brestschneider, 2003.

Roche, Daniel. *Le siècle des lumières en province. Académies et académiciens provinciaux, 1680–1789.* 2 vols. Paris: Mouton, 1978.

———. *Humeurs vagabondes. De la circulation des hommes et de l'utilité des voyages.* Paris: Fayard, 2003.

Romanis, Federico de. "I südlicher Völkerverkehr e la proprietà della terra nell'India antica nelle Ideen di A. H. L. Heeren." *Rivista storia italiana,* n.s. 3 (1999): 798–808.

Rothkrug, Lionel. *Opposition to Louis XIV: The Political and Social Origins of the French Enlightenment.* Princeton, NJ: Princeton University Press, 1965.

Roulin, Jean-Marie. "Chateaubriand: Alexandre à la lumière de la Révolution et de Napoléon." In Franco Biasutti and Alessandra Coppola (eds.), *Alessandro Magno in età moderna,* 255–269. Padova: CLEUP, 2009.

Rozière, Eugène de, and Eugène Chatel. *Table générale et méthodique des mémoires . . . de l'Académie des Inscriptions et Belles-Lettres.* Paris, 1852.

Rudler, Gustave. *La jeunesse de Benjamin Constant: 1767–1794: le disciple du XVIIIe siècle, utilitarisme et pessimisme, Mme de Charrière: d'après de nombreux documents inédits.* Paris: A. Colin, 1908.

———. *Bibliographie critique des œuvres de Benjamin Constant avec documents inédits et Fac-simile.* Paris: Armand Colin, 1909.

Said, Edward. *Orientalism.* New York: Vintage Books, 1994 [1979].

Salas, Charles G. "Ralegh and the Punic Wars." *Journal of the History of Ideas* 57, no. 2 (1996): 195–215.

Séguy, René. *L'Héritage d'Alexandre, essai sur la colonisation, suivi de Considérations sur l'Islam.* Paris: Société d'éditions géographiques, maritimes et coloniales, 1931.

Seth, Catriona. "L'Institut et les prix littéraires." In J.-C. Bonnet (ed.), *L'empire des Muses,* 111–131. Paris: Belin: 2004.

Schiltz, Véronique. "Catherine II, les Turcs et l'antique." In S. Basch, N. Seni, P. Chuvin, M. Espagne, J. Leclant (eds.), *L'orientalisme, les orientalistes et l'empire ottoman de la fin du XVIIIe siècle à la fin du XXe siècle,* 81–120. Paris: Académie des Inscriptions et Lettres, 2011.

Sebastiani, Silvia. *The Scottish Enlightenment: Race, Gender, and the Limits of Progress.* London: Palgrave Macmillan, 2013.

———. "Globalization under Alexander the Great." Review of Briant, *Alexandre des Lumières. Books and Ideas,* September 9, 2013. http://www.booksandideas.net /Globalization-under-Alexander-the.html

Seidl, Barbara. "L'iconografia alessandrina nella Roma dell' 800." In Franco Biasutti and Alessandra Coppola (eds.), *Alessandro Magno in età moderna,* 315–348. Padova: CLEUP, 2009.

Smitten, Jeffrey. "Bibliography of Writings about William Robertson, 1755–1996." In Stuart J. Brown (ed.), *William Robertson and the Expansion of the Empire,* 231–267. Cambridge: Cambridge University Press, 1997.

———. "Robertson's Letters and the Life of Writing." In Stuart J. Brown (ed.), *William Robertson and the Expansion of the Empire,* 36–54. Cambridge: Cambridge University Press, 1997.

Somov, Vladimir A. "Pierre-Charles Levesque, protégé de Diderot et historien de la Russie." *Cahiers du Monde Russe* 42, no. 3 (2002): 275–294.

Spawforth, Anthony. "Symbol of Unity? The Persian-Wars Tradition in the Roman Empire." In S. Hornblower (ed.), *Greek Historiography,* 233–247. Oxford: Clarendon Press, 1994.

———. "Alexander Enlightened." Review of Briant, *Alexandre des Lumières. Histos* (2014): xxv–xxix. http://research.ncl.ac.uk/histos/documents/2015RR05Spaw forthonBriant.pdf.

Spector, Céline. "Montesquieu, l'Europe et les nouvelles figures de l'empire." *Revue Montesquieu* 8 (2005–2006): 17–42.

——. *Montesquieu et l'émergence de l'économie politique*. Paris: Champion, 2006.

Sassi, Maria Michela. "La fredezza dello storico: Christian Gottlob Heyne." *Annali della Scuola Normale di Pisa*, ser. 3, 26, no. 1 (1971): 105–126.

Stamboulis, Giorgio. "La *Dichiarazione dei diritti* di Rigas Velestinlis." *Cromohs* 14 (2009): 1–17. http://www.cromohs.unifi.it/14_2009/stamboulis_rigas.html.

Stela, Vito G. "Linguet *philosophe*." *Studi Settecenteschi* 18 (1998): 89–157.

Sternhell, Zeev. *Les anti-Lumières. Une tradition du XVIIIe siècle à la guerre froide*. Paris: Fayard, 2006; Collection Folio Histoire, Gallimard, 2010.

Stokes, Eric. *The English Utilitarians and India*. Delhi: Oxford University Press, 1959.

Terrel, Jean. "À propos de la conquête: droit et politique chez Montesquieu." *Revue Montesquieu* 8 (2005–2006): 137–150.

Terribile, Claudia. *Del piacere della virtù. Paolo Veronese, Alessandro Magno et il patriziato veneziano*. Venice: Marsilio, 2009.

Thomas, Stephan Alexander. *Makedonien und Preußen. Die Geschichte einer Analogie*. Egelsbach: Hänsel-Hohenhausen, 1994.

Thomson, Ann. *Barbary and Enlightenment: European Attitudes towards the Maghreb in the 18th Century*. Leiden: Brill, 1987.

——. "Diderot, Roubaud et l'esclavage. *Recherches sur Diderot et sur l'Encyclopédie* 35 (2003): 69–93.

——. "L'Europe des Lumières et le monde musulman. Une altérité ambiguë." *Cromohs* 10 (2005): 1–11.

Thouars, Denis. "Benjamin Constant et l'École de Göttingen." In H. E. Boedeker, P. Büttgen, M. Espagne (eds.), *Göttingen vers 1800: l'Europe des Sciences de l'Homme*, 129–154. Paris: Cerf, 2010.

Tolias, George. "Antiquarianism, Patriotism and Empire: Transfers of the Cartography of the Travels of Anarcharsis the Younger in Greece (1788–1811)." *Historical Review* [Athens] 2 (2005): 67–91.

——. Review of Briant, *Alexandre des Lumières*. *Historical Review* 10 (2013): 300–305. http://ejournals.epublishing.ekt.gr/index.php/historicalReview/article/view/4094/3878.

Tolmer, Léon. *Pierre-Daniel Huet (1630–1721). Humaniste-physicien*. Bayeux: Colas, 1949.

Tott, Ferenc (ed.). *Mémoires du baron de Tott sur les Turcs et les Tartares*. Paris: Champion, 2004 [1785].

Ubicicini, Jean-Henri Abdolonyme. "La grande carte de la Grèce." *Revue de géographie* (April 1881): 241–253; (July–December 1881): 9–25.

[UNESCO]. *Rhigas Vélinstélis (1757–1798). Intellectuel et combattant de la liberté*. Proceedings of the International UNESCO Symposium, December 12–13, 1998. Paris: UNESCO/Éditions Desmos, 2002.

Valence, Françoise de. (ed. and trans.). *Voyage en Perse et en Inde (1637–1640). Le journal de Johann Albrecht von Mandelslo*. Paris: Éd. Chandeigne, 2008.

Valensi, Lucette. "Éloge de l'Orient, éloge de l'orientalisme. Le jeu d'échecs d'Anquetil-Duperron." *Revue de l'histoire des religions* 112, no. 4 (1995): 419–452.

——. *The Birth of the Despot: Venice and the Sublime Porte.* Translated by A. Denner. Ithaca, NY: Cornell University Press, 2009 [French 1987].

Valera, Gabriella (ed.). *Scienza dello Stato e metodo storiografico nella Scuola storica di Gottinga.* Naples: Edizioni Scientifiche Italiane, 1980.

Van der Zande, Johann. "Statistik and History in the German Enlightenment." *Journal of the History of Ideas* 71, no. 3 (2010): 411–432.

Van Steen, Gonda. "Enacting History and Patriotic Myth: Aeschylus' *Persians* on the Eve of the Great War of Independence." In E. Bridges, E. Hall, and P. J. Rhodes (eds.), *Cultural Responses to the Persian Wars: Antiquity to the Third Millenium,* 299–329. Oxford: Oxford University Press, 2007.

Vasunia, Phiroze. "Alexander and Asia: Droysen and Grote." In Himanshu Prabha Ray and Daniel T. Potts (eds.), *Memory as History: The Legacy of Alexander in Asia,* 89–102. New Delhi: Aryan Books, 2007.

——. "Alexander Sikandar." In Susan A. Stephen and Phiroze Vasunia (eds.), *Classics and National Cultures,* 302–324. Oxford: Oxford University Press, 2010.

——. *The Classics and Colonial India.* Oxford: Oxford University Press, 2013.

Vatin, Nicolas, and Veinstein, Gilles. *Le sérail ébranlé. Essai sur les morts, dépositions et avènements des* sultans *ottomans XIVe–XIXe siècles.* Paris: Fayard, 2003.

Vaughan, Géraldine. "Un empire écossais? L'Écosse et le monde britannique, 1815–1931." *Histoire & Politique* 11 (2010): 1–13. http://www.histoire-politique.fr/documents/11/dossier/pdf/HP11_Vaughan_pdf_210510.pdf.

Vaughan, Rosie. Introduction to Henry Pottinger, *Travels in Beloochistan and Sinde,* v–x. Karachi: Oxford University Press, 2002 [1816].

Veinstein, Gilles. "La question du despotisme ottoman. La polémique Tott-Peyssonnel." In S. Basch, N. Seni, P. Chuvin, M. Espagne, J. Leclant (eds.), *L'orientalisme, les orientalistes et l'empire ottoman de la fin du XVIIIe siècle à la fin du XXe siècle,* 187–203. Paris: Académie des Inscriptions et Lettres, 2011.

Vidal-Naquet, Pierre. "Les Alexandres." In C. Grell and C. Michel (eds.), *L'école des Princes ou Alexandre disgrâcié,* 7–30. Paris: Les Belles Lettres, 1988.

Vivien de Saint-Martin, Louis. *Histoire de la géographie et des découvertes géographiques depuis les temps les plus reculés jusqu'à nos jours.* Paris: Hachette, 1873.

Vlassopoulos, Kostas. "Imperial Encounters: Discourses on Empire and the Uses of Ancient History during the Eighteenth Century." In Mark Bradley (ed.), *Classics and Imperialism in the British Empire,* 29–53. Oxford: Oxford University Press, 2010.

——. Review of Briant, *Alexandre des Lumières. American Historical Review* (2014): 1345–1346.

Volpilhac-Auger, Catherine, with the collaboration of C. Bustaret. *L'Atelier de Montesquieu.* Naples: Ligouri Editore, 2001.

——. "Montesquieu et l'impérialisme grec: Alexandre ou l'art de la conquête." In *Montesquieu and the Spirit of Modernity,* 49–60. Oxford: Voltaire Foundation, 2002.

——. Review of Briant, *Alexandre des Lumières. Revue française de Science Politique* 64, no. 3 (2014): 593–595.

———. (ed.). *La collection Ad usum Delphini. L'Antiquité au miroir du Grand Siècle.* Grenoble: Ellug-Université Stendhal, 2000.

———. *De l'esprit des loix. Manuscrits.* In *Montesquieu. Œuvres completes,* vols. 3–4. Oxford: Voltaire Foundation, 2008.

———. *Dictionnaire électronique Montesquieu.* http://dictionnaire-montesquieu.ens-lyon.fr/index.php.

———, with the collaboration of Gabriel Sabbagh and Françoise Weil. *Un auteur en quête d'éditeurs? Histoire éditoriale de l'œuvre de Montesquieu (1748–1964).* Lyon: ENS Éditions, 2011.

Waszek, Norbert. "La fondation de l'université de Berlin." In G. Laudin (ed.), *Berlin 1700–1929,* 85–95. Paris: L'Harmattan, 2009.

———. "L'impact des Lumières écossaises sur les sciences de l'homme à Göttingen à travers l'exemple des *Göttingische Gelehrte Anzeigen.*" In H. E. Boedeker, P. Büttgen, and M. Espagne (eds.), *Göttingen vers 1800: l'Europe des Sciences de l'Homme,* 155–190. Paris: Cerf, 2010.

Watson, Wendy. "Tradition and Innovation: Pierre-Henri de Valenciennes and the Neoclassical Landscape." In Michael Marlais, John Varriano, and Wendy M. Watson, *Valenciennes, Daubigny and the Origins of French Landscape Painting,* 22–37. South Hadley, MA: Mount Holyoke College Art Museum, 2004.

Wiesehöfer, Josef. "'Sie haben sich durch ihre Schlechtigkeit selbst überlebt.' Barthold Georg Niebuhr und die Perser der Antike." In T. Stamm-Kulmann, J. Elvert, B. Aschmann, and J. Hohensee (eds.), *Geschichtsbilder. Festschrift für Michael Salewski zum 65. Geburtstag,* 201–211. Stuttgart: F. Steiner, 2003.

———, and Stephan Conermann (eds.). *Carsten Niebuhr (1733–1815) und seine Zeit.* Stuttgart: F. Steiner, 2006.

Yapp, Malcolm, "The Legend of the Great Game." Proceedings of the British Academy, Vol. 111, 179–98. London: The British Academy, 2001.

Zuber, Roger. *Les "Belles Infidèles"et la formation du goût classique en France.* Paris, 1968.

———. *Nicolas Perrot d'Ablancourt. Lettres et Préfaces critiques publiées avec une introduction, des notices et un lexique . . .* Paris: librairie Marcel Didier, 1972.

Notes

Preface

1. I refer to them here in alphabetical order, as they appear in the Bibliography: Bonnet (2013); Bowden (2014); Gaullier-Bougassas (2015); Goulemot (2013); Imbruglia (2013); Lanfranchi (2013); Psilakis (2013); Tolias (2013); Payen (2013); Sebastiani (2013); Spawforth (2014); Vlassopoulos (2014); Volpilhac-Auger (2013).
2. Announced by the author as of 2011–2012, the book was released in Summer 2014. My deepest thanks go to the author for giving me access to her book as a pdf file. Consulting her work led me to simplify certain biographic elements in Chap. 2.
3. Among its reviews see those by R. J. Pranger, in *Mediterranean Quarterly* 21, no. 4 (2010): 93–96, and M. Hamilton in *Journal of Medieval Studies* 88, no. 3 (2013): 754–757.
4. However, I remain perplexed by the conceptual model the author proposes to find in the work of the French philosopher Emmanuel Levinas.
5. See, particularly, the Alexander Redivivus series (General Editors: C. Gaullier-Bougassas, J.-Y. Tilliette, C. Jouanno, and M. Bridges) published by Brepols, which includes the four-volume *La fascination pour Alexandre le Grand dans les littératures européennes (XIe-XVIe siècles)* edited by Gaullier-Bougassas (2014).
6. *Alexandre le Grand au passé et au présent*, Actes Sud, Arles (forthcoming).

Introduction

1. One can really only note a single exception among specialists of Enlightenment literature, which is Volpilhac-Auger's article "Montesquieu et l'impérialisme grec" about Montesquieu's Alexander. On the other hand, the history of Alexander

in the eighteenth century is absent from recent articles on Greek history during the same period; see Ceserani, "Modern Histories of Ancient Greece"; and Murray, "Ancient History in the Eighteenth Century." The same is true of the studies collected in Avlami, Alvar, and Romero-Recio, *Historiographie de l'antiquité et transferts culturels* (with the exception of Koubourlis's contribution on Greece) and of another collection devoted to ancient history in the Age of Enlightenment (Moore, Morris, and Bayliss, *Enlightenment Origins of Ancient History*).

2. I borrow the term "history in equal parts" from Romain Bertrand and his book of the same name (see *L'histoire à parts égales*, 11–22), for a comparable (methodological) fight was and must constantly continue to be fought for the history of the ancient Persian empire to be considered for what it is, rather than what the ancient Greeks said about it or what too many contemporary specialists of the history of Alexander say and, especially, do not say about it (see my *Alexander the Great*, esp. 171–185).

3. See my "Impérialismes antiques et idéologie coloniale dans la France contemporaine"; and, more recently, "'Alexandre et l'hellénisation de l'Asie'"; I also addressed the question in a lecture given at Yale University on November 10, 2011: see "Michael Rostovtzeff, Elias J. Bickerman, and the 'Hellenization of Asia'" (2015). Studies written in preparation for this book are listed in the bibliography under Briant (2005–2012).

4. On this subject see the fundamental article by Escudier, "De Chladenius à Droysen."

5. For confirmation one need only consult the indexes of books by Pagden, *European Encounters* and *Lords of the Sea*; Muthu, *Enlightenment against Empire*; Pitts, *Turn to Empire*; and Osterhammel, *Die Entzauberung Asiens*. Anthony Pagden has included a chapter on Alexander in several recent books (which are thoroughly interesting and even exciting in their overall perspectives): *Peoples and Empire*, 13–27 (referring to Alexander as "the first world conqueror," but unfortunately forgetting that the first global empire was built by the Achaemenids and used as a model by Alexander); *Worlds at War*, chap. 2 "In the Shadow of Alexander," in which, after the Greco-Persian Wars and the classical period (chap. 1 "Perpetual Enmity"), Alexander is mentioned in the context of the opposition between East and West and the Persian empire is included (at least in the shadow of Themistocles and Alexander). None of these books feature any consideration of the question of the construction of images of Alexander in the literature of the Enlightenment (with the exception of a reference in *Worlds at War* [p. 53] to Montesquieu, *Spirit of the Laws* 10.14): this was simply not the author's purpose; the Enlightenment period is treated individually in specific chapters (*People and Empire*, 88–144; *Worlds at War*, chap. 9 "Enlightened Orientalism"). One notes a recently expressed interest among scholars of antiquity and specialists in reception (particularly in Great Britain) in the study of the uses of antiquity in modern and contemporary colonial discourse (e.g., Goff,

Classics and Colonialism; Ataç, "Imperial Lessons from Athens and Sparta"; Hardwick and Gillespie, *Classics in Post-Colonial Worlds;* Bradley, *Classics and Imperialism;* Hall and Vasunia, *India, Greece, and Rome, 1757 to 2007;* yet the example of Alexander in the eighteenth century is never mentioned (the same is true of Centanni's recent article "Alexander the Great," esp. 30 on the eighteenth century). A notable exception is Hagerman's remarkable analysis, "In the Footsteps of the 'Macedonian Conqueror'" (which I return to in Chap. 6 § "British Travelers and Spies in Alexander's Footsteps"); as is Vasunia's recent volume, *Classics and Colonial India,* in which part I is devoted to "Alexander in India" (33–115).

6. Despite the term's ambiguous status (particularly since the publication of Said's *Orientalism*), I am using it without quotation marks. According to my geopolitical acceptation of the word, "Orient" corresponds quite precisely to the area of Darius's former empire, which later became Alexander's, and in the eighteenth century included the Ottoman empire and its dependencies, Persia and the (Western) Mughal empire, as well as Afghanistan and the Central Asian nations ("Tartary") and the neighboring maritime areas (Eastern Mediterranean, Black Sea, Caspian Sea, Aral Sea, Persian Gulf, Red Sea). This is the area referred to by the term "Asia" in the texts inspired by the ancient Greeks' use of the word; to the Greeks, "Asia" referred to the empire of the Great King later conquered by Alexander.

7. Grell and Michel, *L'Ecole des Princes,* 139–211; see also p. 45: "It seemed to us that the texts in this anthology, presented in chronological order, faithfully represent the entire body of works consulted."

8. See Chaussard, *Histoire des expéditions d'Alexandre,* 3:75–155 (chap. 5 "Various Appraisals: French Authors, Historians, Politicians, Moralists, Poets"); also 3:157–304 (chap. 6 "Parallels"); and 1:xii–xlvii ("Review of the Historians of Alexander"), drawing heavily on Sainte-Croix, *Examen critique* (1775); hereafter cited as *Examen critique* followed by the year of publication in parentheses.

9. See Chap. 1 § "Alexander in the Academy" and, in a more detailed form, my *Alexandre des Lumières,* chap. 3.

10. Saint-Martin, *Histoire de la géographie,* 90, 93, 110.

11. For example, see Blair, *History of the Rise and Progress of Geography,* 49ff.

12. See my remarks in "Impérialismes antiques et idéologie coloniale dans la France contemporaine," in which I refer to Demangeon's book (also in my "Alexander and the Persian Empire," 182–184); on geography and colonialism see the studies collected by Godlewska and Smith, *Geography and Empire* (on Demangeon see Claval's article, "Playing with Mirrors," and Sebastiani's marked insistence on this point in "Globalization under Alexander the Great" (n. 1) in her review of *Alexandre des Lumières.*

13. I am specifically thinking of Rigas Velestinlis's research and his *Karta tès Hellados* (1797): see Chap. 10 § "The First of the Hellenes?"

14. See Chap. 5 n. 1.

15. See, in particular, Chap. 6 § "British Travelers and Spies in Alexander's Footsteps."

16. See Chaps. 6–7.

17. On this point see Christophe Charle's strong remarks in "Peut-on écrire une histoire de la culture européenne à l'époque contemporaine?"

18. Regarding Italy see Tolias's critical remarks in his review of *Alexandre des Lumières* (301 n. 3), which I comment on below in Chap. 2 § "Sainte-Croix and the Others" (n. 48); I will add that my Italian diagnosis naturally does not apply to ancient history in general but only to works on Alexander the Great (except as of the discovery of the mosaic of Alexander in Pompeii in 1831: see below, n. 40). Regarding Spain see the regrets expressed by Imbruglia in his review of *Alexandre des Lumières;* I have not carried out additional research for this American edition, with the exception of a discussion of the figure of Alexander at the court of Philip V of Spain in Chap. 1 § "Alexander as an Example of Royal Virtues." I should add that Barletta's 2010 book *Death in Babylon* suggests that research could be conducted on the eighteenth century in Portugal. I hope that in the coming years young researchers will work on the countries that my research only touched on peripherally.

19. See, in particular, the dissertation in Latin by Van der Chys (1828), along with Droysen's very important review in *Jahrbücher für wissenschaftliche Kritik,* 472–480.

20. On the inclusion of Alexander in the neo-Hellenic vision of Greek history before and after 1830 see Chap. 10 § "The First of the Hellenes?"

21. See the fascinating recent study by Schiltz, "Catherine II, les Turcs et l'antique."

22. However, I must add that Svetlana Gorshenina is on the verge of publishing an article on the question of "Alexander the Great and the Russians" (forthcoming).

23. See, in particular, Chap. 6 § "British Travelers and Spies in Alexander's Footsteps."

24. See Chap. 8 § "Geography, Voyages, and Alexander's Conquests: Translations and Original Studies." To a certain extent, my analysis confirms (if it was necessary) the validity of Marchand's criticism of Said's book, which (obviously wrongly) did not include nineteenth-century Germany in its scope and analyses: see Marchand, *German Orientalism,* xviii–xx, 29–52.

25. To borrow Antoine Lilti's excellent expression, "the progressive nationalization of the cultural fields . . . is probably a major phenomenon of the eighteenth century." ("Comment écrit-on l'histoire intellectuelle des Lumières?," esp. 201–204; quote on 202).

26. On this point see, in particular, Chap. 10 § "The Sick Man of Asia."

27. See Chap. 6 § "History of Alexander, Franco-British Translations and Confrontations."

28. On the "Germanization" of this institution following Frederick's death see Laudin's remarks in "De la bourgade à la métropole," 32–34.

29. These were published in *Commentationes Societatis Regiae Scientiarum Gottingensis recentiores.*

30. For example, see his foreword to the first issue of the journal he launched in 1767, *Allgemeine historische Bibliothek,* or his presentation, in the same issue, of a plan for a universal history ("Von historischen Plan"), as well as his reflections on a German historian's duties: "Zufällige Gedanken über die Verdienste der Teutschen um die Historie" (1767); and "Räsonnement über die jetzige Verfassung der Geschichtkunde in Teutschland" (1772). He also wrote about the rules of translation for historical works ("Von der Kunst zu übersetzen" [1767]).

31. See Heyne, *Sammlung antiquarischer Aussäge,* 1:x: "Additionally, I write in German essentially because I hope to be useful"(*Übrigens schreibe ich deutsch, eben aus dem Grunde, weil ich nützlich zu seyn wünsche*).

32. On this subject the explanations for the reader by one of the translators of the English *Universal History* into German (based on a Dutch edition) are particularly interesting: Jacob Baumgarten, preface to *Übersetzung der Allgemeinen Welthistorie,* 8–10.

33. Under this name the author confuses the famous Scottish philosopher (he cites the German translations of the *History of America* and the *Historical Disquisition*) and his namesake, also a Scot: see Chap. 2 § "Alexander in England and Scotland: Manuals and Universal History."

34. Born to a family of English origin, the German Johann Reinhold Forster (father of Georg) translated Bougainville's *Voyage* into English (*A Voyage Round the World* [1772]), and began a translation of William Vincent's *Voyage of Nearchus.*

35. On the translation of Vincent into French see Chap. 6 § "History of Alexander, Franco-British Translations and Confrontations" and Chap. 7 § "Alexander, Promoter of Commerce"; on the failure of the German translation of Vincent see Chap. 8 § "Geography, Voyages, and Alexander's Conquests: Translations and Original Studies."

36. Before changing its name in 1802, the journal was known as *Göttingische Zeitungen von gelehrten Sachen* from 1739 to 1753, then as *Göttingische Anzeigen von gelehrten Sachen* from 1753 to 1802.

37. See Chap. 4 § "Montesquieu's Sources: Huet and His Contemporaries (1667–1716)."

38. I am thinking in particular of Sainte-Croix (see Chaps. 2 and 7), in whose case using 1789 as an interruption is nonsensical (as, for example, in Grell, *Dix-Huitième siècle,* 2:1012–1015, particularly 1015 n. 88: see *Alexandre des Lumières,* 163 and n. 64).

39. Visconti, *Iconographie grecque,* 2:36–42 and 42–43.

40. Edward Daniel Clarke, *Tomb of Alexander.*
41. Outside of the Italian archaeologists (see Bonucci, *Gran musaico di Pompei;* Niccolini, *Quadro in musaico in Pompei;* and Rochette's reviews of Niccolini; for current status see my *Darius in the Shadow of Alexander,* chap. 5 § "Freeze-Frame: Darius in the Naples Mosaic"), one of the first commentators on the mosaic was Goethe, then eighty-two years old. On March 6, 1832, Goethe received a drawing sent by the German archaeologist Wilhelm Johann Karl Zahn in a letter dated February 18, 1832. His answer expressed his wonder at the sight. He returned to the subject in his journal over the following days, and died two weeks later (see Andreae, *Das Alexandermosaik,* 29–36).
42. See my essay "Grote on Alexander," with recent bibliography.
43. On this point see my previous remarks in "Montesquieu, Mably et Alexandre le Grand"; "Retour sur Alexandre," part I, 61–67; "Alexander and the Persian Empire, between 'Decline' and 'Renovation'"; and "Alexander the Great."

1. History, Morals, and Philosophy

1. Mitford, *History of Greece,* 5:48 n. 2.
2. Bacon, *Advancement of Learning,* 59.
3. Aside from the *Life of Alexander,* authors knew the *Apothegms of Kings and Great Commanders* and the two treatises *On the Fortune or the Virtue of Alexander* (also known by their title in Latin translation, *De Fortuna Alexandri*). On the use of the exempla see my *Darius in the Shadow of Alexander,* esp. chap. 3.
4. Christina of Sweden, *Works of Christina of Sweden,* 136–137 (translated from the French [1753]).
5. Samuel Clarke, *Life and Death of Alexander the Great.* Curiously none of the bibliographic indexes consulted mention Clarke's book.
6. Translation quoted: *A Discourse on the History of the Whole World* (1686).
7. Not included in the English translations.
8. Rollin, *Ancient History,* vol. 1, intro.: "The Usefulness of Profane History, Especially with Regard to Religion."
9. See my *Alexandre des Lumières,* 42–45.
10. Brunswick-Oels, *Réflexions critiques* (1764) = *Critical reflections* (1767).
11. On the traditions collected in Josephus see Momigliano's study, "Flavius Josephus and Alexander's Visit to Jerusalem."
12. Rollin, *Ancient History,* vol. 1, preface.
13. This subject, frequently addressed in recent publications and exhibitions, deserves its own specialized monograph, which would be of place here. One of the most exhaustive and best informed works remains the catalog for an exhibition in Thessaloniki (1997–1998), edited by N. Hadjnicolaou, *Alexander the Great in European Art;* also see Chiesa, Stirpe, and Paribeni, *Images of a Legend,* partic-

ularly the very well-informed article by Piemontese, "Heroic Deeds of Alexander the Great" (43–68).

14. See Kirchner's recent analysis of this painting in *Les Reines de Perse*.

15. See also my *Alexandre des Lumières,* 222–227.

16. On this I refer the reader to Grell and Michel's book, *L'école des Princes,* esp. 53–95 and 99–120; see also my *Darius in the Shadow of Alexander,* chap. 12.

17. See Chap. 7 § "Alexander and the Revolution: The Pen and the Paintbrush."

18. Among other examples see Rigas's portrait of Alexander in 1797: see Chap. 10 § "The First of the Hellenes?"

19. See, in particular, the Gobelins tapestries, which were recently exhibited in Paris: *La tenture de l'histoire d'Alexandre le Grand* (2008).

20. Michel, "La permanence du héros," 120.

21. On this subject I have closely followed José Alvarez Lopera's articles, "Philip V of Spain at La Granja Palace" and "Las virtudes del Rey." In the latter article (which is basically a Spanish version of the former), the reader will find color reproductions of the paintings, which were restored and displayed at the 2002–2003 Madrid exhibition. I have also borrowed from Lopera's "Philip V of Spain" for the English translations of the titles of paintings commissioned by Juvarra (captions cited in Spanish in "Las virtudes del Rey," 142).

22. See Piemontese, "Heroic Deeds of Alexander the Great," 50–52.

23. In Spanish, *Virtudes de Su Magestad con les Hechos de Alejandro;* see the reproduction of the manuscript in Fernandez Talaya, "Las pinturas encargadas por Juvarra para la galeria del palacio de La Granja," 48.

24. The painter had the option of illustrating another virtue: "FORTITUDE. He severs the Gordian Knot overcoming the difficulty of the undertaking." Examination of the paintings reveals that he chose GENEROSITY (Lopera, "Las virtudes del Rey," 153, with a reproduction of the canvas painted by F. Imperiali).

25. On this see Grell, "Télémaque et Alexandre."

26. See Chapter 3.

27. To my knowledge the only other example of this scene is in the Room of Alexander at the Villa Giulia in Rome and was painted in the middle of the sixteenth century (Piemontese, "Heroic Deeds of Alexander the Great," 52–53).

28. The scene of the Persian princesses appears to be a tracing of Le Brun's painting: see the photo in Lopera, "Las virtudes del Rey," 146.

29. In the midst of a fierce free-for-all, Alexander (carrying a standard) fights Darius; both are on horseback. Note that this scene of a duel between riders was entirely imagined for the occasion. (On this subject see my remarks in *Darius in the Shadow of Alexander,* chap. 7 § "The Tradition of the Duel between Darius and Alexander."

30. "[His] laudable nature, valour and spirit, show him as another Alexander, seen by the whole universe always to vanquish, never to be vanquished" (T. Puga I Roxas [1708] quoted in Lopera, "Philip V of Spain," 40 n. 12).

31. See Bossuet, *Politics Drawn from the Very Words of Holy Scripture*, bk. 5 § 4, 2nd proposition: "The magnanimity, magnificence and all the great virtues of majesty."

32. Rollin, *Ancient History*, 5:370–382.

33. Ibid., 361–370; see also 181–193: "Alexander's Journey to Jerusalem." The episode was frequently discussed during the seventeenth and eighteenth centuries (see above § "The History of Alexander and History of the People of God" and Chap. 2 § "The History of Alexander in the Revolutionary Upheavals."

34. See Lopera, "Philip V of Spain", 40.

35. Regarding what follows see my *Alexandre des Lumières*, 65–84.

36. "Macedonia (Alexander, King of—)," *Dictionary Historical and Critical*, 4:3–10.

37. On these discussions see also Grafton, *What Was History?* (which does not focus on the history of Alexander).

38. See my *Alexandre des Lumières*, 104–124.

39. Translated into English as *On Printed Lies*.

40. Voltaire, "Alexander," *Philosophical Dictionary*, in *Works of Voltaire*, vol. 3, part I.

41. See also Montesquieu, *My Thoughts*, no. 774.

42. See Volpilhac-Auger, "Montesquieu et l'impérialisme grec."

43. These descriptions are from Grange, "Les réactions d'un adversaire des philosophes," 218.

44. Aside from D. Gay Levy's volume *Ideas and Careers*, note especially the articles by Guerci, "Linguet storico della Grecia e di Roma"; and Stela, "Linguet *philosophe*"; see also my "Histoire du *Siècle d'Alexandre* de Linguet," as well as *Alexandre des Lumières*, 112–124 and 652–653.

45. Linguet, *Histoire du siècle d'Alexandre* (1762), 90–92; (1769), 21–22, 159; hereafter cited as *Siècle d'Alexandre* followed by the year of publication in parentheses.

46. *Siècle d'Alexandre* (1762), 91, 91, 155.

47. Ibid., 164.

48. See my *Alexandre des Lumières*, 84–103.

49. Ameilhon, *Histoire du commerce et de la navigation;* the German Schmidt, who had participated in the competition, also published his dissertation, *De commerciis et navigationibus Ptolemaerum*.

50. Cassini, "De l'origine et du progrès de l'Astronomie."

51. Allusions in ancient sources reveal that Diognetus and Baeton were Alexander's bematists, that is, his "surveyors," responsible for measuring the distances from one point to another over the course of the campaign; the names of Philonides and Amyntas have also been passed down. Aside from a few secondhand citations found in Strabo and Pliny the Elder, their written reports have unfortunately been lost: see Auberger, *Historiens d'Alexandre*, 40–61 ("Les arpenteurs").

52. Lenglet-Dufresnoy, *Méthode* (new ed.), vol. 1, chap. 2, esp. 7ff.; a selection of works devoted to the journeys and geography can be found in *Supplément de la method*, part II, 5–8.

53. Buache, "Recherches géographiques sur l'étendue de l'empire d'Alexandre," 110–123.
54. On d'Anville's archives and current research see http://danville.hypotheses .org/
55. In *Examen critique* (1804), 795.
56. D'Anville, "Mémoire de géographie ancienne," in *Œuvres de M. d'Anville*, 2:1–13.
57. De Vaugondy, *Essai sur l'histoire de la géographie*, 9–10; De Vaugondy, "Géographie," in Diderot and d'Alembert, *Encyclopédie*, 7:608–609; hereafter this encyclopedia is cited as *Encyclopédie*.
58. Rollin, *Histoire ancienne*, bk. 15.19.2 = *Ancient History*, 5:380.
59. Rollin's books on these subjects were compiled in English in a monograph: *History of Arts and Sciences of the Ancients*, 4 vols.; quote from 1:1.
60. Ibid., 4:103.
61. Ibid., 1:66.
62. Gast, *History of Greece*, 136, and n. 44; Lowth, *Isaiah*, 201ff.
63. Huet's life and work have inspired many biographies, of which there is no need to provide a hasty list here: one can instead refer to Tolmer's conventional but very well-informed and detailed *Pierre-Daniel Huet*; see 648–657 and 667–669 on the *Histoire du commerce* and related correspondence. On the Caen Academy see Lux, *Patronage*, esp. 8–16 (on Huet and Colbert's patronage); one will also find a great deal of information and reflection in the book edited by Volpilhac-Auger, *La collection Ad usum Delphini*, esp. 34–60; on Huet and sacred geography see the rich article by Massimi, "Montrer et démontrer."
64. See esp. Chap. 4 § "Montesquieu's Sources: Huet and His Contemporaries (1667–1716)."
65. Huet, *Histoire sommaire du commerce et de la navigation des Anciens, à Monsieur Colbert, Ministre d'Estat*, MS, Bibliothèque Nationale, Suppl. fr. 5307. Barring an oversight on my part, the manuscript has never been commented on. It would be interesting to do a careful study of it. Huet alludes to it in his *Memoirs*, 2:212, without mentioning Colbert's commission: "I had long ago made a commencement of a work upon a subject new to myself, though relating to a common topic—the commerce and navigation of the Ancients; and at leisure hours I had collected many facts worthy of remark, hitherto unnoticed. It was indeed, as yet, a rude and unformed mass, and written in the vernacular tongue, but by means of attention and arrangement, might rise to a work neither useless nor contemptible, provided a vacation were granted me from severer studies; and this, through the divine favour, I afterwards obtained."
66. "Thus have I given your Lordship what I have been able to remember, with my Observations and reflections concerning the History of the Commerce and Navigation of the Ancients. I might have enriched this Work with more ample and curious enquiries but you know my time is not my own, and therefore cannot attribute the disposal of it to that what I have been called to [sic], without

being guilty of some sort of robbery; or at least an infidelity which your example would continually reproach me, by seeing your constant application and indefatigable Industry for the publick welfare and to your duty" (*Histoire sommaire du commerce* MS [1667], 164 = *History of the Commerce* [1717], 265).

67. Huet, *Paradis*, 85–88 = *Paradise*, 61–62; on this see my detailed two-part study "Retour sur Alexandre" (esp. part I, 17–26 on the *Paradis terrestre* and the *Histoire du commerce*). See also "*Katarraktai* of the Tigris: Irrigation-Works, Commerce and Shipping in Elam and Babylonia from Darius to Alexander," in *Kings, Countries and Peoples*), chap. 28 (forthcoming); and Chap. 5 § "The Weight of the Model: The Aborted Debate on Cataracts."

68. Rollin, *History of the Arts and Sciences of the Ancients*, 1:60: "Great revolution in the affairs of commerce."

2. Alexander in Europe

1. See below Chap. 5 § "The Hesitations of the Chevalier de Jaucourt." Naturally scholars of Sainte-Croix's rank never cited the *Encyclopédie*.

2. On Sainte-Croix's life one can now consult Montecalvo's fundamental work, *Baron de Sainte-Croix*, vol. 2: *Biografia*. Montecalvo has provided a detailed account of the scholar's life and work (vol. 2) and edited the entire correspondence (vol. 1).

3. See Montecalvo, "Les relations intellectuelles entre Séguier et le baron de Sainte-Croix."

4. For example, Sainte-Croix, *Mémoire sur le cours de l'Araxe et du Cyrus* (1795).

5. Sainte-Croix, *De l'état et du sort des colonies des anciens peuples* (1779, translated into Italian in 1780); *Observations sur le traité de paix conclu à Paris* (1780); *Histoire des progrès de la puissance navale d'Angleterre* (1782). Boissonade published a complete bibliography of Sainte-Croix's works in his obituary in the *Journal de l'Empire* (April 6, 1809) (=Naudet, *J.-F. Boissonade critique littéraire*, 1:474–475; now see Montecalvo, *Baron de Sainte-Croix*, 1:17–27).

6. See the very precise analysis in Montecalvo, *Baron de Sainte-Croix*, 2:40–42, 46–59, 83–109, 352–379.

7. See *Examen critique* (1771), 30–31; (1804), 86.

8. See below Chap. 7 § "Sainte-Croix and the Alexander of *The Spirit of the Laws*."

9. *Magasin Encyclopédique*, An VII (1799), 7.

10. Translated into English under the title of *Travels of Anarcharsis the Younger in Greece* (6 vols., 1791).

11. Sainte-Croix, "Notice sur la vie et les ouvrages de Jean-Jacques Barthélemy," 80–81, 86; Sainte-Croix, *Éloge historique de J. J. Barthélemy*, 49, 54.

12. See Grafton, *Footnote*.

13. Goldsmith, *General History of the World*, 1:i–xvi = *Collected Works of O. Goldsmith* 5:277–289. On the *General History of the World* see below § "Alexander in England and Scotland: Manuals and Universal History."

14. See C. Seth's article, "L'Institut et les prix littéraires," esp. 124–131 on political passions sparked by the Decennial prizes (no mention of the debates on Sainte-Croix).

15. Anon., *Rapport du Jury . . . pour le jugement des Prix décennaux*, 82.

16. Chénier, "Rapport sur le grand prix de littérature 1810," and his *Tableau historique*, 115; 128–131; on the French Language and Literature Class's deliberations see also Anon., *Rapports et discussions de toutes les Classes de l'Institut de France*, 90–109.

17. Momigliano, "Ancient History and the Antiquarian" and "Gibbon's Contribution to Historical Method" (quote on 460).

18. The first volumes of the *History of Greece* were published from 1784 to 1797; the others followed at a highly irregular rate. Volume 5 (quarto), which included the entire history of Alexander, was published in 1818, when Mitford was nearing seventy-five. Born in 1744 to a family of lawyers, the young Mitford had had to interrupt his law studies at Oxford for health reasons. In 1776–1777, his poor health led him to seek rest in the area near Nice, where he met the Baron de Sainte-Croix on his property at Mormoiron; according to his own account, his host told him that only an Englishman could write a history of Greece, thanks to "a familiar acquaintance with a free constitution"; this scene is passed down by Mitford himself in vol. 5 (p. 48, n. 2). On Mitford, the account by his brother Lord Redesdale in the preface to vol 1. of the posthumous edition of 1838 is of particular interest ("A Short Account of the Author and His Pursuits in Life," ix–xliv); see also Dacier's mixed but generally positive assessment in his *Rapport historique*, 179–180.

19. See Anon., "Remarks on Mr Mitford's View of the Constitution of Macedonia, Contained in the New Volume of His History of Greece."

20. Mitford, *History of Greece*, chap. 43: "State of the Known World, More Especially of Macedonia, when Alexander, son of Philip, Succeeded to the Macedonian Throne" (5[1818]:1–89); compare with Gillies, *History of Ancient Greece*, 2:556–557 ("Liberal Spirit of the Macedonian Government"), to be read with Gillies's French translator's "philosophical perspective": *Histoire de la Grèce ancienne*, 6:122–124 n., and compared with another book by Gillies, *View of the Reign of Frederick*. On this subject see my study "Les débats sur la royauté macédonienne dans l'Europe du XVIIIᵉ siècle."

21. See Anquetil Duperron, *Discours préliminaire ou Introduction au Zend-Avesta*, in *Zend-Avesta*, vol. 1, part I, xi–xii = Deloche, Filliozat, and Filliozat, *Voyage en Inde, 1754–1762*, 79–80.

22. See Sainte-Croix, *Éloge historique de J. J. Barthélemy*, 54.

23. Anon., *Rapports et discussions de toutes les Classes de l'Institut de France*, 135–136.

24. *Examen critique* (1775), 5; see also (1804), 29.

25. See my *Alexandre des Lumières,* 153–157.

26. Sainte-Croix only cites the philosopher twice in the different versions of his *Examen critique:* aside from an explicit allusion in 1771 (p. 49 n.), a parenthetical reference in 1804 is used to contest an interpretation of the itinerary of the Ten Thousand (p. 812).

27. See also Chap. 7.

28. See Arrian, *Anabasis,* 7.28–30.

29. See, in particular, *Examen critique* (1804), 345–354.

30. See Mably, *Observations sur l'histoire de France,* bk. 2, chap. 2, with Morrissey's comments in his *L'empereur à la barbe fleurie,* 297–303. For contemporaries (like Aristotle), "the particular economy" is the domestic economy and is therefore distinct from the "public economy" (see Rousseau, "Economie ou Oeconomie," *Encyclopédie* 5:337). On this passage in Montesquieu and its relationship to an address by Diderot to Frederick of Prussia (Raynal, *Histoire de deux Indes* [1780], 5.10), see also below Chap. 10 § "Oriental Hoarding and European Circulation."

31. *Examen critique* (1775), 65–69.

32. Moyle, *Works of Walter Moyle,* 2:26–39, 64–69.

33. Gillies, *History of Ancient Greece,* 1:608–609 n. 19.

34. Sainte-Croix, *Critical Enquiry,* l:108–113. Vincent's review appeared in a typically Tory periodical, the *British Critic* 3 (1793): 510–517 and 620–629; his opinion on Sainte-Croix's Voltairian ties can be found on pp. 510–511 and 514.

35. Vincent, *Sermon,* 3: see in *Association Papers,* London, 1793, the *Publications printed by order of the Patriotic Association for liberty and property against Republicans and Levellers,* II, 1793, ii: "Short Hints upon Levelling Extracted from Dr. Vincent's Discourse on May 13, 1792," where the opening sentence is expressed in less brutal terms: "All History and all experience prove that, wherever Society exists, there must exist a class of poor"; on this text and its distribution, see the contemporary account by Robert Nares, a friend of Vincent and supporter of the association, "Life of Dr. Vincent," 191–192, and Barrell, *Spirit of Despotism,* pp. 70–72. Burke's antirevolutionary pamphlet *Reflections on the Revolution in France and on the Proceedings in Certain Societies in London relative to This Event* had been published in 1790.

36. See Sainte-Croix, *Remontrances des États du Comté Venaissin* (1784), and *Réflexions sur les États du Comtat-Venaissin* (1791). On this period in Sainte-Croix's life, one can now refer to Montecalvo's meticulous, exhaustive study, *Baron de Sainte-Croix,* 1:177–230.

37. See also Montecalvo's remarks in *Baron de Sainte-Croix,* 1:375–379.

38. See ibid., 1:334–337.

39. See *Examen critique* (1804), 558, and 562 n. 4.

40. Ibid., 541–542 n. 3.

41. On Sainte-Croix during the revolutionary and postrevolutionary periods see Montecalvo, *Baron de Sainte-Croix*, 1:237–270.

42. See the report written by Théophile-Guillaume de Sainte-Croix, *Déclaration de M. de Sainte-Croix;* regarding the events in the Comtat and Avignon see Menou, *Troisième rapport sur Avignon et le Comtat-Venaissin.*

43. See Montecalvo, *Baron de Sainte-Croix*, 1:270–413.

44. See my *Alexandre des Lumières*, 42–45.

45. In his review of *Alexandre des Lumières* Tolias considers that "this exclusion [of Italy] seems too severe. . . . Vico in his influential *Scienza Nuova* (1725) made ample references to Alexander, etc." There are indeed several references to Alexander in this work, but they are most often isolated (see Vico, *New Science* § 46, 103–104, 297); I will simply note that Vico tends to be more influenced by the Plutarchian image of Alexander as unifier of the world through the spread of the Greek language (§ 441) and by the grandiose vision attributed to him (§ 1023: "All the world was a single city of which his phalanx was the citadel," according to a phrase taken directly from Plutarch's *On the Fortune or the Virtue of Alexander*. Overall, I do not have the impression that Vico took particular interest in the figure of Alexander, nor that he contributed to the discussion in a significant manner (the passages on Alexander are not cited in P. Girard's recent book, *Giambattista Vico*), but it is also likely that specific and exhaustive research on the Italian literature of the era (which I did not undertake) would yield much richer findings.

46. See Denina, *Istoria politica e letteraria*, 3:236–242. On the author see the biobibliographic note by Barbier in the *Magasin Encyclopédique* dated January 1814; on Barbier see Brot, "Bibliothèque idéale."

47. I am not aware of any work that provides an analytical and synthetic treatment of Greek history in eighteenth-century England or Scotland: Clarke's treatment (*Greek Studies in England*, 102–111) is extremely basic; critical biographies of most of the British authors mentioned in this chapter are lacking, including of Rennell, Gillies, Vincent, and even Robertson.

48. See *Göttingische Anzeigen von gelehrten Sachen* (1779): 773–776; on the "other" Robertson see particularly Ceserani's article, "Narrative, Interpretation and Plagiarism."

49. On the *Universal History* and its European versions, see the studies by Abbatista and G. Ricuperati cited in the Bibliography.

50. The full account of the conquest is in *Universal History*, 8:494–660.

51. The history of Alexander is in ibid., 3:273–315.

52. Sainte-Croix, *Critical Enquiry*, preface; Mitford, *History of Greece*, 5:231 n. 2. References to Sainte-Croix: one in Robertson, *Historical Disquisition;* five in Gillies, *History of Ancient Greece;* eleven in Vincent, *Voyage of Nearchus;* the book is also cited by Gibbon, *Decline and Fall*, vol. 2, chaps. 26 and 51.

53. See Sebastiani's recent volume, *Scottish Enlightenment*, in which Robertson is often mentioned.
54. Quoted by Gleig in "Life of Dr Robertson," 1:xxxvii.
55. Biographical information in ibid., v–lxxix, and in Buchon, *Œuvres complètes* 1:i–vi (with quotes from several interesting letters between Walpole, Hume, Gibbon, and Voltaire). His work inspired the very important volume edited by Stuart J. Brown, *William Robertson and the Expansion of the Empire*, which includes a bibliography for 1755–1996 (Smitten, "Bibliography"). One of the most illuminating studies remains that by K. O'Brien, *Narratives of Enlightenment*, esp. 92–128 ("William Robertson to the Rescue of Scottish History"), and 129–165 ("Robertson on the Triumph of Europe and Its Empires").
56. Robertson, *History of America*, vol. 1 nn. 2–6 (at the end of the volume). Mably, who had not read the book, denounced this account as no more than a useless display of erudition (*Manière d'écrire l'histoire*=*Œuvres completes*, 12:460–461).
57. Robertson, *Historical Disquisition*, 2–44, and the final section ("Notes and Illustrations", 192–213). This book has recently been studied from different perspectives by G. Carnall ("Contemporary Images of India"), myself ("Alexander the Great and the Enlightenment"), and Brown (*"Historical Disquisition"*).
58. On the Scots' position in the empire see, in particular, Bryant, "Scots in India," and Devine, *Scotland's Empire*, 250–270 ("Colonizing the Indian Empire"); see also the articles by McGilvary, "Scottish Connection with India 1725–1833," and Vaughan, "Un empire écossais?"; on Robertson's knowledge of India see Brown, "William Robertson, Early Orientalism and the *Historical Disquisition* on India of 1791," 295–300; on Robertson's nephews and sons in India see Smitten, "Robertson's Letters and the Life of Writing," 50–53.
59. There is no critical biography of Gillies. On his body of work see the Bibliography, and my "Theme of 'Persian Decadence.'" Gillies is frequently mentioned in C. R. Markham's *Major James Rennell*.
60. On this character see the monograph by Lemny, *Jean-Louis Carra*, esp. 128–133 (on Gillies's translation); see also Constant, *Essai sur les mœurs*.
61. Gillies, *History of Ancient Greece*, 2:674 n. 49.
62. Ibid., vol. 1, preface.
63. See Anon., *Public Characters of 1800–1801*, 179–189: "In the second part of that work, he will probably pursue the history of the Greeks through their foreign conquests, their colonial settlements, their dispersions, their subjugation to the power of strangers, their intercourse with other nations, the reciprocal influences of their transactions on the rest of the world, and of the rest of the world on them, even downward, almost to the present times" (188).
64. The first edition had been published in 1793–1796 and was immediately translated into French.
65. Bernoulli collected in a single book (in three quarto volumes) three translated essays: the first written in Latin by Father Tieffenthaler (a missionary in India)

and entitled *Descriptio Indiae;* the second written in French by Anquetil Duperron (*Recherches historiques et géographiques sur l'Inde*); and the third written in
English by Rennell (*Memoir of Map of Hindoustan*). He translated the essays into
German and French and published them in Berlin. The German and French
versions' title includes a shared introductory subtitle: *Description historique et
géographique de l'Inde / Historisch-geographische Beschreibung von Hindustan.* In
both languages, Bernoulli's translation of Rennell's *Memoir* is in vol. 3 (*La carte
générale de l'Inde / General-Charte von Indien*).

66. On the life and work of Rennell one can consult the dated but useful biography
by Markham (*Major James Rennell*): see 30–64 on his stay in India and his return
to London; 65–81 on his place in the history of geography; 82–99 on his work on
India; 83–122 on his work on Herodotus (*Geographical System of Herodotus*); 122–
145 on his research on the geography of Africa (which I will not discuss here);
and 145–170 on his work on hydrography (research on marine currents). On
d'Anville's "Indian" research as discussed by Rennell see, in particular, *Éclaircissements géographiques;* "Recherches géographiques"; and *Antiquité géographique
de l'Inde.*

67. See Rennell, *Memoir*, II, pp. 31–153, 200–237, 248–249; III, 224, etc.

68. I must report that I have found no trace of this sentence in Gillies, in which "the
voyage of Nearchus" is addressed in only a few lines (*History of Ancient Greece*,
2:655).

69. There are two entries on Vincent in *The General Dictionary containing an historical and critical account of the Lives and Writings of the most eminent persons*, XXX,
London, 1816, pp. 371–387, and in J. P. Neale (illustrated by—), *The History and
Antiquities of the Abbey Church of St. Peter, Westminster*, I, London, 1818, pp. 219–
226; both contributions are based on the best informed article (which has never
been superseded), "The Life of Dr Vincent" by Robert Nares. Several pertinent
studies can be found in Marcotte, *D'Arrien à William Vincent*, particularly a
few interesting biographical details in Buccianti's article "Annotazioni
manoscritte."

70. See above § "The History of Alexander in the Revolution."

71. Montesquieu was already convinced that the book was not by Arrian: see
Volpilhac-Auger, *Atelier de Montesquieu*, 212.

72. Vincent wrote these notes by hand on his personal copy (on this, see Bucciantini, "Annotazioni manoscritte"); a synoptic study with another copy annotated
by Vincent at a later date and currently in the collection of the Bibliothèque
Nationale would be of the highest interest (on the latter copy see Chap. 7 § "Alexander, Promoter of Commerce").

73. Vincent, *Voyage of Nearchus*, 505; see below Chap. 5 § "The Weight of the Model:
The Aborted Debate on the Cataracts."

74. See, in particular, "Major Rennell," in Anon., *Public Characters of 1803–1804*,
514–516.

75. On the French translation see below Chap. 7 § "Alexander, Promoter of Commerce"; on plan(s) for a German translation see Chap. 8 § "Geography, Voyages, and Alexander's Conquests: Translations and Original Studies."

76. On the authors mentioned below see, in particular, Chap. 8, which features analyses and biobibliographical notes.

77. This project is discussed in an exchange of letters between Wolf and Heyne dated from February 24 to March 25, 1784; instead, Heyne pointed Wolf to Sainte-Croix's work on the mysteries of paganism: see Montecalvo, *Baron de Sainte-Croix*, 1:205.

78. On the major figures of Göttingen see Marino, *I maestri della Germania* and his *Praeceptores Germaniae*, as well as Bödeker, Büttgen, and Espagne, *Göttingen vers 1800*; on Heeren, see Becker-Schaum, *Arnold Herrmann Ludwig Heeren* and Muhlack, "De la philologie à l'histoire politique"; on Heyne see Fornaro, "Lo 'Studio degli Antichi'"; "I Greci Barbari di Ch.-G. Heyne"; *I Greci senza lumi;* and "Christian Gottlob Heyne"; and Heidenreich, *Christian Gottlob Heyne*.

79. Aside from Chap. 8, see Chap. 10 § "Oriental Hoarding and European Circulation."

80. An English translation of the lesson is available in *History and Theory* 11 (1972): 321–334.

81. See, for example, Gatterer's *Handbuch der Universalhistorie; Abriß dere Universalhistorie; Weltgeschichte;* and *Versuch einer allgemeinen Weltgeschichte;* Beck's *Anleitung zur genauer Kenntniss;* Schlözer's *Vorstellung seiner Universal-historie;* Schlosser's *Histoire universelle*, etc. See Laudin, "L'histoire comme science de l'homme chez Gatterer et Schlözer."

82. See Baumgarten, preface to *Uebersetzung der Allgemeinen Welthistorie*, vol. 7 (on Alexander, see 7:229–381); Heyne himself participated in the translation-adaptation of the *History of the World* by Guthrie and Gray: *Allgemeine Weltgeschichte*, vol. 16: see Heidenreich, *Christian Gottlob Heyne*, 149–170 (see the review in the *Allgemeine historische Bibliothek* (1767): 233–242—certainly written by Gatterer).

83. See Chap. 10 § "The First European."

84. This was the *Göttingische gelehrte Anzeigen*, known as the *Göttingische Anzeigen von gelehrten Sachen* from 1752 to 1802; it was founded in 1739 under the name of *Göttingische Zeitungen von gelehrten Sachen*. All of the journals published in Göttingen and elsewhere are available digitally on the *Göttinger Digitalisierungszentrum*'s website (http://gdz.sub.uni-goettingen.de/gdz/).

85. Laudin, "Les enjeux allemands de la réception des ouvrages historiques français" (quote on 181); see also (on universal histories) Laudin, "De la *magistra vitae* au tribunal de l'Histoire" (which specifically and extensively discusses Gatterer). On this subject see also N. Waszek's specific study "L'impact des Lumières écossaises … à travers l'exemple des *Göttingische gelehrte Anzeigen*."

86. Schmieder, *Arriani Historia Indica,* xi–xii; see Chap. 8 § "Geography, Voyages, and Alexander's Conquests: Translations and Original Studies."

3. War, Reason, and Civilization

1. Bulwer-Lytton, *Athens: Its Rise and Fall;* I have used the 2004 edition, edited with commentary by Oswyn Murray (see esp. 1–35, 527–532); see also his article "L'invention d'une Athènes romantique et radical" and Demetriou's passages in *George Grote,* 47–51.
2. *Siècle d'Alexandre* (1762), 47; (1769), 97.
3. Schlözer and Schröckh, *Histoire universelle,* 1:245–246.
4. Rollin, *Ancient History,* 5:361–382: The Judgment We Are to Form of Alexander."
5. Montaigne, *Essays,* 3:165; on Montaigne's Alexander see Kupisz, "Alexandre le Grand dans les *Essais* de Montaigne"; and Lombard, "Vieillesse de l'écrivain, jeunesse du conquérant." The figures used by Montaigne and the eighteenth-century authors (particularly C. de Pauw) in discussing the extent of the massacres perpetrated during the Spanish conquest are the subject of illuminating remarks by Michèle Duchet in her *Anthropologie et histoire au siècle des Lumières,* 194–199.
6. "Caesar," in Bayle, *Dictionary Historical and Critical,* n. D; the figure was repeated by *Siècle d'Alexandre* (1762), 2; (1769), 8.
7. "Macedonia, Alexander of," in Bayle, *Dictionary Historical and Critical,* n. L.
8. Abbt, *Vom Verdienste,* 222.
9. Gatterer, *Handbuch der Universalhistorie,* 653–654, with Laudin's remarks in "Les grands hommes de l'Antiquité."
10. See Bossuet, *Politics,* bk. 10, article 1, 3rd proposition: "The first source of such riches is commerce and navigation."
11. See Rollin, *Ancient History,* 5:362.
12. Sainte-Croix, *De l'état et du sort des anciennes colonies,* 231–232.
13. In Raynal, *Histoire des Deux Indes* (1780), 1.xxiv (on Diderot's probable contribution see 2010 ed., pp. 132 n. 536 and 754 §12).
14. Carra, *Essai particulier de politique,* v–vi.
15. Bacon, *Essays,* no. 29, p. 84; see the *Monthly Review, or, Literary Journal* 79 (1788): 673.
16. See Raynal, *Histoire des deux-Indes* (1780), 5.9–10. On Diderot's criticism of the figure of the enlightened despot see Goggi, *Diderot,* 43–49, 117–120, 189–190.
17. The abbé considered that Alexander should be excluded from this category because his conquests were not guided by the "public interest." Voltaire's point of view has often been studied: see, in particular, Rihs, *Voltaire,* 150–162; Inverson, "La guerre, le grand homme et l'histoire selon Voltaire"; as a mere

patchwork of quotes, Christodoulou's "Alexandre le Grand chez Voltaire" is unfortunately very disappointing.

18. Letter 12, "On the Lord Bacon," in Voltaire, *Letters concerning the English Nation*, 71–72.

19. Trans. *Works of Voltaire*, 20:172.

20. *Dictionnaire universel du commerce* (1741), 1:ix.

21. Huet, *Histoire du commerce*, 242–243; also see his 1667 manuscript, *Histoire sommaire du commerce*, 91–92.

22. Trans. *Works of Voltaire*, 35:102.

23. See my study "Des Scythes aux Tartares."

24. The ensuing translations are from Montesquieu, *Spirit of the Laws*.

25. Folard, *Histoire de Polybe*, 1:iii; on the topos of the good and bad courtier, see my *Darius in the Shadow of Alexander*, chap. 7.

26. Folard, *Histoire de Polybe*, 5:281–284.

27. See my detailed analysis in "Montesquieu and His Sources," in *Kings, Countries and Peoples*, chap. 14 (forthcoming).

28. In both of the following examples Montesquieu contests the views expressed by Huet in his *Histoire du commerce*, though he does not mention him by name.

29. On this model see Sabatier, *Versailles ou la figure du roi*, 334–397, and a few reflections in my *Darius in the Shadow of Alexander*, chap. 12 § "From Parmenio to Richelieu."

30. See Volpilhac-Auger's remark in *Œuvres complètes de Montesquieu*, vol. 4 (*De l'esprit des Lois. Brouillons II*), 524–525, 531 (on Huet) and my own comments in *Œuvres complètes de Montesquieu*, vol. 17.

31. With the exception of an interpolated clause in *Spirit of the Laws* (30.25), in the polemic against the Abbé Dubos.

32. See Mably, *Observations sur l'histoire de la Grèce*, 219–220, which explicitly takes position against *Spirit of the Laws*.

33. *Siècle d'Alexandre* (1762), 140–141; (1769), 194–195; the author added an (exceedingly rare) documentary note in the 1769 edition (p. 195 n. 1): "In the enumeration of Darius's troops, Arrian always includes Indians, he even distinguishes those from the mountains and those from the plains."

34. *Siècle d'Alexandre* (1762): 141, 151; (1769): 195–196, 206.

35. The few pages in the 1762 edition (199–124) are given a separate chapter in the 1769 edition: "Voyage d'Alexandre au temple de Jupiter Ammon. S'il est aussi ridicule ou aussi imprudent que les historiens l'ont cru" "Alexander's Journey to the Temple of Jupiter Amon: Whether It Is as Ridiculous or Imprudent as the Historians Have Believed"] (172–178).

36. I have primarily used the most recent and most up-to-date edition, edited by J.-P. Schandeler and P. Crépel with the assistance of numerous collaborators. The "Quatrième époque" of the *Esquisse ou Prospectus* (1793) is on pp. 277–292

and the "Élément de la Quatrième époque" of the *Éléments du Tableau historique* (1793–1794) is on pp. 585–802; on Alexander see pp. 675–679.

37. See Condorcet, *Mémoires sur l'Instruction publique*, as quoted in the Schandeler and Crépel edition, p. 29.

38. *Edinburgh Review* (1755): 1–8; see D. Francesconi's judicious comments in "William Robertson on Historical Causation."

39. See Robertson, *Historical Disquisition*, 12–31.

40. Harris, *Navigantium atque itinerantium Bibliotheca*, 1:390–409 (quote on 390).

41. Gillies, *History of Ancient Greece*, 2:630–631, 658–681.

42. See Gillies, *History of the World*, 1:2–7, 178–199.

43. Gillies, *View of the Reign of Frederick of Prussia*. Unless stated otherwise, quotes are from the first part: *The Parallel of Frederick II of Prussia with Philip II of Macedon* (pp. 1–60).

44. Heyne, Review of Gillies; Anon., Review of Gillies (*Monthly Review, or, Literary Journal*) (quote); Anon., Review of Gillies (*Critical Review, or, Annals of Literature*); Gillies, *Vergleichung zwischen Friedrich dem Zweiten und Philipp, dem Könige von Macedonien*, 53–60. A friend of Immanuel Kant (to whom he dedicated a book on ethics in 1798) and Friedrich August Wolf (with whom he corresponded: see Markner and Veltri, *Friedrich August Wolf*, 76–101), Garve had an excellent command of English and English literature; he translated several books by English and Scottish philosophers such as Adam Smith and Adam Ferguson. This dual proficiency certainly inspired him to make Gillies's book available to his compatriots, though he only translated the first part (*Vergleichung*, 1–53); he reiterated his disagreement with Gillies in a book devoted to Frederick (*Fragmente zur Schilderung*, 1:7). Based on the rarity of the book in German libraries, the fact that is not among the books inventoried in the *Göttingische Anzeigen von gelehrten Sachen*, and S. A. Thomas's surprising oversight (*Makedonien und Preußen*, 10), Garve's translation had little success, including in Germany: see my article "Philipp II" On Garve's work, see the *Lexicon deutscher Dichter und Prosaisten*, II, 1807, pp. 9–39, and *Deutscher Ehren-Temple* (W. Hennings, ed.), 6, 1824, pp. 128–142.

45. See my *Alexandre des Lumières*, 227–233.

46. *Siècle d'Alexandre* (1762), 90; (1769), 144.

47. See Thomas, *Makedonien und Preußen*, 49–90; Carra's translator's note in Gillies, *Histoire de la Grèce* 6:122–123; and my studies "Les débats sur la royauté macédonienne dans l'Europe du XVIIIᵉ siècle" and "Philipp II."

48. *Siècle d'Alexandre* (1762), 144–145; (1769), 198–199.

49. Bougainville, *Parallèle de l'expédition d'Alexandre dans les Indes avec la conquête des mêmes contrées par Tahmas-Kouli-Khan*, 1752, 132–133.

50. Voltaire, *Political Writings*, 153. Voltaire states the number of citizens of Vannes put to death by Caesar as 600 in one text and 2,000 in the other. The second figure is probably due to a mix-up with the number of Tyrians tortured.

51. *Siècle d'Alexandre* (1762), 167–168. The passage was stricken from the 1769 edition, in which the author attempts to rehabilitate "despotic" states.
52. *Siècle d'Alexandre* (1762), 6, 8.
53. Voltaire, *Essai sur les mœurs*, intro., chap. 14.
54. Montesquieu, *My Thoughts*.
55. On the law of war in Montesquieu see J. Terrel's dense analyses in "À propos de la conquête."
56. See, in particular, Bossuet, *Politics*, bk. 2, article 2, 2nd proposition: "To make the right of conquest incontestable, peaceable possession must be added."
57. See Chap. 4 §§ "How to Cement an Empire" and "Conquest and Civilization."

4. A Successful Conquest

1. *Siècle d'Alexandre* (1762), 154–155; (1769), 208–210.
2. On this point see Chap. 10 § "Oriental Hoarding and European Circulation."
3. See Chap. 5 § "The Weight of the Model: The Aborted Debate on Cataracts."
4. See Chap. 3.
5. On India seen by Montesquieu see also R. Minuti's recent article "L'inde dans l'œuvre de Montesquieu."
6. Regarding the manuscripts and history of the writing of bk. 21, see Volpilhac-Auger's analysis in *Œuvres complètes de Montesquieu*, 4:519–572. I must also note that it is out of the question to exhaustively and analytically summarize the considerable bibliography on bk. 21 here: see the recent studies by Larrère, "Montesquieu et l'histoire du commerce"; Spector, *Montesquieu et l'émergence de l'économie politique*, esp. 399–445; and Platania, "Dynamiques des empires et dynamiques du commerce."
7. See Chap. 1 § "Between Divine Providence, Sacred Geography, and History of Commerce." Quotes are from the 1717 edition (*Commerce and Navigation*). Researchers have found Montesquieu and / or his secretary's notes on Huet's book: on this see my comments in *Œuvres complètes de Montesquieu*, vol. 17 (forthcoming).
8. In the 1667 manuscript, an initial (crossed-out) version of the address to Colbert sounded even more concerned, even anxious; Huet hoped that the minister would be "satisfied with a light and superficial exposition."
9. I quote the English edition published in 1695.
10. Dessert and Journet, "Le lobby Colbert," 1312–1316.
11. On this point, see Chapelain's correspondence with Colbert, in which the former states that the book's presence at the Frankfurt fair will reach a vast audience (*Lettres, instructions et mémoires de Colbert*, 2.2, 588–589, 604–609).
12. A parallel can be drawn between Huet's *Histoire du commerce* and a book published in Paris in 1740, *Traité des finances et de la fausse monnaie des Romains*, etc.

which originated from a report given to Colbert by the author Chassipol: see vol. 17 of *Œuvres complètes de Montesquieu* (forthcoming).

13. On Huet and mercantilism see, in particular, Roberto, "'Del commercio del Romani'" and his analysis (pp. 354–361) of Mengotti, *Del commercio dei Romani* (1787). As for the theory that Huet was active in an "agrarian" pressure group with Fleury and Fénelon (a theory developed by Rothkrug, *Opposition,* 275–285, which never refers to the *Histoire du commerce*), it is based on the (highly debatable) assumption that Huet was the author of the *Grand trésor historique et politique des Hollandais dans tous les états et empires du monde* (1712), translated into English from the French 2nd ed. in 1719. To cite only one significant example, Huet's name is never mentioned in C. Larrère's book, *L'invention de l'économie,* including in her analysis of Rothkrug's theories (96–99, 174–176).

14. Quote from Larrère, "Montesquieu et l'histoire du commerce" (p. 322), with which I disagree; it seems to me that the author has made too hasty a reading of Huet's preface, in which such a project is never mentioned.

15. Tolmer, *Pierre-Daniel Huet,* 648 (written without any knowledge of the 1667 report).

16. Huet, *Mémoires=Memoirs,* 2:212.

17. The first number in citations from Huet's manuscript and the *Histoire du commerce* refers to the chapter; the second to the paragraph; titles for paragraphs (or chapter subsections) were already included in the margins of the 1667 manuscript.

18. Quoted from the English translation by R. Van Deman Magoffin (1916).

19. As can also be seen in Friedrich S. Bock's book, *Versuch einer vollständigen Natur und Handlungsgeschichte der Heringe,* Könisgberg, 1769.

20. On the context of the French-English-Dutch debate see the recent book by C.-E. Levillain, *Vaincre Louis XIV,* 42–58.

21. Locke, *History of Navigation,* 365–366; Alexander is referred to as "the founder of the Grecian empire," as was already the case in Samuel Clarke in 1665.

22. Huet, *Commerce and Navigation,* 7.1 ("for long before the time of Alexander, the Egyptians and the Phoenicians had sailed to the Indies"); 11.1 (the Persians' conduct before Alexander); 12.1 ("Persians before Alexander's time"); 13.1 (Arabs before Alexander); 15.1 ("Commerce of the Carthaginians before Alexander"); 16.1 ("Commerce of the Greeks before Alexander").

23. This is reminiscent of what Voltaire wrote in his "Préface historique et critique" to the *Histoire de Russie,* directing his barbs at Rousseau (*Œuvres complètes en ligne,* 46:383–384 and n. 5).

24. Huet was convinced that along with the Phoenicians the Egyptians had been in very ancient times "the most ancient navigators, [and that they] drove a considerable commerce with the Indians" (7.1–2).

25. See Arrian, *Anabasis,* 7.8.7: "During this voyage upstream he removed the weirs (*katarraktai*) in the river and made the stream level throughout; these weirs

had been made by the Persians to prevent anyone sailing up to their country overpowering it by a naval force. All this had been contrived by the Persians, inexpert as they were in maritime matters (*ou nautikoi*); and so these weirs, built up at frequent intervals, made the voyage up the Tigris very difficult. Alexander, however, said that contrivances (*sophismata*) of this kind belonged to those who had no military supremacy; he therefore regarded these safeguards as of no value to himself, and indeed proved them not worth the mention by destroying with ease these labours of the Persians"; see also Strabo (*Geography*, 16.1.9): "Now the Persians (*hoi men oun Persai*), wishing on purpose to prevent voyaging on these rivers for fear of attacks from without (*exothen*), had constructed artificial cataracts (*kateskeuakeisan kataraktas kheiropoietous*), but Alexander (*ho de Alexandros*), when he went against them, destroyed as many of them as he could, and in particular those at Opis."

26. Arc de Sainte-Foix, *Histoire du commerce et de la navigation,* 1:160.

27. Far from being permanent defensive dams against an invasion from the Persian Gulf, these were light, temporary structures that were destroyed by the administration every year during the high tides period; they allowed for fields to be irrigated during low tide; they temporarily hindered navigation but did not prevent it. These observations dash the theory initially suggested by Huet and repeated by nearly all his successors, according to which the Persians had banned all maritime and fluvial commerce: see my demonstration in "Retour sur Alexandre" (parts I and II); *Alexander the Great,* 89–93; and "*Katarraktai* of the Tigris: Irrigation-Works, Commerce and Shipping in Elam and Babylonia from Darius to Alexander," in *Kings, Countries and Peoples*, chap. 28 (forthcoming).

28. See his *Huetania* § 110: "Comparaison d'Alexandre, d'Annibal, de Scipion et de César"; in the same volume (§ 63), Huet hails the importance of the founding of Alexandria, displaying no concern for consistency, given the extent to which the two images coexist: "When Alexander ruined Tyre and built Alexandria, he did not only seek to punish the Tyrians, but also realized a project based on very wise policy."

29. Written in the same period (1671–1672), François Bernier's *Travels in the Mogul Empire* includes a "Letter to Monseigneur Colbert, concerning the extent of Hindoustan, the currency towards, and final absorption of gold and silver in that country, its resources, armies, the administration of justice, and the principal cause of the decline of the States of Asia" (improved English edition, 1891, 200–238).

30. Lucas, *Voyages de Paul Lucas fait en MDCCXIV etc. par ordre de Louis XIV dans la Turquie, l'Asie, Sourie, Palestine, Haute et Basse-Egypte,* 3: 169–170.

31. Rollin, *History of Arts and Sciences of the Ancients,* 1:50, 53, 60.

32. See the "list of artists who flourished in this century" in Voltaire, *Le siècle de Louis XIV.*

33. Voltaire, *Conseils à un journaliste sur la philosophie, l'histoire, le théâtre*. Voltaire tirelessly repeated more or less rounded-out versions of this remark until 1776 (*Bible enfin expliquée*). Note that there is no mention of Iskenderun in Huet's book.

34. This text will be published in vol. 17 of the *Œuvres complètes de Montesquieu* (forthcoming), with my commentary; see Volpilhac-Auger, "Alexandre et l'impérialisme grec," 61.

35. See the edition with commentary by Françoise Weil and Catherine Larrère in *Œuvres complètes de Montesquieu*, 2:319–364.

36. Arrian, *Anabasis*, 7.28.3; Montesquieu's use of the passage was strongly decried by Sainte-Croix: see Chap. 7 § "Sainte-Croix and the Alexander of *The Spirit of the Laws*."

37. The fifth French edition was translated into English under the title *Critical Reflections on Poetry, Painting and Music, etc.*, 3 volumes, London, J. Nourse, 1748.

38. Montesquieu, *The Spirit of the Laws*, XXX.24.

39. On the very French context of the Montesquieu-Dubos debate see Nicolet, *Fabrique d'une nation*, 56–96, esp. 89–96.

40. See 10.14: "After the conquest, he abandoned all the prejudices that had served him to execute it," namely the advice he had received from Aristotle "to treat the Greeks like masters and the Persians like slaves" (at this point, Montesquieu refers to Plutarch's *On the Fortune or the Virtue of Alexander* in a note).

41. Montesquieu, *The Spirit of the Laws*, X.14.

42. Arrian mentions that when they followed the coast to the north, toward Persia, "for the first time the Greeks saw cultivated trees and men who lived there not entirely like wild animals" (*Indica*, 27.2). A little further along, a village's inhabitants bring "gifts of hospitality (*xenia*)" to the coastline for them, namely "tuna cooked in a pie dish . . . a few cakes and fruits of the date palm. . . . These are the last of the Ichthyophagi, and they are the first that the Greeks saw cooking their food."

43. I have primarily drawn from the studies (which I cite in the body of the text) by G. Goggi, "Le mot civilisation et ses domaines d'application, 1757 à 1760," and R. Monnier, "Usages d'un couple d'antonymes," but also the studies collected by B. Binoche in *Les équivoques de la civilisation*; on the word in the context of French missions in America in the eighteenth century see Havard, "'Les forcer à devenir cytoyens,'" esp. 994–997. On Alexander, my commentary qualifies the opinion expressed by Volpilhac-Auger ("Montesquieu et l'impérialisme grec," n. 12), according to which "Montesquieu does not take much interest in the 'civilizing' aspect of the Hellenic conquest, unlike Voltaire."

44. Lacombe de Prézel, *Progrès du commerce*, 12; on all these issues see also my treatment in *État et pasteurs au Moyen-Orient ancien*, 25–30.

45. Montesquieu referred to Strabo in a note. Drawing on information supplied by Onesicritus (one of Alexander's companion-witnesses), Strabo (11.11.3) had

reported these "disconcerting mores: the men, due to their old age, were thrown to dogs specially raised for this, which were called 'gravediggers' in the country's language. . . . Alexander is said to have put an end to this custom." The passage merits a brief explanation. The ancient authors (Strabo is not the only one allude to it) were referring to the funeral rites of Central Asia (without always being perfectly aware that they were doing so or perfectly understanding these rites); here, excarnation was practiced rather than inhumation; to this end, the dead were left in "towers of silence" in which animals ate their flesh; the bones were then piously gathered and left in ossuaries.

5. Affirming and Contesting the Model

1. See, for example, Arc de Sainte-Foix, *Histoire du commerce et de la navigation* (the "Preliminary Address" includes an interesting response to the difficulties of reading and understanding *The Spirit of the Laws*; the Persians are discussed in chap. 6; the Macedonians in chap. 13 of vol. 2); Lacombe de Prézel, *Les progrès du commerce*; Schlözer, *Versuch einer allgemeinen Geschichte*; Schmidt, *De commerciis et navigationibus Ptolemaerum*; Ameilhon, *Histoire du commerce et de la navigation*; Eichhorn, *Geschichte des ostindischen Handels vor Mohammed*; Robertson, *Historical Disquisition*; Berghaus, *Geschichte der Schiffahrtskunde*; Vincent, *Voyage of Nearchus*; see also Jullien du Ruet, *Tableau chronologique*; Malouet, *Considérations historiques* (no mention of Alexander), and Heeren's numerous studies on antique commerce (see below Chap. 8). I note in passing that Alexander is also mentioned in histories of the navy, such as the one by Boismêlé, *Histoire générale de la marine, contenant son origine chez tous les peuples du monde* [*General history of the navy containing its origin among all the peoples of the world*], I, 1744, pp. 133–145.

2. D'Alembert|Mallet, "Navigation," *Encyclopédie* 11:54; see also Anon., "Memoirs of Navigation and Commerce since the Earliest Periods", *Naval Chronicle* (January–July 1789), 177–195 (which primarily deals with Carthage), and MacPherson, *Annals of Commerce*, 1:71–75.

3. Schlözer, *Versuch*, 40, 84 (the author is somewhat critical of Huet [11–12] but draws on him abundantly; he cites the 1748 edition of *The Spirit of the Laws*); Schmidt, *De commerciis et navigationibus*, 174–176 n., he also quotes Huet at length (265–266).

4. Ameilhon, *Commerce et navigation des Égyptiens*, 6 n. c, 40–50, 187 (on the populations of the Gulf).

5. The *Tableau chronologique* is an enormous quarto over nine hundred pages long, full of endless cumulative, erudite notes that often nearly fill the page; the author acknowledges the help he received from Letronne, "M. Mentelle's student," everything concerning Alexander's marches and itineraries. There are many

discussions of Alexander throughout the entire book (see index, xxxv–xxxviii). The author himself is not well known and to my knowledge has never been the subject of a biographical sketch (see also Chap. 7 § "Alexander, Promoter of Commerce"). The author has read a great deal, but often too hastily; see, for example, pp. 499–500, where, in discussing Alexandria, he refers to Vincent but is in reality paraphrasing Huet, and where he criticizes Montesquieu for misunderstanding Alexander's policy, which is presented as follows in the index: "M. has doubts about Alexander's commercial policy."

6. See Chap. 2 § "Alexander in England and Scotland: Manuals and Universal History."

7. On Robertson, India's commerce, and the cataracts see my "Alexander the Great and the Enlightenment" and "Retour sur Alexandre," part I, 35–41; Robertson was alone in repeating the theories Montesquieu suggested to explain the Persians' aversion for the waters of the rivers and seas, which he considered to be due to a religious taboo: see Robertson, *Recherches historiques sur l'Inde ancienne,* 1:516 and 575 n. 9 (refers directly to Hyde, without citing Montesquieu). The only place this explanation is later found is in an essay by an author who had read Robertson, J.-M. Le Père, "Mémoire sur la communication des mers des Indes à la Méditerranée."

8. Bourlet de Vauxcelles, Review of Vincent, *Voyage de Néarque,* 123. The review appeared in *Paris dans l'année,* an antirevolutionary journal published in London beginning in 1795 under the direction of Jean-Gabriel Peltier: see his editorial in *Paris dans l'année* (1795): 3–40. I note in passing that Vincent cites the 1748 edition of *The Spirit of the Laws:* see p. 6 n. d, on Alexandria.

9. On the French translation see Chap. 7 § "Alexander, Promoter of Commerce"; on translation projects in Germany see Chap. 8 § "Geography, Voyages, and Alexander's Conquests: Translations and Original Studies."

10. This first part of the article is sometimes attributed to Diderot. If this were the case, the philosopher's statements subsequent to the *Histoire des Deux-Indes* would indicate a complete change of mind (see below § "Diderot, the *Histoire des deux Indes,* and Alexander's Conquests"): while an evolution of the sort is not out of the question, some of Diderot's subsequent judgments regarding Alexander are not particularly laudatory (see, for example, *Encyclopédie* 2:800: "Alexander [made himself] famous . . . by ravaging Asia").

11. Amyot, *Œuvres morales et meslées,* 1:307. The English translation below is taken from F. C. Babbit in the Loeb Classical Library (*Plutarch's Moralia,* 4 [1936]).

12. "Étranger," 6:71; also "Hospitalité," 8:315.

13. *Siècle d'Alexandre* (1762), 165–168; (1769), 218–220.

14. *Siècle d'Alexandre* (1762); this passage was excised from the 1769 edition (p. 220).

15. Robertson, *Historical Disquisition,* 25–26; Gillies, *History of Ancient Greece,* 2:660–661, 670.

16. On this see my very detailed study in "Retour sur Alexandre" (parts I and II), in which I introduce and analyze the pertinent European literature from c. 1580 to 2007, and to which I refer the reader for the details of my demonstration; see particularly part I, 41–56 ("Témoignages textuels, récits de voyage et expertise géographique "), and part II, 161–171 ("Défense du territoire et irrigation des terres: suite et reprise du débat"); on the religious explanation provided by Montesquieu, see part I, 29–31 and 38–39 (Robertson); see a partial English translation in "The *Katarraktai* of the Tigris: Irrigation-Works, Commerce and Shipping in Elam and Babylonia from Darius to Alexander," in *Kings, Countries and Peoples,* chap. 28 (forthcoming).

17. Carsten Niebuhr, *Reisenbeschreibung,* 2:37 = *Voyage,* p. 307 and n.; on Niebuhr (1733–1815) see his *Éloge* published in *Histoire et mémoires de l'Institut royal de France. Académie des Inscriptions et Belles-Lettres* [*History and memoirs of the Royal Institute of France*], VII, 1804, p. 160–174, and the studies collected by J. Wiesehöfer and S. Conermann in *Carsten Niebuhr und seine Zeit* (see also my "Retour sur Alexandre," part I, 44–46); see also the recent book by L. J. Baack, 2014.

18. Gillies, *History of Ancient Greece,* 2:658; Gillies, *History of the World,* 1:192–193 nn.

19. Mannert, *Geographie,* 5:367–375. See Heeren's statements in the *Commentationes Societatis Regiae Scientiarum Gottingensis recentiores* in 1791 and 1793 ("Commentatio de Graecorum de India notitia"), his review of Robertson in *Bibliothek der alten Litteratur und Kunst,* and his review of Vincent in *Göttingische Anzeigen von gelehrten Sachen* (see my "Retour sur Alexandre," part II, 48–49, 53–56); see also below Chap. 8 § "Alexander the Great in Heeren and Schlosser."

20. Gillies, *History of the World,* 1:193–194.

21. Heeren, "De Graecorum de India noticia" (1793), 71.

22. *Examen critique* (1804), 538–540; Rollin, *Ancient History,* 5:353.

23. Williams, *Life and Actions of Alexander the Great,* 349–352; see also his *Two Essays on the Geography of Ancient Asia,* 27–28 (in which he essentially deals with locating the city of Opis); Chesney, *Expedition,* 2:362; on both see my "Retour sur Alexandre," part I, 50–52, and part II, 163–169.

24. Rollin sidesteps the problem. Sainte-Croix only briefly refers to the question in *Examen critique* (1775), 293, but does not take a position; while Huet (*Paradis terrestre*), Vincent, and Niebuhr are cited in additional notes to the 1804 edition (p. 857), this is not in reference to the cataracts but the hydraulic work Alexander undertook in Babylon. On Grote (1794–1871) and Alexander see my "Alexandre et l'hellénisation de l'Asie," 18–23 and n. 32; and "Grote on Alexander."

25. See my "Retour sur Alexandre", part II, 170ff. on the conditions of the resumption of discussions from c. 1950 to 2005; see also on these subjects my recent update in *Alexander the Great and His Empire,* 83–96. The only exception is MacPherson's note, *Annals of Commerce,* 1:74–75, which, in all likelihood and without ever citing him, closely follows Vincent, but also does not draw any

particular inference from the observation, which it exclusively credits to the travelers Tavernier and Niebuhr; MacPherson's pages on Alexander (1:71–75) were themselves ignored by historians: not a great loss, one must admit.

26. See Chap. 3 § "From the Ancients to the Moderns."

27. See Chap. 7.

28. See Chap. 8.

29. See Chap. 6.

30. *Siècle d'Alexandre* (1762), 159–171; (1769), 212–224.

31. See, in particular, Raynal, *Histoire des deux-indes,* 5.10; the argument is due to Diderot: see Raynal, *Histoire philosophique* (2010), 500–502, 764; and Goggi, *Diderot,* 43–49.

32. Maréchal, *Apologues modernes,* 28; d'Holbach, *La Morale universelle,* 3:250; see Israel, *Revolution of the Mind,* 124–153.

33. The legend of Manco Cápac was well known in Europe. In 1763 Le Blanc had written a play entitled *Manco-Capac, premier Inca du Pérou,* which was revived in 1782 (see Grimm's commentaries in the *Correspondance littéraire* dated January 1782).

34. Garve, *Sur l'accord de la morale avec la politique,* 117–119 (Gustavus Adolphus); 132–133 (Alexander; German ed. 1788, p. 80); 221–222 (Peter the Great).

35. On the man and his place in the birth of European Orientalism see primarily G. Abbatista's essay, "'Barbarie' et 'sauvagerie' in un contributo di Anquetil-Duperron," with L. Valensi's very pertinent critical remarks, "Éloge de l'Orient," from which I drew inspiration; see also Osterhammel, *Entzauberung Asiens,* 293–296.

36. Polybius, *Histories,* 10.27.3: "Media is surrounded by Greek cities founded on Alexander's initiative in order to protect it from neighboring barbarians."

37. See my *États et pasteurs au Moyen-Orient ancien,* 9–56 and 94–112; on the conception of nomadism in the eighteenth century see Osterhammel, *Entzauberung Asiens,* 264–271.

38. Anquetil Duperron, "Recherches sur les migrations des Mardes," 113.

39. See Levesque, *Histoire des différents peuples,* which completes his *Histoire de Russie,* I–V, 1782.

40. Information found in the archives of the Collège de France.

41. Levesque, *Études de l'histoire ancienne,* 3:385–472 (Alexander's reign); 468–470 (assessment); see also Chap. 7 § "Alexander, Promoter of Commerce."

42. On the image of Peter the Great in Levesque, see V. A. Somov's remarks in "Pierre-Charles Levesque, protégé de Diderot et historien de la Russie," 284–285.

43. Mably, *De l'étude de l'histoire,* part III, chap. 3 = *Œuvres completes,* 12:288–289.

44. Levesque, *Éloge historique de M. l'abbé de Mably.* Levesque's text was a response to a "call for submissions" by the Académie Royale des Inscriptions et Belles-Lettres. The prize awarded by the Académie had been founded by the Abbé

Raynal (the "person who does not want to be known" in Levesque's subtitle); Levesque shared the prize with the Abbé Brizard.

45. "Tyr," *Encyclopédie*, 16:783: "These are the excellent reflections of the author of *The Spirit of the Laws*."

46. Montesquieu, *Spirit of the Laws* 21.6; *Siècle d'Alexandre* (1762), 51, 208; (1769), 101–102, 272.

47. Huet, *Histoire du commerce*, chaps. 8 and 17.1.

48. The 1780 edition is considerably expanded on this point. It is hard to know whether or not Raynal wrote these additions. What does seem certain, however, is that the preceding paragraph (. . . "That is commerce, that is commerce!") is by Diderot: see Raynal, *Histoire philosophique* (2010), 1:24 nn. 7 and 8.

49. See Chap. 3 § "Forgiveness and Atonement: Voltaire and Linguet's Perspective."

50. Schlözer, *Versuch einer allgemeinen Geschichte;* on the author see Peters, *Altes Reich und Europa;* on the book see pp. 46–53 (no reference to Alexander, who does not directly concern Peters); on Michaelis see Marchand, *German Orientalism*, 38–43.

51. On his reading of Huet and Montesquieu see, in particular, the foreword (*Vorrede*); see p. 40 for his use of the expression from *The Spirit of the Laws* (without referring to Montesquieu): "After his conquests, commerce took an entirely different turn (*Durch seine Eroberungen bekam die Handlung einen ganz andern Lauf*)."

52. Berghaus, *Geschichte der Schiffahrtskunde*, vol. 1, 1–2, 343–350 on the history of Tyre and its fall.

53. See Herder, *Outlines*, 86–92, excerpts.

54. See Chap. 8 § "Christian Gottlob Heyne: From European Wars to Alexander's Campaigns."

55. For example, *Robinson Crusoe* (1719); *Captain Singleton* (1720); *Molly Flanders* (1721); *Colonel Jack* (1722), etc. On the relationship between maritime adventures, piracy, and imperialism in Defoe see Downie, "Defoe, Imperialism and the Travel Books Reconsidered" (which does not dwell on his treatment of Alexander); see also D. Carey's analyses in "Reading Contrapuntally"; on his position regarding the Moors and the Turks see Matar, *Turks, Moors and Englishmen*, 170–172. Defoe is curiously absent from A. Thomson's very interesting book (*Barbary and Enlightenment*), which admittedly is primarily based on texts dating from c. 1770 to 1830 and a reflection on the genesis of the French expedition to Algiers; I will simply note that some of the calls to conquest issued by the Englishmen J. G. Jackson (in 1818) and L. Goldsmith (*Barbary and Enlightenment*, 136–138) resemble certain polemical arguments made by Defoe as early as 1725–1726.

56. On this last point see Salas, "Raleigh and the Punic Wars."

57. See Defoe, *Plan for English Commerce*, 10.

58. See Anon., "Memoirs of Navigation and Commerce," 194–195: "The Phoenicians and their descendants the Carthaginians deserve our admiration, in first reducing commerce to a science, and in carrying navigation to such a state of perfection"; yet on the other hand, "the British navy moves in the greatness of its strength, not to confine, or selfishly to seclude advantages from any particular country; but to support and to secure the greatest of blessings, in defending the cause of real liberty throughout the world."

59. For example, Séran de la Tour, *Parallèle de la conduite des Carthaginois*; Sainte-Croix, *De l'état et du sort des colonies*, 298ff.; Anquetil Duperron, *Plan*, xi, etc. In his *Histoire des revolutions*, Chateaubriand frequently compares (in heavily contradictory statements) Tyre and Holland, and Carthage and England: see part I, chaps. 31 and 35 (*Parallèle de Carthage et de l'Angleterre*), and 53–54 (*Tyr. La Hollande*).

60. English trans. D. Bindon.

61. *Encyclopédie*, 7: 716–721; 7.855–857; 8.181; 8. 183; 8.279.

62. "Estime (Droit naturel)," *Encyclopédie*, 5:1003.

63. On Jaucourt's life and his contribution to the *Encyclopédie* see Haechler, *L'Encyclopédie de Diderot et de Jaucourt*, 399–462, 498–500; see also Ehrard, *Lumières et esclavage*, 169–181.

64. He wrote more than eighty toponymic articles (cities, regions, battles, etc.), in which references to Alexander are most often quick, even allusive.

65. See, for example, the article "Grecs" (*Encyclopédie*, 7.914): "While it is true that victory gave him everything, [Alexander] did everything to obtain victory, and perhaps he is the only usurper who can claim to have made the family he overthrew shed tears for him"; see *Spirit of the Laws*, 10.14.

66. Delia, "Crime et châtiment," 469.

67. *Examen critique* (1804), 278–282.

68. Quoting the expression used in *The Spirit of the Laws* ("'Admirable thing!' said M. de Montesquieu"), but also the original collection ("*See* the collection by M. Barbeyrac, *art.* 112"), Jaucourt notes: "This article of the treaty could only concern the Carthaginians established on the island, who were masters of the western part of the country; for human sacrifices still persisted in Carthage" ("Victime humaine," *Encyclopédie*, 17:242). However, Damilaville closely adheres to Montesquieu's position in the article on "Population" (13:93).

69. "Grecs|Histoire ancienne|Littérature," *Encyclopédie*, 7:915. See also Chap. 9 § "The End of History?"

70. "Étrangers," *Encyclopédie*, 6:71; see also "Hospitalité," 8:315: "A beautiful trait of the life of Alexander is that edict by which he declared that the good people of every country are kin to one another & that only bad people were excluded from this honor."

71. See my *Alexandre des Lumières*, 304–307, and Chap. 7, *in fine*.

72. "Mahométisme," *Encyclopédie*, 9:864.

73. The bibliography on Raynal is vast; G. Bancarel cites selections from it in his introduction to the 2006 reprint of the 1780 edition (*Histoire philosophique,* 1:9–38), and in the introductions and notes to the 2010 critical edition of bks. 1–5 (vol. 1); see also the publication by L. Versini of Diderot's fragments on the history of the two Indies (*Diderot. Œuvres,* 3:579–759), and now especially Goggi, *Diderot,* as well as his other specialized study "Collaboration de Diderot." Due to the multitude of editions in different formats, I will refer to the work not according to its pagination, but to the numbering of the books and chapters: for example, 1.11 or 5.1. The English translation used here is (for the most part) the one published in Edinburgh and Glasgow under the title *A Philosophical History of the Settlements and Trade of the Europeans in the East and West Indies* in 1804; I also consulted J. Justamond's translation (same title), published in London in 1777.

74. Huet, *Histoire du commerce,* 97–101 (Alexander); Ameilhon, *Commerce des Égyptiens,* 53ff. (Ptolemies).

75. On this, see (no references to antiquity) the studies by Benot in *Les Lumières, l'esclavage, la colonization,* 107–195, and Muthu in *Enlightenment against Empire,* 72–121; lastly, M. Platania's reflections in "Relire l'histoire coloniale au XVIIIe siècle."

76. Sandracottos/Chandragupta, the founder of the Maurya dynasty, was well known through the classical sources. He seized the Indus Valley after Alexander's death, then, following a treaty with Seleucus (in 303 BC), he extended his sovereignty to the countries of the Eastern Iranian Plateau (what Strabo calls Arianè).

77. On Diderot's use of Roubaud in the *Histoire des deux-Indes* (on slavery) see Thomson, "Diderot, Roubaud et l'esclavage."

6. Lessons of Empire, from the Thames to the Indus

1. On the use of the figure of Alexander in Camões and the Spanish authors one can now consult Barletta, *Death in Babylon.*

2. De Castanheda, *Historia do descobrimento e conquista de India,* [1552], 1833 ed., dedicated to King John III.

3. Grotius, *Mare liberum,* chap. 2.

4. See, for example, Le Vayer, *Jugements sur les anciens,* 90: "Arrian did not fail to give us a far more accurate situation of several places in the Oriental Indies than Ptolemy, as the modern Accounts by the Portuguese have shown us with certainty."

5. On the book and its author see Chap. 2 § "William Vincent and *The Voyage of Nearchus.*"

6. See Chap. 7 § "Alexander, Promoter of Commerce" and Chap. 8 § "Geography, Voyages, and Alexander's Conquests."

7. Anon., Review of Vincent (*European Magazine, and London Review*).

8. Anon., Review of Vincent (*Monthly Review, or, Literary Journal*).

9. The anonymous review is entitled "On the Ancient and Modern Navigation of India: From Dr. Vincent's Voyage of Nearchus." (The *Annual Register* was founded in 1758 and edited by Edmund Burke until at least 1768. It continues to this day.)

10. *The London Review and Literary Journal*, March 1797, p. 169.

11. Anon., Review of Vincent (*British Critic*). It is not unlikely that the review was written by a close friend of Vincent's: Robert Nares, one of the journal's directors.

12. See Chap. 2 § "James Rennell, Alexander's Conquest, and Establishing the Map of India."

13. The note is omitted in the 1783 edition, p. v n.

14. On Dalrymple see "Biographical Memoir of Alexander Dalrymple Esq.," *Naval Chronicle* 35 (1816): 177–204; he is often mentioned in Markham's book, *Major James Rennell;* see its index, p. 230.

15. The map is in the Gosselin collection in the Bibliothèque Nationale's Maps and Plans Department (GE E-183) under the title *Esquisse de l'angle sud-est de la côte de Perse, dessinée pour cet ouvrage par le capitaine A. Blair,* engraving by Tardieu, 1797. It had been published previously by J. McCluer in *Account of the Navigation. between India and the Gulph of Persia* (1786).

16. Langlès, *Voyages dans l'Inde et en Perse;* see Franklin, *Observations Made on a Tour from Bengal to Persia.*

17. Charles-Pierre Claret, Comte de Fleurieu (1738–1810), was well known for his works on nautical science and his high office in the navy's administration. He had also taken an interest in ancient navigation and voyages, but the book he was preparing on the subject was never published: see the biographical sketch published by C. Delambre in *Mémoires de l'Académie des Sciences de l'Institut de France* (1812): lxxiii–xc.

18. Gosselin, "Recherches," 69–70.

19. The quotes are taken from the cartographic appendix published by Barbié du Bocage in the 1804 edition of Sainte-Croix's *Examen critique,* 796–797.

20. Ibid., 744–748, and *Examen critique* (1775), 250–264: "On Nearchus's Navigation,"

21. See Chap. 7 § "Alexander, Promoter of Commerce."

22. Sainte-Croix, *De l'état et du sort des colonies;* Sainte-Croix, *Observations;* Vincent, *Sermon;* Vincent, Review of Clayton, 514: see Chap. 2 § "The History of Alexander in the Revolutionary Upheavals" and my *Alexandre des Lumières,* 159–172.

23. Anquetil Duperron, *L'Inde en rapport avec l'Europe* 1:i–ii; Anquetil Duperron, "Plan d'administration pour l'Inde," lxiv.

24. Rennell, *Geographical System of Herodotus.*
25. R. Nares, "Life of Dr. Vincent," *British Critique,* July 1816, pp. 208, 210.
26. In the *Courrier d'Egypte,* no. 33, dated Thermidor, Year 7 (1799), Volney expressed his skepticism; he underlined Bonaparte's inability to go to India: "he cannot by sea . . . even less so by land; for this gazettes' route by the Euphrates, the deserts of Persia and the Indus is a folly that even a caravan of Arabs would not consider; and a French army lives more expensively; and anyhow the political situation has now changed" (3-4).
27. Van der Chys, *Commentarius geographicus,* xviii; see Droysen's important review of this work.
28. Williams, *Two Essays, on the Geography of Ancient Asia,* 2.
29. Hagerman, "In the Footsteps of the 'Macedonian Conqueror,'" esp. 348-352 and 379-390 ("British 'Alexanders' in India"); the author primarily studies examples from the second half of the nineteenth century.
30. Anon., Review of Vincent (*Monthly Review, or, Literary Journal*), 265; *Bibliothèque britannique ou recueil extrait des ouvrages anglais périodiques et autres,* xi, in Geneva, Year VII, p. 185.
31. See *Paris pendant l'année* 31 (1801), 195. On the Gardane mission and the Treaty of Finkelstein see Driault, *La politique orientale de Napoléon,* 170-185 and 309-342; and Amini, *Napoleon and Persia,* 70-180; the author naturally also deals with Malcolm's missions to Persia, (chaps. 4 and 12) as well as those carried out by Jones (chap. 19).
32. See Pottinger, *Travels in Baloochistan and Sinde,* 9, 263-264, 267, 381-385, 390, etc.; see also 403-423 ("Appendix: Abstract of Captain Christie's Journal"). Pottinger's account was cited and used by Barthold Georg Niebuhr in his lectures of 1826-1829: see *Vorträge,* 2:497.
33. On Malcolm's life and his missions in Persia one can consult the highly conventional biography by J. W. Kaye, *Life and Correspondence,* and, more recently, R. Pasley's *'Send Malcolm!';* on those accompanying Malcolm on the 1810 mission see Kaye, vol. 2, chap. 1; also Malcolm, *History of Persia,* 1:x-xi; on Kinneir see "Memoir of Sir John Macdonald Kinneir", in *Asiatic Journal and Monthly Register for British and Foreign India, China and Australasia,* n.s., 4 (January-April 1831): 144-146; on Pottinger see the biography by his homonymous descendant, *Sir Henry Pottinger,* esp. 1-62; on Burnes see André, "Alexander Burnes" and W. Dalrymple, *The Return of a King.* All these characters are obviously very present in Peter Hopkirk's famous book *The Great Game,* to be read alongside M. Yapp's warning about the terminology and concept: "The Legend of the Great Game." On Kinneir and Monteith's voyages of exploration in Persia see the text and maps by A. Gabriel, *Die Erforschung Persiens,* 134-136, adapted here *Fig. 13.* During the same period, British diplomats and travelers contributed to a more accurate knowledge of ancient sites, particularly that of Persepolis: on this see Errington and Curtis, *From Persepolis to the Punjab,* 2007.

34. Kinneir, *Geographical Memoir,* appendix.

35. On the Bombay government's growing hold on the Gulf see Allen, "State of Masquat in the Gulf and East Africa 1785–1829" and my remarks in "Retour sur Alexandre," part II, 182–183.

36. "It is perhaps unnecessary to remark that this Dissertation was written before the downfall of Napoleon and the eventful changes in Europe, which, by the aggrandizement of Russia, have endangered the safety of our eastern possessions" (Kinneir, *Journey,* 512 n.).

37. Ibid., esp. 107–161 (Alexander's marches to Issus) and 512–539 (*Dissertation on the Invasion of India*). For example, William Tooke had suggested the possibility of launching an expedition against India from Egypt in 1798. Kinneir's book was warmly reviewed by Letronne (Review of Kinneir).

38. Hopkins, *Dangers of British India from French Invasion.*

39. Elphinstone, *Account, of the Kingdom of Caubul,* 80.

40. See Alexander Burnes, *Travels to Bokhara,* 3:10–15, 35–36, 61–62, 115, 128–133, 228, 231–232, 284–285, etc., and Hagerman's "In the Footsteps of the 'Macedonian Conqueror,'" 381–385.

41. James Burnes, *Narrative, of a Visit to the Court of Sinde,* 136–141 ("Remarks on Alexander's Route"); quote on 137.

42. Chesney, *Expedition for the Survey of the Rivers Euphrates and Tigris;* Chesney, *Narrative of the Euphrates Expedition;* see also my discussion in "Retour sur Alexandre," part II, 163–167.

43. William Mitford, *The History of Greece,* vol. 5, 436.

44. *The Classical Review* XXV (April–July 1821): 167. On this review see also Chap. 2 § "What Is a Philosopher Historian?"

45. Note that Vincent made certain to add "the primary cause, *however remote ...*" (my italics).

46. See Francesconi, "William Robertson on Historical Causation and Unintended Consequences"; see also (on Germany), Reill, *German Enlightenment,* 100ff.

47. This subject is dealt with throughout the volume edited by S. J. Brown, *William Robertson and the Expansion of the Empire;* among the most informative articles on the *Historical Disquisition* see especially Carnall, "Robertson"; I contributed to the discussion with "William Robertson"; see lastly Brown, "William Robertson." See also K. O'Brien's extremely well articulated *Narratives of Enlightenment,* esp. chap. 5 ("Robertson on the Triumph of Europe and Its Empires," 129–165).

48. Montaigne, *Essais,* 3.6; for a contrary position, see 2.26; on the development of Montaigne's position see Dezemeiris, "Annotations inédites de Montaigne," and, more recently, Kupisz, "Alexandre dans les *Essais* de Montaigne" and Lombard, "Montaigne et Alexandre le Grand."

49. In Bernoulli's French translation (*Description historique et géographique de l'Inde,* vol. 3, part I, 25 n. a), Rennell added a vindictive commentary against "people

who would have risked losing India to ensure a certain degree of imaginary liberty to the Natives of the land, [but who] are not adverse to lending their assistance to put the poor Africans in the chains of slavery"; see also Carnall's remarks, "Robertson and Contemporary Images of India," 228–229.

50. On the trial and the people involved see, in particular, Pitts, *Turn to Empire,* 59–100, and Dirks, *Scandal of Empire.*

51. Burke, *Speeches,* 2:430–432, and the more recent annotated edition by Peter Marshall, *Writings and Speeches of Edmund Burke,* vol. 7.

52. See Embree, *Charles Grant,* 237.

53. Barthold Georg Niebuhr, *Vorträge,* 2:499.

54. On Charles Grant and his *Observations* see the biography by H. Morris, *The Life of Charles Grant,* 174–193, and especially the study by A. T. Embree, *Charles Grant,* esp. chap. 11 ("Interpreter of the Indian Response," 231–260), as well as the analyses respectively developed by E. Stokes (*English Utilitarians,* 25ff. ("Liberalism and the Policy of Assimilation"), and G. Abbatista (*James Mill e il problema indiano,* 65–77); also see Carnall, "Robertson and Contemporary Images of India," 218–221. These provide a detailed analysis of the protagonists (including James Mill), their ideas, and the London networks (particularly "the Clapham sect"), which I do not go into here. However, none of these authors has noted Grant and Mitchell's use of the precedent of Alexander, which I highlight here; on these issues, also see the interesting discussion by Hagerman, "In the Footsteps of the 'Macedonian Conqueror,'" 357–366, which emphasizes Mill's position, but also omits any reference to Grant and Mitchell's polemics against Robertson's position.

55. Mitchell, *Essay,* 15.

56. See Grant, *Observations,* 202–206.

57. See Mitchell, *Essay,* esp. 68–74.

58. Hopkins, *Dangers of British India from French Invasion,* 57–64. The author may have been thinking of one of the plans attributed to Alexander, which consisted in "proceeding to groupings of cities and transfers of populations from Asia to Europe and vice versa, etc." (Diodorus of Sicily, *Library of History,* 18.4.4).

7. Alexander in France from the Revolution to the Restoration

1. See Grell, *Le Dix-huitième siècle, et l'antiquité,* 1:469–478; Vidal-Naquet, "La place de la Grèce dans la Révolution"; Paoletti, *Benjamin Constant,* chap. 1 ("Le vertige du passé"), which also emphasizes the radical change brought by Thermidor in this regard.

2. See my study "Montesquieu, Mably et Alexandre le Grand."

3. See Gaulmier, "Volney et ses Leçons d'histoire" and his *L'idéologue Volney,* 305–310, 324–345; on the context of Volney's presentation (against revolutionary classicism) see Paoletti, *Benjamin Constant,* 58–65.
4. On Bonaparte's reading see Chuquet, *Jeunesse de Napoléon,* 1:102ff.; 2:2ff.; Assali, *Napoléon et l'Antiquité,* 102ff.
5. [Bossuet], *Extraits de l'Histoire Universelle;* I consulted an 1818 reprint; the passages on Alexander (pp. 179–180) are extremely disparaging, as they had been in the *Discourse on Universal History.*
6. Bonaparte, *Discours de Lyon* [1791], E. Driault (ed.), Paris, 1929, 33.
7. Ibid., 91–92; aside from Driault's introduction see Chuquet's analysis in *Jeunesse de Napoléon,* 2:210–223.
8. On this appellation see the entry "peintre de batailles," in the *Encyclopédie,* 12:266 (author unknown): "Name given to a *painter* who specifically dedicates himself to this kind of work. In a composition of this kind, there must be much fire and action in the figures & in the horses. This is why one must prefer a strong and vigorous manner, free strokes, and a jerky taste over a finished work, a delicate brush, and an overly accomplished design." There follows a list of painters of this category, in which Gamelin is obviously not included, given the publication date.
9. See Musée de Carcassonne, *Jacques Gamelin,* nos. 45–64; nos. 44–45, 55–56 depict Alexander; on no. 44 (Alexander and his soldiers dying of thirst) see my *Darius in the Shadow of Alexander,* chap. 8 § "Iron Helmet, Silver Vessels."
10. C. Michel refers to this example in "La permanence du héros," 100, but does not develop the subject I discuss here.
11. Arrian, *Anabasis,* 6.29.11.
12. See my *Alexandre des Lumières,* 295, with color plates of the paintings by Il Grechetto (Castiglione: 1609–1664); by Glauber, known as Polidor (1646–1726; in the collection of the Musée des Beaux-Arts de Nantes, the painting is entitled: *Alexandre visitant le tombeau de Darius* [*Alexander Visiting the Tomb of Darius*]); and by Collin de Vermont (1663–1761).
13. On Valenciennes and this painting see Gallo, "Pierre-Henri de Valenciennes," and a few words in Frankfort, "The Alexander Mountain"; however, I have not found any commentary specific to the painting *Alexandre au tombeau de Cyrus* [*Alexander at the Tomb of Cyrus*]. On the art of landscape in Valenciennes see Watson, "Tradition and Innovation" (no reference to the latter painting).
14. See the catalog (by Jean-Marcel Hombert) for the exhibition *L'égyptomanie dans l'art occidental,* ACR Éditions, Courbevois (Paris), 1989, esp. 228ff. on the imaginary world created by painters in the second half of the eighteenth century (no mention of Valenciennes's painting): "In a curious mix of styles, pyramids and sphinxes appear out of the clouds, and imaginary tombs decorated with pseudo-hieroglyphics are peopled with worrisome characters wearing the

nemes" (228). Valenciennes's painting is not included because it was in a private collection at the time. It can now be seen at the Art Institute of Chicago.

15. *Siècle d'Alexandre* (1762), 106–107.

16. See Chap. 2 § "What Is a Philosopher Historian?"

17. The exception relates to a question considered of secondary importance by Montesquieu: the speed of Alexander's marches (*Spirit of the Laws,* 10.14). See *Examen critique* (1775), 101–106; (1804), 232.

18. See *Examen critique* (1775), 260–261 (date of the monsoon).

19. Expanded on in *Examen critique* (1804), 278–282, in a highly ironic tone, the critique of Montesquieu's interpretation of the "loi de Gélon" ("law of Gelo") (*Spirit of the Laws,* 10.5, on the prohibition of human sacrifices in Carthage) was infinitely more courteous and moderate when introduced in the 1779 edition (*De l'état et du sort des colonies,* 28–29).

20. *Examen critique* (1775), 99 (= *Critical Enquiry,* 1:171–172); (1804), 403.

21. Saint-Croix, *De l'état et du sort des colonies,* 293.

22. *Examen critique* (1775), 96; (1804), 401 (to which Sainte-Croix adds that the term should be taken "figuratively," since he has just shown that the Macedonians did not erect trophies after their victories). Berghaus uses the same terminology in *Geschichte der Schiffahrtskunde,* 1:549, in which he explicitly sides with Mably against Montesquieu.

23. Mably, *Observations* (1766), 230–231; I have provided a detailed analysis of the grounds for Mably's counterattack elsewhere ("Montesquieu, Mably, et Alexandre le Grand").

24. *Examen critique* (1804), 402.

25. Ibid., 285–286; see earlier *Examen critique* (1775), 70–71.

26. See, in particular, *Siècle d'Alexandre* (1762), 27–41; (1769), 51–86.

27. Mably, *Observations* (1766), 232–233; see *Observations*(1749), 205.

28. Mably, *De l'étude de l'histoire,* 18; see my remarks in *Revue Montesquieu* 2005–2006, p. 177 (§ "Alexandre sans le commerce de l'Inde").

29. Saint-Croix, *De l'état et du sort des colonies,* 9, referring to the Phoenicians, who systematically massacred "those peoples [who] refused to traffic with them and got in the way of their installations."

30. *Examen critique* (1775), 64.

31. Here Sainte-Croix quotes Vincent, *Voyage de Néarque,* 6 (the 1800 French translation).

32. See Plutarch, *Life of Alexander,* 66.2: "He landed and sacrificed to the gods, and . . . prayed that no man after him might pass beyond the bounds of his expedition."

33. *Examen critique* (1775), 140; (1804), p. 379.

34. *Examen critique* (1775), 140; (1804), 372–373.

35. See, for example, Baillet, *Des enfants devenus célèbres,* 11–20.

36. Ricard, *Œuvres morales de Plutarque,* 4:259–306.

37. La Harpe, *Lycée ou cours de literature*, 4 :144–145; the series began publication in 1786. (The author's name is sometimes spelled Laharpe.)

38. *Examen critique* (1804), 370, and esp. 83–86 (opposition with Augustus); in the 1775 edition, the author expresses doubts regarding the discourses' authenticity (30–31).

39. In his 1779 *De l'état et du sort des colonies* (which is violently hostile to British colonization), Sainte-Croix states that he had read Raynal's writings on the subject.

40. *Examen critique* (1775), 96; (1804), 481, 487. The English author mentioned on p. 738 is Rennell, whose *Memoir* is quoted in Boucheseiche's translation (1:5, 18).

41. Vancouver, *Voyage of Discovery; to the North Pacific Ocean and round the World*; the book was quickly translated into French (*Voyages de découvertes à l'océan pacifique du Nord et autour du monde*, 3 vols., Year 8).

42. On this text by Curtius Rufus (7.8.22–30) and the diverging commentaries it elicited in the seventeenth and eighteenth centuries, see my study "Des Scythes aux Tartares," in which Sainte-Croix's commentary is considered as part of a group of writings.

43. See Guyon, *Histoire des empires* 4:434 n. i: "I saw a harangue by these Savages of Canada addressed to the Intendant of Quebec in 1726, every bit as beautiful as this one"; Crèvecoeur, *Voyage dans la Haute-Pennsylvanie, et dans l'état de New-York* 1801, pp. 124–125 n. (on this work see Plet, *Une géographie*; Lafitau, *Mœurs des Sauvages amériquains*, 1:18, 41, 92.

44. See Voltaire, *Histoire de l'empire de Russie*, part II, chap. XVI=*Complete Works*, 47:923–924.

45. Rollin, *Histoire ancienne*, 1:v–vi; xx (Saint-Albin Berville).

46. See my *Alexandre des Lumières*, 304–307.

47. Commonly called the *Dictionnaire universel françois et latin* (1771) 1:223; the text is identical to the entry in the 1752 edition.

48. On the lives of the two brothers Joseph-François (1767–1839) and Louis-Gabriel (1773–1858) and on the *Biographie universelle*, see the entries devoted to each man in it and the *Discours préliminaire* at the beginning of the first volume of the 1811 edition (vii–xviii); see also the study by J.-F. Burger, "La *Biographie universelle* des frères Michaud."

49. In a note (*Biographie universelle* [1811], 1:507), Louis-Gabriel Michaud mentioned that he had "been helped in writing this article by the scholarly M. Clavier." According to the entry on "Jean-François Michaud" in the dictionary (p. 217), the article on "Alexander the Great" had initially been "written by Clavier, who did not want to have it attributed it to him because cuts had been made."

50. This would change by the 1842 edition of the *Biographie universelle*: see below § "Commerce, Colonization, Civilization."

51. Heyne, *Göttingische gelehrte Anzeigen* 1803, pp. 740–743; Heyne ironically states that he envies an author who can so easily write explanatory notes by servilely

copying entire passages from modern authors into his commentaries. Boissonade ("Histoire des expéditions d'Alexandre") lays the biting irony on thick: "M. Chaussard has done no harm to science; he has left it where others brought it. He compiles opinions, but has none of his own. . . . He has done even less to prove his knowledge of Greek than his erudition," etc. Boissonade also wrote a highly positive review of the *Examen critique* (1804) (see his "Sur l'Examen critique" and "De Sainte-Croix").

52. Chaussard, *Histoire,* I:xlvii. In the explanatory notes, the citations from Vincent are identified by the initial B, a somewhat confusing reference to the name of the French translator Billecocq.

53. New edition by S. Montecalvo, *Baron de Sainte-Croix,* 1:371, no. 286.

54. On Daunou see the *Notice* written by B. Guérard, republished in 1853.

55. Quotes taken from Daunou, *Cours d'études historiques,* 12:653–674; the author also presents his point of view by commenting on Boileau's famous *Satire* 8 (which Voltaire claimed had succeeded in enraging Charles XII): see Daunou, *Œuvres complètes de Boileau Despréaux,* 1:xvi–xvii and 135ff.

56. On Constant's education one can still consult Rudler's *La jeunesse de Benjamin Constant,* esp. 157ff., and now the study by Klooke, *Benjamin Constant,* esp. 181ff.; on Constant's stays in Göttingen see Thouars, "Benjamin Constant et l'École de Göttingen"; on his translation of Gillies (*Essai sur les mœurs des temps héroïques*) see Rudler, *Bibliographie critique,* 44–46, and Paoletti, *Benjamin Constant,* 239–241. *L'esprit de conquête* (1813) is cited from the edition by Klooke and Fink, *Œuvres complètes de B. Constant,* ser. 1, 8:527–598.

57. Constant, *Du polythéisme romain,* 1:141–142 (chap. 10): *De l'influence des conquêtes d'Alexandre sur la décadence du Polythéisme* [*On the Influence of Alexander's Conquests on the Decadence of Polytheism*].

58. A systematic study of this question can be found in Roulin, "Chateaubriand."

59. Thiers's book is quoted from the translation by D. Forbes Campbell and John Stebbing, *History of the Consulate,* 12:399–433 (excerpts).

60. See my *Alexandre des Lumières,* 144–147.

61. To my knowledge the existence of unpublished letters and manuscripts related to this copy has never been noted, though it is duly mentioned in the Bibliothèque Nationale records (RES 4–02–88). The marginal notes are primarily by Vincent; others were suggested to him by Samuel Horsley and Harford Jones; they were all handwritten by the author. The copy also includes an unpublished letter from Heyne to Vincent, which I discuss below (Chap. 8 § "Geography, Voyages and Conquests of Alexander": translations and original studies).—I have since learned that there is a second copy annotated by Vincent between 1809 and 1815. It is in the collection of the Westminster Library in London; the first study of it has just been published; see Bucciantini, "Annotazioni manoscritte" and Chap. 2 § "William Vincent and *The Voyage of Nearchus,*" with n. 52.

62. Born in 1765, a jurist and lawyer, and a "constitutional monarchist" during the revolution, he was imprisoned, but survived thanks to 9 Thermidor; he died in 1829. He translated several works from English, as well as Latin classics. A specific biobibliographic presentation can be found in J.-M. Quérard, *La France Littéraire*, 1:506–511.

63. Ramusio, *Delle navigazione e viaggi*, 263–264 (now see Milanesi, "Neaco come fone nelle *Navigazioni* di Giovanni Ramusio"); Harris and Campbell, *Navigantium atque itinerantium Bibliotheca*, 1:400–409.

64. Boucher de la Richarderie, *Bibliothèque universelle des voyages*, 1:15–31; on this publication and its representativeness see the detailed analysis by D. Roche, *Humeurs vagabondes*, 21–38; Mentelle and Malte-Brun, *Géographie mathématique, physique et politique de toutes les parties du monde*; Malte-Brun, *Précis de géographie universelle*, vol. 1, bk. 8. Delisle de Sale, *Histoire philosophique du monde primitive*, 6:305–308.

65. Eschassériaux, *Tableau politique de l'Europe*, 40.

66. See *Mémoires de l'Institut National des Sciences et des Arts. Sciences morales et politiques*, 2nd ser., 4 (1803): 26–70; summary of Gosselin's paper in the *Magazin Encyclopédique* 6th year, vol. VI, 1801, pp. 389–391.

67. On this journal see Hazard, "Le Spectateur du Nord."

68. *Analyse raisonnée de l'Histoire de France*, 398; see Roulin, "Chateaubriand," 262–263.

69. Michaud, Joseph-François, *Histoire, des progrès et de la chûte de l'empire de Mysore*, 1:1–29, 152–160 (Egyptian Expedition); 2:423–430 (Alexander).

70. On this point it is interesting to note that the article on "Alexander the Great" written by his brother (and Clavier) for the *Biographie* (1811) follows in Sainte-Croix's footsteps but does not say a word about *The Voyage of Nearchus*.

71. He is referring to the argument in the introduction to bk. 1, which ends with the famous exclamation: "It's commerce, it's commerce!"

72. For evidence one need only look at the entry for "Alexander the Great" in the index (*Tableau chronologique*, xxv–xxxviii).

73. See the book edited by J.-C. Bonnet, *L'empire des Muses*, in which Alexander does not actually feature much, including in the articles devoted to antiquity. The reader will recall that in his youth, Bonaparte had clearly expressed his profound hostility to the Macedonian conqueror: see above § "Alexander and the Revolution: The Pen and the Paintbrush."

74. Lamberti, *Alessandro in Armozia*; Guingené, Review of Lamberti.

75. See Allen, "State of Masquat."

76. See above § "Alexander and the Revolution."

77. On the execution of the sculpture see primarily D. Ternois, "Napoléon et la décoration du palais du Monte-Cavallo en 1811–1813," 1970, and Jørnaes, "Thorvaldsen's "'Triumph of Alexander' in the Palazzo del Quirinale", 1991; also see P.

Calmeyer's doubts in "Die Orientalen auf Thorvaldsens Alexanderfries", 1990; and lastly Seidl, "L'iconografia alessandrina."

78. See Anon., *Correspondance,* 14, 19, 151.

79. Henri Stendhal, *The Charterhouse of Parma,* trans. John Sturrock (Penguin: London, 2006), 7.

80. Flaubert, *Voyage dans les Pyrénées et en Corse 1840 [Travels in the Pyrenees and in Corsica 1840], Ed. Entente, Paris, 1983, p. 107.*

81. *Moniteur,* March 19, 1805, cited in Morrissey, "Charlemagne et la légende impériale," 344.

82. See below Chap. 10 § "After Alexander?"

83. Las Cases, *Mémorial,* 1:436, 462.

84. Gourgaud, *Sainte-Hélène,* 1:161; 2:191.

85. Ibid., 1:162.

86. Ibid., 2:337–338.

87. Ibid., 2:435–436.

88. Las Cases, *Mémorial,* 2:303.

89. See, for example, Hopkins, *Dangers of British India from French Invasion,* 58–59.

90. See Anon., "Projet d'une expédition dans l'Inde, par terre," *Paris pendant l'année 31* (1801): 195–202 (quote on 199).

91. See above Chap. 5 § "An Inexpiable Debt?"

92. See, for example, Volpilhac-Auger, *L'Atelier de Montesquieu,* 43–67. For a synthetic approach see the article on "Colonies" by G. Barrera in the *Dictionnaire Montesquieu:* http://dictionnaire-montesquieu.ens-lyon.fr/index.php?id=320.

93. His name is also spelled Désiré Raoul-Rochette.

94. Poirson and Cayx's 1820 report *Commission de l'instruction publique. Programme pour l'enseignement de l'histoire ancienne dans les collèges royaux* called for twelve chapters to cover the period from Egypt to the fall of Syracuse at the hand of the Romans. Chap. 11 was devoted to "the Power of Macedonia," with two passages on Alexander, including a negative assessment of one episode: "Through his recklessness, he lost three fourths of his army in the deserts of Gedrosia" (p. 19). This negative appraisal did not appear in the 1827 volume (p. 369).

95. See *Cours d'études pour la section des Lettres rédigé conformément aux programmes des Lycées et aux programmes pour l'examen du Baccalauréat ès-lettres du 3 août 1857* Paris, Dezobry et Magdeleine et Cie, n.d., pp. 76–86 (long quote from *Spirit of the Laws* 10.14 on 84–85); Delalleau de Bailliencourt, *Cours normal d'histoire grecque,* 108–123. Also see the vigorous indictment of Sainte-Croix and his theories by P. Van Limburg Brouwer, who (also citing Montesquieu) considers that "Sainte-Croix knows historians far better than the history of Alexander, and his judgment of the veracity of these historians themselves is often absolutely false" (*Histoire de la civilisation morale et religieuse des Grecs,* vol. 5, part II, 34).

8. German Alexanders

1. This text was published in the *Göttingische gelehrte Anzeigen* (June 24, 1805): 993–996; a French translation-paraphrase by A. L. Millin can be found in the "Nouvelles littéraires" of the *Magasin Encyclopédique*, no. 3 (1806): 373–379. The dissertation focused on Alexander *(De Alexandro Magno id agente, ut totum terrarrum orbem mutuis commerciis jungeret)* was published in Göttingen in 1805, then reprinted in Heyne's *Opuscula Academica Collecta*, 6:330–362. It has never been given an in-depth commentary.

2. See Chap. 5 § "Alexander and Tyre: The Phoenician Mirage."

3. See Heidenreich, *Heyne*, 197–252; on the Göttingen intelligentsia's reservations about the revolution (with the exception of Georg Forster) see Marino, *I maestri della Germania*, 358–371, and his *Praeceptores Germaniae*, 384–409. On Georg Forster see primarily the introduction by Gilli, *Un révolutionnaire allemande*, 5–48, and, on p. 432, a letter dated December 10, 1792, in which he refers to Heyne in the following terms: "The good old man in Göttingen makes me very sad. But he is only an aristocrat because he doesn't live 50 miles further south."

4. See Heyne, Review of Feßler; and Heyne, Review of Chaussard; on the former see Heidenreich, *Heyne*, 359–360.

5. Pownall, *Treatise*, esp. *on the Study of Antiquities*, esp. 89–94 (quote on 90); Heyne, Review of Pownall.

6. Heyne, Review of Sainte-Croix.

7. The letters were published as supplements to the *Göttingische gelehrte Anzeigen* 1803/1, inserted between pp 1024 and 1025 (additions to vol. 102 of the GGA).

8. Laudin, "Les grands hommes de l'Antiquité," 221.

9. "Description de la révolution à Mayence," in Gilli, *Un révolutionnaire allemand*, 141.

10. Herder, *Outlines*, 92. On Herder's position regarding the European empires of his time see Muthu, *Enlightenment against Empire*, 210–258; for a synoptic analysis (though not comprehensive) of Diderot and Herder's pages see the enlightening Pagden, *European Encounters*, 141–181. I note in passing that the *Histoire des deux Indes* was translated into German in 1783.

11. Berghaus, *Geschichte der Schiffahrtskunde*. On his use of *The Spirit of the Laws* on the history of Alexander see, in particular, 1:548 n. *.

12. On this point see the analysis by Heidenreich, *Heyne*, 248–252. The text from the 1763 conference on the Ptolemaic dynasty *(De genio Saeculi Ptolemaerum)* was published in his *Opuscula* 1:76–134; on this text see the French paraphrase published in 1806 by Jean-François Boissonade, and the contextual analysis by Bravo, *Droysen*, 61–63, 239.

13. On these two articles see also Chap. 10 § "Oriental Hoarding and European Circulation."

14. Barthold Georg Niebuhr, *Demosthenis erste philippische Rede*.

15. See Quillien, *G. von Humboldt,* esp. 65–69; on the man and his work see also Fuhrmann, "Wilhelm von Humboldt"; a text he delivered to the Academy of Prussia in 1821 ("Über die Aufgabe des Geschichtschreibers") can be read in English translation as "On the Historian's Task," *History and Theory* 6 (1967): 57–71.

16. Wolf, *Darstellung der Alterthumswissenschaft;* on this book and its author see Gigante, "Il ruolo del Wolf"; Cerasuolo, *"La Esposizione";* Markner and Veltri, *Friedrich August Wolf;* Leghissa, *Incorpore l'antico,* 11–47; and the recent article by Maufroy "Friedrich August Wolf."

17. Quotes from Leghissa, "L'antiquité grecque," 215 and 220. On the founding of the University of Berlin see Waszek, "Fondation"; on Goethe in Weimar at this time see Delinière, *Weimar à l'époque de Goethe,* 201–219.

18. Barthold Georg, *Vorträge,* 2:423 = *Lectures,* 2:403.

19. Constant, *De la religion* 1:136. Concerning Sainte-Croix, Constant is targeting his studies on religion here.

20. For example, Heeren, *Handbuch der Geschichte des Alterthums* (1810), 272 = *Manual* (1854), 174: "contains more than the title implies"; Heyne, Review of Sainte-Croix; Bredow, *Handbuch,* 411 n. 2; Schlosser, *Histoire universelle* 2:3–22; 3:7–32 (very many citations and references); Droysen, Review of Van der Chys, 472 (Droysen refers to the *Examen critique* in this review as "the first fundamental work [*erste grundliche Werk*] on the history of Alexander"); Droysen, *Geschichte des Hellenismus,* 1:xiii; Hoffmann, *Die Alterthumswissenschaft,* 439 (cites Droysen's *Geschichte Alexanders des Grossen* and the 1804 *Examen critique* side by side: the first is mentioned without commentary, while the second is referred to as the principal work [*Hauptwerk*] on the history of Alexander).

21. Barthold Georg Niebuhr, "Ueber das zweyte Buch der Oekonomika unter den aristotelischen Schriften", 1812; see its use by Schlosser, *Histoire universelle,* 3:13–18, and below § "Alexander the Great in Heeren and Schlosser."

22. Barthold Georg Niebuhr, *Vorträge über alte Geschichte* (posthumous volumes prepared by his son Marcus based on lecture notes); translated into English as *Lectures on Ancient History,* of which vol. 2 includes the history of Sparta and Athens, as well as the history of the conquest of Alexander (Lectures 74–80). The division into chapters (lectures) is specific to the English version; I use it to facilitate references, but I have corrected the sometimes loose translation.

23. Barthold Georg Niebuhr, *Vorträge,* 2:508: "Er wollte nich Asien griechisch, sondern Griechenland persisch machen" = *Lectures,* 3:482–483: "His intention was not to hellenise Asia, but to make Greece Persian." On Niebuhr's position on the Orient see Chap. 10 § The Sick Man of Asia.

24. See my *Alexandre des Lumières,* 227–233.

25. Fichte, *Addresses,* no. 13, 230; on the political context in which Fichte delivered these addresses see Losurdo, "Fichte et la question nationale allemande."

26. The expression was used by Edmund Burke in a letter sent to Robertson in 1777 after the publication of his *History of America;* it represents all the work by all

the scholars of the Republic of Letters in their quest for exhaustive knowledge of all the countries and populations in the world: see Osterhammel, *Entzauberung Asien,* 18–21.

27. Sprengel, *Geschichte der Maratten;* Sprengel, *Geschichte der wichtigsten geographischen Entdeckungen* (1792). On Sprengel see a short but useful discussion in Dharampal-Frick, "Entre Orientalisme des Lumières," 18–19 ("Sprengel, témoin ambivalent de l'histoire coloniale britannique" ["Sprengel, Ambivalent Witness to British Colonial History"]); for his part Osterhammel, *Entzauberung Asien,* presents Sprengel as "the indefatigable laborer-adaptor of information from overseas *(der unermüdliche Verarbeiter von Nachrichten aus Übersee)*" (231).

28. On Forster (the younger) see Promies "Georg Forster"; on Humboldt's travels see Pagden's *European Encounters,* 8–10; on his view of Alexander see his book published in 1847 and translated into English in 1849 as *Cosmos: A Sketch of a Physical Description of the Universe;* in chap. 2 of vol. 2 (*Expedition of the Macedonians under Alexander the Great,* 519–535), Humboldt borrowed Droysen's entire image of Alexander and his civilizing enterprise.

29. On this point see the interesting remarks by Osterhammel, *Entzauberung Asien,* 192–196. Besides those names cited by the author, in the field of political philosophy one could add Christian Garve, a translator of many Scottish authors (MacFarlane, Payley, Adam Smith, Ferguson, Gillies).

30. On all these points I owe a great deal to reading L. Kontler's "William Robertson and His German Audience," and "Mankind and Its Histories," and Dharampal-Frick, "Entre Orientalisme des Lumières et idéalisme révolutionnaire"; on other aspects of Forster see Gilli, *Un révolutionnaire allemande.*

31. See his short note in the *Göttingische Anzeigen von gelehrten Sachen,* June 1792, p. 1032, in which he describes the *Historical Disquisition* as "a work as entertaining as it is instructive" (*ein eben so unterhaltendes als belehrendes Werk*).

32. Though it is difficult to explain the reasons for its presence (did Vincent accidentally forget it or purposely leave it?), the letter was inserted in the signed copy of the English version that Vincent sent to his French translator (Billecocq) in December 1800, and which Billecocq donated to the Bibliothèque Nationale in 1804, after adding his own handwritten dedication (see above Chap. 3 § "Alexander, Promoter of Commerce"); the librarians pasted the letter on the inside of the binding.

33. Though it implies that Vincent did not read the review with much attention, the error is understandable, given that Heyne's letter to Vincent indicates that he personally sent the review to the author and that, in keeping with the general practice of the time, the *Gottingische Anzeigen*'s reviews were anonymous. This probably explains why it is not mentioned in the publication lists compiled by recent biographers of Heeren (Becker-Schaum, *Arnold Herrmann Ludwig Heeren,* 468–474) and Heyne (Heidenreich, *Christian Gottlob Heyne,* 604–605). However, a handwritten note on the copy at the Göttingen library (which can be

consulted online on the Göttinger Digitalisierungszentrum website) mentions the reviewer's name (Heeren); the reviewer's astute knowledge of the issues addressed and the barely veiled reference to his own works clearly confirm his identity. Heeren refers to himself in the third person, as "a local scholar" (*ein hiesiger Gelehrter*). Given his dual role as head of the university library and editor in chief of the journal, Heyne is nearly certainly responsible for the handwritten additions. [After I had written this note, I realized that this observation regarding the author of the handwritten notes was previously made by G. Valera (*Scienza dello Stato,* ciii), based on her analysis of the periodical from Heyne's copies in the collection of the Göttingen library, which are those now available online.]

34. One hypothesis is that the publication of Billecocq's French translation in 1800 (financed by public funds from the government) dissuaded the German bookseller from investing too much money in a publication made all the more onerous by the market shares already taken by the English and French editions. Research in private and public archives in Magdeburg may one day provide an answer to this question.

35. Bredow, *Untersuchungen,* 715–797. First published in 1799 (like Heeren's), his *Handbuch der alten Geschichte* was issued in a fifth edition in 1816.

36. Regarding Heeren's biographical, pedagogical, and scientific histories, I refer the reader once and for all to the fundamental monograph by Becker-Schaum, *Arnold Hermann Ludwig Heeren,* esp. 87–210. Also see Marino, *I maestri della Germania,* 1975, pp. 318–328; the studies compiled in *Rivista Storica Italiana* (1999), and the texts introduced and translated into Italian by G. Valera, *Scienza dello Stato,* 323ff. On *Staatistik,* see *Scienza dello Stato,* 189–203 (Italian translation of passages from Schlözer's pioneering work *Theorie der Statistik,* 1804 ed.), and Peters, *Altes Reich und Europa,* 207–256 (Schlözer and statistics); on Heeren's *Staatistik* courses in Göttingen see Becker-Schaum, *Arnold Hermann Ludwig Heeren,* 321–366; and, lastly, Van der Zande, "Staatistik" and Garner, "Économie."

37. Heeren, *Ideen*; vol. 1 of the first edition was published in a French translation in 1800 under the title *Idées sur les relations politiques et commerciales des anciens peuples de l'Afrique*; this is the translation I have quoted from (p. 7). The following French edition (1830) would be published under the title *De la politique et du commerce des peuples de l'Antiquité.*

38. See, in particular, Heeren, "Commentatio de Graecorum," 68–71, with my commentary in "Retour sur Alexandre," part I, 39–41 and 53–56.

39. See Heeren, Review of Robertson, esp. 106–107.

40. Heeren, "Commentatio de prisca Sinus"; the study had been announced and summarized in *Göttingische Anzeigen von gelehrten Sachen* (July 1796): 1041–1043.

41. Heeren, *Handbuch der Geschichte des Alterthums* (1828), 253=*Manual* (1854), 177.

42. *Ideen,* First Part, Second Chapter, 4th Edition, 1824, p. 229, note=*Historical Researches,* 2:221 n. 3; however, Vincent is cited at 1:27 n. g, as well as in an appendix

"on the most ancient navigation of the Persian gulf" (*Historical Researches*, 2:416) because one of his remarks confirms what Heeren had written.

43. Heeren, Review of Vincent (1801) and Review of Vincent (1806).

44. French trans.: *De la politique et du commerce des peuples de l'Antiquité* (1830); English trans.: *Historical Researches into the Politics, Intercourse and Trade of the Principal Nations of Antiquity* (1833). See Anon., Review of Heeren, which the author closes by wishing that English scholars would seek inspiration in this kind of work; however, the 1796 edition had been torn apart in *British Critique* 10 (1798): 455–459, in which the reviewer firmly rejected the possibility of an English translation; instead he advised Heeren to collaborate with Rennell. Published in a Jena journal in 1812 (= *Kleine Schriften* 2:107–158), Niebuhr's criticism focused on Heeren's method in his volume of Greek history (*Ideen*, 3.1): see Marcone, "La polemica."

45. In France see Delalleau de Bailliencourt's textbook *Cours normal d'Histoire grecque*, which refers to many French authors (Bossuet, Rollin, Montesquieu, Barthélemy, Sainte-Croix, Daunou, Cayx and Poirson), as well as the Englishman George Grote, who regularly drew on Heeren in his discussions of the Persians and Alexander (see Briant, "Grote on Alexander"). In chaps. 14–15, which Delalleau devotes to Alexander, Heeren is used to support the author's views on Alexander's accession to the throne (p. 111), on Alexandria (p. 115, note), on the expedition to India (p. 120: quote), and on the union of the empire's subjects through marriages and commercials ties (p. 121: quote).

46. The quotes and references are from / to the 1854 *Manual*.

47. Schlosser, *Universalhistorische Uebersicht der Geschichte des Alten Welt une ihrer Cultur = Histoire universelle de l'Antiquité*, vols. 2–3. On the particularly original passages see the commentary on a passage by Polyenus on the king's table (3:2–4).

48. Droysen, *Geschichte des Hellenismus*, 1:ix.

49. See his *Geschichte des Luxus der Athenienser*. His academic title at Göttingen was "Lehrer der Weltweisheit" ("Teacher of Philosophy") (see Gierl, "Christoph Meiners").

50. The list of seminars attended by Droysen is provided (with their titles) by Bravo, *Philologie, histoire*, 170–171 (in chronological order), and by Hackel, *Philologue*, 21 (by professor name).

51. Droysen, Review of Van der Chys, in which the author already clearly sets forth his conception of Alexander and his work.

52. Ritter, "Über Alexander des Großen Feldzug am Indischen Kaukasus" (many references to English and Scottish authors, to Sainte-Croix, to Forster, to Van der Chys).

53. Lassen, *Commentatio geographica. atque historica*, 1827.

54. Hegel, *Vorlesungen*, 332–334; see Biasutti, "Alessandro Magno nella Philosophie-geschichte di Hegel."

9. After Alexander?

1. English trans. *Works of Voltaire,* 12:5.
2. See below § "Voltaire and the 'Hellenists' of Jerusalem."
3. "Siècles, les quatre," *Encyclopédie,* 15:172.
4. "Grecs|Histoire ancienne|Littérature," *Encyclopédie,* 7:914.
5. The following quotes are from the introduction to *Siècle d'Alexandre* (1762), 1–13; (1769), 7–22.
6. On this point see Chap. 10 § "Oriental Hoarding and European Circulation."
7. *Siècle d'Alexandre* (1762), 205–207; (1769), 270–272: "The Hottentots, the Kaffir, lived before they knew our eaux-de-vie. . . . The greater part of our citizens who still do not know the name of chocolate and a thousand other more pernicious drugs, would undoubtedly have survived, even if a handful of European pleasure-seekers had not discovered them!" See also his vehement denunciations of the voyages and enterprises of the Europeans of his time in his *Annales politiques, civiles et littéraires du dix-huitième siècle,* volume five, at London, 1779, pp. 504–518.
8. *Siècle d'Alexandre* (1762), 161; (1769), 213–214 (Frederick's name was added alongside Marcus Aurelius's in 1769); on Plutarch see (1762), 160: "It is undoubtedly not on reasoning of this kind that the admiration we ordinarily have for Plutarch is founded. One might as well claim that Muhammad and the Caliphs his successors were the most eloquent of all men because they converted a large part of the world to their law. They preached the Koran the way Alexander taught Philosophy, weapons in hand"=(1769), 213.
9. Moutonnet de Clairfons, *Réflexions sur les siècles d'Alexandre, d'Auguste, de Léon X et de Louis XIV.*
10. Stanyan, *Grecian History* (1751), vol. 2 (the preface does not have page numbers).
11. Grote, *History of Greece,* vol. 12. On Grote and Alexander in relation to Droysen and the Englishman Thirwall see my study "Alexander et l'hellénisation de l'Asie," 18–23, and Vasunia, "Alexander and Asia."
12. On these points see my detailed study "Grote on Alexander."
13. Gast, *History of Greece* (1793), "Author's Preface," xxx–xxi; a devastating assessment of Alexander, II, pp. 171–172; on pages xxviii–xxxii (vol. I), the author defines what he calls the five periods of Greek history.
14. *Vorträge,* 3:1–3 ("Ueber die spätere griechische Geschichte im Allgemeine")=*Lectures,* 3:1.
15. See above Chap. 7 § "Commerce, Colonization, and Civilization."
16. Levesque, *Études de l'histoire ancienne,* 3:385.
17. Rochette, *Histoire critique,* 4:4–6, 98–99.
18. Mably, *Observations sur les Grecs,* 195, 200–201; *Observations sur l'histoire de la Grèce,* 226–227 (reference to Machiavelli), 229–230; on Mably's position on the

Alexander of *The Spirit of the Laws,* see my study "Montesquieu, Mably et Alexandre le Grand."

19. See Chap. 5 § "The Hesitations of the Chevalier de Jaucourt."

20. "Grecs|Histoire ancienne|Littérature," *Encyclopédie,* 7:915.

21. Iselin, *Über die Geschichte der Menscheit* (1764); and esp. the 2nd ed. (1770), chap. 18, 206–211; on Iselin and the European context of his reflection see Reill, *German Enlightenment,* 65–69; on Herder's opposition to his theories see Cambiano, "Herder et la jeunesse de l'antiquité."

22. Heeren, *Idées,* 1:9; see Heeren, *Manual* (1854), 262: "Seleucus was one of the few followers of Alexander who had any genius for the arts of peace. He either founded or embellished a vast number of cities, the most important of which were the capital, Antiochia in Syria, and the two Seleucias, one on the Tigris, the other on the Orontes: the flourishing prosperity of several of these places was the result of the restoration of eastern trade; new channels for which appear to have been opened at this period on the main streams of Asia, and more particularly on the Oxus"; see p. 223: "Though a soldier by profession, Ptolemy was highly accomplished, was himself a writer, and had a genius for all the arts of peace, which he fostered with the openhanded liberality of a king." Robertson, *Historical Disquisition,* 27–88.

23. Gillies, *History of Ancient Greece,* 2:687 n. 31.

24. Ibid., 2:680.

25. Ibid., 2:679 n. 57.

26. "Orateurs grecs," *Encyclopédie,* 11:563–565.

27. *Examen critique* (1775), 1–5 (excerpts)=*Critical Enquiry* 1:1–5.

28. *Examen critique* (1775), 15=*Critical Enquiry* 1:19–20); *Examen critique* (1804), 47–51.

29. See, for example, in France, the Poirson and Cayx manual *Précis de l'histoire ancienne,* in which the "fifth age" is entitled "Founding of a Powerful Empire in Macedonia and in Greece by Philip II, Father of Alexander. Conquest of the Persian Monarchy by Alexander. Temporary Joining of Macedon, Greece and Persia (Period of One Hundred and Thirty-Seven Years, 360–323)." Significantly chap. 41, which is entitled "On Letters, Sciences and Arts among the Greeks from the Heroic Ages to the Age of Alexander," ends with the beginning of Alexander's reign (p. 267).

30. Gillies, *History of the World;* on the book's presentation of Alexander and his achievements see Chap. 2 § "John Gillies, Alexander, and Hellenistic History"; the quotes in the body of the text are from vol. 1, 1–2, 178–224.

31. Visconti, *Iconographie ancienne,* 2:31. All the authors refer to a famous passage in Diodorus of Sicily (bk. 18.4) traditionally called "Alexander's Last Plans." The army allegedly followed Perdiccas's suggestion to refuse to execute these plans. Whether the plans actually existed had already been the subject of a bitter controversy that has remained constant into the twenty-first century. Nonetheless, critics of Alexander used the passage as confirmation of their analysis. For

example, Mably wrote that "[nothing] in these Memoirs indicates the views of the Founder of a lasting monarchy; they only contain the projects of a vain man who wishes to surprise mankind and a power-hungry man who cannot tire of making conquests" (*Observations sur l'histoire de la Grèce*, 229).

32. Rochette, *Histoire critique*, 4:119–120.

33. Herder, *Ideen zur Philosophie der Geschichte der Menscheit*, bk. 13, chap. 8 = *Outlines*, 388–389. Advocated by Herder, the geopolitical realigning of the Seleucid kingdom had earlier been presented by Montesquieu in chap. 5 of the *Considérations:* see my remarks in "Montesquieu, Mably et Alexandre le Grand," 180–181.

34. Rochette, *Histoire critique*, 4 :108, 118–119).

35. Courier, *Œuvres*, 276; see text reprinted in Montecalvo, *Baron de Sainte-Croix*, 1:371 (no. 286).

36. See Chap. 8 § "Christian G. Heyne: From European Wars to Alexander's Campaigns."

37. Ph. Roget, "Historiens allemands contemporains," 1867, p. 92.

38. Quote from Droysen, *Geschichte des Hellenismus*, 2:566–567 (announcing a more thorough study on "the literary and scientific movement," which he never wrote); the English translation is from the French translation by Roget in his "Historiens allemands contemporains," 235. Roget chooses to side with Grote (see his second article in the same periodical, 1867, p. 92).

39. See above Chap. 2 § "The History of Alexander in the Revolution."

40. Rollin, *Ancient History* 5:192 (bk. 15.7).

41. See above Chap. 1 § "The History of Alexander and the History of the People of God."

42. See Rollin, *Histoire ancienne* (1821), 6:379–383 (passage not translated in the English editions).

43. Bossuet, *Discourse*, 438.

44. I do not think this phrasing is found earlier in Voltaire, though it is in Linguet; I am therefore led to wonder whether by introducing it with the words "it has not been enough noted that . . . ," Voltaire is indirectly recognizing his debt without mentioning the author by name.

45. On Heyne and Herder see Bravo, *Droysen*, 151 and 239–240. The case of Gillies, which I have added, is nonetheless quite different: in his *History of Ancient Greece*, 2:679 n. 57, he mentions that in his opinion "the Greek language must have been understood by all ranks of men in Judea, since the inspired writers employed it in propagating the gospel, which was first preached to the Jews," but this is a mere observation, which he does not go on to interpret.

46. Bickerman, "L'européanisation de l'Orient classique," 382–383. The article and its author are succinctly presented in the Introduction to this volume, which includes a quote from the passage. I have studied the contemporary resonances of the author's thought elsewhere: see "Alexandre et l'hellénisation de l'Asie," 42–44, and mainly "Michael Rostovtzeff"; Bickerman's article has been

translated into English by A. Kuhrt in the same volume (Bickerman 2015). On discussions of the term "Hellenists" see R. Bichler's historiographic clarification, *"Hellenismus,"* 22–32.

47. Momigliano, "J. G. Droysen." Along with the Momigliano texts cited, one should mention another text too often overlooked, Droysen's review of Van der Chys's *Commentarius* (1828): referring to the consequences of the conquest, Droysen writes that Alexander "had, in ten years, founded Hellenistic life *(das hellenistische Leben),* from which Christianity would one day blossom *(aus dem einst das Christenthum erblühen sollte)*" (p. 471). On all these questions (which are outside of the scope of this book), I refer the reader to the indispensable book by B. Bravo, *Droysen,* esp. 222–224, 273–274.

48. Émile Ruelle, about whom I have found no biographical details other than those attributed to him in the translation ("professor at the Collège Royal de Henri IV, former inspector of the académie de Montpellier"), should not be confused with the canon Charles-Émile Ruelle (1833–1912), a very famous Hellenist. In the foreword (pp. v–viii), Ruelle emphasizes the originality of his work and insists on the fact that he and his assistant "corrected the errors and filled in the gaps in Gillies's book" (which explains the "citation" from Jouffroy). However, he does not mention that Gillies's book had already been translated by Carra in 1788.

49. Ruelle and Huillard-Brihales, *Histoire résumée des temps anciens* (1845), 2:248–249.

50. On the man and his position at *Le Globe,* see the studies by Goblot, *Documents pour servir à l'histoire de la presse,* 97–103, and *La jeune France libérale,* esp. 281–304 on Jouffroy and the philosophy of history. Goethe especially enjoyed reading *Le Globe:* see Valentin, *Johann Wolfgang Goethe,* 27, 37, 232.

51. Information on his teaching was found in the (thin) file in the archives of the Collège de France. On the man see also the editor's preface (by P. Damiron) to Jouffroy's *Nouveaux mélanges philosophiques.*

52. On this see the recent articles by E. Hall ("Aeschylus' *Persians* and Images of Islam") and G. Van Steen ("The *Persians* and the Greek War of Independence").

53. Jouffroy published several articles on Greece in *Le Globe:* see Goblot, *Documents pour servir à l'histoire de la presse,* 97–103.

54. Hegel, *Vorlesungen,* 268–272.

10. Alexander, Europe, and the Immobile Orient

1. Levesque, *Études de l'histoire ancienne,* 3:385.
2. See Spawforth, "Symbol of Unity?"
3. See Raby, "Mehmed the Conqueror's Greek Scriptorium."
4. Mentioned by K. Buraselis (*Archèognôsia* 8, 1993–1994, p. 130, n. 35) through a reference to a book (in Greek) by Sn. Euanggelatos, *Istoria tou theatrou en Kephallènia (1600–1900),* Athens, 1970, p. 15ff. *(non vidi)*; in the same note, Buraselis

refers to the designation *Persai* applied to the Turks by certain Byzantine writers. On the representation of Cephalonia see details and context in Hall, "Aeschylus' Persians," 178; on the popularity of the *Persians* in the circles of neo-Hellenic classicism see Clogg, "Classics and the Movement for Greek Independence," 41–42. On this see also Momigliano, *Polybius between the English and the Turks.*

5. "Histoire," *Encyclopédie*, 8:222.

6. See Paviot, *Les ducs de Bourgogne, la Croisade et l'Orient,* and Blondeau, *Un conquérant pour quatre ducs,* esp. 231–255.

7. Gaudenzio, *I fatti d'Alessandro il Grande,* 206–207.

8. See Plutarch, *On the Fortune or the Virtue of Alexander,* 1.7: "When Demaratus the Corinthian had seen Alexander in Susa, he exclaimed with tears of joy that all the Greeks who had died before that hour had been deprived of a great joy, since they had not seen Alexander seated on the throne of Darius."

9. Fénelon, *Œuvres de Fénelon,* I, Paris, Didot, 1845, p. 4.

10. On the idea of the Crusade and images of the Ottoman during this period in Europe see Poumarède, *Pour en finir avec la Croisade,* 50ff. and 123, as well as Valensi's reflections in *Birth of the Despot.*

11. Gatterer, "Vom historischen Plan," 46–47 ("Hauptepisoden in dem Leben dieses Räubers"); *Handbuch der Universalhistorie* (1765), 633–654, esp. 653–654; *Abriss der Universalhistorie,* 282–283.

12. Gatterer, "Vom historischen Plan," 47: "Der Sitz der Herrschaft ist nun erstmal in Europa"; *Weltgeschichte,* 2:84: "Und so kam denn durch Alexander . . . die Weltherrschaft von den Asiaten zum erstmal an die Europäer."

13. See Chap. 8 § "Greek History, the History of Alexander, and German Identity," and below § "The Sick Man of Asia."

14. Barthold Georg Niebuhr, *Vorträge* 2:418: "Die Herrschaft Europa's über Asien. . . . Er hat zuerst die Europäer siegreich in den Orient geführt"=*Lectures,* 3:399.

15. Heeren, *Historical Researches,* 1:356.

16. Williams, *Alexander the Great,* 1–2.

17. On this period in Ottoman history one can easily consult Robert Mantran's chapter, "Les débuts de la Question d'Orient (1774–1839)"; see also Driault, *La Question d'Orient,* 50–60, 104–133 (he begins his introduction with an evocation of Alexander's conquests). Regarding plans for colonization, I am referring to Lamartine; I take the liberty of referring the reader to my study "De Thémistocle à Lamartine," 173–191 and 175–176.

18. The first volume (1826) was published under the pseudonym of Sylvain Phalantée because the author (Pierre David) then held the official French position of consul general for Asia in Smyrna (he served as an intermediary in the acquisition of the statue that became famous as the *Venus de Milo;* he was also the "founder of the Academy of Smyrna"); in 1827 he published a similarly fashioned *Athènes assiégée.* The bibliography of political philhellenism is vast: see,

for example, the 2005 issue of *Revue germanique internationale* on the subject (*Philhellénisme et transferts culturels dans l'Europe du XIXᵉ siècle*); the books by Marchand, *Down from Olympus*, Angelomatis-Tsougarakis, *Eve of the Greek Revival*, and Hamilakis, *Nation and Its Ruins* (esp. 57–123); and several studies collected in Bridges, Hall, and Rhodes, *Cultural Responses to the Persian Wars*. A list of philhellenic pamphlets is available at the website of the Messolonghi Byron Society: http://www.messolonghibyronsociety.gr/index.php/en/collection-of -philhellenic-pamphlets.html. Visual representations of the Greek revolt in France are pertinently studied in Athanassoglou-Kallmyer, *French Images from the Greek War of Independence,* which also effectively brings to light (pp. 35–37) the way the Liberals (including the paper *Le Globe*) assimilated the Greek war of independence to their own struggle against the Ultras.

19. See Montesquieu, *Persian Letters,* 67: "That is a true description of this empire, which inside two hundred years will be the scene of the triumphs of some conqueror"—as predicted by Usbek in a letter sent "to his friend Rustam, the 2d of the moon of Rammaddan 1711."

20. On Korais and the Greek Enlightenment see, in particular, the volume edited by Kitromilidès, *Adamantios Korais and the European Enlightenment* (with his introduction "Adamantios Korais and the Dilemmas of Liberal Nationalism"); on the general cultural context (including efforts in translation) see also Clogg's fine article, "Classics and the Movement for Greek Independence" (pp. 26–33 on Korais).

21. Korais, *Mémoire*, 6.

22. On Alexander's gradual reintegration into the history of Greece as it was written in the modern era see the explanations and interpretations in Koubourlis, *La formation de l'histoire nationale grecque,* esp. 53–71 and 316–320. The author has summarized some of his ideas in the article "Les péripéties de l'intégration des anciens Macédoniens"; see also his "European Historiographical Influences upon the Young Konstantinos Paparrigopoulos"; the following pages borrow some of his ideas, with additions based on my supplementary reading, particularly on Rigas.

23. On Paparrigopoulos and the "Great Idea" see Kitromilidès, "On the Intellectual Content of Greek Nationalism," and Koubourlis, "European Historiographical Influences upon the Young Konstantinos Paparrigopoulos"; on the approaches of Paparrigopoulos, Droysen, and Grote to the question of Hellenization see a few remarks in my article "Alexandre et l'hellénisation de l'Asie," 40–42.

24. On the man and his work, A. Dascalakis's books remain fundamental (*Rhigas Velestinlis* and *Les Œuvres de Rhigas Velestinlis*); some of his works have been translated into French (Rhigas Velestinlis, *Œuvres Révolutionnaires*, Athens, 2002, with an introduction by D. Karabéropoulos). See also the studies by Kitromilidès, "Itineraries in the World of the Enlightenment" and *Enlightenment and Revolution,* 201ff. The bicentennial of Velestinlis's arrest by the Austrian authorities

in Trieste and of his subsequent execution in Belgrade by the Ottoman authorities (1798) generated several symposiums about him; aside from the symposium at UNESCO (*Rigas Velestinlis [1757–1798]. Intellectuel et combattant de la liberté*) (*Rigas Velestinlis [1757–1798]: Intellectual and Freedom Fighter*), 2002, others
were held in Greece and Trieste (see analysis in *Annales historiques de la Révolution française* no. 319 (2000): 127–140). I should also mention that the Wikipedia
entry on "Rigas" has recently been published with author names and sources
(Fr. Miller-A. F. Vandome-J. McBrewster, *Rigas*, VDM Publishing House, 2010).

25. *Florilegium of Physics for Sharp-Minded and Knowledge-Loving Greeks*; see Kitrom-
    ilides, *Enlightenment and Revolution*, 202–204.

26. See Dascalakis, *Rhigas Velestinlis*, 49: "On the last page of the *Elements of physics*,
    one finds an announcement providing the following information: 'If a patriot
    wants to go to the trouble of translating a book to make himself useful to the
    Nation, he should not tackle *The Spirit of the Laws* by Monsieur de Montesquieu,
    because I have already translated half of this volume and it will be printed as
    soon as I am finished.'" On Montesquieu's influence in Greece see Apostol-
    opoulos, "La fortune de Montesquieu en Grèce dans la seconde moitié du XVIIIe
    siècle"; and Argyropoulos, "Présence de Montesquieu en Grèce de la Révolution
    française à l'indépendance grecque."

27. On this map see Ubicini's study "La grande carte de la Grèce"; the more recent
    study by Guiomar and Lorain, "La carte de Grèce de Rigas et le nom de la Grèce";
    and the studies published in a special edition (vol. 3, 2008) of the periodical *e-
    Perimetron* (http://www.e-perimetron.org); on mutual influence and cultural
    transfers between the *Voyage d'Anacharsis* and the reflections of the Greek En-
    lightenment (primarily Rigas), see the remarkable article by G. Tolias, "Anti-
    quarianism, Patriotism and Empire."

28. See the institutional proposal written by Rigas: *Nouveau statut politique* (in Das-
    calakis, *Œuvres*, 75), and, on this text, the commentaries by Kitromilides, "An
    Enlightenment Perspective," and Stamboulis, "La *Dichiarazione di diritti* di
    Rigas Velestinlis." As early as 1881, Jean-Henri Abdolonyme Ubicini clearly
    pointed out the difference with what would later be known as the Great Idea:
    "Rigas imagined nothing better for the emancipated Orient than the re-
    establishment of the small republics of ancient Greece. This was probably his
    ideal, as of all the philhellenes of his time, king and philosophers" ("La Grande
    Carte," 18).

29. Cited by D. Karabéropoulos in Velestinlis, *Œuvres révolutionnaires*, 27.

30. Every work on Rigas includes commentary (to varying degrees of detail) on the
    Portrait. The most detailed and accurate commentary is that by O. Gratziou,
    "Monophyllo" (1982, Greek); a more accessible article is Karabéropoulos, *O
    Mégas Alexandros tou Règa Belestinlè*.

31. Rigas's borrowing from Kleiner was earlier recognized by Gratziou, "Mono-
    phyllo," 136–137. Today the engraved stone is at the Hermitage Museum in Saint

Petersburg. My study of the ways images were copied and circulated was presented at a conference in Athens on March 10, 2014, under the title "Alexandre le Grand, l'Europe et la Grèce: l'empreinte des Lumières." It will be published in the near future.

32. One can wonder (without coming to a definitive answer) whether Rigas, who had begun to translate Montesquieu, might not have been influenced, even partially, by the positive image of Alexander developed in *The Spirit of the Laws.*

33. Korais, *Mémoire,* 20–23.

34. Korais, *Appel aux Grecs,* 41.

35. Tolias, "Antiquarianism, Patriotism and Empire," 85 n. 52; same note, with supplementary material, in Rigas, *Karta tès Hellados,* 115 n. 52; www.e-perimetron .org; see also Guiomar and Lorain, "La carte de Grèce," 117–118 (on the club and the spear).

36. *Preußische Jahrbücher* 130 (1908), 384: "Die heutige Zustand der Türkei mit den leßten Zeiten des alten Perserreich."

37. Heeren, *Handbuch* (1799), vii–viii = *Manual* (1854), viii–ix.

38. A stele from the canal opened by Darius I between the Nile and the Red Sea in about 500 BC was discovered and then published by its discoverer, F.-M. de Rozière in "Notice sur les ruines d'un monument persépolitain" (1809); the article is also a good summary of knowledge of cuneiform at the time; see § 7: "Quelques observations sur l'écriture persépolitaine." In presenting a vase inscribed in cuneiform, the Comte de Caylus does not fail to mention that it bears an inscription in the Persepolitan type (*Recueil d'Antiquités,* 5:80).

39. Herder, *Outlines,* 327.

40. On cross-fertilization between Brisson and Chardin see references in my article "Theme of 'Persian Decadence'"; see also my "Montesquieu et ses sources." On the Heeren-Herder polemic see Herder's *Persepolis* (published in 1787) and Heeren's response, "Über Herder's Persepolis," in *Ideen* (1817), vol. 1, part I, 450–459, and his review in *Historical Researches,* 2:401–413 (which drew on the publications of British travelers such as Ker Porter, Morier, and Kinneir).

41. Mill, *History of British India,* 248–249; Maillet, *Description de l'Égypte,* vol. 1, Letter 11, 105–106.

42. Heeren, *Historical Researches,* 1:23, in an opening section entitled *Asia* (pp. 1–79). There is no need to cite all the studies on "Asian despotism" that have since flourished.

43. Rollin, *Ancient History,* bk. 6, chap. 1 § 1.

44. Machiavelli, *Prince,* chap. 4: "Why the Kingdom of Darius, Conquered by Alexander, Did Not, on Alexander's Death, Rebel against His Successors."

45. Febvre, *L'état présent de la Turquie,* article 19: "Des causes qui affaiblissent et diminuent la puissance du Turc." Naturally, the author refers to the prophecy of Daniel, which inspired the theory of the "four empires." On the "four empires"

explanation of the Ottoman empire given in Venice and Europe see Valensi, *Venise et la Sublime Porte*, 59–70.

46. Ricaut, *History*, bk. 3, chap. 1: "On the Present State of the Military Discipline in General among the Turks" (pp. 322–323). See Jaucourt, "Turquie," *Encyclopédie* 16:759. On Ricaut (or Rycaut) in Montesquieu and other eighteenth-century authors see Thomson, "L'Europe des Lumières et le monde musulman."

47. Ricaut, *History*, bk. 1, chap. 18: "The Several Arts the Turks Use to Increase Their People Is a Principal Policy, without Which the Greatness of Their Empire Cannot Continue nor Be Increased."

48. See, for example (aside from Ricaut), Mably, *Observations on the Manners, Government, and Policy of the Greeks*, 126 ("Nature never produces large branches upon small stems.... The first blast of wind would rent to pieces a tree whose branches should be larger than the trunk"); Montesquieu, *Persian Letters* no. 121 ("An empire can be compared to a tree with branches which, if they spread too far, take all the sap from the trunk, and do nothing but provide shade"); Herder, *Outlines*, 325 ("The root of the Persian empire was so small and its branches so extensive that it must of necessity fall to the ground"); Volney, *Considerations on the War with the Turks*, 82 ("weakness and decay of the Turkish empire . . . [like] aged trees, which, under an appearance of verdure and a few branches, conceal a rotten trunk, etc.").

49. I have previously discussed these issues in "Histoire et idéologie," "Alexander and the Persian Empire," and "Theme of 'Persian Decadence,'" as well as in *Darius in the Shadow of Alexander*. My aim here is not to deal with the historiographic subject of "Persian decadence" in extenso, but to establish the bases of frequently made comparisons between past and present.

50. See Chap. 1 § "Return to the Sources."

51. Linguet, *Siècle d'Alexandre* (1762), 105–106; (1769), 158.

52. See Bossuet earlier: "They would find in the army the same magnificence and delicacies as in those places where the Court made its ordinary stay, so that the Kings marched with their wives, their concubines, their eunuchs, and whatsoever else might contribute to their pleasures" (*Discourse on the History of the World*, 488–489). On this subject, based on a famous passage from Quintus Curtius (3.3.8–25), see the texts and commentaries in *Darius in the Shadow of Alexander*, chap. 8: "Iron Helmet, Silver Vessels."

53. Justin (*Epitome of the Philippic History of Pompeius Trogus* 10.1–2) attributed the plot to the young prince and fifty of his brothers, who were soon put to death.

54. Montesquieu, *Spirit of the Laws*, 5.14: "How the Laws Are Relative to the Principle of Despotic Government." On these dynastic crises and their resolution in Istanbul see Vatin and Veinstein, *Le sérail ébranlé*, 72–79; in the Achaemenid empire see my *From Cyrus to Alexander*, 769–780.

55. On views of the "despotic seraglio" in Europe see the remarkable essay by A. Grosrichard, *The Sultan's Court*, whose analysis deserves to be supported by many Greek texts beyond those of Aristotle.

56. Herder, *Outlines,* 326–327.

57. Arrian, *Anabasis,* 2.11.10.

58. The translation quoted here is from *The Works of M. de Voltaire,* translated from the French, vol. 21:165–169.

59. I have discussed this in "Des Scythes aux Tartares," in which additional references are listed. The tsar's campaign in Persia is recounted by Voltaire in the second part of *Histoire de Russie,* chap. 16: "Des conquêtes en Perse"=*Œuvres completes,* 47:913–930. This is not the place to pick up the discussion of Voltaire's methods of investigation or his real or supposed positions; on this see Michel Mervaud's long and remarkable introduction to his edition of *Histoire de Russie* (*Œuvres complètes* 46:85–380) and the article by Christiane and Michel Mervaud ("Le Pierre le Grand et la Russie de Voltaire") in which the authors refute the theories of A. Lortholary in his *Mirage russe en France.* On Catherine II's use of Greek antiquity in facing the Turks see the study by V. Schiltz, "Catherine II, les Turcs et l'antique."

60. Barthold Georg Niebuhr, *Vorträge,* 2:374–399; in the English version (quoted here), this passage is found in Lectures 70–71 (*Lectures,* 359–382). On Niebuhr's position regarding the ancient Persians see Wiesehöfer, "Barthold Georg Niebuhr und die Perser der Antike."

61. Heeren, *Manual* (1854), 80–81.

62. Heeren, *Historical Researches,* 1:356, 428, 442. On this subject see also the studies collected in Bridges, Hall, and Rhodes, *Cultural Responses to the Persian Wars,* particularly the articles by Hall and Van Steen.

63. See, for example, Flathe, *Geschichte Makedoniens,* 1:277 n. 1; 278 n. 1; 347 n. 2. As for Schlosser, he proposed comparisons with "the exploits of Hernan Cortés or Francisco Pizarro against Mexico and Peru, or the English war in India," from which he drew identical inferences: "Here too, one sees innumerable masses of peoples without moral power, without military knowledge, and these masses also flee before a small number of practiced and valiant warriors, despite the fact that they must defend their native land against them" (*Histoire de l'antiquité,* 2:432–433).

64. Droysen, *Geschichte Alexanders des Grossen,* 100.

65. Compare this with what Hegel says of the reasons for the fall of the Persian empire in his lectures: "It was not the effeminacy of the Persians . . . that ruined them, but the unwieldy, unorganized character of their host as matched against Greek organization, i.e. the superior principle overcame the inferior" (*Lectures on the Philosophy of History,* 232).

66. Droysen, *Geschichte Alexanders des Grossen* (1833), p. 101: "Das großeste Reich der neueren Zeit." The text of the 1877 edition ("wie das Reich der Osmanen lange genug den Beweis gegeben hat") is quoted from the French trans., *Histoire de l'hellénisme,* 1:180. Does the difference in wording imply that Droysen thought that reforms—particularly those carried out by Abdülmecid (1839–1861)—had

left the Ottoman empire in a better state in 1877 than at the beginning of the 1830s?

67. Volney, *Considerations on the War with the Turks,* 32.

68. Attributed to L. B., the article is entitled "Considérations sur l'Égypte, la Syrie et la puissance des Anglais dans l'Inde," 74–86.

69. Bourlet de Vauxcelles, Review of Vincent, 121.

70. See Chap. 5 § "The Weight of the Model: The Aborted Debate on Cataracts."

71. Heeren, Review of Vincent, 667.

72. Gillies, *History of Ancient Greece,* 2:574–575.

73. *Journal des savants* 1792, p. 198.

74. *Chant de guerre des Grecs qui combattent en Égypte pour la cause de la liberté;* the title page indicates that it was published in a bilingual Greek-French edition in the Greek printing shop in Egypt; in fact, it was printed in Paris.

75. Maillet, *Description de l'Égypte,* Letter 4: "Description de la ville d'Alexandrie ancienne et moderne, des monuments qu'elle renferme et en particulier de la colonne de Pompée." On eighteenth-century travelers to Egypt see Carré, *Voyageurs et écrivains français,* 1:39–143, and Lamy and Bruwier, *L'égyptologie avant Champollion,* 141–235.

76. Lucas, *Voyages de Paul Lucas,* 3:169–170.

77. Savary, *Le parfait négociant,* 469–471.

78. Leibniz, *Projet d'expédition d'Égypte,* 29–30; see Hentsch, *L'Orient imaginaire,* 137–142.

79. See "Sur une ancienne communication de la Méditerranée avec la Mer Rouge," *Histoire de l'Académie des Sciences* (1703): 83–86.

80. Tott, *Memoirs of the Baron de Tott,* 1:9–10; 3:235–236, and 257–260 on the Red Sea canal.

81. Gillies, *History of Ancient Greece,* 2:611 (with n. 29): "Such was the sagacity of his choice that, within the space of twenty years, Alexandria rose to distinguished eminence among the cities of Egypt and the East, and continued, through all subsequent ages of antiquity, the principal bond of union, the seat of correspondence and commerce, among the civilized nations of the earth."

82. Linguet, "Préparatifs de la guerre contre les Turcs," esp. 240–244.

83. Vincent, *Voyage of Nearchus;* see above Chap. 6 §§ "From Nearchus to the East India Company" and "History of Alexander: Franco-British Translations and Confrontations."

84. On the *Description de l'Égypte* and the "Orientalist" ideology that underpinned it and that it conveyed, and on the history and European representations of the Suez Canal, see the now famous passages by Edward Said in *Orientalism,* 79–88.

85. Quoted by Lassus, *L'Égypte, une aventure savante,* 52.

86. Girard, "Mémoire sur l'agriculture et le commerce." Like *La Décade philosophique* in France, "*La Décade égyptienne* [*Egyptian Ten-Day Week*] is the Ideologues

movement's principal tool for propagation" (Boulad-Ayoub, "L'Institut d'Égypte et *La Décade égyptienne.*")

87. Le Père, "Mémoire sur la communication," 7–8; the report's introduction is entitled: *Examen des différentes voies qu'a suivies le commerce des Indes; avantages généraux et particuliers de celle de l'Égypte par l'ancien canal de communication de la Méditerranée à la mer Rouge. [Examination of the Different Routes Taken by the Commerce of the Indies; General and Particular Advantages of the Egyptian Route by the Ancient Canal from the Mediterranean to the Red Sea].*

88. See, for example, de Lesseps, *Percement de l'Isthme de Suez,* 1–40.

89. This idea is a found in a great number of articles in the *Encyclopédie:* see the articles on "Anatomie" (1:411); "Aristotélisme" (1:654); "Cabinet d'histoire naturelle" (2:489); "Géographie" (7:609); "Eau" (5:206); "Antiquité" (1:516); "Astronomie" (1:785); "Bibliothèque" (2:229); "Chaldéens. Philosophie des—" (3:22); and "Chronologie sacrée" (3:392). See also Chap. 1 § "Alexander in the Academy," with the citation from Cassini, *Œuvres diverses,* 13–14.

90. From a toast delivered during a banquet in Cairo in the presence of Bonaparte: see Charles-Roux, *Bonaparte gouverneur d'Égypte,* 185. Another toast emphasized the specificity of the French conquest (including, implicitly, in comparison to the Alexander of *The Spirit of the Laws*): "We give the world the first example of a conqueror legislator. Until us, the victors always adopted the laws of the vanquished. Let us achieve the triumph of Reason over them, more difficult than that of arms, and prove ourselves as superior to the other nations as Bonaparte is to Genghis!" On the alliance between scholars and soldiers see also, for example, Sonnini, *Travels,* 1:xxi: "Europe attentive, and the East astonished, were looking with eyes full of curiosity and inquietude towards Egypt, which France covered with her legions, and with the fertile resources of her genius, with combatants as well as with artists and men of science."

91. Brisson, *De regio Persarum principatu,* 156–162; Potter, *Archaeologia Graeca* (1706) in the German translation by Raumbach, *Griechische Archäologie,* 3:186–188; Boeckh refers to Potter-Raumbach in his *Staatshaltung der Athener,* 1:12 n. 32.

92. Heyne, "Opum regni Macedonici auctarum, attritarum et eversarum, caussae probabiles"; see above Chap. 8 § "Christian Gottlob Heyne: From European Wars to Alexander's Campaigns."

93. On this plunder and its financial and symbolic value in the British imperial imagination and the history of the East India Company see the interesting remarks by Yasanoff, "Collectors of Empire," esp. 123–128.

94. Heyne, "Repentina auri argentique affluentia quasnam rerum vicissitudines attulerit, ex historiarum antiquarum fide disputatur."

95. Levesque, *Études de l'histoire ancienne,* 1:220–221.

96. Barthélemy, *Travels of Anacharsis the Younger:* "Fragments of a Letter of Anacharsis" (in chap. 61); Claustre, *Histoire de Thamas-Kouli-Kan,* 433–437. (A more detailed inventory of the plunder taken by the Persian king can be found

in Fraser, *History of Nadir-Shah,* 220–223); Maurice, *Bullion and Coined Money,* 93–101. In François Bernier's *Travels in the Mogul Empire* (original French ed. 1671–1672), the subject of hoarding is discussed in his "Letter to Monseigneur Colbert, concerning the Extent of Hindoustan, the Currency towards, and Final Absorption of Gold and Silver in that Country, Its Resources, Armies, the Administration of Justice, and the Principal Cause of the Decline of the States of Asia" (improved English trans. by A. Constable, pp. 200–238). Claustre implicitly but very clearly positions himself in Bernier's footsteps: "It has long been said that Hindustan is the abyss of all the treasures in the Universe etc." (*Histoire de Thamas-Kouli-Kan,* 434).

97. On the decisive nature of the concept of circulation among seventeenth- and eighteenth-century economists see Meyssonier, *La balance et l'horloge,* 45, 215, 221, and Larrère, *L'invention de l'économie,* 107–109, which both underline that the metaphor of blood circulation was found very early: as of 1588 in Davanzatti, according to Meyssonier, who (pp. 45 and 211ff.) also shows that a shift occurs with Véron de Forbonnais (1755): circulation no longer solely consists of a monetary flow, but a flow of expenses: "He replaces the mercantilist metaphor of the currency-blood with that of a river overflowing its banks, irrigating the plains and fertilizing them, especially as the water level will have been higher" (221). Circulation is therefore "the general movement of exchanges in which commodities are permanently transformed into money and money into commodities" (215).

98. See *Histoire des deux Indes* (2010), 1:500 n. 146 and 501.

99. Boeckh, *Staatshaltung der Athener,* 1:1–15; see Boeckh, *Public Economy of the Athenians,* 12ff.

100. Droysen, *Geschichte Alexanders des Grossen,* 539; see my "Alexander and the Persian Empire."

Conclusion

1. Boulanger, *Histoire d'Alexandre* (before 1759); Bury, *Histoire de Philippe et d'Alexandre* (1760); Linguet, *Siècle d'Alexandre* (1762), (1769); Feßler, *Alexander der Eroberer* (1797); Samuel Clarke, *Life and Death of Alexander the Great* (1665); Williams, *Life and Actions of Alexander the Great* (1829).

2. Bickerman, "L'européanisation de l'Orient classique," 381 (trans. Amélie Kuhrt); I have commented on Bickerman's paper at length in "Michael Rostovtzeff, Elias J. Bickerman and the 'Hellenization of Asia.'"

3. On Bonaparte's expedition, see Said, *Orientalism,* 80–88. The author says very little on "pre-Napoleonic orientalism," particularly concerning Antiquity; I note that he alludes to "Alexander—king warrior, *scientific conqueror*" (58; my italics), apparently without taking a comprehensive view of the expression or trying to

establish a link with the "scientific" nature of Bonaparte's expedition. I have borrowed the term "proto-orientalism" (*Proto-Orientalismus*) from Osterhammel, *Entzauberung*, 412; this is the reality analyzed under the term "Enlightened Orientalism" by Pagden in *Worlds at War*, 267–313. See, especially, the very important pages in S. Marchand, *German Orientalism*, chap. 1 "Orientalism and the *Longue Durée*," 15–28.

4. On Gillies's position see my "The Theme of 'Persian Decadence' in Eighteenth-Century European Historiography."

5. Barthold Georg Niebuhr *Lectures*, 3:482.

6. On the use of the image of the European island see my remarks in "Colonisation hellénistique et populations indigenes"; on the problem of Hellenization vs. Orientalization, see my "Alexandre et 'l'hellénisation de l'Asie.'"

7. Heeren, *Handbuch* (1799), 268; *Handbuch* (1828), 254 ("der Erhebung über alle Nationalvorurtheile")=*Manual* (1854), 178.

8. *Manual* (1858), 258=*Handbuch* (1828), 266 (. . . "Beweis, wie wenig von einer gewaltsamen Mischung der Völker zu erwarten steht, wenn sie durch den Untergang des Nationellen bei den Einzelnen erkauft wird")=*Manual* (1854), 185–186. This sentence is not in the first edition of 1799 (p. 281), where Heeren instead insists on the permanent state of war and military character of colonies; he even considers that the condition of Asia during the successors' wars has "many points of comparison with that of Germany during the Thirty Years' War." This comparison, particularly demeaning to the Hellenistic era (especially coming from a German), was not included in the 1828 edition, but Heeren's generally critical opinion of the consequences of the conquests and colonization remained.

9. Heeren, *Handbuch der Geschichte des Europäischen Staatsystems*, in *Historische Werke* 9:417: "Sie wäre das Grab Deutscher Cultur und Europäer Freiheit"=*Manual* (1858), 480; see Marino, *Maestri della Germania*, 319. Marino states that Heeren's declaration "is in perfect agreement with his entire political reflection, which was fundamentally in keeping with Montesquieu"; see my "Montesquieu, Mably et Alexandre le Grand," 184–185. On Heeren's involvement in the history of Europe in his time see Becker-Schaum, *Arnold Herrmann Ludwig Heeren*, 211ff.

10. Droysen, *Geschichte des Hellenismus*, 2:753 ("die trostlosen Mißgestalten der Colonialsysteme") and 754 ("der Aushebung des Unterschiedes zwischen Siegern und Besiegten, von dem Prinzip wahrhafter Ausgleichung und Verschmelzung ausging")=*Histoire de l'Hellénisme*, 2:775–777.

11. This expression is taken from Commandant Reynaud, "Alexandre le Grand colonisateur" (see my "Impérialisme antique et idéologie coloniale dans la France contemporaine"; R. Séguy used the same example (the French protectorate in Morocco) in 1931 in *L'héritage d'Alexandre* to argue that Alexander was a perfect precedent for French colonial methods (referring to *Spirit of the Laws* [10.13–14]);

see also these works by Jurien de la Gravière: *L'Asie sans maître,* v ("I call a legitimate conquest any conquest whose result is a better fate for the vanquished")
and xxii–xxiii (another reference to Montesquieu); *L'héritage de Darius,* 388
("Which of the two [Alexander or Julian], I ask both our soldiers and our philosophers, should we consider imitating in Algeria?"); and *La conquête de l'Inde,*
431–432 ("Our Persians and our Bactrians of Africa"). One of the last historians
of Alexander to refer to Voltaire and Montesquieu was Georges Radet, *Alexandre le Grand,* 133, 413, 422. On these questions see my "Michael Rostovtzeff,
Elias J. Bickerman and the "Hellenization of Asia."

Acknowledgments

1. I list them here in alphabetical order, as they appear in the bibliography at the
   end of the volume: Bonnet (2013); Bowden (2014); Goulemot (2013); Imbruglia
   (2013); Lanfranchi (2013); Tolias (2013); Payen (2013); Sebastiani (2013); Spawforth (2015); Volpilhac-Auger (2013).

Acknowledgments

I would like to repeat the acknowledgments at the beginning of the French edition, which expressed my thanks to all those who encouraged me to see this project through over eight years of work. Today my thanks must also go to those who reviewed the French edition.[1] Whether scholars of antiquity or the modern era, these writers honestly stated what this book could contribute to our understanding of the Enlightenment and the historiography of Alexander the Great. I would also like to thank those colleagues who invited me to present and discuss the book in various European cities and universities, including Montpellier (2012), Fribourg (2013), Reims (2013), Florence (2013), Athens and Thessaloniki (2014), and Uppsala (2014), as well as at Princeton in March 2012, a few months before the French edition was published.

This American translation would not have seen the day had it not been for the insightful interest of Sharmila Sen, Executive Editor-at-Large at Harvard University Press, to whom I also owe the American edition of *Darius in the Shadow of Alexander* (2015); the patient attention of Heather Hughes, Assistant Editor for Humanities; and the talent of translator Nicholas Elliott. I give them my most sincere thanks.

Index

tactics of France, 261–262. See also *specific leaders*
Military Fanfare (Marathon), 331
Mill, James, 319
Mitchell, John, 217–219
Mitford, William, 19, 57–58, 71, 122, 212
Modern Geography (Philippides and Constantas), 312
Modern Lives (Robertson), 72
Momigliano, Arnaldo, 3, 56–57, 75, 301
Montaigne, Michel Eyquem de, 95
Montesquieu, Charles-Louis de Secondat: critical erudition by, 37–38; *Reflection on the Universal Monarchy in Europe,* 96, 150; *Pensées,* 98–99, 110; *Spicilège,* 104; on Charles XII, 105–106; use of Arrian by, 109–110, 151–152, 154–155; sources of, 137–147; Huet and, 147–149; on Phoenicians, 174; on history of empires, 321, 323–324. See also *Spirit of the Laws, The* (Montesquieu)
Moutonnet de Clairfons, Julien-Jacques, 286
Moyle, Walter, 63, 65
Mystères du Paganisme (Sainte-Croix), 51

Nadir Shah, 42, 80, 124, 125, 335, 336
Napoléon. *See* Bonaparte, Napoléon
Nares, Robert, 83, 86, 202
navigation and commerce, 139–146, 158–161, 197–199. *See also* exploration and discovery
Nearchus, 84. See also *Voyage of Nearchus, The* (Vincent)
Nearchus's Journal, 84
Netherlands, 141–142, 174, 270; Alexander scholarship from, 8, 12, 311
Newberry, John, 71
Niebuhr, Barthold Georg, 264–270; influence of, 15, 87; criticism by, 216, 276, 309–310; on Greek history, 288; use of Ottoman Empire analogy, 326–327
Niebuhr, Carsten, 164–166, 264
Nouveau dictionnaire historique (Chaudon), 237
Nouveau statut politique (Rigas), 317

Observations on the State of Society among the Asiatic Subjects of Great-Britain (Grant), 217
Observations sur les Grecs (Mably), 221
Of the Dominion of Ownership of the Sea (Selden), 12
Old and New Testament (Prideaux), 28
On Alexander and His Plans for Putting All the Parts of the Universe in Mutual Communication (Heyne), 259–260
On the Fortune or the Virtue of Alexander (Plutarch), 54, 152, 156, 217
On the Immense Treasures in bullion and Coined Money of the Ancient Sovereigns of Asia (Maurice), 337
Os Lusiadas (Camões), 193–194
Ottoman Empire, 319–321, 323–324, 326–328

Palmyra, 118, 128–129, 328
Paradis terrestre (Huet), 14
Parisot, Vincent, 257–258
Patriotic Association for Liberty and Property against Republicans and Levellers, 64
Patriotic Hymn (Rigas), 314
peace, 96, 183. *See also* military arts
Pensées (Montesquieu), 98–99, 110
Periplus of the Erythrean Sea (Vincent): publication of, 83, 274; dedication in, 195; on commerce, 202; reception of, 204, 244, 264, 276
Persepolis: destruction of, 22, 61, 132, 319; wealth of, 133, 285, 335, 337; prominence of, 311, 318
Persian Empire: description of army, 107; battle logistics of, 108; maritime commerce of, 144–145; river engineering by, 164–165; Jouffroy on, 304; moral decadence of, 321–322, 326–327; strength of, 323–324; analogy with Ottoman Empire, 326–328
Peter the Great (Peter I), 24, 102–103, 222
Philip, Duke of Anjou, 31, 32
Philip II, King of Macedon, 74, 121–123, 264, 267–269, 335
Philip II, King of Spain, 94
Philip IV, King of Spain, 23